Solutions Manual for
Algebra 1

An Incremental Development

Third Edition

John H. Saxon, Jr.

SAXON PUBLISHERS, INC.

Algebra 1: An Incremental Development
Third Edition
Solutions Manual

Printed in the United States of America.

ISBN: 1-56577-137-0

Prepress Manager: J. Travis Rose

Production Coordinator: Joan Coleman

4 5 6 7 8 9 10 862 13 12 11 10 09 08 07

┌─── *Reaching us via the Internet* ───┐

www.saxonpublishers.com

E-mail: info@saxonpublishers.com

Preface

This manual contains solutions to every problem in the third edition of John Saxon's *Algebra 1* textbook. The solutions are designed to be representative of students' work, but please keep in mind that many problems will have more than one correct solution. We have attempted to stay as close as possible to the methods and procedures outlined in the textbook. Early solutions of problems of a particular type contain every step. Later solutions omit simpler steps. The final answers are set in boldface for ease of grading.

The following Saxon employees were instrumental in the development of this solutions manual, and we gratefully acknowledge their contributions: Edward Burr, Adriana Maxwell, Paul Kerr, and Erin McCain for working the solutions and proofreading the various revisions; Serena Freeberg and Letha Steinbron for typesetting the manual; Travis Southern for creating the graphics; and Emerson Mounger for producing the cover art.

We also thank teacher-consultant James Sellers for providing us with the initial draft of the solutions on which this manual is based.

Problem Set 1

1. $\dfrac{1}{5} + \dfrac{2}{5} = \dfrac{3}{5}$

2. $\dfrac{3}{8} - \dfrac{2}{8} = \dfrac{1}{8}$

3. $\dfrac{4}{3} - \dfrac{1}{3} + \dfrac{2}{3} = \dfrac{3}{3} + \dfrac{2}{3} = \dfrac{5}{3} = 1\dfrac{2}{3}$

4. $\dfrac{1}{3} + \dfrac{1}{5} = \dfrac{5}{15} + \dfrac{3}{15} = \dfrac{8}{15}$

5. $\dfrac{3}{8} - \dfrac{1}{5} = \dfrac{15}{40} - \dfrac{8}{40} = \dfrac{7}{40}$

6. $\dfrac{2}{3} - \dfrac{1}{8} = \dfrac{16}{24} - \dfrac{3}{24} = \dfrac{13}{24}$

7. $\dfrac{1}{13} + \dfrac{1}{5} = \dfrac{5}{65} + \dfrac{13}{65} = \dfrac{18}{65}$

8. $\dfrac{14}{15} - \dfrac{2}{3} = \dfrac{14}{15} - \dfrac{10}{15} = \dfrac{4}{15}$

9. $\dfrac{5}{9} + \dfrac{2}{5} = \dfrac{25}{45} + \dfrac{18}{45} = \dfrac{43}{45}$

10. $\dfrac{14}{17} - \dfrac{6}{34} = \dfrac{28}{34} - \dfrac{6}{34} = \dfrac{22}{34} = \dfrac{11}{17}$

11. $\dfrac{5}{13} + \dfrac{1}{26} = \dfrac{10}{26} + \dfrac{1}{26} = \dfrac{11}{26}$

12. $\dfrac{4}{7} - \dfrac{2}{5} = \dfrac{20}{35} - \dfrac{14}{35} = \dfrac{6}{35}$

13. $\dfrac{4}{7} + \dfrac{1}{8} + \dfrac{1}{2} = \dfrac{32}{56} + \dfrac{7}{56} + \dfrac{28}{56} = \dfrac{67}{56} = 1\dfrac{11}{56}$

14. $\dfrac{3}{5} + \dfrac{1}{8} + \dfrac{1}{8} = \dfrac{24}{40} + \dfrac{5}{40} + \dfrac{5}{40} = \dfrac{34}{40} = \dfrac{17}{20}$

15. $\dfrac{5}{11} - \dfrac{1}{6} + \dfrac{2}{3} = \dfrac{30}{66} - \dfrac{11}{66} + \dfrac{44}{66} = \dfrac{63}{66} = \dfrac{21}{22}$

16. $2\dfrac{1}{2} + 3\dfrac{1}{5} = 2\dfrac{5}{10} + 3\dfrac{2}{10} = 5\dfrac{7}{10}$

17. $7\dfrac{3}{8} + 6\dfrac{1}{3} = 7\dfrac{9}{24} + 6\dfrac{8}{24} = 13\dfrac{17}{24}$

18. $1\dfrac{1}{8} + 7\dfrac{2}{5} = 1\dfrac{5}{40} + 7\dfrac{16}{40} = 8\dfrac{21}{40}$

19. $15\dfrac{1}{3} - 7\dfrac{4}{5} = 15\dfrac{5}{15} - 7\dfrac{12}{15} = 14\dfrac{20}{15} - 7\dfrac{12}{15}$
$= 7\dfrac{8}{15}$

20. $42\dfrac{3}{8} - 21\dfrac{3}{4} = 42\dfrac{3}{8} - 21\dfrac{6}{8} = 41\dfrac{11}{8} - 21\dfrac{6}{8}$
$= 20\dfrac{5}{8}$

21. $22\dfrac{2}{5} - 13\dfrac{7}{15} = 22\dfrac{6}{15} - 13\dfrac{7}{15}$
$= 21\dfrac{21}{15} - 13\dfrac{7}{15} = 8\dfrac{14}{15}$

22. $42\dfrac{1}{11} - 18\dfrac{2}{3} = 42\dfrac{3}{33} - 18\dfrac{22}{33}$
$= 41\dfrac{36}{33} - 18\dfrac{22}{33} = 23\dfrac{14}{33}$

23. $78\dfrac{2}{5} - 14\dfrac{7}{10} = 78\dfrac{4}{10} - 14\dfrac{7}{10}$
$= 77\dfrac{14}{10} - 14\dfrac{7}{10} = 63\dfrac{7}{10}$

24. $43\dfrac{1}{13} - 6\dfrac{5}{8} = 43\dfrac{8}{104} - 6\dfrac{65}{104}$
$= 42\dfrac{112}{104} - 6\dfrac{65}{104} = 36\dfrac{47}{104}$

25. $21\dfrac{1}{5} - 15\dfrac{7}{13} = 21\dfrac{13}{65} - 15\dfrac{35}{65}$
$= 20\dfrac{78}{65} - 15\dfrac{35}{65} = 5\dfrac{43}{65}$

26. $21\dfrac{2}{19} - 7\dfrac{7}{10} = 21\dfrac{20}{190} - 7\dfrac{133}{190}$
$= 20\dfrac{210}{190} - 7\dfrac{133}{190} = 13\dfrac{77}{190}$

27. $43\dfrac{3}{17} - 21\dfrac{9}{10} = 43\dfrac{30}{170} - 21\dfrac{153}{170}$
$= 42\dfrac{200}{170} - 21\dfrac{153}{170} = 21\dfrac{47}{170}$

28. $7\dfrac{1}{8} + 5\dfrac{2}{7} = 7\dfrac{7}{56} + 5\dfrac{16}{56} = 12\dfrac{23}{56}$ units

29. $42\dfrac{1}{7} - 24\dfrac{2}{11} = 42\dfrac{11}{77} - 24\dfrac{14}{77}$
$= 41\dfrac{88}{77} - 24\dfrac{14}{77} = 17\dfrac{74}{77}$ units

30. $12\dfrac{11}{16} - 3\dfrac{5}{8} = 12\dfrac{11}{16} - 3\dfrac{10}{16} = 9\dfrac{1}{16}$ units

Practice 2

a. $x = 180 - 55 - 55 = \mathbf{70}$

b. Since angles opposite sides of equal length have equal measure, $x = \mathbf{40}.$

$y = 180 - 40 - 40$

$y = \mathbf{100}$

c. Since angles opposite sides of equal length have equal measure, x and y are equivalent.

$180 - 112 = 68$

$68 \div 2 = 34$

$x = \mathbf{34};\ y = \mathbf{34}$

Problem Set 2

1. **Right angles**

2. **Straight angle**

3. **An acute angle is an angle that is smaller than a right angle.**

4. **An obtuse angle is an angle that is larger than a right angle, but smaller than a straight angle.**

5. (a) **90°**

   (b) **180°**

   (c) **360°**

6. **Equilateral polygons**

7. **Equiangular polygons**

8. **Regular polygons**

9. (a) **A right triangle is a triangle that contains one right angle.**

   (b) **An acute triangle is a triangle that contains three acute angles.**

   (c) **An obtuse triangle is a triangle that contains one obtuse angle.**

   (d) **An equiangular triangle is a triangle that contains three angles of equal measure.**

10. (a) **An isosceles triangle is a triangle that has at least two sides of equal length.**

    (b) **An equilateral triangle is a triangle that contains three sides of equal length.**

    (c) **A scalene triangle is a triangle that contains three sides of unequal length.**

11. $x = 180 - 80 - 50 = \mathbf{50}$

12. $y = 180 - 100 - 40 = \mathbf{40}$

13. $\dfrac{1}{3} + \dfrac{4}{9} = \dfrac{3}{9} + \dfrac{4}{9} = \dfrac{\mathbf{7}}{\mathbf{9}}$

14. $\dfrac{3}{5} + \dfrac{2}{7} = \dfrac{21}{35} + \dfrac{10}{35} = \dfrac{\mathbf{31}}{\mathbf{35}}$

15. $\dfrac{3}{4} - \dfrac{5}{12} = \dfrac{9}{12} - \dfrac{5}{12} = \dfrac{4}{12} = \dfrac{\mathbf{1}}{\mathbf{3}}$

16. $\dfrac{2}{3} + \dfrac{1}{15} = \dfrac{10}{15} + \dfrac{1}{15} = \dfrac{\mathbf{11}}{\mathbf{15}}$

17. $\dfrac{9}{14} - \dfrac{1}{2} + \dfrac{3}{7} = \dfrac{9}{14} - \dfrac{7}{14} + \dfrac{6}{14}$

    $= \dfrac{2}{14} + \dfrac{6}{14} = \dfrac{8}{14} = \dfrac{\mathbf{4}}{\mathbf{7}}$

18. $5\dfrac{1}{3} + 1\dfrac{1}{6} = 5\dfrac{2}{6} + 1\dfrac{1}{6} = 6\dfrac{3}{6} = \mathbf{6\dfrac{1}{2}}$

19. $3\dfrac{1}{8} + 4\dfrac{1}{2} = 3\dfrac{1}{8} + 4\dfrac{4}{8} = \mathbf{7\dfrac{5}{8}}$

20. $5\dfrac{2}{5} + 7\dfrac{7}{10} = 5\dfrac{4}{10} + 7\dfrac{7}{10} = 12\dfrac{11}{10} = \mathbf{13\dfrac{1}{10}}$

21. $9\dfrac{1}{3} + 3\dfrac{3}{5} = 9\dfrac{5}{15} + 3\dfrac{9}{15} = \mathbf{12\dfrac{14}{15}}$

22. $9\dfrac{3}{5} + 5\dfrac{2}{3} = 9\dfrac{9}{15} + 5\dfrac{10}{15} = 14\dfrac{19}{15} = \mathbf{15\dfrac{4}{15}}$

23. $23\dfrac{7}{10} - 14\dfrac{2}{5} = 23\dfrac{7}{10} - 14\dfrac{4}{10} = \mathbf{9\dfrac{3}{10}}$

24. $22\dfrac{2}{5} - 14\dfrac{4}{15} = 22\dfrac{6}{15} - 14\dfrac{4}{15} = \mathbf{8\dfrac{2}{15}}$

25. $8\dfrac{2}{5} - 5\dfrac{1}{3} = 8\dfrac{6}{15} - 5\dfrac{5}{15} = \mathbf{3\dfrac{1}{15}}$

26. $4\dfrac{2}{3} - 1\dfrac{5}{6} = 4\dfrac{4}{6} - 1\dfrac{5}{6} = 3\dfrac{10}{6} - 1\dfrac{5}{6} = \mathbf{2\dfrac{5}{6}}$

27. $14\dfrac{1}{2} - 12\dfrac{2}{3} = 14\dfrac{3}{6} - 12\dfrac{4}{6} = 13\dfrac{9}{6} - 12\dfrac{4}{6}$

    $= \mathbf{1\dfrac{5}{6}}$

28. $2\dfrac{1}{3} + 5\dfrac{2}{9} = 2\dfrac{3}{9} + 5\dfrac{2}{9} = \mathbf{7\dfrac{5}{9}}$ cm

29. $16\frac{3}{4} - 9\frac{7}{8} = 16\frac{6}{8} - 9\frac{7}{8} = 15\frac{14}{8} - 9\frac{7}{8}$

$\qquad = 6\frac{7}{8}$ m

30. $10\frac{1}{5} - 4\frac{2}{3} = 10\frac{3}{15} - 4\frac{10}{15} = 9\frac{18}{15} - 4\frac{10}{15}$

$\qquad = 5\frac{8}{15}$ **units**

Practice 3

a. $P = (10 + 5 + 10 + 5)$ cm $= \mathbf{30\ cm}$

b. $l = 12$ m $\div\ 4 = \mathbf{3\ m}$

c. $P = (5 + 2 + 2 + 6 + 2 + 4 + 5 + 12)$ km
$\qquad = \mathbf{38\ km}$

d. $C = 2\pi r = 2\pi(5$ in.$) = \mathbf{10\pi}$ **in.** $= \mathbf{31.4\ in.}$

e. $P = \left(6 + 6 + 6 + \dfrac{2\pi(3)}{2}\right)$ ft
$\qquad = (18 + 3\pi)$ **ft** $= \mathbf{27.42\ ft}$

Problem Set 3

1. **180°**

2. (a) Each angle measures **60°**.

  (b) Each angle measures **60°**.

3. **The angles opposite the sides of equal length have equal measures.**

4. **The sides opposite the angles of equal measure have equal lengths.**

5. **Parallelogram**

6. **Trapezoid**

7. $P = (12 + 8 + 12 + 8)$ in. $= \mathbf{40\ in.}$

8. $l = 16$ ft $\div\ 4 = \mathbf{4\ ft}$

9. $C = 2\pi r = 2\pi\,(6$ cm$) = \mathbf{12\pi}$ **cm** $= \mathbf{37.68\ cm}$

10. $C = \pi D = \pi(8$ m$) = \mathbf{8\pi}$ **m** $= \mathbf{25.12\ m}$

11. $P = (20 + 8 + 10 + 17 + 10 + 25)$ in.
$\qquad = \mathbf{90\ in.}$

12. $P = (5 + 15 + 10 + 10 + 15 + 25)$ in.
$\qquad = \mathbf{80\ in.}$

13. $P = \left(4 + 4 + 4 + \dfrac{2\pi(2)}{2}\right)$ in.
$\qquad = (12 + 2\pi)$ **in.** $= \mathbf{18.28\ in.}$

14. $P = \left(10 + 6 + 10 + \dfrac{2\pi(3)}{2}\right)$ in.
$\qquad = (26 + 3\pi)$ **in.** $= \mathbf{35.42\ in.}$

15. $x = 180 - 60 - 60 = \mathbf{60}$

16. $y = 180 - 110 - 35 = \mathbf{35}$

17. $\dfrac{1}{2} + \dfrac{5}{18} = \dfrac{9}{18} + \dfrac{5}{18} = \dfrac{14}{18} = \mathbf{\dfrac{7}{9}}$

18. $\dfrac{11}{12} - \dfrac{3}{4} = \dfrac{11}{12} - \dfrac{9}{12} = \dfrac{2}{12} = \mathbf{\dfrac{1}{6}}$

19. $\dfrac{8}{15} + \dfrac{2}{3} - \dfrac{1}{5} = \dfrac{8}{15} + \dfrac{10}{15} - \dfrac{3}{15} = \dfrac{15}{15} = \mathbf{1}$

20. $5\frac{2}{3} + 1\frac{7}{12} = 5\frac{8}{12} + 1\frac{7}{12} = 6\frac{15}{12} = 7\frac{3}{12}$
$\qquad = \mathbf{7\frac{1}{4}}$

21. $7\frac{5}{6} + 4\frac{1}{18} = 7\frac{15}{18} + 4\frac{1}{18} = 11\frac{16}{18} = \mathbf{11\frac{8}{9}}$

22. $6\frac{3}{5} + 14\frac{9}{10} = 6\frac{6}{10} + 14\frac{9}{10} = 20\frac{15}{10}$
$\qquad = 21\frac{5}{10} = \mathbf{21\frac{1}{2}}$

23. $4\frac{7}{8} + 3\frac{3}{16} = 4\frac{14}{16} + 3\frac{3}{16} = 7\frac{17}{16} = \mathbf{8\frac{1}{16}}$

24. $5\frac{1}{8} + 8\frac{3}{7} = 5\frac{7}{56} + 8\frac{24}{56} = \mathbf{13\frac{31}{56}}$

25. $4\frac{3}{5} - 3\frac{4}{15} = 4\frac{9}{15} - 3\frac{4}{15} = 1\frac{5}{15} = \mathbf{1\frac{1}{3}}$

26. $15\frac{2}{3} - 4\frac{5}{11} = 15\frac{22}{33} - 4\frac{15}{33} = \mathbf{11\frac{7}{33}}$

27. $7\frac{5}{6} - 6\frac{11}{12} = 7\frac{10}{12} - 6\frac{11}{12} = 6\frac{22}{12} - 6\frac{11}{12}$
$\qquad = \mathbf{\dfrac{11}{12}}$

28. $33\frac{5}{8} - 7\frac{11}{16} = 33\frac{10}{16} - 7\frac{11}{16} = 32\frac{26}{16} - 7\frac{11}{16}$

$= 25\frac{15}{16}$

29. $14\frac{1}{3} + 12\frac{2}{5} = 14\frac{5}{15} + 12\frac{6}{15} = 26\frac{11}{15}$ ft

30. $7\frac{2}{3} - 4\frac{1}{2} = 7\frac{4}{6} - 4\frac{3}{6} = 3\frac{1}{6}$ yd

Practice 4

a. $4\frac{1}{2} \times 2\frac{4}{5} = \frac{9}{2} \times \frac{14}{5} = \frac{63}{5} = 12\frac{3}{5}$

b. $3\frac{1}{4} \div 1\frac{3}{8} = \frac{13}{4} \div \frac{11}{8} = \frac{13}{4} \times \frac{8}{11} = \frac{26}{11}$

$= 2\frac{4}{11}$

c.   47.123
       8.416
   + 705.4
   ———————
   760.939

d.   800.62
   −   75.88
   ———————
   724.74

e.   47.05
   ×   6.42
   ————
      9410
    18820
    28230
   ————————
   302.0610

f.   100.7
   4⟌402.8
       4
      ——
      2 8
      2 8

g. $75 \text{ ft} \times \frac{12 \text{ in.}}{1 \text{ ft}} \times \frac{2.54 \text{ cm}}{1 \text{ in.}} = \textbf{75(12)(2.54) cm}$

$= \textbf{2286 cm}$

h. $450 \text{ in.} \times \frac{1 \text{ ft}}{12 \text{ in.}} \times \frac{1 \text{ mi}}{5280 \text{ ft}} = \frac{450}{(12)(5280)} \text{ mi}$

$= \textbf{0.0071 mi}$

Problem Set 4

1. A number is an idea. A numeral is a symbol used to express the idea of a number.

2. (a) **Decimal system**

   (b) **The Hindus of India**

   (c) **0, 1, 2, 3, 4, 5, 6, 7, 8, 9**

3. (a) **1, 2, 3, 4, 5, ...**

   (b) **1, 2, 3, 4, 5, ...**

4. A positive real number is any number that can be used to describe a physical distance greater than zero.

5. (a) **A rectangle is a parallelogram with four right angles.**

   (b) **A rhombus is an equilateral parallelogram.**

   (c) **A square is a rhombus with four right angles.**

   (d) **Yes**

6. $20 \text{ in.} \times \frac{2.54 \text{ cm}}{1 \text{ in.}} = \textbf{20(2.54) cm} = \textbf{50.8 cm}$

7. $25 \text{ ft} \times \frac{12 \text{ in.}}{1 \text{ ft}} \times \frac{2.54 \text{ cm}}{1 \text{ in.}} = \textbf{25(12)(2.54) cm}$

$= \textbf{762 cm}$

8. $P = (16 + 9 + 16 + 9) \text{ cm} = \textbf{50 cm}$

9. $l = 24 \text{ m} \div 4 = \textbf{6 m}$

10. $C = 2\pi r = 2\pi(8 \text{ in.}) = \textbf{16}\boldsymbol{\pi}\textbf{ in.} = \textbf{50.24 in.}$

11. $C = \pi D = \pi(10 \text{ ft}) = \textbf{10}\boldsymbol{\pi}\textbf{ ft} = \textbf{31.4 ft}$

12. $P = (15 + 4 + 6 + 8 + 9 + 12) \text{ cm} = \textbf{54 cm}$

13. $P = (25 + 30 + 12 + 22 + 13 + 8) \text{ cm}$

$= \textbf{110 cm}$

14. $P = \left(8 + 8 + 8 + \frac{2\pi(4)}{2}\right) \text{ cm}$

$= (24 + 4\pi) \text{ cm} = \textbf{36.56 cm}$

15. $P = \left(7 + 10 + 7 + \frac{2\pi(5)}{2}\right) \text{ cm}$

$= (24 + 5\pi) \text{ cm} = \textbf{39.7 cm}$

16. $x = 180 - 70 - 55 = \textbf{55}$

17. $\dfrac{17}{24} - \dfrac{1}{4} - \dfrac{1}{8} = \dfrac{17}{24} - \dfrac{6}{24} - \dfrac{3}{24}$

$\qquad = \dfrac{11}{24} - \dfrac{3}{24} = \dfrac{8}{24} = \dfrac{1}{3}$

18. $8\dfrac{1}{4} + 5\dfrac{3}{8} = 8\dfrac{2}{8} + 5\dfrac{3}{8} = 13\dfrac{5}{8}$

19. $8\dfrac{1}{4} - 5\dfrac{3}{8} = 8\dfrac{2}{8} - 5\dfrac{3}{8} = 7\dfrac{10}{8} - 5\dfrac{3}{8} = 2\dfrac{7}{8}$

20. $95\dfrac{1}{8} - 4\dfrac{13}{16} = 95\dfrac{2}{16} - 4\dfrac{13}{16} = 94\dfrac{18}{16} - 4\dfrac{13}{16}$

$\qquad = 90\dfrac{5}{16}$

21. $\dfrac{4}{3} \times \dfrac{7}{2} \times \dfrac{9}{5} = \dfrac{42}{5} = 8\dfrac{2}{5}$

22. $4\dfrac{1}{2} \times 6\dfrac{2}{3} = \dfrac{9}{2} \times \dfrac{20}{3} = 30$

23. $4\dfrac{1}{2} \div 6\dfrac{2}{3} = \dfrac{9}{2} \div \dfrac{20}{3} = \dfrac{9}{2} \times \dfrac{3}{20} = \dfrac{27}{40}$

24. $\dfrac{14\frac{2}{3}}{3\frac{1}{4}} = \dfrac{44}{3} \div \dfrac{13}{4} = \dfrac{44}{3} \times \dfrac{4}{13} = \dfrac{176}{39}$

$\qquad = 4\dfrac{20}{39}$

25. $\begin{array}{r} 6.0018 \\ + \ 0.03121 \\ \hline \mathbf{6.03301} \end{array}$

26. $\begin{array}{r} 8.0146 \\ - \ 0.03251 \\ \hline \mathbf{7.98209} \end{array}$

27. $\begin{array}{r} 16.04 \\ \times \ \ 3.46 \\ \hline 9624 \\ 6416 \\ 4812 \\ \hline \mathbf{55.4984} \end{array}$

28. $\begin{array}{r} 44 \\ 123\overline{)5412} \\ \underline{492} \\ 492 \\ \underline{492} \end{array}$

29. $3\dfrac{1}{2} + 10\dfrac{3}{8} = 3\dfrac{4}{8} + 10\dfrac{3}{8} = 13\dfrac{7}{8} \text{ m}$

30. $15\dfrac{2}{3} - 10\dfrac{1}{6} = 15\dfrac{4}{6} - 10\dfrac{1}{6} = 5\dfrac{3}{6} = 5\dfrac{1}{2} \text{ km}$

Practice 5

a. $|-4| = \mathbf{4}$

b. $|4.2| = \mathbf{4.2}$

c. $-|10 - 6| = -|4| = \mathbf{-4}$

d. $-|-14 + 6| = -|-8| = \mathbf{-8}$

e. **+5**

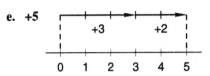

f. **−1**

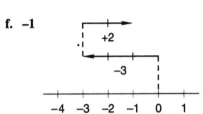

g. **−3**

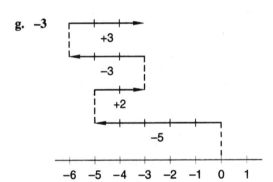

Problem Set 5

1. (a) **{1, 2, 3, 4, 5, ...}**

(b) **{0, 1, 2, 3, 4, 5, ...}**

(c) **{..., −3, −2, −1, 0, 1, 2, 3, ...}**

2. **Origin**

3. (a) **A dot on the number line that represents the location of the number**

(b) **The number that the point represents**

(c) **The greater number is further to the right-hand side on the number line.**

4. $|-8| = \mathbf{8}$

5. $|+8| = \mathbf{8}$

6. $|-12| = \mathbf{12}$

7. $-|15 - 5| = -|10| = \mathbf{-10}$

8. $-|-15 + 5| = -|-10| = \mathbf{-10}$

9. $|12 - 30| = |-18| = \mathbf{18}$

10. **-5**

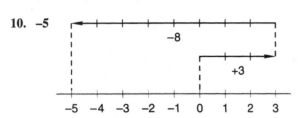

11. **+1**

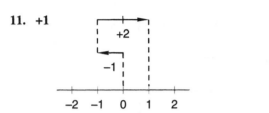

12. **+7**

13. **+2**

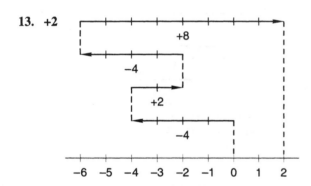

14. $28 \text{ cm} \times \dfrac{1 \text{ in.}}{2.54 \text{ cm}} = \dfrac{\mathbf{28}}{\mathbf{2.54}} \text{ in.} = \mathbf{11.02 \text{ in.}}$

15. $42 \text{ cm} \times \dfrac{1 \text{ in.}}{2.54 \text{ cm}} \times \dfrac{1 \text{ ft}}{12 \text{ in.}} = \dfrac{\mathbf{42}}{\mathbf{(2.54)(12)}} \text{ ft}$

    $= \mathbf{1.38 \text{ ft}}$

16. $P = (22 + 13 + 22 + 13) \text{ in.} = \mathbf{70 \text{ in.}}$

17. $C = 2\pi r = 2\pi(10 \text{ ft}) = 20\pi \text{ ft} = \mathbf{62.8 \text{ ft}}$

18. $P = (10 + 18 + 15 + 4 + 5 + 14) \text{ yd} = \mathbf{66 \text{ yd}}$

19. $P = \left(12 + 12 + 12 + \dfrac{2\pi(6)}{2}\right) \text{yd}$

    $= (36 + 6\pi) \text{ yd} = \mathbf{54.84 \text{ yd}}$

20. $y = 180 - 120 - 30 = \mathbf{30}$

21. $6\dfrac{2}{3} + 7\dfrac{4}{9} = 6\dfrac{6}{9} + 7\dfrac{4}{9} = 13\dfrac{10}{9} = \mathbf{14\dfrac{1}{9}}$

22. $95\dfrac{1}{8} - 4\dfrac{13}{16} = 95\dfrac{2}{16} - 4\dfrac{13}{16}$

    $= 94\dfrac{18}{16} - 4\dfrac{13}{16} = \mathbf{90\dfrac{5}{16}}$

23. $4\dfrac{1}{2} \times 2\dfrac{2}{3} = \dfrac{9}{2} \times \dfrac{8}{3} = \mathbf{12}$

24. $4\dfrac{1}{2} \div 7\dfrac{3}{8} = \dfrac{9}{2} \div \dfrac{59}{8} = \dfrac{9}{2} \times \dfrac{8}{59} = \mathbf{\dfrac{36}{59}}$

25. $\dfrac{7\dfrac{1}{8}}{4\dfrac{2}{5}} = \dfrac{57}{8} \div \dfrac{22}{5} = \dfrac{57}{8} \times \dfrac{5}{22} = \dfrac{285}{176}$

    $= \mathbf{1\dfrac{109}{176}}$

26.
$$\begin{array}{r} 23.0106 \\ +\ \ 0.1094 \\ \hline \mathbf{23.1200} \end{array}$$

27.
$$\begin{array}{r} 48.2 \\ -\ 13.34 \\ \hline \mathbf{34.86} \end{array}$$

28.
$$\begin{array}{r} 8.08 \\ \times\ 0.120 \\ \hline 000 \\ 1616 \\ 808 \\ \hline \mathbf{0.96960} \end{array}$$

29.
$$\begin{array}{r} \mathbf{4.003} \\ 212\overline{)848.636} \\ \underline{848} \\ 636 \\ \underline{636} \end{array}$$

30. $18\dfrac{2}{5} - 6\dfrac{1}{15} = 18\dfrac{6}{15} - 6\dfrac{1}{15} = 12\dfrac{5}{15}$

    $= \mathbf{12\dfrac{1}{3} \text{ mi}}$

Practice 6

a. $-5 - 2 + 7 - 6$

   $= (-5) + (-2) + (+7) + (-6) = \mathbf{-6}$

b. $-4 - |-2| - 6 + (-5)$

   $= (-4) + (-2) + (-6) + (-5) = \mathbf{-17}$

c. $-|-8| - 3 + 5 - 11$

   $= (-8) + (-3) + (+5) + (-11) = \mathbf{-17}$

d. $-8 + |-6| - |5| - 7$
  $= (-8) + (+6) + (-5) + (-7) = \mathbf{-14}$

Problem Set 6

1. **Add the absolute values of the numbers and give the result the same sign as that of the numbers.**

2. **Take the difference of the absolute values of the numbers and give it the sign of the number whose absolute value is greater.**

3. **Commutative property** of addition

4. (a) **Sum**

   (b) **Difference**

   (c) **Product**

   (d) **Quotient**

5. $|-5| = \mathbf{5}$

6. $-|10 - 7| = -|3| = \mathbf{-3}$

7. $|3 - 6| = |-3| = \mathbf{3}$

8. **–1**

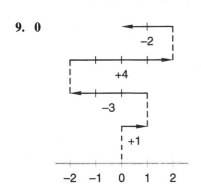

9. **0**

10. $34\,\text{m} \times \dfrac{100\,\text{cm}}{1\,\text{m}} = \mathbf{34(100)\,cm = 3400\,cm}$

11. $6\,\text{mi} \times \dfrac{5280\,\text{ft}}{1\,\text{mi}} \times \dfrac{12\,\text{in.}}{1\,\text{ft}} = \mathbf{6(5280)(12)\,in.}$
    $= \mathbf{380{,}160\ in.}$

12. $l = 36\,\text{cm} \div 4 = \mathbf{9\,cm}$

13. $C = \pi D = \pi(14\,\text{m}) = 14\pi\,\text{m} = \mathbf{43.96\,m}$

14. $(+3) + (-14) = \mathbf{-11}$

15. $(-3) + (-14) = \mathbf{-17}$

16. $(-5) + (4) + (-3) + (+8)$
    $= (-5) + (+4) + (-3) + (+8) = \mathbf{4}$

17. $(-3) + (+2) + (-2) + |-2|$
    $= (-3) + (+2) + (-2) + (+2) = \mathbf{-1}$

18. $-2 + 11 - 4 + 3 - 8$
    $= (-2) + (+11) + (-4) + (+3) + (-8) = \mathbf{0}$

19. $-5 - 11 + 20 - 14 + 5$
    $= (-5) + (-11) + (+20) + (-14) + (+5) = \mathbf{-5}$

20. $-4 - 3 + 2 - 4 - 3 - 8$
    $= (-4) + (-3) + (+2) + (-4) + (-3) + (-8)$
    $= \mathbf{-20}$

21. $7 - 3 + 2 - 11 + 4 - 5 + 3$
    $= (+7) + (-3) + (+2) + (-11) + (+4)$
    $\quad + (-5) + (+3)$
    $= \mathbf{-3}$

22. $-7 + (-8) + 3 = (-7) + (-8) + (+3) = \mathbf{-12}$

23. $-7 + (-3) + 4 - 3 + (-2)$
    $= (-7) + (-3) + (+4) + (-3) + (-2) = \mathbf{-11}$

24. $-4 - 2 + (+8) + |-5|$
    $= (-4) + (-2) + (+8) + (+5) = \mathbf{7}$

25. $+|-2 - 3| - 4 + (-8) = +|-5| + (-4) + (-8)$
    $= (+5) + (-4) + (-8) = \mathbf{-7}$

26. $P = (12 + 15 + 10 + 4 + 2 + 11)\,\text{km} = \mathbf{54\,km}$

27. $P = \left(20 + 10 + 20 + \dfrac{2\pi(5)}{2}\right)\text{km}$
    $= (50 + 5\pi)\,\text{km} = \mathbf{65.7\,km}$

28. $x = 180 - 50 - 65 = \mathbf{65}$

29. $\dfrac{21}{5} \times \dfrac{15}{7} \times \dfrac{4}{9} = \mathbf{4}$

30. $25\dfrac{3}{4} - 20\dfrac{1}{20} = 25\dfrac{15}{20} - 20\dfrac{1}{20}$
    $= 5\dfrac{14}{20} = \mathbf{5\dfrac{7}{10}\ in.}$

Practice 7

a. $-(-3) - (-4) = (+3) + (+4) = \mathbf{7}$

b. $+(-5) + [-(-6)] = (-5) + (+6) = \mathbf{1}$

c. $-(+6) - (-8) + 7 - (-3) + (-5)$

$= (-6) + (+8) + (+7) + (+3) + (-5) = \mathbf{7}$

d. $-(-3) - [-(-4)] + [-(-6)]$

$= (+3) + (-4) + (+6) = \mathbf{5}$

Problem Set 7

1. (a) **–2**

(b) **2**

(c) **0**

2. **Additive inverse**

3. (a) **{1, 2, 3, 4, ...}**

(b) **{0, 1, 2, 3, 4, ...}**

(c) **{..., –3, –2, –1, 0, 1, 2, 3, ...}**

4. $-(+4) = (-4) = \mathbf{-4}$

5. $-(-4) = (+4) = \mathbf{4}$

6. $-[-(-4)] = (-4) = \mathbf{-4}$

7. $-\left\{-[-(-4)]\right\} = (+4) = \mathbf{4}$

8. $2200 \text{ cm} \times \dfrac{1 \text{ m}}{100 \text{ cm}} = \dfrac{\mathbf{2200}}{\mathbf{100}} \text{ m} = \mathbf{22 \text{ m}}$

9. $3000 \text{ in.} \times \dfrac{1 \text{ ft}}{12 \text{ in.}} \times \dfrac{1 \text{ mi}}{5280 \text{ ft}} = \dfrac{3000}{(12)(5280)} \text{ mi}$

$= \mathbf{0.047 \text{ mi}}$

10. $P = (32 + 16 + 32 + 16) \text{ in.} = \mathbf{96 \text{ in.}}$

11. $C = 2\pi r = 2\pi(12 \text{ ft}) = \mathbf{24\pi \text{ ft}} = \mathbf{75.36 \text{ ft}}$

12. $+7 - (-3) + (-2) = (+7) + (+3) + (-2) = \mathbf{8}$

13. $-3 + (-2) - (-3) = (-3) + (-2) + (+3) = \mathbf{-2}$

14. $-(-3) - [-(-4)] - 2 + 7$

$= (+3) + (-4) + (-2) + (+7) = \mathbf{4}$

15. $-2 - (-3) - \left\{-[-(-4)]\right\}$

$= (-2) + (+3) + (+4) = \mathbf{5}$

16. $-(-2) - |-2| = (+2) + (-2) = \mathbf{0}$

17. $-|-10| - (-10) = (-10) + (+10) = \mathbf{0}$

18. $-3 - (-3) + |-3| = (-3) + (+3) + (+3) = \mathbf{3}$

19. $-2 - [-(-6)] + |-5| = (-2) + (-6) + (+5) = \mathbf{-3}$

20. $-|-3 - 2| - (-3) - 2 - 5$

$= -|-5| + (+3) + (-2) + (-5)$

$= (-5) + (+3) + (-2) + (-5) = \mathbf{-9}$

21. $|-2 - 5 - 7| - (-4) = |-14| + 4$

$= (+14) + (+4) = \mathbf{18}$

22.

$A + C = 50$

$B + D = 62$

$P = 50 + 62 + A + B + C + D$

$= 50 + 62 + (A + C) + (B + D)$

$= 50 + 62 + 50 + 62 = \mathbf{224 \text{ yd}}$

23. $P = \left(5 + 16 + 5 + \dfrac{2\pi(8)}{2}\right) \text{ yd}$

$= (26 + 8\pi) \text{ yd} = \mathbf{51.12 \text{ yd}}$

24. $x = 180 - 90 - 60 = \mathbf{30}$

25. $5\dfrac{1}{2} + 7\dfrac{3}{8} - 1\dfrac{1}{4} = 5\dfrac{4}{8} + 7\dfrac{3}{8} - 1\dfrac{2}{8}$

$= 12\dfrac{7}{8} - 1\dfrac{2}{8} = \mathbf{11\dfrac{5}{8}}$

26. $1\dfrac{3}{5} \times 12\dfrac{1}{2} = \dfrac{8}{5} \times \dfrac{25}{2} = \mathbf{20}$

27. $4\dfrac{1}{4} \div 3\dfrac{2}{5} = \dfrac{17}{4} \div \dfrac{17}{5} = \dfrac{17}{4} \times \dfrac{5}{17} = \dfrac{5}{4}$

$= \mathbf{1\dfrac{1}{4}}$

28.
$$\begin{array}{r} 0.00143 \\ 0.012 \\ 443.6 \\ +\quad 0.0007 \\ \hline \mathbf{443.61413} \end{array}$$

29.
$$\begin{array}{r} 3.628 \\ \times\ 0.0404 \\ \hline 14512 \\ 14512\quad \\ \hline \mathbf{0.1465712} \end{array}$$

30. $16\dfrac{2}{3} + 5\dfrac{5}{6} = 16\dfrac{4}{6} + 5\dfrac{5}{6} = 21\dfrac{9}{6} = 22\dfrac{3}{6}$

$= \mathbf{22\dfrac{1}{2} \text{ cm}}$

Practice 8

a.

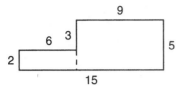

Area = (2 in.)(6 in.) + (9 in.)(5 in.)

= 12 in.^{2} + 45 in.^{2} = **57 in.^{2}**

b.

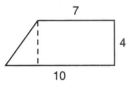

Area = $\frac{1}{2}$(3 ft)(4 ft) + (7 ft)(4 ft)

= 6 ft^2 + 28 ft^2 = **34 ft^2**

c. Area = πr^2 = π(5 cm)^2 = **25π cm^2 = 78.5 cm^2**

d.

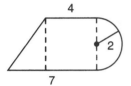

Area = $\frac{1}{2}$(3 m)(4 m) + (4 m)(4 m) + $\frac{1}{2}\pi$(2 m)^2

= 6 m^2 + 16 m^2 + $\frac{1}{2}\pi$(4 m^2)

= **(22 + 2π) m^2 = 28.28 m^2**

Problem Set 8

1. (a) $-\dfrac{1}{2}$

(b) $\dfrac{1}{2}$

(c) **0**

2. Additive inverse

3. Right angles

4. Straight angle

5. 36 ft × $\dfrac{12 \text{ in.}}{1 \text{ ft}}$ × $\dfrac{2.54 \text{ cm}}{1 \text{ in.}}$ = **36(12)(2.54) cm**

= **1097.28 cm**

6. 44 in. × $\dfrac{2.54 \text{ cm}}{1 \text{ in.}}$ × $\dfrac{1 \text{ m}}{100 \text{ cm}}$ = $\dfrac{44(2.54)}{(100)}$ m

= **1.12 m**

7. $P = 2l + 2w$

30 cm = 2(10 cm) + 2w

30 cm = 20 cm + 2w

30 cm − 20 cm = 2w

10 cm = 2w

$w = \dfrac{10 \text{ cm}}{2}$

$w =$ **5 cm**

8. $A = lw = $ (5 m)(4 m) = **20 m^2**

9. $C = 2\pi r = 2\pi$(3 in.) = **6π in. = 18.84 in.**

10. $A = \pi r^2 = \pi$(4 ft)^2 = **16π ft^2 = 50.24 ft^2**

11. −(−4) + (−2) − (−3) = (+4) + (−2) + (+3) = **5**

12. −3 + (−3) + (−6) − 2

= (−3) + (−3) + (−6) + (−2) = **−14**

13. −7 + 3 − 2 − 5 + (−6)

= (−7) + (+3) + (−2) + (−5) + (−6) = **−17**

14. 5 − 3 − (−2) − [−(−3)]

= (+5) + (−3) + (+2) + (−3) = **1**

15. −|−2| − (−2) = (−2) + (+2) = **0**

16. −|−2| + |2| − (−2) = (−2) + (+2) + (+2) = **2**

17. 7 − 4 − 5 + 12 − 2 − |−2|

= (+7) + (−4) + (−5) + (+12) + (−2) + (−2)

= **6**

18. |−4 − 3| − 2 + 7 − (−3)

= (+7) + (−2) + (+7) + (+3) = **15**

19. 5 − |−2 + 5| − (−3) + 2

= (+5) + (−3) + (+3) + (+2) = **7**

20. 4 − 3 − (−2) − |12 − 3 + 4|

= (+4) + (−3) + (+2) + (−13) = **−10**

21.

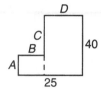

$A + C = 40$

$B + D = 25$

$P = 40 + 25 + A + B + C + D$

$\quad = 40 + 25 + (A + C) + (B + D)$

$\quad = 40 + 25 + 40 + 25 = \textbf{130 yd}$

22. $P = \left(7 + 14 + 7 + \dfrac{2\pi(7)}{2}\right)$ yd

$\quad = (28 + 7\pi)$ **yd** $=$ **49.98 yd**

23.

Area $= (6\text{ cm})(3\text{ cm}) + (4\text{ cm})(3\text{ cm})$

$\quad\quad = 18\text{ cm}^2 + 12\text{ cm}^2 = \textbf{30 cm}^2$

24. Area $= \dfrac{1}{2}(8\text{ cm})(6\text{ cm}) = \textbf{24 cm}^2$

25. $y = 180 - 90 - 45 = \textbf{45}$

26. $8\dfrac{1}{18} - 2\dfrac{1}{6} - 4\dfrac{1}{3} = 8\dfrac{1}{18} - 2\dfrac{3}{18} - 4\dfrac{6}{18}$

$\quad = 7\dfrac{19}{18} - 2\dfrac{3}{18} - 4\dfrac{6}{18} = 5\dfrac{16}{18} - 4\dfrac{6}{18}$

$\quad = 1\dfrac{10}{18} = \mathbf{1\dfrac{5}{9}}$

27. $3\dfrac{2}{3} \times 1\dfrac{4}{5} \times 2\dfrac{3}{11} = \dfrac{11}{3} \times \dfrac{9}{5} \times \dfrac{25}{11} = \textbf{15}$

28.
$$\begin{array}{r} 4.016 \\ + \ 0.984 \\ \hline \textbf{5.000} \end{array}$$

29.
$$\begin{array}{r} \textbf{0.02} \\ 416\overline{)8.32} \\ \underline{8\ 32} \end{array}$$

30. $33\dfrac{1}{3} - 5\dfrac{5}{6} = 33\dfrac{2}{6} - 5\dfrac{5}{6} = 32\dfrac{8}{6} - 5\dfrac{5}{6}$

$\quad = 27\dfrac{3}{6} = \mathbf{27\dfrac{1}{2}}$ **m**

Practice 9

a. $-4(2) = \textbf{-8}$

b. $3(-2) = \textbf{-6}$

c. $-4(+3) = \textbf{-12}$

d. $(-3)(-5) = \textbf{15}$

e. $\dfrac{4}{2} = \textbf{2}$

f. $\dfrac{-6}{3} = \textbf{-2}$

g. $\dfrac{8}{-4} = \textbf{-2}$

h. $\dfrac{-16}{-2} = \textbf{8}$

Problem Set 9

1. (a) **Positive number**

  (b) **Negative number**

2. (a) **–3**

  (b) **3**

  (c) **0**

3. The **opposite** of the number

4. $(2)(5) = \textbf{10}$

5. $-5(+2) = \textbf{-10}$

6. $5(-2) = \textbf{-10}$

7. $(-3)(-5) = \textbf{15}$

8. $-(2)(-3) = \textbf{6}$

9. $\dfrac{6}{3} = \textbf{2}$

10. $\dfrac{-18}{3} = \textbf{-6}$

11. $\dfrac{8}{-4} = \textbf{-2}$

12. $\dfrac{-16}{-2} = \textbf{8}$

13. $320 \text{ cm} \times \dfrac{1 \text{ in.}}{2.54 \text{ cm}} \times \dfrac{1 \text{ ft}}{12 \text{ in.}} = \dfrac{320}{(2.54)(12)} \text{ ft}$

    $= \mathbf{10.50 \text{ ft}}$

14. $65 \text{ m} \times \dfrac{100 \text{ cm}}{1 \text{ m}} \times \dfrac{1 \text{ in.}}{2.54 \text{ cm}} = \dfrac{65(100)}{(2.54)} \text{ in.}$

    $= \mathbf{2559.06 \text{ in.}}$

15.
$$P = 2l + 2w$$
$$40 \text{ in.} = 2l + 2(8 \text{ in.})$$
$$40 \text{ in.} = 2l + 16 \text{ in.}$$
$$40 \text{ in.} - 16 \text{ in.} = 2l$$
$$24 \text{ in.} = 2l$$
$$l = \dfrac{24 \text{ in.}}{2}$$
$$l = \mathbf{12 \text{ in.}}$$

16.
$$A = S^2$$
$$9 \text{ ft}^2 = S^2$$

    Each side is **3 ft** because $3 \text{ ft} \times 3 \text{ ft} = 9 \text{ ft}^2$.

17. $A = \pi r^2 = \pi(5 \text{ yd})^2 = 25\pi \text{ yd}^2 = \mathbf{78.5 \text{ yd}^2}$

18. $-6 - 4 - (3) - (-3) + 3$

    $= (-6) + (-4) + (-3) + (+3) + (+3) = \mathbf{-7}$

19. $-6 + (-3) - [-(-2)] + 7$

    $= (-6) + (-3) + (-2) + (+7) = \mathbf{-4}$

20. $-|-6| - [-(-2)] + 5 = (-6) + (-2) + (+5) = \mathbf{-3}$

21. $-7 - 4 - (-3) + |-3|$

    $= (-7) + (-4) + (+3) + (+3) = \mathbf{-5}$

22. $-3 + (-3) - (-5) - |7|$

    $= (-3) + (-3) + (+5) + (-7) = \mathbf{-8}$

23. $-|-5 + 3 - 2| + 2 = -|-4| + 2$

    $= (-4) + (+2) = \mathbf{-2}$

24. $P = (30 + 25 + 14 + 15 + 16 + 10) \text{ cm}$

    $= \mathbf{110 \text{ cm}}$

25. $P = \left(20 + 20 + 20 + \dfrac{2\pi(10)}{2}\right) \text{ cm}$

    $= \mathbf{(60 + 10\pi) \text{ cm} = 91.4 \text{ cm}}$

26.

    $\text{Area} = (2 \text{ m})(7 \text{ m}) + (5 \text{ m})(8 \text{ m})$

    $= 14 \text{ m}^2 + 40 \text{ m}^2 = \mathbf{54 \text{ m}^2}$

27. $\text{Area} = \dfrac{1}{2}(5 \text{ m})(6 \text{ m}) = \mathbf{15 \text{ m}^2}$

28.
```
   52.3
 - 15.26
  ------
  37.04
```

29.
```
    4.03
 × 0.220
 -------
   000
   806
  806
 -------
 0.88660
```

30. $20\dfrac{5}{12} - 6\dfrac{1}{4} = 20\dfrac{5}{12} - 6\dfrac{3}{12} = 14\dfrac{2}{12}$

    $= \mathbf{14\dfrac{1}{6} \text{ km}}$

Practice 10

a. $\dfrac{-3 - 2}{-2 + 8 - 6} = \dfrac{-5}{0}$, which is **undefined**

b. $\dfrac{-8 + 6 + 2}{8 - 4 - 4} = \dfrac{0}{0}$, which is **indeterminate**

c. $-(-4)(-1)(-4) = \mathbf{16}$

d. $2(-6)(10)(-2) = \mathbf{240}$

e. $44 \text{ mi} \cdot \text{mi} \times \dfrac{5280 \text{ ft}}{1 \text{ mi}} \times \dfrac{5280 \text{ ft}}{1 \text{ mi}}$

   $= \mathbf{44(5280)^2 \text{ ft}^2 = 1,226,649,600 \text{ ft}^2}$

f. $3500 \text{ cm} \cdot \text{cm} \times \dfrac{1 \text{ m}}{100 \text{ cm}} \times \dfrac{1 \text{ m}}{100 \text{ cm}}$

   $= \dfrac{3500}{(100)^2} \text{ m}^2 = \mathbf{0.35 \text{ m}^2}$

Problem Set 10

1. **Commutative property** of multiplication

2. (a) **Subtraction**

   (b) **Addition**

   (c) **Division**

   (d) **Multiplication**

3. (a) $-\dfrac{1}{3}$

   (b) $\dfrac{1}{3}$

   (c) **0**

4. The **opposite** of the number

5. $-2(3)(4) = \mathbf{-24}$

6. $-4(3)(-2) = \mathbf{24}$

7. $4(-3)(-4) = \mathbf{48}$

8. $\dfrac{-2 + 3}{4 - 5 + 3} = \dfrac{1}{4 - 5 + 3} = \dfrac{1}{2}$

9. $\dfrac{4 + 7 - 6}{2 + 7 - 3} = \dfrac{5}{2 + 7 - 3} = \dfrac{5}{6}$

10. $\dfrac{-3 + 6 - 1}{-2 + 4 - 2} = \dfrac{2}{-2 + 4 - 2} = \dfrac{2}{0}$

    which is **undefined**

11. $50 \text{ in.} \times \dfrac{2.54 \text{ cm}}{1 \text{ in.}} = 50(2.54) \text{ cm} = \mathbf{127\ cm}$

12. $48 \text{ in.} \cdot \text{ in.} \times \dfrac{2.54 \text{ cm}}{1 \text{ in.}} \times \dfrac{2.54 \text{ cm}}{1 \text{ in.}}$

    $= \mathbf{48(2.54)^2\ cm^2 = 309.68\ cm^2}$

13.
$$P = 2l + 2w$$
$$28 \text{ cm} = 2(9 \text{ cm}) + 2w$$
$$28 \text{ cm} = 18 \text{ cm} + 2w$$
$$28 \text{ cm} - 18 \text{ cm} = 2w$$
$$10 \text{ cm} = 2w$$
$$w = \dfrac{10 \text{ cm}}{2}$$
$$w = \mathbf{5\ cm}$$

14. $A = (15 \text{ m})(8 \text{ m}) = \mathbf{120\ m^2}$

15. $C = \pi D = \pi(16 \text{ in.}) = 16\pi \text{ in.} = \mathbf{50.24\ in.}$

16. $A = \pi r^2 = \pi(6 \text{ ft})^2 = 36\pi \text{ ft}^2 = \mathbf{113.04\ ft^2}$

17. $\dfrac{-8}{2} = \mathbf{-4}$

18. $\dfrac{9}{-3} = \mathbf{-3}$

19. $3 - (-4) + (-3) - (-4)$
    $= (+3) + (+4) + (-3) + (+4) = \mathbf{8}$

20. $-[-(-4)] - (-3) + 2 = (-4) + (+3) + (+2) = \mathbf{1}$

21. $-|-3 - 2| + (-5) = -|-5| + (-5)$
    $= (-5) + (-5) = \mathbf{-10}$

22. $-\{-[-(-2)]\} - |-4 - 2| = (+2) + (-6) = \mathbf{-4}$

23. $3 - |-2 - 3| + (-6) - (-3)$
    $= (+3) + (-5) + (-6) + (+3) = \mathbf{-5}$

24. $P = (31 + 26 + 10 + 18 + 11 + 18 + 10$
    $+ \ 26) \text{ yd}$
    $= \mathbf{150\ yd}$

25.

$A = (12 \text{ cm})(5 \text{ cm}) + (10 \text{ cm})(8 \text{ cm})$
$= 60 \text{ cm}^2 + 80 \text{ cm}^2 = \mathbf{140\ cm^2}$

26. $A = \dfrac{1}{2}(8 \text{ cm})(5 \text{ cm}) = \mathbf{20\ cm^2}$

27. $A = (4 \text{ cm})(4 \text{ cm}) + \dfrac{1}{2}\pi(2 \text{ cm})^2$

    $= 16 \text{ cm}^2 + \dfrac{1}{2}\pi(4 \text{ cm}^2)$

    $= (16 + 2\pi) \text{ cm}^2 = \mathbf{22.28\ cm^2}$

28. $\dfrac{3\frac{3}{5}}{2\frac{7}{10}} = \dfrac{18}{5} \div \dfrac{27}{10} = \dfrac{18}{5} \times \dfrac{10}{27} = \dfrac{4}{3} = \mathbf{1\dfrac{1}{3}}$

29.
$$
\begin{array}{r}
3.03 \\
28\overline{)84.84} \\
\underline{84} \\
84 \\
\underline{84}
\end{array}
$$

30. $3\dfrac{8}{21} + 3\dfrac{2}{7} = 3\dfrac{8}{21} + 3\dfrac{6}{21} = 6\dfrac{14}{21} = \mathbf{6\dfrac{2}{3}\ m}$

Practice 11

a. $6 \cdot 3 - 4(5)(6) = 18 - 120 = \mathbf{-102}$

b. $3 \cdot 5 + 2 + 4(-2) = 15 + 2 - 8 = \mathbf{9}$

c. $2 \cdot 4 - 3 \cdot 2 - 7 + 5 \cdot 2 = 8 - 6 - 7 + 10$
   $= \mathbf{5}$

d. $13 - 4(-5) - 3(10) = 13 + 20 - 30 = \mathbf{3}$

Problem Set 11

1. (a) $\dfrac{1}{2}$

    (b) $-\dfrac{1}{2}$

    (c) **1**

2. Multiplicative inverse

3. The only real number that does not have a reciprocal is **zero** because **division by zero is undefined.**

4. Yes

5. An acute angle is an angle that is smaller than a right angle.

6. An obtuse angle is an angle that is larger than a right angle and smaller than a straight angle.

7. $25 \text{ m} \times \dfrac{100 \text{ cm}}{1 \text{ m}} = 25(100) \text{ cm} = \mathbf{2500 \text{ cm}}$

8. $40 \text{ m} \cdot \text{m} \times \dfrac{100 \text{ cm}}{1 \text{ m}} \times \dfrac{100 \text{ cm}}{1 \text{ m}} = 40(100)^2 \text{ cm}^2$

    $= \mathbf{400{,}000 \text{ cm}^2}$

9. $l = 49 \text{ in.} \div 4 = \mathbf{12\dfrac{1}{4} \text{ in.}}$

10. $A = S^2$

    $16 \text{ ft}^2 = S^2$

    Each side is **4 ft** because $4 \text{ ft} \times 4 \text{ ft} = 16 \text{ ft}^2$.

11. $r = D \div 2 = 14 \text{ yd} \div 2 = 7 \text{ yd}$

    $A = \pi r^2 = \pi(7 \text{ yd})^2 = \mathbf{49\pi \text{ yd}^2} = \mathbf{153.86 \text{ yd}^2}$

12. $6 - 8 + 2(3) = 6 - 8 + 6 = \mathbf{4}$

13. $-2 - 3(+6) = -2 - 18 = \mathbf{-20}$

14. $3 - 2 \cdot 4 + 3 \cdot 2 = 3 - 8 + 6 = \mathbf{1}$

15. $-3(-2)(-3) - 2 = -18 - 2 = \mathbf{-20}$

16. $-4(-3) + (-2)(-5) = 12 + 10 = \mathbf{22}$

17. $-2 - 2(-2) + (-2)(-2) = -2 + 4 + 4 = \mathbf{6}$

18. $(-5) - (-5) + 2(-2) + 4 = -5 + 5 - 4 + 4 = \mathbf{0}$

19. $-3 - (-2) + (-3) - 2(-2) = -3 + 2 - 3 + 4 = \mathbf{0}$

20. $(-2)(-2)(-2) - |-8| = -8 - 8 = \mathbf{-16}$

21. $-(-5) + (-2) + (-5)|-3| = 5 - 2 + (-5)(3)$

    $= 3 - 15 = \mathbf{-12}$

22. $4 + |-3 - 1| + (-3) - (-2)$

    $= 4 + |-4| - 3 + 2 = 4 + 4 - 3 + 2 = \mathbf{7}$

23. $3(-2) - |-3 + 6| + 9 - 7(-2)$

    $= -6 - |3| + 9 + 14 = -6 - 3 + 9 + 14 = \mathbf{14}$

24. $\dfrac{-3 + 5}{4 - 6 + 5} = \dfrac{2}{4 - 6 + 5} = \dfrac{2}{-2 + 5} = \mathbf{\dfrac{2}{3}}$

25. $\dfrac{-6 + 4 + 2}{-2 + 5 + 3} = \dfrac{-2 + 2}{3 + 3} = \dfrac{0}{6} = \mathbf{0}$

26. $P = \left(15 + 8 + 15 + \dfrac{2\pi(4)}{2}\right) \text{ cm}$

    $= (38 + 4\pi) \text{ cm} = \mathbf{50.56 \text{ cm}}$

27.

    $A = (5 \text{ m})(8 \text{ m}) + (10 \text{ m})(14 \text{ m})$

    $= 40 \text{ m}^2 + 140 \text{ m}^2 = \mathbf{180 \text{ m}^2}$

28. $A = \dfrac{1}{2}(10 \text{ m})(7 \text{ m}) = \mathbf{35 \text{ m}^2}$

29. Area $= \text{Area}_{\text{rectangle}} - \text{Area}_{\text{square}}$

    $= (8 \text{ in.})(11 \text{ in.}) - (5 \text{ in.})(5 \text{ in.})$

    $= 88 \text{ in.}^2 - 25 \text{ in.}^2 = \mathbf{63 \text{ in.}^2}$

30. $26\dfrac{1}{2} - 8\dfrac{3}{10} = 26\dfrac{5}{10} - 8\dfrac{3}{10} = 18\dfrac{2}{10} = \mathbf{18\dfrac{1}{5} \text{ ft}}$

Practice 12

a. $(-3 - 2)(-4 - 1) = (-5)(-5) = \mathbf{25}$

b. $(6 - 2) - (4 - 6) = 4 - (-2) = 4 + 2 = \mathbf{6}$

c. $-5(-3 - 3) + 2(1 - 3) = -5(-6) + 2(-2)$

    $= 30 - 4 = \mathbf{26}$

d. $\dfrac{-3(10 - 8) - (-4)}{4 - 3(-3) - 13} = \dfrac{-3(2) + 4}{4 + 9 - 13} = \dfrac{-6 + 4}{13 - 13}$

    $= \dfrac{-2}{0}$, which is **undefined**

Problem Set 12

1. (a) **2**

   (b) **–2**

   (c) **1**

2. **Multiplicative inverse**

3. The only real number that does not have a reciprocal is **zero** because **division by zero is undefined.**

4. **No**

5. (a) **90°**

   (b) **180°**

   (c) **360°**

6. $80 \text{ ft} \times \dfrac{12 \text{ in.}}{1 \text{ ft}} \times \dfrac{2.54 \text{ cm}}{1 \text{ in.}} = \textbf{80(12)(2.54) cm}$

   $= \textbf{2438.4 cm}$

7. $12 \text{ ft} \cdot \text{ft} \times \dfrac{12 \text{ in.}}{1 \text{ ft}} \times \dfrac{12 \text{ in.}}{1 \text{ ft}} = \textbf{12(12)}^2 \textbf{ in.}^2$

   $= \textbf{1728 in.}^2$

8. $A = lw$

   $18 \text{ cm}^2 = (6 \text{ cm})w$

   $w = \dfrac{18 \text{ cm}^2}{6 \text{ cm}}$

   $w = \textbf{3 cm}$

9. $C = 2\pi r$

   $6\pi \text{ m} = 2\pi r$

   $6(3.14) \text{ m} = 2(3.14)r$

   $18.84 \text{ m} = 6.28r$

   $r = \dfrac{18.84 \text{ m}}{6.28}$

   $r = \textbf{3 m}$

10. $(-4 + 7) + (-3 - 2) = 3 + (-5) = \textbf{–2}$

11. $(-3 - 2) - (-6 + 2) = -5 - (-4) = -5 + 4$

    $= \textbf{–1}$

12. $(-2 - 2)(-3 - 4) = (-4)(-7) = \textbf{28}$

13. $4(8 + 4) + 7(10 - 8) = 4(12) + 7(2)$

    $= 48 + 14 = \textbf{62}$

14. $5(9 + 2) - (-4)(5 + 1) = 5(11) + 4(6)$

    $= 55 + 24 = \textbf{79}$

15. $-3(-6 - 2) + 3(-2 + 5) = -3(-8) + 3(3)$

    $= 24 + 9 = \textbf{33}$

16. $-2(-5 - 7) - 3(-8 + 2) = -2(-12) - 3(-6)$

    $= 24 + 18 = \textbf{42}$

17. $(-3 - 2)(-2)(-2 - 2) = (-5)(-2)(-4) = \textbf{–40}$

18. $(6 - 2)(-3 - 5) - (-5) = (4)(-8) + 5$

    $= -32 + 5 = \textbf{–27}$

19. $-8 - 4 - (-2) - (+2)(-3) = -12 + 2 + 6 = \textbf{–4}$

20. $\dfrac{1}{4}(8 - 4) - 5(8 - 2) - 2 = \dfrac{1}{4}(4) - 5(6) - 2$

    $= 1 - 30 - 2 = \textbf{–31}$

21. $5(12 + 2) - 6(-3 + 8) - (2 + 3)$

    $= 5(14) - 6(5) - 5 = 70 - 30 - 5 = \textbf{35}$

22. $(2 - 3)(-8 + 2) + |-3 + 5| = (-1)(-6) + |2|$

    $= 6 + 2 = \textbf{8}$

23. $-|-2 - 5 + 3|(5 - 2) = -|-4|(3) = -4(3) = \textbf{–12}$

24. $4 - \dfrac{(+12)}{(-3)} + 2 = 4 - (-4) + 2 = 4 + 4 + 2$

    $= \textbf{10}$

25. $\dfrac{-4(5 - 2) - (-8)}{3 - (-3)(3)} = \dfrac{-4(3) + 8}{3 + 9} = \dfrac{-12 + 8}{12}$

    $= \dfrac{-4}{12} = -\dfrac{1}{3}$

26. $P = \left(8 + 10 + 8 + \dfrac{2\pi(5)}{2}\right) \text{ km}$

    $= \textbf{(26 + 5}\boldsymbol{\pi}\textbf{) km} = \textbf{41.7 km}$

27.

    $A = (6 \text{ in.})(7 \text{ in.}) + (17 \text{ in.})(6 \text{ in.})$

    $= 42 \text{ in.}^2 + 102 \text{ in.}^2 = \textbf{144 in.}^2$

28.

    $A = (6 \text{ in.})(4 \text{ in.}) + \dfrac{1}{2}(3 \text{ in.})(4 \text{ in.})$

    $= 24 \text{ in.}^2 + 6 \text{ in.}^2 = \textbf{30 in.}^2$

29. Area = Area$_{\text{large rectangle}}$ − Area$_{\text{small rectangle}}$

$= (14\,\text{ft})(6\,\text{ft}) - (7\,\text{ft})(2\,\text{ft})$

$= 84\,\text{ft}^2 - 14\,\text{ft}^2 = \mathbf{70\,ft^2}$

30. $y = 180 - 90 - 30 = \mathbf{60}$

Practice 13

a. $3\{2[(-4 - 3)(-8 - 2) - 4]\}$

$= 3\{2[(-7)(-10) - 4]\}$

$= 3[2(70 - 4)] = 3[2(66)] = \mathbf{396}$

b. $\dfrac{-3\{[(-4 - 1)3] - 5\}}{2(4 - 7)} = \dfrac{-3\{[(-5)3] - 5\}}{2(-3)}$

$= \dfrac{-3(-15 - 5)}{-6} = \dfrac{-3(-20)}{-6} = \dfrac{60}{-6} = \mathbf{-10}$

c. $(-2)(-2)(-3)(-3) = \mathbf{36}$

d. $-\{-[-(-2)]\} = \mathbf{2}$

e. The product is a **negative number** because **the number of negative signs in the product is odd.**

Problem Set 13

1. **Negative number**

2. (a) $\dfrac{1}{3}$

(b) $-\dfrac{1}{3}$

(c) **1**

3. **Reciprocal**

4. The only real number that does not have a multiplicative inverse is **zero** because **division by zero is undefined.**

5. **Equilateral polygons**

6. $60\,\text{mi} \times \dfrac{5280\,\text{ft}}{1\,\text{mi}} \times \dfrac{12\,\text{in.}}{1\,\text{ft}} = \mathbf{60(5280)(12)\,in.}$

$= \mathbf{3,801,600\,in.}$

7. $125\,\text{mi} \cdot \text{mi} \times \dfrac{5280\,\text{ft}}{1\,\text{mi}} \times \dfrac{5280\,\text{ft}}{1\,\text{mi}}$

$= \mathbf{125(5280)^2\,ft^2 = 3,484,800,000\,ft^2}$

8. $A = lw$

$35\,\text{cm}^2 = l(5\,\text{cm})$

$l = \dfrac{35\,\text{cm}^2}{5\,\text{cm}}$

$l = \mathbf{7\,cm}$

9. $r = D \div 2 = 6\,\text{m} \div 2 = 3\,\text{m}$

$A = \pi r^2 = \pi(3\,\text{m})^2 = 9\pi\,\text{m}^2 = \mathbf{28.26\,m^2}$

10. $-[-(-2)] = \mathbf{-2}$

11. $-\{-[-(-3)]\} = \mathbf{3}$

12. $(-3 - 2) - (5 + 2) = -5 - 7 = \mathbf{-12}$

13. $(-3 + 5)(2 - 3) = (2)(-1) = \mathbf{-2}$

14. $-2(-6 - 3) + \dfrac{0}{5} = -2(-9) + 0 = \mathbf{18}$

15. $-2 + (-2) - (-4)5 = -4 + 20 = \mathbf{16}$

16. $-3 - (2) + (-2) - (-3)(-2) = -3 - 2 - 2 - 6$

$= \mathbf{-13}$

17. $-5(-3 - 2) + (-2) - (-3 - 4)$

$= -5(-5) - 2 - (-7) = 25 - 2 + 7 = \mathbf{30}$

18. $(-2)(-3)(-4 + 2) - (3 + 1) = 6(-2) - 4$

$= -12 - 4 = \mathbf{-16}$

19. $-2 - (-2) - |-2|(2) = -2 + 2 - 4 = \mathbf{-4}$

20. $\dfrac{-6}{-10} + (-3)(-2) + 3|-4 - 2|$

$= \dfrac{3}{5} + 6 + 3(6) = \dfrac{3}{5} + 6 + 18 = \mathbf{24\dfrac{3}{5}}$

21. $(-7) - [-(-2)]5 = -7 - 2(5) = -7 - 10 = \mathbf{-17}$

22. $-3 - [-(-2)] + (-3)(5) = -3 - 2 - 15 = \mathbf{-20}$

23. $\dfrac{-2(-6) - 2}{-3 + (-7 + 2)} = \dfrac{12 - 2}{-3 + (-5)} = \dfrac{10}{-8} = -\dfrac{5}{4}$

$= \mathbf{-1\dfrac{1}{4}}$

24. $\dfrac{4 + 2 - 3(2)}{3(2) - 6} = \dfrac{6 - 6}{6 - 6} = \dfrac{0}{0}$

which is **indeterminate**

25. $P = (34 + 20 + 17 + 16 + 12 + 16 + 5$

$+ 20)\,\text{in.}$

$= \mathbf{140\,in.}$

26.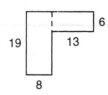

$$\text{Area} = (19 \text{ ft})(8 \text{ ft}) + (13 \text{ ft})(6 \text{ ft})$$
$$= 152 \text{ ft}^2 + 78 \text{ ft}^2 = \mathbf{230 \text{ ft}^2}$$

27.

$$\text{Area} = \frac{1}{2}(6 \text{ ft})(8 \text{ ft}) + (5 \text{ ft})(8 \text{ ft})$$
$$= 24 \text{ ft}^2 + 40 \text{ ft}^2 = \mathbf{64 \text{ ft}^2}$$

28. $\text{Area} = (8 \text{ ft})(6 \text{ ft}) + \frac{1}{2}\pi(3 \text{ ft})^2$

$$= 48 \text{ ft}^2 + \frac{1}{2}\pi(9) \text{ ft}^2$$

$$= \left(48 + \frac{9\pi}{2}\right) \text{ ft}^2 = \mathbf{62.13 \text{ ft}^2}$$

29. $\text{Area} = \text{Area}_{\text{rectangle}} - \text{Area}_{\text{triangle}}$

$$= (12 \text{ yd})(7 \text{ yd}) - \frac{1}{2}(7 \text{ yd})(4 \text{ yd})$$

$$= 84 \text{ yd}^2 - 14 \text{ yd}^2 = \mathbf{70 \text{ yd}^2}$$

30. $15\frac{4}{5} - 4\frac{2}{15} = 15\frac{12}{15} - 4\frac{2}{15} = 11\frac{10}{15} = \mathbf{11\frac{2}{3} \text{ mi}}$

Practice 14

a. $x - xy = -2 - (-2)(3) = -2 + 6 = \mathbf{4}$

b. $a - (ab - a) = -4 - [(-4)(-2) - (-4)]$
$$= -4 - (8 + 4) = -4 - 12 = \mathbf{-16}$$

c. $x - ab(a - b) = -3 - (-2)(-4)[-2 - (-4)]$
$$= -3 - 8(-2 + 4) = -3 - 8(2) = -3 - 16$$
$$= \mathbf{-19}$$

d. $-xa(a + x) + x$
$$= -(-4)(-2)[(-2) + (-4)] + (-4)$$
$$= -8(-6) + (-4) = 48 - 4 = \mathbf{44}$$

Problem Set 14

1. A numerical expression contains only numbers. An algebraic expression may contain numbers and may contain letters.

2. The value of an expression is the number it represents.

3. (a) A variable of an algebraic expression is a letter that represents an unspecified number.

   (b) A variable

4. Positive number

5. Equiangular polygons

6. $300 \text{ in.} \times \dfrac{2.54 \text{ cm}}{1 \text{ in.}} \times \dfrac{1 \text{ m}}{100 \text{ cm}} = \dfrac{300(2.54)}{(100)} \text{ m}$
$$= \mathbf{7.62 \text{ m}}$$

7. $100 \text{ yd} \cdot \text{yd} \times \dfrac{3 \text{ ft}}{1 \text{ yd}} \times \dfrac{3 \text{ ft}}{1 \text{ yd}} = 100(3)^2 \text{ ft}^2$
$$= \mathbf{900 \text{ ft}^2}$$

8. $A = lw$
$$44 \text{ in.}^2 = (11 \text{ in.})w$$
$$w = \frac{44 \text{ in.}^2}{11 \text{ in.}}$$
$$w = \mathbf{4 \text{ in.}}$$

9. $C = 2\pi r$
$$8\pi \text{ ft} = 2\pi r$$
$$8(3.14) \text{ ft} = 2(3.14)r$$
$$25.12 \text{ ft} = 6.28r$$
$$r = \frac{25.12 \text{ ft}}{6.28}$$
$$r = \mathbf{4 \text{ ft}}$$

10. $xm - 2m = (-2)(-3) - 2(-3) = 6 + 6 = \mathbf{12}$

11. $ma - m - a = (-2)(-4) - (-2) - (-4)$
$$= 8 + 2 + 4 = \mathbf{14}$$

12. $2abc - 3ab = 2(2)(-3)(4) - 3(2)(-3)$
$$= -48 + 18 = \mathbf{-30}$$

13. $-x(a + b) = -4[-3 + (-5)] = -4(-8) = \mathbf{32}$

14. $-a + b + ab = -(-5) + (-2) + (-5)(-2)$
$$= 5 - 2 + 10 = \mathbf{13}$$

15. $x - y(a - x) = -3 - 4[4 - (-3)]$
$$= -3 - 4(7) = -3 - 28 = \mathbf{-31}$$

16. $-(m - x)(a - mx) = -[3 - (-4)][-2 - 3(-4)]$
$$= (-7)(-2 + 12) = (-7)(10) = \mathbf{-70}$$

17. $-xa(x + a) - a = -2(-4)[2 + (-4)] - (-4)$
$$= 8(-2) + 4 = -16 + 4 = \mathbf{-12}$$

18. $-xy - (-x + y) = -(-3)(-4) - [-(-3) + (-4)]$
    $= -12 - (3 - 4) = -12 - (-1) = -12 + 1 = \mathbf{-11}$

19. $-2(-1 - 4)(5 - 6) + 3 = -2(-5)(-1) + 3$
    $= -10 + 3 = \mathbf{-7}$

20. $-4 - [-(-5)] + |-6| = -4 - 5 + 6 = \mathbf{-3}$

21. $-|-3|(2 - 5) - [-(-3)] = -3(-3) - 3$
    $= 9 - 3 = \mathbf{6}$

22. $-2[-3(-2 - 5)(3)] = -2[-3(-7)(3)] = -2(63)$
    $= \mathbf{-126}$

23. $\dfrac{-2[-(-3)]}{(-2)(-4 + 3)} = \dfrac{-2(3)}{(-2)(-1)} = \dfrac{-6}{2} = \mathbf{-3}$

24. $\dfrac{(-5 - 2) + (-3 - 2)}{-3 - (-2)} = \dfrac{-7 + (-5)}{-3 + 2} = \dfrac{-12}{-1} = \mathbf{12}$

25. $P = \left(16 + 18 + 16 + \dfrac{2\pi(9)}{2}\right)$ yd
    $= \mathbf{(50 + 9\pi)}$ **yd** $= \mathbf{78.26}$ **yd**

26.

    $A = (20\text{ cm})(10\text{ cm}) + (40\text{ cm})(10\text{ cm})$
    $= 200\text{ cm}^2 + 400\text{ cm}^2 = \mathbf{600\ cm^2}$

27. $A = (5\text{ cm})(4\text{ cm}) + \dfrac{\pi(2\text{ cm})^2}{2}$
    $= \mathbf{(20 + 2\pi)\ cm^2} = \mathbf{26.28\ cm^2}$

28. Area $=$ Area$_{\text{large triangle}}$ $-$ Area$_{\text{small triangle}}$
    $= \dfrac{1}{2}(16\text{ m})(8\text{ m}) - \dfrac{1}{2}(4\text{ m})(2\text{ m})$
    $= 64\text{ m}^2 - 4\text{ m}^2 = \mathbf{60\ m^2}$

29. $x = 180 - 130 - 25 = \mathbf{25}$

30.
$$\begin{array}{r} 0.06 \\ 102\overline{)6.12} \\ \underline{6\ 12} \end{array}$$

Practice 15

a. $S.A. = 2(\text{Area}_{\text{top}}) + 2(\text{Area}_{\text{front}}) + 2(\text{Area}_{\text{side}})$
    $= 2(4\text{ in.} \times 3\text{ in.}) + 2(2\text{ in.} \times 4\text{ in.})$
    $+ 2(2\text{ in.} \times 3\text{ in.})$
    $= 2(12\text{ in.}^2) + 2(8\text{ in.}^2) + 2(6\text{ in.}^2)$
    $= 24\text{ in.}^2 + 16\text{ in.}^2 + 12\text{ in.}^2$
    $= \mathbf{52\ in.^2}$

b. $S.A. = 2(\text{Area}_{\text{triangle}}) + \text{Area}_{\text{bottom}} + \text{Area}_{\text{back}}$
    $+ \text{Area}_{\text{top}}$
    $= 2\left[\dfrac{1}{2}(8\text{ ft} \times 6\text{ ft})\right] + (8\text{ ft} \times 12\text{ ft})$
    $+ (6\text{ ft} \times 12\text{ ft}) + (10\text{ ft} \times 12\text{ ft})$
    $= 2(24\text{ ft}^2) + 96\text{ ft}^2 + 72\text{ ft}^2 + 120\text{ ft}^2$
    $= 48\text{ ft}^2 + 288\text{ ft}^2$
    $= \mathbf{336\ ft^2}$

c. $S.A. = 2(\text{Area}_{\text{base}}) + \text{Lateral Surface Area}$
    $= 2[\pi(20\text{ cm})^2] + (\text{Perimeter}_{\text{base}})(\text{Length})$
    $= 800\pi\text{ cm}^2 + [2\pi(20\text{ cm})](200\text{ cm})$
    $= 800\pi\text{ cm}^2 + 8000\pi\text{ cm}^2$
    $= \mathbf{8800\pi\ cm^2} = \mathbf{27{,}632\ cm^2}$

d. $S.A. = 2(\text{Area}_{\text{base}}) + \text{Lateral Surface Area}$
    $= 2\left[\dfrac{1}{2}(6\text{ m} \times 8\text{ m}) + \dfrac{1}{2}\pi(3\text{ m})^2\right]$
    $+ (\text{Perimeter}_{\text{base}})(\text{Height})$
    $= 2\left(24\text{ m}^2 + \dfrac{9\pi}{2}\text{ m}^2\right)$
    $+ \left(10\text{ m} + 8\text{ m} + \dfrac{2\pi(3)}{2}\text{ m}\right)(10\text{ m})$
    $= 2\left(24\text{ m}^2 + \dfrac{9\pi}{2}\text{ m}^2\right)$
    $+ (18\text{ m} + 3\pi\text{ m})(10\text{ m})$
    $= 48\text{ m}^2 + 9\pi\text{ m}^2 + 180\text{ m}^2 + 30\pi\text{ m}^2$
    $= \mathbf{(228 + 39\pi)\ m^2} = \mathbf{350.46\ m^2}$

Problem Set 15

1. (a) **Surface area**

   (b) To find the lateral surface area of a right solid, **multiply the perimeter of a base by the height of the right solid.**

2. (a) **3**

   (b) **–3**

   (c) **1**

3. **Reciprocal**

4. The only real number that does not have a multiplicative inverse is **zero** because **division by zero is undefined.**

5. $112\text{ ft} \times \dfrac{12\text{ in.}}{1\text{ ft}} \times \dfrac{2.54\text{ cm}}{1\text{ in.}}$
   $= 112(12)(2.54)\text{ cm} = \mathbf{3413.76\ cm}$

6. $60 \text{ km} \cdot \text{km} \times \dfrac{1000 \text{ m}}{1 \text{ km}} \times \dfrac{1000 \text{ m}}{1 \text{ km}}$

$= 60(1000)^2 \text{ m}^2 = \mathbf{60{,}000{,}000 \text{ m}^2}$

7. $\qquad A = lw$

$72 \text{ cm}^2 = (6 \text{ cm})w$

$w = \dfrac{72 \text{ cm}^2}{6 \text{ cm}}$

$w = \mathbf{12 \text{ cm}}$

8. $A = \dfrac{1}{2}(12 \text{ m})(9 \text{ m}) = \mathbf{54 \text{ m}^2}$

9. $r = D \div 2 = 16 \text{ km} \div 2 = 8 \text{ km}$

$A = \pi r^2 = \pi(8 \text{ km})^2 = \mathbf{64\pi \text{ km}^2} = \mathbf{200.96 \text{ km}^2}$

10. $a - ab = 2 - 2(-3) = 2 - (-6) = 2 + 6 = \mathbf{8}$

11. $xy - 3y = 2(4) - 3(4) = 8 - 12 = \mathbf{-4}$

12. $2ab - 3abc = 2(-1)(2) - 3(-1)(2)(3)$

$= -4 + 18 = \mathbf{14}$

13. $-x(a - b) = -(-2)[3 - (-1)] = 2(4) = \mathbf{8}$

14. $-x - (-a + b) = -3 - [-(-2) + 4]$

$= -3 - (2 + 4) = -3 - 6 = \mathbf{-9}$

15. $(x - y)(y - x) = (-2 - 3)[3 - (-2)]$

$= (-5)(5) = \mathbf{-25}$

16. $(-x) + (-y) = [-(-3)] + (-2) = 3 + (-2) = \mathbf{1}$

17. $-c - (p - c) = -2 - (-5 - 2) = -2 - (-7)$

$= -2 + 7 = \mathbf{5}$

18. $(a - x)(ma - x) = [-3 - (-4)][5(-3) - (-4)]$

$= (-3 + 4)(-15 + 4) = (1)(-11) = \mathbf{-11}$

19. $-2(-6 - 1 - 2) - (-2 + 7)$

$= -2(-9) - (5) = 18 - 5 = \mathbf{13}$

20. $-|-11| + (-3)|-3 + 5| = -11 - 3(2)$

$= -11 - 6 = \mathbf{-17}$

21. $-3(-3)(-2 - 5 + |-11|) = 9(-7 + 11)$

$= 9(4) = \mathbf{36}$

22. $-3\{[(-5 - 2)](-1)\} = -3[(-7)(-1)] = -3(7)$

$= \mathbf{-21}$

23. $\dfrac{-4 - (-1 - 3)}{-7 - (-9 + 2)} = \dfrac{-4 - (-4)}{-7 - (-7)} = \dfrac{0}{0}$

which is **indeterminate**

24. $\dfrac{3(-5 + 2) + 6(-4 + 10) - 2}{(10 - 2) + 7 + 5}$

$= \dfrac{3(-3) + 6(6) - 2}{8 + 7 + 5} = \dfrac{-9 + 36 - 2}{20}$

$= \dfrac{25}{20} = \dfrac{5}{4} = \mathbf{1\dfrac{1}{4}}$

25. $P = (25 + 35 + 25 + 6 + 15 + 13 + 15$

$\qquad + 16) \text{ in.}$

$\quad = \mathbf{150 \text{ in.}}$

26. $A = (7 \text{ ft})(10 \text{ ft}) + \dfrac{\pi(5 \text{ ft})^2}{2}$

$= 70 \text{ ft}^2 + \dfrac{25\pi \text{ ft}^2}{2}$

$= \left(70 + \dfrac{25\pi}{2}\right) \text{ ft}^2 = \mathbf{109.25 \text{ ft}^2}$

27. $-2\dfrac{2}{3} + 2\dfrac{3}{5} = 2\dfrac{3}{5} - 2\dfrac{2}{3} = 2\dfrac{9}{15} - 2\dfrac{10}{15}$

$= -\dfrac{1}{15}$

28. $\dfrac{4\dfrac{2}{3}}{-3\dfrac{1}{9}} = \dfrac{14}{3} \div -\dfrac{28}{9} = \dfrac{14}{3} \times \dfrac{-9}{28} = -\dfrac{3}{2}$

$= -1\dfrac{1}{2}$

29. $5\dfrac{1}{3} + 8\dfrac{5}{12} = 5\dfrac{4}{12} + 8\dfrac{5}{12} = 13\dfrac{9}{12} = \mathbf{13\dfrac{3}{4} \text{ yd}}$

30. $S.A. = 2(\text{Area}_{\text{top}}) + 2(\text{Area}_{\text{front}}) + 2(\text{Area}_{\text{side}})$

$= 2(6 \text{ cm} \times 8 \text{ cm}) + 2(4 \text{ cm} \times 8 \text{ cm})$

$\quad + 2(4 \text{ cm} \times 6 \text{ cm})$

$= 2(48 \text{ cm}^2) + 2(32 \text{ cm}^2) + 2(24 \text{ cm}^2)$

$= 96 \text{ cm}^2 + 64 \text{ cm}^2 + 48 \text{ cm}^2$

$= \mathbf{208 \text{ cm}^2}$

Practice 16

a. $-a[-a(p - a)] = -2[-2(-4 - 2)]$

$= -2[-2(-6)] = -2(12) = \mathbf{-24}$

b. $pa[-p(-a)] = -2(-4)\{-(-2)[-(-4)]\}$

$= 8[2(4)] = 8(8) = \mathbf{64}$

c. $-x[-x(x - a) - (a - x)]$

$= -(-2)\{-(-2)[-2 - (-5)] - [-5 - (-2)]\}$

$= 2[2(-2 + 5) - (-5 + 2)]$

$= 2[2(3) - (-3)] = 2(6 + 3) = 2(9) = \mathbf{18}$

Problem Set 16

1. **Negative number**

2. (a) **Sum**

   (b) **Difference**

   (c) **Product**

   (d) **Quotient**

3. **Regular polygons**

4. $100 \text{ cm} \times \dfrac{1 \text{ in.}}{2.54 \text{ cm}} = \dfrac{100}{2.54} \text{ in.} = \mathbf{39.37 \text{ in.}}$

5. $152 \text{ cm} \cdot \text{cm} \times \dfrac{1 \text{ in.}}{2.54 \text{ cm}} \times \dfrac{1 \text{ in.}}{2.54 \text{ cm}}$

   $= \dfrac{152}{(2.54)^2} \text{ in.}^2 = \mathbf{23.56 \text{ in.}^2}$

6. $P = (31 + 11 + 31 + 11) \text{ in.} = \mathbf{84 \text{ in.}}$

7. $A = (17 \text{ ft})(13 \text{ ft}) = \mathbf{221 \text{ ft}^2}$

8. $A = \pi r^2 = \pi(9 \text{ yd})^2 = \mathbf{81\pi \text{ yd}^2} = \mathbf{254.34 \text{ yd}^2}$

9. $x - xy = -2 - (-2)(-3) = -2 - 6 = \mathbf{-8}$

10. $x(x - y) = -2[-2 - (-3)] = -2(-2 + 3)$

    $= -2(1) = \mathbf{-2}$

11. $(x - y)(y - x) = [2 - (-3)](-3 - 2)$

    $= (2 + 3)(-5) = 5(-5) = \mathbf{-25}$

12. $(x - y) - (x - y) = (-2 - 3) - (-2 - 3)$

    $= -5 - (-5) = -5 + 5 = \mathbf{0}$

13. $-xa(x - a) = -4(-2)[4 - (-2)] = 8(4 + 2)$

    $= 8(6) = \mathbf{48}$

14. $(-x + a) - (x - a) = [-(-4) + 5] - (-4 - 5)$

    $= (4 + 5) - (-9) = 9 - (-9) = 9 + 9 = \mathbf{18}$

15. $(p - x)(a - px) = [2 - (-4)][-3 - 2(-4)]$

    $= (2 + 4)(-3 + 8) = 6(5) = \mathbf{30}$

16. $-a[-a(x - a)] = -(-2)\{-(-2)[3 - (-2)]\}$

    $= 2[2(3 + 2)] = 2[2(5)] = 2(10) = \mathbf{20}$

17. $-a[(-x - a) - (x - y)]$

    $= -(-3)\{[-4 - (-3)] - [4 - (-5)]\}$

    $= 3[(-4 + 3) - (4 + 5)] = 3(-1 - 9)$

    $= 3(-10) = \mathbf{-30}$

18. $-3(-1 - 2)(4 - 5) + 6 = -3(-3)(-1) + 6$

    $= -9 + 6 = \mathbf{-3}$

19. $-2 + (-3) - |-5 + 2|3 = -5 - |-3|3$

    $= -5 - (3)3 = -5 - 9 = \mathbf{-14}$

20. $4[2(3 - 2) - (6 - 4)] = 4[2(1) - 2]$

    $= 4(2 - 2) = 4(0) = \mathbf{0}$

21. $-2(-4) - \{-[-(-6)]\} = 8 + 6 = \mathbf{14}$

22. $\dfrac{3(-2) - 5}{-3(-2)} = \dfrac{-6 - 5}{6} = \dfrac{-11}{6} = \mathbf{-1\dfrac{5}{6}}$

23. $\dfrac{-3(-6 - 2) + 5}{-3(-2 + 1)} = \dfrac{-3(-8) + 5}{-3(-1)} = \dfrac{24 + 5}{3}$

    $= \dfrac{29}{3} = \mathbf{9\dfrac{2}{3}}$

24. $P = \left(7 + 20 + 7 + \dfrac{2\pi(10)}{2}\right) \text{mi}$

    $= \mathbf{(34 + 10\pi) \text{ mi}} = \mathbf{65.4 \text{ mi}}$

25. $A = \dfrac{1}{2}(12 \text{ cm})(16 \text{ cm}) = \mathbf{96 \text{ cm}^2}$

26. $\text{Area} = \text{Area}_{\text{rectangle}} - \text{Area}_{\text{circle}}$

    $= (12 \text{ m} \times 20 \text{ m}) - [\pi(6 \text{ m})^2]$

    $= 240 \text{ m}^2 - 36\pi \text{ m}^2$

    $= \mathbf{(240 - 36\pi) \text{ m}^2} = \mathbf{126.96 \text{ m}^2}$

27. $y = 180 - 40 - 40 = \mathbf{100}$

28. $1\dfrac{7}{12} + 5\dfrac{5}{6} - 4\dfrac{2}{3} = 1\dfrac{7}{12} + 5\dfrac{10}{12} - 4\dfrac{8}{12}$

    $= 6\dfrac{17}{12} - 4\dfrac{8}{12} = 2\dfrac{9}{12} = \mathbf{2\dfrac{3}{4}}$

29. $2\dfrac{2}{5} \times 11\dfrac{2}{3} = \dfrac{12}{5} \times \dfrac{35}{3} = \mathbf{28}$

30. $S.A. = 2\left(\text{Area}_{\text{triangle}}\right) + \text{Area}_{\text{bottom}} + \text{Area}_{\text{side}}$

    $+ \text{Area}_{\text{top}}$

    $= 2\left[\dfrac{1}{2}(3 \text{ km} \times 4 \text{ km})\right] + (8 \text{ km} \times 4 \text{ km})$

    $+ (3 \text{ km} \times 8 \text{ km}) + (8 \text{ km} \times 5 \text{ km})$

    $= 2\left[\dfrac{1}{2}(12 \text{ km}^2)\right] + 32 \text{ km}^2 + 24 \text{ km}^2$

    $+ 40 \text{ km}^2$

    $= 2(6 \text{ km}^2) + 96 \text{ km}^2$

    $= 12 \text{ km}^2 + 96 \text{ km}^2$

    $= \mathbf{108 \text{ km}^2}$

Practice 17

a. $4(5 - 3) = 4(2) = \mathbf{8}$

b. $4(5 - 3) = 4(5) + 4(-3) = 20 - 12 = \mathbf{8}$

c. $a(b + c) = \mathbf{ab + ac}$

d. $4(6 - 2 + 5 - 7)$
$= 4(6) + 4(-2) + 4(5) + 4(-7)$
$= 24 - 8 + 20 - 28 = \mathbf{8}$

e. $2m(xy - 3p) = 2m(xy) + 2m(-3p) = \mathbf{2mxy - 6mp}$

f. $xy(a + b - 2c) = xy(a) + xy(b) + xy(-2c)$
$= \mathbf{axy + bxy - 2cxy}$

Problem Set 17

1. **The coefficient of an expression is any one factor of the expression, or any product of factors of the expression.**

2. (a) **A numerical coefficient of an expression is a coefficient that consists of numerals only.**

   (b) **A literal coefficient of an expression is a coefficient that consists of variables or letters only.**

3. **Commutative property of addition**

4. **Commutative property of multiplication**

5. $250 \text{ cm} \times \dfrac{1 \text{ m}}{100 \text{ cm}} = \dfrac{\mathbf{250}}{\mathbf{100}} \text{ m} = \mathbf{2.5 \text{ m}}$

6. $5000 \text{ cm} \cdot \text{cm} \times \dfrac{1 \text{ m}}{100 \text{ cm}} \times \dfrac{1 \text{ m}}{100 \text{ cm}}$

   $= \dfrac{\mathbf{5000}}{(100)^2} \text{ m}^2 = \mathbf{0.5 \text{ m}^2}$

7. $P = 4S$
   $64 \text{ cm} = 4S$
   $S = \dfrac{64 \text{ cm}}{4}$
   $S = \mathbf{16 \text{ cm}}$

8. $A = S^2$
   $25 \text{ m}^2 = S^2$
   Each side is **5 m** because $5 \text{ m} \times 5 \text{ m} = 25 \text{ m}^2$.

9. $A = \dfrac{1}{2}(6 \text{ in.})(8 \text{ in.}) = \mathbf{24 \text{ in.}^2}$

10. $-7(-8 + 3) = (-7)(-8) + (-7)(3) = 56 - 21 = \mathbf{35}$

11. $5(-3 - 6) = 5(-3) + 5(-6) = -15 - 30 = \mathbf{-45}$

12. $mx(ab - b) = (mx)(ab) + (mx)(-b)$
    $= \mathbf{mxab - mxb}$

13. $-4y(d + cx) = (-4y)(d) + (-4y)(cx)$
    $= \mathbf{-4yd - 4ycx}$

14. $(a + bc)2x = a(2x) + bc(2x) = \mathbf{2xa + 2xbc}$

15. $3a(x + 2y) = 3a(x) + 3a(2y) = \mathbf{3ax + 6ay}$

16. $-a(a - b) = -(-2)[-2 - (-7)] = 2(-2 + 7)$
    $= 2(5) = \mathbf{10}$

17. $(x - y) - (y - x) = [-2 - (-4)] - [-4 - (-2)]$
    $= (-2 + 4) - (-4 + 2) = 2 - (-2)$
    $= 2 + 2 = \mathbf{4}$

18. $x - 2a(-a) = 4 - 2(-3)[-(-3)]$
    $= 4 + 6(3) = 4 + 18 = \mathbf{22}$

19. $-x(a - xa) = -(-4)[-3 - (-4)(-3)] = 4(-3 - 12)$
    $= 4(-15) = \mathbf{-60}$

20. $-y[-ay - (xy)] = -(-3)[-(-2)(-3) - 2(-3)]$
    $= 3(-6 + 6) = 3(0) = \mathbf{0}$

21. $4[(2 - 4) - (6 - 3)] = 4(-2 - 3)$
    $= 4(-5) = \mathbf{-20}$

22. $-[-(-3)] - 2(-2) + (-3) = -3 + 4 - 3 = \mathbf{-2}$

23. $-|-2| + (-3) - 3 - (-4 - 2)$
    $= -2 - 3 - 3 - (-6) = -2 - 3 - 3 + 6 = \mathbf{-2}$

24. $-5(-2)(-2 - 3) - (-|-2|) = -5(-2)(-5) + |-2|$
    $= -50 + 2 = \mathbf{-48}$

25. $\dfrac{3 - (-2)(4)}{5 - (-3)} = \dfrac{3 - (-8)}{5 + 3} = \dfrac{3 + 8}{8} = \dfrac{11}{8} = \mathbf{1\dfrac{3}{8}}$

26. $\dfrac{3 + 7(-3)}{-6 - 2(-3)} = \dfrac{3 - 21}{-6 + 6} = \dfrac{-18}{0}$, which is **undefined**

27. $P = (31 + 26 + 16 + 18 + 9 + 18 + 6 + 26) \text{ ft}$
    $= \mathbf{150 \text{ ft}}$

28. $A = (5 \text{ yd} \times 8 \text{ yd}) + \dfrac{1}{2}\pi(4 \text{ yd})^2$

    $= 40 \text{ yd}^2 + \dfrac{1}{2}\pi(16 \text{ yd}^2)$

    $= \mathbf{(40 + 8\pi) \text{ yd}^2 = 65.12 \text{ yd}^2}$

29. $4\dfrac{1}{2} + 2\dfrac{3}{8} + 5\dfrac{1}{8} = 4\dfrac{4}{8} + 2\dfrac{3}{8} + 5\dfrac{1}{8}$

$= 6\dfrac{7}{8} + 5\dfrac{1}{8} = 11\dfrac{8}{8} = \mathbf{12\ mi}$

30. $S.A. = 2\left(\text{Area}_{\text{base}}\right) + \text{Lateral Surface Area}$

$= 2\left[\pi(2\ \text{cm})^2\right] + \left(\text{Perimeter}_{\text{base}}\right)(\text{Height})$

$= 2\left(4\pi\ \text{cm}^2\right) + \left[2\pi(2\ \text{cm})\right](4\ \text{cm})$

$= 8\pi\ \text{cm}^2 + 16\pi\ \text{cm}^2$

$= \mathbf{24\pi\ cm^2} = \mathbf{75.36\ cm^2}$

Practice 18

a. $-2xy + 3x + 4 - 4yx - 2x = \mathbf{-6xy + x + 4}$

b. $2xyz + 3xy - 5zyx = \mathbf{-3xyz + 3xy}$

c. $3yac - 2ac + 6acy = \mathbf{9acy - 2ac}$

d. $4 - x - 2xy + 3x - 7yx = \mathbf{4 + 2x - 9xy}$

Problem Set 18

1. A term of an algebraic expression is a single symbol, a product, or a quotient.

2. Terms of an algebraic expression can be called like terms when they have the same variables in the same or equivalent forms.

3. (a), (c), (d)

4. $a(b + c) = ab + ac$

5. $1500\ \text{cm} \times \dfrac{1\ \text{in.}}{2.54\ \text{cm}} \times \dfrac{1\ \text{ft}}{12\ \text{in.}} = \dfrac{1500}{(2.54)(12)}\ \text{ft}$

$= \mathbf{49.21\ ft}$

6. $1250\ \text{in.} \cdot \text{in.} \times \dfrac{1\ \text{ft}}{12\ \text{in.}} \times \dfrac{1\ \text{ft}}{12\ \text{in.}}$

$= \dfrac{1250}{(12)^2}\ \text{ft}^2 = \mathbf{8.68\ ft^2}$

7. $P = 2l + 2w$

$76\ \text{in.} = 2(22\ \text{in.}) + 2w$

$76\ \text{in.} = 44\ \text{in.} + 2w$

$76\ \text{in.} - 44\ \text{in.} = 2w$

$32\ \text{in.} = 2w$

$w = \dfrac{32\ \text{in.}}{2}$

$w = \mathbf{16\ in.}$

8. $A = \pi r^2 = \pi(9\ \text{ft})^2 = 81\pi\ \text{ft}^2 = \mathbf{254.34\ ft^2}$

9. $3xyz + 2zxy - 7zyx + 2xy = \mathbf{-2xyz + 2xy}$

10. $4x + 3 - 2xy - 5x - 7 + 4yx$

$= -x + 3 + 2xy - 7 = \mathbf{-x - 4 + 2xy}$

11. $(4 + 2y)x = 4x + 2yx = \mathbf{4x + 2xy}$

12. $3x(y - 2m) = 3xy + 3x(-2m) = \mathbf{3xy - 6mx}$

13. $2p(xy - 3k) = 2p(xy) + 2p(-3k) = \mathbf{2pxy - 6pk}$

14. $-a(x - a) = -(-3)\left[6 - (-3)\right]$

$= 3(6 + 3) = 3(9) = \mathbf{27}$

15. $-x - (-a)(a - x) = -(-2) - (-4)\left[4 - (-2)\right]$

$= 2 + 4(4 + 2) = 2 + 4(6) = 2 + 24 = \mathbf{26}$

16. $-p(-x) - px = -(-3)(-4) - (-3)(4)$

$= -12 + 12 = \mathbf{0}$

17. $-x(-y) - xy = -3\left[-(-2)\right] - 3(-2) = -6 + 6 = \mathbf{0}$

18. $(-a)(b)(-a + b) = -6(-3)\left[-6 + (-3)\right]$

$= 18(-9) = \mathbf{-162}$

19. $-6 - 2(-3)(-1) - 5(3 - 2 - 2)$

$= -6 - 6 - 5(-1) = -6 - 6 + 5 = \mathbf{-7}$

20. $-\left\{3(-2)(-4 + 2) - \left[3 - (-2)\right]\right\}$

$= -\left[-6(-2) - (3 + 2)\right] = -(12 - 5)$

$= -(7) = \mathbf{-7}$

21. $-4 - (-2) - \left[-(-2)\right] - |-3|$

$= -4 + 2 - 2 - 3 = \mathbf{-7}$

22. $-3 - 2(-4 + 7) - 5 - |-2 - 5|$

$= -3 - 2(3) - 5 - 7 = -3 - 6 - 5 - 7 = \mathbf{-21}$

23. $\dfrac{-2(-3 + 7)}{(-2)(-3)} = \dfrac{-2(4)}{6} = \dfrac{-8}{6} = \dfrac{-4}{3} = \mathbf{-1\dfrac{1}{3}}$

24. $\dfrac{-2 - 2(3) + 10}{3 - (-2)(-3)} = \dfrac{-2 - 6 + 10}{3 - 6} = \dfrac{2}{-3} = \mathbf{-\dfrac{2}{3}}$

25. $P = \left(6 + 24 + 6 + \dfrac{2\pi(12)}{2}\right)\ \text{yd}$

$= (36 + 12\pi)\ \text{yd} = \mathbf{73.68\ yd}$

26. $A = \dfrac{1}{2}(9\ \text{cm})(12\ \text{cm}) = \mathbf{54\ cm^2}$

27. $\text{Area} = \text{Area}_{\text{triangle}} - \text{Area}_{\text{circle}}$

$= \dfrac{1}{2}(8\ \text{m} \times 16\ \text{m}) - \left[\pi(3\ \text{m})^2\right]$

$= 64\ \text{m}^2 - 9\pi\ \text{m}^2$

$= \mathbf{(64 - 9\pi)\ m^2} = \mathbf{35.74\ m^2}$

28.
$$\begin{array}{r} 0.304 \\ \times\ 12.5 \\ \hline 1520 \\ 608\ \\ 304\ \ \\ \hline 3.8000 \end{array}$$

29.
$$\begin{array}{r} 2.03 \\ 46\overline{)93.38} \\ 92\ \ \ \\ \hline 1\,38 \\ 1\,38 \\ \hline \end{array}$$

30. $S.A. = 2\big(\text{Area}_{\text{top}}\big) + 2\big(\text{Area}_{\text{side}}\big) + 2\big(\text{Area}_{\text{front}}\big)$
$= 2(20 \text{ in.} \times 21 \text{ in.}) + 2(10 \text{ in.} \times 20 \text{ in.})$
$\qquad + 2(10 \text{ in.} \times 21 \text{ in.})$
$= 2\big(420 \text{ in.}^2\big) + 2\big(200 \text{ in.}^2\big) + 2\big(210 \text{ in.}^2\big)$
$= 840 \text{ in.}^2 + 400 \text{ in.}^2 + 420 \text{ in.}^2$
$= \textbf{1660 in.}^2$

Practice 19

a. $(-2)^2 = \textbf{4}$

b. $-2^2 = \textbf{-4}$

c. $-3^3 - (-2)^2 - 2^2 = -27 - 4 - 4 = \textbf{-35}$

d. $\sqrt[3]{-64} = \textbf{-4}$

e. $(-3)^3 + \sqrt[3]{-27} = -27 - 3 = \textbf{-30}$

f. $-3^2 - \sqrt[3]{-8} - \sqrt{16} = -9 - (-2) - 4$
$= -9 + 2 - 4 = \textbf{-11}$

g. $x^2z^3y = (-3)^2(-2)^3(-2) = 9(-8)(-2) = \textbf{144}$

h. $b^2 - 4ac = (-4)^2 - 4(-3)(-5) = 16 - 60 = \textbf{-44}$

Problem Set 19

1. **Like terms**

2. **Positive number**

3. (a) **A right triangle is a triangle that contains one right angle.**

(b) **An acute triangle is a triangle that contains three acute angles.**

(c) **An obtuse triangle is a triangle that contains one obtuse angle.**

(d) **An equiangular triangle is a triangle in which all angles have equal measure.**

4. $10{,}000 \text{ in.} \times \dfrac{1 \text{ ft}}{12 \text{ in.}} \times \dfrac{1 \text{ mi}}{5280 \text{ ft}} = \dfrac{10{,}000}{(12)(5280)} \text{ mi}$
$= \textbf{0.16 mi}$

5. $15{,}000 \text{ ft} \cdot \text{ ft} \times \dfrac{1 \text{ mi}}{5280 \text{ ft}} \times \dfrac{1 \text{ mi}}{5280 \text{ ft}}$
$= \dfrac{15{,}000}{(5280)^2} \text{ mi}^2 = \textbf{0.00054 mi}^2$

6. $A = lw$
$92 \text{ cm}^2 = (23 \text{ cm})w$
$w = \dfrac{92 \text{ cm}^2}{23 \text{ cm}}$
$w = \textbf{4 cm}$

7. $A = \dfrac{1}{2}(9 \text{ m})(14 \text{ m}) = \textbf{63 m}^2$

8. $(-4)^2 = \textbf{16}$

9. $-4^2 = \textbf{-16}$

10. $-2^2 + (-2)^2 = -4 + 4 = \textbf{0}$

11. $-3^2 - (-3)^2 = -9 - 9 = \textbf{-18}$

12. $\sqrt[3]{8} = \textbf{2}$

13. $\sqrt[3]{-8} = \textbf{-2}$

14. $x^2y^3z = (3)^2(-2)^3(4) = (9)(-8)(4) = \textbf{-288}$

15. $-x^2 - y^3 = -(-3)^2 - (-2)^3 = -9 - (-8)$
$= -9 + 8 = \textbf{-1}$

16. $xym - 3ymx - 4xmy - 3my + 2ym$
$= \textbf{-6mxy} - \textbf{my}$

17. $a - 3 - 7a + 2a - 6ax + 4xa - 5$
$= \textbf{-4a} - \textbf{8} - \textbf{2ax}$

18. $x(4 - ap) = 4x + x(-ap) = \textbf{4x} - \textbf{xap}$

19. $(5p - 2c)4xy = 4xy(5p) + 4xy(-2c)$
$= \textbf{20pxy} - \textbf{8cxy}$

20. $4k(2c - a + 3m) = 4k(2c) + 4k(-a) + 4k(3m)$
$= \textbf{8kc} - \textbf{4ka} + \textbf{12km}$

21. $-x(a - 3x) + x = -4[3 - 3(4)] + 4$
$= -4(3 - 12) + 4 = -4(-9) + 4 = 36 + 4 = \textbf{40}$

22. $-(a - x)(x - a) = -(-5 - 3)[3 - (-5)]$
$= -(-8)(3 + 5) = (8)(8) = \textbf{64}$

23. $-a[(x - a) + (2x + a)]$

$= -(-4)\{[3 - (-4)] + [2(3) + (-4)]\}$

$= 4[(3 + 4) + (6 - 4)] = 4(7 + 2) = 4(9) = \mathbf{36}$

24. $-3(4 - 3) - 3 - |-3| = -3(1) - 3 - 3 = \mathbf{-9}$

25. $\dfrac{8 + 2 - 3(2)}{3(2) - 6} = \dfrac{10 - 6}{6 - 6} = \dfrac{4}{0}$, which is **undefined**

26.

$A + B + C = 30$

$20 + D - 11 = 30$

$D = 30 - 20 + 11$

$D = 21$

$P = 30 + 30 + A + 20 + B + 11 + C + D$

$= 30 + 30 + 20 + 11 + (A + B + C) + D$

$= 30 + 30 + 20 + 11 + 30 + 21$

$= \mathbf{142\ km}$

27. $A = (12\text{ in.})(8\text{ in.}) + \dfrac{\pi(4\text{ in.})^2}{2}$

$= (96 + 8\pi)\text{ in.}^2 = \mathbf{121.12\ in.^2}$

28. $9\dfrac{2}{15} - 3\dfrac{1}{5} - 3\dfrac{1}{3} = 9\dfrac{2}{15} - 3\dfrac{3}{15} - 3\dfrac{5}{15}$

$= 8\dfrac{17}{15} - 3\dfrac{3}{15} - 3\dfrac{5}{15} = 5\dfrac{14}{15} - 3\dfrac{5}{15}$

$= 2\dfrac{9}{15} = \mathbf{2\dfrac{3}{5}}$

29.
```
        4.002
   304 )1216.608
        1216
           608
           608
```

30. $S.A. = 2(\text{Area}_{\text{triangle}}) + \text{Area}_{\text{top}} + \text{Area}_{\text{bottom}}$

$\qquad + \text{Area}_{\text{side}}$

$= 2\left[\dfrac{1}{2}(6\text{ ft} \times 8\text{ ft})\right] + (10\text{ ft} \times 15\text{ ft})$

$\qquad + (15\text{ ft} \times 8\text{ ft}) + (6\text{ ft} \times 15\text{ ft})$

$= 2(24\text{ ft}^2) + 150\text{ ft}^2 + 120\text{ ft}^2 + 90\text{ ft}^2$

$= 48\text{ ft}^2 + 360\text{ ft}^2$

$= \mathbf{408\ ft^2}$

Practice 20

a. $V = (\text{Area}_{\text{base}})(\text{Height})$

$= \left[(4\text{ in.} \times 10\text{ in.}) + \dfrac{1}{2}\pi(2\text{ in.})^2\right](10\text{ in.})$

$= (40\text{ in.}^2 + 2\pi\text{ in.}^2)(10\text{ in.})$

$= (400 + 20\pi)\text{ in.}^3 = \mathbf{462.8\ in.^3}$

b. $V = (\text{Area}_{\text{base}})(\text{Length})$

$= [\pi(6\text{ ft})^2](20\text{ ft})$

$= (36\pi\text{ ft}^2)(20\text{ ft})$

$= 720\pi\text{ ft}^3 = \mathbf{2260.8\ ft^3}$

c. $V = (\text{Area}_{\text{base}})(\text{Height})$

$= (50\text{ cm}^2)(12\text{ cm})$

$= \mathbf{600\ cm^3}$

Problem Set 20

1. **(a), (d)**

2. **No**

3. (a) **{1, 2, 3, ...}**

(b) **{0, 1, 2, 3, ...}**

(c) **{..., –3, –2, –1, 0, 1, 2, 3, ...}**

4. $50\text{ m} \times \dfrac{100\text{ cm}}{1\text{ m}} \times \dfrac{1\text{ in.}}{2.54\text{ cm}} = \dfrac{50(100)}{(2.54)}\text{ in.}$

$= \mathbf{1968.50\ in.}$

5. $600\text{ ft} \cdot \text{ft} \times \dfrac{1\text{ yd}}{3\text{ ft}} \times \dfrac{1\text{ yd}}{3\text{ ft}} = \dfrac{600}{(3)^2}\text{ yd}^2$

$= \mathbf{66.67\ yd^2}$

6. $\qquad\qquad P = 2l + 2w$

$110\text{ in.} = 2l + 2(14\text{ in.})$

$110\text{ in.} = 2l + 28\text{ in.}$

$110\text{ in.} - 28\text{ in.} = 2l$

$82\text{ in.} = 2l$

$l = \dfrac{82\text{ in.}}{2}$

$l = \mathbf{41\ in.}$

7. $\qquad\qquad C = 2\pi r$

$10\pi\text{ ft} = 2\pi r$

$\dfrac{10\pi\text{ ft}}{2\pi\text{ ft}} = r$

$r = \mathbf{5\ ft}$

8. $3^2 + (-3)^2 = 9 + 9 = \mathbf{18}$

9. $-2^2 + (-4)^2 = -4 + 16 = \mathbf{12}$

10. $-2^3 + (-2)^3 = -8 + (-8) = \mathbf{-16}$

11. $-(-3)^2 - (-2)^3 = -9 - (-8) = -9 + 8 = \mathbf{-1}$

12. $\sqrt[3]{-27} = \mathbf{-3}$

13. $(-3)^3 - \sqrt[3]{-27} = -27 - (-3) = -27 + 3 = \mathbf{-24}$

14. $xz^2y^3 = 2(-3)^2(-2)^3 = 2(9)(-8) = \mathbf{-144}$

15. $a^2 - b^2a = (-2)^2 - 3^2(-2) = 4 - 9(-2)$
   $= 4 - (-18) = 4 + 18 = \mathbf{22}$

16. $5 - x + xy - 3yx - 2 + 2x = \mathbf{3 + x - 2xy}$

17. $-3pxk + pkx - 3kpx - kp - 3kx$
   $= \mathbf{-5kpx - kp - 3kx}$

18. $-3(-x - 4) = (-3)(-x) + (-3)(-4) = \mathbf{3x + 12}$

19. $(4 - 2p)4x = 4x(4) + 4x(-2p) = \mathbf{16x - 8px}$

20. $2x(a - 3p + 2) = 2x(a) + 2x(-3p) + 2x(2)$
   $= \mathbf{2ax - 6px + 4x}$

21. $-p(-a + 2p) + p = -(-3)[-2 + 2(-3)] + (-3)$
   $= 3(-2 - 6) + (-3) = 3(-8) - 3$
   $= -24 - 3 = \mathbf{-27}$

22. $k(ak - 4a) + k = -3[2(-3) - 4(2)] + (-3)$
   $= -3(-6 - 8) - 3 = -3(-14) - 3$
   $= 42 - 3 = \mathbf{39}$

23. $a(x - a) + |x| = -2[-3 - (-2)] + |-3|$
   $= -2(-3 + 2) + 3 = -2(-1) + 3 = 2 + 3 = \mathbf{5}$

24. $2[-3(-2 - 4)(3 - 2)] = 2[-3(-6)(1)]$
   $= 2(18) = \mathbf{36}$

25. $\dfrac{(-4)(-3 + 7)(-1)}{(7 - 4 - 1)(2 - 3)} = \dfrac{(-4)(4)(-1)}{(2)(-1)} = \dfrac{16}{-2} = \mathbf{-8}$

26. $P = \left(10 + 10 + \dfrac{2\pi(4)}{2} + \dfrac{2\pi(4)}{2}\right)$ cm
   $= (20 + 4\pi + 4\pi)$ cm
   $= (20 + 8\pi)$ cm $= \mathbf{45.12}$ **cm**

27. $A = \dfrac{1}{2}(8 \text{ m})(15 \text{ m}) = \mathbf{60 \ m^2}$

28. Area = Area$_{\text{rectangle}}$ − Area$_{\text{triangle}}$
   $= (10 \text{ km} \times 8 \text{ km}) - \dfrac{1}{2}(8 \text{ km} \times 5 \text{ km})$
   $= 80 \text{ km}^2 - 20 \text{ km}^2$
   $= \mathbf{60 \ km^2}$

29. $5\dfrac{1}{2} + 12\dfrac{3}{10} + 3\dfrac{2}{5} = 5\dfrac{5}{10} + 12\dfrac{3}{10} + 3\dfrac{4}{10}$
   $= 20\dfrac{12}{10} = 21\dfrac{2}{10} = \mathbf{21\dfrac{1}{5}}$ **in.**

30. $V = \left(\text{Area}_{\text{base}}\right)(\text{Height})$
   $= \left(45 \text{ ft}^2\right)(10 \text{ ft})$
   $= \mathbf{450 \ ft^3}$

Practice 21

a. $xyx^4x^3y^5 = xx^4x^3yy^5 = \mathbf{x^8y^6}$

b. $x^3xy^2y^5x^7mm = x^3xx^7y^2y^5mm = \mathbf{x^{11}y^7m^2}$

c. $2x^2y^3 + xy - 8y^3x^2 - 5yx = \mathbf{-6x^2y^3 - 4xy}$

d. $x^6y + yx^6 + 3xy - 5xy^6 = \mathbf{2x^6y + 3xy - 5xy^6}$

Problem Set 21

1. **Negative number**

2. $a(b + c) = \mathbf{ab + ac}$

3. (a) **An isosceles triangle is a triangle that has at least two sides of equal length.**

   (b) **An equilateral triangle is a triangle that contains three sides of equal length.**

   (c) **A scalene triangle is a triangle that contains three sides of unequal length.**

4. $366 \text{ cm} \times \dfrac{1 \text{ in.}}{2.54 \text{ cm}} \times \dfrac{1 \text{ ft}}{12 \text{ in.}} = \dfrac{\mathbf{366}}{\mathbf{(2.54)(12)}}$ **ft**
   $= \mathbf{12.01}$ **ft**

5. $5000 \text{ m} \cdot \text{m} \times \dfrac{1 \text{ km}}{1000 \text{ m}} \times \dfrac{1 \text{ km}}{1000 \text{ m}}$
   $= \dfrac{\mathbf{5000}}{\mathbf{(1000)^2}} \text{ km}^2 = \mathbf{0.005 \ km^2}$

6. $A = lw$

$95 \text{ cm}^2 = l(5 \text{ cm})$

$l = \dfrac{95 \text{ cm}^2}{5 \text{ cm}}$

$l = \textbf{19 cm}$

7. $A = \pi r^2 = \pi(10 \text{ m})^2 = \textbf{100}\boldsymbol{\pi} \textbf{ m}^2 = \textbf{314 m}^2$

8. $x^2 yyyx^3 yx = x^2 x^3 xyyyy = \boldsymbol{x^6 y^4}$

9. $xm^2 xm^3 x^3 m = m^2 m^3 mxxx^3 = \boldsymbol{m^6 x^5}$

10. $ky^2 k^3 k^2 y^5 = kk^3 k^2 y^2 y^5 = \boldsymbol{k^6 y^7}$

11. $a^2 ba^2 b^3 ab^4 = a^2 a^2 abb^3 b^4 = \boldsymbol{a^5 b^8}$

12. $4xyz - 3yz + zxy = \boldsymbol{5xyz - 3yz}$

13. $7 - 3k - 2k + 2kx - xk + 8 = \boldsymbol{15 - 5k + kx}$

14. $3ab^2 - 2ab + 5b^2 a - ba = \boldsymbol{8ab^2 - 3ab}$

15. $x^2 - 3yx + 2yx^2 - 2xy + yx$

$= \boldsymbol{x^2 - 4xy + 2x^2 y}$

16. $5(2 - 4p) = 5(2) + 5(-4p) = \boldsymbol{10 - 20p}$

17. $x(3p - 2y) = x(3p) + x(-2y) = \boldsymbol{3px - 2xy}$

18. $(3 - 2b)a = 3a + (-2b)a = \boldsymbol{3a - 2ab}$

19. $(a - x)(x - a) = (-3 - 4)[4 - (-3)]$

$= -7(4 + 3) = -7(7) = \boldsymbol{-49}$

20. $m(x - m) - |x| = -3[-4 - (-3)] - |-4|$

$= -3(-4 + 3) - 4 = -3(-1) - 4 = 3 - 4 = \boldsymbol{-1}$

21. $x^2 - y^2 = (-3)^2 - (-2)^2 = 9 - 4 = \boldsymbol{5}$

22. $-5 - (-5)^2 - 3 + (-2) = -5 - 25 - 3 - 2$

$= \boldsymbol{-35}$

23. $-3^2 - 2^2 - (-3)^3 - \sqrt[3]{-8}$

$= -9 - 4 - (-27) - (-2)$

$= -9 - 4 + 27 + 2 = \boldsymbol{16}$

24. $\dfrac{3 - [-(-3)]}{-(-2)} = \dfrac{3 - 3}{2} = \dfrac{0}{2} = \boldsymbol{0}$

25. $\dfrac{5(-6 + 4) + 7(-3 + 9)}{(5 - 3) + 6} = \dfrac{5(-2) + 7(6)}{2 + 6}$

$= \dfrac{-10 + 42}{8} = \dfrac{32}{8} = \boldsymbol{4}$

26.

$B + C + D = 40$

$35 + A - 15 = 40$

$A = 40 - 35 + 15$

$A = 20$

$P = 40 + 40 + A + B + 15 + C + 35 + D$

$= 40 + 40 + 15 + 35 + A + (B + C + D)$

$= 40 + 40 + 15 + 35 + 20 + 40$

$= \textbf{190 in.}$

27. $A = (5 \text{ ft})(10 \text{ ft}) + \dfrac{1}{2}(10 \text{ ft})(5 \text{ ft})$

$= 50 \text{ ft}^2 + 25 \text{ ft}^2 = \textbf{75 ft}^2$

28. $\dfrac{-1\frac{3}{4}}{2\frac{1}{3}} = -\dfrac{7}{4} \div \dfrac{7}{3} = -\dfrac{7}{4} \times \dfrac{3}{7} = -\dfrac{3}{4}$

29.
$$\begin{array}{r} 0.012 \\ \times\ 0.004 \\ \hline \textbf{0.000048} \end{array}$$

30. $S.A. = 2\left(\text{Area}_{\text{base}}\right) + \text{Lateral Surface Area}$

$= 2\left[\pi(3 \text{ yd})^2\right] + \left(\text{Perimeter}_{\text{base}}\right)(\text{Length})$

$= 2\left(9\pi \text{ yd}^2\right) + [2\pi(3 \text{ yd})](10 \text{ yd})$

$= 18\pi \text{ yd}^2 + (6\pi \text{ yd})(10 \text{ yd})$

$= 18\pi \text{ yd}^2 + 60\pi \text{ yd}^2$

$= \textbf{78}\boldsymbol{\pi} \textbf{ yd}^2 = \textbf{244.92 yd}^2$

Practice 22

a. $(-2) - 2 = 0 \qquad 2 - 2 = 0$

$-4 \neq 0 \qquad\qquad 0 = 0$

Therefore, **2 satisfies the equation.**

b. $(-2)^2 + 7(-2) = -10 \qquad (-5)^2 + 7(-5) = -10$

$4 - 14 = -10 \qquad\qquad 25 - 35 = -10$

$-10 = -10 \qquad\qquad\quad -10 = -10$

Therefore, **-2 and -5 are roots of the equation.**

Problem Set 22

1. (a) **An equation is an algebraic statement consisting of two algebraic expressions connected by an equals sign.**

   (b) **A conditional equation is an equation whose truth or falsity depends on the replacement values of the variables within it.**

2. **Roots**

3. **(a), (b), (d)**

4. $72 \text{ in.} \times \dfrac{2.54 \text{ cm}}{1 \text{ in.}} = 72(2.54) \text{ cm} = \textbf{182.88 cm}$

5. $55 \text{ m} \cdot \text{m} \times \dfrac{100 \text{ cm}}{1 \text{ m}} \times \dfrac{100 \text{ cm}}{1 \text{ m}} = 55(100)^2 \text{ cm}^2$
   $= \textbf{550,000 cm}^2$

6.
$$P = 2l + 2w$$
$$124 \text{ cm} = 2(45 \text{ cm}) + 2w$$
$$124 \text{ cm} = 90 \text{ cm} + 2w$$
$$124 \text{ cm} - 90 \text{ cm} = 2w$$
$$34 \text{ cm} = 2w$$
$$w = \frac{34 \text{ cm}}{2}$$
$$w = \textbf{17 cm}$$

7.
$$A = \pi r^2$$
$$4\pi \text{ m}^2 = \pi r^2$$
$$4(3.14) \text{ m}^2 = (3.14)r^2$$
$$12.56 \text{ m}^2 = 3.14 r^2$$
$$\frac{12.56 \text{ m}^2}{3.14} = r^2$$
$$4 \text{ m}^2 = r^2$$
The radius is **2 m** because $2 \text{ m} \times 2 \text{ m} = 4 \text{ m}^2$.

8. $(-1) - 1 = 0 \qquad 1 - 1 = 0$
   $\qquad -2 \neq 0 \qquad\quad 0 = 0$
   Therefore, **1 satisfies the equation.**

9. $(-3)^2 - (-3) = 12 \qquad (2)^2 - 2 = 12$
   $\qquad 9 + 3 = 12 \qquad\quad 4 - 2 = 12$
   $\qquad\quad 12 = 12 \qquad\qquad 2 \neq 12$
   Therefore, **–3 is the root of the equation.**

10. $x^2xxy^2xy^3 = x^2xxxy^2y^3 = \textbf{x}^5\textbf{y}^5$

11. $a^2aba^3b^2a^5 = a^2aa^3a^5bb^2 = \textbf{a}^{11}\textbf{b}^3$

12. $p^2m^5ypp^3my^2 = p^2pp^3m^5myy^2 = \textbf{p}^6\textbf{m}^6\textbf{y}^3$

13. $4p^2x^2kpx^3k^2k = 4p^2pkk^2kx^2x^3 = \textbf{4p}^3\textbf{k}^4\textbf{x}^5$

14. $-8 - py + 2yp + 4 - y = \textbf{–4 + py – y}$

15. $m + 4 + 3m - 6 - 2m + mc - 4mc$
    $= \textbf{2m – 2 – 3mc}$

16. $xy - 3xy^2 + 5y^2x - 4xy = \textbf{–3xy + 2xy}^2$

17. $-3x^2ym + 7x - 5ymx^2 + 16x = \textbf{–8mx}^2\textbf{y + 23x}$

18. $a(3x - 2) = a(3x) + a(-2) = \textbf{3ax – 2a}$

19. $4xy(5 - 2a) = 4xy(5) + 4xy(-2a)$
    $= \textbf{20xy – 8axy}$

20. $2x(4a + b - 3m) = 2x(4a) + 2x(b) + 2x(-3m)$
    $= \textbf{8ax + 2bx – 6mx}$

21. $cy(cx - y) = -2(3)[-2(-3) - 3]$
    $= -6(6 - 3) = -6(3) = \textbf{–18}$

22. $|x - a| - a(-x) = |4 - 3| - 3(-4)$
    $= 1 + 12 = \textbf{13}$

23. $a - b(a^2 - b) = -2 - 3[(-2)^2 - 3]$
    $= -2 - 3(4 - 3) = -2 - 3(1) = -2 - 3 = \textbf{–5}$

24. $(-3)^3 + (-2)^3 - |-2| = -27 - 8 - 2 = \textbf{–37}$

25. $-3^2 - (-2)^2 + \sqrt[3]{-27} = -9 - 4 - 3 = \textbf{–16}$

26. $P = \left(4 + 4 + 4 + \dfrac{2\pi(2)}{2}\right) \text{km}$
    $= (12 + 2\pi) \text{ km} = \textbf{18.28 km}$

27.

$A = (2 \text{ in.} \times 4 \text{ in.}) + (2 \text{ in.} \times 4 \text{ in.})$
$\qquad + (2 \text{ in.} \times 4 \text{ in.})$
$= 8 \text{ in.}^2 + 8 \text{ in.}^2 + 8 \text{ in.}^2$
$= \textbf{24 in.}^2$

28. $\text{Area} = \text{Area}_{\text{triangle}} - \text{Area}_{\text{circle}}$
    $= \dfrac{1}{2}(15 \text{ ft})(20 \text{ ft}) - \pi(5 \text{ ft})^2$
    $= 150 \text{ ft}^2 - 25\pi \text{ ft}^2$
    $= (150 - 25\pi) \text{ ft}^2 = \textbf{71.5 ft}^2$

29. $x = 180 - 115 - 45 = \textbf{20}$

30. $\text{Volume} = (\text{Area}_{\text{base}})(\text{Height})$
    $= \left[\dfrac{1}{2}(9 \text{ in.})(6 \text{ in.})\right](10 \text{ in.})$
    $= (27 \text{ in.}^2)(10 \text{ in.})$
    $= \textbf{270 in.}^3$

Practice 23

a. $x + 5 = 17$
$\underline{ -5 \quad -5}$
$x = \mathbf{12}$

b. $k - 27 = -38$
$\underline{ +27 \quad +27}$
$k = \mathbf{-11}$

c. $x - \dfrac{1}{2} = \dfrac{3}{8}$
$\underline{ +\dfrac{1}{2} \quad +\dfrac{1}{2}}$
$x \quad = \dfrac{3}{8} + \dfrac{1}{2}$
$x = \dfrac{3}{8} + \dfrac{4}{8}$
$x = \dfrac{\mathbf{7}}{\mathbf{8}}$

d. $d + 4\dfrac{1}{7} = 3\dfrac{1}{6}$
$\underline{ -4\dfrac{1}{7} \quad -4\dfrac{1}{7}}$
$d \quad = 3\dfrac{1}{6} - 4\dfrac{1}{7}$
$d = \dfrac{19}{6} - \dfrac{29}{7}$
$d = \dfrac{133}{42} - \dfrac{174}{42}$
$d = -\dfrac{\mathbf{41}}{\mathbf{42}}$

Problem Set 23

1. To solve an equation means to find the value(s) of the unknown that makes the equation true.

2. Two equations are said to be equivalent if every solution of either one of the equations is also a solution of the other equation.

3. **180°**

4. $150 \text{ m} \times \dfrac{100 \text{ cm}}{1 \text{ m}} = \mathbf{150(100)}$ **cm** $= \mathbf{15{,}000}$ **cm**

5. $116 \text{ in.} \cdot \text{in.} \times \dfrac{2.54 \text{ cm}}{1 \text{ in.}} \times \dfrac{2.54 \text{ cm}}{1 \text{ in.}}$
$= \mathbf{116(2.54)^2 \text{ cm}^2 = 748.39 \text{ cm}^2}$

6. $A = lw$
$209 \text{ in.}^2 = (19 \text{ in.})w$
$w = \dfrac{209 \text{ in.}^2}{19 \text{ in.}}$
$w = \mathbf{11 \text{ in.}}$

7. $A = \pi r^2$
$9\pi \text{ ft}^2 = \pi r^2$
$9(3.14) \text{ ft}^2 = (3.14)r^2$
$28.26 \text{ ft}^2 = 3.14 r^2$
$\dfrac{28.26 \text{ ft}^2}{3.14} = r^2$
$9 \text{ ft}^2 = r^2$
The radius is **3 ft** because $3 \text{ ft} \times 3 \text{ ft} = 9 \text{ ft}^2$.

8. $x - 4 = 10$
$\underline{ +4 \quad +4}$
$x = \mathbf{14}$

9. $x + \dfrac{1}{5} = -\dfrac{1}{10}$
$\underline{ -\dfrac{1}{5} \quad -\dfrac{1}{5}}$
$x \quad = -\dfrac{1}{10} - \dfrac{1}{5}$
$x = -\dfrac{1}{10} - \dfrac{2}{10}$
$x = -\dfrac{\mathbf{3}}{\mathbf{10}}$

10. $x + 1\dfrac{1}{4} = -\dfrac{5}{8}$
$\underline{ -1\dfrac{1}{4} \quad -1\dfrac{1}{4}}$
$x \quad = -\dfrac{5}{8} - 1\dfrac{1}{4}$
$x = -\dfrac{5}{8} - \dfrac{5}{4}$
$x = -\dfrac{5}{8} - \dfrac{10}{8}$
$x = -\dfrac{\mathbf{15}}{\mathbf{8}}$

11. $(-2) + 2 = 0 \qquad 2 + 2 = 0$
$\qquad 0 = 0 \qquad\qquad 4 \neq 0$
Therefore, **−2 satisfies the equation.**

12. $(-2)^2 - 2(-2) = 3 \qquad (3)^2 - 2(3) = 3$
$\qquad 4 + 4 = 3 \qquad\qquad 9 - 6 = 3$
$\qquad\qquad 8 \neq 3 \qquad\qquad\qquad 3 = 3$
Therefore, **3 is a root of the equation.**

13. $x^2ym^5x^2y^4 = m^5x^2x^2yy^4 = \boldsymbol{m^5x^4y^5}$

14. $x^3y^2myxm = mmx^3xy^2y = \boldsymbol{m^2x^4y^3}$

15. $xxx^2yyy^3xy = xxx^2xyyy^3y = \boldsymbol{x^5y^6}$

16. $-4 + 7x - 3x - 5 + 2x - 4x = \boldsymbol{-9 + 2x}$

17. $p^2xy - 3yp^2x + 2xp^2y - 5 = \boldsymbol{-5}$

18. $4x(a + 2b) = 4x(a) + 4x(2b) = \boldsymbol{4ax + 8bx}$

19. $(2x + 4)3 = (2x)3 + (4)3 = \boldsymbol{6x + 12}$

20. $4px(my - 3ab) = 4px(my) + 4px(-3ab)$
$= \boldsymbol{4mypx - 12abpx}$

21. $x(x - y) - y = -2(-2 - 3) - 3$
$= -2(-5) - 3 = 10 - 3 = \boldsymbol{7}$

22. $(a - b)(b - x) = [3 - (-3)](-3 - 2)$
$= (3 + 3)(-5) = (6)(-5) = \boldsymbol{-30}$

23. $x^3 - a(a - b) = (-2)^3 - 3(3 - 3)$
$= -8 - 3(0) = \boldsymbol{-8}$

24. $-3^2 - (-3)^2 + \sqrt[5]{32} = -9 - (9) + 2$
$= -18 + 2 = \boldsymbol{-16}$

25. $\dfrac{-3 - 4(4) - 6}{10 + (-5)(-4)} = \dfrac{-3 - 16 - 6}{10 + 20} = \dfrac{-25}{30} = \boldsymbol{-\dfrac{5}{6}}$

26. $P = \left(\dfrac{2\pi(6)}{2} + 13 + \dfrac{2\pi(6)}{2} + 13 \right)$ yd
$= \boldsymbol{(26 + 12\pi)}$ **yd** $= \boldsymbol{63.68}$ **yd**

27. $A = (25 \text{ cm} \times 8 \text{ cm}) + \dfrac{1}{2}(25 \text{ cm} \times 10 \text{ cm})$
$= 200 \text{ cm}^2 + 125 \text{ cm}^2 = \boldsymbol{325 \text{ cm}^2}$

28. $3\dfrac{3}{7} \times 3\dfrac{1}{16} = \dfrac{24}{7} \times \dfrac{49}{16} = \dfrac{21}{2} = \boldsymbol{10\dfrac{1}{2}}$

29. $\dfrac{3\frac{1}{5}}{-2\frac{2}{15}} = \dfrac{\frac{16}{5}}{-\frac{32}{15}} = \dfrac{16}{5} \times \dfrac{-15}{32} = \dfrac{-3}{2} = \boldsymbol{-1\dfrac{1}{2}}$

30. $S.A. = 2\left(\text{Area}_{\text{front}}\right) + 2\left(\text{Area}_{\text{top}}\right) + 2\left(\text{Area}_{\text{side}}\right)$
$= 2(2 \text{ m} \times 2 \text{ m}) + 2(2 \text{ m} \times 2 \text{ m})$
$+ 2(2 \text{ m} \times 2 \text{ m})$
$= 2\left(4 \text{ m}^2\right) + 2\left(4 \text{ m}^2\right) + 2\left(4 \text{ m}^2\right)$
$= 8 \text{ m}^2 + 8 \text{ m}^2 + 8 \text{ m}^2$
$= \boldsymbol{24 \text{ m}^2}$

Practice 24

a. $\dfrac{3}{5}x = 27$

$\dfrac{\frac{3}{5}x}{\frac{3}{5}} = \dfrac{27}{\frac{3}{5}}$

$x = \dfrac{27}{\frac{3}{5}}$

$x = 27 \cdot \dfrac{5}{3}$

$x = \boldsymbol{45}$

b. $3\dfrac{1}{5}y = 32$

$\dfrac{3\frac{1}{5}y}{3\frac{1}{5}} = \dfrac{32}{3\frac{1}{5}}$

$y = \dfrac{32}{\frac{16}{5}}$

$y = 32 \cdot \dfrac{5}{16}$

$y = \boldsymbol{10}$

c. $\dfrac{x}{\frac{1}{4}} = 20$

$\dfrac{\frac{1}{4}x}{\frac{1}{4}} = 20 \cdot \dfrac{1}{4}$

$x = 20 \cdot \dfrac{1}{4}$

$x = \boldsymbol{5}$

d. $\dfrac{x}{2\frac{1}{4}} = 5$

$\dfrac{2\frac{1}{4}x}{2\frac{1}{4}} = 5 \cdot 2\dfrac{1}{4}$

$x = 5 \cdot \dfrac{9}{4}$

$x = \dfrac{45}{4}$

Problem Set 24

1. Positive number

2. (b), (c)

3. (a) **60°**

   (b) **60°**

4. $280 \text{ mi} \times \dfrac{5280 \text{ ft}}{1 \text{ mi}} \times \dfrac{12 \text{ in.}}{1 \text{ ft}} = \textbf{280(5280)(12) in.}$

   $= \textbf{17,740,800 in.}$

5. $45 \text{ ft} \cdot \text{ft} \times \dfrac{12 \text{ in.}}{1 \text{ ft}} \times \dfrac{12 \text{ in.}}{1 \text{ ft}} = \textbf{45(12)}^2 \textbf{ in.}^2$

   $= \textbf{6480 in.}^2$

6. $A = \dfrac{1}{2}(24 \text{ cm})(18 \text{ cm}) = \textbf{216 cm}^2$

7.
$$C = 2\pi r$$
$$12\pi \text{ m} = 2\pi r$$
$$12(3.14) \text{ m} = 2(3.14)r$$
$$37.68 \text{ m} = 6.28r$$
$$r = \dfrac{37.68 \text{ m}}{6.28}$$
$$r = \textbf{6 m}$$

8. $x + 5 = 7$
$$\underline{-5 \quad -5}$$
$$x = \textbf{2}$$

9. $y - 3 = 2$
$$\underline{+3 \quad +3}$$
$$y = \textbf{5}$$

10. $x - \dfrac{1}{4} = \dfrac{7}{8}$
$$\underline{+\dfrac{1}{4} \quad +\dfrac{1}{4}}$$
$$x \quad = \dfrac{7}{8} + \dfrac{1}{4}$$
$$x = \dfrac{7}{8} + \dfrac{2}{8}$$
$$x = \dfrac{\textbf{9}}{\textbf{8}}$$

11. $y - \dfrac{1}{2} = -2\dfrac{1}{2}$
$$\underline{+\dfrac{1}{2} \quad \quad +\dfrac{1}{2}}$$
$$y \quad = -2\dfrac{1}{2} + \dfrac{1}{2}$$
$$y = -\dfrac{5}{2} + \dfrac{1}{2}$$
$$y = -\dfrac{4}{2}$$
$$y = \textbf{-2}$$

12. $x + \dfrac{1}{2} = 2\dfrac{1}{5}$
$$\underline{-\dfrac{1}{2} \quad \quad -\dfrac{1}{2}}$$
$$x \quad = 2\dfrac{1}{5} - \dfrac{1}{2}$$
$$x = \dfrac{11}{5} - \dfrac{1}{2}$$
$$x = \dfrac{22}{10} - \dfrac{5}{10}$$
$$x = \dfrac{\textbf{17}}{\textbf{10}}$$

13. $2x = 20$
$$\dfrac{2x}{2} = \dfrac{20}{2}$$
$$x = \textbf{10}$$

14. $3x = 4\dfrac{1}{2}$
$$\dfrac{3x}{3} = \dfrac{4\dfrac{1}{2}}{3}$$
$$x = \dfrac{\dfrac{9}{2}}{3}$$
$$x = \dfrac{9}{2} \cdot \dfrac{1}{3}$$
$$x = \dfrac{\textbf{3}}{\textbf{2}}$$

15. $\dfrac{x}{3} = 5$
$$3 \cdot \dfrac{x}{3} = 5 \cdot 3$$
$$x = \textbf{15}$$

16. $\dfrac{x}{\frac{1}{2}} = 4$

$\dfrac{\frac{1}{2}x}{\frac{1}{2}} = 4 \cdot \dfrac{1}{2}$

$x = 2$

17. $(-5) - 5 = 0 \qquad 5 - 5 = 0$
$\qquad\qquad -10 \neq 0 \qquad\qquad 0 = 0$

Therefore, **5 satisfies the equation.**

18. $m^2xyp^2x^3y^5 = m^2p^2xx^3yy^5 = \boldsymbol{m^2p^2x^4y^6}$

19. $3p^2xxypp^3xy^2 = 3p^2pp^3xxxyy^2 = \boldsymbol{3p^6x^3y^3}$

20. $a + 3 - 2a - 5a + 5 - a = 8 - 7a = \boldsymbol{-7a + 8}$

21. $-3x^2ym + 5myx^2 - 2my^2x = \boldsymbol{2mx^2y - 2mxy^2}$

22. $(3a - 5p)xy = (3a)xy + (-5p)xy = \boldsymbol{3axy - 5pxy}$

23. $(-x)^3 - y = [-(-2)]^3 - 4 = 2^3 - 4 = 8 - 4$
$\quad = \boldsymbol{4}$

24. $a^3 - (a - b) + |a - b|$
$\quad = (-2)^3 - (-2 - 3) + |-2 - 3|$
$\quad = -8 - (-5) + |-5| = -8 + 5 + 5 = \boldsymbol{2}$

25. $-2\{-5(-3 + 4) - [3 - (-4)]\}$
$\quad = -2[-5(1) - (3 + 4)] = -2(-5 - 7)$
$\quad = -2(-12) = \boldsymbol{24}$

26. $(-2)^3 - (-2)^2 - 5 + \sqrt[3]{-64} = -8 - 4 - 5 - 4$
$\quad = \boldsymbol{-21}$

27.

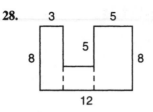

$A + B + C = 8$
$P = 12 + 8 + 4 + A + 4 + B + 4 + C$
$\quad = 12 + 8 + 4 + 4 + 4 + (A + B + C)$
$\quad = 12 + 8 + 4 + 4 + 4 + 8$
$\quad = \boldsymbol{40\ km}$

28.

$A = (3\ \text{in.} \times 8\ \text{in.}) + (5\ \text{in.} \times 8\ \text{in.})$
$\qquad + (3\ \text{in.} \times 4\ \text{in.})$
$\quad = 24\ \text{in.}^2 + 40\ \text{in.}^2 + 12\ \text{in.}^2$
$\quad = \boldsymbol{76\ \text{in.}^2}$

29. $\text{Area} = \text{Area}_{\text{triangle}} - \text{Area}_{\text{circle}}$
$\qquad = \dfrac{1}{2}(16\ \text{ft})(13\ \text{ft}) - \pi(4\ \text{ft})^2$
$\qquad = 104\ \text{ft}^2 - 16\pi\ \text{ft}^2$
$\qquad = \boldsymbol{(104 - 16\pi)\ \text{ft}^2 = 53.76\ \text{ft}^2}$

30. $V = \left(\text{Area}_{\text{base}}\right)(\text{Height})$
$\quad = \left(95\ \text{cm}^2\right)(16\ \text{cm}) = \boldsymbol{1520\ \text{cm}^3}$

Practice 25

a. $\dfrac{2}{5}x - \dfrac{3}{10} = \dfrac{1}{2}$

$\qquad\quad +\dfrac{3}{10} \quad +\dfrac{3}{10}$

$\dfrac{2}{5}x \qquad = \dfrac{8}{10}$

$\dfrac{5}{2} \cdot \dfrac{2}{5}x = \dfrac{8}{10} \cdot \dfrac{5}{2}$

$\qquad\quad x = \dfrac{4}{2}$

$\qquad\quad x = 2$

b. $2\dfrac{1}{4}x + \dfrac{3}{7} = \dfrac{5}{14}$

$\qquad\qquad -\dfrac{3}{7} \quad -\dfrac{3}{7}$

$2\dfrac{1}{4}x \qquad = -\dfrac{1}{14}$

$\dfrac{9}{4}x = -\dfrac{1}{14}$

$\dfrac{4}{9} \cdot \dfrac{9}{4}x = -\dfrac{1}{14} \cdot \dfrac{4}{9}$

$\qquad\quad x = -\dfrac{2}{63}$

c.
$$1.2 = -1.4 + 20x$$
$$\underline{+1.4 \quad\quad +1.4}$$
$$2.6 = \quad\quad\quad 20x$$

$$\frac{20x}{20} = \frac{2.6}{20}$$

$$x = \mathbf{0.13}$$

d.
$$0.7x - 0.4 = 0.16$$
$$\underline{\quad\quad +0.4 \quad +0.4}$$
$$0.7x \quad\quad = 0.56$$

$$\frac{0.7x}{0.7} = \frac{0.56}{0.7}$$

$$x = \mathbf{0.8}$$

Problem Set 25

1. **(a), (d)**

2. (a) **Subtraction**

    (b) **Addition**

    (c) **Division**

    (d) **Multiplication**

3. $508 \text{ cm} \times \dfrac{1 \text{ in.}}{2.54 \text{ cm}} = \dfrac{\mathbf{508}}{\mathbf{2.54}} \text{ in.} = \mathbf{200 \text{ in.}}$

4. $15{,}000 \text{ cm} \cdot \text{cm} \times \dfrac{1 \text{ m}}{100 \text{ cm}} \times \dfrac{1 \text{ m}}{100 \text{ cm}}$

$= \dfrac{\mathbf{15{,}000}}{\mathbf{(100)^2}} \text{ m}^2 = \mathbf{1.5 \text{ m}^2}$

5.
$$A = S^2$$
$$9 \text{ cm}^2 = S^2$$

Each side is 3 cm because $3 \text{ cm} \times 3 \text{ cm} = 9 \text{ cm}^2$.

$$P = 4S = 4(3 \text{ cm}) = \mathbf{12 \text{ cm}}$$

6.
$$x - 5 = 3$$
$$\underline{\quad +5 \quad +5}$$
$$x = \mathbf{8}$$

7.
$$x + \frac{1}{2} = \frac{2}{3}$$
$$\underline{\quad -\frac{1}{2} \quad -\frac{1}{2}}$$
$$x \quad\quad = \frac{2}{3} - \frac{1}{2}$$
$$x = \frac{4}{6} - \frac{3}{6}$$
$$x = \mathbf{\frac{1}{6}}$$

8.
$$x + 3\frac{1}{3} = 5$$
$$\underline{\quad -3\frac{1}{3} \quad -3\frac{1}{3}}$$
$$x \quad\quad = 5 - 3\frac{1}{3}$$
$$x = \frac{15}{3} - \frac{10}{3}$$
$$x = \mathbf{\frac{5}{3}}$$

9.
$$4x = 2\frac{2}{3}$$
$$\frac{4x}{4} = \frac{2\frac{2}{3}}{4}$$
$$x = \frac{\frac{8}{3}}{4}$$
$$x = \frac{8}{3} \cdot \frac{1}{4}$$
$$x = \mathbf{\frac{2}{3}}$$

10.
$$2x + 3 = 11$$
$$\underline{\quad -3 \quad -3}$$
$$2x \quad = 8$$
$$\frac{2x}{2} = \frac{8}{2}$$
$$x = \mathbf{4}$$

11.
$$3x - 4 = 10$$
$$\underline{\quad +4 \quad +4}$$
$$3x \quad = 14$$
$$\frac{3x}{3} = \frac{14}{3}$$
$$x = \mathbf{\frac{14}{3}}$$

12.
$$-2x - 2 = 10$$
$$\underline{\quad +2 \quad +2}$$
$$-2x \quad = 12$$
$$\frac{-2x}{-2} = \frac{12}{-2}$$
$$x = \mathbf{-6}$$

13.
$$\frac{1}{8}m - \frac{1}{4} = \frac{3}{4}$$
$$\underline{\quad +\frac{1}{4} \quad +\frac{1}{4}}$$
$$\frac{1}{8}m \quad = 1$$
$$\frac{8}{1} \cdot \frac{1}{8}m = 1 \cdot \frac{8}{1}$$
$$m = \mathbf{8}$$

14. $0.5x - 0.2 = 0.15$

$$\underline{ +0.2 \quad +0.2}$$

$0.5x \qquad = 0.35$

$$\frac{0.5x}{0.5} = \frac{0.35}{0.5}$$

$x = \mathbf{0.7}$

15. (a) **1**

(b) **1**

(c) **Yes**

(d) **Yes**

16. $(-2)^2 - 2(-2) = 8 \qquad (4)^2 - 2(4) = 8$

$\qquad\quad 4 + 4 = 8 \qquad\qquad 16 - 8 = 8$

$\qquad\qquad 8 = 8 \qquad\qquad\quad 8 = 8$

Therefore, **−2 and 4 are roots of the equation.**

17. $x^2 k x k^2 x^2 y k x^2 = k k^2 k x^2 x x^2 x^2 y = \mathbf{k^4 x^7 y}$

18. $aaa^3 b x a^2 b^3 abx^4 = aaa^3 a^2 abb^3 bxx^4 = \mathbf{a^8 b^5 x^5}$

19. $6c - 6 - 2c - 5 - 3c + 7 = \mathbf{c - 4}$

20. $a^2 xx + a^2 x^2 - 3x^2 aa = a^2 x^2 + a^2 x^2 - 3a^2 x^2$

$= \mathbf{-a^2 x^2}$

21. $4x(2y - 3 + 2a) = 4x(2y) + 4x(-3) + 4x(2a)$

$= \mathbf{8xy - 12x + 8ax}$

22. $-b(b - a) = -1[1 - (-2)] = -1(1 + 2)$

$= -1(3) = \mathbf{-3}$

23. $a(a^3 - b) - b = -2[(-2)^3 - 3] - 3$

$= -2(-8 - 3) - 3 = -2(-11) - 3$

$= 22 - 3 = \mathbf{19}$

24. $-3^2 + (-3)^3 - 4 - \sqrt[3]{27} = -9 - 27 - 4 - 3$

$= \mathbf{-43}$

25. $\dfrac{20 - 8 + (-6)(-2)}{8(-5) + 10} = \dfrac{20 - 8 + 12}{-40 + 10} = \dfrac{24}{-30}$

$= \mathbf{-\dfrac{4}{5}}$

26. $P = 5 \text{ m} + 5 \text{ m} + 5 \text{ m} + \dfrac{2\pi\left(\dfrac{5}{2}\right)}{2} \text{ m}$

$= \left(15 + \dfrac{5\pi}{2}\right) \text{ m} = \mathbf{22.85 \text{ m}}$

27.

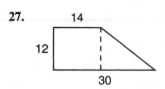

$A = (14 \text{ km})(12 \text{ km}) + \dfrac{1}{2}(16 \text{ km})(12 \text{ km})$

$= 168 \text{ km}^2 + 96 \text{ km}^2 = \mathbf{264 \text{ km}^2}$

28. $y = 180 - 110 - 48 = \mathbf{22}$

29. $\begin{array}{r} \mathbf{0.02} \\ 318\overline{)6.36} \\ \underline{6\,36} \end{array}$

30. $S.A. = 2\left(\text{Area}_{\text{triangle}}\right) + \text{Area}_{\text{top}} + \text{Area}_{\text{bottom}}$

$\qquad\qquad + \text{Area}_{\text{side}}$

$= 2\left[\dfrac{1}{2}(12 \text{ in.} \times 9 \text{ in.})\right] + (15 \text{ in.} \times 10 \text{ in.})$

$\qquad + (12 \text{ in.} \times 10 \text{ in.}) + (9 \text{ in.} \times 10 \text{ in.})$

$= 2(54 \text{ in.}^2) + 150 \text{ in.}^2 + 120 \text{ in.}^2 + 90 \text{ in.}^2$

$= 108 \text{ in.}^2 + 360 \text{ in.}^2$

$= \mathbf{468 \text{ in.}^2}$

Practice 26

a. $3m - 7m = 8m - 6$

$-4m = 8m - 6$

$$\underline{-8m \quad -8m}$$

$-12m = \qquad -6$

$$\frac{-12m}{-12} = \frac{-6}{-12}$$

$m = \dfrac{1}{2}$

b. $5 - 6p = 9p - 7 + 8p - 3 + 2p$

$5 - 6p = 19p - 10$

$$\underline{-19p \quad -19p}$$

$5 - 25p = \qquad -10$

$$\underline{-5 \qquad\qquad\qquad -5}$$

$-25p = \qquad -15$

$$\frac{-25p}{-25} = \frac{-15}{-25}$$

$p = \dfrac{3}{5}$

c. $2x + 3x + 4x - 5 = 2 + 3 + 4x$

$$9x - 5 = 5 + 4x$$
$$\underline{-4x \qquad\qquad -4x}$$
$$5x - 5 = 5$$
$$\underline{\qquad +5 \quad +5}$$
$$5x \qquad = 10$$
$$\frac{5x}{5} = \frac{10}{5}$$
$$x = \mathbf{2}$$

d. $3p + 7 - (-3) = p + (-2)$

$$3p + 10 = p - 2$$
$$\underline{-p \qquad\qquad -p}$$
$$2p + 10 = -2$$
$$\underline{\quad -10 \qquad -10}$$
$$2p \qquad = -12$$
$$\frac{2p}{2} = \frac{-12}{2}$$
$$p = \mathbf{-6}$$

Problem Set 26

1. **Negative number**

2. (a) $\{1, 2, 3, \ldots\}$

(b) $\{0, 1, 2, 3, \ldots\}$

(c) $\{\ldots, -3, -2, -1, 0, 1, 2, 3, \ldots\}$

3. $1000 \text{ cm} \times \dfrac{1 \text{ m}}{100 \text{ cm}} = \dfrac{\mathbf{1000}}{\mathbf{100}} \text{ m} = \mathbf{10\ m}$

4. $525 \text{ cm} \cdot \text{cm} \times \dfrac{1 \text{ in.}}{2.54 \text{ cm}} \times \dfrac{1 \text{ in.}}{2.54 \text{ cm}}$

$= \dfrac{\mathbf{525}}{\mathbf{(2.54)^2}} \text{ in.}^2 = \mathbf{81.38\ in.^2}$

5. $A = \dfrac{1}{2}(15 \text{ in.})(12 \text{ in.}) = \mathbf{90\ in.^2}$

6.
$$A = \pi r^2$$
$$16\pi \text{ ft}^2 = \pi r^2$$
$$16(3.14) \text{ ft}^2 = (3.14)r^2$$
$$50.24 \text{ ft}^2 = 3.14 r^2$$
$$\frac{50.24 \text{ ft}^2}{3.14} = r^2$$
$$16 \text{ ft}^2 = r^2$$

The radius is **4 ft** because $4 \text{ ft} \times 4 \text{ ft} = 16 \text{ ft}^2$.

7. $k - \dfrac{2}{3} = 3\dfrac{1}{3}$

$$\underline{\quad +\frac{2}{3} \qquad +\frac{2}{3}}$$
$$k \qquad = 3\frac{1}{3} + \frac{2}{3}$$
$$k = \mathbf{4}$$

8. $7x = 49$

$$\frac{7x}{7} = \frac{49}{7}$$
$$x = \mathbf{7}$$

9. $2\dfrac{1}{2}x = \dfrac{3}{7}$

$$\frac{2\frac{1}{2}x}{2\frac{1}{2}} = \frac{\frac{3}{7}}{2\frac{1}{2}}$$
$$x = \frac{\frac{3}{7}}{\frac{5}{2}}$$
$$x = \frac{3}{7} \cdot \frac{2}{5}$$
$$x = \frac{\mathbf{6}}{\mathbf{35}}$$

10. $3x - 4 = 7$

$$\underline{\quad +4 \qquad +4}$$
$$3x \qquad = 11$$
$$\frac{3x}{3} = \frac{11}{3}$$
$$x = \frac{\mathbf{11}}{\mathbf{3}}$$

11. $-3y + \dfrac{1}{2} = \dfrac{5}{7}$

$$\underline{\quad -\frac{1}{2} \qquad -\frac{1}{2}}$$
$$-3y \qquad = \frac{3}{14}$$
$$\frac{-3y}{-3} = \frac{\frac{3}{14}}{-3}$$
$$y = \frac{3}{14} \cdot -\frac{1}{3}$$
$$y = -\frac{\mathbf{1}}{\mathbf{14}}$$

12.
$$0.4x - 0.3 = -0.14$$
$$\underline{+0.3 \qquad +0.3}$$
$$0.4x \qquad = 0.16$$
$$\frac{0.4x}{0.4} = \frac{0.16}{0.4}$$
$$x = \mathbf{0.4}$$

13.
$$3x - 2 = 6x + 4$$
$$\underline{-6x \qquad -6x}$$
$$-3x - 2 = \qquad 4$$
$$\underline{+2 \qquad +2}$$
$$-3x \qquad = \qquad 6$$
$$\frac{-3x}{-3} = \frac{6}{-3}$$
$$x = \mathbf{-2}$$

14.
$$2x + x + 3 = x + 2 - 5$$
$$3x + 3 = x - 3$$
$$\underline{-x \qquad -x}$$
$$2x + 3 = \qquad -3$$
$$\underline{-3 \qquad -3}$$
$$2x \qquad = \qquad -6$$
$$\frac{2x}{2} = \frac{-6}{2}$$
$$x = \mathbf{-3}$$

15.
$$-m - 6m + 4 = -2m - 5$$
$$-7m + 4 = -2m - 5$$
$$\underline{+2m \qquad\quad +2m}$$
$$-5m + 4 = \qquad -5$$
$$\underline{-4 \qquad\qquad -4}$$
$$-5m \qquad = \qquad -9$$
$$\frac{-5m}{-5} = \frac{-9}{-5}$$
$$m = \mathbf{\frac{9}{5}}$$

16. (a) **10**

(b) **10**

(c) **Yes**

(d) **Yes**

17.
$$(-7) + 7 = 0 \qquad (7) + 7 = 0$$
$$0 = 0 \qquad\qquad 14 \neq 0$$

Therefore, **−7 satisfies the equation.**

18. $m^2 y^5 m y y^3 m^3 = m^2 m m^3 y^5 y y^3 = \mathbf{m^6 y^9}$

19. $k^5 m m m^2 k^2 m^2 k^3 a a^2 = a a^2 k^5 k^2 k^3 m m m^2 m^2$
$= \mathbf{a^3 k^{10} m^6}$

20. $a - ax + 2xa - 3a - 3 = \mathbf{-2a + ax - 3}$

21. $a^2bc + 2bc - bca^2 + 5ca^2b - 3cb = \mathbf{5a^2bc - bc}$

22. $4(7 - 3x^2) = 4(7) + 4(-3x^2) = \mathbf{28 - 12x^2}$

23. $x(y - a) + a(y - x)$
$= -3[2 - (-1)] + (-1)[2 - (-3)]$
$= -3(2 + 1) - 1(2 + 3) = -3(3) - 1(5)$
$= -9 - 5 = \mathbf{-14}$

24. $a(-a^2 + b) - |b - a|$
$= -2[-(-2)^2 + 4] - |4 - (-2)|$
$= -2(-4 + 4) - |4 + 2| = -2(0) - 6 = \mathbf{-6}$

25. $-4(-3 + 2) - 3 - (-4) - |-3 + 2|$
$= -4(-1) - 3 + 4 - |-1| = 4 - 3 + 4 - 1 = \mathbf{4}$

26. $-3^2 - (-3)^3 + (-2) - \sqrt[3]{-125}$
$= -9 - (-27) - 2 - (-5)$
$= -9 + 27 - 2 + 5 = \mathbf{21}$

27. $P = (500 + 620 + 400 + 210 + 100 + 410)$ mi
$= \mathbf{2240 \ mi}$

28. $A = \frac{1}{2}(9 \text{ cm})(12 \text{ cm}) = \mathbf{54 \ cm^2}$

29. $4\frac{2}{3} + 5\frac{1}{4} + 9\frac{1}{12} = 4\frac{8}{12} + 5\frac{3}{12} + 9\frac{1}{12}$
$= 18\frac{12}{12} = \mathbf{19 \ m}$

30. $V = (\text{Area}_{\text{base}})(\text{Height})$
$= [\pi(2 \text{ km})^2](6 \text{ km})$
$= \mathbf{24\pi \ km^3} = \mathbf{75.36 \ km^3}$

Practice 27

a. $xy^2(y^2p - p) = (xy^2)(y^2p) + (xy^2)(-p)$
$= \mathbf{xy^4p - xy^2p}$

b. $(xy - x)2xy = (2xy)(xy) + (2xy)(-x)$
$= \mathbf{2x^2y^2 - 2x^2y}$

c. $3xp^3(p^5 - x^2p^8) = (3xp^3)(p^5) + (3xp^3)(-x^2p^8)$
$= \mathbf{3xp^8 - 3x^3p^{11}}$

d. $2x^2m^2(m^2 - 4m)$
$= (2x^2m^2)(m^2) + (2x^2m^2)(-4m)$
$= \mathbf{2x^2m^4 - 8x^2m^3}$

e.
$$0.08x - 0.1 = 16.7$$
$$8x - 10 = 1670$$
$$8x = 1680$$
$$x = \mathbf{210}$$

f. $0.7m + 0.6m = 3.4$

$\qquad 7m + 6m = 34$

$\qquad\qquad 13m = 34$

$\qquad\qquad\quad m = \dfrac{34}{13}$

$\qquad\qquad\quad m = 2\dfrac{8}{13}$

Problem Set 27

1. **(a), (c), (d)**

2. **The angles opposite the sides of equal length have equal measures.**

3. $63{,}400$ in. $\times \dfrac{1\text{ ft}}{12\text{ in.}} \times \dfrac{1\text{ mi}}{5280\text{ ft}} = \dfrac{63{,}400}{(12)(5280)}$ mi

$\quad = \mathbf{1.00\ mi}$

4. 5800 in. $\cdot$ in. $\times \dfrac{1\text{ ft}}{12\text{ in.}} \times \dfrac{1\text{ ft}}{12\text{ in.}} = \dfrac{5800}{(12)^2}$ ft^2

$\quad = \mathbf{40.28\ ft^2}$

5. $\qquad P = 4S$

$\quad 12\text{ cm} = 4S$

$\qquad\quad S = \dfrac{12\text{ cm}}{4}$

$\qquad\quad S = 3\text{ cm}$

$\quad A = S^2 = (3\text{ cm})^2 = \mathbf{9\ cm^2}$

6. $x - \dfrac{1}{4} = \dfrac{5}{8}$

$\quad \underline{+\dfrac{1}{4} \quad +\dfrac{1}{4}}$

$\quad x \qquad = \dfrac{5}{8} + \dfrac{1}{4}$

$\qquad\quad x = \dfrac{7}{8}$

7. $1\dfrac{1}{2}y = 6\dfrac{3}{4}$

$\quad \dfrac{1\frac{1}{2}y}{1\frac{1}{2}} = \dfrac{6\frac{3}{4}}{1\frac{1}{2}}$

$\qquad y = \dfrac{\frac{27}{4}}{\frac{3}{2}}$

$\qquad y = \dfrac{27}{4} \cdot \dfrac{2}{3}$

$\qquad y = \dfrac{9}{2}$

8. $\dfrac{x}{3\frac{1}{2}} = 4$

$\quad \dfrac{3\frac{1}{2}x}{3\frac{1}{2}} = 4 \cdot 3\dfrac{1}{2}$

$\qquad\quad x = 4 \cdot \dfrac{7}{2}$

$\qquad\quad x = \mathbf{14}$

9. $\dfrac{1}{2}x + \dfrac{3}{4} = -\dfrac{3}{8}$

$\qquad \underline{\quad -\dfrac{3}{4} \qquad -\dfrac{3}{4}}$

$\qquad \dfrac{1}{2}x \qquad = -\dfrac{9}{8}$

$\quad \dfrac{2}{1} \cdot \dfrac{1}{2}x = -\dfrac{9}{8} \cdot \dfrac{2}{1}$

$\qquad\qquad x = -\dfrac{9}{4}$

10. $0.02m + 0.2 = 1.4$

$\quad\ 2m + 20 = 140$

$\qquad\qquad 2m = 120$

$\qquad\qquad\ m = \mathbf{60}$

11. $0.4x - 0.2 = -0.12$

$\quad 40x - 20 = -12$

$\qquad\quad 40x = 8$

$\qquad\qquad x = \dfrac{8}{40}$

$\qquad\qquad x = \mathbf{0.2}$

12. $5x - 3 - 2 = 3x - 2 + x$

$\qquad 5x - 5 = 4x - 2$

$\quad \underline{-4x \qquad\ -4x}$

$\qquad\ x - 5 = \qquad -2$

$\qquad \underline{\ +5 \qquad\qquad +5}$

$\qquad\qquad x = 3$

13. $x + 3 - 5 - 2x = x - 3 - 7x$

$\qquad\quad -x - 2 = -6x - 3$

$\qquad \underline{+6x \qquad\qquad +6x}$

$\qquad\ 5x - 2 = \qquad -3$

$\qquad \underline{\ +2 \qquad\qquad +2}$

$\qquad\ 5x \qquad = \qquad -1$

$\qquad\qquad \dfrac{5x}{5} = \dfrac{-1}{5}$

$\qquad\qquad\ x = -\dfrac{1}{5}$

14. $m + 4m - 2 - 2m = 2m + 2 - 3$

$$3m - 2 = 2m - 1$$

$$\underline{-2m \qquad\quad -2m}$$

$$\begin{array}{rr} m - 2 = & -1 \\ \underline{+2 \qquad} & \underline{+2} \\ m = & 1 \end{array}$$

15. (a) **–1**

    (b) **–1**

    (c) **Yes**

    (d) **Yes**

16. $(-3)^2 + 2(-3) = 3 \qquad (1)^2 + 2(1) = 3$

$$9 - 6 = 3 \qquad\qquad 1 + 2 = 3$$

$$3 = 3 \qquad\qquad\quad 3 = 3$$

    Therefore, **–3 and 1 are roots of the equation.**

17. $p^2xyy^2x^2yx^2x = p^2xx^2x^2xyy^2y = \mathbf{p^2x^6y^4}$

18. $3p^2x^4yp^5xxyy^2 = 3p^2p^5x^4xxyyy^2 = \mathbf{3p^7x^6y^4}$

19. $-4x + x^2 - 3x - 5 + 7x^2 = \mathbf{-7x + 8x^2 - 5}$

20. $xyp^2 - 4p^2xy + 5xp^2y - 7yxp^2 = \mathbf{-5p^2xy}$

21. $4x^2(ax - 2) = (4x^2)(ax) + (4x^2)(-2)$

$$= \mathbf{4ax^3 - 8x^2}$$

22. $(a - b) + (-a)^2 = (-3 - 6) + [-(-3)]^2$

$$= -9 + 9 = \mathbf{0}$$

23. $-(-p)^2 + (p - x) = -[-(-2)]^2 + (-2 - 5)$

$$= -(2)^2 - 7 = -4 - 7 = \mathbf{-11}$$

24. $-3^2 - 3(3^2 - 4) - \sqrt[4]{16} - |-7 + 2|$

$$= -9 - 3(9 - 4) - 2 - |-5|$$

$$= -9 - 3(5) - 2 - 5 = -9 - 15 - 2 - 5 = \mathbf{-31}$$

25. $\dfrac{-6 - (-2 - 3) + 1}{4 - (-3) - 7} = \dfrac{-6 - (-5) + 1}{4 + 3 - 7}$

$$= \dfrac{0}{0}, \text{ which is } \mathbf{indeterminate}$$

26. $P = (14 + 10 + 14 + 10)\,\text{m} = \mathbf{48\ m}$

27. $A = (12\ \text{km} \times 7\ \text{km}) + \dfrac{1}{2}(12\ \text{km} \times 11\ \text{km})$

$$= 84\ \text{km}^2 + 66\ \text{km}^2 = \mathbf{150\ km^2}$$

28. $\text{Area} = \text{Area}_{\text{rectangle}} - \text{Area}_{\text{triangle}}$

$$= (9\ \text{in.} \times 8\ \text{in.}) - \left[\dfrac{1}{2}(6\ \text{in.} \times 3\ \text{in.})\right]$$

$$= 72\ \text{in.}^2 - 9\ \text{in.}^2$$

$$= \mathbf{63\ in.^2}$$

29. Since angles opposite sides of equal length have equal measure, $x = \mathbf{50}$.

$$y = 180 - 50 - 50$$

$$\mathbf{y = 80}$$

30. $S.A. = 2(\text{Area}_{\text{base}}) + \text{Lateral Surface Area}$

$$= 2[\pi(4\ \text{ft})^2] + (\text{Perimeter}_{\text{base}})(\text{Height})$$

$$= 2(16\pi\ \text{ft}^2) + [2\pi(4\ \text{ft})](7\ \text{ft})$$

$$= 32\pi\ \text{ft}^2 + (8\pi\ \text{ft})(7\ \text{ft})$$

$$= 32\pi\ \text{ft}^2 + 56\pi\ \text{ft}^2$$

$$= \mathbf{88\pi\ ft^2 = 276.32\ ft^2}$$

Practice 28

a. $\dfrac{4}{3}WN = 64$

     $\dfrac{3}{4} \cdot \dfrac{4}{3}WN = 64 \cdot \dfrac{3}{4}$

          $WN = \mathbf{48}$

b. $3\dfrac{1}{5}WN = 48$

     $\dfrac{16}{5}WN = 48$

     $\dfrac{5}{16} \cdot \dfrac{16}{5}WN = 48 \cdot \dfrac{5}{16}$

          $WN = \mathbf{15}$

c. $WF(60) = 48$

     $\dfrac{WF \cdot 60}{60} = \dfrac{48}{60}$

          $WF = \dfrac{\mathbf{4}}{\mathbf{5}}$

d. $\left(4\dfrac{1}{2}\right)(220) = WN$

          $WN = \dfrac{9}{2} \cdot 220$

          $WN = \mathbf{990}$

e. $f(x) = x^2 - 3$

     $f(-1) = (-1)^2 - 3 = 1 - 3 = \mathbf{-2}$

f. $g(x) = x(x^2 - 3)$

     $g(2) = 2(2^2 - 3) = 2(4 - 3) = 2(1) = \mathbf{2}$

Problem Set 28

1. **Negative number**

2. **The sides opposite the angles of equal measure have equal lengths.**

3. $3938 \text{ in.} \times \dfrac{2.54 \text{ cm}}{1 \text{ in.}} \times \dfrac{1 \text{ m}}{100 \text{ cm}} = \dfrac{3938(2.54)}{(100)} \text{ m}$

    $= \mathbf{100.03 \text{ m}}$

4. $200 \text{ km} \cdot \text{km} \times \dfrac{1000 \text{ m}}{1 \text{ km}} \times \dfrac{1000 \text{ m}}{1 \text{ km}}$

    $= \mathbf{200(1000)^2 \ m^2 = 200{,}000{,}000 \ m^2}$

5.
$$A = \pi r^2$$
$$25\pi \text{ in.}^2 = \pi r^2$$
$$25(3.14) \text{ in.}^2 = (3.14)r^2$$
$$78.5 \text{ in.}^2 = 3.14 r^2$$
$$\dfrac{78.5 \text{ in.}^2}{3.14} = r^2$$
$$25 \text{ in.}^2 = r^2$$

The radius is 5 in. because $5 \text{ in.} \times 5 \text{ in.} = 25 \text{ in.}^2$.

$D = 2r = 2(5 \text{ in.}) = \mathbf{10 \ in.}$

6.
$$\tfrac{2}{5}WN = 40$$
$$\tfrac{5}{2} \cdot \tfrac{2}{5}WN = 40 \cdot \tfrac{5}{2}$$
$$WN = \mathbf{100}$$

7.
$$WF(30) = 25$$
$$\dfrac{WF \cdot 30}{30} = \dfrac{25}{30}$$
$$WF = \mathbf{\dfrac{5}{6}}$$

8. $f(x) = x + 1$
$f(2) = 2 + 1 = \mathbf{3}$

9. $g(x) = 2x + 1$
$g(-1) = 2(-1) + 1 = -2 + 1 = \mathbf{-1}$

10. $\quad 3x = 18$
$$\dfrac{3x}{3} = \dfrac{18}{3}$$
$$x = \mathbf{6}$$

11. $2x - 3 = -9$
$$\underline{\quad +3 \quad +3 \quad}$$
$$2x \quad\;\; = -6$$
$$\dfrac{2x}{2} = \dfrac{-6}{2}$$
$$x = \mathbf{-3}$$

12. $\tfrac{1}{5}x + \tfrac{1}{2} = 2\tfrac{1}{10}$
$$\underline{\quad -\tfrac{1}{2} \quad\;\; -\tfrac{1}{2} \quad}$$
$$\tfrac{1}{5}x \quad\;\; = 1\tfrac{6}{10}$$
$$\tfrac{5}{1} \cdot \tfrac{1}{5}x = 1\tfrac{6}{10} \cdot \tfrac{5}{1}$$
$$x = \dfrac{16}{10} \cdot \dfrac{5}{1}$$
$$x = \dfrac{16}{2}$$
$$x = \mathbf{8}$$

13. $0.05x - 0.3 = 1.8$
$$5x - 30 = 180$$
$$5x = 210$$
$$x = \mathbf{42}$$

14. $x - 2 - 2x = 3 - x + 4x$
$$-x - 2 = 3x + 3$$
$$\underline{-3x \qquad\quad -3x \qquad}$$
$$-4x - 2 = \qquad 3$$
$$\underline{\quad\;\; +2 \qquad\quad +2 \quad}$$
$$-4x \quad\;\; = \qquad 5$$
$$\dfrac{-4x}{-4} = \dfrac{5}{-4}$$
$$x = \mathbf{-\dfrac{5}{4}}$$

15. $3y - y + 2y - 5 = 7 - 2y + 5$
$$4y - 5 = -2y + 12$$
$$\underline{+2y \qquad\quad +2y \qquad}$$
$$6y - 5 = \qquad 12$$
$$\underline{\quad\;\; +5 \qquad\quad +5 \quad}$$
$$6y \quad\;\; = \qquad 17$$
$$\dfrac{6y}{6} = \dfrac{17}{6}$$
$$y = \mathbf{\dfrac{17}{6}}$$

16. (a) **6**

    (b) **6**

    (c) **Yes**

    (d) **Yes**

17. $(-10) - 10 = 0 \qquad 10 - 10 = 0$
$$\quad\;\; -20 \neq 0 \qquad\qquad 0 = 0$$
Therefore, **10 satisfies the equation.**

18. $y^5 x^2 y^3 y x y^2 = x^2 x y^5 y^3 y y^2 = \mathbf{x^3 y^{11}}$

19. $m^2 m y y^2 m^3 y m = m^2 m m^3 m y y^2 y = \mathbf{m^7 y^4}$

20. $pc - 4cp + c - p + 7pc - 7c =$ **$4cp - 6c - p$**

21. $xym^2 + 3xy^2m - 4m^2xy + 5mxy^2$
$= -3m^2xy + 8mxy^2$

22. $x^2y(x^3 - xyz^3) = (x^2y)(x^3) + (x^2y)(-xyz^3)$
$= x^5y - x^3y^2z^3$

23. $p(a) - xp(-a) = -2(3) - 4(-2)(-3)$
$= -6 - 24 = -30$

24. $x^3y(x - y) = (-3)^3(1)(-3 - 1) = -27(-4) = 108$

25. $-4(-7 + 5)(-2) - |-2 - 5| = -4(-2)(-2) - |-7|$
$= -16 - 7 = -23$

26. $-3^2 + (-2)^3 - \sqrt[4]{81} = -9 - 8 - 3 = -20$

27. $P = \left(5 + 3 + 5 + 3 + \dfrac{2\pi(3)}{2}\right)$ ft
$= (16 + 3\pi)$ ft $= 25.42$ ft

28.

$A = (10 \text{ mi} \times 24 \text{ mi}) + \dfrac{1}{2}(18 \text{ mi} \times 24 \text{ mi})$
$= 240 \text{ mi}^2 + 216 \text{ mi}^2$
$= 456 \text{ mi}^2$

29. Since the sides opposite the angles of equal measure have equal lengths, $x = 5$.

30. $V = (\text{Area}_{\text{base}})(\text{Height})$
$= \left[\dfrac{1}{2}(8 \text{ cm} \times 13 \text{ cm})\right](12 \text{ cm})$
$= (52 \text{ cm}^2)(12 \text{ cm})$
$= 624 \text{ cm}^3$

Practice 29

a. $\dfrac{1}{2^{-3}} = 2^3 = 8$

b. $(-4)^{-2} = \dfrac{1}{(-4)^2} = \dfrac{1}{16}$

c. $\dfrac{1}{(-3)^{-2}} = (-3)^2 = 9$

d. $8^0 = 1$

e. $-8^0 = -1$

f. $(-3)^0 = 1$

g. $(p + m + k^2)^0 = 1$

h. $x^{-3}y^{-8}y^5x^4zx^2z^5 = x^{-3}x^4x^2y^{-8}y^5zz^5 = x^3y^{-3}z^6$

i. $x^6y^{-3}x^2y^3 = x^6x^2y^{-3}y^3 = x^8y^0 = x^8$

j. $2x^{-2}y^3(x^2y - 3x^{-1}y^{-3})$
$= 2x^{-2}y^3(x^2y) + 2x^{-2}y^3(-3x^{-1}y^{-3})$
$= 2x^{-2}x^2y^3y - 6x^{-2}x^{-1}y^3y^{-3}$
$= 2x^0y^4 - 6x^{-3}y^0 = 2y^4 - 6x^{-3}$

Problem Set 29

1. (a), (b)

2. Parallelogram

3. $500 \text{ ft} \times \dfrac{12 \text{ in.}}{1 \text{ ft}} \times \dfrac{2.54 \text{ cm}}{1 \text{ in.}} = 500(12)(2.54)$ cm
$= 15{,}240$ cm

4. $180 \text{ yd} \cdot \text{yd} \times \dfrac{3 \text{ ft}}{1 \text{ yd}} \times \dfrac{3 \text{ ft}}{1 \text{ yd}} = 180(3)^2 \text{ ft}^2$
$= 1620 \text{ ft}^2$

5. $A = S^2$
$16 \text{ in.}^2 = S^2$
Each side is 4 in. because $4 \text{ in.} \times 4 \text{ in.} = 16 \text{ in.}^2$.
$P = 4S = 4(4 \text{ in.}) = 16 \text{ in.}$

6. $2^{-2} = \dfrac{1}{2^2} = \dfrac{1}{4}$

7. $\dfrac{1}{4^{-2}} = 4^2 = 16$

8. $3^0 = 1$

9. $2\dfrac{1}{4}WN = 72$
$\dfrac{9}{4}WN = 72$
$\dfrac{4}{9} \cdot \dfrac{9}{4}WN = 72 \cdot \dfrac{4}{9}$
$WN = 32$

10. $\left(3\frac{1}{8}\right)(72) = WN$

$$WN = \frac{25}{8} \cdot 72$$

$$WN = \mathbf{225}$$

11. $f(x) = 2x - 1$

$f(3) = 2(3) - 1 = 6 - 1 = \mathbf{5}$

12. $g(x) = 3x + 2$

$g(-2) = 3(-2) + 2 = -6 + 2 = \mathbf{-4}$

13. $-x = 3$

$$\frac{-x}{-1} = \frac{3}{-1}$$

$$x = \mathbf{-3}$$

14. $\dfrac{y}{2\frac{1}{3}} = 6$

$$\frac{2\frac{1}{3}y}{2\frac{1}{3}} = 6 \cdot 2\frac{1}{3}$$

$$y = 6 \cdot \frac{7}{3}$$

$$y = \mathbf{14}$$

15. $\dfrac{1}{4}x + \dfrac{1}{2} = \dfrac{7}{8}$

$$\underline{\quad -\frac{1}{2} \quad -\frac{1}{2}}$$

$$\frac{1}{4}x = \frac{3}{8}$$

$$\frac{4}{1} \cdot \frac{1}{4}x = \frac{3}{8} \cdot \frac{4}{1}$$

$$x = \frac{\mathbf{3}}{\mathbf{2}}$$

16. $0.002k + 0.04 = 2.04$

$2k + 40 = 2040$

$2k = 2000$

$k = \mathbf{1000}$

17. $3x + 5 - x = x + 5$

$2x + 5 = x + 5$

$\underline{-x \qquad -x}$

$\underline{x + 5 = \qquad 5}$

$\underline{-5 \qquad -5}$

$x = \mathbf{0}$

18. $3m - 2 - m = -2 + m - 5$

$2m - 2 = m - 7$

$\underline{-m \qquad -m}$

$\underline{m - 2 = \qquad -7}$

$\underline{+2 \qquad +2}$

$m = \mathbf{-5}$

19. $x^5m^2x^{-3}m^{-4} = m^2m^{-4}x^5x^{-3} = \mathbf{m^{-2}x^2}$

20. $a^3b^{-4}a^{-3}b^6 = a^3a^{-3}b^{-4}b^6 = a^0b^2 = \mathbf{b^2}$

21. $4x^2yp - 7px^2y + 3ypx^2 - 4 = \mathbf{-4}$

22. $x^2y^3(3xy - 5y) = (x^2y^3)(3xy) + (x^2y^3)(-5y)$

$= \mathbf{3x^3y^4 - 5x^2y^4}$

23. $x^{-2}y(x^2y + 2x^3y^0) = (x^{-2}y)(x^2y) + (x^{-2}y)(2x^3)$

$= x^0y^2 + 2x^1y = \mathbf{y^2 + 2xy}$

24. $4x(a + x)(-x) = 4(-3)[2 + (-3)][-(-3)]$

$= -12(-1)(3) = \mathbf{36}$

25. $a^2 - (a + b) - |-a^3|$

$= (-2)^2 - (-2 + 3) - |-(-2)^3|$

$= 4 - (1) - 8 = \mathbf{-5}$

26. $\dfrac{2^2 - 3^2 - 4^2}{(-3)^2} = \dfrac{4 - 9 - 16}{9} = -\dfrac{21}{9} = -\dfrac{\mathbf{7}}{\mathbf{3}}$

27. $P = (46 + 29 + 46 + 21 + 11 + 19)\,\text{ft} = \mathbf{172\ ft}$

28. $A = (12\,\text{mi} \times 8\,\text{mi}) + \dfrac{1}{2}(12\,\text{mi} \times 4\,\text{mi})$

$= 96\,\text{mi}^2 + 24\,\text{mi}^2 = \mathbf{120\ mi^2}$

29. $\text{Area} = \text{Area}_{\text{triangle}} - \text{Area}_{\text{circle}}$

$= \dfrac{1}{2}(16\,\text{cm} \times 8\,\text{cm}) - \pi(3\,\text{cm})^2$

$= 64\,\text{cm}^2 - 9\pi\,\text{cm}^2$

$= \mathbf{(64 - 9\pi)\ cm^2 = 35.74\ cm^2}$

30. $S.A. = 2\left(\text{Area}_{\text{front}}\right) + 2\left(\text{Area}_{\text{side}}\right) + 2\left(\text{Area}_{\text{top}}\right)$

$= 2(4\,\text{m} \times 3\,\text{m}) + 2(3\,\text{m} \times 3\,\text{m})$

$+ 2(4\,\text{m} \times 3\,\text{m})$

$= 2(12\,\text{m}^2) + 2(9\,\text{m}^2) + 2(12\,\text{m}^2)$

$= 24\,\text{m}^2 + 18\,\text{m}^2 + 24\,\text{m}^2$

$= \mathbf{66\ m^2}$

Practice 30

a. $5(3N - 5)$

b. $3(N - 50)$

c. $5N - 13$

d. $3(-N - 7)$

e. $0.16WN = 10.24$

$$\frac{0.16WN}{0.16} = \frac{10.24}{0.16}$$

$$WN = \mathbf{64}$$

f. $WD(80) = 60$

$$\frac{WD \cdot 80}{80} = \frac{60}{80}$$

$$WD = \frac{3}{4}$$

$$WD = \mathbf{0.75}$$

g. $(0.48)(8) = WN$

$$WN = \mathbf{3.84}$$

Problem Set 30

1. **Positive number**

2. **Trapezoid**

3. $10{,}000 \text{ ft} \times \dfrac{12 \text{ in.}}{1 \text{ ft}} \times \dfrac{2.54 \text{ cm}}{1 \text{ in.}}$

  $= \mathbf{10{,}000(12)(2.54) \text{ cm} = 304{,}800 \text{ cm}}$

4. $135 \text{ mi} \cdot \text{mi} \times \dfrac{5280 \text{ ft}}{1 \text{ mi}} \times \dfrac{5280 \text{ ft}}{1 \text{ mi}}$

  $= \mathbf{135(5280)^2 \text{ ft}^2 = 3{,}763{,}584{,}000 \text{ ft}^2}$

5. $A = \pi r^2$

     $36\pi \text{ cm}^2 = \pi r^2$

  $36(3.14) \text{ cm}^2 = (3.14)r^2$

    $113.04 \text{ cm}^2 = 3.14r^2$

    $\dfrac{113.04 \text{ cm}^2}{3.14} = r^2$

       $36 \text{ cm}^2 = r^2$

The radius is 6 cm because $6 \text{ cm} \times 6 \text{ cm} = 36 \text{ cm}^2$.

$D = 2r = 2(6 \text{ cm}) = \mathbf{12 \text{ cm}}$

6. $\mathbf{5N - 8}$

7. $\mathbf{3(-N - 7)}$

8. $0.18WN = 4.68$

$$\frac{0.18WN}{0.18} = \frac{4.68}{0.18}$$

$$WN = \mathbf{26}$$

9. $WD(60) = 45$

$$\frac{WD \cdot 60}{60} = \frac{45}{60}$$

$$WD = \frac{3}{4}$$

$$WD = \mathbf{0.75}$$

10. $(-3)^{-2} = \dfrac{1}{(-3)^2} = \dfrac{\mathbf{1}}{\mathbf{9}}$

11. $\dfrac{1}{(-3)^{-3}} = (-3)^3 = \mathbf{-27}$

12. $-3^0 = \mathbf{-1}$

13. $3\frac{1}{4}WN = 91$

       $\dfrac{13}{4}WN = 91$

  $\dfrac{4}{13} \cdot \dfrac{13}{4}WN = 91 \cdot \dfrac{4}{13}$

          $WN = \mathbf{28}$

14. $\left(\dfrac{7}{3}\right)(42) = WN$

        $WN = \mathbf{98}$

15. $f(x) = 3x - 5$

  $f(-2) = 3(-2) - 5 = -6 - 5 = \mathbf{-11}$

16. $g(x) = 4x + 2$

  $g(2) = 4(2) + 2 = 8 + 2 = \mathbf{10}$

17. $3x - 7 = 42$

$$\frac{\quad +7 \quad +7}{3x \quad\;\; = 49}$$

$$\frac{3x}{3} = \frac{49}{3}$$

$$x = \mathbf{\frac{49}{3}}$$

18. $\dfrac{3}{4}y = 4\frac{7}{8}$

  $\dfrac{4}{3} \cdot \dfrac{3}{4}y = \dfrac{39}{8} \cdot \dfrac{4}{3}$

         $y = \dfrac{\mathbf{13}}{\mathbf{2}}$

19. $\frac{1}{2}x + \frac{1}{2} = 2\frac{1}{5}$

$\phantom{\frac{1}{2}x}\;\; \underline{-\frac{1}{2} \quad -\frac{1}{2}}$

$\frac{1}{2}x \qquad = 1\frac{7}{10}$

$\frac{2}{1} \cdot \frac{1}{2}x = 1\frac{7}{10} \cdot \frac{2}{1}$

$\qquad x = \frac{17}{10} \cdot \frac{2}{1}$

$\qquad x = \mathbf{\frac{17}{5}}$

20. $0.03x - 0.6 = 2.4$

$\qquad 3x - 60 = 240$

$\qquad 3x = 300$

$\qquad x = \mathbf{100}$

21. $7p - 15 = 4p - 5 + p$

$7p - 15 = 5p - 5$

$\underline{-5p \qquad\quad -5p}$

$2p - 15 = \qquad -5$

$\underline{\;+15 \qquad\quad +15}$

$2p \quad = \qquad 10$

$\frac{2p}{2} = \frac{10}{2}$

$p = \mathbf{5}$

22. $x^{-5}y^5axy^3a^{-3} = aa^{-3}x^{-5}xy^5y^3 = \mathbf{a^{-2}x^{-4}y^8}$

23. $m^2p^{-4}m^{-2}p^6 = m^2m^{-2}p^{-4}p^6 = m^0p^2 = \mathbf{p^2}$

24. $5m^2x^2y - 2x^2m^2y + 8m^2y^2x = \mathbf{3m^2x^2y + 8m^2xy^2}$

25. $x^{-4}y^0(x^4 - 3y^2x^5p^0)$

$= (x^{-4}y^0)(x^4) + (x^{-4}y^0)(-3y^2x^5p^0)$

$= x^0y^0 - 3x^{-4}x^5y^2 = \mathbf{1 - 3xy^2}$

26. $-c(ac - a) = -4[-3(4) - (-3)] = -4(-12 + 3)$

$= -4(-9) = \mathbf{36}$

27. $-n(n - m) - |m^2| = -(-4)(-4 - 3) - |3^2|$

$= 4(-7) - 9 = -28 - 9 = \mathbf{-37}$

28. $P = \left(18 + 12 + 18 + 12 + \frac{2\pi(12)}{2}\right)$ m

$\quad = \mathbf{(60 + 12\pi)\ m = 97.68\ m}$

29. $A = \frac{1}{2}(15\text{ km})(20\text{ km}) = \mathbf{150\ km^2}$

30. $V = (\text{Area}_{\text{base}})(\text{Length})$

$\quad = [\pi(4\text{ in.})^2](10\text{ in.})$

$\quad = (16\pi\text{ in.}^2)(10\text{ in.})$

$\quad = \mathbf{160\pi\ in.^3 = 502.4\ in.^3}$

Practice 31

a. $-3(2 - c) = c - 2$

$-6 + 3c = c - 2$

$\underline{-c \quad -c}$

$-6 + 2c = \qquad -2$

$\underline{+6 \qquad\qquad +6}$

$\qquad 2c = \qquad 4$

$\qquad c = \mathbf{2}$

b. $-(6c - 5) = 4(7c - 8) + 3$

$-6c + 5 = 28c - 32 + 3$

$-6c + 5 = 28c - 29$

$\underline{-28c \qquad\quad -28c}$

$-34c + 5 = \qquad -29$

$\underline{-5 \qquad\quad -5}$

$-34c \quad = \qquad -34$

$\qquad c = \mathbf{1}$

c. $-(7 - 9)z - 6z = 8(-6 + 2)$

$2z - 6z = 8(-4)$

$-4z = -32$

$z = \mathbf{8}$

Problem Set 31

1. **(a), (c)**

2. (a) **A rectangle is a parallelogram with four angles of equal measure.**

(b) **A rhombus is a parallelogram with four sides of equal length.**

(c) **A square is a rhombus with four angles of equal measure.**

(d) **Yes**

3. $20\text{ m} \times \frac{100\text{ cm}}{1\text{ m}} \times \frac{1\text{ in.}}{2.54\text{ cm}} = \mathbf{\frac{20(100)}{(2.54)}}$ **in.**

$= \mathbf{787.40\ in.}$

4. $1800\text{ m} \cdot \text{m} \times \frac{1\text{ km}}{1000\text{ m}} \times \frac{1\text{ km}}{1000\text{ m}}$

$= \mathbf{\frac{1800}{(1000)^2}\ km^2 = 0.0018\ km^2}$

5. $P = 4S$

$20\text{ in.} = 4S$

$\frac{20\text{ in.}}{4} = S$

$5\text{ in.} = S$

$A = S^2 = (5\text{ in.})^2 = \mathbf{25\ in.^2}$

6. $7(N - 5)$

7. $2(-N) - 7$

8. $7N - 51$

9. $4N - 15$

10. $0.21WN = 7.98$

$$\frac{0.21WN}{0.21} = \frac{7.98}{0.21}$$

$$WN = \textbf{38}$$

11. $(0.32)(62) = WN$

$$WN = \textbf{19.84}$$

12. $2^{-4} = \dfrac{1}{2^4} = \dfrac{\textbf{1}}{\textbf{16}}$

13. $\dfrac{1}{3^{-2}} = 3^2 = \textbf{9}$

14. $(-4)^0 = \textbf{1}$

15. $WF(60) = 42$

$$\frac{WF \cdot 60}{60} = \frac{42}{60}$$

$$WF = \frac{\textbf{7}}{\textbf{10}}$$

16. $\left(5\dfrac{1}{3}\right)(120) = WN$

$$WN = \frac{16}{3} \cdot 120$$

$$WN = \textbf{640}$$

17. $f(x) = -2x + 3$

$f(3) = -2(3) + 3 = -6 + 3 = \textbf{-3}$

18. $5k - 4 = -30$

$$\frac{+4 \qquad +4}{5k \quad = -26}$$

$$k = -\frac{\textbf{26}}{\textbf{5}}$$

19. $3\dfrac{1}{3}x - \dfrac{1}{2} = 5$

$$\frac{+\dfrac{1}{2} \qquad +\dfrac{1}{2}}{3\dfrac{1}{3}x \qquad = 5\dfrac{1}{2}}$$

$$\frac{3\dfrac{1}{3}x}{3\dfrac{1}{3}} = \frac{5\dfrac{1}{2}}{3\dfrac{1}{3}}$$

$$x = \frac{\dfrac{11}{2}}{\dfrac{10}{3}}$$

$$x = \frac{11}{2} \cdot \frac{3}{10}$$

$$x = \frac{\textbf{33}}{\textbf{20}}$$

20. $0.002k + 0.02 = 2.06$

$$2k + 20 = 2060$$

$$2k = 2040$$

$$k = \textbf{1020}$$

21. $3(p - 2) = p + 7$

$$3p - 6 = p + 7$$

$$\frac{-p \qquad\quad -p}{2p - 6 = \qquad 7}$$

$$\frac{+6 \qquad\quad +6}{2p \quad = \qquad 13}$$

$$p = \frac{\textbf{13}}{\textbf{2}}$$

22. $2(3x - 5) = 7x + 2$

$$6x - 10 = 7x + 2$$

$$\frac{-7x \qquad\quad -7x}{-x - 10 = \qquad 2}$$

$$\frac{+10 \qquad\quad +10}{-x \quad = \qquad 12}$$

$$x = \textbf{-12}$$

23. $(-1)^2 + 5(-1) = -4 \qquad (4)^2 + 5(4) = -4$

$\qquad\quad 1 - 5 = -4 \qquad\qquad 16 + 20 = -4$

$\qquad\qquad -4 = -4 \qquad\qquad\quad 36 \neq -4$

Therefore, **-1 is a root of the equation.**

24. $xmp^{-2} - 4p^{-2}xm + 6p^{-2}mx - 5mx$

$= \textbf{3}\boldsymbol{mp^{-2}x} - \textbf{5}\boldsymbol{mx}$

25. $p^0x^{-1}(x - 2x^0) = (p^0x^{-1})(x) + (p^0x^{-1})(-2x^0)$

$= p^0x^0 - 2p^0x^{-1} = \textbf{1} - \textbf{2}\boldsymbol{x^{-1}}$

26. $y^0x^{-4}(x^4 - 5y^4x^4)$
$= (y^0x^{-4})(x^4) + (y^0x^{-4})(-5y^4x^4)$
$= y^0x^0 - 5x^0y^4 = \mathbf{1 - 5y^4}$

27. $-a^2 - 3a(a - b) = -(-2)^2 - 3(-2)[-2 - (-1)]$
$= -4 + 6(-2 + 1) = -4 + 6(-1) = -4 - 6$
$= \mathbf{-10}$

28. $-c(ac - a^0) = -4[-3(4) - (-3)^0] = -4(-12 - 1)$
$= -4(-13) = \mathbf{52}$

29. $P = \left(10 + 6 + 10 + \dfrac{2\pi(3)}{2}\right)$ ft
$= (26 + 3\pi) \text{ ft} = \mathbf{35.42 \text{ ft}}$

30. $V = \left(\text{Area}_{\text{base}}\right)(\text{Height})$
$= (58 \text{ cm}^2)(15 \text{ cm}) = \mathbf{870 \text{ cm}^3}$

Practice 32

a. $4N - 8 = 92$
$ \underline{+8 \quad +8}$
$4N = 100$
$N = \mathbf{25}$

$4(25) - 8 = 92$
$100 - 8 = 92$
$ 92 = 92 \qquad \text{Check}$

b. $4N - 12 = 2(-N)$
$4N - 12 = -2N$
$\underline{+2N \quad +2N}$
$6N - 12 = 0$
$\underline{ +12 \quad +12}$
$6N = 12$
$N = \mathbf{2}$

$4(2) - 12 = 2(-2)$
$8 - 12 = -4$
$ -4 = -4 \qquad \text{Check}$

Problem Set 32

1. (a) **Surface area**

(b) **Multiply the perimeter of a base by the height of the right solid.**

2. (a) **Natural numbers (or counting numbers)**

(b) **Whole numbers**

(c) **Integers**

3. $1828 \text{ cm} \times \dfrac{1 \text{ in.}}{2.54 \text{ cm}} \times \dfrac{1 \text{ ft}}{12 \text{ in.}} = \dfrac{1828}{(2.54)(12)} \text{ ft}$
$= \mathbf{59.97 \text{ ft}}$

4. $57 \text{ ft} \cdot \text{ft} \times \dfrac{1 \text{ yd}}{3 \text{ ft}} \times \dfrac{1 \text{ yd}}{3 \text{ ft}} = \dfrac{57}{(3)^2} \text{ yd}^2 = \mathbf{6.33 \text{ yd}^2}$

5. $ C = 2\pi r$
$ 14\pi \text{ cm} = 2\pi r$
$14(3.14) \text{ cm} = 2(3.14)r$
$ 43.96 \text{ cm} = 6.28r$
$ \dfrac{43.96 \text{ cm}}{6.28} = r$
$ 7 \text{ cm} = r$
$D = 2r = 2(7 \text{ cm}) = \mathbf{14 \text{ cm}}$

6. $2N + 17 = 55$
$ \underline{-17 \quad -17}$
$2N = 38$
$N = \mathbf{19}$

7. $2N - 16 = 84$
$ \underline{+16 \quad +16}$
$2N = 100$
$N = \mathbf{50}$

8. $DP(25) = 1.25$
$\dfrac{DP \cdot 25}{25} = \dfrac{1.25}{25}$
$DP = \mathbf{0.05}$

9. $(-5)^{-2} = \dfrac{1}{(-5)^2} = \mathbf{\dfrac{1}{25}}$

10. $\dfrac{1}{(-4)^{-3}} = (-4)^3 = \mathbf{-64}$

11. $-5^0 = \mathbf{-1}$

12. $\left(2\dfrac{1}{9}\right)WN = 76$
$\dfrac{2\dfrac{1}{9}WN}{2\dfrac{1}{9}} = \dfrac{76}{2\dfrac{1}{9}}$
$WN = \dfrac{76}{\dfrac{19}{9}}$
$WN = 76 \cdot \dfrac{9}{19}$
$WN = \mathbf{36}$

13. $g(x) = -5x - 4$

$g(-5) = -5(-5) - 4 = 25 - 4 = \textbf{21}$

14. $2\frac{1}{2}x - 5 = 15$

$\underline{\quad\quad +5 \quad +5}$

$2\frac{1}{2}x \quad = 20$

$\dfrac{2\frac{1}{2}x}{2\frac{1}{2}} = \dfrac{20}{2\frac{1}{2}}$

$x = \dfrac{20}{\frac{5}{2}}$

$x = 20 \cdot \dfrac{2}{5}$

$x = \textbf{8}$

15. $2\frac{1}{4}k + \frac{1}{4} = \frac{1}{8}$

$\underline{\quad -\frac{1}{4} \quad -\frac{1}{4}}$

$2\frac{1}{4}k \quad = -\frac{1}{8}$

$\dfrac{2\frac{1}{4}k}{2\frac{1}{4}} = \dfrac{-\frac{1}{8}}{2\frac{1}{4}}$

$k = \dfrac{-\frac{1}{8}}{\frac{9}{4}}$

$k = -\dfrac{1}{8} \cdot \dfrac{4}{9}$

$k = -\dfrac{\textbf{1}}{\textbf{18}}$

16. $0.025x + 0.03 = 1.03$

$25x + 30 = 1030$

$25x = 1000$

$x = \textbf{40}$

17. $3p - 4 - 6 = -2(p - 5)$

$3p - 10 = -2p + 10$

$\underline{+2p \quad\quad\quad +2p}$

$5p - 10 = \quad\quad 10$

$\underline{\quad +10 \quad\quad +10}$

$5p \quad = \quad 20$

$p = \textbf{4}$

18. $-(x - 3) - 2(x - 4) = 7$

$-x + 3 - 2x + 8 = 7$

$-3x + 11 = 7$

$\underline{\quad -11 \quad -11}$

$-3x \quad = -4$

$x = \dfrac{\textbf{4}}{\textbf{3}}$

19. (a) **4**

(b) **−4**

(c) **No**

(d) **No**

20. $k^2p^{-4}y - 5k^2yp^{-4} + 2yk^2p^{-4} - 5k^2yp^{-4}$

$= \textbf{−7}k^2p^{-4}y$

21. $2x^{-2}y^0(x^2y^0 - 4x^{-6}y^4)$

$= (2x^{-2}y^0)(x^2y^0) + (2x^{-2}y^0)(-4x^{-6}y^4)$

$= 2x^0y^0 - 8x^{-8}y^4 = \textbf{2 − 8}x^{-8}y^4$

22. $(x^2 - 4x^5y^{-5})3p^0x^{-2}$

$= (3p^0x^{-2})(x^2) + (3p^0x^{-2})(-4x^5y^{-5})$

$= 3p^0x^0 - 12p^0x^3y^{-5} = \textbf{3 − 12}x^3y^{-5}$

23. $-a^3(a^0 - b) = -(-2)^3[(-2)^0 - 4]$

$= 8(1 - 4) = 8(-3) = \textbf{−24}$

24. $x(x^0 - y)(y - 2x) = -3[(-3)^0 - 5][5 - 2(-3)]$

$= -3(1 - 5)(5 + 6) = -3(-4)(11) = \textbf{132}$

25. $-3^2 + (-3)^3 - 3^0 - |-3 - 3|$

$= -9 - 27 - 1 - 6 = \textbf{−43}$

26. $\dfrac{-3[5(-2 - 1) - (6 - 3)]}{2(-3 - 4)} = \dfrac{-3[5(-3) - 3]}{2(-7)}$

$= \dfrac{-3(-15 - 3)}{-14} = \dfrac{-3(-18)}{-14} = \dfrac{54}{-14} = -\dfrac{\textbf{27}}{\textbf{7}}$

27.

Area $= A_1 + A_2$

$= \dfrac{1}{2}(20 \text{ m} \times 5 \text{ m}) + \dfrac{1}{2}(20 \text{ m} \times 5 \text{ m})$

$= \dfrac{1}{2}(100 \text{ m}^2) + \dfrac{1}{2}(100 \text{ m}^2)$

$= 50 \text{ m}^2 + 50 \text{ m}^2$

$= \textbf{100 m}^2$

28.
$$-46 \overline{)\begin{array}{r} -2.03 \\ 93.38 \end{array}}$$
$$\begin{array}{r} 92 \\ \hline 1\ 38 \\ 1\ 38 \end{array}$$

29. $14\dfrac{2}{5} - 4\dfrac{3}{10} - 3\dfrac{1}{2} = 14\dfrac{4}{10} - 4\dfrac{3}{10} - 3\dfrac{5}{10}$

$= 10\dfrac{1}{10} - 3\dfrac{5}{10} = 9\dfrac{11}{10} - 3\dfrac{5}{10} = 6\dfrac{6}{10}$

$= 6\dfrac{3}{5}$ **km**

30.

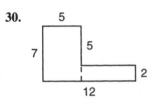

$S.A. = 2\left(\text{Area}_{\text{base}}\right) + \text{Lateral Surface Area}$
$= 2[(7 \text{ in.} \times 5 \text{ in.}) + (7 \text{ in.} \times 2 \text{ in.})]$
$\quad + \left(\text{Perimeter}_{\text{base}}\right)(\text{Height})$
$= 2\left(35 \text{ in.}^2 + 14 \text{ in.}^2\right)$
$\quad + [(12 + 7 + 5 + 5 + 7 + 2) \text{ in.}$
$\quad\quad \cdot (10 \text{ in.})]$
$= 2\left(49 \text{ in.}^2\right) + (38 \text{ in.})(10 \text{ in.})$
$= 98 \text{ in.}^2 + 380 \text{ in.}^2$
$= \mathbf{478 \text{ in.}^2}$

Practice 33

a.
$$\begin{array}{r} 8N = -N + 36 \\ +N \quad\quad +N \\ \hline 9N = \quad\quad 36 \end{array}$$
$N = \mathbf{4}$

$8(4) = -4 + 36$
$32 = 32 \quad$ Check

b. $2(N + 6) = N + 10$
$$\begin{array}{r} 2N + 12 = N + 10 \\ -N \quad\quad -N \\ \hline N + 12 = \quad\quad 10 \\ -12 \quad\quad -12 \\ \hline N = \mathbf{-2} \end{array}$$
$2(-2 + 6) = -2 + 10$
$\quad\quad 2(4) = 8$
$\quad\quad\quad\quad 8 = 8 \quad$ Check

c. $108 \quad \dfrac{108}{2} = 54 \quad \dfrac{54}{2} = 27 \quad \dfrac{27}{3} = 9$

$\dfrac{9}{3} = 3 \quad \mathbf{2 \cdot 2 \cdot 3 \cdot 3 \cdot 3}$

d. $400 \quad \dfrac{400}{2} = 200 \quad \dfrac{200}{2} = 100$

$\dfrac{100}{2} = 50 \quad \dfrac{50}{2} = 25 \quad \dfrac{25}{5} = 5$

$\mathbf{2 \cdot 2 \cdot 2 \cdot 2 \cdot 5 \cdot 5}$

Problem Set 33

1. Negative number

2. The angles opposite the sides of equal length have equal measures.

3. $9140 \text{ cm} \times \dfrac{1 \text{ in.}}{2.54 \text{ cm}} \times \dfrac{1 \text{ ft}}{12 \text{ in.}} = \dfrac{9140}{(2.54)(12)}$ **ft**

$= \mathbf{299.87 \text{ ft}}$

4. $28,000 \text{ ft} \cdot \text{ft} \times \dfrac{1 \text{ mi}}{5280 \text{ ft}} \times \dfrac{1 \text{ mi}}{5280 \text{ ft}}$

$= \dfrac{28,000}{(5280)^2} \text{ mi}^2 = \mathbf{0.0010 \text{ mi}^2}$

5. $\quad\quad A = lw$
$24 \text{ cm}^2 = (8 \text{ cm})w$
$\dfrac{24 \text{ cm}^2}{8 \text{ cm}} = w$
$\quad 3 \text{ cm} = w$

$P = 2l + 2w$
$P = 2(8 \text{ cm}) + 2(3 \text{ cm})$
$P = 16 \text{ cm} + 6 \text{ cm}$
$P = \mathbf{22 \text{ cm}}$

6. $\quad 3N - 15 = 2(-N)$
$$\begin{array}{r} 3N - 15 = -2N \\ +2N \quad\quad +2N \\ \hline 5N - 15 = \quad 0 \\ +15 \quad +15 \\ \hline 5N \quad\quad = 15 \end{array}$$
$N = \mathbf{3}$

7. $2N = -104 - 36$
$2N = -140$
$N = \mathbf{-70}$

8. $60 \quad \dfrac{60}{2} = 30 \quad \dfrac{30}{2} = 15 \quad \dfrac{15}{3} = 5$

$\mathbf{2 \cdot 2 \cdot 3 \cdot 5}$

9. $105 \quad \dfrac{105}{3} = 35 \quad \dfrac{35}{5} = 7 \quad \mathbf{3 \cdot 5 \cdot 7}$

10. $(1.025)(50) = WN$

$\qquad WN = \mathbf{51.25}$

11. $2^{-3} = \dfrac{1}{2^3} = \dfrac{\mathbf{1}}{\mathbf{8}}$

12. $(-3)^{-3} = \dfrac{1}{(-3)^3} = -\dfrac{\mathbf{1}}{\mathbf{27}}$

13. $(-6)^0 = \mathbf{1}$

14. $\left(2\dfrac{5}{8}\right)(32) = WN$

$\qquad WN = \left(\dfrac{21}{8}\right)(32)$

$\qquad WN = \mathbf{84}$

15. $h(x) = -9x - 3$

$\qquad h(3) = -9(3) - 3 = -27 - 3 = \mathbf{-30}$

16. $\dfrac{5}{8}x - 3 = \dfrac{1}{2}$

$\qquad \dfrac{+3 \quad +3}{\dfrac{5}{8}x \qquad = 3\dfrac{1}{2}}$

$\qquad \dfrac{\dfrac{5}{8}x}{\dfrac{5}{8}} = \dfrac{3\dfrac{1}{2}}{\dfrac{5}{8}}$

$\qquad x = \dfrac{7}{2} \cdot \dfrac{8}{5}$

$\qquad x = \dfrac{\mathbf{28}}{\mathbf{5}}$

17. $\dfrac{1}{8}y + 10 = 14\dfrac{1}{4}$

$\qquad \dfrac{-10 \quad -10}{\dfrac{1}{8}y \qquad = 4\dfrac{1}{4}}$

$\qquad \dfrac{\dfrac{1}{8}y}{\dfrac{1}{8}} = \dfrac{4\dfrac{1}{4}}{\dfrac{1}{8}}$

$\qquad y = \dfrac{17}{4} \cdot \dfrac{8}{1}$

$\qquad y = \mathbf{34}$

18. $0.005p + 1.4 = 0.005$

$\qquad 5p + 1400 = 5$

$\qquad 5p = -1395$

$\qquad p = \mathbf{-279}$

19. $k + 4 - 5(k + 2) = 3k - 2$

$\qquad k + 4 - 5k - 10 = 3k - 2$

$\qquad -4k - 6 = 3k - 2$

$\qquad \dfrac{-3k \qquad -3k}{-7k - 6 = \qquad -2}$

$\qquad \dfrac{+6 \qquad +6}{-7k \qquad = \qquad 4}$

$\qquad k = -\dfrac{\mathbf{4}}{\mathbf{7}}$

20. $x - 4(x - 3) + 7 = 6 - (x - 4)$

$\qquad x - 4x + 12 + 7 = 6 - x + 4$

$\qquad -3x + 19 = 10 - x$

$\qquad \dfrac{+x \qquad\qquad +x}{-2x + 19 = 10}$

$\qquad \dfrac{-19 \quad -19}{-2x \qquad = -9}$

$\qquad x = \dfrac{\mathbf{9}}{\mathbf{2}}$

21. $-3x^{-2}y^2x^5 + 6x^3y^{-2}y^4 - 3x^3y^2 + 5x^2y^3$

$\qquad = -3x^3y^2 + 6x^3y^2 - 3x^3y^2 + 5x^2y^3 = \mathbf{5x^2y^3}$

22. $2x^{-2}\left(x^{-2}y^0 + x^2y^5p^0\right)$

$\qquad = \left(2x^{-2}\right)\left(x^{-2}y^0\right) + \left(2x^{-2}\right)\left(x^2y^5p^0\right) = \mathbf{2x^{-4} + 2y^5}$

23. $\left(4p^{-2} - 3x^{-3}p^5\right)p^2x^0$

$\qquad = \left(p^2\right)\left(4p^{-2}\right) + \left(p^2\right)\left(-3x^{-3}p^5\right) = \mathbf{4 - 3p^7x^{-3}}$

24. $m - (-m)\left(m^0 - a\right) = -2 - [-(-2)]\left[(-2)^0 - 3\right]$

$\qquad = -2 - 2(1 - 3) = -2 - 2(-2) = -2 + 4 = \mathbf{2}$

25. $a^3x - \left|x^3\right| = (-3)^3(-2) - \left|(-2)^3\right|$

$\qquad = (-27)(-2) - 8 = 54 - 8 = \mathbf{46}$

26. $-2(-3) - (-4)^0(-3)|-5 - 2| = 6 - (-3)|-7|$

$\qquad = 6 + 3(7) = 6 + 21 = \mathbf{27}$

27. $(-2)^3 - (-2)^2 - 5 + \sqrt[3]{-64} = -8 - 4 - 5 - 4$

$\qquad = \mathbf{-21}$

28.

$\text{Area} = A_1 + A_2$

$\qquad = \dfrac{1}{2}(7\text{ m} \times 4\text{ m}) + \dfrac{1}{2}(13\text{ m} \times 4\text{ m})$

$\qquad = \dfrac{1}{2}\left(28\text{ m}^2\right) + \dfrac{1}{2}\left(52\text{ m}^2\right)$

$\qquad = 14\text{ m}^2 + 26\text{ m}^2$

$\qquad = \mathbf{40\text{ m}^2}$

29. Area = Area$_{\text{outer circle}}$ − Area$_{\text{inner circle}}$

= $\left[\pi(16\text{ in.})^2\right]$ − $\left[\pi(10\text{ in.})^2\right]$

= 256π in.^{2} − 100π in.^{2}

= **156π in.^{2} = 489.84 in.^{2}**

30. Since angles opposite sides of equal length have equal measure, **$x = 70$.**

$y = 180 - 70 - 70$

$y = 40$

Practice 34

a. $6x^2y^3m - 14xy^5m^2 + 24x^{10}y^6m^4$

The GCF is **$2xy^3m$.**

b. $5a^2b^2c^2 + 60a^3b^3c^3 - 30a^4b^4c^4$

The GCF is **$5a^2b^2c^2$.**

c. $12xy^5p - 16x^6y^2p^{16} + 28x^3yp^5$

The GCF is **$4xyp$.**

Problem Set 34

1. **(a), (c)**

2. $C = \pi D$

$C \div D = \dfrac{C}{D} = \dfrac{\pi D}{D} = \pi$

3. 85,000 in. × $\dfrac{2.54\text{ cm}}{1\text{ in.}}$ × $\dfrac{1\text{ m}}{100\text{ cm}}$ × $\dfrac{1\text{ km}}{1000\text{ m}}$

= $\dfrac{\mathbf{85,000(2.54)}}{\mathbf{(100)(1000)}}$ **km = 2.16 km**

4. 3200 in. · in. × $\dfrac{2.54\text{ cm}}{1\text{ in.}}$ × $\dfrac{2.54\text{ cm}}{1\text{ in.}}$

× $\dfrac{1\text{ m}}{100\text{ cm}}$ × $\dfrac{1\text{ m}}{100\text{ cm}}$ = $\dfrac{\mathbf{3200(2.54)^2}}{\mathbf{(100)^2}}$ **m^2**

= **2.06 m^2**

5. (a) $C = 2\pi r = 2\pi(12\text{ in.}) = $ **24π in. = 75.36 in.**

(b) $A = \pi r^2 = \pi(12\text{ in.})^2 = $ **144π in.^{2} = 452.16 in.^{2}**

6. $N - 24 = 3(-N)$

$N - 24 = -3N$

$\underline{+3N \qquad\quad +3N}$

$4N - 24 = \quad 0$

$\underline{\qquad +24 \quad +24}$

$4N \qquad = 24$

$N = 6$

7. $6N = 56 - N$

$\underline{+N \qquad\quad +N}$

$7N = 56$

$N = 8$

8. 90 $\quad \dfrac{90}{2} = 45 \qquad \dfrac{45}{3} = 15 \qquad \dfrac{15}{3} = 5$

$2 \cdot 3 \cdot 3 \cdot 5$

9. 216 $\quad \dfrac{216}{2} = 108 \qquad \dfrac{108}{2} = 54 \qquad \dfrac{54}{2} = 27$

$\dfrac{27}{3} = 9 \qquad \dfrac{9}{3} = 3 \qquad \mathbf{2 \cdot 2 \cdot 2 \cdot 3 \cdot 3 \cdot 3}$

10. $0.125WN = 5.25$

$\dfrac{0.125WN}{0.125} = \dfrac{5.25}{0.125}$

$WN = \mathbf{42}$

11. $(-5)^{-3} = \dfrac{1}{(-5)^3} = -\dfrac{1}{\mathbf{125}}$

12. $\dfrac{1}{(-5)^{-2}} = (-5)^2 = \mathbf{25}$

13. $-8^0 = \mathbf{-1}$

14. $WF\left(2\dfrac{1}{4}\right) = \dfrac{3}{4}$

$\dfrac{WF \cdot 2\frac{1}{4}}{2\frac{1}{4}} = \dfrac{\frac{3}{4}}{2\frac{1}{4}}$

$WF = \dfrac{3}{4} \cdot \dfrac{4}{9}$

$WF = \dfrac{\mathbf{1}}{\mathbf{3}}$

15. $f(x) = 7 - 2x$

$f(2) = 7 - 2(2) = 7 - 4 = \mathbf{3}$

16. $3\dfrac{1}{2} + 2\dfrac{1}{4}x = 1\dfrac{1}{4}$

$\underline{-3\dfrac{1}{2} \qquad\qquad -3\dfrac{1}{2}}$

$2\dfrac{1}{4}x = -2\dfrac{1}{4}$

$\dfrac{2\frac{1}{4}x}{2\frac{1}{4}} = \dfrac{-2\frac{1}{4}}{2\frac{1}{4}}$

$x = \mathbf{-1}$

17. $0.3 + 0.06x = 6.9$

$30 + 6x = 690$

$6x = 660$

$x = \mathbf{110}$

18. $8 - k + 2(4 - 2k) = k + 2k$

$8 - k + 8 - 4k = 3k$

$16 - 5k = 3k$

$\underline{+5k \quad +5k}$

$16 \quad = 8k$

$k = \mathbf{2}$

19. $3(x - 2) + (2x + 5) = x + 7$

$3x - 6 + 2x + 5 = x + 7$

$5x - 1 = x + 7$

$\underline{-x \qquad -x}$

$4x - 1 = \qquad 7$

$\underline{+1 \qquad +1}$

$4x \quad = \quad 8$

$x = \mathbf{2}$

20. $4ab^2c^4 - 2a^2b^3c^2 + 6a^3b^4c$

The GCF is $\mathbf{2ab^2c}$.

21. $5x^2y^5m^2 - 10xy^2m^2 + 15x^2y^4m^2$

The GCF is $\mathbf{5xy^2m^2}$.

22. $3xy - 2x^2yx^{-1} + 5x^3x^{-2}y^3y^{-2} + 5xxxx^{-2}y$

$= 3xy - 2xy + 5xy + 5xy = \mathbf{11xy}$

23. $4x^{-3}y^2(x^3y^{-2} - 2x^4y^{-2})$

$= (4x^{-3}y^2)(x^3y^{-2}) + (4x^{-3}y^2)(-2x^4y^{-2}) = \mathbf{4 - 8x}$

24. $(y^{-5} - 2y^7x^5)x^0y^5 = (x^0y^5)(y^{-5}) + (x^0y^5)(-2y^7x^5)$

$= \mathbf{1 - 2x^5y^{12}}$

25. $-x^0 - a(x - 2a) = -(-5)^0 - 3[-5 - 2(3)]$

$= -1 - 3(-11) = \mathbf{32}$

26. $a^2 - a^3 - a^4 = (-2)^2 - (-2)^3 - (-2)^4$

$= 4 + 8 - 16 = \mathbf{-4}$

27. $-3^2 + (-3)^3 - 3^0 - |-3 - 3|$

$= -9 - 27 - 1 - 6 = \mathbf{-43}$

28. $\dfrac{-7(-4 - 6)}{-(-4) - [-(-6)]} = \dfrac{-7(-10)}{4 - 6} = \dfrac{70}{-2} = \mathbf{-35}$

29. $P = (16 + 6 + 16 + 6)\ \text{ft} = \mathbf{44\ ft}$

30.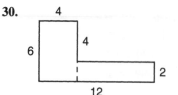

Volume $= \left(\text{Area}_{\text{base}}\right)(\text{Height})$

$= [(6\,\text{cm} \times 4\,\text{cm}) + (8\,\text{cm} \times 2\,\text{cm})](6\,\text{cm})$

$= \left(24\ \text{cm}^2 + 16\ \text{cm}^2\right)(6\ \text{cm})$

$= \left(40\ \text{cm}^2\right)(6\ \text{cm})$

$= \mathbf{240\ cm^3}$

Practice 35

a. $15a^2z^8 - 35z^5a = \mathbf{5az^5(3az^3 - 7)}$

b. $2a^2b^2 + 2a^3b^2 + 2a^3b^6 = \mathbf{2a^2b^2(1 + a + ab^4)}$

c. $\dfrac{4 - 4x}{4} = \dfrac{4(1 - x)}{4} = \mathbf{1 - x}$

d. $\dfrac{7x - 49x^2}{7x} = \dfrac{7x(1 - 7x)}{7x} = \mathbf{1 - 7x}$

Problem Set 35

1. (a) **Surface area**

(b) To find the lateral surface area of a right solid, **multiply the perimeter of a base by the height of the right solid.**

2. $6\ \text{ft} \times \dfrac{12\ \text{in.}}{1\ \text{ft}} \times \dfrac{2.54\ \text{cm}}{1\ \text{in.}} \times \dfrac{1\ \text{m}}{100\ \text{cm}}$

$= \dfrac{6(12)(2.54)}{(100)}\ \mathbf{m} = \mathbf{1.83\ m}$

3. $20\ \text{ft} \cdot \text{ft} \times \dfrac{12\ \text{in.}}{1\ \text{ft}} \times \dfrac{12\ \text{in.}}{1\ \text{ft}} \times \dfrac{2.54\ \text{cm}}{1\ \text{in.}}$

$\times \dfrac{2.54\ \text{cm}}{1\ \text{in.}} = 20(12)^2(2.54)^2\ \mathbf{cm^2}$

$= \mathbf{18,580.61\ cm^2}$

4.
$$P = 2l + 2w$$
$$32\text{ cm} = 2(10\text{ cm}) + 2w$$
$$32\text{ cm} = 20\text{ cm} + 2w$$
$$32\text{ cm} - 20\text{ cm} = 2w$$
$$12\text{ cm} = 2w$$
$$\frac{12\text{ cm}}{2} = w$$
$$6\text{ cm} = w$$

$$A = lw$$
$$A = (10\text{ cm})(6\text{ cm})$$
$$A = \mathbf{60\text{ cm}^2}$$

5.
$$4N = 7N + 9$$
$$\underline{-7N \quad -7N}$$
$$-3N = \quad\quad 9$$
$$N = \mathbf{-3}$$

6.
$$2(2N - 12) = -N + 11$$
$$4N - 24 = -N + 11$$
$$\underline{+N \quad\quad\quad +N}$$
$$5N - 24 = \quad\quad 11$$
$$\underline{+24 \quad\quad\quad +24}$$
$$5N \quad = \quad\quad 35$$
$$N = \mathbf{7}$$

7. 160 $\frac{160}{2} = 80$ $\frac{80}{2} = 40$ $\frac{40}{2} = 20$

$\frac{20}{2} = 10$ $\frac{10}{2} = 5$ $\mathbf{2 \cdot 2 \cdot 2 \cdot 2 \cdot 2 \cdot 5}$

8. 294 $\frac{294}{2} = 147$ $\frac{147}{3} = 49$ $\frac{49}{7} = 7$

$\mathbf{2 \cdot 3 \cdot 7 \cdot 7}$

9.
$$DP(36) = 20.88$$
$$\frac{DP \cdot 36}{36} = \frac{20.88}{36}$$
$$DP = \mathbf{0.58}$$

10. $2^{-4} = \dfrac{1}{2^4} = \mathbf{\dfrac{1}{16}}$

11. $\dfrac{1}{3^{-3}} = 3^3 = \mathbf{27}$

12. $\left(3\frac{1}{5}\right)\left(3\frac{1}{8}\right) = WN$

$$WN = \frac{16}{5} \cdot \frac{25}{8}$$
$$WN = \mathbf{10}$$

13.
$$g(x) = -3 + 6x$$
$$g(-2) = -3 + 6(-2) = -3 - 12 = \mathbf{-15}$$

14.
$$4\frac{1}{2}y - \frac{1}{6} = 1\frac{1}{3}$$
$$\underline{+\frac{1}{6} \quad +\frac{1}{6}}$$
$$4\frac{1}{2}y \quad = 1\frac{1}{2}$$

$$\frac{4\frac{1}{2}y}{4\frac{1}{2}} = \frac{1\frac{1}{2}}{4\frac{1}{2}}$$

$$y = \frac{\frac{3}{2}}{\frac{9}{2}}$$

$$y = \frac{3}{2} \cdot \frac{2}{9}$$

$$y = \mathbf{\frac{1}{3}}$$

15.
$$0.8m + 0.4m = 4.8$$
$$8m + 4m = 48$$
$$12m = 48$$
$$m = \mathbf{4}$$

16.
$$3(-k - 4) + 6 = k + 7$$
$$-3k - 12 + 6 = k + 7$$
$$-3k - 6 = k + 7$$
$$\underline{-k \quad\quad -k}$$
$$-4k - 6 = \quad\quad 7$$
$$\underline{+6 \quad\quad\quad +6}$$
$$-4k \quad = \quad\quad 13$$
$$k = \mathbf{-\frac{13}{4}}$$

17.
$$x - 4 - 2x + 5 = 3(2x - 4)$$
$$-x + 1 = 6x - 12$$
$$\underline{-6x \quad\quad -6x}$$
$$-7x + 1 = \quad\quad -12$$
$$\underline{-1 \quad\quad\quad -1}$$
$$-7x \quad = \quad\quad -13$$
$$x = \mathbf{\frac{13}{7}}$$

18. $(-1)^2 - 4(-1) = -3$ $(3)^2 - 4(3) = -3$
          $1 + 4 = -3$ $9 - 12 = -3$
             $5 \neq -3$ $-3 = -3$

Therefore, **3 is a root of the equation.**

19. $3x^4y^2p - 6x^2y^5p^4 = \mathbf{3x^2y^2p(x^2 - 2y^3p^3)}$

20. $6a^3x^2m^5 + 2a^4x^5m^5 + 4a^2x^2m$

$= 2a^2x^2m(3am^4 + a^2x^3m^4 + 2)$

21. $\dfrac{4x + 4}{4} = \dfrac{4(x + 1)}{4} = x + 1$

22. $\dfrac{4x - 16x^2}{4x} = \dfrac{4x(1 - 4x)}{4x} = 1 - 4x$

23. $3x^2xyy^3y^{-1} + 2x^2xyyy - 4x^{-2}yx^5y^2 + 7x^2$

$= 3x^3y^3 + 2x^3y^3 - 4x^3y^3 + 7x^2 = x^3y^3 + 7x^2$

24. $p^0x^2y(x^3y^{-1} - 3x^5y^{-2})$

$= (x^2y)(x^3y^{-1}) + (x^2y)(-3x^5y^{-2}) = x^5 - 3x^7y^{-1}$

25. $(p^5y^5 - y^{-5})p^0y^5 = (y^5)(p^5y^5) + (y^5)(-y^{-5})$

$= p^5y^{10} - 1$

26. $a^2 - a^3 - a^4 = (-1)^2 - (-1)^3 - (-1)^4$

$= 1 + 1 - 1 = 1$

27. $x(y - xy^0) = -2[4 - (-2)(4)^0]$

$= -2[4 - (-2)(1)] = -2(4 + 2) = -2(6) = -12$

28. $A = \dfrac{1}{2}(3\text{ m})(4\text{ m}) + \dfrac{1}{2}\pi(2\text{ m})^2$

$= 6\text{ m}^2 + 2\pi\text{ m}^2$

$= (6 + 2\pi)\text{ m}^2 = 12.28\text{ m}^2$

29. $-3^2 + (-6)^0 - \sqrt[4]{16} + |2 - 7|$

$= -9 + 1 - 2 + 5 = -5$

30. $S.A. = 2(\text{Area}_{\text{base}}) + \text{Lateral Surface Area}$

$= 2[(4\text{ in.} \times 8\text{ in.}) + (5\text{ in.} \times 6\text{ in.})]$

$\quad + (\text{Perimeter}_{\text{base}})(\text{Height})$

$= 2(32\text{ in.}^2 + 30\text{ in.}^2)$

$\quad + [(10 + 8 + 4 + 3 + 6 + 5)\text{ in.}$

$\qquad \cdot (15\text{ in.})]$

$= 2(62\text{ in.}^2) + [(36\text{ in.})(15\text{ in.})]$

$= 124\text{ in.}^2 + 540\text{ in.}^2$

$= 664\text{ in.}^2$

Practice 36

a. $\dfrac{x^2}{y}\left(\dfrac{x^2}{y} - \dfrac{3y^2}{m}\right) = \dfrac{x^2}{y}\left(\dfrac{x^2}{y}\right) + \dfrac{x^2}{y}\left(\dfrac{-3y^2}{m}\right)$

$= \dfrac{x^4}{y^2} - \dfrac{3x^2y}{m}$

b. $\dfrac{am}{b^2}\left(\dfrac{xm}{ab} - 3ab + \dfrac{6m}{b^2}\right)$

$= \dfrac{am}{b^2}\left(\dfrac{xm}{ab}\right) + \dfrac{am}{b^2}(-3ab) + \dfrac{am}{b^2}\left(\dfrac{6m}{b^2}\right)$

$= \dfrac{m^2x}{b^3} - \dfrac{3a^2m}{b} + \dfrac{6am^2}{b^4}$

c. $-4^{-2} = \dfrac{-1}{4^2} = -\dfrac{1}{16}$

d. $\dfrac{1}{-4^{-2}} = \dfrac{4^2}{-1} = -16$

e. $-(-4)^{-3} = \dfrac{-1}{(-4)^3} = \dfrac{-1}{-64} = \dfrac{1}{64}$

f. $\dfrac{1}{-(-4)^{-3}} = \dfrac{(-4)^3}{-1} = \dfrac{-64}{-1} = 64$

Problem Set 36

1. (b), (d)

2. The sides opposite the angles of equal measure have equal lengths.

3. $80\text{ yd} \times \dfrac{3\text{ ft}}{1\text{ yd}} \times \dfrac{12\text{ in.}}{1\text{ ft}} \times \dfrac{2.54\text{ cm}}{1\text{ in.}}$

$= 80(3)(12)(2.54)\text{ cm} = 7315.2\text{ cm}$

4. $36\text{ yd} \cdot \text{yd} \times \dfrac{3\text{ ft}}{1\text{ yd}} \times \dfrac{3\text{ ft}}{1\text{ yd}} \times \dfrac{12\text{ in.}}{1\text{ ft}} \times \dfrac{12\text{ in.}}{1\text{ ft}}$

$= 36(3)^2(12)^2\text{ in.}^2 = 46{,}656\text{ in.}^2$

5. (a) $C = \pi D = 18\pi\text{ cm} = 56.52\text{ cm}$

(b) $A = \pi r^2 = \pi(9\text{ cm})^2 = 81\pi\text{ cm}^2 = 254.34\text{ cm}^2$

6.

$N - 21 = 2(-N)$

$N - 21 = -2N$

$\underline{+2N \qquad\qquad +2N}$

$3N - 21 = 0$

$\underline{\quad +21 \quad +21}$

$3N \qquad = 21$

$N = 7$

7.

$7N = 2(-N) - 18$

$7N = -2N - 18$

$\underline{+2N \quad +2N}$

$9N = \qquad -18$

$N = -2$

8. 250 $\qquad \dfrac{250}{2} = 125 \qquad \dfrac{125}{5} = 25 \qquad \dfrac{25}{5} = 5$

$2 \cdot 5 \cdot 5 \cdot 5$

9. $-2^{-2} = \dfrac{-1}{2^2} = -\dfrac{1}{4}$

10. $\dfrac{1}{-2^{-2}} = \dfrac{2^2}{-1} = -4$

11. $\left(2\dfrac{5}{8}\right)WN = 14$

$$\dfrac{2\dfrac{5}{8}WN}{2\dfrac{5}{8}} = \dfrac{14}{2\dfrac{5}{8}}$$

$$WN = \dfrac{14}{\dfrac{21}{8}}$$

$$WN = 14 \cdot \dfrac{8}{21}$$

$$WN = \dfrac{16}{3}$$

$$WN = \mathbf{5\dfrac{1}{3}}$$

12. $h(x) = -4 - 7x$

$h(-3) = -4 - 7(-3) = -4 + 21 = \mathbf{17}$

13. $-5\dfrac{1}{2} + 2\dfrac{2}{5}p = 7\dfrac{1}{4}$

$\quad\dfrac{+5\dfrac{1}{2} \qquad\qquad +5\dfrac{1}{2}}{\qquad 2\dfrac{2}{5}p = 12\dfrac{3}{4}}$

$$\dfrac{2\dfrac{2}{5}p}{2\dfrac{2}{5}} = \dfrac{12\dfrac{3}{4}}{2\dfrac{2}{5}}$$

$$p = \dfrac{\dfrac{51}{4}}{\dfrac{12}{5}}$$

$$p = \dfrac{51}{4} \cdot \dfrac{5}{12}$$

$$p = \dfrac{85}{16}$$

14. $m - 0.4m + 1.5 = 5.7$

$\qquad 0.6m + 1.5 = 5.7$

$\qquad\quad 6m + 15 = 57$

$\qquad\qquad\quad 6m = 42$

$\qquad\qquad\qquad m = 7$

15. $x - (3x - 2) + 5 = 2x + 4$

$x - 3x + 2 + 5 = 2x + 4$

$\quad -2x + 7 = 2x + 4$

$\dfrac{\quad -2x \qquad\qquad -2x}{\quad -4x + 7 = \qquad\quad 4}$

$\dfrac{\qquad\quad -7 \qquad\qquad -7}{\quad -4x \quad = \qquad\quad -3}$

$$x = \dfrac{3}{4}$$

16. $-p - 4 - (2p - 5) = 4 + 2(p + 3)$

$-p - 4 - 2p + 5 = 4 + 2p + 6$

$\quad -3p + 1 = 2p + 10$

$\dfrac{\quad -2p \qquad\quad -2p}{\quad -5p + 1 = \qquad 10}$

$\dfrac{\qquad\quad -1 \qquad\qquad -1}{\quad -5p \quad = \qquad\quad 9}$

$$p = -\dfrac{9}{5}$$

17. $4a^2xy^4p - 6a^2x^4 = 2a^2x\left(2y^4p - 3x^3\right)$

18. $3a^2x^4y^6 + 9ax^2y^4 - 6x^4a^2y^5z$
$= 3ax^2y^4\left(ax^2y^2 + 3 - 2ax^2yz\right)$

19. $\dfrac{2 - 6x}{2} = \dfrac{2(1 - 3x)}{2} = 1 - 3x$

20. $\dfrac{9x^2 - 3x}{3x} = \dfrac{3x(3x - 1)}{3x} = 3x - 1$

21. $2x^4y^{-3} - 3x^2x^2y^{-7}y^4 + 6x^3xy^{-1}y^{-3} + x^2x^2y^{-3}y^{-1}$
$= -x^4y^{-3} + 7x^4y^{-4}$

22. $3x^4y^2\left(xy^{-4} - 3x^{-4}y^5\right) = 3x^5y^{-2} - 9y^7$

23. $\dfrac{x}{z}\left(\dfrac{15y}{x} - \dfrac{4x}{y}\right) = \dfrac{x}{z}\left(\dfrac{15y}{x}\right) + \dfrac{x}{z}\left(\dfrac{-4x}{y}\right)$
$= \dfrac{15y}{z} - \dfrac{4x^2}{yz}$

24. $k^3 - k(a)^2 = (-3)^3 - (-3)(2)^2 = -27 + 3(4)$
$= -27 + 12 = \mathbf{-15}$

25. $m\left(a^0 - ma\right)(-m) + \left|m^2 - 2\right|$
$= 2[1 - 2(-4)](-2) + |4 - 2|$
$= 2(1 + 8)(-2) + 2$
$= 2(9)(-2) + 2 = -36 + 2 = \mathbf{-34}$

26. $-3^3 - 3^2 - (-3)^4 - \left|-3^2 - 3\right|$
$= -27 - 9 - 81 - 12 = \mathbf{-129}$

27. $\dfrac{-5(-5 - 4)}{-2^0(-8 - 1)} = \dfrac{-5(-9)}{-1(-9)} = 5$

28. $P = (40 + 20 + 40 + 20)$ m $= \mathbf{120\ m}$

29. Area $=$ Area$_{circle}$ $-$ Area$_{trapezoid}$

$= \pi(4\text{ in.})^2$

$\qquad - \left[(3\text{ in.} \times 4\text{ in.}) + \dfrac{1}{2}(4\text{ in.} \times 2\text{ in.}) \right]$

$= 16\pi\text{ in.}^2 - \left(12\text{ in.}^2 + 4\text{ in.}^2 \right)$

$= 16\pi\text{ in.}^2 - 16\text{ in.}^2$

$= (\mathbf{16\pi - 16})\text{ in.}^2 = \mathbf{34.24\ in.}^2$

30. The sides opposite the angles of equal measure have equal lengths. Therefore, $y = \mathbf{8.}$

Practice 37

a. $x \le 5$

b. $x > 4$

Problem Set 37

1. $3N + 70 = -50$

$\quad\dfrac{-70 \qquad -70}{3N \qquad = -120}$

$\qquad\qquad N = \mathbf{-40}$

2. $3N + 7 = N + 23$

$\quad\dfrac{-N \qquad\quad -N}{2N + 7 = \qquad 23}$

$\quad\dfrac{\quad -7 \qquad\quad -7}{2N \quad = \qquad 16}$

$\qquad\qquad N = \mathbf{8}$

3. $17\text{ mi} \times \dfrac{5280\text{ ft}}{1\text{ mi}} \times \dfrac{12\text{ in.}}{1\text{ ft}} \times \dfrac{2.54\text{ cm}}{1\text{ in.}}$

$= 17(5280)(12)(2.54)\text{ cm} = \mathbf{2,735,884.8\ cm}$

4. $200\text{ mi} \cdot \text{mi} \times \dfrac{5280\text{ ft}}{1\text{ mi}} \times \dfrac{5280\text{ ft}}{1\text{ mi}} \times \dfrac{12\text{ in.}}{1\text{ ft}}$

$\times \dfrac{12\text{ in.}}{1\text{ ft}} = 200(5280)^2(12)^2\text{ in.}^2$

$= \mathbf{802,897,920,000\ in.}^2$

5. $\qquad A = lw$

$54\text{ in.}^2 = (9\text{ in.})w$

$\qquad w = \dfrac{54\text{ in.}^2}{9\text{ in.}}$

$\qquad w = 6\text{ in.}$

$P = 2l + 2w$

$\quad = 2(9\text{ in.}) + 2(6\text{ in.})$

$\quad = 18\text{ in.} + 12\text{ in.}$

$\quad = \mathbf{30\ in.}$

6. $x > 3$

7. $x \ge 2$

8. $360 \qquad \dfrac{360}{2} = 180 \qquad \dfrac{180}{2} = 90 \qquad \dfrac{90}{2} = 45$

$\dfrac{45}{3} = 15 \qquad \dfrac{15}{3} = 5 \qquad \mathbf{2 \cdot 2 \cdot 2 \cdot 3 \cdot 3 \cdot 5}$

9. $-(-2)^{-2} = \dfrac{-1}{(-2)^2} = \mathbf{-\dfrac{1}{4}}$

10. $\dfrac{1}{-(-2)^{-2}} = \dfrac{(-2)^2}{-1} = \dfrac{4}{-1} = \mathbf{-4}$

11. $WD(0.42) = 0.00504$

$\dfrac{WD \cdot 0.42}{0.42} = \dfrac{0.00504}{0.42}$

$WD = \mathbf{0.012}$

12. $f(x) = x^2 + 1$

$f(3) = (3)^2 + 1 = 9 + 1 = \mathbf{10}$

13. $-\dfrac{1}{3} + 2\dfrac{1}{2}p = 3$

$\dfrac{+\dfrac{1}{3} \qquad\qquad\qquad +\dfrac{1}{3}}{\qquad 2\dfrac{1}{2}p = 3\dfrac{1}{3}}$

$\dfrac{2\dfrac{1}{2}p}{2\dfrac{1}{2}} = \dfrac{3\dfrac{1}{3}}{2\dfrac{1}{2}}$

$p = \dfrac{\dfrac{10}{3}}{\dfrac{5}{2}}$

$p = \dfrac{10}{3} \cdot \dfrac{2}{5}$

$p = \dfrac{\mathbf{4}}{\mathbf{3}}$

14. $-n + 0.4n + 1.8 = -4.2$

$-0.6n + 1.8 = -4.2$

$-6n + 18 = -42$

$-6n = -60$

$n = \mathbf{10}$

15. $-3m - 3 + 5m - 2 = -(2m + 3)$

$$2m - 5 = -2m - 3$$

$$\frac{+2m \qquad\qquad +2m}{4m - 5 = \qquad -3}$$

$$\frac{+5 \qquad\qquad +5}{4m \qquad = \qquad 2}$$

$$m = \frac{2}{4}$$

$$m = \frac{1}{2}$$

16. $x - 3(x - 2) = 7x - (2x + 5)$

$$x - 3x + 6 = 7x - 2x - 5$$

$$-2x + 6 = 5x - 5$$

$$\frac{-5x \qquad\qquad -5x}{-7x + 6 = \qquad -5}$$

$$\frac{-6 \qquad\qquad -6}{-7x \qquad = \qquad -11}$$

$$x = \frac{11}{7}$$

17. (a) **5**

(b) **–5**

(c) **No**

(d) **No**

18. $12a^2x^5y^7 - 3ax^2y^2 = \mathbf{3ax^2y^2(4ax^3y^5 - 1)}$

19. $15a^5x^4y^6 + 3a^4x^3y^7 - 9a^2x^6y$
$= \mathbf{3a^2x^3y(5a^3xy^5 + a^2y^6 - 3x^3)}$

20. $\dfrac{2x + 6}{2} = \dfrac{2(x + 3)}{2} = \mathbf{x + 3}$

21. $\dfrac{4x^2 - 4x}{4x} = \dfrac{4x(x - 1)}{4x} = \mathbf{x - 1}$

22. $3xxy^2x^{-2} - 2xx^{-1}yy + 5y^2 - 6x^2 - 4x^2xxx^{-2}$
$= \mathbf{6y^2 - 10x^2}$

23. $(x^3y^0 - p^0x^2y^4)x^{-3} = x^3y^0x^{-3} - p^0x^2y^4x^{-3}$
$= \mathbf{1 - x^{-1}y^4}$

24. $\dfrac{ax}{c^2}\left(\dfrac{b^4}{xk} - 2b^2\right) = \dfrac{axb^4}{c^2xk} - \dfrac{2axb^2}{c^2}$

$= \mathbf{\dfrac{ab^4}{c^2k} - \dfrac{2axb^2}{c^2}}$

25. $a^2 - a^0(a - ab) = (-3)^2 - [(-3) - (-3)(5)]$
$= 9 - (-3 + 15) = 9 - 12 = \mathbf{-3}$

26. $-k - kp^0 - (-pk^2) = -(-3) - (-3) - [-2(-3)^2]$
$= 3 + 3 + 2(9) = 6 + 18 = \mathbf{24}$

27. $2^2 - 2^3 - (-3)^2 + \sqrt[4]{81} = 4 - 8 - 9 + 3$
$= \mathbf{-10}$

28. $\dfrac{-(-3 + 7) + 4^0}{(-2)(3 - 5)} = \dfrac{-4 + 1}{(-2)(-2)} = \mathbf{-\dfrac{3}{4}}$

29. $P = \left(20 + 20 + \dfrac{2\pi(8)}{2} + \dfrac{2\pi(8)}{2}\right)$ cm

$= \mathbf{(40 + 16\pi)}$ **cm** $= \mathbf{90.24}$ **cm**

30.

Volume $= (\text{Area}_{\text{base}})(\text{Height})$
$= [(6 \text{ m} \times 12 \text{ m}) + (5 \text{ m} \times 4 \text{ m})](8 \text{ m})$
$= (72 \text{ m}^2 + 20 \text{ m}^2)(8 \text{ m})$
$= (92 \text{ m}^2)(8 \text{ m}) = \mathbf{736 \text{ m}^3}$

Practice 38

a. $\dfrac{714}{M} = \dfrac{7}{2}$

$$7M = 714 \cdot 2$$

$$\dfrac{7M}{7} = \dfrac{714 \cdot 2}{7}$$

$$M = \mathbf{204}$$

b. $\dfrac{C}{18,000} = \dfrac{5}{9}$

$$9C = 18,000 \cdot 5$$

$$\dfrac{9C}{9} = \dfrac{18,000 \cdot 5}{9}$$

$$C = \mathbf{10,000}$$

Problem Set 38

1. $\dfrac{R}{600} = \dfrac{13}{5}$

$$5R = 600 \cdot 13$$

$$\dfrac{5R}{5} = \dfrac{600 \cdot 13}{5}$$

$$R = \mathbf{1560}$$

2. $5N + 8 = -42$

$$\frac{-8 \qquad -8}{5N \qquad = -50}$$

$$N = \mathbf{-10}$$

3. $2(3N + 60) = -N + 155$

$$6N + 120 = -N + 155$$

$$\underline{+N \qquad\qquad\quad +N}$$

$$\overline{7N + 120 = \qquad\quad 155}$$

$$\underline{-120 \qquad\qquad -120}$$

$$\overline{7N \qquad = \qquad\quad 35}$$

$$N = 5$$

4. **Negative number**

5. $49 \text{ m} \times \dfrac{100 \text{ cm}}{1 \text{ m}} \times \dfrac{1 \text{ in.}}{2.54 \text{ cm}} \times \dfrac{1 \text{ ft}}{12 \text{ in.}}$

$= \dfrac{49(100)}{(2.54)(12)} \text{ ft} = \mathbf{160.76 \text{ ft}}$

6. (a) $\qquad\qquad A = \pi r^2$

$$36\pi \text{ cm}^2 = \pi r^2$$

$$36(3.14) \text{ cm}^2 = (3.14)r^2$$

$$113.04 \text{ cm}^2 = 3.14 r^2$$

$$\dfrac{113.04 \text{ cm}^2}{3.14} = r^2$$

$$36 \text{ cm}^2 = r^2$$

The radius is **6 cm** because
$6 \text{ cm} \times 6 \text{ cm} = 36 \text{ cm}^2$.

(b) $C = 2\pi r = 2\pi(6 \text{ cm}) = \mathbf{12\pi \text{ cm}} = \mathbf{37.68 \text{ cm}}$

7. $x < 2$

8. $x \le -2$

9. $(-6)^{-2} = \dfrac{1}{(-6)^2} = \dfrac{1}{36}$

10. $-5^{-2} = \dfrac{-1}{5^2} = -\dfrac{1}{25}$

11. $WF\left(3\dfrac{3}{4}\right) = 22\dfrac{1}{2}$

$$\dfrac{WF \cdot 3\frac{3}{4}}{3\frac{3}{4}} = \dfrac{22\frac{1}{2}}{3\frac{3}{4}}$$

$$WF = \dfrac{\frac{45}{2}}{\frac{15}{4}}$$

$$WF = \dfrac{45}{2} \cdot \dfrac{4}{15}$$

$$WF = 6$$

12. $g(x) = x^2 - 2$

$g(-2) = (-2)^2 - 2 = 4 - 2 = 2$

13. $3\dfrac{1}{2}k + \dfrac{3}{4} = -\dfrac{7}{8}$

$$\underline{\qquad -\dfrac{3}{4} \qquad -\dfrac{3}{4}}$$

$$3\dfrac{1}{2}k \qquad = -\dfrac{13}{8}$$

$$\dfrac{3\frac{1}{2}k}{3\frac{1}{2}} = \dfrac{-\frac{13}{8}}{3\frac{1}{2}}$$

$$k = -\dfrac{13}{8} \cdot \dfrac{2}{7}$$

$$k = -\dfrac{13}{28}$$

14. $0.3k + 0.85k - 2 = 2.6$

$$1.15k - 2 = 2.6$$

$$115k - 200 = 260$$

$$115k = 460$$

$$k = 4$$

15. $2(3p - 2) - (p + 4) = 3p$

$$6p - 4 - p - 4 = 3p$$

$$5p - 8 = 3p$$

$$\underline{-3p \qquad\qquad -3p}$$

$$\overline{2p - 8 = 0}$$

$$\underline{\qquad +8 \quad +8}$$

$$\overline{2p}$$

$$p - 4$$

16. $3(x - 2) - (2x + 5) = -2x + 10$

$$3x - 6 - 2x - 5 = -2x + 10$$

$$x - 11 = -2x + 10$$

$$\underline{+2x \qquad\qquad +2x}$$

$$\overline{3x - 11 = \qquad\quad 10}$$

$$\underline{\quad +11 \qquad\qquad +11}$$

$$\overline{3x \qquad = \qquad\quad 21}$$

$$x = 7$$

17. $4a^2x^3y^5 - 8a^4x^2y^4 = 4a^2x^2y^4(xy - 2a^2)$

18. $6a^2xm^6 - 18a^5x^3m^5 = 6a^2xm^5(m - 3a^3x^2)$

19. $\dfrac{3x - 9}{3} = \dfrac{3(x - 3)}{3} = x - 3$

20. $\dfrac{5x^2 - 25x}{5x} = \dfrac{5x(x - 5)}{5x} = x - 5$

21. $xy - 3yx + 7x^3y^2x^{-2}y^{-1} - 2x^2yy^5y^{-4}y^{-1}x^{-1}$

$= xy - 3xy + 7xy - 2xy = \mathbf{3xy}$

22. $3x^0y^{-3}(4y^3z - 7x^2) = \mathbf{12z - 21x^2y^{-3}}$

23. $\dfrac{ax}{c^2}\left(\dfrac{ax^2}{c} - \dfrac{3c^2a}{x^3}\right) = \dfrac{axax^2}{c^2c} - \dfrac{3axc^2a}{c^2x^3}$

$= \dfrac{a^2x^3}{c^3} - \dfrac{3a^2c^2x}{c^2x^3} = \dfrac{\boldsymbol{a^2x^3}}{\boldsymbol{c^3}} - \dfrac{\boldsymbol{3a^2}}{\boldsymbol{x^2}}$

24. $k^2 - k^3\left(km^0\right) = (-3)^2 - (-3)^3(-3)$

$= 9 - (-27)(-3) = 9 - 81 = \boldsymbol{-72}$

25. $-n\left(n^0 - m\right) - \left|2 - m^2\right|$

$= -(-4)\left[1 - (-2)\right] - \left|2 - 4\right| = 4(1 + 2) - 2$

$= 4(3) - 2 = 12 - 2 = \boldsymbol{10}$

26. $-3^3 - 3^2 - (-3)^2 - \left|-2^2\right| = -27 - 9 - 9 - |-4|$

$= -27 - 9 - 9 - 4 = \boldsymbol{-49}$

27. $\dfrac{-4\left(3^0 - 6\right)(-2)}{-4 - (-3)(-2) - 5} = \dfrac{-4(1 - 6)(-2)}{-4 - 6 - 5}$

$= \dfrac{-4(-5)(-2)}{-15} = \dfrac{-40}{-15} = \dfrac{\boldsymbol{8}}{\boldsymbol{3}}$

28. $A = \dfrac{1}{2}(12\text{ m})(16\text{ m}) + \dfrac{1}{2}\pi(10\text{ m})^2$

$= 96\text{ m}^2 + 50\pi\text{ m}^2$

$= (96 + 50\pi)\text{ m}^2 = \boldsymbol{253\text{ m}^2}$

29. $8\dfrac{3}{4} - 2\dfrac{1}{3} - 3\dfrac{1}{2} = 8\dfrac{9}{12} - 2\dfrac{4}{12} - 3\dfrac{6}{12}$

$= 6\dfrac{5}{12} - 3\dfrac{6}{12} = 5\dfrac{17}{12} - 3\dfrac{6}{12} = \boldsymbol{2\dfrac{11}{12}}$ **in.**

30. $S.A. = 2\left(\text{Area}_{\text{triangle}}\right) + \text{Area}_{\text{top}} + \text{Area}_{\text{side}}$

$\quad\quad + \text{Area}_{\text{bottom}}$

$= 2\left[\dfrac{1}{2}(12\text{ ft} \times 16\text{ ft})\right] + (20\text{ ft} \times 15\text{ ft})$

$\quad + (12\text{ ft} \times 15\text{ ft}) + (16\text{ ft} \times 15\text{ ft})$

$= 2\left(96\text{ ft}^2\right) + 300\text{ ft}^2 + 180\text{ ft}^2 + 240\text{ ft}^2$

$= 192\text{ ft}^2 + 720\text{ ft}^2 = \boldsymbol{912\text{ ft}^2}$

Practice 39

a. $W = 3$

$L = 2$

$T = 5$

(a) $\dfrac{W}{L} = \dfrac{3}{2}$ (b) $\dfrac{W}{T} = \dfrac{3}{5}$ (c) $\dfrac{L}{T} = \dfrac{2}{5}$

For this problem, we will use equation (b).

$\dfrac{W}{65} = \dfrac{3}{5}$

$5W = 65 \cdot 3$

$\dfrac{5W}{5} = \dfrac{65 \cdot 3}{5}$

$W = \boldsymbol{39}$

b. $H = 23$

$E = 7$

$T = 30$

(a) $\dfrac{H}{E} = \dfrac{23}{7}$ (b) $\dfrac{H}{T} = \dfrac{23}{30}$ (c) $\dfrac{E}{T} = \dfrac{7}{30}$

For this problem, we will use equation (c).

$\dfrac{E}{930} = \dfrac{7}{30}$

$30E = 930 \cdot 7$

$\dfrac{30E}{30} = \dfrac{930 \cdot 7}{30}$

$E = \boldsymbol{217}$

c. $x \not\geq 2$

d. $x \geq -1;\ x \not< -1$

Problem Set 39

1. $\dfrac{B}{S} = \dfrac{15}{7}$

$\dfrac{105}{S} = \dfrac{15}{7}$

$15S = 105 \cdot 7$

$\dfrac{15S}{15} = \dfrac{105 \cdot 7}{15}$

$S = \boldsymbol{49}$

2. $W = 7$

$B = 10$

$T = 17$

(a) $\dfrac{W}{B} = \dfrac{7}{10}$ (b) $\dfrac{W}{T} = \dfrac{7}{17}$ (c) $\dfrac{B}{T} = \dfrac{10}{17}$

For this problem, we will use equation (b).

$\dfrac{W}{136} = \dfrac{7}{17}$

$17W = 136 \cdot 7$

$\dfrac{17W}{17} = \dfrac{136 \cdot 7}{17}$

$W = \boldsymbol{56}$

3. $6N - 5 = -35$

$\dfrac{+5 \quad\quad +5}{6N \quad\ = -30}$

$N = \boldsymbol{-5}$

4. $3(5N + 9) = -N + 11$

$$15N + 27 = -N + 11$$

$$\begin{array}{r} +N \qquad\qquad +N \\ \hline 16N + 27 = \qquad 11 \\ \underline{\quad -27 \qquad\qquad -27 \quad} \\ 16N \qquad = \qquad -16 \end{array}$$

$$N = \mathbf{-1}$$

5. $300 \text{ km} \times \dfrac{1000 \text{ m}}{1 \text{ km}} \times \dfrac{100 \text{ cm}}{1 \text{ m}} \times \dfrac{1 \text{ in.}}{2.54 \text{ cm}}$

$= \dfrac{300(1000)(100)}{(2.54)} \text{ in.} = \mathbf{11{,}811{,}023.62 \text{ in.}}$

6.
$$P = 2l + 2w$$
$$56 \text{ cm} = 2(18 \text{ cm}) + 2w$$
$$56 \text{ cm} = 36 \text{ cm} + 2w$$
$$56 \text{ cm} - 36 \text{ cm} = 2w$$
$$20 \text{ cm} = 2w$$
$$10 \text{ cm} = w$$

$$A = lw$$
$$A = (18 \text{ cm})(10 \text{ cm})$$
$$A = \mathbf{180 \text{ cm}^2}$$

7. $x < 1$

8. $x \not> 1$

9. 450 $\dfrac{450}{2} = 225$ $\dfrac{225}{3} = 75$ $\dfrac{75}{3} = 25$

$\dfrac{25}{5} = 5$ $\mathbf{2 \cdot 3 \cdot 3 \cdot 5 \cdot 5}$

10. **(b), (c)**

11. $(-7)^0 = \mathbf{1}$

12. $\dfrac{1}{-3^{-2}} = \dfrac{3^2}{-1} = \mathbf{-9}$

13. $h(x) = 2 - x^2$

$h(4) = 2 - 4^2 = 2 - 16 = \mathbf{-14}$

14. $-\dfrac{7}{8} + 2\dfrac{3}{4}x = \dfrac{1}{2}$

$$\begin{array}{r} +\dfrac{7}{8} \qquad\qquad +\dfrac{7}{8} \\ \hline 2\dfrac{3}{4}x = \dfrac{11}{8} \end{array}$$

$$\dfrac{2\dfrac{3}{4}x}{2\dfrac{3}{4}} = \dfrac{\dfrac{11}{8}}{2\dfrac{3}{4}}$$

$$x = \dfrac{11}{8} \cdot \dfrac{4}{11}$$

$$x = \dfrac{1}{2}$$

15. $0.1p - 0.2p + 2 = -4.6$

$$-0.1p + 2 = -4.6$$
$$-1p + 20 = -46$$
$$-p = -66$$
$$p = \mathbf{66}$$

16. $5(x - 2) - (-x + 3) = 7$

$$5x - 10 + x - 3 = 7$$
$$6x - 13 = 7$$
$$\begin{array}{r} +13 \quad +13 \\ \hline 6x \qquad = 20 \end{array}$$
$$x = \dfrac{20}{6}$$
$$x = \dfrac{\mathbf{10}}{\mathbf{3}}$$

17. $-5(p - 4) - 3(-2 - p) = p - 2$

$$-5p + 20 + 6 + 3p = p - 2$$
$$-2p + 26 = p - 2$$
$$\begin{array}{r} -p \qquad\qquad -p \\ \hline -3p + 26 = \qquad -2 \\ \underline{\quad -26 \qquad\qquad -26 \quad} \\ -3p \qquad = \qquad -28 \end{array}$$
$$p = \dfrac{\mathbf{28}}{\mathbf{3}}$$

18. $3x^2y^3z^5 - 9xy^6z^6 = \mathbf{3xy^3z^5(x - 3y^3z)}$

19. $4x^2y - 12xy^2 + 24x^3y^3 = \mathbf{4xy(x - 3y + 6x^2y^2)}$

20. $\dfrac{7x + 7}{7} = \dfrac{7(x + 1)}{7} = \mathbf{x + 1}$

21. $\dfrac{9x - 3x^2}{3x} = \dfrac{3x(3 - x)}{3x} = \mathbf{3 - x}$

22. $3x^4x^{-3}y^0 + xy^0y^{-2}y^2 - 7x^3x^{-2}x^0y^0$

$= 3x + x - 7x = \mathbf{-3x}$

23. $\left(y^{-5} + 3x^5y^2\right)x^0y^5 = y^{-5}y^5 + 3x^5y^2y^5$

   $= \mathbf{1 + 3x^5y^7}$

24. $\left(\dfrac{a^2}{x} - \dfrac{2x}{a}\right)\dfrac{4x^2}{a} = \dfrac{4a^2x^2}{ax} - \dfrac{8x^3}{a^2}$

   $= \mathbf{4ax - \dfrac{8x^3}{a^2}}$

25. $m^2 - \left(m - p^0\right) = 2^2 - (2 - 1) = 4 - 1 = \mathbf{3}$

26. $a^2b^0 - (a - b) - \left|a^3\right|$

   $= (-2)^2 - [-2 - (-1)] - \left|(-2)^3\right|$

   $= 4 - (-2 + 1) - 8 = 4 + 1 - 8 = \mathbf{-3}$

27. $3^2 - 3^3 - 3^0 + \left|-3^0\right| = 9 - 27 - 1 + 1 = \mathbf{-18}$

28. $\dfrac{4(-2 - 3) - 4^0}{-2(-4 + 6) - 3} = \dfrac{4(-5) - 1}{-2(2) - 3} = \dfrac{-20 - 1}{-4 - 3}$

   $= \dfrac{-21}{-7} = \mathbf{3}$

29. $P = \left(30 + 20 + 30 + \dfrac{2\pi(10)}{2}\right)$ m

   $= (80 + 10\pi)\,\text{m} = \mathbf{111.4\ m}$

30. Volume $= \left(\text{Area}_{\text{base}}\right)(\text{Height})$

   $= \left[\dfrac{1}{2}(14\ \text{in.} \times 6\ \text{in.})\right](15\ \text{in.})$

   $= \left(42\ \text{in.}^2\right)(15\ \text{in.})$

   $= \mathbf{630\ in.^3}$

Practice 40

a. $\dfrac{x^{-6}y^4z^5}{x^{-6}y^5z^2} = x^{-6}y^4z^5x^6y^{-5}z^{-2} = x^0y^{-1}z^3 = \boldsymbol{y^{-1}z^3}$

b. $\dfrac{m^4p^3z^{10}d}{m^{-2}p^4z^{-6}d^{-2}} = m^4p^3z^{10}dm^2p^{-4}z^6d^2$

   $= \boldsymbol{m^6p^{-1}z^{16}d^3}$

c. $\dfrac{z^{-3}}{m}\left(\dfrac{x^4}{m^2} - \dfrac{3z}{m}\right) = \dfrac{z^{-3}x^4}{m^3} - \dfrac{3z^{-2}}{m^2}$

   $= \boldsymbol{z^{-3}x^4m^{-3} - 3z^{-2}m^{-2}}$

d. $\left(\dfrac{m^{-5}}{w^4x} - \dfrac{cw^2}{x^3m}\right)\dfrac{m^{-2}}{3cm} = \dfrac{m^{-7}}{3w^4xcm} - \dfrac{cw^2m^{-2}}{3x^3cm^2}$

   $= \dfrac{m^{-8}w^{-4}x^{-1}c^{-1}}{3} - \dfrac{w^2x^{-3}m^{-4}}{3}$

Problem Set 40

1. $\dfrac{78}{M} = \dfrac{13}{6}$

   $13M = 78 \cdot 6$

   $\dfrac{13M}{13} = \dfrac{78 \cdot 6}{13}$

   $M = \mathbf{36}$

2. $GS = 7$

   $TS = 11$

   $T = 18$

   (a) $\dfrac{GS}{TS} = \dfrac{7}{11}$ (b) $\dfrac{GS}{T} = \dfrac{7}{18}$ (c) $\dfrac{TS}{T} = \dfrac{11}{18}$

   For this problem, we will use equation (b).

   $\dfrac{GS}{2520} = \dfrac{7}{18}$

   $18GS = 2520 \cdot 7$

   $\dfrac{18GS}{18} = \dfrac{2520 \cdot 7}{18}$

   $GS = \mathbf{980}$

3. $4(N - 6) = 20$

   $4N - 24 = 20$

   $\underline{+24 \quad\ +24}$

   $4N \qquad = 44$

   $N = \mathbf{11}$

4. $3(4N + 6) = -N + 5$

   $12N + 18 = -N + 5$

   $\underline{+N \qquad\quad +N}$

   $13N + 18 = \qquad 5$

   $\underline{\quad -18 \qquad\ -18}$

   $13N \qquad = \quad -13$

   $N = \mathbf{-1}$

5. $30\,\text{m} \cdot \text{m} \times \dfrac{100\ \text{cm}}{1\ \text{m}} \times \dfrac{100\ \text{cm}}{1\ \text{m}} \times \dfrac{1\ \text{in.}}{2.54\ \text{cm}}$

   $\times \dfrac{1\ \text{in.}}{2.54\ \text{cm}} = \dfrac{30(100)^2}{(2.54)^2}\ \text{in.}^2 = \mathbf{46{,}500.09\ in.^2}$

6. $x \le 1;\ x \not> 1$

7. **(b), (d)**

8. $-(-3)^{-3} = \dfrac{-1}{(-3)^3} = \dfrac{-1}{-27} = \dfrac{\mathbf{1}}{\mathbf{27}}$

9. $\dfrac{1}{-(-3)^{-3}} = \dfrac{(-3)^3}{-1} = \dfrac{-27}{-1} = \mathbf{27}$

10.　$(1.05)(0.043) = WN$

　　　　$WN = \textbf{0.04515}$

11.　$f(x) = -x^2 + 5$

　　　$f(5) = -5^2 + 5 = -25 + 5 = \textbf{-20}$

12.　$\dfrac{3}{4} + \dfrac{1}{2}x + 2 = 0$

　　　　$\dfrac{1}{2}x + 2\dfrac{3}{4} = 0$

　　　　$\dfrac{-2\dfrac{3}{4} \quad -2\dfrac{3}{4}}{\dfrac{1}{2}x \qquad = -2\dfrac{3}{4}}$

　　　　$\dfrac{\frac{1}{2}x}{\frac{1}{2}} = \dfrac{-2\frac{3}{4}}{\frac{1}{2}}$

　　　　$x = -\dfrac{11}{4} \cdot \dfrac{2}{1}$

　　　　$x = -\dfrac{\textbf{11}}{\textbf{2}}$

13.　$1.3p + 0.3p - 2 = 1.2$

　　　　$1.6p - 2 = 1.2$

　　　　$16p - 20 = 12$

　　　　$16p = 32$

　　　　$p = \textbf{2}$

14.　$p - 3(p - 4) = 2 + (2p + 5)$

　　　$p - 3p + 12 = 2 + 2p + 5$

　　　$-2p + 12 = 2p + 7$

　　　$\dfrac{-2p \qquad -2p}{-4p + 12 = \qquad 7}$

　　　$\dfrac{\qquad -12 \qquad -12}{-4p \qquad = \qquad -5}$

　　　　$p = \dfrac{\textbf{5}}{\textbf{4}}$

15.　$2(5 - x) - (-2)(x - 3) = -(3x - 4)$

　　　$10 - 2x + 2x - 6 = -3x + 4$

　　　　　$4 = -3x + 4$

　　　　$\dfrac{-4 \qquad\qquad -4}{0 = -3x}$

　　　　　$x = \textbf{0}$

16.　$4a^2xy^4p - 6a^2x^4 = \textbf{2}\textbf{\textit{a}}^\textbf{2}\textbf{\textit{x}}\left(\textbf{2}\textbf{\textit{y}}^\textbf{4}\textbf{\textit{p}} - \textbf{3}\textbf{\textit{x}}^\textbf{3}\right)$

17.　$3a^2x^4y^6 + 9ax^2y^4 - 6x^4a^2y^5z$

　　　$= \textbf{3}\textbf{\textit{ax}}^\textbf{2}\textbf{\textit{y}}^\textbf{4}\left(\textbf{\textit{ax}}^\textbf{2}\textbf{\textit{y}}^\textbf{2} + \textbf{3} - \textbf{2}\textbf{\textit{ax}}^\textbf{2}\textbf{\textit{yz}}\right)$

18.　$\dfrac{6x - 36x^2}{6x} = \dfrac{6x(1 - 6x)}{6x} = \textbf{1} - \textbf{6}\textbf{\textit{x}}$

19.　$\dfrac{4xy + 16xy^2}{4xy} = \dfrac{4xy(1 + 4y)}{4xy} = \textbf{1} + \textbf{4}\textbf{\textit{y}}$

20.　$\dfrac{x^3y^2}{xy^4} = x^3y^2x^{-1}y^{-4} = \textbf{\textit{x}}^\textbf{2}\textbf{\textit{y}}^\textbf{-2}$

21.　$\dfrac{x^3y^{-3}z}{z^5x^2y} = x^3y^{-3}zz^{-5}x^{-2}y^{-1} = \textbf{\textit{xy}}^\textbf{-4}\textbf{\textit{z}}^\textbf{-4}$

22.　$\dfrac{m^{-2}}{b}\left(\dfrac{b^2}{m^3} - \dfrac{4am^2}{b^4}\right) = \dfrac{m^{-2}b^2}{bm^3} - \dfrac{4m^{-2}am^2}{bb^4}$

　　　$= m^{-5}b - 4ab^{-5} = \textbf{\textit{bm}}^\textbf{-5} - \textbf{4}\textbf{\textit{ab}}^\textbf{-5}$

23.　$\left(\dfrac{x^{-4}}{a^3} - \dfrac{a^3}{x}\right)\dfrac{a^{-3}}{x} = \dfrac{x^{-4}a^{-3}}{a^3x} - \dfrac{a^3a^{-3}}{xx}$

　　　$= \textbf{\textit{a}}^\textbf{-6}\textbf{\textit{x}}^\textbf{-5} - \textbf{\textit{x}}^\textbf{-2}$

24.　$-3x^2x^0xy^2 + 2x^3yy^0y^{-3}y^4 + 5x^3x^{-6}y^0y^3y^{-5}$

　　　$= -3x^3y^2 + 2x^3y^2 + 5x^{-3}y^{-2} = \textbf{-}\textbf{\textit{x}}^\textbf{3}\textbf{\textit{y}}^\textbf{2} + \textbf{5}\textbf{\textit{x}}^\textbf{-3}\textbf{\textit{y}}^\textbf{-2}$

25.　$a\left(b^0 - ab\right) = 3[1 - 3(-5)]$

　　　$= 3(1 + 15) = 3(16) = \textbf{48}$

26.　$\left(m - x^2\right)x - |m - x|$

　　　$= \left[-3 - (-2)^2\right](-2) - \left|-3 - (-2)\right|$

　　　$= (-3 - 4)(-2) - |-1| = (-7)(-2) - 1$

　　　$= 14 - 1 = \textbf{13}$

27.　$-3^3 - 2^2 - 4^3 - \left|-2^2 - 2\right|$

　　　$= -27 - 4 - 64 - |-6| = -27 - 4 - 64 - 6$

　　　$= \textbf{-101}$

28.　$\dfrac{-3^2 + 4^2 + 3^3}{2(-5 + 2) - 3^0} = \dfrac{-9 + 16 + 27}{2(-3) - 1} = \dfrac{34}{-7}$

　　　$= -\dfrac{\textbf{34}}{\textbf{7}}$

29.　Area $=$ Area$_\text{trapezoid}$ $-$ Area$_\text{circle}$

　　　$= \left[(30 \text{ cm} \times 24 \text{ cm}) + \dfrac{1}{2}(24 \text{ cm} \times 18 \text{ cm})\right]$

　　　　$- \left[\pi(12 \text{ cm})^2\right]$

　　　$= \left(720 \text{ cm}^2 + 216 \text{ cm}^2\right) - 144\pi \text{ cm}^2$

　　　$= 936 \text{ cm}^2 - 144\pi \text{ cm}^2$

　　　$= \textbf{(936} - \textbf{144}\boldsymbol{\pi}\textbf{) cm}^\textbf{2} = \textbf{483.84 cm}^\textbf{2}$

30.　Since angles opposite sides of equal length have equal measure, $x = \textbf{55}$.

　　　$y = 180 - 55 - 55$

　　　$y = \textbf{70}$

Practice 41

a. $x^{-2}y + \dfrac{3y}{x^2} - 5xy = x^{-2}y + 3x^{-2}y - 5xy$

$= 4x^{-2}y - 5xy$

b. $\dfrac{a^{-8}b^2}{b^{-9}} - \dfrac{4b^{11}}{a^8} + \dfrac{6b^{11}}{a^8 b^5}$

$= a^{-8}b^{11} - 4a^{-8}b^{11} + 6a^{-8}b^6$

$= -3a^{-8}b^{11} + 6a^{-8}b^6$

c. $x + 7 = 2$

$\underline{\quad -7 \quad -7 \quad}$

$x = -5$

$x + 3 = -5 + 3 = -2$

d. $x - 6 = 4$

$\underline{\quad +6 \quad +6 \quad}$

$x = 10$

$x - 5 = 10 - 5 = 5$

Problem Set 41

1. $\dfrac{B}{R} = \dfrac{15}{9}$

$\dfrac{75}{R} = \dfrac{15}{9}$

$15R = 75 \cdot 9$

$\dfrac{15}{15}R = \dfrac{75 \cdot 9}{15}$

$R = 45$

2. $-3N - 5 = 2(-N) - 25$

$-3N - 5 = -2N - 25$

$\underline{+2N \qquad\quad +2N \qquad\qquad}$

$-N - 5 = \qquad -25$

$\underline{\quad +5 \qquad\qquad +5 \qquad}$

$-N \quad = \qquad -20$

$N = 20$

3. (a) **Natural numbers (or counting numbers)**

(b) **Whole numbers**

(c) **Integers**

4. $40 \text{ m} \times \dfrac{100 \text{ cm}}{1 \text{ m}} \times \dfrac{1 \text{ in.}}{2.54 \text{ cm}} \times \dfrac{1 \text{ ft}}{12 \text{ in.}}$

$= \dfrac{40(100)}{(2.54)(12)} \text{ ft} = \textbf{131.23 ft}$

5. (a) $A = \pi r^2$

$25 \text{ in.}^2 = (3.14)r^2$

$\dfrac{(3.14)r^2}{3.14} = \dfrac{25 \text{ in.}^2}{3.14}$

$r^2 = 7.96 \text{ in.}^2$

$r = \sqrt{7.96 \text{ in.}^2}$

$r = \textbf{2.82 in.}$

(b) $C = 2\pi r$

$C = 2\pi(2.82 \text{ in.}) = \textbf{5.64}\pi \textbf{ in.} = \textbf{17.71 in.}$

6. $x > 1$

7. $x \not< 1$

8. $270 \qquad \dfrac{270}{2} = 135 \qquad \dfrac{135}{3} = 45$

$\dfrac{45}{3} = 15 \qquad \dfrac{15}{3} = 5$

$\mathbf{2 \cdot 3 \cdot 3 \cdot 3 \cdot 5}$

9. $g(x) = -x^2 - 10$

$g(-4) = -(-4)^2 - 10 = -16 - 10 = \textbf{-26}$

10. $3\dfrac{3}{4}n - \dfrac{9}{16} = 2\dfrac{1}{4}$

$\underline{\qquad\quad +\dfrac{9}{16} \quad +\dfrac{9}{16} \quad}$

$3\dfrac{3}{4}n \qquad\quad = 2\dfrac{13}{16}$

$\dfrac{3\dfrac{3}{4}n}{3\dfrac{3}{4}} = \dfrac{2\dfrac{13}{16}}{3\dfrac{3}{4}}$

$n = \dfrac{45}{16} \cdot \dfrac{4}{15}$

$n = \dfrac{3}{4}$

11. $0.3 + 0.06p + 0.02 - 0.02p = 4$

$0.04p + 0.32 = 4$

$4p + 32 = 400$

$4p = 368$

$p = \textbf{92}$

12. $-x - 2(-x - 3) = -4 - x$

$\quad -x + 2x + 6 = -4 - x$

$\quad\quad\quad x + 6 = -4 - x$

$\quad\quad \underline{+x \qquad\qquad +x}$

$\quad\quad\quad 2x + 6 = -4$

$\quad\quad\quad \underline{-6 \quad -6}$

$\quad\quad\quad 2x \quad\quad = -10$

$\quad\quad\quad\quad x = -5$

13. $3(-2x - 2 - 3) - (-x + 2) = -2(x + 1)$

$\quad -6x - 6 - 9 + x - 2 = -2x - 2$

$\quad\quad\quad\quad -5x - 17 = -2x - 2$

$\quad\quad\quad\quad \underline{+2x \qquad\quad +2x}$

$\quad\quad\quad\quad -3x - 17 = \qquad -2$

$\quad\quad\quad\quad \underline{\quad +17 \qquad\quad +17}$

$\quad\quad\quad\quad -3x \qquad = \qquad 15$

$\quad\quad\quad\quad\quad\quad x = -5$

14. $x + 4 = 6$

$\quad \underline{-4 \quad -4}$

$\quad\quad x = 2$

$\quad x - 7 = 2 - 7 = -5$

15. $3x^2y^5p^6 - 9x^2y^4p^3 + 12x^2yp^4$

$\quad = 3x^2yp^3(y^4p^3 - 3y^3 + 4p)$

16. $2x^2y^2 - 6y^2x^4 - 12xy^5 = 2xy^2(x - 3x^3 - 6y^3)$

17. $\dfrac{5xy + 20xy^2}{5xy} = \dfrac{5xy(1 + 4y)}{5xy} = 1 + 4y$

18. $\dfrac{k^2x - k^3x}{k^2x} = \dfrac{k^2x(1 - k)}{k^2x} = 1 - k$

19. $\dfrac{x^2y^5}{x^4y^{-3}} = \dfrac{1}{x^4y^{-3}x^{-2}y^{-5}} = \dfrac{1}{x^2y^{-8}}$

20. $\dfrac{x^{-4}y^{-3}p^2}{x^{-5}yp^4} = \dfrac{1}{x^{-5}yp^4x^4y^3p^{-2}} = \dfrac{1}{x^{-1}y^4p^2}$

21. $\dfrac{x^{-2}}{y}\left(\dfrac{xz}{y} - \dfrac{1}{y^{-4}}\right) = \dfrac{x^{-2}xz}{y^2} - \dfrac{x^{-2}}{y^{-3}}$

$\quad = \dfrac{x^{-1}z}{y^2} - \dfrac{x^{-2}}{y^{-3}} = \dfrac{1}{xy^2z^{-1}} - \dfrac{1}{x^2y^{-3}}$

22. $\left(\dfrac{a}{b} - \dfrac{2b}{a}\right)\dfrac{a^{-2}}{b^{-2}} = \dfrac{aa^{-2}}{bb^{-2}} - \dfrac{2a^{-2}b}{ab^{-2}}$

$\quad = \dfrac{a^{-1}}{b^{-1}} - \dfrac{2a^{-2}b}{ab^{-2}} = \dfrac{1}{ab^{-1}} - \dfrac{2}{a^3b^{-3}}$

23. $x^2y^2y^{-2}pp^0 - 4xxy^0p - 3x^4x^{-2}yy^{-1}p$

$\quad = x^2p - 4x^2p - 3x^2p = -6x^2p$

24. $\dfrac{m^2}{y^2} - \dfrac{3y^{-2}}{m^{-2}} = \dfrac{m^2}{y^2} - \dfrac{3m^2}{y^2} = \dfrac{-2m^2}{y^2}$

$\quad = -2m^2y^{-2}$

25. $b - (-c^0) - b^3 = -2 - (-1) - (-2)^3$

$\quad = -2 + 1 + 8 = 7$

26. $k^3 - (k - c)|k - c|$

$\quad = (-2)^3 - (-2 - 3)|-2 - 3| = -8 - (-5)|-5|$

$\quad = -8 + 5(5) = -8 + 25 = 17$

27. $\dfrac{1}{4^{-2}} - \sqrt[3]{-27} = 4^2 - (-3) = 16 + 3 = 19$

28. $\dfrac{-3^2 + 4^2 - 5(4 - 2)}{3^0(5 - 2)} = \dfrac{-9 + 16 - 5(2)}{3}$

$\quad = \dfrac{-9 + 16 - 10}{3} = \dfrac{-3}{3} = -1$

29. $A = \left[\dfrac{1}{2}(8 \text{ ft} \times 6 \text{ ft})\right] + \left[\dfrac{1}{2}\pi(3 \text{ ft})^2\right]$

$\quad = 24 \text{ ft}^2 + \dfrac{9\pi}{2} \text{ ft}^2$

$\quad = \left(24 + \dfrac{9\pi}{2}\right) \text{ ft}^2 = 38.13 \text{ ft}^2$

30. $S.A. = 2(\text{Area}_{base}) + \text{Lateral Surface Area}$

$\quad = 2[\pi(2 \text{ cm})^2] + (\text{Perimeter}_{base})(\text{Length})$

$\quad = 2(4\pi \text{ cm}^2) + [2\pi(2 \text{ cm})](12 \text{ cm})$

$\quad = 8\pi \text{ cm}^2 + (4\pi \text{ cm})(12 \text{ cm})$

$\quad = 8\pi \text{ cm}^2 + 48\pi \text{ cm}^2$

$\quad = 56\pi \text{ cm}^2 = 175.84 \text{ cm}^2$

Practice 42

a. $8y - 13x - 8 = \quad 4$

$\quad \underline{+13x + 8 \quad +8 + 13x}$

$\quad 8y \qquad\quad = 12 + 13x$

$\quad\quad \dfrac{8y}{8} = \dfrac{12}{8} + \dfrac{13x}{8}$

$\quad\quad\quad y = \dfrac{13}{8}x + \dfrac{3}{2}$

b. $8p + 3w = \quad w - 15 - 2p$

$\quad \underline{+2p - 3w \quad -3w \qquad\quad +2p}$

$\quad 10p \qquad = -2w - 15$

$\quad\quad \dfrac{10p}{10} = \dfrac{-2w}{10} - \dfrac{15}{10}$

$\quad\quad\quad p = -\dfrac{1}{5}w - \dfrac{3}{2}$

Problem Set 42

1. $A = 9$

$W = 5$

$T = 14$

(a) $\dfrac{A}{W} = \dfrac{9}{5}$ (b) $\dfrac{A}{T} = \dfrac{9}{14}$ (c) $\dfrac{W}{T} = \dfrac{5}{14}$

For this problem, we will use equation (b).

$$\frac{A}{1428} = \frac{9}{14}$$

$$14A = 9 \cdot 1428$$

$$\frac{14A}{14} = \frac{9 \cdot 1428}{14}$$

$$A = \mathbf{918}$$

2. $4(2N - 3) = 28$

$$8N - 12 = 28$$

$$\underline{\quad +12 \quad +12}$$

$$\overline{8N \qquad = 40}$$

$$N = \mathbf{5}$$

3. **Negative number**

4. $58 \text{ cm} \cdot \text{cm} \times \dfrac{1 \text{ in.}}{2.54 \text{ cm}} \times \dfrac{1 \text{ in.}}{2.54 \text{ cm}} \times \dfrac{1 \text{ ft}}{12 \text{ in.}}$

$\times \dfrac{1 \text{ ft}}{12 \text{ in.}} = \dfrac{58}{(2.54)^2 (12)^2} \text{ ft}^2 = \mathbf{0.062 \text{ ft}^2}$

5. $A = S^2$

$25 \text{ cm}^2 = S^2$

Each side is 5 cm because $5 \text{ cm} \times 5 \text{ cm} = 25 \text{ cm}^2$.

$P = 4S = 4(5 \text{ cm}) = \mathbf{20 \text{ cm}}$

6. $x > 1; \ x \nleq 1$

7. $\left(5\dfrac{7}{10}\right) WN = 9\dfrac{1}{2}$

$$\frac{5\dfrac{7}{10} \, WN}{5\dfrac{7}{10}} = \frac{9\dfrac{1}{2}}{5\dfrac{7}{10}}$$

$$WN = \frac{19}{2} \cdot \frac{10}{57}$$

$$WN = \mathbf{\frac{5}{3}}$$

8. $h(x) = -2x^2 + 3$

$h(3) = -2(3)^2 + 3$

$= -2(9) + 3$

$= -18 + 3 = \mathbf{-15}$

9. $2\dfrac{1}{3}x + 5 = 19$

$$\underline{\quad -5 \quad -5}$$

$$2\dfrac{1}{3}x \quad = 14$$

$$\frac{2\dfrac{1}{3}x}{2\dfrac{1}{3}} = \frac{14}{2\dfrac{1}{3}}$$

$$x = \frac{14}{1} \cdot \frac{3}{7}$$

$$x = \mathbf{6}$$

10. $0.4k + 0.4k - 0.02 = 4.02$

$$0.8k - 0.02 = 4.02$$

$$80k - 2 = 402$$

$$80k = 404$$

$$k = \mathbf{5.05}$$

11. $3p - 2(p - 4) = 7p + 6$

$$3p - 2p + 8 = 7p + 6$$

$$p + 8 = 7p + 6$$

$$\underline{-7p \qquad -7p}$$

$$\overline{-6p + 8 = \qquad 6}$$

$$\underline{\quad -8 \qquad -8}$$

$$\overline{-6p \qquad = \quad -2}$$

$$p = \mathbf{\frac{1}{3}}$$

12. $4(x - 2) - 4x = -(3x + 2)$

$$4x - 8 - 4x = -3x - 2$$

$$-8 = -3x - 2$$

$$\underline{+2 \qquad\qquad +2}$$

$$\overline{-6 = -3x}$$

$$x = \mathbf{2}$$

13. $x - 6 = 3$

$$\underline{\quad +6 \quad +6}$$

$$\overline{x = 9}$$

$x + 2 = 9 + 2 = \mathbf{11}$

14.

$$3x + 2y = 5 - y$$

$$\underline{-5 \qquad\qquad -2y \quad -5 - 2y}$$

$$\overline{-5 + 3x \qquad = \qquad -3y}$$

$$\frac{-3y}{-3} = \frac{3x}{-3} - \frac{5}{-3}$$

$$y = \mathbf{-x + \frac{5}{3}}$$

15. $-2y + 6y - x - 4 = 0$

$4y - x - 4 = 0$

$\underline{+x + 4 \quad\quad +x + 4}$

$4y \quad\quad\quad = x + 4$

$\dfrac{4y}{4} = \dfrac{x}{4} + \dfrac{4}{4}$

$y = \dfrac{1}{4}x + 1$

16. $4x^2m^5y - 2x^4m^3y^3 = \mathbf{2x^2m^3y(2m^2 - x^2y^2)}$

17. $4m^2x^5 - 2m^2x^2 + 6m^5x^2$

$= \mathbf{2m^2x^2(2x^3 - 1 + 3m^3)}$

18. $\dfrac{3xy - 9x^2y^2}{3xy} = \dfrac{3xy(1 - 3xy)}{3xy} = \mathbf{1 - 3xy}$

19. $\dfrac{x^2ym + xym}{xym} = \dfrac{xym(x + 1)}{xym} = \mathbf{x + 1}$

20. $\dfrac{x^5y^5mm^{-2}}{xx^3y^{-3}m^4} = \dfrac{x^5y^5m^{-1}}{x^4y^{-3}m^4} = x^5x^{-4}y^5y^3m^{-1}m^{-4}$

$= xy^8m^{-5} = \dfrac{\mathbf{xy^8}}{\mathbf{m^5}}$

21. $\dfrac{x^2xyp^{-5}}{p^{-3}p^{-4}y^{-4}} = \dfrac{x^3yp^{-5}}{p^{-7}y^{-4}} = x^3yp^{-5}p^7y^4 = \mathbf{x^3y^5p^2}$

22. $x^2z^{-2}\left(\dfrac{x^4z^{-4}}{x} - \dfrac{3z^2}{x^2}\right)$

$= \dfrac{x^2z^{-2}x^4z^{-4}}{x} - \dfrac{3x^2z^{-2}z^2}{x^2}$

$= x^5z^{-6} - 3 = \dfrac{\mathbf{x^5}}{\mathbf{z^6}} - \mathbf{3}$

23. $5yxx^0p^2 - p^2y^2y^{-1}x + 2p^2p^0yx - 3p^2y^2y^{-1}x$

$= 5yxp^2 - yxp^2 + 2yxp^2 - 3yxp^2$

$= 3yxp^2 = \mathbf{3p^2xy}$

24. $\dfrac{3x^{-2}x^3y}{y^{-4}} - 2xy^5 = 3xy^5 - 2xy^5 = xy^5$

$= \dfrac{\mathbf{1}}{\mathbf{x^{-1}y^{-5}}}$

25. $x(x^0 - y) + |xy| = -2(1 - 5) + |-10|$

$= -2(-4) + 10 = 8 + 10 = \mathbf{18}$

26. $c + 2 = 6$

$\underline{ -2 \quad -2}$

$c = 4$

$k^3 - (k - c) = (-2)^3 - (-2 - 4) = -8 - (-6)$

$= -8 + 6 = \mathbf{-2}$

27. $\dfrac{1}{-3^{-2}} - \sqrt[3]{8} = -3^2 - 2 = -9 - 2 = \mathbf{-11}$

28. $\dfrac{-3^2 - (-3)^3 - 3}{-3(-3)(+3)} = \dfrac{-9 + 27 - 3}{27} = \dfrac{15}{27} = \dfrac{\mathbf{5}}{\mathbf{9}}$

29. $P = \left(20 + 20 + \dfrac{2\pi(10)}{2} + \dfrac{2\pi(10)}{2}\right)$ m

$= (40 + 20\pi)$ m $= \mathbf{102.8}$ **m**

30. $V = (\text{Area}_{\text{base}})(\text{Height})$

$= [\pi(10 \text{ in.})^2](20 \text{ in.})$

$= (100\pi \text{ in.}^2)(20 \text{ in.})$

$= \mathbf{2000\pi \text{ in.}^3} = \mathbf{6280 \text{ in.}^3}$

Practice 43

a. $14 = 2 \cdot 7 \quad\quad 20 = 2 \cdot 2 \cdot 5$

$30 = 2 \cdot 3 \cdot 5$

$\text{LCM} = 2 \cdot 2 \cdot 3 \cdot 5 \cdot 7 = \mathbf{420}$

b. $75 = 3 \cdot 5 \cdot 5 \quad\quad 120 = 2 \cdot 2 \cdot 2 \cdot 3 \cdot 5$

$315 = 3 \cdot 3 \cdot 5 \cdot 7$

$\text{LCM} = 2 \cdot 2 \cdot 2 \cdot 3 \cdot 3 \cdot 5 \cdot 5 \cdot 7 = \mathbf{12{,}600}$

c. $4a^3b^4 = 2 \cdot 2 \cdot a \cdot a \cdot a \cdot b \cdot b \cdot b \cdot b$

$6a^{10}b^2 = 2 \cdot 3 \cdot a \cdot a \cdot a \cdot a \cdot a \cdot a \cdot a$

$\phantom{6a^{10}b^2 = } \cdot a \cdot a \cdot b \cdot b$

$\text{LCM} = 2 \cdot 2 \cdot 3 \cdot a \cdot a \cdot a \cdot a \cdot a \cdot a \cdot a$

$\phantom{\text{LCM} = } \cdot a \cdot a \cdot b \cdot b \cdot b \cdot b$

$= \mathbf{12a^{10}b^4}$

d. $12x^4y^2m^3 = 2 \cdot 2 \cdot 3 \cdot x \cdot x \cdot x \cdot x \cdot y \cdot y$

$ \cdot m \cdot m \cdot m$

$20x^6ym^3 = 2 \cdot 2 \cdot 5 \cdot x \cdot x \cdot x \cdot x \cdot x \cdot x \cdot y$

$ \cdot m \cdot m \cdot m$

$\text{LCM} = 2 \cdot 2 \cdot 3 \cdot 5 \cdot x \cdot x \cdot x \cdot x \cdot x \cdot x$

$\phantom{\text{LCM} = } \cdot y \cdot y \cdot m \cdot m \cdot m$

$= \mathbf{60x^6y^2m^3}$

Problem Set 43

1. $\dfrac{I}{S} = \dfrac{6}{17}$

$\dfrac{I}{136} = \dfrac{6}{17}$

$17I = 6 \cdot 136$

$\dfrac{17I}{17} = \dfrac{6 \cdot 136}{17}$

$I = \mathbf{48}$

2.
$$7N + 7 = 9N - 1$$
$$\underline{-9N \qquad\qquad -9N}$$
$$-2N + 7 = \qquad -1$$
$$\underline{\qquad -7 \qquad\qquad -7}$$
$$-2N \qquad = \qquad -8$$
$$N = \mathbf{4}$$

3. $500 \text{ cm} \times \dfrac{1 \text{ in.}}{2.54 \text{ cm}} \times \dfrac{1 \text{ ft}}{12 \text{ in.}} \times \dfrac{1 \text{ yd}}{3 \text{ ft}}$

$= \dfrac{\mathbf{500}}{\mathbf{(2.54)(12)(3)}} \text{ yd} = \mathbf{5.47 \text{ yd}}$

4. $x \geq 1$

5. $x \nleq 1$

6. $f(x) = -3x^2 + 7$
$f(-3) = -3(-3)^2 + 7$
$\qquad = -3(9) + 7$
$\qquad = -27 + 7 = \mathbf{-20}$

7. $\dfrac{1}{2} + \dfrac{3}{8}x - 5 = 10\dfrac{1}{2}$

$\dfrac{3}{8}x - 4\dfrac{1}{2} = 10\dfrac{1}{2}$

$\underline{\quad +4\dfrac{1}{2} \qquad +4\dfrac{1}{2}}$

$\dfrac{3}{8}x \qquad = 15$

$\dfrac{\frac{3}{8}x}{\frac{3}{8}} = \dfrac{15}{\frac{3}{8}}$

$x = \dfrac{15}{1} \cdot \dfrac{8}{3}$

$x = \mathbf{40}$

8. $0.02x - 4 - 0.01x - 2 = -6.3$
$\qquad\qquad 0.01x - 6 = -6.3$
$\qquad\qquad x - 600 = -630$
$\qquad\qquad\qquad x = \mathbf{-30}$

9. $2p - 5(p - 4) = 2p + 12$
$2p - 5p + 20 = 2p + 12$
$-3p + 20 = 2p + 12$
$\underline{-2p \qquad\qquad -2p}$
$-5p + 20 = \qquad 12$
$\underline{\qquad -20 \qquad\qquad -20}$
$-5p \qquad = \qquad -8$
$p = \dfrac{\mathbf{8}}{\mathbf{5}}$

10. $x - 5x + 4(x - 2) = 3x - 8$
$x - 5x + 4x - 8 = 3x - 8$
$3x - 8 = -8$
$\underline{\qquad +8 \quad +8}$
$3x \quad = \quad 0$
$x = \mathbf{0}$

11. $x - 4 + 2x = 8$
$3x - 4 = 8$
$\underline{\quad +4 \quad +4}$
$3x \quad = 12$
$x = 4$
$x + 3 = 4 + 3 = \mathbf{7}$

12. $x + 3y - 4 = 0$
$\underline{-x \qquad +4 \quad -x + 4}$
$3y \qquad = -x + 4$
$\dfrac{3y}{3} = \dfrac{-x}{3} + \dfrac{4}{3}$
$y = -\dfrac{1}{3}x + \dfrac{4}{3}$

13. $4 + 2x + 2y - 3 = 5$
$2x + 2y + 1 = 5$
$\underline{-2x \qquad\quad -1 \quad -1 - 2x}$
$2y \qquad = 4 - 2x$
$\dfrac{2y}{2} = \dfrac{4}{2} - \dfrac{2x}{2}$
$y = 2 - x$
$y = \mathbf{-x + 2}$

14. $12 = 2 \cdot 2 \cdot 3 \qquad 16 = 2 \cdot 2 \cdot 2 \cdot 2$
$50 = 2 \cdot 5 \cdot 5$
LCM $= 2 \cdot 2 \cdot 2 \cdot 2 \cdot 3 \cdot 5 \cdot 5 = \mathbf{1200}$

15. $4a^2b^2 = 2 \cdot 2 \cdot a \cdot a \cdot b \cdot b$
$8a^3b = 2 \cdot 2 \cdot 2 \cdot a \cdot a \cdot a \cdot b$
LCM $= 2 \cdot 2 \cdot 2 \cdot a \cdot a \cdot a \cdot b \cdot b = \mathbf{8a^3b^2}$

16. $6k^5m^2 - 2mk^3 - mk = \mathbf{mk(6mk^4 - 2k^2 - 1)}$

17. $x^4y^2m - x^3y^3m^2 + 5x^6y^2m^2$
$= \mathbf{x^3y^2m(x - ym + 5x^3m)}$

18. $\dfrac{4px^2 - 8px}{px} = \dfrac{px(4x - 8)}{px} = \mathbf{4x - 8}$

19. $\dfrac{x^2y - xy}{xym} = \dfrac{xy(x - 1)}{xym} = \dfrac{\mathbf{x - 1}}{\mathbf{m}}$

20. $\dfrac{x^5yx^{-7}y^2}{x^4yy^3x^3} = \dfrac{x^{-2}y^3}{x^7y^4} = x^{-2}y^3x^{-7}y^{-4} = \mathbf{x^{-9}y^{-1}}$

21. $\dfrac{x^{-2}y^{-6}m}{x^5y^5m^{-4}} = \dfrac{x^{-2}y^{-6}x^{-5}y^{-5}}{m^{-1}m^{-4}} = \dfrac{x^{-7}y^{-11}}{m^{-5}}$

22. $m^{-2}z^4\left(m^2z^{-4} - \dfrac{3m^6z}{z^4}\right)$

$= m^{-2}z^4m^2z^{-4} - \dfrac{3m^{-2}z^4m^6z}{z^4}$

$= 1 - 3m^4z = \mathbf{1 - \dfrac{3}{m^{-4}z^{-1}}}$

23. $-x^3x^{-3}ym^2 + 6yy^0m^2x^0 - 3x^2y^2y^{-1}m^2 + 9yxxm^2$

$= -ym^2 + 6ym^2 - 3x^2ym^2 + 9x^2ym^2$

$= \mathbf{5m^2y + 6m^2x^2y}$

24. $\dfrac{3m^{-1}y^2}{m^{-2}} - \dfrac{5m^2y^2}{x^2} + \dfrac{my^2}{m^{-1}x^2}$

$= 3m^{-1}m^2y^2 - \dfrac{5m^2y^2}{x^2} + \dfrac{m^2y^2}{x^2}$

$= \mathbf{3my^2 - \dfrac{4m^2y^2}{x^2}}$

25. $m + 3 = -2$

$\dfrac{-3 \quad -3}{m = -5}$

$|m| - (m - x) = |-5| - (-5 - 3)$

$= 5 - (-8) = 5 + 8 = \mathbf{13}$

26. $y + 4 = 8$

$\dfrac{-4 \quad -4}{y = 4}$

$|x| - x(y)(-x) = |-2| - (-2)(4)[-(-2)]$

$= 2 + 2(4)(2) = 2 + 16 = \mathbf{18}$

27. $\dfrac{1}{4^{-3}} - \sqrt[5]{-32} = 4^3 - (-2) = 64 + 2 = \mathbf{66}$

28. $\dfrac{-2^0(-5 - 7)(-3) - |-4|}{-2[-(-6)]} = \dfrac{-(-12)(-3) - 4}{-12}$

$= \dfrac{-36 - 4}{-12} = \dfrac{-40}{-12} = \mathbf{\dfrac{10}{3}}$

29.

Area $= A_1 + A_2$

$= \left[\dfrac{1}{2}(24 \text{ in.} \times 5 \text{ in.})\right] + \left[\dfrac{1}{2}(24 \text{ in.} \times 5 \text{ in.})\right]$

$= 60 \text{ in.}^2 + 60 \text{ in.}^2$

$= \mathbf{120 \text{ in.}^2}$

30. $S.A. = 2(\text{Area}_{\text{base}}) + \text{Lateral Surface Area}$

$= 2\left[(4 \text{ ft} \times 4 \text{ ft}) + \dfrac{1}{2}\pi(2 \text{ ft})^2\right]$

$+ (\text{Perimeter}_{\text{base}})(\text{Height})$

$= 2(16 \text{ ft}^2 + 2\pi \text{ ft}^2)$

$+ \left(4 \text{ ft} + 4 \text{ ft} + 4 \text{ ft} + \dfrac{2\pi(2 \text{ ft})}{2}\right)(10 \text{ ft})$

$= 32 \text{ ft}^2 + 4\pi \text{ ft}^2 + (12 \text{ ft} + 2\pi \text{ ft})(10 \text{ ft})$

$= 32 \text{ ft}^2 + 4\pi \text{ ft}^2 + 120 \text{ ft}^2 + 20\pi \text{ ft}^2$

$= \mathbf{(152 + 24\pi) \text{ ft}^2 = 227.36 \text{ ft}^2}$

Practice 44

a. $\dfrac{4m - 2}{3m + 2} + \dfrac{6m - 4}{3m + 2} = \dfrac{4m - 2 + 6m - 4}{3m + 2}$

$= \mathbf{\dfrac{10m - 6}{3m + 2}}$

b. $\dfrac{9}{xy^3 + m} - \dfrac{7ap}{xy^3 + m} = \mathbf{\dfrac{9 - 7ap}{xy^3 + m}}$

c. $\dfrac{x}{m^3} + \dfrac{1}{c^3} + \dfrac{a}{m^4}$

$= \dfrac{xmc^3}{m^4c^3} + \dfrac{m^4}{m^4c^3} + \dfrac{ac^3}{m^4c^3}$

$= \mathbf{\dfrac{xmc^3 + m^4 + ac^3}{m^4c^3}}$

d. $\dfrac{m}{p^2} + \dfrac{3}{p^3} - 4 = \dfrac{mp}{p^3} + \dfrac{3}{p^3} - \dfrac{4p^3}{p^3}$

$= \mathbf{\dfrac{mp + 3 - 4p^3}{p^3}}$

Problem Set 44

1. $\dfrac{P}{T} = \dfrac{14}{17}$

$\dfrac{P}{2244} = \dfrac{14}{17}$

$17P = 14 \cdot 2244$

$\dfrac{17P}{17} = \dfrac{14 \cdot 2244}{17}$

$P = \mathbf{1848}$

2. $9(N - 3) = 36$

$9N - 27 = 36$

$\dfrac{+27 \quad +27}{9N \quad = 63}$

$N = \mathbf{7}$

3. $170 \text{ in.} \cdot \text{in.} \times \dfrac{1 \text{ ft}}{12 \text{ in.}} \times \dfrac{1 \text{ ft}}{12 \text{ in.}} \times \dfrac{1 \text{ yd}}{3 \text{ ft}} \times \dfrac{1 \text{ yd}}{3 \text{ ft}}$

$= \dfrac{170}{(12)^2 (3)^2} \text{ yd}^2 = \mathbf{0.13 \text{ yd}^2}$

4. $\quad P = 4S$

$52 \text{ in.} = 4S$

$13 \text{ in.} = S$

$A = S^2 = (13 \text{ in.})^2 = \mathbf{169 \text{ in.}^2}$

5. $\boldsymbol{x < -2; \ x \not\geq -2}$

6. $168 \quad \dfrac{168}{2} = 84 \quad \dfrac{84}{2} = 42 \quad \dfrac{42}{2} = 21$

$\dfrac{21}{3} = 7 \quad \mathbf{2 \cdot 2 \cdot 2 \cdot 3 \cdot 7}$

7. $g(x) = x(x + 1)$

$g(-4) = -4(-4 + 1) = -4(-3) = \mathbf{12}$

8. $\dfrac{1}{4} + \dfrac{2}{5}x + 1 = 2\dfrac{1}{4}$

$\dfrac{2}{5}x + 1\dfrac{1}{4} = 2\dfrac{1}{4}$

$\dfrac{-1\dfrac{1}{4} \quad -1\dfrac{1}{4}}{}$

$\dfrac{2}{5}x \qquad = 1$

$\dfrac{\frac{2}{5}x}{\frac{2}{5}} = \dfrac{1}{\frac{2}{5}}$

$x = \dfrac{1}{1} \cdot \dfrac{5}{2}$

$x = \dfrac{5}{2}$

9. $0.004m - 0.001m + 0.002 = -0.004$

$0.003m + 0.002 = -0.004$

$3m + 2 = -4$

$3m = -6$

$m = \mathbf{-2}$

10. $3(-x - 4) = 2x + 3(x - 5)$

$-3x - 12 = 2x + 3x - 15$

$-3x - 12 = 5x - 15$

$\dfrac{-5x \qquad\qquad -5x}{}$

$\overline{-8x - 12 = \qquad -15}$

$\dfrac{+12 \qquad\qquad +12}{}$

$\overline{-8x \qquad = \qquad -3}$

$x = \dfrac{3}{8}$

---

11. $5p - 6(2p + 1) = -4p - 2$

$5p - 12p - 6 = -4p - 2$

$-7p - 6 = -4p - 2$

$\dfrac{+4p \qquad\qquad +4p}{}$

$\overline{-3p - 6 = \qquad -2}$

$\dfrac{+6 \qquad\qquad +6}{}$

$\overline{-3p \qquad = \qquad 4}$

$p = -\dfrac{4}{3}$

12. $x + 3 - 4x = 12$

$-3x + 3 = 12$

$\dfrac{-3 \quad -3}{}$

$\overline{-3x \quad = \quad 9}$

$x = -3$

$2x - 1 = 2(-3) - 1 = -6 - 1 = \mathbf{-7}$

13. $3y - 2x - 7 = 0$

$\dfrac{+2x + 7 \quad +2x + 7}{}$

$\overline{3y \qquad = 2x + 7}$

$\dfrac{3y}{3} = \dfrac{2x}{3} + \dfrac{7}{3}$

$y = \dfrac{2}{3}x + \dfrac{7}{3}$

14. $3x - 3y + 4 = y - 4$

$\dfrac{-y - 4 \quad -y - 4}{}$

$\overline{3x - 4y \quad = \quad -8}$

$\dfrac{-3x \qquad\qquad\qquad -3x}{}$

$\overline{-4y \quad = \quad -8 - 3x}$

$\dfrac{-4y}{-4} = \dfrac{-8}{-4} - \dfrac{3x}{-4}$

$y = 2 + \dfrac{3}{4}x$

$y = \dfrac{3}{4}x + 2$

15. $8 = 2 \cdot 2 \cdot 2 \qquad 30 = 2 \cdot 3 \cdot 5$

$75 = 3 \cdot 5 \cdot 5$

$\text{LCM} = 2 \cdot 2 \cdot 2 \cdot 3 \cdot 5 \cdot 5 = \mathbf{600}$

16. $4w^2y^3 = 2 \cdot 2 \cdot w \cdot w \cdot y \cdot y \cdot y$

$6wy^2 = 2 \cdot 3 \cdot w \cdot y \cdot y$

$\text{LCM} = 2 \cdot 2 \cdot 3 \cdot w \cdot w \cdot y \cdot y \cdot y = \mathbf{12w^2y^3}$

17. $\dfrac{2x + m}{3x^2 m} + \dfrac{x + 3m}{3x^2 m} = \dfrac{2x + m + x + 3m}{3x^2 m}$

$= \dfrac{\mathbf{3x + 4m}}{\mathbf{3x^2 m}}$

18. $\dfrac{3}{a} + \dfrac{1}{b} + \dfrac{1}{3} = \dfrac{9b}{3ab} + \dfrac{3a}{3ab} + \dfrac{ab}{3ab}$

$= \dfrac{\mathbf{9b + 3a + ab}}{\mathbf{3ab}}$

19. $8x^5y^2z - 16x^2y^2z^2 - xyz$

$= xyz(8x^4y - 16xyz - 1)$

20. $\dfrac{5x^2y^2 - 25x^3y^3}{x^2y^2} = \dfrac{x^2y^2(5 - 25xy)}{x^2y^2}$

$= 5 - 25xy$

21. $\dfrac{p^5p^{-4}z^2}{z^{-5}zp^3} = pz^2z^5z^{-1}p^{-3} = p^{-2}z^6$

22. $\dfrac{akp^2p^4}{a^{-3}a^5p^5k^4} = akp^6a^3a^{-5}p^{-5}k^{-4} = a^{-1}k^{-3}p$

23. $\left(\dfrac{m^2}{y^{-1}} + 4m^5y^6\right)m^{-2}y$

$= \dfrac{m^2m^{-2}y}{y^{-1}} + 4m^5y^6m^{-2}y = m^0y^2 + 4m^3y^7$

$= y^2 + 4m^3y^7$

24. $4aaxxy^{-3} - \dfrac{2a^2x^2}{y^3} - \dfrac{a^3x^2}{ay^3}$

$= \dfrac{4a^2x^2}{y^3} - \dfrac{2a^2x^2}{y^3} - \dfrac{a^2x^2}{y^3} = \dfrac{a^2x^2}{y^3}$

$= \dfrac{y^{-3}}{a^{-2}x^{-2}}$

25. $x - 3 = 2$

$\underline{\quad +3 \quad +3}$

$x = 5$

$x - (-y^0) - y^2 = 5 - (-1) - (-2)^2$

$= 5 + 1 - 4 = 2$

26. $m - 3m^{-2} = -3 - 3(-3)^{-2} = -3 - \dfrac{3}{(-3)^2}$

$= -3 - \dfrac{3}{9} = -\dfrac{10}{3}$

27. $\dfrac{1}{(-4)^{-3}} - \sqrt[3]{64} = (-4)^3 - 4 = -64 - 4 = -68$

28. $\dfrac{-(-2-5)-(-3-6)}{-2^0(-4)(-2)+(-3)^0(-1)(-8)} = \dfrac{7+9}{-8+8}$

$= \dfrac{16}{0}$, which is **undefined**

29. Area $=$ Area$_{\text{parallelogram}}$ $-$ Area$_{\text{circle}}$

$= \left[\dfrac{1}{2}(8 \text{ ft} \times 6 \text{ ft}) + \dfrac{1}{2}(8 \text{ ft} \times 6 \text{ ft})\right]$

$\quad - \left[\pi(2 \text{ ft})^2\right]$

$= (24 \text{ ft}^2 + 24 \text{ ft}^2) - 4\pi \text{ ft}^2$

$= (48 - 4\pi) \text{ ft}^2 = 35.44 \text{ ft}^2$

30. $10\dfrac{7}{18} - 2\dfrac{1}{3} - 4\dfrac{2}{9} = 10\dfrac{7}{18} - 2\dfrac{6}{18} - 4\dfrac{4}{18}$

$= 8\dfrac{1}{18} - 4\dfrac{4}{18} = 7\dfrac{19}{18} - 4\dfrac{4}{18} = 3\dfrac{15}{18}$

$= 3\dfrac{5}{6} \text{ mi}$

Practice 45

a. Range $= 12 - 3 = 9$

Median $= \dfrac{8 + 9}{2} = 8.5$

Mode $= 9$

Mean $= \dfrac{3 + 8 + 7 + 4 + 9 + 10 + 12 + 9}{8}$

$= \dfrac{62}{8} = 7.75$

b. Range $= 96 - 66 = 30$

Median $= 81$

Mode $= 81$

Mean $= (81 + 79 + 96 + 66 + 81 + 70 + 89$
$\quad + 80 + 92) \div 9 = 734 \div 9$
$= 81.56$

c. $\dfrac{2 + 4 + 7 + x}{4} = 8$

$13 + x = 32$

$x = 19$

Problem Set 45

1. $\dfrac{A}{D} = \dfrac{5}{18}$

$\dfrac{125}{D} = \dfrac{5}{18}$

$5D = 18 \cdot 125$

$\dfrac{5D}{5} = \dfrac{18 \cdot 125}{5}$

$D = 450$

2. Range $= 12 - 5 = 7$

Median $= 7$

Mode $= 6$

Mean $= \dfrac{5 + 6 + 9 + 6 + 12 + 8 + 7}{7}$

$= \dfrac{53}{7} = 7.57$

3. $80{,}500 \text{ cm} \times \dfrac{1 \text{ in.}}{2.54 \text{ cm}} \times \dfrac{1 \text{ ft}}{12 \text{ in.}} \times \dfrac{1 \text{ mi}}{5280 \text{ ft}}$

$= \dfrac{80{,}500}{(2.54)(12)(5280)} \text{ mi} = \mathbf{0.50 \text{ mi}}$

4. (a) $\qquad A = \pi r^2$

$36 \text{ cm}^2 = (3.14)r^2$

$\dfrac{(3.14)r^2}{3.14} = \dfrac{36 \text{ cm}^2}{3.14}$

$r^2 = 11.46 \text{ cm}^2$

$r = \sqrt{11.46 \text{ cm}^2}$

$r = \mathbf{3.39 \text{ cm}}$

(b) $C = 2\pi r$

$C = 2\pi(3.39 \text{ cm}) = \mathbf{6.78\pi \text{ cm}} = \mathbf{21.29 \text{ cm}}$

5. $x < 3$

6. $x \not\geq -2$

7. $h(x) = x(x - 10)$

$h(5) = 5(5 - 10) = 5(-5) = \mathbf{-25}$

8. $\dfrac{1}{3} + \dfrac{5}{12}x - 2 = 6\dfrac{2}{3}$

$\dfrac{5}{12}x - 1\dfrac{2}{3} = 6\dfrac{2}{3}$

$\dfrac{+1\dfrac{2}{3} \quad +1\dfrac{2}{3}}{\dfrac{5}{12}x \qquad = 8\dfrac{1}{3}}$

$\dfrac{\frac{5}{12}x}{\frac{5}{12}} = \dfrac{8\frac{1}{3}}{\frac{5}{12}}$

$x = \dfrac{25}{3} \cdot \dfrac{12}{5}$

$x = \mathbf{20}$

9. $0.004k - 0.002 + 0.002k = 4$

$0.006k - 0.002 = 4$

$6k - 2 = 4000$

$6k = 4002$

$k = \mathbf{667}$

10. $7(x - 3) - 6x + 4 = 2 - (x + 3)$

$7x - 21 - 6x + 4 = 2 - x - 3$

$x - 17 = -x - 1$

$\dfrac{+x + 17 \quad +x + 17}{2x \qquad = \qquad 16}$

$x = \mathbf{8}$

11. $5p - 4p - (p - 2) = 3(p + 4)$

$p - p + 2 = 3p + 12$

$3p + 12 = 2$

$\dfrac{-12 \quad -12}{3p \qquad = -10}$

$p = \mathbf{-\dfrac{10}{3}}$

12. $x - 4 + 2x - 5 = 6$

$3x - 9 = 6$

$\dfrac{+9 \quad +9}{3x \quad = 15}$

$x = 5$

$3x - 2 = 3(5) - 2 = 15 - 2 = \mathbf{13}$

13. $3x + 2y = 5$

$\dfrac{-3x \qquad\qquad -3x}{2y = -3x + 5}$

$\dfrac{2y}{2} = \dfrac{-3x}{2} + \dfrac{5}{2}$

$y = \mathbf{-\dfrac{3}{2}x + \dfrac{5}{2}}$

14. $2x - 5y + 4 = 0$

$\dfrac{-2x \qquad -4 \quad -2x - 4}{-5y \qquad = -2x - 4}$

$\dfrac{-5y}{-5} = \dfrac{-2x}{-5} - \dfrac{4}{-5}$

$y = \mathbf{\dfrac{2}{5}x + \dfrac{4}{5}}$

15. $18 = 2 \cdot 3 \cdot 3 \qquad 27 = 3 \cdot 3 \cdot 3$

$45 = 3 \cdot 3 \cdot 5$

$\text{LCM} = 2 \cdot 3 \cdot 3 \cdot 3 \cdot 5 = \mathbf{270}$

16. $8a^4m^2x = 2 \cdot 2 \cdot 2 \cdot a \cdot a \cdot a \cdot a \cdot m \cdot m \cdot x$

$12a^3m^3x = 2 \cdot 2 \cdot 3 \cdot a \cdot a \cdot a \cdot m \cdot m$

$\cdot\, m \cdot x$

$\text{LCM} = 2 \cdot 2 \cdot 2 \cdot 3 \cdot a \cdot a \cdot a \cdot a \cdot m \cdot m$

$\cdot\, m \cdot x$

$= \mathbf{24a^4m^3x}$

17. $\dfrac{4x+2}{3a^2m} - \dfrac{x-1}{3a^2m} = \dfrac{4x+2-(x-1)}{3a^2m}$

$= \dfrac{4x+2-x+1}{3a^2m} = \dfrac{3x+3}{3a^2m} = \dfrac{3(x+1)}{3a^2m}$

$= \dfrac{x+1}{a^2m}$

18. $\dfrac{5}{x} + \dfrac{1}{y} + \dfrac{1}{4} = \dfrac{20y}{4xy} + \dfrac{4x}{4xy} + \dfrac{xy}{4xy}$

$= \dfrac{20y+4x+xy}{4xy}$

19. $3a^2b^4c^5 - 6a^2b^6c^6 = 3a^2b^4c^5(1-2b^2c)$

20. $\dfrac{k^4p - 2k^5p^2}{k^4p} = \dfrac{k^4p(1-2kp)}{k^4p} = 1-2kp$

21. $\dfrac{k^5m^2}{k^7m^{-5}} = \dfrac{1}{k^7m^{-5}k^{-5}m^{-2}} = \dfrac{1}{k^2m^{-7}}$

22. $\dfrac{a^2bc^{-2}c^5}{a^2b^{-3}a^2c^3} = \dfrac{a^2bc^3}{a^4b^{-3}c^3}$

$= \dfrac{1}{a^4b^{-3}c^3a^{-2}b^{-1}c^{-3}} = \dfrac{1}{a^2b^{-4}}$

23. $\dfrac{x^{-2}p^0}{y^4}\left(\dfrac{x^2}{p^4} - x^4p^6\right)$

$= \dfrac{x^{-2}p^0x^2}{y^4p^4} - \dfrac{x^{-2}p^0x^4p^6}{y^4}$

$= \dfrac{1}{y^4p^4} - \dfrac{x^2p^6}{y^4} = \dfrac{1}{p^4y^4} - \dfrac{1}{x^{-2}p^{-6}y^4}$

24. $xy^2 - \dfrac{3xy}{y^{-1}} + \dfrac{2x^0y^2}{x^{-1}} - \dfrac{4x^2}{y^2} + 2x^2y^{-2}$

$= xy^2 - 3xy^2 + 2xy^2 - 4x^2y^{-2} + 2x^2y^{-2}$

$= -2x^2y^{-2}$

25. $|x-y| + |y-x| = |2-5| + |5-2|$

$= 3+3 = 6$

26. $xa - a(x^{-2} - xa) = 3(-1) - (-1)[3^{-2} - 3(-1)]$

$= -3 + \left(\dfrac{1}{9} + 3\right) = \dfrac{1}{9}$

27. $\dfrac{1}{-(-3)^{-3}} - \sqrt[3]{-27} = \dfrac{(-3)^3}{-1} - \sqrt[3]{-27}$

$= \dfrac{-27}{-1} - (-3) = 27 + 3 = 30$

28. $\dfrac{-4\left[(-2+5) - (-3+8^0)\right]}{-2^0|5-1|}$

$= \dfrac{-4[3-(-3+1)]}{-4} = 3+3-1 = 5$

29. $P = 5\dfrac{2}{7}\text{ m} + 5\dfrac{2}{7}\text{ m} + 2\dfrac{3}{14}\text{ m} + 2\dfrac{3}{14}\text{ m}$

$= 10\dfrac{4}{7}\text{ m} + 4\dfrac{6}{14}\text{ m}$

$= 10\dfrac{4}{7}\text{ m} + 4\dfrac{3}{7}\text{ m}$

$= 14\dfrac{7}{7}\text{ m} = \mathbf{15\ m}$

30. Volume $= (\text{Area}_{\text{base}})(\text{Height})$

$= \left[(6\text{ in.} \times 4\text{ in.}) + \dfrac{1}{2}\pi(2\text{ in.})^2\right](8\text{ in.})$

$= (24\text{ in.}^2 + 2\pi\text{ in.}^2)(8\text{ in.})$

$= (192 + 16\pi)\text{ in.}^3 = \mathbf{242.24\ in.^3}$

Practice 46

a. $-5 < x \le 4$

b. $-7 < x < -2$

c. $-3 < x \le 2$

d. $-2 \le x < 5$

Problem Set 46

1. $(2N-7) + 8 = -N + 16$

$2N + 1 = -N + 16$

$\underline{+N \qquad\qquad +N}$

$3N + 1 = \qquad +16$

$\underline{-1 \qquad\qquad -1}$

$3N \qquad = \qquad 15$

$N = \mathbf{5}$

2. Range $= 98 - 64 = \mathbf{34}$

Median $= \mathbf{83}$

Mode $= \mathbf{83}$

Mean $= (92 + 72 + 83 + 64 + 98 + 83 + 94$

$+ 89 + 78) \div 9$

$= 753 \div 9 = \mathbf{83.67}$

3. $42{,}000\text{ in.} \cdot \text{in.} \times \dfrac{1\text{ ft}}{12\text{ in.}} \times \dfrac{1\text{ ft}}{12\text{ in.}} \times \dfrac{1\text{ mi}}{5280\text{ ft}}$

$\times \dfrac{1\text{ mi}}{5280\text{ ft}} = \dfrac{42{,}000}{(12)^2(5280)^2}\text{ mi}^2 = \mathbf{0.000010\ mi^2}$

                                    Algebra 1, **Third Edition**

4. $A = lw$

  $221 \text{ in.}^2 = l(13 \text{ in.})$

  $l = \dfrac{221 \text{ in.}^2}{13 \text{ in.}}$

  $l = 17 \text{ in.}$

  $P = 2l + 2w$

  $= 2(17 \text{ in.}) + 2(13 \text{ in.})$

  $= 34 \text{ in.} + 26 \text{ in.}$

  $= \textbf{60 in.}$

5. $x \geq -3;\ x \nless -3$

6. $-3 < x < 2$

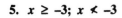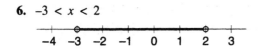

7. $(DP)(41.25) = 2.475$

  $DP = \dfrac{2.475}{41.25}$

  $DP = \textbf{0.06}$

8. $f(x) = x(6 - x)$

  $f(-5) = -5[6 - (-5)]$

  $= -5(6 + 5)$

  $= -5(11) = \textbf{-55}$

9. $\dfrac{2}{3} - \dfrac{4}{9}x + 1 = 2\dfrac{7}{9}$

  $-\dfrac{4}{9}x + \dfrac{5}{3} = 2\dfrac{7}{9}$

  $\phantom{-\dfrac{4}{9}x} \dfrac{-\dfrac{5}{3} \quad -\dfrac{5}{3}}{}$

  $-\dfrac{4}{9}x \quad = 1\dfrac{1}{9}$

  $\dfrac{\dfrac{-4}{9}x}{\dfrac{-4}{9}} = \dfrac{1\dfrac{1}{9}}{\dfrac{-4}{9}}$

  $x = \dfrac{10}{9} \cdot -\dfrac{9}{4}$

  $x = -\dfrac{10}{4}$

  $x = -\dfrac{\textbf{5}}{\textbf{2}}$

10. $0.06 + 0.06x = -0.042$

  $60 + 60x = -42$

  $60x = -102$

  $x = \textbf{-1.7}$

11. $5x - 4(2x - 2) = 5 - x$

  $5x - 8x + 8 = 5 - x$

  $-3x + 8 = 5 - x$

  $\dfrac{+x \qquad\qquad +x}{}$

  $-2x + 8 = 5$

  $\dfrac{-8 \quad -8}{}$

  $-2x \quad = -3$

  $x = \dfrac{\textbf{3}}{\textbf{2}}$

12. $3x - 4 + x - 6 = 10$

  $4x - 10 = 10$

  $\dfrac{+10 \quad +10}{}$

  $4x \quad = 20$

  $x = 5$

  $2x - 4 = 2(5) - 4 = 10 - 4 = \textbf{6}$

13. $5x + 4 = 3y$

  $\dfrac{3y}{3} = \dfrac{5x}{3} + \dfrac{4}{3}$

  $y = \dfrac{5}{3}x + \dfrac{4}{3}$

14. $2y - 5 - x = 0$

  $\dfrac{+5 + x \quad +5 + x}{}$

  $2y \qquad = 5 + x$

  $\dfrac{2y}{2} = \dfrac{5}{2} + \dfrac{x}{2}$

  $y = \dfrac{1}{2}x + \dfrac{5}{2}$

15. $45 = 3 \cdot 3 \cdot 5 \qquad 75 = 3 \cdot 5 \cdot 5$

  $125 = 5 \cdot 5 \cdot 5$

  $\text{LCM} = 3 \cdot 3 \cdot 5 \cdot 5 \cdot 5 = \textbf{1125}$

16. $5x^5y^3z = 5 \cdot x \cdot x \cdot x \cdot x \cdot x \cdot y \cdot y \cdot y \cdot z$

  $6x^3y^4z^2 = 2 \cdot 3 \cdot x \cdot x \cdot x \cdot y \cdot y \cdot y \cdot y$

  $\cdot z \cdot z$

  $\text{LCM} = 2 \cdot 3 \cdot 5 \cdot x \cdot x \cdot x \cdot x \cdot x \cdot y \cdot y \cdot y$

  $\cdot y \cdot z \cdot z$

  $= \textbf{30}x^5y^4z^2$

17. $\dfrac{7}{x^2 + y} - \dfrac{4}{x^2 + y} + \dfrac{3}{x^2 + y} = \dfrac{7 - 4 + 3}{x^2 + y}$

  $= \dfrac{\textbf{6}}{x^2 + y}$

18. $\dfrac{a}{4d^2} + \dfrac{5}{d} + \dfrac{b}{d^3} = \dfrac{ad}{4d^3} + \dfrac{5(4d^2)}{4d^3} + \dfrac{4b}{4d^3}$

  $= \dfrac{ad + 20d^2 + 4b}{4d^3}$

19. $3x^2yz - 4zyx^2 + 2xyz^2 = xyz(3x - 4x + 2z)$

    $= xyz(-x + 2z)$

20. $\dfrac{a^3b - 2a^2b^2}{a^2b} = \dfrac{a^2b(a - 2b)}{a^2b} = a - 2b$

21. $\dfrac{m^4p^5}{p^{-3}m^6} = m^4p^5p^3m^{-6} = m^{-2}p^8 = \dfrac{p^8}{m^2}$

22. $\dfrac{xxx^3y^5y^{-2}}{x^{-3}yy^{-6}} = \dfrac{x^5y^3}{x^{-3}y^{-5}} = x^5y^3x^3y^5 = x^8y^8$

23. $\left(\dfrac{a^2}{x^{-1}} - 4a^6x^4\right)\dfrac{a^{-2}}{x} = \dfrac{a^2a^{-2}}{x^{-1}x} - \dfrac{4a^6x^4a^{-2}}{x}$

    $= \dfrac{a^0}{x^0} - 4a^4x^3 = 1 - 4a^4x^3$

24. $4m^2y^{-2} - \dfrac{2mmy^{-2}}{x} + \dfrac{3m^2x^{-1}}{y^2} - 3mmyy^{-3}$

    $= \dfrac{4}{m^{-2}y^2} - \dfrac{2}{m^{-2}y^2x} + \dfrac{3}{m^{-2}y^2x} - \dfrac{3}{m^{-2}y^2}$

    $= \dfrac{1}{m^{-2}y^2} + \dfrac{1}{m^{-2}xy^2}$

25. $|x - y| - |y - x| = |5 - 2| - |2 - 5|$

    $= 3 - 3 = 0$

26. $-a^{-3}(a - a^2x) = -(-2)^{-3}[-2 - (-2)^2 4]$

    $= \dfrac{-1}{-8}[-2 - 4(4)] = \dfrac{1}{8}(-2 - 16) = \dfrac{-18}{8} = -\dfrac{9}{4}$

27. $-2^4 + \dfrac{1}{-(-2)^3} + \sqrt[3]{64} = -16 + \dfrac{1}{8} + 4$

    $= -12 + \dfrac{1}{8} = -11\dfrac{7}{8} = -\dfrac{95}{8}$

28. $\dfrac{-2\left[(-3 + 2)(-3 + 5^0)\right]}{|-4 - 1| - (-6)^0} = \dfrac{-2[(-1)(-3 + 1)]}{|-5| - 1}$

    $= \dfrac{-2[(-1)(-2)]}{5 - 1} = \dfrac{-4}{4} = -1$

29.

![Trapezoid with top side 10, right height 8, bottom side 13, divided by a diagonal into regions A_1 and A_2]

$A = A_1 + A_2$

    $= \dfrac{1}{2}(10 \text{ ft} \times 8 \text{ ft}) + \dfrac{1}{2}(13 \text{ ft} \times 8 \text{ ft})$

    $= 40 \text{ ft}^2 + 52 \text{ ft}^2 = \textbf{92 ft}^2$

30. $S.A. = 2(\text{Area}_{\text{base}}) + \text{Lateral Surface Area}$

    $= 2\left[(12 \text{ cm} \times 12 \text{ cm}) + \dfrac{1}{2}\pi(6 \text{ cm})^2\right]$

    $+ (\text{Perimeter}_{\text{base}})(\text{Height})$

    $= 2(144 \text{ cm}^2 + 18\pi \text{ cm}^2)$

    $+ \left(12 \text{ cm} + 12 \text{ cm} + 12 \text{ cm} + \dfrac{2\pi(6 \text{ cm})}{2}\right)$

    $\cdot 30 \text{ cm}$

    $= 288 \text{ cm}^2 + 36\pi \text{ cm}^2 + (36 \text{ cm} + 6\pi \text{ cm})$

    $\cdot 30 \text{ cm}$

    $= 288 \text{ cm}^2 + 36\pi \text{ cm}^2 + 1080 \text{ cm}^2$

    $+ 180\pi \text{ cm}^2$

    $= \textbf{(1368 + 216}\pi\textbf{) cm}^2 = \textbf{2046.24 cm}^2$

Practice 47

a. $\dfrac{20}{100} \cdot WN = 800$

    $\dfrac{100}{20} \cdot \dfrac{20}{100}WN = 800 \cdot \dfrac{100}{20}$

             $WN = \dfrac{80{,}000}{20}$

             $WN = \textbf{4000}$

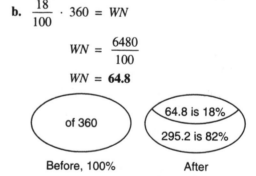

of 4000   800 is 20%

                       3200 is 80%

Before, 100%   After

b. $\dfrac{18}{100} \cdot 360 = WN$

         $WN = \dfrac{6480}{100}$

         $WN = \textbf{64.8}$

of 360   64.8 is 18%

                      295.2 is 82%

Before, 100%   After

c. $\dfrac{270}{100} \cdot 80 = WN$

         $WN = \dfrac{21{,}600}{100}$

         $WN = \textbf{216}$

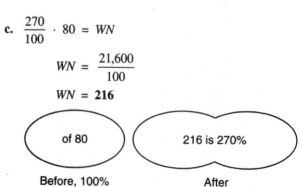

of 80   216 is 270%

Before, 100%   After

d. $\dfrac{190}{100} \cdot 20 = WN$

$WN = 1.9 \cdot 20$

$WN = \textbf{38}$

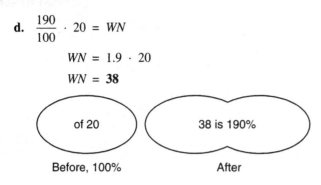

of 20

38 is 190%

Before, 100%   After

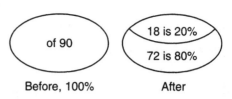

of 90

18 is 20%

72 is 80%

Before, 100%   After

Problem Set 47

1. $\dfrac{H}{T} = \dfrac{2}{21}$

$\dfrac{H}{84,000} = \dfrac{2}{21}$

$21H = 2 \cdot 84,000$

$H = \dfrac{2 \cdot 84,000}{21}$

$H = \textbf{8000 farthings}$

2. $\dfrac{4 + 7 + x}{3} = 10$

$11 + x = 30$

$x = \textbf{19}$

3. $42 \text{ ft} \times \dfrac{12 \text{ in.}}{1 \text{ ft}} \times \dfrac{2.54 \text{ cm}}{1 \text{ in.}} \times \dfrac{1 \text{ m}}{100 \text{ cm}}$

$= \dfrac{\textbf{42(12)(2.54)}}{\textbf{(100)}} \text{ m} = \textbf{12.80 m}$

4. (a) $C = 2\pi r$

$16\pi \text{ cm} = 2\pi r$

$16(3.14) \text{ cm} = 2(3.14)r$

$50.24 \text{ cm} = 6.28r$

$r = \dfrac{50.24 \text{ cm}}{6.28}$

$r = \textbf{8 cm}$

(b) $A = \pi r^2$

$A = \pi(8 \text{ cm})^2 = \textbf{64}\boldsymbol{\pi} \textbf{ cm}^2 = \textbf{200.96 cm}^2$

5. $\dfrac{20}{100} \cdot WN = 18$

$\dfrac{100}{20} \cdot \dfrac{20}{100}WN = 18 \cdot \dfrac{100}{20}$

$WN = \dfrac{1800}{20}$

$WN = \textbf{90}$

6. $\dfrac{140}{100} \cdot 70 = WN$

$WN = \dfrac{9800}{100}$

$WN = \textbf{98}$

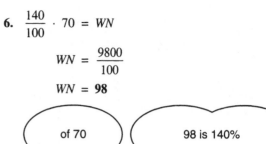

of 70

98 is 140%

Before, 100%   After

7. $-3 < x \le 2$

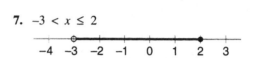

8. $g(x) = -x(1 - x)$

$g(10) = -10(1 - 10) = -10(-9) = \textbf{90}$

9. $2\dfrac{1}{3}k - 4 = 17$

$\underline{\quad +4 \quad +4 \quad}$

$2\dfrac{1}{3}k \quad\;\; = 21$

$k = \dfrac{21}{2\dfrac{1}{3}}$

$k = \dfrac{21}{1} \cdot \dfrac{3}{7}$

$k = \textbf{9}$

10. $-4.2 + 0.02x - 0.4 = 0.03x$

$-420 + 2x - 40 = 3x$

$-460 + 2x = 3x$

$-x = 460$

$x = \textbf{-460}$

11. $-2^0 - |-3| - 2^2 - (3 - x) = -(-3)^3$

$-1 - 3 - 4 - 3 + x = -(-27)$

$-11 + x = 27$

$\underline{+11 \qquad +11}$

$x = \textbf{38}$

12. $5x - 9 + x - 3 = 6$

$6x - 12 = \;\; 6$

$\underline{\quad +12 \quad +12}$

$6x \qquad = 18$

$x = 3$

$9 - 3x = 9 - 3(3) = 9 - 9 = \textbf{0}$

13. $\quad 2x + 4y = \qquad 6$

$\dfrac{-2x \qquad\qquad -2x}{4y = -2x + 6}$

$\dfrac{4y}{4} = \dfrac{-2x}{4} + \dfrac{6}{4}$

$y = -\dfrac{1}{2}x + \dfrac{3}{2}$

14. $\quad 5x - 3y + 5 = 2y - 5$

$\dfrac{-2y - 5 \qquad -2y - 5}{5x - 5y \quad = \qquad -10}$

$\dfrac{-5x \qquad\qquad -5x}{-5y \quad = -5x - 10}$

$\dfrac{-5y}{-5} = \dfrac{-5x}{-5} - \dfrac{10}{-5}$

$y = x + 2$

15. $\quad 18 = 2 \cdot 3 \cdot 3 \qquad 35 = 5 \cdot 7$

$40 = 2 \cdot 2 \cdot 2 \cdot 5$

LCM $= 2 \cdot 2 \cdot 2 \cdot 3 \cdot 3 \cdot 5 \cdot 7 =$ **2520**

16. $\quad 2 = 2 \qquad c^2 = c \cdot c \qquad c^3 = c \cdot c \cdot c$

LCM $= 2 \cdot c \cdot c \cdot c =$ **$2c^3$**

17. $\quad \dfrac{a}{b} + \dfrac{c^2 - a}{b} + \dfrac{4}{b} = \dfrac{a + c^2 - a + 4}{b}$

$= \dfrac{c^2 + 4}{b}$

18. $\quad \dfrac{4}{a} + \dfrac{c}{4a} + 5 = \dfrac{16}{4a} + \dfrac{c}{4a} + \dfrac{20a}{4a}$

$= \dfrac{16 + c + 20a}{4a}$

19. $\quad 5x^2y^5m^2 - 10x^4y^2m^3 =$ **$5x^2y^2m^2(y^3 - 2x^2m)$**

20. $\quad \dfrac{4a^2x - ax^2y}{ax} = \dfrac{ax(4a - xy)}{ax} =$ **$4a - xy$**

21. $\quad \dfrac{x^2xyy^{-4}}{x^4y^{-5}} = \dfrac{x^3y^{-3}}{x^4y^{-5}} = \dfrac{x^3x^{-4}}{y^3y^{-5}} =$ **$\dfrac{x^{-1}}{y^{-2}}$**

22. $\quad \dfrac{mm^2p^3y^{-3}}{m^{-3}m^{-2}p^{-3}y^4} = \dfrac{m^3p^3y^{-3}}{m^{-5}p^{-3}y^4}$

$= \dfrac{y^{-3}y^{-4}}{m^{-5}p^{-3}m^{-3}p^{-3}} =$ **$\dfrac{y^{-7}}{m^{-8}p^{-6}}$**

23. $\quad \dfrac{x^{-2}}{y^{-3}}\left(\dfrac{x^2}{y^3} - \dfrac{ax^3}{y^{-4}}\right) = \dfrac{x^{-2}x^2}{y^{-3}y^3} - \dfrac{ax^{-2}x^3}{y^{-3}y^{-4}}$

$= \dfrac{x^0}{y^0} - \dfrac{ax}{y^{-7}} = 1 - \dfrac{1}{a^{-1}x^{-1}y^{-7}}$

24. $\quad 5m^2k^5 - \dfrac{3m^3k^6}{mk} - 4mmk^6k^{-1} + \dfrac{3m^2m^0}{k^{-5}}$

$= 5m^2k^5 - 3m^2k^5 - 4m^2k^5 + 3m^2k^5 =$ **k^5m^2**

25. $\quad -x - |xa|(x^0 - a) = -(-2) - \big|-2(-3)\big|\big[1 - (-3)\big]$

$= 2 - 6(1 + 3) = 2 - 6(4) = 2 - 24 =$ **-22**

26. $\quad a^{-2}(2a - a^{-3}) = (-3)^{-2}\big[2(-3) - (-3)^{-3}\big]$

$= \dfrac{1}{9}\left(-6 + \dfrac{1}{27}\right) = \dfrac{-6}{9} + \dfrac{1}{243} = \dfrac{-162}{243} + \dfrac{1}{243}$

$= -\dfrac{\mathbf{161}}{\mathbf{243}}$

27. $\quad \dfrac{1}{-3^{-3}} - (-5)^0 + \sqrt[5]{32} = -27 - 1 + 2 =$ **-26**

28. $\quad \dfrac{-2^2\big[(-4 - 6^0)(5 - 3^0)\big]}{|-6| \cdot [-(-2)]}$

$= \dfrac{-4[(-4 - 1)(5 - 1)]}{6 - 2} = \dfrac{-4(-5)(4)}{4} =$ **20**

29. $\quad P = \left(4\dfrac{1}{4} + 3\dfrac{5}{6} + 9\dfrac{1}{2} + 12\dfrac{5}{12}\right)m$

$= \left(4\dfrac{3}{12} + 3\dfrac{10}{12} + 9\dfrac{6}{12} + 12\dfrac{5}{12}\right)m$

$= 28\dfrac{24}{12}\,m =$ **30 m**

30. Volume $= \big(\text{Area}_{\text{base}}\big)(\text{Height})$

$= \left[(10 \text{ in.} \times 8 \text{ in.}) + \dfrac{1}{2}\pi(4 \text{ in.})^2\right](7 \text{ in.})$

$= \big(80 \text{ in.}^2 + 8\pi \text{ in.}^2\big)(7 \text{ in.})$

$=$ **$(560 + 56\pi)$ in.^{3}** $= $ **735.84 in.^{3}**

Practice 48

a. $-\big(3x^5 + 6x^4 - 7x^3 - 5\big)$

$+ \big(x^5 - x^4 + 3x^2 - 2x - 8\big)$

$= -3x^5 - 6x^4 + 7x^3 + 5 + x^5 - x^4 + 3x^2$

$- 2x - 8$

$= \mathbf{-2x^5 - 7x^4 + 7x^3 + 3x^2 - 2x - 3}$

b. $\big(3x^2 + x^4 - 6x + 2\big)$

$- \big(15x^4 + 2x^3 - 6x^2 + 5x - 3\big)$

$= 3x^2 + x^4 - 6x + 2 - 15x^4 - 2x^3 + 6x^2 - 5x$

$+ 3$

$= \mathbf{-14x^4 - 2x^3 + 9x^2 - 11x + 5}$

Problem Set 48

1. $3N + 5 = -55$

$\underline{\quad -5 \qquad -5\quad}$

$3N \qquad = -60$

$N = \mathbf{-20}$

2. Range $= 12 - 2 = \mathbf{10}$

Median $= \dfrac{7 + 8}{2} = \mathbf{7.5}$

Mode $= \mathbf{11}$

Mean $= \dfrac{8 + 11 + 5 + 7 + 11 + 2 + 12 + 4}{8}$

$= \dfrac{60}{8} = \mathbf{7.5}$

3. $28{,}000 \text{ in.} \cdot \text{in.} \times \dfrac{2.54 \text{ cm}}{1 \text{ in.}} \times \dfrac{2.54 \text{ cm}}{1 \text{ in.}}$

$\times \dfrac{1 \text{ m}}{100 \text{ cm}} \times \dfrac{1 \text{ m}}{100 \text{ cm}} \times \dfrac{1 \text{ km}}{1000 \text{ m}} \times \dfrac{1 \text{ km}}{1000 \text{ m}}$

$= \dfrac{28{,}000(2.54)^2}{(100)^2 (1000)^2} \text{ km}^2 = \mathbf{0.000018 \text{ km}^2}$

4. $P = 2l + 2w$

$66 \text{ in.} = 2l + 2(11 \text{ in.})$

$66 \text{ in.} = 2l + 22 \text{ in.}$

$44 \text{ in.} = 2l$

$22 \text{ in.} = l$

$A = lw = (22 \text{ in.})(11 \text{ in.}) = \mathbf{242 \text{ in.}^2}$

5. $\dfrac{WP}{100} \cdot 160 = 88$

$\dfrac{100}{160} \cdot \dfrac{WP}{100} \cdot 160 = 88 \cdot \dfrac{100}{160}$

$WP = \dfrac{8800}{160}$

$WP = \mathbf{55\%}$

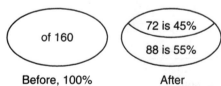

of 160   72 is 45%

88 is 55%

Before, 100%   After

6. $\dfrac{240}{100} \cdot 25 = WN$

$WN = 2.4 \cdot 25$

$WN = \mathbf{60}$

of 25   60 is 240%

Before, 100%   After

7. $-2 \le x < 3$

8. $315 \qquad \dfrac{315}{3} = 105 \qquad \dfrac{105}{3} = 35 \qquad \dfrac{35}{5} = 7$

$\mathbf{3 \cdot 3 \cdot 5 \cdot 7}$

9. $h(x) = \dfrac{1}{x}$

$h(4) = \dfrac{\mathbf{1}}{\mathbf{4}}$

10. $-4\dfrac{3}{4} + 3\dfrac{3}{5}x = 13\dfrac{1}{4}$

$\underline{+4\dfrac{3}{4} \qquad\qquad +4\dfrac{3}{4}}$

$3\dfrac{3}{5}x = 18$

$\dfrac{3\dfrac{3}{5}x}{3\dfrac{3}{5}} = \dfrac{18}{3\dfrac{3}{5}}$

$x = \dfrac{18}{1} \cdot \dfrac{5}{18}$

$x = \mathbf{5}$

11. $0.2p + 2.2 + 2.2p = 4.36$

$20p + 220 + 220p = 436$

$240p = 216$

$p = \mathbf{0.9}$

12. $(-2)^3(-x - 4) - |-4| = -2(x + 7^0)$

$-8(-x - 4) - 4 = -2x - 2$

$8x + 32 - 4 = -2x - 2$

$8x + 28 = -2x - 2$

$\underline{+2x \qquad\qquad +2x}$

$10x + 28 = \qquad -2$

$\underline{\quad -28 \qquad\qquad -28}$

$10x \qquad = \qquad -30$

$x = \mathbf{-3}$

13. $x + 3 = 4$

$\underline{-3 \quad -3}$

$x = 1$

$x^2 - 19 = (1)^2 - 19 = 1 - 19 = \mathbf{-18}$

14. $6y + x - 4y - 6 + 5x = 0$

$2y - 6 + 6x = 0$

$\underline{\qquad +6 - 6x \quad +6 - 6x}$

$2y \qquad\qquad = 6 - 6x$

$\dfrac{2y}{2} = \dfrac{6}{2} - \dfrac{6x}{2}$

$y = \mathbf{-3x + 3}$

15. $8 = 2 \cdot 2 \cdot 2$ $36 = 2 \cdot 2 \cdot 3 \cdot 3$

$75 = 3 \cdot 5 \cdot 5$

$LCM = 2 \cdot 2 \cdot 2 \cdot 3 \cdot 3 \cdot 5 \cdot 5 = \mathbf{1800}$

16. $\dfrac{1}{3} + \dfrac{2}{5} + \dfrac{3}{10} = \dfrac{10}{30} + \dfrac{12}{30} + \dfrac{9}{30} = \dfrac{\mathbf{31}}{\mathbf{30}}$

17. $\dfrac{a}{x} + \dfrac{b}{c^2 x^2} + d = \dfrac{ac^2 x}{c^2 x^2} + \dfrac{b}{c^2 x^2} + \dfrac{dc^2 x^2}{c^2 x^2}$

$= \dfrac{ac^2 x + b + dc^2 x^2}{c^2 x^2}$

18. $(4x^3 + x^2 + 3) + (x^3 + 2x^2 + 1)$

$= \mathbf{5x^3 + 3x^2 + 4}$

19. $4x^2 y^5 p^2 - 3x^5 y^4 p^2 = \mathbf{x^2 y^4 p^2(4y - 3x^3)}$

20. $\dfrac{x^3 y^2 k - x^2 yk}{x^2 yk} = \dfrac{x^2 yk(xy - 1)}{x^2 yk} = \mathbf{xy - 1}$

21. $\dfrac{xx^{-3} y^5 x^0}{x^2 y^{-3} xy^2} = \dfrac{x^{-2} y^5}{x^3 y^{-1}} = \mathbf{x^{-5} y^6}$

22. $\dfrac{kp^2 k^{-1} p^{-3} p^{-4}}{k^2 pp^2 k^{-5}} = \dfrac{p^{-5}}{k^{-3} p^3} = \mathbf{k^3 p^{-8}}$

23. $\left(\dfrac{x^2}{yp^{-4}} - \dfrac{x^2 y}{p^{-4}} \right) \dfrac{x^{-2}}{y^4 p} = \dfrac{x^2 x^{-2}}{yp^{-4} y^4 p} - \dfrac{x^2 yx^{-2}}{p^{-4} y^4 p}$

$= \dfrac{1}{p^{-3} y^5} - \dfrac{y}{p^{-3} y^4} = \mathbf{p^3 y^{-5} - p^3 y^{-3}}$

24. $\dfrac{7my^0}{ym^0} - \dfrac{3m^2 y}{my^2} - \dfrac{5m^{-3} m^4}{y^{-3} y^4} + \dfrac{2ymm}{my^2}$

$= \dfrac{7m}{y} - \dfrac{3m}{y} - \dfrac{5m}{y} + \dfrac{2m}{y} = \dfrac{m}{y} = \dfrac{y^{-1}}{m^{-1}}$

25. $\dfrac{\begin{array}{l} y + 1 = 4 \\ -1 \; -1 \end{array}}{y = 3}$

$x - y^2(x^0 - y) = -2 - 3^2(1 - 3) = -2 - 9(-2)$

$= -2 + 18 = \mathbf{16}$

26. $\dfrac{\begin{array}{l} x + 2 = 4 \\ -2 \; -2 \end{array}}{x = 2}$

$-p^{-2} - (p^2 - x) = -(-3)^{-2} - \left[(-3)^2 - 2 \right]$

$= -\dfrac{1}{9} - (9 - 2) = -\dfrac{1}{9} - 7 = -7\dfrac{1}{9} = -\dfrac{\mathbf{64}}{\mathbf{9}}$

27. $-\dfrac{1}{(-4)^{-2}} - \sqrt[3]{-27} = -(-4)^2 - (-3)$

$= -16 + 3 = \mathbf{-13}$

28. $\dfrac{(-6)^0 \left[(-4 - 2^0) + (9 - 2^2) \right]}{|-2| - |-6|} = \dfrac{1[(-5) + 5]}{2 - 6}$

$= \dfrac{0}{-4} = \mathbf{0}$

29. Area $= \text{Area}_{\text{trapezoid}} - \text{Area}_{\text{triangle}}$

$= \left[\dfrac{1}{2}(17 \text{ ft} \times 6 \text{ ft}) + \dfrac{1}{2}(11 \text{ ft} \times 6 \text{ ft}) \right]$

$\quad - \left[\dfrac{1}{2}(3 \text{ ft} \times 4 \text{ ft}) \right]$

$= 51 \text{ ft}^2 + 33 \text{ ft}^2 - 6 \text{ ft}^2$

$= \mathbf{78 \text{ ft}^2}$

30. Since angles opposite sides of equal length have equal measure, x and y are equivalent.

$180 - 140 = 40$

$40 \div 2 = 20$

$\mathbf{x = 20; \; y = 20}$

Practice 49

a. $(5x + 3)(2x - 4) = 10x^2 - 20x + 6x - 12$

$= \mathbf{10x^2 - 14x - 12}$

b. $(5x - 6)^2 = (5x - 6)(5x - 6)$

$= 25x^2 - 30x - 30x + 36 = \mathbf{25x^2 - 60x + 36}$

c. $(3x - 1)(x^2 - 2x + 3)$

$= 3x^3 - 6x^2 + 9x - x^2 + 2x - 3$

$= \mathbf{3x^3 - 7x^2 + 11x - 3}$

Problem Set 49

1. $\dfrac{\text{Tri}}{\text{Total}} = \dfrac{3}{17}$

$\dfrac{\text{Tri}}{3400} = \dfrac{3}{17}$

$17\text{Tri} = 3 \cdot 3400$

$\text{Tri} = \dfrac{3 \cdot 3400}{17}$

$\text{Tri} = \mathbf{600}$

2. Range $= 97 - 62 = \mathbf{35}$

Median $= \dfrac{71 + 78}{2} = \mathbf{74.5}$

Mode $= \mathbf{71}$

Mean $= (62 + 67 + 71 + 71 + 71 + 78 + 85$

$\quad + 89 + 94 + 97) \div 10$

$= 785 \div 10 = \mathbf{78.5}$

3. $10{,}000 \text{ ft} \times \dfrac{12 \text{ in.}}{1 \text{ ft}} \times \dfrac{2.54 \text{ cm}}{1 \text{ in.}} \times \dfrac{1 \text{ m}}{100 \text{ cm}}$

$\times \dfrac{1 \text{ km}}{1000 \text{ m}} = \dfrac{10{,}000(12)(2.54)}{(100)(1000)} \text{ km} = \mathbf{3.05 \text{ km}}$

4. (a) $C = \pi D = \pi(22 \text{ in.}) = \mathbf{22\pi \text{ in.}} = \mathbf{69.08 \text{ in.}}$

(b) $A = \pi r^2$

$= \pi(11 \text{ in.})^2 = \mathbf{121\pi \text{ in.}^2} = \mathbf{379.94 \text{ in.}^2}$

5. $\dfrac{25}{100} \cdot 200 = WN$

$WN = \dfrac{5000}{100}$

$WN = \mathbf{50}$

6. $\dfrac{WP}{100} \cdot 80 = 208$

$\dfrac{100}{80} \cdot \dfrac{WP}{100} \cdot 80 = 208 \cdot \dfrac{100}{80}$

$WP = \dfrac{20{,}800}{80}$

$WP = \mathbf{260\%}$

7. $-3 < x \le 6$

8. $WF\left(5\dfrac{5}{8}\right) = 2\dfrac{1}{4}$

$\dfrac{WF \cdot 5\dfrac{5}{8}}{5\dfrac{5}{8}} = \dfrac{2\dfrac{1}{4}}{5\dfrac{5}{8}}$

$WF = \dfrac{9}{4} \cdot \dfrac{8}{45}$

$WF = \mathbf{\dfrac{2}{5}}$

9. $f(x) = -\dfrac{1}{x}$

$f(5) = \mathbf{-\dfrac{1}{5}}$

10. $\dfrac{1}{5} + \dfrac{3}{25}x - 3 = 2\dfrac{3}{5}$

$\dfrac{3}{25}x - 2\dfrac{4}{5} = 2\dfrac{3}{5}$

$\underline{+2\dfrac{4}{5} \quad\quad +2\dfrac{4}{5}}$

$\dfrac{3}{25}x \quad\quad = 5\dfrac{2}{5}$

$\dfrac{\dfrac{3}{25}x}{\dfrac{3}{25}} = \dfrac{5\dfrac{2}{5}}{\dfrac{3}{25}}$

$x = \dfrac{27}{5} \cdot \dfrac{25}{3}$

$x = \mathbf{45}$

11. $0.04x + 0.2 - 0.4x = 0.38$

$4x + 20 - 40x = 38$

$-36x = 18$

$x = \dfrac{18}{-36}$

$x = -\dfrac{1}{2}$

$x = \mathbf{-0.5}$

12. $(-2)^3(-x - 4) - |-2| - 3^2 = -2(x - 4) - x$

$-8(-x - 4) - 2 - 9 = -2x + 8 - x$

$8x + 32 - 11 = -3x + 8$

$8x + 21 = -3x + 8$

$\underline{+3x \quad\quad\quad +3x}$

$\underline{11x + 21 = \quad\quad 8}$

$\underline{\quad\quad -21 \quad\quad -21}$

$11x \quad = \quad -13$

$x = \mathbf{-\dfrac{13}{11}}$

13. $x + 4 = \quad 3$

$\underline{\quad -4 \quad -4}$

$x = -1$

$x^2 - 11 = (-1)^2 - 11 = 1 - 11 = \mathbf{-10}$

14. $b^3 = b \cdot b \cdot b \quad\quad b^2 c = b \cdot b \cdot c$

$b^2 c^2 = b \cdot b \cdot c \cdot c$

$\text{LCM} = b \cdot b \cdot b \cdot c \cdot c = \mathbf{b^3 c^2}$

15. $\dfrac{3}{4} + \dfrac{2}{5} - \dfrac{3}{20} = \dfrac{15}{20} + \dfrac{8}{20} - \dfrac{3}{20} = \dfrac{20}{20} = \mathbf{1}$

16. $\dfrac{ad}{4d^3} + \dfrac{8}{d} + \dfrac{mx}{d^4} = \dfrac{ad^2}{4d^4} + \dfrac{8(4d^3)}{4d^4} + \dfrac{4mx}{4d^4}$

$= \mathbf{\dfrac{ad^2 + 32d^3 + 4mx}{4d^4}}$

17. $(2x^4 - x^2 + 5) - (x^4 - x^3 + 2x^2)$
$= 2x^4 - x^2 + 5 - x^4 + x^3 - 2x^2$
$= \mathbf{x^4 + x^3 - 3x^2 + 5}$

18. $(2x + 3)(x - 2) = 2x^2 - 4x + 3x - 6$
$= \mathbf{2x^2 - x - 6}$

19. $(2x + 1)^2 = (2x + 1)(2x + 1)$
$= 4x^2 + 2x + 2x + 1 = \mathbf{4x^2 + 4x + 1}$

20. $8m^3x^2y^4p - 4m^2xpm = \mathbf{4m^3px(2xy^4 - 1)}$

21. $\dfrac{m^2xym^3x^{-5}}{yy^{-4}m^{-3}x^2} = \dfrac{m^5x^{-4}y}{y^{-3}m^{-3}x^2} = \dfrac{1}{\mathbf{m^{-8}x^6y^{-4}}}$

22. $\dfrac{x^2y^{-2}m^{-5}y^0}{xxy^2y^{-5}x^{-3}} = \dfrac{x^2y^{-2}m^{-5}}{x^{-1}y^{-3}} = \dfrac{1}{\mathbf{m^5x^{-3}y^{-1}}}$

23. $\dfrac{x^{-1}}{y}\left(\dfrac{y}{x} - \dfrac{3xy^{-5}}{p^6}\right) = \dfrac{yx^{-1}}{xy} - \dfrac{3x^0y^{-5}}{p^6y}$
$= \dfrac{1}{x^2} - \dfrac{3}{p^6y^6}$

24. $\dfrac{x^2y}{p^{-3}} - \dfrac{4x^2p^3}{y^{-1}} - \dfrac{2xp}{y^{-1}p^2} - \dfrac{5y}{p^{-3}x^{-2}}$
$= p^3x^2y - 4p^3x^2y - 2p^{-1}xy - 5p^3x^2y$
$= \mathbf{-8p^3x^2y - 2p^{-1}xy}$

25. $x + 2 = -2$
$\underline{-2\quad -2}$
$x = -4$

$-p^2 - p^{-3}(xp^0) = -(-2)^2 - (-2)^{-3}(-4)$
$= -4 - \dfrac{1}{(-2)^3}(-4) = -4 + \dfrac{1}{8}(-4) = -4 - \dfrac{1}{2}$
$= -4\dfrac{1}{2} = \mathbf{-\dfrac{9}{2}}$

26. $x + 1 = -1$
$\underline{-1\quad -1}$
$x = -2$

$-x - x^{-2} - xy^{-2} = -(-2) - (-2)^{-2} - (-2)(2)^{-2}$
$= 2 - \dfrac{1}{(-2)^2} + \dfrac{2}{2^2} = 2 - \dfrac{1}{4} + \dfrac{2}{4} = \mathbf{\dfrac{9}{4}}$

27. $\dfrac{1}{-(-3)^{-2}} - \sqrt[3]{-64} = \dfrac{(-3)^2}{-1} - (-4)$
$= -9 + 4 = \mathbf{-5}$

28. $-2\left[(-4 - 3^0)(5 - 2) - (-6)\right] - \sqrt[3]{-125}$
$= -2[(-5)(3) + 6] - (-5) = -2(-9) + 5$
$= 18 + 5 = \mathbf{23}$

29. $A = \dfrac{1}{2}(3\text{ ft} \times 4\text{ ft}) + (4\text{ ft} \times 4\text{ ft}) + \dfrac{1}{2}\pi(2\text{ ft})^2$
$= 6\text{ ft}^2 + 16\text{ ft}^2 + 2\pi\text{ ft}^2$
$= \mathbf{(22 + 2\pi)\text{ ft}^2 = 28.28\text{ ft}^2}$

30. $S.A. = 2(\text{Area}_{\text{base}}) + \text{Lateral Surface Area}$
$= 2\left[\pi(8\text{ yd})^2\right] + (\text{Perimeter}_{\text{base}})(\text{Height})$
$= 128\pi\text{ yd}^2 + [2\pi(8\text{ yd})](12\text{ yd})$
$= 128\pi\text{ yd}^2 + 192\pi\text{ yd}^2$
$= \mathbf{320\pi\text{ yd}^2 = 1004.8\text{ yd}^2}$

Practice 50

a.

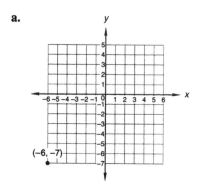

$(-6, -7)$

b.

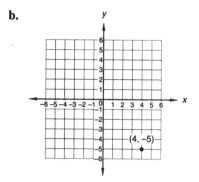

$(4, -5)$

Problem Set 50

1. $4(-N) - 3 = N + 27$
$-4N - 3 = N + 27$
$\underline{-N + 3\quad -N + 3}$
$-5N = 30$
$N = \mathbf{-6}$

2. $\dfrac{5 + 8 + 13 + x}{4} = 9$
$26 + x = 36$
$x = \mathbf{10}$

3. $15 \text{ km} \cdot \text{km} \times \dfrac{1000 \text{ m}}{1 \text{ km}} \times \dfrac{1000 \text{ m}}{1 \text{ km}} \times \dfrac{100 \text{ cm}}{1 \text{ m}}$

$\times \dfrac{100 \text{ cm}}{1 \text{ m}} \times \dfrac{1 \text{ in.}}{2.54 \text{ cm}} \times \dfrac{1 \text{ in.}}{2.54 \text{ cm}}$

$= \dfrac{15(1000)^2 (100)^2}{(2.54)^2} \text{ in.}^2 = \textbf{23,250,046,500 in.}^2$

4. $\dfrac{80}{100} \cdot WN = 1120$

$\dfrac{100}{80} \cdot \dfrac{80}{100} WN = 1120 \cdot \dfrac{100}{80}$

$WN = \textbf{1400}$

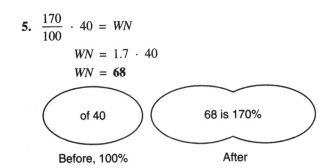

of 1400   280 is 20%   1120 is 80%

Before, 100%   After

5. $\dfrac{170}{100} \cdot 40 = WN$

$WN = 1.7 \cdot 40$

$WN = \textbf{68}$

of 40   68 is 170%

Before, 100%   After

6. $-5 \le x < 1$

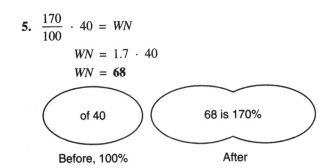

7. $1155 \qquad \dfrac{1155}{3} = 385 \qquad \dfrac{385}{5} = 77 \qquad \dfrac{77}{7} = 11$

$\textbf{3} \cdot \textbf{5} \cdot \textbf{7} \cdot \textbf{11}$

8. $g(x) = -\dfrac{1}{x}$

$g(-6) = \dfrac{-1}{-6} = \dfrac{\textbf{1}}{\textbf{6}}$

9. $\dfrac{2}{7} - \dfrac{1}{14}x + 2 = 3\dfrac{1}{14}$

$-\dfrac{1}{14}x + 2\dfrac{2}{7} = 3\dfrac{1}{14}$

$\dfrac{-2\dfrac{2}{7} \quad -2\dfrac{2}{7}}{-\dfrac{1}{14}x \qquad = \dfrac{11}{14}}$

$\dfrac{-\dfrac{1}{14}x}{-\dfrac{1}{14}} = \dfrac{\dfrac{11}{14}}{-\dfrac{1}{14}}$

$x = \dfrac{11}{14} \cdot -\dfrac{14}{1}$

$x = \textbf{-11}$

10. $0.3z - 0.02z + 0.2 = 1.18$

$30z - 2z + 20 = 118$

$28z = 98$

$z = \textbf{3.5}$

11. $(-2)^3\left(-k - |-3|\right) - (-2) - 2k = k - 3^2$

$-8(-k - 3) + 2 - 2k = k - 9$

$8k + 24 + 2 - 2k = k - 9$

$6k + 26 = k - 9$

$\dfrac{-k - 26 \quad -k - 26}{5k \qquad = \quad -35}$

$k = \textbf{-7}$

12. $7p + 3w = w - 12 - 3p$

$\dfrac{+3p - 3w \quad -3w \qquad + 3p}{10p \qquad = -2w - 12}$

$\dfrac{10p}{10} = \dfrac{-2w}{10} - \dfrac{12}{10}$

$p = -\dfrac{\textbf{1}}{\textbf{5}}w - \dfrac{\textbf{6}}{\textbf{5}}$

13. $x = x \qquad c^2 x^2 = c \cdot c \cdot x \cdot x$

$cdx = c \cdot d \cdot x$

$\text{LCM} = c \cdot c \cdot x \cdot x \cdot d = \textbf{c}^2\textbf{x}^2\textbf{d}$

14.

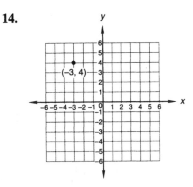

15.

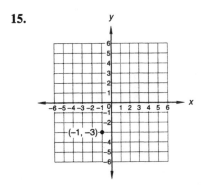

16. $\dfrac{3}{7} + \dfrac{8}{9} - \dfrac{1}{3} = \dfrac{27}{63} + \dfrac{56}{63} - \dfrac{21}{63} = \dfrac{\textbf{62}}{\textbf{63}}$

17. $\dfrac{4}{x^2} + \dfrac{6}{2x^3} - \dfrac{3}{4x^4} = \dfrac{16x^2}{4x^4} + \dfrac{12x}{4x^4} - \dfrac{3}{4x^4}$

$= \dfrac{\textbf{16}x^2 + \textbf{12}x - \textbf{3}}{\textbf{4}x^4}$

18. $\left(2x^5 + x^3 + 4x - 1\right) - \left(x^5 + 2x^3 - x + 2\right)$

$= 2x^5 + x^3 + 4x - 1 - x^5 - 2x^3 + x - 2$

$= \mathbf{x^5 - x^3 + 5x - 3}$

19. $(2x - 1)^2 = (2x - 1)(2x - 1)$

$= 4x^2 - 2x - 2x + 1 = \mathbf{4x^2 - 4x + 1}$

20. $(x + 1)\left(x^2 - 2x + 3\right)$

$= x^3 - 2x^2 + 3x + x^2 - 2x + 3$

$= \mathbf{x^3 - x^2 + x + 3}$

21. $\dfrac{3x^4 - 3x^2}{3x^2} = \dfrac{3x^2\left(x^2 - 1\right)}{3x^2} = \mathbf{x^2 - 1}$

22. $\dfrac{x^{-4}yy^{-3}x^0x^2}{x^{-3}y^3y^2x^{-4}} = \dfrac{x^{-2}y^{-2}}{x^{-7}y^5} = \dfrac{\mathbf{x^5}}{\mathbf{y^7}}$

23. $\left(\dfrac{ax^{-5}}{y^{-2}} + \dfrac{4x^3}{ay^2}\right)\dfrac{x^5}{ay^2} = \dfrac{ax^{-5}x^5}{y^{-2}ay^2} + \dfrac{4x^8}{ay^2ay^2}$

$= \dfrac{a}{a} + \dfrac{4x^8}{a^2y^4} = \mathbf{1 + \dfrac{4x^8}{a^2y^4}}$

24. $\dfrac{m^2xx^0}{y^{-1}} - \dfrac{3m^2y}{x^{-1}y^0} + 5mmyx - \dfrac{4x^2ym^2}{x}$

$= m^2xy - 3m^2xy + 5m^2xy - 4m^2xy$

$= -m^2xy = -\dfrac{\mathbf{1}}{\mathbf{m^{-2}x^{-1}y^{-1}}}$

25. $\begin{array}{ll} x + 2 = 1 & y + 3 = -1 \\ \underline{-2\quad -2} & \underline{-3\quad -3} \\ x = -1 & y = -4 \end{array}$

$-x\left(x - y^0\right)|y| = -(-1)(-1 - 1)|-4| = -2(4) = \mathbf{-8}$

26. $ab^0\left(a^{-3} - b^{-2}\right) = -2\left[(-2)^{-3} - (2)^{-2}\right]$

$= -2\left(-\dfrac{1}{8} - \dfrac{1}{4}\right) = -2\left(-\dfrac{3}{8}\right) = \dfrac{\mathbf{3}}{\mathbf{4}}$

27. $\dfrac{1}{-4^{-2}} - |-2| - \sqrt[5]{-243} = \dfrac{4^2}{-1} - 2 - (-3)$

$= -16 - 2 + 3 = \mathbf{-15}$

28. $P = \left(10 + 10 + \dfrac{2\pi(5)}{2} + \dfrac{2\pi(5)}{2}\right)$ cm

$= (20 + 10\pi)$ cm $= \mathbf{51.4}$ **cm**

29. $A = (32 \text{ in.})(12 \text{ in.}) = \mathbf{384 \text{ in.}^2}$

30. Volume $= \left(\text{Area}_{\text{base}}\right)(\text{Height})$

$= \left[\dfrac{1}{2}(6 \text{ m} \times 8 \text{ m}) + \dfrac{1}{2}\pi(4 \text{ m})^2\right](12 \text{ m})$

$= \left(24 \text{ m}^2 + 8\pi \text{ m}^2\right)(12 \text{ m})$

$= (288 + 96\pi) \text{ m}^3 = \mathbf{589.44 \text{ m}^3}$

Practice 51

a. $y = -x + 1$

x	0	1	–2
y	1	0	3

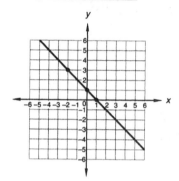

b. $y = -\dfrac{1}{3}x + 2$

x	0	3	–3
y	2	1	3

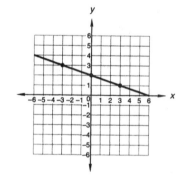

c. $x = 3$

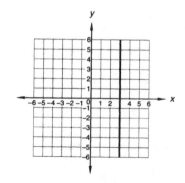

d. $y = -4$

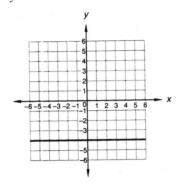

Problem Set 51

1. $\quad \dfrac{R}{T} = \dfrac{5}{12}$

$\quad \dfrac{R}{1080} = \dfrac{5}{12}$

$\quad 12R = 5 \cdot 1080$

$\quad R = \dfrac{5 \cdot 1080}{12}$

$\quad R = \mathbf{450}$

2. Range $= 28 - 4 = \mathbf{24}$

Median $= \mathbf{15}$

Mode $= \mathbf{15}$

Mean $= (4 + 6 + 8 + 14 + 15 + 15 + 18$

$\qquad + 23 + 28) \div 9$

$\qquad = 131 \div 9 = \mathbf{14.56}$

3. $10 \text{ km} \times \dfrac{1000 \text{ m}}{1 \text{ km}} \times \dfrac{100 \text{ cm}}{1 \text{ m}} \times \dfrac{1 \text{ in.}}{2.54 \text{ cm}}$

$\times \dfrac{1 \text{ ft}}{12 \text{ in.}} = \dfrac{\mathbf{10(1000)(100)}}{\mathbf{(2.54)(12)}} \text{ ft} = \mathbf{32{,}808.40 \text{ ft}}$

4. (a) $\quad C = 2\pi r$

$\quad 20 \text{ cm} = 2(3.14)r$

$\quad r = \dfrac{20 \text{ cm}}{6.28}$

$\quad r = \mathbf{3.18 \text{ cm}}$

(b) $A = \pi r^2$

$A = \pi(3.18 \text{ cm})^2 = \mathbf{10.11\pi \text{ cm}^2} = \mathbf{31.75 \text{ cm}^2}$

5. $\quad \dfrac{WP}{100} \cdot 8300 = 996$

$\dfrac{100}{8300} \cdot \dfrac{WP}{100} \cdot 8300 = 996 \cdot \dfrac{100}{8300}$

$\qquad WP = \mathbf{12\%}$

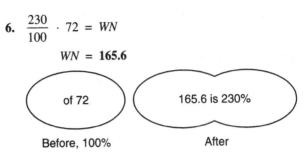

Before, 100%   After

6. $\dfrac{230}{100} \cdot 72 = WN$

$\qquad WN = \mathbf{165.6}$

of 72   165.6 is 230%

Before, 100%   After

7. $x \not\le 3$

$\qquad$
1 2 3 4 5

8. $\quad h(x) = \dfrac{1}{x}$

$h\left(-\dfrac{1}{2}\right) = \dfrac{1}{-\dfrac{1}{2}} = \dfrac{1}{1} \cdot -\dfrac{2}{1} = \mathbf{-2}$

9. $\quad -1\dfrac{2}{9} + 2\dfrac{1}{5}p = -\dfrac{1}{3}$

$\quad +1\dfrac{2}{9} \qquad\qquad +1\dfrac{2}{9}$

$\qquad\qquad 2\dfrac{1}{5}p = \dfrac{8}{9}$

$\qquad \dfrac{2\dfrac{1}{5}p}{2\dfrac{1}{5}} = \dfrac{\dfrac{8}{9}}{2\dfrac{1}{5}}$

$\qquad\qquad p = \dfrac{8}{9} \cdot \dfrac{5}{11}$

$\qquad\qquad p = \dfrac{\mathbf{40}}{\mathbf{99}}$

10. $0.4x - 0.02x + 1.396 = 0.598$

$\qquad 0.38x + 1.396 = 0.598$

$\qquad 380x + 1396 = 598$

$\qquad\qquad 380x = -798$

$\qquad\qquad\quad x = \mathbf{-2.1}$

11. $3x - [-(-2)]x + (-3)(x + 2) = 5x + (-7)$

$\qquad 3x - 2x - 3x - 6 = 5x - 7$

$\qquad\qquad -2x - 6 = 5x - 7$

$\qquad\quad \dfrac{-5x \qquad\qquad -5x}{-7x - 6 = \qquad -7}$

$\qquad\quad \dfrac{+6 \qquad\qquad +6}{-7x \qquad = \qquad -1}$

$\qquad\qquad\qquad x = \dfrac{\mathbf{1}}{\mathbf{7}}$

12. $x + 9 = 3$
$$\frac{-9 \quad -9}{x = -6}$$

$-x^2 + 4 = -(-6)^2 + 4 = -36 + 4 = \mathbf{-32}$

13. $4x^2 = 2 \cdot 2 \cdot x \cdot x \qquad yx^2 = y \cdot x \cdot x$

$8m^3x^2 = 2 \cdot 2 \cdot 2 \cdot m \cdot m \cdot m \cdot x \cdot x$

$\text{LCM} = 2 \cdot 2 \cdot 2 \cdot m \cdot m \cdot m \cdot x \cdot x \cdot y$

$\quad = \mathbf{8m^3x^2y}$

14. $y = x - 3$

x	0	1	4
y	-3	-2	1

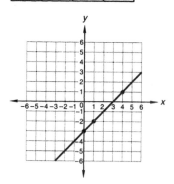

15. $x = 2$

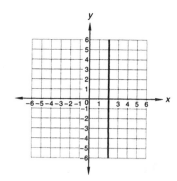

16. $\dfrac{4}{x^2} + \dfrac{c}{4x^3} + m = \dfrac{4(4x)}{4x^3} + \dfrac{c}{4x^3} + \dfrac{m(4x^3)}{4x^3}$

$= \mathbf{\dfrac{16x + c + 4mx^3}{4x^3}}$

17. $\dfrac{1}{2a^3} + \dfrac{3}{4ab^2} + \dfrac{c}{8a^2b^2}$

$= \dfrac{4b^2}{8a^3b^2} + \dfrac{3(2a^2)}{8a^3b^2} + \dfrac{c(a)}{8a^3b^2}$

$= \mathbf{\dfrac{4b^2 + 6a^2 + ac}{8a^3b^2}}$

18. $\left(3x^4 - 2x^3 - x - 2\right) + \left(x^4 + x^3 - 4x + 5\right)$

$= 3x^4 - 2x^3 - x - 2 + x^4 + x^3 - 4x + 5$

$= \mathbf{4x^4 - x^3 - 5x + 3}$

19. $(2x + 4)(5x - 3) = 10x^2 - 6x + 20x - 12$

$= \mathbf{10x^2 + 14x - 12}$

20. $(x + 3)^2 = (x + 3)(x + 3) = x^2 + 3x + 3x + 9$

$= \mathbf{x^2 + 6x + 9}$

21. $4k^2pz - 6k^3p^2z^5 - 2k^2p^2z^2 - 4kp$

$= \mathbf{2kp\left(2kz - 3k^2pz^5 - kpz^2 - 2\right)}$

22. $\dfrac{x^3y^{-4}p^0y^4p^2}{x^4xx^{-7}y^2p^4} = \dfrac{x^3p^2}{x^{-2}y^2p^4} = \dfrac{p^{-2}y^{-2}}{x^{-5}}$

$= \mathbf{\dfrac{y^{-2}p^{-2}}{x^{-5}}}$

23. $\dfrac{x^{-4}}{y^4}\left(\dfrac{x^{-4}}{y^4} - \dfrac{x^2}{ay^2}\right) = \dfrac{x^{-8}}{y^8} - \dfrac{x^{-2}}{ay^6}$

$= x^{-8}y^{-8} - x^{-2}a^{-1}y^{-6} = \mathbf{x^{-8}y^{-8} - a^{-1}x^{-2}y^{-6}}$

24. $\dfrac{x^2y}{p^{-3}} - \dfrac{4x^2p^3}{y^{-1}} - \dfrac{2xp}{y^{-1}p^{-2}} - \dfrac{5y}{p^{-3}x^{-2}}$

$= p^3x^2y - 4p^3x^2y - 2p^3xy - 5p^3x^2y$

$= \mathbf{-8p^3x^2y - 2p^3xy}$

25. $a + 2 = -1 \qquad x + 1 = 2$
$$\frac{-2 \quad -2}{a = -3} \qquad \frac{-1 \quad -1}{x = 1}$$

$-|xa|\left(a - xa^0\right) = -|1(-3)|(-3 - 1) = -3(-4)$

$= \mathbf{12}$

26. $x^0y\left(y^{-2} - x^{-3}\right) = -2\left[(-2)^{-2} - (-2)^{-3}\right]$

$= -2\left(\dfrac{1}{4} - \dfrac{1}{-8}\right) = -2\left(\dfrac{1}{4} + \dfrac{1}{8}\right) = -2\left(\dfrac{3}{8}\right) = \mathbf{-\dfrac{3}{4}}$

27. $27(-3)^{-3} - 5^2 - \sqrt[3]{-125} = \dfrac{27}{-27} - 25 - (-5)$

$= -1 - 25 + 5 = \mathbf{-21}$

28. $A = \dfrac{1}{2}(80 \text{ in.})(60 \text{ in.}) = \mathbf{2400 \text{ in.}^2}$

29. $A = \text{Area}_{\text{rectangle}} - \text{Area}_{\text{semicircle}}$

$= (6 \text{ in.})(4 \text{ in.}) - \dfrac{1}{2}\pi(2 \text{ in.})^2$

$= \mathbf{(24 - 2\pi) \text{ in.}^2 = 17.72 \text{ in.}^2}$

30. $S.A. = 2\left(\text{Area}_{\text{base}}\right) + \text{Lateral Surface Area}$

$= 2\left[\pi(24 \text{ ft})^2\right] + \left(\text{Perimeter}_{\text{base}}\right)(\text{Height})$

$= 2\left(576\pi \text{ ft}^2\right) + \left[2\pi(24 \text{ ft})\right](20 \text{ ft})$

$= 1152\pi \text{ ft}^2 + 960\pi \text{ ft}^2$

$= \mathbf{2112\pi \text{ ft}^2 = 6631.68 \text{ ft}^2}$

Practice 52

a. $\dfrac{x}{y} - b + \dfrac{c + d}{m}$

$= \dfrac{mx}{my} - \dfrac{b(my)}{my} + \dfrac{y(c + d)}{my}$

$= \dfrac{xm - bmy + y(c + d)}{my}$

b. $\dfrac{5b + c}{a + b} - \dfrac{x}{b} + c$

$= \dfrac{b(5b + c)}{b(a + b)} - \dfrac{x(a + b)}{b(a + b)} + \dfrac{cb(a + b)}{b(a + b)}$

$= \dfrac{b(5b + c) - x(a + b) + cb(a + b)}{b(a + b)}$

c. Overall Average $= \dfrac{(5 \times 10) + (10 \times 25)}{5 + 10}$

$= \dfrac{50 + 250}{15}$

$= \dfrac{300}{15} = \mathbf{20\ lb}$

Problem Set 52

1. $2(3N - 5) = 2N - 14$

$6N - 10 = 2N - 14$

$\underline{-2N \qquad\qquad -2N}$

$4N - 10 = \qquad -14$

$\underline{\quad +10 \qquad\qquad +10}$

$4N \quad = \qquad -4$

$N = \mathbf{-1}$

2. Overall Average $= \dfrac{(6 \times 15) + (14 \times 30)}{6 + 14}$

$= \dfrac{90 + 420}{20}$

$= \dfrac{510}{20} = \mathbf{25.5\ lb}$

3. $70\ \text{ft} \cdot \text{ft} \times \dfrac{12\ \text{in.}}{1\ \text{ft}} \times \dfrac{12\ \text{in.}}{1\ \text{ft}} \times \dfrac{2.54\ \text{cm}}{1\ \text{in.}}$

$\times \dfrac{2.54\ \text{cm}}{1\ \text{in.}} \times \dfrac{1\ \text{m}}{100\ \text{cm}} \times \dfrac{1\ \text{m}}{100\ \text{cm}}$

$= \dfrac{70(12)^2 (2.54)^2}{(100)^2}\ \text{m}^2 = \mathbf{6.50\ m^2}$

4. $\dfrac{16}{100} \cdot 4200 = WN$

$WN = \dfrac{67{,}200}{100}$

$WN = \mathbf{672}$

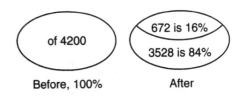

Before, 100%   After

5. $\dfrac{WP}{100} \cdot 50 = 700$

$\dfrac{100}{50} \cdot \dfrac{WP}{100} \cdot 50 = 700 \cdot \dfrac{100}{50}$

$WP = \mathbf{1400\%}$

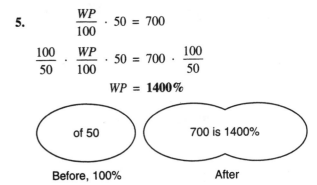

Before, 100%   After

6. $x > -4$

     -6   -5   -4   -3   -2

7. $(DP)7 = 14.14$

$DP = \dfrac{14.14}{7}$

$DP = \mathbf{2.02}$

8. $f(x) = -\dfrac{1}{x}$

$f\left(-\dfrac{2}{3}\right) = \dfrac{-1}{-\dfrac{2}{3}} = \dfrac{-1}{1} \cdot \dfrac{-3}{2} = \dfrac{\mathbf{3}}{\mathbf{2}}$

9. $2\dfrac{1}{5}x - \dfrac{1}{3} = -15$

$\underline{\qquad +\dfrac{1}{3} \qquad +\dfrac{1}{3}}$

$2\dfrac{1}{5}x \qquad = -14\dfrac{2}{3}$

$\dfrac{2\dfrac{1}{5}x}{2\dfrac{1}{5}} = \dfrac{-14\dfrac{2}{3}}{2\dfrac{1}{5}}$

$x = \dfrac{-44}{3} \cdot \dfrac{5}{11}$

$x = -\dfrac{\mathbf{20}}{\mathbf{3}}$

10. $0.2k - 4.21 - 0.8k = 2(-k + 0.1)$

$-0.6k - 4.21 = -2k + 0.2$

$-60k - 421 = -200k + 20$

$140k = 441$

$k = \mathbf{3.15}$

11. $-2[(-k - 3)(-2) - 3] = (-3 - 3k)(-2)^3 - 3^2$

$$-2(2k + 6 - 3) = 24 + 24k - 9$$

$$-4k - 6 = 24k + 15$$

$$\underline{-24k \qquad\qquad -24k}$$

$$\overline{-28k - 6 = \qquad\qquad 15}$$

$$\underline{\qquad\quad +6 \qquad\qquad +6}$$

$$\overline{-28k \qquad = \qquad 21}$$

$$k = -\frac{3}{4}$$

12. $5p + a - 10 = p - 5a$

$$\underline{-p - a + 10 \quad -p - a + 10}$$

$$\overline{4p \qquad\qquad = \qquad -6a + 10}$$

$$\frac{4p}{4} = \frac{-6a}{4} + \frac{10}{4}$$

$$p = -\frac{3}{2}a + \frac{5}{2}$$

13. $21 = 3 \cdot 7 \qquad 24 = 2 \cdot 2 \cdot 2 \cdot 3$

$$60 = 2 \cdot 2 \cdot 3 \cdot 5$$

$$\text{LCM} = 2 \cdot 2 \cdot 2 \cdot 3 \cdot 5 \cdot 7 = \mathbf{840}$$

14. $y = -2x + 4$

x	0	1	4
y	4	2	-4

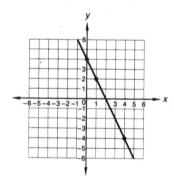

15. $y = 3$

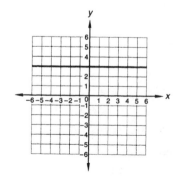

16. $\dfrac{4}{a^2b^2} - \dfrac{c}{ad} - \dfrac{m}{a^3b}$

$$= \frac{4ad}{a^3b^2d} - \frac{c(a^2b^2)}{a^3b^2d} - \frac{m(bd)}{a^3b^2d}$$

$$= \frac{4ad - ca^2b^2 - mbd}{a^3b^2d}$$

17. $\dfrac{2x + a}{a + b} + \dfrac{d}{x} = \dfrac{x(2x + a)}{x(a + b)} + \dfrac{d(a + b)}{x(a + b)}$

$$= \frac{x(2x + a) + d(a + b)}{x(a + b)}$$

18. $\left(3x^3 - x^2 + 2x + 5\right) - 2\left(x^3 + 2x^2 - x - 3\right)$

$$= 3x^3 - x^2 + 2x + 5 - 2x^3 - 4x^2 + 2x + 6$$

$$= \mathbf{x^3 - 5x^2 + 4x + 11}$$

19. $(5x - 3)^2 = (5x - 3)(5x - 3)$

$$= 25x^2 - 15x - 15x + 9 = \mathbf{25x^2 - 30x + 9}$$

20. $(x + 1)\left(5x^2 + 12x + 7\right)$

$$= 5x^3 + 12x^2 + 7x + 5x^2 + 12x + 7$$

$$= \mathbf{5x^3 + 17x^2 + 19x + 7}$$

21. $\dfrac{6xay - 24xay^2}{6xay} = \dfrac{6xay(1 - 4y)}{6xay} = \mathbf{1 - 4y}$

22. $\dfrac{m^2 p^4 x^{-2} x^2 x^0 p^6}{m^2 p^{-4} x^0 p^0 x^2} = \dfrac{m^2 p^{10}}{m^2 p^{-4} x^2} = \mathbf{p^{14} x^{-2}}$

23. $\dfrac{x}{y^{-1}}\left(\dfrac{x}{y} - \dfrac{3x^2}{xy}\right) = x^2 - \dfrac{3x^3}{x} = x^2 - 3x^2$

$$= \mathbf{-2x^2}$$

24. $\dfrac{3x^2 y^{-2}}{m^5} - \dfrac{3x^2 y^2}{m^5} - \dfrac{4xx^3 m^{-5}}{x^2 y^2} + \dfrac{6m^{-5}}{x^{-2}y^{-2}}$

$$= \frac{3m^{-5}y^{-2}}{x^{-2}} - \frac{3m^{-5}}{x^{-2}y^{-2}} - \frac{4m^{-5}y^{-2}}{x^{-2}} + \frac{6m^{-5}}{x^{-2}y^{-2}}$$

$$= -\frac{m^{-5}y^{-2}}{x^{-2}} + \frac{3m^{-5}}{x^{-2}y^{-2}}$$

25. $y + 1 = -3$

$$\underline{-1 \quad -1}$$

$$\overline{y = -4}$$

$$|x - y||y - x| = |-3 - (-4)||-4 - (-3)|$$

$$= |1||-1| = \mathbf{1}$$

26. $p^{-2}\left(a^{-5} - y\right) = 2^{-2}\left[(-1)^{-5} - (-4)\right]$

$$= \frac{1}{4}(-1 + 4) = \frac{3}{4}$$

27. $\dfrac{8(-2)^{-3} - 27(-3)^{-3}}{|3| - |-3|} = \dfrac{8\left(-\dfrac{1}{8}\right) - 27\left(-\dfrac{1}{27}\right)}{3 - 3}$

$$= \frac{-1 + 1}{0} = \frac{0}{0}, \text{ which is } \mathbf{indeterminate}$$

28. $P = (30 + 25 + 30 + 25)$ cm $= $ **110 cm**

29. $A = \dfrac{1}{2}(48 \text{ in.})(20 \text{ in.}) = $ **480 in.^{2}**

30. Volume $= \left(\text{Area}_{\text{base}}\right)(\text{Height})$

$= \left[\dfrac{1}{2}(20 \text{ m})(20 \text{ m}) + \dfrac{1}{2}\pi(10 \text{ m})^2\right](30 \text{ m})$

$= \left(200 \text{ m}^2 + 50\pi \text{ m}^2\right)(30 \text{ m})$

$= (6000 + 1500\pi) \text{ m}^3 = $ **10,710 m^3**

Practice 53

a. $\left(\dfrac{3^0 y^{-2} z^5}{x^3}\right)^{-3} = \dfrac{3^0 y^6 z^{-15}}{x^{-9}} = $ **$x^9 y^6 z^{-15}$**

b. $\left(\dfrac{x^2 y^{-2}}{3m^4 k}\right)^{-2}\left(\dfrac{y^{-2}m}{x^3 k}\right)^2 = \dfrac{x^{-4}y^4}{3^{-2}m^{-8}k^{-2}}\left(\dfrac{y^{-4}m^2}{x^6 k^2}\right)$

$= \dfrac{9x^{-4}m^2}{m^{-8}x^6} = $ **$9m^{10}x^{-10}$**

c. 75 in. $\cdot$ in. $\cdot$ in. $\times \dfrac{2.54 \text{ cm}}{1 \text{ in.}} \times \dfrac{2.54 \text{ cm}}{1 \text{ in.}}$

$\times \dfrac{2.54 \text{ cm}}{1 \text{ in.}} = 75(2.54)^3 \text{ cm}^3 = $ **1229.03 cm^3**

d. 28 m $\cdot$ m $\cdot$ m $\times \dfrac{100 \text{ cm}}{1 \text{ m}} \times \dfrac{100 \text{ cm}}{1 \text{ m}} \times \dfrac{100 \text{ cm}}{1 \text{ m}}$

$\times \dfrac{1 \text{ in.}}{2.54 \text{ cm}} \times \dfrac{1 \text{ in.}}{2.54 \text{ cm}} \times \dfrac{1 \text{ in.}}{2.54 \text{ cm}}$

$= \dfrac{28(100)^3}{(2.54)^3} \text{ in.}^3 = $ **1,708,664.84 in.^{3}**

Problem Set 53

1. $\dfrac{P}{T} = \dfrac{3}{16}$

$\dfrac{P}{6816} = \dfrac{3}{16}$

$16P = 3 \cdot 6816$

$P = \dfrac{3 \cdot 6816}{16}$

$P = $ **1278**

2. Overall Average $= \dfrac{(3 \times 135) + (97 \times 163)}{3 + 97}$

$= \dfrac{405 + 15811}{100}$

$= \dfrac{16,216}{100} = $ **162.16 lb**

3. 50 in. $\cdot$ in. $\cdot$ in. $\times \dfrac{2.54 \text{ cm}}{1 \text{ in.}} \times \dfrac{2.54 \text{ cm}}{1 \text{ in.}}$

$\times \dfrac{2.54 \text{ cm}}{1 \text{ in.}} = 50(2.54)^3 \text{ cm}^3 = $ **819.35 cm^3**

4. $\dfrac{65}{100} \cdot WN = 260$

$\dfrac{100}{65} \cdot \dfrac{65}{100} \cdot WN = 260 \cdot \dfrac{100}{65}$

$WN = $ **400**

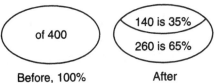

Before, 100%   After

of 400   140 is 35%   260 is 65%

5. $\dfrac{190}{100} \cdot 30 = WN$

$WN = $ **57**

of 30   57 is 190%

Before, 100%   After

6. **$x < 5$; $x \not\geq 5$**

7. 990 $\dfrac{990}{2} = 495$ $\dfrac{495}{3} = 165$

$\dfrac{165}{3} = 55$ $\dfrac{55}{5} = 11$ **$2 \cdot 3 \cdot 3 \cdot 5 \cdot 11$**

8. $g(x) = x^{-1}$

$g\left(-\dfrac{3}{5}\right) = \left(-\dfrac{3}{5}\right)^{-1} = $ **$-\dfrac{5}{3}$**

9. $3\dfrac{1}{8}p + 2\dfrac{1}{4} = \dfrac{1}{6}$

$\dfrac{-2\dfrac{1}{4} \quad\quad -2\dfrac{1}{4}}{3\dfrac{1}{8}p \quad\quad = -2\dfrac{1}{12}}$

$\dfrac{3\dfrac{1}{8}p}{3\dfrac{1}{8}} = \dfrac{-2\dfrac{1}{12}}{3\dfrac{1}{8}}$

$p = \dfrac{-25}{12} \cdot \dfrac{8}{25}$

$p = $ **$-\dfrac{2}{3}$**

10. $-(-3)^3 - |-2| - 2^2 - (-k - 3) = -4^2 - (3k - 4)$

$27 - 2 - 4 + k + 3 = -16 - 3k + 4$

$k + 24 = -3k - 12$

$\underline{+3k \qquad\qquad +3k}$

$\overline{4k + 24 = \qquad -12}$

$\underline{\qquad -24 \qquad\quad -24}$

$\overline{4k \qquad = \qquad -36}$

$k = -9$

11. $x + 1 = 4 \qquad\qquad y - 2 = 3$

$\qquad x = 3 \qquad\qquad\quad y = 5$

$x^2 - y^2 = (3)^2 - (5)^2 = 9 - 25 = -16$

12. $2c^2 = 2 \cdot c \cdot c \qquad 4c^3 = 2 \cdot 2 \cdot c \cdot c \cdot c$

$3c^4 = 3 \cdot c \cdot c \cdot c \cdot c$

$\text{LCM} = 2 \cdot 2 \cdot 3 \cdot c \cdot c \cdot c \cdot c = 12c^4$

13. $y = \dfrac{1}{3}x - 3$

x	0	3	-3
y	-3	-2	-4

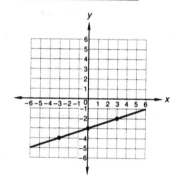

14. $x = -1$

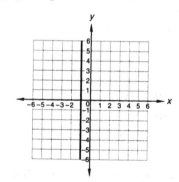

15. $\dfrac{m}{p^2 k} - \dfrac{4a}{3pk} + \dfrac{6}{5pk^2}$

$= \dfrac{15km}{15p^2k^2} - \dfrac{4a(5pk)}{15p^2k^2} + \dfrac{6(3p)}{15p^2k^2}$

$= \dfrac{15km - 20apk + 18p}{15p^2k^2}$

16. $\dfrac{a}{b + c} - \dfrac{4x}{b^2} = \dfrac{a(b^2)}{b^2(b + c)} - \dfrac{4x(b + c)}{b^2(b + c)}$

$= \dfrac{ab^2 - 4x(b + c)}{b^2(b + c)}$

17. $(7x^5 + 4x^2 - 2x) - 2(3x^4 + 2x^2 + x - 4)$

$= 7x^5 + 4x^2 - 2x - 6x^4 - 4x^2 - 2x + 8$

$= 7x^5 - 6x^4 - 4x + 8$

18. $(x + 3)(3x - 4) = 3x^2 - 4x + 9x - 12$

$= 3x^2 + 5x - 12$

19. $(2x + 7)(2x - 7) = 4x^2 - 14x + 14x - 49$

$= 4x^2 - 49$

20. $9k^2bm^4 - 3kb^4m^2 + 12kb^3m^3$

$= 3kbm^2(3km^2 - b^3 + 4b^2m)$

21. $(x^2y^{-3}z^{-1})^2 = x^4y^{-6}z^{-2}$

22. $\left(\dfrac{xy^{-3}}{m^4}\right)^{-2} = \dfrac{x^{-2}y^6}{m^{-8}} = m^8x^{-2}y^6 = x^{-2}y^6m^8$

23. $\left(\dfrac{x^2m^2}{3} - \dfrac{5x^5p^0}{m^{-4}}\right)\dfrac{3x^{-2}y^0}{m^2} = \dfrac{m^2}{m^2} - \dfrac{15x^3}{m^{-2}}$

$= 1 - \dfrac{15}{m^{-2}x^{-3}} = 1 - \dfrac{15}{x^{-3}m^{-2}}$

24. $\dfrac{xx^0}{y} - \dfrac{3x^2x^{-1}y^2}{x^0y^3} + \dfrac{2x^2}{xy^2} - \dfrac{4xxy^{-1}}{xyy^0}$

$= \dfrac{x}{y} - \dfrac{3x}{y} + \dfrac{2x}{y^2} - \dfrac{4x}{y^2} = \dfrac{-2x}{y} - \dfrac{2x}{y^2}$

$= -2xy^{-1} - 2xy^{-2}$

25. $x + 3 = 1$

$\underline{-3 \quad -3}$

$\overline{x = -2}$

$x^{-3} - x^{-2} - x^{-1} = (-2)^{-3} - (-2)^{-2} - (-2)^{-1}$

$= -\dfrac{1}{8} - \dfrac{1}{4} - \dfrac{1}{-2} = -\dfrac{1}{8} - \dfrac{1}{4} + \dfrac{1}{2} = \dfrac{1}{8}$

26. $b + 1 = -2$

$\underline{-1 \quad -1}$

$\overline{b = -3}$

$|a + b||a - b| = |2 - 3||2 - (-3)| = 1 \cdot 5 = 5$

27. $\dfrac{1}{(-2)^{-3}} + \dfrac{1}{2^{-3}} + \sqrt[3]{27} = -8 + 8 + 3 = 3$

28. $P = (50 + 25 + 50 + 25)\text{ cm} = 150\text{ cm} = 1.5\text{ m}$

29. $A = \dfrac{1}{2}(25\text{ in.})(12\text{ in.}) + \dfrac{1}{2}\pi(12\text{ in.})^2$

$= (150 + 72\pi)\text{ in.}^2 = 376.08\text{ in.}^2$

30. $S.A. = 2(\text{Area}_{\text{top}}) + 2(\text{Area}_{\text{front}}) + 2(\text{Area}_{\text{side}})$
$= 2(15 \text{ ft} \times 30 \text{ ft}) + 2(5 \text{ ft} \times 30 \text{ ft})$
$\quad + 2(5 \text{ ft} \times 15 \text{ ft})$
$= 2(450 \text{ ft}^2) + 2(150 \text{ ft}^2) + 2(75 \text{ ft}^2)$
$= 900 \text{ ft}^2 + 300 \text{ ft}^2 + 150 \text{ ft}^2$
$= \mathbf{1350 \text{ ft}^2}$

Practice 54

a. $\begin{cases} 2x + 3y = 24 \\ x = 4y - 10 \end{cases}$

$2x + 3y = 24$
$2(4y - 10) + 3y = 24$
$8y - 20 + 3y = 24$
$11y - 20 = 24$
$11y = 44$
$y = 4$

$x = 4y - 10$
$x = 4(4) - 10$
$x = 16 - 10$
$x = 6$

Thus the solution is the ordered pair **(6, 4)**.

b. $\begin{cases} y = x + 7 \\ x + 2y = -16 \end{cases}$

$x + 2y = -16$
$x + 2(x + 7) = -16$
$x + 2x + 14 = -16$
$3x + 14 = -16$
$3x = -30$
$x = -10$

$y = x + 7$
$y = -10 + 7$
$y = -3$

Thus the solution is the ordered pair **(–10, –3)**.

Problem Set 54

1. $-3(2N + 5) = -57$
$-6N - 15 = -57$
$\underline{\quad +15 \quad +15}$
$\overline{-6N \quad = -42}$
$N = \mathbf{7}$

2. Overall Average $= \dfrac{(2 \times 90) + (8 \times 95)}{2 + 8}$

$= \dfrac{180 + 760}{10} = \dfrac{940}{10} = \mathbf{94}$

3. $140 \text{ cm} \cdot \text{cm} \cdot \text{cm} \times \dfrac{1 \text{ in.}}{2.54 \text{ cm}} \times \dfrac{1 \text{ in.}}{2.54 \text{ cm}}$

$\times \dfrac{1 \text{ in.}}{2.54 \text{ cm}} = \dfrac{140}{(2.54)^3} \text{ in.}^3 = \mathbf{8.54 \text{ in.}^3}$

4. $\dfrac{WP}{100} \cdot 860 = 43$

$\dfrac{100}{860} \cdot \dfrac{WP}{100} \cdot 860 = 43 \cdot \dfrac{100}{860}$

$WP = \mathbf{5\%}$

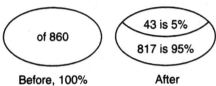

Before, 100%   After

5. $\dfrac{240}{100} \cdot 76 = WN$

$WN = \dfrac{18{,}240}{100}$

$WN = \mathbf{182.4}$

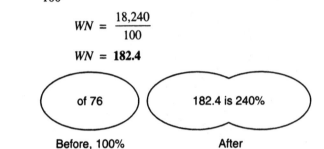

Before, 100%   After

6. $-4 < x \le 3$

-5 -4 -3 -2 -1 0 1 2 3 4

7. $h(x) = -x^{-1}$

$h\left(\dfrac{2}{5}\right) = -\left(\dfrac{2}{5}\right)^{-1} = -\dfrac{5}{2}$

8. $-(0.2 - 0.4z) - 0.4 = z - 1.47$
$-0.2 + 0.4z - 0.4 = z - 1.47$
$-20 + 40z - 40 = 100z - 147$
$40z - 60 = 100z - 147$
$-60z = -87$
$z = \mathbf{1.45}$

9. $-\left[-|-3|(-2 - m) - 4\right] = -2\left[(-3 - m) - 2m\right]$
$3(-2 - m) + 4 = 6 + 2m + 4m$
$-6 - 3m + 4 = 6 + 6m$
$-3m - 2 = 6m + 6$
$\underline{-6m + 2 \quad -6m + 2}$
$\overline{-9m \quad = \quad 8}$

$m = -\dfrac{8}{9}$

10. $\begin{cases} 2x + y = 7 \\ x = -3y + 11 \end{cases}$

$$2x + y = 7$$
$$2(-3y + 11) + y = 7$$
$$-6y + 22 + y = 7$$
$$-5y = -15$$
$$y = 3$$

$$x = -3y + 11$$
$$x = -3(3) + 11$$
$$x = -9 + 11$$
$$x = 2$$

Thus the solution is the ordered pair **(2, 3)**.

11. $\begin{cases} 2x + 3y = 4 \\ y = 2x + 4 \end{cases}$

$$2x + 3y = 4$$
$$2x + 3(2x + 4) = 4$$
$$2x + 6x + 12 = 4$$
$$8x = -8$$
$$x = -1$$

$$y = 2x + 4$$
$$y = 2(-1) + 4$$
$$y = -2 + 4$$
$$y = 2$$

Thus the solution is the ordered pair **(–1, 2)**.

12. $15 = 3 \cdot 5 \qquad 175 = 5 \cdot 5 \cdot 7$
$225 = 3 \cdot 3 \cdot 5 \cdot 5$
$LCM = 3 \cdot 3 \cdot 5 \cdot 5 \cdot 7 = \mathbf{1575}$

13. $y = 3x - 4$

x	0	1	2
y	–4	–1	2

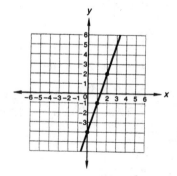

14. $y = -3$

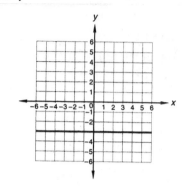

15. $\dfrac{x}{mc} + \dfrac{b}{c} - \dfrac{2}{kc^2}$

$$= \dfrac{x(kc)}{mkc^2} + \dfrac{b(mkc)}{mkc^2} - \dfrac{2m}{mkc^2}$$

$$= \dfrac{xkc + bkcm - 2m}{kc^2m}$$

16. $\dfrac{4}{x - y} - \dfrac{3}{y} = \dfrac{4y}{y(x - y)} - \dfrac{3(x - y)}{y(x - y)}$

$$= \dfrac{4y - 3(x - y)}{y(x - y)} = \dfrac{4y - 3x + 3y}{y(x - y)}$$

$$= \dfrac{7y - 3x}{y(x - y)}$$

17. $\left(-2x^3 + 4x^2 - x + 1\right) - \left(x^2 - 6x - 3\right)$
$= -2x^3 + 4x^2 - x + 1 - x^2 + 6x + 3$
$= \mathbf{-2x^3 + 3x^2 + 5x + 4}$

18. $(4x - 2)^2 = (4x - 2)(4x - 2)$
$= 16x^2 - 8x - 8x + 4$
$= \mathbf{16x^2 - 16x + 4}$

19. $(x + 1)\left(x^2 - 2x + 5\right)$
$= x^3 - 2x^2 + 5x + x^2 - 2x + 5$
$= \mathbf{x^3 - x^2 + 3x + 5}$

20. $\dfrac{3ap^2m - 6ap^2m^2}{3ap^2m} = \dfrac{3ap^2m(1 - 2m)}{3ap^2m} = \mathbf{1 - 2m}$

21. $\left(2^0 a^{-3} b^4 z^2\right)^{-4} = a^{12}b^{-16}z^{-8} = \dfrac{1}{a^{-12}b^{16}z^8}$

22. $\left(\dfrac{3^0 x^{-5}y^2}{z^2}\right)^5 = \dfrac{x^{-25}y^{10}}{z^{10}} = \dfrac{1}{x^{25}y^{-10}z^{10}}$

23. $\dfrac{x^2 y^0 p}{m^{-2}}\left(\dfrac{p^{-3}m^2}{k} - \dfrac{p^0 pm^2}{x^2}\right)$

$= \dfrac{x^2 p^{-2}m^2}{km^{-2}} - \dfrac{x^2 p^2 m^2}{m^{-2}x^2}$

$= \dfrac{x^2 m^4}{p^2 k} - p^2 m^4$

24. $a^2 k^2 y^{-1} - \dfrac{4k^2}{a^{-2}y} + \dfrac{2k^2 a}{a^{-1}y} - \dfrac{6k^{-4}}{k^2 y}$

$= \dfrac{1}{a^{-2}k^{-2}y} - \dfrac{4}{a^{-2}k^{-2}y} + \dfrac{2}{a^{-2}k^{-2}y} - \dfrac{6}{k^6 y}$

$= -\dfrac{1}{a^{-2}k^{-2}y} - \dfrac{6}{k^6 y}$

25. $\begin{array}{r} 2x + 8 = 16 \\ \underline{-8 \quad -8} \\ 2x \quad = 8 \\ x = 4 \end{array}$

$a^{-3} - a(x - a) = (-2)^{-3} - (-2)[4 - (-2)]$

$= -\dfrac{1}{8} + 2(6) = 12 - \dfrac{1}{8} = 11\dfrac{7}{8} = \dfrac{95}{8}$

26. $\begin{array}{r} 2y - 5 = -11 \\ \underline{+5 \quad +5} \\ 2y \quad = -6 \\ y = -3 \end{array}$

$x^2 - xy^{-2} - (-y)^{-2} = 3^2 - 3(-3)^{-2} - [-(-3)]^{-2}$

$= 9 - \dfrac{3}{9} - \dfrac{1}{9} = 9 - \dfrac{4}{9} = 8\dfrac{5}{9} = \dfrac{77}{9}$

27. $\dfrac{1}{-2^{-3}} - \dfrac{1}{(-3)^{-3}} + \dfrac{1}{4^{-3}} + \sqrt[3]{64}$

$= -8 - (-27) + 64 + 4$

$= -8 + 27 + 64 + 4 = \mathbf{87}$

28. $P = \left(4 + 3 + 2 + 1 + 2 + 2 + \dfrac{2\pi(3)}{2}\right)$ cm

$= (14 + 3\pi)$ cm $= \mathbf{23.42}$ cm

29.

$A = (2\,\text{m})(1\,\text{m}) + (2\,\text{m})(1\,\text{m}) = \mathbf{4\ m^2}$

30. Volume $= \left(\text{Area}_{\text{base}}\right)(\text{Height})$

$= \left[(20\,\text{m})(12\,\text{m}) + \dfrac{1}{2}(16\,\text{m})(12\,\text{m})\right](20\,\text{m})$

$= \left(240\,\text{m}^2 + 96\,\text{m}^2\right)(20\,\text{m})$

$= \left(336\,\text{m}^2\right)(20\,\text{m})$

$= \mathbf{6720\ m^3}$

Practice 55

a. $\dfrac{\frac{x}{m}}{d} = \dfrac{\frac{x}{m} \cdot \frac{1}{d}}{\frac{d}{1} \cdot \frac{1}{d}} = \dfrac{\frac{x}{md}}{1} = \dfrac{x}{md}$

b. $\dfrac{\frac{1}{r}}{\frac{1}{z}} = \dfrac{\frac{1}{r} \cdot \frac{z}{1}}{\frac{1}{z} \cdot \frac{z}{1}} = \dfrac{\frac{z}{r}}{1} = \dfrac{z}{r}$

c. $\dfrac{\frac{n}{a}}{\frac{b}{d}} = \dfrac{\frac{n}{a} \cdot \frac{d}{b}}{\frac{b}{d} \cdot \frac{d}{b}} = \dfrac{\frac{nd}{ab}}{1} = \dfrac{nd}{ab}$

d. $\dfrac{\frac{w}{1}}{\frac{1}{w+c}} = \dfrac{\frac{w}{1} \cdot \frac{w+c}{1}}{\frac{1}{w+c} \cdot \frac{w+c}{1}} = \dfrac{w(w+c)}{1}$

$= w(w+c)$

Problem Set 55

1. $\dfrac{R}{T} = \dfrac{7}{9}$

$\dfrac{R}{324} = \dfrac{7}{9}$

$9R = 7 \cdot 324$

$R = \dfrac{7 \cdot 324}{9}$

$R = \mathbf{252}$

2. Overall Average $= \dfrac{(5 \times 200) + (20 \times 400)}{5 + 20}$

$= \dfrac{1000 + 8000}{25}$

$= \dfrac{9000}{25} = \mathbf{360}$

3. $24{,}000\ \text{in.} \cdot \text{in.} \cdot \text{in.} \times \dfrac{1\,\text{ft}}{12\,\text{in.}} \times \dfrac{1\,\text{ft}}{12\,\text{in.}} \times \dfrac{1\,\text{ft}}{12\,\text{in.}}$

$\times \dfrac{1\,\text{yd}}{3\,\text{ft}} \times \dfrac{1\,\text{yd}}{3\,\text{ft}} \times \dfrac{1\,\text{yd}}{3\,\text{ft}}$

$= \dfrac{24{,}000}{(12)^3 (3)^3}\ \text{yd}^3 = \mathbf{0.51\ yd^3}$

4. $\dfrac{38}{100} \cdot 700 = WN$

$WN = \dfrac{26,600}{100}$

$WN = \mathbf{266}$

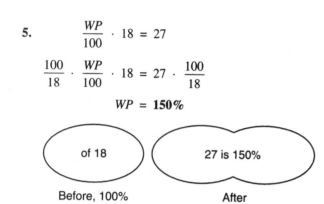

of 700

266 is 38%

434 is 62%

Before, 100%   After

5. $\dfrac{WP}{100} \cdot 18 = 27$

$\dfrac{100}{18} \cdot \dfrac{WP}{100} \cdot 18 = 27 \cdot \dfrac{100}{18}$

$WP = \mathbf{150\%}$

of 18

27 is 150%

Before, 100%   After

6. $0 \le x < 4$

-1 0 1 2 3 4 5

7. $f(x) = \dfrac{1}{x^2}$

$f(-2) = \dfrac{1}{(-2)^2} = \dfrac{1}{4}$

8. $\dfrac{1}{3} + 5\dfrac{1}{3}k + 3\dfrac{2}{9} = 0$

$5\dfrac{1}{3}k + 3\dfrac{5}{9} = 0$

$\qquad -3\dfrac{5}{9} \quad -3\dfrac{5}{9}$

$5\dfrac{1}{3}k \quad = -3\dfrac{5}{9}$

$\dfrac{5\dfrac{1}{3}k}{5\dfrac{1}{3}} = \dfrac{-3\dfrac{5}{9}}{5\dfrac{1}{3}}$

$k = \dfrac{-32}{9} \cdot \dfrac{3}{16}$

$k = -\dfrac{2}{3}$

9. $-[-(-k)] - (-2)(-2 + k) = -k - (4k + 3)$

$-k + 2(-2 + k) = -k - 4k - 3$

$-k - 4 + 2k = -5k - 3$

$k - 4 = -5k - 3$

$\underline{+5k + 4 \qquad +5k + 4}$

$6k \quad = \quad 1$

$k = \dfrac{1}{6}$

10. $\dfrac{\dfrac{m}{n}}{z} = \dfrac{\dfrac{m}{n} \cdot \dfrac{1}{z}}{\dfrac{z}{1} \cdot \dfrac{1}{z}} = \dfrac{\dfrac{m}{nz}}{1} = \dfrac{m}{nz}$

11. $\dfrac{\dfrac{m+1}{n}}{\dfrac{n}{d}} = \dfrac{\dfrac{m+1}{1} \cdot \dfrac{d}{n}}{\dfrac{n}{d} \cdot \dfrac{d}{n}} = \dfrac{\dfrac{d(m+1)}{n}}{1}$

$= \dfrac{d(m+1)}{n}$

12. $\begin{cases} 3x + 2y = 7 \\ x = 7 - 3y \end{cases}$

$3x + 2y = 7$

$3(7 - 3y) + 2y = 7$

$21 - 9y + 2y = 7$

$21 - 7y = 7$

$-7y = -14$

$y = 2$

$x = 7 - 3y$

$x = 7 - 3(2)$

$x = 7 - 6$

$x = 1$

Thus the solution is the ordered pair $(\mathbf{1, 2})$.

13. $\begin{cases} x + 2y = -6 \\ y = 3x + 4 \end{cases}$

$x + 2y = -6$

$x + 2(3x + 4) = -6$

$x + 6x + 8 = -6$

$7x + 8 = -6$

$7x = -14$

$x = -2$

$y = 3x + 4$

$y = 3(-2) + 4$

$y = -6 + 4$

$y = -2$

Thus the solution is the ordered pair $(\mathbf{-2, -2})$.

14. $2x^2 = 2 \cdot x \cdot x$ $4x^2y = 2 \cdot 2 \cdot x \cdot x \cdot y$

$8x^3p = 2 \cdot 2 \cdot 2 \cdot x \cdot x \cdot x \cdot p$

LCM $= 2 \cdot 2 \cdot 2 \cdot x \cdot x \cdot x \cdot y \cdot p = \mathbf{8x^3py}$

15. $y = 2x + 2$

x	0	1	–2
y	2	4	–2

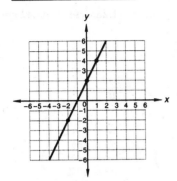

16. $x = -1\dfrac{1}{2}$

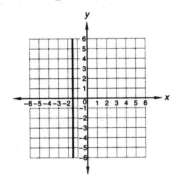

17. $\dfrac{3}{2x^2y} - \dfrac{ab}{4x^3y} - c$

$= \dfrac{3(2x)}{4x^3y} - \dfrac{ab}{4x^3y} - \dfrac{c(4x^3y)}{4x^3y}$

$= \dfrac{6x - ab - 4x^3yc}{4x^3y}$

18. $\dfrac{a}{x^2} - \dfrac{m}{x + y} = \dfrac{a(x + y)}{x^2(x + y)} - \dfrac{mx^2}{x^2(x + y)}$

$= \dfrac{a(x + y) - mx^2}{x^2(x + y)}$

19. $-(4x^5 + x^3 - 5x + 2) + (x^5 - 2x^3 - 3x + 3)$

$= -4x^5 - x^3 + 5x - 2 + x^5 - 2x^3 - 3x + 3$

$= -3x^5 - 3x^3 + 2x + 1$

20. $(4x - 2)(3x + 5) = 12x^2 + 20x - 6x - 10$

$= \mathbf{12x^2 + 14x - 10}$

21. $x^2ym - 4x^2ym^3 + 2x^4y^3m^6$

$= x^2ym(1 - 4m^2 + 2x^2y^2m^5)$

22. $(2x^2y^{-2}z)^{-2}(xy)^4 = 2^{-2}x^{-4}y^4z^{-2}x^4y^4 = \dfrac{y^8}{4z^2}$

23. $\left(\dfrac{3x^{-3}y^4z^3}{p^5}\right)^{-3} = \dfrac{3^{-3}x^9y^{-12}z^{-9}}{p^{-15}} = \dfrac{x^9p^{15}}{27y^{12}z^9}$

24. $\left(\dfrac{p^{-3}m^2}{k} - \dfrac{p^0pm^2}{x^2}\right)\dfrac{x^2y^0p}{m^2}$

$= \dfrac{p^{-3}m^2x^2p}{km^2} - \dfrac{pm^2x^2p}{m^2x^2} = \dfrac{p^{-2}x^2}{k} - p^2$

$= \dfrac{p^{-2}k^{-1}}{x^{-2}} - \dfrac{1}{p^{-2}}$

25. $mx^0x - \dfrac{3m^0}{m^{-1}x^{-1}} + \dfrac{4m^2m^{-1}x}{m^2xx} + \dfrac{5m^2x^{-1}}{mx^{-2}}$

$= mx - 3mx + \dfrac{4}{mx} + 5mx = \mathbf{3mx} + \dfrac{\mathbf{4}}{\mathbf{mx}}$

26. $2x - 5 = 9$

$\quad \underline{+5 \quad +5}$

$2x \quad\; = 14$

$\quad x = 7$

$(xa - a)(-a^{-4}x) = [7(-3) - (-3)][-(-3)^{-4}(7)]$

$= (-21 + 3)\left(-\dfrac{7}{81}\right) = (-18)\left(-\dfrac{7}{81}\right) = \dfrac{\mathbf{14}}{\mathbf{9}}$

27. $\dfrac{1}{-2^{-4}} + |-4||-4| - \sqrt[3]{125} = -16 + 16 - 5$

$= \mathbf{-5}$

28. $P = (280 + 200 + 280 + 200)\,\text{cm}$

$= 960\,\text{cm} = \mathbf{9.6\,m}$

29. $A = \dfrac{1}{2}(15\text{ in.} \times 9\text{ in.}) + \dfrac{1}{2}(15\text{ in.} \times 9\text{ in.})$

$= 67\dfrac{1}{2}\text{ in.}^2 + 67\dfrac{1}{2}\text{ in.}^2$

$= \mathbf{135\ in.^2}$

30. $S.A. = 2(\text{Area}_{\text{triangle}}) + 2(\text{Area}_{\text{side}}) + \text{Area}_{\text{bottom}}$

$= 2\left[\dfrac{1}{2}(8\text{ ft} \times 3\text{ ft})\right] + 2(5\text{ ft} \times 10\text{ ft})$

$\quad + (10\text{ ft} \times 8\text{ ft})$

$= 2(12\text{ ft}^2) + 2(50\text{ ft}^2) + 80\text{ ft}^2$

$= 24\text{ ft}^2 + 100\text{ ft}^2 + 80\text{ ft}^2$

$= \mathbf{204\ ft^2}$

Practice 56

a. $K = \{0, 1, 3, 5, 9\}$

b. (a) **True,** because 5 is a member of B.

    (b) **True,** because 5 is not a member of C.

    (c) **True,** because 0 is a member of A.

    (d) **False,** because 3 is a member of C.

c.
$$2x - 3y = 6$$
$$\underline{-2x \qquad\qquad -2x}$$
$$-3y = 6 - 2x$$
$$y = -2 + \frac{2}{3}x$$
$$y = \frac{2}{3}x - 2$$

x	0	3	-3
y	-2	0	-4

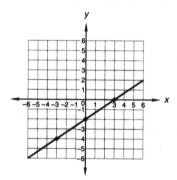

Problem Set 56

1.
$$3N + 13 = 2(-N) - 12$$
$$3N + 13 = -2N - 12$$
$$\underline{+2N - 13 \qquad +2N - 13}$$
$$5N \quad = \quad -25$$
$$N = -5$$

2. $30 \text{ yd} \cdot \text{yd} \cdot \text{yd} \times \dfrac{3 \text{ ft}}{1 \text{ yd}} \times \dfrac{3 \text{ ft}}{1 \text{ yd}} \times \dfrac{3 \text{ ft}}{1 \text{ yd}}$

$\times \dfrac{12 \text{ in.}}{1 \text{ ft}} \times \dfrac{12 \text{ in.}}{1 \text{ ft}} \times \dfrac{12 \text{ in.}}{1 \text{ ft}}$

$= 30(3)^3(12)^3 \text{ in.}^3 = \textbf{1,399,680 in.}^3$

3. $K = \{0, 2, 4, 6, 8, 10\}$

4. (a) **False,** because 0 is not a member of A.

    (b) **True,** because 1 is not a member of B.

    (c) **True,** because 2 is a member of C.

    (d) **False,** because 3 is a member of A.

5. (a)
$$A = \pi r^2$$
$$100 \text{ cm}^2 = (3.14)r^2$$
$$r^2 = \frac{100 \text{ cm}^2}{3.14}$$
$$r^2 = 31.85 \text{ cm}^2$$
$$r = \sqrt{31.85 \text{ cm}^2}$$
$$r = \textbf{5.64 cm}$$

    (b) $C = 2\pi r$

        $= 2\pi(5.64 \text{ cm}) = \textbf{11.28}\pi \textbf{ cm} = \textbf{35.42 cm}$

6.
$$\frac{40}{100} \cdot WN = 22$$
$$\frac{100}{40} \cdot \frac{40}{100}WN = 22 \cdot \frac{100}{40}$$
$$WN = \textbf{55}$$

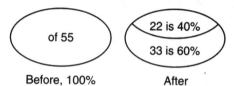

Before, 100%   After

7. $WN = \dfrac{180}{100} \cdot 55$

$WN = \textbf{99}$

Before, 100%   After

8. $-5 < x \le -1$

9.
$$g(x) = \frac{1}{x^2}$$
$$g\left(-\frac{1}{3}\right) = \frac{1}{\left(-\frac{1}{3}\right)^2} = \frac{1}{\frac{1}{9}} = \textbf{9}$$

10. $-3(-2 - x) - 3^2 - |-2| = -(-2x - 3)$
$$6 + 3x - 9 - 2 = 2x + 3$$
$$3x - 5 = 2x + 3$$
$$\underline{-2x + 5 \quad -2x + 5}$$
$$x = \textbf{8}$$

11.
$$-x - 11 = -9 \qquad a + 1 = 1$$
$$\underline{+11 \quad +11} \qquad\quad \underline{-1 \quad -1}$$
$$-x \quad = 2 \qquad\qquad a = 0$$
$$x = -2$$
$$x^2 - 2a = (-2)^2 - 2(0) = 4 - 0 = \textbf{4}$$

12. $\dfrac{\frac{am}{n}}{\frac{x}{dc}} = \dfrac{\frac{am}{n} \cdot \frac{dc}{x}}{\frac{x}{dc} \cdot \frac{dc}{x}} = \dfrac{\frac{amdc}{nx}}{1} = \dfrac{\textbf{amdc}}{\textbf{nx}}$

13. $\dfrac{\frac{x}{c}}{x+y} = \dfrac{\frac{x}{c}\cdot\frac{1}{x+y}}{\frac{x+y}{1}\cdot\frac{1}{x+y}} = \dfrac{\frac{x}{c(x+y)}}{1}$

$= \dfrac{x}{c(x+y)}$

14. $\begin{cases} 2x - 2y = 18 \\ x = 6 - 2y \end{cases}$

$2x - 2y = 18$

$2(6 - 2y) - 2y = 18$

$12 - 4y - 2y = 18$

$12 - 6y = 18$

$-6y = 6$

$y = -1$

$x = 6 - 2y$

$x = 6 - 2(-1)$

$x = 6 + 2$

$x = 8$

Thus the solution is the ordered pair **(8, –1)**.

15. $\begin{cases} 3x - y = 4 \\ y = 6 - 2x \end{cases}$

$3x - y = 4$

$3x - (6 - 2x) = 4$

$3x - 6 + 2x = 4$

$5x - 6 = 4$

$5x = 10$

$x = 2$

$y = 6 - 2x$

$y = 6 - 2(2)$

$y = 6 - 4$

$y = 2$

Thus the solution is the ordered pair **(2, 2)**.

16. $y = -\dfrac{1}{2}x + 4$

x	0	2	-2
y	4	3	5

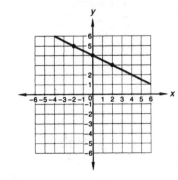

17. $3y + 2x = 3$

$\dfrac{-2x \qquad\qquad -2x}{3y \qquad = 3 - 2x}$

$y = 1 - \dfrac{2}{3}x$

$y = -\dfrac{2}{3}x + 1$

x	0	3	-3
y	1	-1	3

18. $\dfrac{4}{2x^2} - \dfrac{3}{4x^2 p} + \dfrac{2a}{8x^3 p}$

$= \dfrac{4}{2x^2} - \dfrac{3}{4x^2 p} + \dfrac{a}{4x^3 p}$

$= \dfrac{4(2xp)}{4x^3 p} - \dfrac{3x}{4x^3 p} + \dfrac{a}{4x^3 p}$

$= \dfrac{8xp}{4x^3 p} - \dfrac{3x}{4x^3 p} + \dfrac{a}{4x^3 p} = \dfrac{8xp - 3x + a}{4x^3 p}$

19. $\dfrac{m}{b(b+c)} - \dfrac{k}{b} = \dfrac{m}{b(b+c)} - \dfrac{k(b+c)}{b(b+c)}$

$= \dfrac{m - k(b+c)}{b(b+c)}$

20. $4(x^2 - 3x + 5) - 2(x^2 - 2x - 4)$
$- (x^2 - 3x + 3)$
$= 4x^2 - 12x + 20 - 2x^2 + 4x + 8 - x^2$
$+ 3x - 3$
$= x^2 - 5x + 25$

21. $(3 - x)^2 = (3 - x)(3 - x) = 9 - 3x - 3x + x^2$
$= x^2 - 6x + 9$

22. $(5x^{-3}y^{-2})^2(x^0 y^{-1})^{-4} = 25x^{-6}y^{-4}y^4 = 25x^{-6}$

23. $\left(\dfrac{x^2 y^{-1} m^{-3}}{2p^{-4}}\right)^3 = \dfrac{x^6 y^{-3} m^{-9}}{8p^{-12}} = \dfrac{y^{-3} m^{-9}}{8x^{-6} p^{-12}}$

24. $\dfrac{x^{-4}y}{p^2}\left(\dfrac{y^{-1}}{x^4} + \dfrac{2x^{-4}p^{-2}}{y^{-1}}\right)$

$= \dfrac{x^{-4}yy^{-1}}{p^2x^4} + \dfrac{2x^{-4}yx^{-4}p^{-2}}{p^2y^{-1}}$

$= p^{-2}x^{-8} + 2x^{-8}p^{-4}y^2$

25. $\dfrac{xyz^0}{z} - \dfrac{7x^2y^2}{xyz} + \dfrac{2x^3x^{-2}yz^{-2}}{z^{-1}x^0} + \dfrac{5xy^{-1}y^0}{zy^{-2}}$

$= \dfrac{xy}{z} - \dfrac{7xy}{z} + \dfrac{2xy}{z} + \dfrac{5xy}{z} = \dfrac{xy}{z} = \dfrac{z^{-1}}{x^{-1}y^{-1}}$

26. $3x + 8 = -10$

$\dfrac{-8 \quad\quad -8}{3x \quad\quad = -18}$

$x = -6$

$|x|(y^{-4} - y^{-3} - y^{-2})$

$= |-6|[(-1)^{-4} - (-1)^{-3} - (-1)^{-2}]$

$= 6(1 + 1 - 1) = 6$

27. $-\{3(-3 \times 2^0)[-(3 - 2)(-2)] - |4|\} + \sqrt[3]{64}$

$= -\{3(-3)[(-1)(-2)] - 4\} + 4$

$= -[(-9)(2) - 4] + 4 = 22 + 4 = 26$

28. $A = \dfrac{1}{2}(7 \text{ cm} \times 40 \text{ cm}) + (40 \text{ cm} \times 15 \text{ cm})$

$= 140 \text{ cm}^2 + 600 \text{ cm}^2$

$= 740 \text{ cm}^2$

29. Since angles opposite sides of equal lengths have equal measures, $x = 65$.

$y = 180 - 65 - 65$

$y = 50$

30. $V = \left(\text{Area}_{base}\right)(\text{Height})$

$= \left[\dfrac{1}{2}(12 \text{ m} \times 24 \text{ m}) + (24 \text{ m} \times 10 \text{ m})\right](11 \text{ m})$

$= \left(144 \text{ m}^2 + 240 \text{ m}^2\right)(11 \text{ m})$

$= \left(384 \text{ m}^2\right)(11 \text{ m})$

$= 4224 \text{ m}^3$

Practice 57

a. $ax^{-1} - by^{-2} = \dfrac{a}{x} - \dfrac{b}{y^2} = \dfrac{ay^2}{xy^2} - \dfrac{bx}{xy^2}$

$= \dfrac{ay^2 - bx}{xy^2}$

b. $a^{-3}xy^{-1} - bx^{-2} = \dfrac{x}{a^3y} - \dfrac{b}{x^2}$

$= \dfrac{x(x^2)}{a^3x^2y} - \dfrac{b(a^3y)}{a^3x^2y} = \dfrac{x^3 - a^3by}{a^3x^2y}$

Problem Set 57

1. $\dfrac{L}{T} = \dfrac{14}{27}$

$\dfrac{L}{1080} = \dfrac{14}{27}$

$27L = 14 \cdot 1080$

$L = \dfrac{14 \cdot 1080}{27}$

$L = 560$

2. Range $= 832 - 740 = $ **92 kg**

Median $= \dfrac{760 + 790}{2} = $ **775 kg**

Mode $= $ **745 kg**

Mean $= (790 + 832 + 745 + 804 + 804 + 745$

$+ 810 + 760 + 740 + 745) \div 10$

$= 7775 \div 10 = $ **777.5 kg**

3. $8400 \text{ in.} \cdot \text{in.} \cdot \text{in.} \times \dfrac{1 \text{ ft}}{12 \text{ in.}} \times \dfrac{1 \text{ ft}}{12 \text{ in.}} \times \dfrac{1 \text{ ft}}{12 \text{ in.}}$

$= \dfrac{8400}{(12)^3} \text{ ft}^3 = $ **4.86 ft³**

4. $L = \{-7, -5, -3, -1, 1, 3, 5, 7\}$

5. (a) **True,** because 1 is not a member of A.

(b) **True,** because 5 is a member of B.

(c) **False,** because 6 is a member of C.

(d) **False,** because 4 is not a member of B.

6. $\dfrac{WP}{100} \cdot 180 = 36$

$\dfrac{100}{180} \cdot \dfrac{WP}{100} \cdot 180 = 36 \cdot \dfrac{100}{180}$

$WP = $ **20%**

of 180 | 36 is 20%
144 is 80%

Before, 100% | After

7. $-4 \le x \le 2$

8. $h(x) = -\dfrac{2}{x^2}$

$h(-2) = -\dfrac{2}{(-2)^2} = -\dfrac{2}{4} = -\dfrac{1}{2}$

9. $0.02 + 0.02x - 0.4 - 0.4x = 3.116$

$\qquad -0.38x - 0.38 = 3.116$

$\qquad -380x - 380 = 3116$

$\qquad -380x = 3496$

$\qquad x = -9.2$

10. $\dfrac{\frac{1}{a}}{\frac{x}{1}} = \dfrac{\frac{1}{a} \cdot \frac{1}{x}}{\frac{x}{1} \cdot \frac{1}{x}} = \dfrac{\frac{1}{ax}}{1} = \dfrac{1}{ax}$

11. $\dfrac{\frac{b}{c}}{\frac{1}{a+b}} = \dfrac{\frac{b}{c} \cdot \frac{a+b}{1}}{\frac{1}{a+b} \cdot \frac{a+b}{1}} = \dfrac{\frac{b(a+b)}{c}}{1}$

$\quad = \dfrac{b(a+b)}{c}$

12. $\begin{cases} x + y = 6 \\ x = 9 - 2y \end{cases}$

$\qquad x + y = 6$

$\qquad (9 - 2y) + y = 6$

$\qquad 9 - y = 6$

$\qquad -y = -3$

$\qquad y = 3$

$x = 9 - 2y$

$x = 9 - 2(3)$

$x = 9 - 6$

$x = 3$

Thus the solution is the ordered pair **(3, 3)**.

13. $\begin{cases} 5x - 3y = 6 \\ y = 2x + 3 \end{cases}$

$\qquad 5x - 3y = 6$

$\quad 5x - 3(2x + 3) = 6$

$\qquad 5x - 6x - 9 = 6$

$\qquad -x - 9 = 6$

$\qquad -x = 15$

$\qquad x = -15$

$y = 2x + 3$

$y = 2(-15) + 3$

$y = -30 + 3$

$y = -27$

Thus the solution is the ordered pair **(-15, -27)**.

14. $y = -3x - 2$

x	0	1	-1
y	-2	-5	1

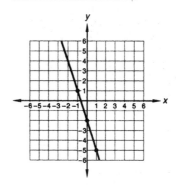

15. $4y + 8x = 12$

$\dfrac{-8x \qquad\qquad -8x}{4y \qquad = 12 - 8x}$

$\qquad y = 3 - 2x$

$\qquad y = -2x + 3$

x	0	1	3
y	3	1	-3

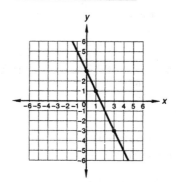

16. $4 - \dfrac{7}{a} + \dfrac{a+b}{a^2} = \dfrac{4a^2}{a^2} - \dfrac{7a}{a^2} + \dfrac{a+b}{a^2}$

$\quad = \dfrac{4a^2 - 7a + a + b}{a^2} = \dfrac{4a^2 - 6a + b}{a^2}$

17. $\dfrac{a}{x^2y} + 4a - \dfrac{m}{x+y}$

$\quad = \dfrac{a(x+y)}{x^2y(x+y)} + \dfrac{4ax^2y(x+y)}{x^2y(x+y)} - \dfrac{mx^2y}{x^2y(x+y)}$

$\quad = \dfrac{a(x+y) + 4ax^2y(x+y) - mx^2y}{x^2y(x+y)}$

18. $xy^{-1} + az = \dfrac{x}{y} + az = \dfrac{x}{y} + \dfrac{azy}{y} = \dfrac{x+azy}{y}$

19. $x^{-1} + ay^{-1} = \dfrac{1}{x} + \dfrac{a}{y} = \dfrac{y}{xy} + \dfrac{ax}{xy} = \dfrac{y+ax}{xy}$

20. $5(x^4 - 2x^3 + x^2 - 1) - 2(x^3 + 3x^2 + 1)$
$+ (2x^2 - x - 3)$
$= 5x^4 - 10x^3 + 5x^2 - 5 - 2x^3 - 6x^2 - 2$
$+ 2x^2 - x - 3$
$= \mathbf{5x^4 - 12x^3 + x^2 - x - 10}$

21. $(2x - 3)(2x^2 - 3x + 4)$
$= 4x^3 - 6x^2 + 8x - 6x^2 + 9x - 12$
$= \mathbf{4x^3 - 12x^2 + 17x - 12}$

22. $xx(x^2)^{-2}(x^2)(x^{-3}y^0)^5 = x^2x^{-4}x^2x^{-15} = \mathbf{x^{-15}}$

23. $\left(\dfrac{3x^{-2}y^5}{p^{-3}}\right)^{-2}\left(\dfrac{3x^{-2}}{y}\right)^2 = \dfrac{x^4y^{-10}}{9p^6}\left(\dfrac{9x^{-4}}{y^2}\right)$
$= \dfrac{y^{-10}}{p^6y^2} = p^{-6}y^{-12} = \mathbf{y^{-12}p^{-6}}$

24. $\left(\dfrac{x^2y^0}{2y^{-1}} - \dfrac{4x^{-2}}{x^0y}\right)\dfrac{2x^{-2}}{y} = \dfrac{x^2(2x^{-2})}{2y^{-1}y} - \dfrac{8x^{-4}}{y^2}$
$= \mathbf{1 - \dfrac{8}{x^4y^2}}$

25. $x^2(p^5)^2y - \dfrac{3x^2p^{10}}{y^{-1}} + \dfrac{4x^3p^8y}{x^2p^{-2}} - \dfrac{2p^{10}}{x^{-1}y^{-1}}$
$= x^2p^{10}y - 3x^2p^{10}y + 4xp^{10}y - 2xp^{10}y$
$= \mathbf{-2x^2p^{10}y + 2xp^{10}y}$

26. $\begin{array}{cc} 2x - 1 = 1 & 2y + 1 = -1 \\ \underline{+1 \quad +1} & \underline{-1 \quad -1} \\ 2x = 2 & 2y = -2 \\ x = 1 & y = -1 \end{array}$

$(x^2 + y^{-2})(x^{-2} - y^2)$
$= [1^2 + (-1)^{-2}][(1)^{-2} - (-1)^2]$
$= (1 + 1)(1 - 1) = 2(0) = \mathbf{0}$

27. $\sqrt[3]{8} - \sqrt[4]{16} + \sqrt[5]{32} - \sqrt[6]{64}$
$= 2 - 2 + 2 - 2 = \mathbf{0}$

28. $P = (100 + 300 + 100 + 300)\,\text{cm} = \mathbf{800\ cm}$

29. $A = \dfrac{1}{2}(35\ \text{in.} \times 16\ \text{in.}) + \dfrac{1}{2}\pi(16\ \text{in.})^2$
$= (280 + 128\pi)\,\text{in.}^2 = \mathbf{681.92\ in.^2}$

30. $S.A. = 2(\text{Area}_\text{base}) + \text{Lateral Surface Area}$
$= 2\left[(20\ \text{ft} \times 15\ \text{ft}) + \dfrac{1}{2}(15\ \text{ft} \times 20\ \text{ft})\right]$
$+ (\text{Perimeter}_\text{base})(\text{Height})$
$= 2(300\ \text{ft}^2 + 150\ \text{ft}^2)$
$+ (30\ \text{ft} + 20\ \text{ft} + 15\ \text{ft} + 25\ \text{ft})(10\ \text{ft})$
$= 600\ \text{ft}^2 + 300\ \text{ft}^2 + (90\ \text{ft})(10\ \text{ft})$
$= 900\ \text{ft}^2 + 900\ \text{ft}^2$
$= \mathbf{1800\ ft^2}$

Practice 58

a. $\dfrac{WP}{100} \cdot 160 = 32$

$\dfrac{100}{160} \cdot \dfrac{WP}{100} \cdot 160 = 32 \cdot \dfrac{100}{160}$

$WP = \mathbf{20\%}$

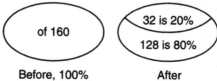

b. $\dfrac{70}{100} \cdot 2400 = WN$

$WN = \mathbf{1680}$

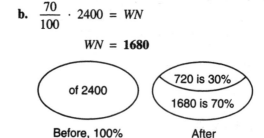

c. $\dfrac{250}{100} \cdot 40 = WN$

$WN = \mathbf{100}$

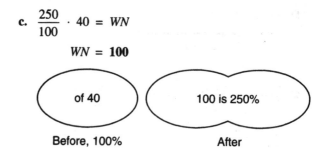

Problem Set 58

1. $\dfrac{15}{100} \cdot B = 2100$

$\dfrac{100}{15} \cdot \dfrac{15}{100} \cdot B = 2100 \cdot \dfrac{100}{15}$

$B = \mathbf{14,000}$

2. $\dfrac{160}{100} \cdot H = 128$

$\dfrac{100}{160} \cdot \dfrac{160}{100} \cdot H = 128 \cdot \dfrac{100}{160}$

$H = \mathbf{80\ lb}$

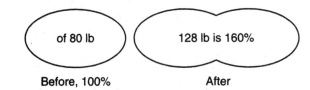

of 80 lb   128 lb is 160%

Before, 100%   After

3. $N(-5) + 6 = 3(-N) - 2$

$-5N + 6 = -3N - 2$

$\underline{+3N - 6 \quad +3N - 6}$

$-2N \quad = \quad -8$

$N = \mathbf{4}$

4. Overall average $= \dfrac{(7 \times 21) + (3 \times 11)}{7 + 3}$

$= \dfrac{147 + 33}{10}$

$= \dfrac{180}{10} = \mathbf{18}$

5. $K = \{-5, -4, -3, -2, -1\}$

6. $-6 \le x \le -2$

$$-7 \quad -6 \quad -5 \quad -4 \quad -3 \quad -2 \quad -1$$

7. $2310 \qquad \dfrac{2310}{2} = 1155 \qquad \dfrac{1155}{3} = 385$

$\dfrac{385}{5} = 77 \qquad \dfrac{77}{7} = 11 \qquad \mathbf{2 \cdot 3 \cdot 5 \cdot 7 \cdot 11}$

8. $f(x) = \sqrt{x}$

$f(4) = \sqrt{4} = \mathbf{2}$

9. $-2[(-3 - 2) - 2(-2 + m)] = -3m - 4^2 - |-2|$

$-2(-5 + 4 - 2m) = -3m - 16 - 2$

$10 - 8 + 4m = -3m - 18$

$4m + 2 = -3m - 18$

$\underline{+3m - 2 \quad +3m - 2}$

$7m \quad = \quad -20$

$m = -\dfrac{20}{7}$

10. $\dfrac{\dfrac{1}{x + y}}{\dfrac{a}{b}} = \dfrac{\dfrac{1}{x + y} \cdot \dfrac{b}{a}}{\dfrac{a}{b} \cdot \dfrac{b}{a}} = \dfrac{\dfrac{b}{a(x + y)}}{1}$

$= \dfrac{b}{a(x + y)}$

11. $\dfrac{\dfrac{m}{a}}{\dfrac{a}{mc^2}} = \dfrac{\dfrac{m}{1} \cdot \dfrac{mc^2}{a}}{\dfrac{a}{mc^2} \cdot \dfrac{mc^2}{a}} = \dfrac{\dfrac{m^2c^2}{a}}{1} = \dfrac{m^2c^2}{a}$

12. $\begin{cases} 2x + 3y = 8 \\ x = y - 1 \end{cases}$

$2x + 3y = 8$

$2(y - 1) + 3y = 8$

$2y - 2 + 3y = 8$

$5y - 2 = 8$

$5y = 10$

$y = 2$

$x = y - 1$

$x = 2 - 1$

$x = 1$

Thus the solution is the ordered pair $\mathbf{(1, 2)}$.

13. $\begin{cases} 3x - y = 3 \\ y = 2x - 1 \end{cases}$

$3x - y = 3$

$3x - (2x - 1) = 3$

$3x - 2x + 1 = 3$

$x + 1 = 3$

$x = 2$

$y = 2x - 1$

$y = 2(2) - 1$

$y = 4 - 1$

$y = 3$

Thus the solution is the ordered pair $\mathbf{(2, 3)}$.

14. $y = \dfrac{1}{2}x - 2$

x	0	2	-2
y	-2	-1	-3

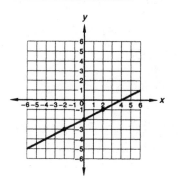

15. $3y + x = -9$

$$\frac{-x \qquad -x}{3y \quad = -9 - x}$$

$$y = -3 - \frac{1}{3}x$$

$$y = -\frac{1}{3}x - 3$$

x	0	3	–3
y	–3	–4	–2

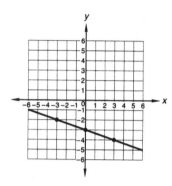

16. $-3x + \dfrac{2}{xp^2} - \dfrac{5x}{x^3 p}$

$$= -3x + \frac{2}{xp^2} - \frac{5}{x^2 p}$$

$$= \frac{-3x(x^2 p^2)}{x^2 p^2} + \frac{2(x)}{x^2 p^2} - \frac{5(p)}{x^2 p^2}$$

$$= \frac{-3x^3 p^2}{x^2 p^2} + \frac{2x}{x^2 p^2} - \frac{5p}{x^2 p^2}$$

$$= \frac{-3x^3 p^2 + 2x - 5p}{x^2 p^2}$$

17. $\dfrac{4}{x+y} - \dfrac{3}{y^2} = \dfrac{4y^2}{(x+y)y^2} - \dfrac{3(x+y)}{(x+y)y^2}$

$$= \frac{4y^2 - 3(x+y)}{y^2(x+y)}$$

18. $ayx^{-1} + bz = \dfrac{ay}{x} + bz = \dfrac{ay}{x} + \dfrac{bzx}{x}$

$$= \frac{ay + bzx}{x}$$

19. $a^{-2}x^{-1} + bz^{-1} = \dfrac{1}{a^2 x} + \dfrac{b}{z} = \dfrac{z}{a^2 xz} + \dfrac{ba^2 x}{a^2 xz}$

$$= \frac{z + ba^2 x}{a^2 xz}$$

20. $2(-x^5 - 3x^3 + x - 2) - 3(x^5 - 2x^3 - x + 1)$

$= -2x^5 - 6x^3 + 2x - 4 - 3x^5 + 6x^3 + 3x - 3$

$= \mathbf{-5x^5 + 5x - 7}$

21. $(2x - 4)(x - 3) = 2x^2 - 6x - 4x + 12$

$= \mathbf{2x^2 - 10x + 12}$

22. $x(x^2)(x^3)^{-3}(y^2 y^0)^{-4} = xx^2 x^{-9} y^{-8} = x^{-6} y^{-8}$

$$= \frac{1}{x^6 y^8}$$

23. $\dfrac{(x^2)^{-3}(yx)^2 x^0}{x^2 y^{-2}(xy^{-2})^3} = \dfrac{x^{-6} y^2 x^2}{x^2 y^{-2} x^3 y^{-6}} = \dfrac{x^{-4} y^2}{x^5 y^{-8}}$

$$= \frac{1}{x^9 y^{-10}}$$

24. $\dfrac{x^{-2}}{4m^2 k^{-2}}\left(\dfrac{4x^2}{m^{-2}k^2} - \dfrac{8m^{-2}k}{x^{-2}m^0}\right)$

$$= \frac{4x^{-2}x^2}{4m^2 k^{-2} m^{-2} k^2} - \frac{8x^{-2}m^{-2}k}{4m^2 k^{-2} x^{-2}}$$

$$= 1 - \frac{2m^{-2}k}{m^2 k^{-2}} = \mathbf{1 - \frac{2k^3}{m^4}}$$

25. $3(xy)^2 m - \dfrac{2m}{(x^{-1}y^{-1})^2} + \dfrac{4x^2 y^2}{m^{-1}} - \dfrac{3x^3 y^3 m^{-1}}{xym^{-2}}$

$= 3x^2 y^2 m - 2x^2 y^2 m + 4x^2 y^2 m - 3x^2 y^2 m$

$= 2x^2 y^2 m = \mathbf{\dfrac{2}{x^{-2} y^{-2} m^{-1}}}$

26.

$2 - 3x = 5$	$1 - 2y = 5$
$\underline{-2 \qquad -2}$	$\underline{-1 \qquad -1}$
$-3x = 3$	$-2y = 4$
$x = -1$	$y = -2$

$(|x| - |y|)(|y| - |x|)$
$= (|-1| - |-2|)(|-2| - |-1|)$
$= (1 - 2)(2 - 1) = \mathbf{-1}$

27. $\sqrt[3]{-1} + \sqrt[3]{-8} + \sqrt[3]{-27} + \sqrt[3]{-64} + \sqrt[3]{-125}$

$= -1 - 2 - 3 - 4 - 5 = \mathbf{-15}$

28. $P = (20 + 12 + 15 + 19 + 20 + 46)$ in.

$= 132$ in.

$132 \text{ in.} \cdot \dfrac{1 \text{ ft}}{12 \text{ in.}} = \mathbf{11 \text{ ft}}$

29. Area $= \dfrac{1}{2}(12 \text{ cm} \times 8 \text{ cm}) + \dfrac{1}{2}(8 \text{ cm} \times 8 \text{ cm})$

$= 48 \text{ cm}^2 + 32 \text{ cm}^2$

$= \mathbf{80 \text{ cm}^2}$

30. Volume $= (\text{Area}_{\text{base}})(\text{Height})$

$= \left[(32 \text{ m} \times 10 \text{ m}) + \dfrac{1}{2}(20 \text{ m} \times 15 \text{ m})\right]$

$\times (16 \text{ m})$

$= (320 \text{ m}^2 + 150 \text{ m}^2)(16 \text{ m})$

$= (470 \text{ m}^2)(16 \text{ m})$

$= \mathbf{7520 \text{ m}^3}$

Practice 59

a. $\begin{cases} x - 3y = -7 \\ 2x - 3y = 4 \end{cases}$

$x - 3y = -7$

$\dfrac{+3y \qquad\qquad +3y}{x \qquad\quad = -7 + 3y}$

$2x - 3y = 4$

$2(-7 + 3y) - 3y = 4$

$-14 + 6y - 3y = 4$

$-14 + 3y = 4$

$3y = 18$

$y = 6$

$x - 3y = -7$

$x - 3(6) = -7$

$x - 18 = -7$

$x = 11$

Thus the solution is the ordered pair **(11, 6)**.

b. $\begin{cases} 4x - y = 41 \\ 2x + y = 25 \end{cases}$

$4x - y = 41$

$\dfrac{-4x \qquad\qquad -4x}{-y = 41 - 4x}$

$y = -41 + 4x$

$2x + y = 25$

$2x + (-41 + 4x) = 25$

$6x - 41 = 25$

$6x = 66$

$x = 11$

$4x - y = 41$

$4(11) - y = 41$

$44 - y = 41$

$-y = -3$

$y = 3$

Thus the solution is the ordered pair **(11, 3)**.

Problem Set 59

1. $\dfrac{65}{100} \cdot WN = 247$

$\dfrac{100}{65} \cdot \dfrac{65}{100} \cdot WN = 247 \cdot \dfrac{100}{65}$

$WN = \textbf{\$380}$

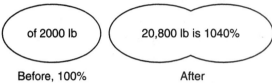

Before, 100%   After

2. $\dfrac{1040}{100} \cdot B = 20{,}800$

$\dfrac{100}{1040} \cdot \dfrac{1040}{100} \cdot B = 20{,}800 \cdot \dfrac{100}{1040}$

$B = \textbf{2000 lb}$

of 2000 lb   20,800 lb is 1040%

Before, 100%   After

3. $\dfrac{L}{T} = \dfrac{7}{9}$

$\dfrac{L}{1098} = \dfrac{7}{9}$

$9L = 7 \cdot 1098$

$L = \dfrac{7 \cdot 1098}{9}$

$L = \textbf{854}$

4. (a) **True,** because -3 is a member of A.

(b) **False,** because -2 is not a member of B.

(c) **False,** because 2 is a member of C.

(d) **False,** because 3 is a member of C.

5. $\mathbf{0 < x < 6}$

6. $2.625(WN) = 8.00625$

$\dfrac{2.625\,WN}{2.625} = \dfrac{8.00625}{2.625}$

$WN = \textbf{3.05}$

7. $g(x) = -\sqrt{x}$

$g(9) = -\sqrt{9} = \textbf{-3}$

8. $1.591 + 0.003k - 0.002 + 0.002k = -(0.003 - k)$

$0.005k + 1.589 = -0.003 + k$

$5k + 1589 = -3 + 1000k$

$-995k = -1592$

$k = \textbf{1.6}$

9. $\dfrac{\dfrac{1}{x}}{\dfrac{1}{a}} = \dfrac{\dfrac{1}{x} \cdot \dfrac{1}{a}}{\dfrac{a}{1} \cdot \dfrac{1}{a}} = \dfrac{\dfrac{1}{xa}}{1} = \dfrac{1}{xa}$

10. $\dfrac{x + y}{\dfrac{1}{c}} = \dfrac{\dfrac{x + y}{1} \cdot \dfrac{c}{1}}{\dfrac{1}{c} \cdot \dfrac{c}{1}} = \dfrac{c(x + y)}{1} = c(x + y)$

11. $\begin{cases} 2x - 3y = 5 \\ x = -2y - 8 \end{cases}$

$$2x - 3y = 5$$
$$2(-2y - 8) - 3y = 5$$
$$-4y - 16 - 3y = 5$$
$$-7y - 16 = 5$$
$$-7y = 21$$
$$y = -3$$

$$x = -2y - 8$$
$$x = -2(-3) - 8$$
$$x = 6 - 8$$
$$x = -2$$

Thus the solution is the ordered pair **(–2, –3)**.

12. $\begin{cases} x + 2y = 5 \\ 3x - y = 1 \end{cases}$

$$x + 2y = 5$$
$$\underline{ -2y \qquad\quad -2y}$$
$$x = 5 - 2y$$

$$3x - y = 1$$
$$3(5 - 2y) - y = 1$$
$$15 - 6y - y = 1$$
$$15 - 7y = 1$$
$$-7y = -14$$
$$y = 2$$

$$x + 2y = 5$$
$$x + 2(2) = 5$$
$$x + 4 = 5$$
$$x = 1$$

Thus the solution is the ordered pair **(1, 2)**.

13. $y = -3\dfrac{1}{2}$

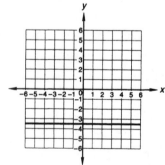

14. $4y - 4x = 8$
$$\underline{+4x \qquad\qquad +4x}$$
$$4y = 8 + 4x$$
$$y = 2 + x$$
$$y = x + 2$$

x	0	1	–4
y	2	3	–2

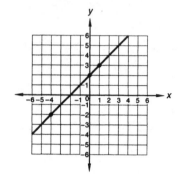

15. $\dfrac{-x}{a^2 b} + \dfrac{a - b}{b} = \dfrac{-x}{a^2 b} + \dfrac{a^2(a - b)}{a^2 b}$

$$= \dfrac{-x + a^2(a - b)}{a^2 b}$$

16. $\dfrac{m}{k(k + c)} + \dfrac{m}{k} = \dfrac{m}{k(k + c)} + \dfrac{m(k + c)}{k(k + c)}$

$$= \dfrac{m + m(k + c)}{k(k + c)}$$

17. $bx + cy^{-1} = bx + \dfrac{c}{y} = \dfrac{bxy}{y} + \dfrac{c}{y} = \dfrac{bxy + c}{y}$

18. $x^{-1}ay^{-2} - bz^{-1} = \dfrac{a}{xy^2} - \dfrac{b}{z} = \dfrac{az}{xy^2 z} - \dfrac{bxy^2}{xy^2 z}$

$$= \dfrac{az - bxy^2}{xy^2 z}$$

19. $4(x^2 - 3x + 5) - 2(x^3 + 2x^2 - 4)$
$$- \ (2x^4 - 3x^3 + x^2 + 3)$$
$$= 4x^2 - 12x + 20 - 2x^3 - 4x^2 + 8 - 2x^4$$
$$+ \ 3x^3 - x^2 - 3$$
$$= \mathbf{-2x^4 + x^3 - x^2 - 12x + 25}$$

20. $(-5x - 2)(-x + 4) = 5x^2 - 20x + 2x - 8$
$$= \mathbf{5x^2 - 18x - 8}$$

21. $12x^4yp^3 - 4x^3y^2pz - 8x^2p^2y^2$
$$= \mathbf{4x^2 py(3x^2 p^2 - xyz - 2py)}$$

22. $(4x^0 y^2 m)^{-2}(2y^{-4} m^0 x)^4 = (4^{-2}y^{-4}m^{-2})(2^4 y^{-16} x^4)$
$$= \dfrac{16}{16}y^{-4}m^{-2}y^{-16}x^4 = \dfrac{x^4}{m^2 y^{20}} = \mathbf{\dfrac{x^4}{y^{20} m^2}}$$

23. $\dfrac{(x^2)^{-3}(yx)^2 x^0}{x^2 y^{-2}(xy^{-2})^3} = \dfrac{x^{-6}y^2 x^2}{x^2 y^{-2} x^3 y^{-6}} = \dfrac{x^{-4}y^2}{x^5 y^{-8}}$

$$= \mathbf{\dfrac{y^{10}}{x^9}}$$

24. $\left(\dfrac{4p^2}{m^2b^3} - \dfrac{4m^{-2}}{ab^2p}\right)\dfrac{p^{-3}m^2}{4a^{-1}b^{-3}}$

$= \dfrac{4p^{-1}m^2}{4m^2a^{-1}} - \dfrac{4p^{-3}}{4b^{-1}p} = \dfrac{p^{-1}}{a^{-1}} - \dfrac{p^{-4}}{b^{-1}}$

25. $\dfrac{4\left(a^{-1}b^2\right)^2}{a^0b^2} + \dfrac{2aab^0}{\left(a^{-1}b\right)^{-2}} - \dfrac{5a^3a^{-1}b^0}{\left(ab^{-1}\right)^2}$

$- \dfrac{3\left(a^0a^3\right)^{-2}}{a^{-4}b^{-2}}$

$= \dfrac{4a^{-2}b^4}{b^2} + \dfrac{2a^2}{a^2b^{-2}} - \dfrac{5a^2}{a^2b^{-2}} - \dfrac{3a^{-6}}{a^{-4}b^{-2}}$

$= 4a^{-2}b^2 + 2b^2 - 5b^2 - 3a^{-2}b^2$

$= a^{-2}b^2 - 3b^2 = \dfrac{b^2}{a^2} - 3b^2$

26.

$\begin{array}{ll} 1 - 2x = 3 & 6 + 5y = -4 \\ \underline{-1 \qquad -1} & \underline{-6 \qquad\quad -6} \\ \;\;-2x = 2 & \;\;5y = -10 \\ \quad\;\; x = -1 & \quad\;\; y = -2 \end{array}$

$x^{-1}y^{-2} - x^{-2}y^{-3} = (-1)^{-1}(-2)^{-2} - (-1)^{-2}(-2)^{-3}$

$= -1\left(\dfrac{1}{4}\right) - (+1)\left(-\dfrac{1}{8}\right) = -\dfrac{1}{4} + \dfrac{1}{8} = -\dfrac{1}{8}$

27. $2^0|1 - 4| - (-3)^0|1 - 5| - 4^0|1 - 6| + \sqrt[3]{-27}$

$= 3 - 4 - 5 - 3 = -9$

28.

Area $= A_1 + A_2 + A_3$

$= (0.9\text{ m} \times 1.3\text{ m}) + (0.6\text{ m} \times 0.6\text{ m})$

$\quad + (0.4\text{ m} \times 0.6\text{ m})$

$= 1.17\text{ m}^2 + 0.36\text{ m}^2 + 0.24\text{ m}^2$

$= \mathbf{1.77\text{ m}^2}$

29. Area $= $ Area$_{\text{parallelogram}} - $ Area$_{\text{circle}}$

$= \left[\dfrac{1}{2}(40\text{ in.} \times 18\text{ in.}) + \dfrac{1}{2}(40\text{ in.} \times 18\text{ in.})\right]$

$\quad - \pi(6\text{ in.})^2$

$= \left(360\text{ in.}^2 + 360\text{ in.}^2\right) - 36\pi\text{ in.}^2$

$= (720 - 36\pi)\text{ in.}^2 = \mathbf{606.96\text{ in.}^2}$

30. Since angles opposite sides of equal length have equal measure, angles x and y are equivalent.

$180 - 110 = 70$

$70 \div 2 = 35$

$x = 35;\; y = 35$

Practice 60

a. $V = \left(\text{Area}_{\text{base}}\right)(\text{Height})$

$\quad = \left(34\text{ in.}^2\right)(12\text{ in.}) = \mathbf{408\text{ in.}^3}$

b. Lateral $S.A. = \left(\text{Perimeter}_{\text{base}}\right)(\text{Height})$

$\quad = (12\text{ ft} + 12\text{ ft} + 12\text{ ft} + 12\text{ ft}$

$\quad\;\; + 12\text{ ft})(16\text{ ft})$

$\quad = (60\text{ ft})(16\text{ ft}) = \mathbf{960\text{ ft}^2}$

Problem Set 60

1.

$\dfrac{160}{100} \cdot F = 440$

$\dfrac{100}{160} \cdot \dfrac{160}{100} \cdot F = 440 \cdot \dfrac{100}{160}$

$F = \mathbf{275}$

2.

$\begin{array}{l} 2N + 5 = -N - 13 \\ \underline{+N - 5 \quad\; +N - \;\,5} \\ 3N \quad\;\; = \quad\;\; -18 \\ \quad\; N = \mathbf{-6} \end{array}$

3. Overall average $= \dfrac{(5 \times 6.5) + (15 \times 4.5)}{5 + 15}$

$= \dfrac{32.5 + 67.5}{20}$

$= \dfrac{100}{20} = \mathbf{5}$

4. $L = \{\mathbf{-12, -8, -4, 0, 4, 8, 12}\}$

5. (a) $A = \pi r^2$

$200\text{ in.}^2 = (3.14)r^2$

$r^2 = \dfrac{200\text{ in.}^2}{3.14}$

$r^2 = 63.69\text{ in.}^2$

$r = \sqrt{63.69\text{ in.}^2}$

$r = \mathbf{7.98\text{ in.}}$

(b) $C = 2\pi r$

$= 2\pi(7.98\text{ in.}) = \mathbf{15.96\pi\text{ in.} = 50.11\text{ in.}}$

6. $\mathbf{3 < x < 6}$

7. $h(x) = |x|$

$h(-4) = |-4| = \mathbf{4}$

8. $2\dfrac{1}{2} + 3\dfrac{1}{16}k + \dfrac{1}{8} = 0$

$$3\dfrac{1}{16}k + 2\dfrac{5}{8} = 0$$

$$\dfrac{-2\dfrac{5}{8} \qquad -2\dfrac{5}{8}}{3\dfrac{1}{16}k \qquad\quad = -2\dfrac{5}{8}}$$

$$\dfrac{3\dfrac{1}{16}k}{3\dfrac{1}{16}} = \dfrac{-2\dfrac{5}{8}}{3\dfrac{1}{16}}$$

$$k = -\dfrac{21}{8} \cdot \dfrac{16}{49}$$

$$k = -\dfrac{6}{7}$$

9. $2x + 5 = -5$ $3y + 5 = -10$

$$\dfrac{-5 \quad\; -5}{2x \qquad = -10} \qquad \dfrac{-5 \quad\; -5}{3y \qquad = -15}$$

$$x = -5 \qquad\qquad y = -5$$

$$x^3 - y^3 = (-5)^3 - (-5)^3 = -125 - (-125) = \mathbf{0}$$

10. $\dfrac{\dfrac{a}{b}}{\dfrac{1}{x}} = \dfrac{\dfrac{a}{b} \cdot \dfrac{x}{1}}{\dfrac{1}{x} \cdot \dfrac{x}{1}} = \dfrac{\dfrac{ax}{b}}{1} = \dfrac{ax}{b}$

11. $\dfrac{\dfrac{x}{1}}{\dfrac{1}{a+b}} = \dfrac{\dfrac{x}{1} \cdot \dfrac{a+b}{1}}{\dfrac{1}{a+b} \cdot \dfrac{a+b}{1}} = \dfrac{x(a+b)}{1}$

     $= x(a+b)$

12. $\begin{cases} x = -19 - 6y \\ 2x + 3y = -11 \end{cases}$

$$2x + 3y = -11$$
$$2(-19 - 6y) + 3y = -11$$
$$-38 - 12y + 3y = -11$$
$$-38 - 9y = -11$$
$$-9y = 27$$
$$y = -3$$

$$x = -19 - 6y$$
$$x = -19 - 6(-3)$$
$$x = -19 + 18$$
$$x = -1$$

Thus the solution is the ordered pair **(–1, –3)**.

13. $\begin{cases} 4x + y = -5 \\ 2x - y = -1 \end{cases}$

$$\dfrac{4x + y = -5}{-4x \qquad\qquad -4x}$$
$$y = -5 - 4x$$

$$2x - y = -1$$
$$2x - (-4x - 5) = -1$$
$$2x + 4x + 5 = -1$$
$$6x + 5 = -1$$
$$6x = -6$$
$$x = -1$$

$$4x + y = -5$$
$$4(-1) + y = -5$$
$$-4 + y = -5$$
$$y = -1$$

Thus the solution is the ordered pair **(–1, –1)**.

14. $y = -2x - 5$

x	0	-2	-4
y	-5	-1	3

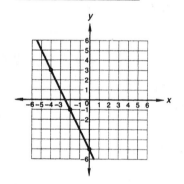

15. $3x + 2y = 6$

$$\dfrac{-3x \qquad\qquad -3x}{2y = 6 - 3x}$$

$$y = 3 - \dfrac{3}{2}x$$

$$y = -\dfrac{3}{2}x + 3$$

x	0	2	4
y	3	0	-3

16. $\dfrac{3ax}{m} + \dfrac{4x}{am^2} + \dfrac{2}{mx}$

$= \dfrac{3ax(amx)}{am^2x} + \dfrac{4xx}{am^2x} + \dfrac{2(am)}{am^2x}$

$= \dfrac{3a^2x^2m + 4x^2 + 2am}{am^2x}$

17. $\dfrac{x}{x+y} + y = \dfrac{x}{x+y} + \dfrac{y(x+y)}{x+y}$

$= \dfrac{x + y(x+y)}{x+y}$

18. $2x^{-1} + 3y^{-2} = \dfrac{2}{x} + \dfrac{3}{y^2} = \dfrac{2y^2}{xy^2} + \dfrac{3x}{xy^2}$

$= \dfrac{2y^2 + 3x}{xy^2}$

19. $x^{-2}y^{-1} - 4z^{-2} = \dfrac{1}{x^2y} - \dfrac{4}{z^2}$

$= \dfrac{z^2}{x^2yz^2} - \dfrac{4x^2y}{x^2yz^2} = \dfrac{z^2 - 4x^2y}{x^2yz^2}$

20. $5(-x^5 + 3x^3 - x + 2)$
$+ 3(x^5 - 3x^3 - x^2 + x - 3)$
$= -5x^5 + 15x^3 - 5x + 10 + 3x^5 - 9x^3 - 3x^2$
$+ 3x - 9$
$= -2x^5 + 6x^3 - 3x^2 - 2x + 1$

21. $(2x - 3)(3x^2 - 2x + 2)$
$= 6x^3 - 4x^2 + 4x - 9x^2 + 6x - 6$
$= 6x^3 - 13x^2 + 10x - 6$

22. $(2m^2x^{-3}y^0)^{-4}(4m^3y^{-1}x^{-5})^2$
$= (2^{-4}m^{-8}x^{12})(4^2m^6y^{-2}x^{-10})$
$= \dfrac{16}{16}m^{-8}x^{12}m^6y^{-2}x^{-10} = m^{-2}x^2y^{-2}$
$= \dfrac{m^{-2}y^{-2}}{x^{-2}}$

23. $\left(\dfrac{x^2p^2}{p^0y^{-2}}\right)^{-2} \dfrac{(y^{-2})^{-2}}{y^0p^{-3}} = \dfrac{x^{-4}p^{-4}}{y^4} \cdot \dfrac{y^4}{p^{-3}} = x^{-4}p^{-1}$

24. $\dfrac{x^{-5}y^0}{2p^{-2}y^{-1}}\left(\dfrac{2y^{-2}}{x^{-3}} - \dfrac{4x^5}{p^2}\right)$

$= \dfrac{2x^{-5}y^{-2}}{2p^{-2}y^{-1}x^{-3}} - \dfrac{4}{2y^{-1}} = \dfrac{x^{-2}y^{-1}}{p^{-2}} - \dfrac{2}{y^{-1}}$

$= x^{-2}p^2y^{-1} - 2y$

25. $2(xy^2)^{-1} - \dfrac{9x^{-2}y^{-3}}{(x^0y)^{-2}} + \dfrac{(3y)^2\,x^{-4}}{x^{-2}y^3} - \dfrac{(y^{-1}x)^2}{x^3}$
$= 2x^{-1}y^{-2} - 9x^{-2}y^{-1} + 9x^{-2}y^{-1} - x^{-1}y^{-2}$
$= x^{-1}y^{-2}$

26. $(|x| + |y|)(|x| - |y|)$
$= (|-4| + |-5|)(|-4| - |-5|)$
$= (4 + 5)(4 - 5) = -9$

27. $\sqrt[4]{16}(1 - |-2|) - \sqrt[4]{81}(2 - |-3|)$
$= 2(1 - 2) - 3(2 - 3) = -2 + 3 = 1$

28.

$P = (18 + 10 + 18 + 6 + 6 + 10)$ in. $=$ **68 in.**

29. $A = (12 \text{ cm} \times 24 \text{ cm}) + \dfrac{1}{2}\pi(6 \text{ cm})^2$

$\qquad + \dfrac{1}{2}\pi(6 \text{ cm})^2$

$= 288 \text{ cm}^2 + 18\pi \text{ cm}^2 + 18\pi \text{ cm}^2$

$= (288 + 36\pi) \text{ cm}^2 = $ **401.04 cm²**

30. $V = (\text{Area}_{\text{base}})(\text{Height})$
$= (30 \text{ m}^2)(12 \text{ m}) = $ **360 m³**

Practice 61

a. (1) **True. All of set B is contained in set A.**

(2) **False. None of set B is contained in set C.**

(3) **True. All of set C is contained in set A.**

b. Rationals, reals

c. Rationals, reals

d. Naturals, wholes, integers, rationals, reals

e. Irrationals, reals

f. Integers, rationals, reals

Problem Set 61

1. $\dfrac{P}{T} = \dfrac{13}{15}$

$\dfrac{P}{315} = \dfrac{13}{15}$

$15P = 13 \cdot 315$

$P = \dfrac{13 \cdot 315}{15}$

$P = 273$

2. Overall average $= \dfrac{(6 \times 80) + (4 \times 90)}{6 + 4}$

$= \dfrac{480 + 360}{10}$

$= \dfrac{840}{10} = \mathbf{84\%}$

3. $\dfrac{240}{100} \cdot 1400 = WN$

$WN = 240 \cdot 14$

$WN = \mathbf{3360 \ lb}$

of 1400 lb	3360 lb is 240%
Before, 100%	After

4. $\dfrac{15}{100} \cdot F = 120$

$\dfrac{100}{15} \cdot \dfrac{15}{100} \cdot F = 120 \cdot \dfrac{100}{15}$

$F = \mathbf{800}$

of 800	120 is 15%
	680 is 85%
Before, 100%	After

5. Range $= 16 - 6 = \mathbf{10}$

Median $= \mathbf{8}$

Mode $= \mathbf{8}$

Mean $= (6 + 7 + 7 + 8 + 8 + 8 + 10 + 11$
$+ \ 12 + 13 + 16) \div 11$
$= 106 \div 11 = \mathbf{9.64}$

6. $x \not\geq -2$

7. $6\dfrac{4}{5}(WN) = 1\dfrac{7}{10}$

$\dfrac{6\frac{4}{5}WN}{6\frac{4}{5}} = \dfrac{1\frac{7}{10}}{6\frac{4}{5}}$

$WN = \dfrac{17}{10} \cdot \dfrac{5}{34}$

$WN = \dfrac{\mathbf{1}}{\mathbf{4}}$

8. (a) **Integers, rationals, reals**

(b) **Irrationals, reals**

9. (a) **Rationals, reals**

(b) **Wholes, integers, rationals, reals**

10. (a) **True. The set of rational numbers is a subset of the set of real numbers.**

(b) **False. The set of rational numbers contains numbers that are not in the set of integers.**

11. (a) **False. Zero, a member of set A, is not a member of set B.**

(b) **True. All members of set C are members of set B.**

(c) **False. Zero is a member of set A.**

(d) **True. Two is a member of set C.**

12. $-[-(-2p)] - 3(-3p + 15) = -(-4)(p - 12)$

$-2p + 9p - 45 = 4p - 48$

$7p - 45 = 4p - 48$

$\dfrac{-4p + 45 \quad -4p + 45}{3p \quad = \quad -3}$

$p = \mathbf{-1}$

13. $x^{-1}y - y^{-1} = \dfrac{y}{x} - \dfrac{1}{y} = \dfrac{y^2}{xy} - \dfrac{x}{xy} = \dfrac{\mathbf{y^2 - x}}{\mathbf{xy}}$

14. $\dfrac{\frac{a}{b}}{c + x} = \dfrac{\frac{a}{b} \cdot \frac{1}{c+x}}{\frac{c+x}{1} \cdot \frac{1}{c+x}} = \dfrac{\frac{a}{b(c+x)}}{1}$

$= \dfrac{\mathbf{a}}{\mathbf{b(c + x)}}$

15. $\dfrac{\frac{a}{b}}{\frac{b}{c+x}} = \dfrac{\frac{a}{1} \cdot \frac{c+x}{b}}{\frac{b}{c+x} \cdot \frac{c+x}{b}} = \dfrac{\frac{a(c+x)}{b}}{1}$

$= \dfrac{\mathbf{a(c + x)}}{\mathbf{b}}$

16. $\begin{cases} 4x + y = -5 \\ 2x - y = -1 \end{cases}$

$4x + y = -5$

$y = -4x - 5$

$2x - y = -1$

$2x - (-4x - 5) = -1$

$2x + 4x + 5 = -1$

$6x + 5 = -1$

$6x = -6$

$x = -1$

$4x + y = -5$

$4(-1) + y = -5$

$-4 + y = -5$

$y = -1$

Thus the solution is the ordered pair **$(-1, -1)$**.

17. $\begin{cases} x - 3y = -7 \\ 3x + y = -1 \end{cases}$

$$x - 3y = -7$$

$$x = 3y - 7$$

$$3x + y = -1$$

$$3(3y - 7) + y = -1$$

$$9y - 21 + y = -1$$

$$10y - 21 = -1$$

$$10y = 20$$

$$y = 2$$

$$x - 3y = -7$$

$$x - 3(2) = -7$$

$$x - 6 = -7$$

$$x = -1$$

Thus the solution is the ordered pair **(–1, 2)**.

18. $y = -3x$

x	0	1	-1
y	0	-3	3

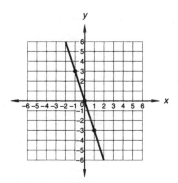

19. $y = 3x$

x	0	1	-1
y	0	3	-3

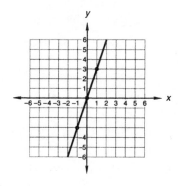

20. $4 + 3x - y = 0$

$$y = 3x + 4$$

x	0	-1	-2
y	4	1	-2

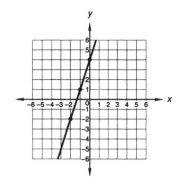

21. $\dfrac{4xy}{a} + \dfrac{4y}{ab^2} + \dfrac{2}{ab} = \dfrac{4xyb^2}{ab^2} + \dfrac{4y}{ab^2} + \dfrac{2b}{ab^2}$

$$= \dfrac{4xyb^2 + 4y + 2b}{ab^2}$$

22. $my + \dfrac{p}{y} = \dfrac{my^2}{y} + \dfrac{p}{y} = \dfrac{my^2 + p}{y}$

23. $(4x - 3)(x + 2) = 4x^2 + 8x - 3x - 6$

$$= \mathbf{4x^2 + 5x - 6}$$

24. $(4x + 3)^2 = (4x + 3)(4x + 3)$

$$= 16x^2 + 12x + 12x + 9 = \mathbf{16x^2 + 24x + 9}$$

25. $\dfrac{a^0 x^2 x^0}{m^2 y^0 m^{-2}} = \dfrac{x^2}{1} = \mathbf{x^2}$

26. $\dfrac{(x^2 y^0)^2 y^0 k^2}{(2x^2 k^5)^{-4} y} = \dfrac{x^4 k^2}{2^{-4} x^{-8} k^{-20} y} = \dfrac{\mathbf{16x^{12} k^{22}}}{\mathbf{y}}$

27. $20x^2 m^5 k^6 - 10x^3 m^4 k^4 + 30x^5 m^4 k^6$

$$= \mathbf{10x^2 m^4 k^4 (2mk^2 - x + 3x^3 k^2)}$$

28. $-2\left[(3 + |-5|) - 6^0 (-2 - 1)\right] - (-2)^3 + \sqrt[3]{-8}$

$$= -2[8 - (-3)] + 8 - 2 = -22 + 8 - 2 = \mathbf{-16}$$

29. $P = \left(12 + 24 + 12 + \dfrac{2\pi(6)}{2} + \dfrac{2\pi(6)}{2}\right)$ in.

$$= (48 + 12\pi) \text{ in.} = \mathbf{85.68 \text{ in.}}$$

30. Lateral $S.A. = \left(\text{Perimeter}_{\text{base}}\right)(\text{Height})$

$$= (6 \text{ ft} + 6 \text{ ft} + 6 \text{ ft} + 6 \text{ ft} + 6 \text{ ft})$$

$$\times 13 \text{ ft}$$

$$= (30 \text{ ft})(13 \text{ ft}) = \mathbf{390 \text{ ft}^2}$$

Practice 62

a. $\sqrt{17} = $ **4.1231**

b. Since $5^2 = 25$ and $6^2 = 36$, the number whose square is 27 must lie between **5 and 6.**

c. $\sqrt[3]{-27} = $ **–3**

d. $\sqrt{81} - \sqrt{144} = 9 - 12 = $ **–3**

e. $-1^2 + (-2)^2 \pm \sqrt{9} = -1 + 4 \pm 3 = 3 \pm 3$
   $= $ **0, 6**

Problem Set 62

1. Overall average $= \dfrac{(100 \times 1000) + (120 \times 725)}{100 + 120}$

   $= \dfrac{100{,}000 + 87{,}000}{220}$

   $= \dfrac{187{,}000}{220} = $ **850 lb**

2. $\dfrac{128}{100} \cdot D = 3840$

   $\dfrac{100}{128} \cdot \dfrac{128}{100} \cdot D = 3840 \cdot \dfrac{100}{128}$

   $D = $ **3000 units**

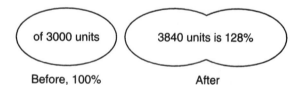

Before, 100%   After

of 3000 units   3840 units is 128%

3. $\dfrac{72}{100} \cdot P = 324$

   $\dfrac{100}{72} \cdot \dfrac{72}{100} \cdot P = 324 \cdot \dfrac{100}{72}$

   $P = $ **$450**

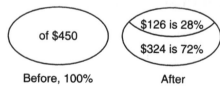

Before, 100%   After

of $450 $126 is 28% $324 is 72%

4. Range $= 103 - 97 = $ **6**

   Median $= $ **100**

   Mode $= $ **100**

   Mean $= (97 + 98 + 99 + 100 + 100 + 101$
   $+ 102 + 103) \div 8$
   $= 800 \div 8 = $ **100**

5. (a) **Naturals, wholes, integers, rationals, reals**

   (b) **Irrationals, reals**

6. (a) $\sqrt{9} + \sqrt{16} = 3 + 4 = $ **7**

   (b) $\sqrt{225} - \sqrt{169} = 15 - 13 = $ **2**

7. Since $7^2 = 49$ and $8^2 = 64$, the number whose square is 57 must lie between **7 and 8.**

8. $\sqrt{19} = $ **4.3589**

9. $-2^2 + 3^2 \pm \sqrt{4} = -4 + 9 \pm 2 = 5 \pm 2 = $ **3, 7**

10. (a) **False. Some real numbers are not rational numbers.**

   (b) **True. The set of irrational numbers is a subset of the set of real numbers.**

11. $-k(-2 - 3) - (-2)(-k - 5)$
   $\qquad\qquad = -2 - (-2k + 4) + \sqrt[3]{-27}$
   $2k + 3k - 2k - 10 = -2 + 2k - 4 - 3$
   $\qquad 3k - 10 = 2k - 9$
   $\qquad \underline{-2k + 10 \quad -2k + 10}$
   $\qquad\qquad k = 1$

12. $\dfrac{\frac{m}{x+y}}{\frac{a}{x+y}} = \dfrac{\frac{m}{x+y}}{\frac{a}{x+y}} \cdot \dfrac{\frac{x+y}{a}}{\frac{x+y}{a}} = \dfrac{\frac{m(x+y)}{a(x+y)}}{1} = \dfrac{m}{a}$

13. $\dfrac{\frac{m}{x+y}}{\frac{m}{x}} = \dfrac{\frac{m}{x+y}}{\frac{m}{x}} \cdot \dfrac{\frac{x}{m}}{\frac{x}{m}} = \dfrac{\frac{mx}{m(x+y)}}{1} = \dfrac{x}{x+y}$

14. $2a^{-1} + 4b^{-2} = \dfrac{2}{a} + \dfrac{4}{b^2} = \dfrac{2b^2}{ab^2} + \dfrac{4a}{ab^2}$

   $= \dfrac{2b^2 + 4a}{ab^2}$

15. $\begin{cases} 5x - 3y = 1 \\ 7x - y = -5 \end{cases}$

   $7x - y = -5$
   $\quad -y = -7x - 5$
   $\quad\; y = 7x + 5$

   $\quad 5x - 3y = 1$
   $5x - 3(7x + 5) = 1$
   $5x - 21x - 15 = 1$
   $\quad -16x = 16$
   $\quad\;\; x = -1$

$$7x - y = -5$$
$$7(-1) - y = -5$$
$$-7 - y = -5$$
$$-y = 2$$
$$y = -2$$

Thus the solution is the ordered pair **(–1, –2)**.

16. $\begin{cases} 5x + 2y = -21 \\ -2x + y = 3 \end{cases}$

$$-2x + y = 3$$
$$y = 2x + 3$$
$$5x + 2y = -21$$
$$5x + 2(2x + 3) = -21$$
$$5x + 4x + 6 = -21$$
$$9x + 6 = -21$$
$$9x = -27$$
$$x = -3$$
$$-2x + y = 3$$
$$-2(-3) + y = 3$$
$$6 + y = 3$$
$$y = -3$$

Thus the solution is the ordered pair **(–3, –3)**.

17. $y = 2$

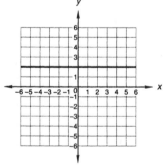

18. $y = -3$

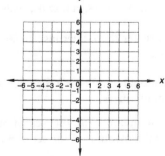

19. $y - x + 1 = 0$

$$y = x - 1$$

x	0	1	-3
y	-1	0	-4

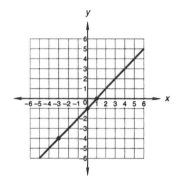

20. $\dfrac{a}{x^2 y} + \dfrac{m + c}{y^2} - \dfrac{c}{x^2}$

$$= \dfrac{ay}{x^2 y^2} + \dfrac{x^2(m + c)}{x^2 y^2} - \dfrac{cy^2}{x^2 y^2}$$

$$= \dfrac{ay + x^2(m + c) - cy^2}{x^2 y^2}$$

21. $1 + \dfrac{y}{x} = \dfrac{x}{x} + \dfrac{y}{x} = \dfrac{x + y}{x}$

22. $9x^3 y m^5 + 6m^2 y^4 p^4 - 3y^3 m^3$
$$= 3y m^2 \left(3x^3 m^3 + 2y^3 p^4 - y^2 m\right)$$

23. $\dfrac{4kp + 4kpx}{4kp} = \dfrac{4kp(1 + x)}{4kp} = \mathbf{1 + x}$

24. $\dfrac{a^{-2} p^2 a (a^0)^2}{(a^{-3})^2 (p^{-2})^{-2}} = \dfrac{a^{-1} p^2}{a^{-6} p^4} = \dfrac{a^5}{p^2}$

25. $mx(x^0 y) m^2 x^2 (y^2) = \mathbf{m^3 x^3 y^3}$

26. $-\dfrac{x^{-3}}{y} \left(\dfrac{x^3}{y^{-1}} - \dfrac{3x^{-3}}{y^2} + \dfrac{4x^2}{y^{-3}} \right)$

$$= -\dfrac{x^0}{y^0} + \dfrac{3x^{-6}}{y^3} - \dfrac{4x^{-1}}{y^{-2}}$$

$$= \mathbf{-1} + \dfrac{\mathbf{3}}{x^6 y^3} - \dfrac{4y^2}{x}$$

27. $-2^0 x^2 y^2 x^{-2} + \dfrac{3y^2}{x^2} - \dfrac{4x^{-2}}{y^{-2}} + 5y^2$

$$= -y^2 + \dfrac{3y^2}{x^2} - \dfrac{4y^2}{x^2} + 5y^2 = 4y^2 - \dfrac{y^2}{x^2}$$

$$= \mathbf{4y^2 - x^{-2} y^2}$$

28.
$$2 - 3a = 8 \qquad 4b + 4 = 0$$
$$\underline{-2 \qquad -2} \qquad \underline{-4 \quad -4}$$
$$-3a = 6 \qquad 4b = -4$$
$$a = -2 \qquad b = -1$$

$$a^{-2}b^{-3} - a^2b^3 = (-2)^{-2}(-1)^{-3} - (-2)^2(-1)^3$$
$$= \frac{1}{4}(-1) - (4)(-1) = 4 - \frac{1}{4} = 3\frac{3}{4} = \mathbf{\frac{15}{4}}$$

29. $A = \text{Area}_{\text{triangle}} - \text{Area}_{\text{circle}}$
$$= \frac{1}{2}(36 \text{ cm} \times 20 \text{ cm}) - \pi(6 \text{ cm})^2$$
$$= \mathbf{(360 - 36\pi) \text{ cm}^2 = 246.96 \text{ cm}^2}$$

30. $V = \left(\text{Area}_{\text{base}}\right)(\text{Height})$
$$= (6 \text{ m} \times 10 \text{ m})(20 \text{ m})$$
$$= \left(60 \text{ m}^2\right)(20 \text{ m})$$
$$= \mathbf{1200 \text{ m}^3}$$

Practice 63

a. $\sqrt{75} = \sqrt{3 \cdot 5 \cdot 5} = \sqrt{3}\sqrt{5}\sqrt{5} = \sqrt{3}\,(5)$
$$= \mathbf{5\sqrt{3}}$$

b. $\sqrt{200} = \sqrt{2 \cdot 2 \cdot 2 \cdot 5 \cdot 5}$
$$= \sqrt{2}\sqrt{2}\sqrt{2}\sqrt{5}\sqrt{5} = (2)\sqrt{2}\,(5) = \mathbf{10\sqrt{2}}$$

c. $\sqrt{189} = \sqrt{3 \cdot 3 \cdot 3 \cdot 7}$
$$= \sqrt{3}\sqrt{3}\sqrt{3}\sqrt{7} = (3)\sqrt{3}\sqrt{7} = \mathbf{3\sqrt{21}}$$

d. $0.1\overline{6} = \mathbf{\dfrac{1}{6}}$

Problem Set 63

1. $-3(-N) - 7 = N + 1$
$$3N - 7 = N + 1$$
$$\underline{-N + 7 \quad -N + 7}$$
$$\frac{2N}{} = 8$$
$$N = \mathbf{4}$$

2.
$$\frac{17}{100} \cdot WN = 1020$$
$$\frac{100}{17} \cdot \frac{17}{100} \cdot WN = 1020 \cdot \frac{100}{17}$$
$$WN = \mathbf{6000}$$

Before, 100%   After

3.
$$\frac{3}{100} \cdot 1200 = R$$
$$R = 3 \cdot 12$$
$$R = \mathbf{36}$$

Before, 100%   After

4. Overall average $= \dfrac{(70 \times 90) + (30 \times 100)}{70 + 30}$
$$= \frac{6300 + 3000}{100}$$
$$= \frac{9300}{100} = \mathbf{93 \text{ lb}}$$

5. $1.05(WN) = 4.221$
$$\frac{1.05WN}{1.05} = \frac{4.221}{1.05}$$
$$WN = \mathbf{4.02}$$

6. $8 \text{ yd} \cdot \text{yd} \cdot \text{yd} \times \dfrac{3 \text{ ft}}{1 \text{ yd}} \times \dfrac{3 \text{ ft}}{1 \text{ yd}} \times \dfrac{3 \text{ ft}}{1 \text{ yd}}$

$\times \dfrac{12 \text{ in.}}{1 \text{ ft}} \times \dfrac{12 \text{ in.}}{1 \text{ ft}} \times \dfrac{12 \text{ in.}}{1 \text{ ft}} \times \dfrac{2.54 \text{ cm}}{1 \text{ in.}}$

$\times \dfrac{2.54 \text{ cm}}{1 \text{ in.}} \times \dfrac{2.54 \text{ cm}}{1 \text{ in.}} \times \dfrac{1 \text{ m}}{100 \text{ cm}} \times \dfrac{1 \text{ m}}{100 \text{ cm}}$

$\times \dfrac{1 \text{ m}}{100 \text{ cm}} = \dfrac{8(3)^3(12)^3(2.54)^3}{(100)^3} \text{ m}^3 = \mathbf{6.12 \text{ m}^3}$

7. $\sqrt{300} = \sqrt{2 \cdot 2 \cdot 3 \cdot 5 \cdot 5}$
$$= \sqrt{2}\sqrt{2}\sqrt{3}\sqrt{5}\sqrt{5} = (2)\sqrt{3}\,(5) = \mathbf{10\sqrt{3}}$$

8. $\sqrt{50} = \sqrt{2 \cdot 5 \cdot 5} = \sqrt{2}\sqrt{5}\sqrt{5} = \sqrt{2}\,(5)$
$$= \mathbf{5\sqrt{2}}$$

9. (a) **Rational**

(b) **Rational**

(c) **Irrational**

(d) **Rational**

10. (a) **Rationals, reals**

(b) **Naturals, wholes, integers, rationals, reals**

11. $\sqrt{\mathbf{16.0000001}}$ **is greater than 4 because 16.0000001 is greater than 4^2.**

12. (a) **False. No irrational number is a member of the set of rational numbers.**

(b) **False. Zero, a member of the set of whole numbers, is not a member of the set of natural numbers.**

13. (a) $\sqrt{225} - \sqrt{25} = 15 - 5 = \mathbf{10}$

(b) $\sqrt{49} + \sqrt{81} - \sqrt{36} = 7 + 9 - 6 = \mathbf{10}$

14. Since $7^2 = 49$ and $8^2 = 64$, the number whose square is 55 must lie between **7 and 8.**

15. $\sqrt{29} = \mathbf{5.3852}$

16. $\begin{cases} x - 2y = 8 \\ 2y - 3x = -4 \end{cases}$

$x - 2y = 8$

$\quad x = 2y + 8$

$\quad\quad 2y - 3x = -4$

$\quad 2y - 3(2y + 8) = -4$

$\quad 2y - 6y - 24 = -4$

$\quad\quad\quad\quad -4y = 20$

$\quad\quad\quad\quad\quad y = -5$

$\quad x - 2y = 8$

$\quad x - 2(-5) = 8$

$\quad\quad x + 10 = 8$

$\quad\quad\quad\quad x = -2$

Thus the solution is the ordered pair **(–2, –5).**

17. $\begin{cases} 5x - 4y = -6 \\ x - 2y = -6 \end{cases}$

$x - 2y = -6$

$\quad x = 2y - 6$

$\quad\quad 5x - 4y = -6$

$5(2y - 6) - 4y = -6$

$10y - 30 - 4y = -6$

$\quad\quad 6y - 30 = -6$

$\quad\quad\quad\quad 6y = 24$

$\quad\quad\quad\quad\quad y = 4$

$\quad x - 2y = -6$

$\quad x - 2(4) = -6$

$\quad\quad x - 8 = -6$

$\quad\quad\quad\quad x = 2$

Thus the solution is the ordered pair **(2, 4).**

18. $\mathbf{-1 < x \le 5}$

19. $y = -2x$

x	0	1	-2
y	0	-2	4

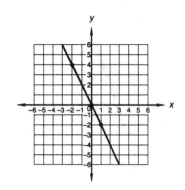

20. $y - 2x = 2$

$\quad y = 2x + 2$

x	0	1	-2
y	2	4	-2

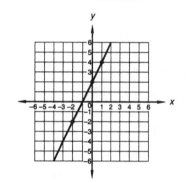

21. $\dfrac{\dfrac{a}{1}}{\dfrac{1}{a+b}} = \dfrac{\dfrac{a}{1} \cdot \dfrac{a+b}{1}}{\dfrac{1}{a+b} \cdot \dfrac{a+b}{1}} = \dfrac{a(a+b)}{1}$

$= a(a + b)$

22. $\dfrac{\dfrac{x}{1}}{\dfrac{x+y}{x}} = \dfrac{\dfrac{x}{1} \cdot \dfrac{x}{x+y}}{\dfrac{x+y}{x} \cdot \dfrac{x}{x+y}} = \dfrac{\dfrac{x^2}{x+y}}{1} = \dfrac{x^2}{x+y}$

23. $5(x^3 - 2x^2 - 7x) - 3(x^4 + 3x^2 - 4)$
$\quad + 2(x^5 - 3x^2 - 2x + 1)$
$= 5x^3 - 10x^2 - 35x - 3x^4 - 9x^2 + 12 + 2x^5$
$\quad - 6x^2 - 4x + 2$
$= \mathbf{2x^5 - 3x^4 + 5x^3 - 25x^2 - 39x + 14}$

24. $15m^2x^5k^4 - 5m^6x^6k^6 + 20m^4xk^5$
$= \mathbf{5m^2xk^4(3x^4 - m^4x^5k^2 + 4m^2k)}$

25. $\dfrac{3x^2m^5(2x^4m^2)}{3x^2m^5m^{-4}} = \dfrac{2x^4m^2}{m^{-4}} = \mathbf{2x^4m^6}$

26. $\left(\dfrac{3x^{-2}}{y^{-3}}\right)^{-2}\left(\dfrac{x^4}{y^6}\right)^2 = \dfrac{3^{-2}x^4}{y^6}\left(\dfrac{x^8}{y^{12}}\right) = \dfrac{x^{12}}{\mathbf{9y^{18}}}$

27. $m^{-2}xy^{-1} + mx^{-1} = \dfrac{x}{m^2y} + \dfrac{m}{x}$

$= \dfrac{x^2}{m^2xy} + \dfrac{m^3y}{m^2xy} = \dfrac{x^2 + m^3y}{m^2xy} = \dfrac{x^2 + m^3y}{m^2yx}$

28. $2x + 5 = 1$

$\dfrac{-5 \quad -5}{2x \quad = -4}$

$x = -2$

$-x^0 - x^2(x^0)^{-3} - \sqrt[3]{-y} = -1 - (-2)^2(1) - \sqrt[3]{-64}$

$= -1 - 4 + 4 = \mathbf{-1}$

29. $A = \text{Area}_{\text{rectangle}} - \text{Area}_{\text{semicircle}}$

$= (12 \text{ in.} \times 8 \text{ in.}) - \dfrac{1}{2}\pi (4 \text{ in.})^2$

$= \mathbf{(96 - 8\pi) \text{ in.}^2 = 70.88 \text{ in.}^2}$

30. $S.A. = 2\left(\text{Area}_{\text{base}}\right) + \text{Lateral Surface Area}$

$= 2\left[(9 \text{ ft} \times 12 \text{ ft}) + \dfrac{1}{2}(12 \text{ ft} \times 9 \text{ ft})\right]$

$\quad + \left(\text{Perimeter}_{\text{base}}\right)(\text{Height})$

$= 2\left(108 \text{ ft}^2 + 54 \text{ ft}^2\right) + (24 \text{ ft} + 9 \text{ ft} + 12 \text{ ft}$

$\quad + 15 \text{ ft})(25 \text{ ft})$

$= 2\left(162 \text{ ft}^2\right) + (60 \text{ ft})(25 \text{ ft})$

$= 324 \text{ ft}^2 + 1500 \text{ ft}^2$

$= \mathbf{1824 \text{ ft}^2}$

Practice 64

a. $x \nleq -2; \ D = \{\text{Positive Integers}\}$

b. $x \nleq 4; \ D = \{\text{Reals}\}$

c. $x - 5 \nless 0; \ D = \{\text{Integers}\}$

$x - 5 \nless 0$

$\dfrac{+5 \quad +5}{x \nless 5}$

d. $x + 2 < 5; \ D = \{\text{Integers}\}$

$x + 2 < 5$

$\dfrac{-2 \quad -2}{x < 3}$

Problem Set 64

1. $\dfrac{380}{100} \cdot 30,000 = WN$

$WN = 380 \cdot 300$

$WN = \mathbf{114,000}$

| of 30,000 | 114,000 is 380% |
| Before, 100% | After |

2. $\dfrac{60}{100} \cdot T = 3600$

$\dfrac{100}{60} \cdot \dfrac{60}{100} \cdot T = 3600 \cdot \dfrac{100}{60}$

$T = \mathbf{6000}$

of 6000	2400 is 40%
	3600 is 60%
Before, 100%	After

3. $\dfrac{40}{100} \cdot M = 184$

$\dfrac{100}{40} \cdot \dfrac{40}{100} \cdot M = 184 \cdot \dfrac{100}{40}$

$M = \mathbf{460}$

of 460	184 is 40%
	276 is 60%
Before, 100%	After

4. Overall average $= \dfrac{(6 \times 1000) + (3 \times 700)}{6 + 3}$

$= \dfrac{6000 + 2100}{9}$

$= \dfrac{8100}{9} = \mathbf{\$900}$

5. Range $= 11 - 2 = \mathbf{9}$

Median $= \dfrac{6 + 8}{2} = \mathbf{7}$

Mode $= \mathbf{5 \text{ and } 11}$

Mean $= (2 + 4 + 5 + 5 + 6 + 8 + 9 + 10$

$\quad + 11 + 11) \div 10$

$= 71 \div 10 = \mathbf{7.1}$

6. $x - 2 \not< -1;\ D = \{\text{Reals}\}$

$$x - 2 \not< -1$$
$$\underline{+2 \quad +2}$$
$$x \not< 1$$

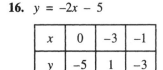

7. $x > -4;\ D = \{\textbf{Integers}\}$

Other answers are possible.

8. $\sqrt{72} = \sqrt{2 \cdot 2 \cdot 2 \cdot 3 \cdot 3} = \sqrt{2}\sqrt{2}\sqrt{2}\sqrt{3}\sqrt{3}$

$= (2)\sqrt{2}(3) = \mathbf{6\sqrt{2}}$

9. (a) Since $4^2 = 16$ and $5^2 = 25$, the number whose square is 23 must lie between **4 and 5.**

(b) $\sqrt{23} = \mathbf{4.796}$

10. (a) **Rationals, reals**

(b) **Irrationals, reals**

(c) **Rationals, reals**

11. $\sqrt{400} + \sqrt{225} - \sqrt{81} - \sqrt{100}$

$= 20 + 15 - 9 - 10 = \mathbf{16}$

12. (a) **True. Every natural number is a member of the set of whole numbers.**

(b) **False. Zero, a member of the set of whole numbers, is not a member of the set of natural numbers.**

13. $\begin{cases} 3x - 2y = 15 \\ 5x + y = 12 \end{cases}$

$$5x + y = 12$$
$$y = -5x + 12$$

$$3x - 2y = 15$$
$$3x - 2(-5x + 12) = 15$$
$$3x + 10x - 24 = 15$$
$$13x - 24 = 15$$
$$13x = 39$$
$$x = 3$$

$$5x + y = 12$$
$$5(3) + y = 12$$
$$15 + y = 12$$
$$y = -3$$

Thus the solution is the ordered pair **(3, –3).**

14. $\begin{cases} y + 2x = 12 \\ x + 2y = 12 \end{cases}$

$$y + 2x = 12$$
$$y = -2x + 12$$

$$x + 2y = 12$$
$$x + 2(-2x + 12) = 12$$
$$x - 4x + 24 = 12$$
$$-3x + 24 = 12$$
$$-3x = -12$$
$$x = 4$$

$$y + 2x = 12$$
$$y + 2(4) = 12$$
$$y + 8 = 12$$
$$y = 4$$

Thus the solution is the ordered pair **(4, 4).**

15. $y = -2x + 5$

x	0	2	4
y	5	1	–3

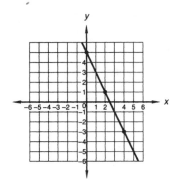

16. $y = -2x - 5$

x	0	–3	–1
y	–5	1	–3

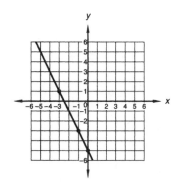

17. $g(x) = \left(x^2 - 3x\right)(x - 2)$

$g(-2) = \left[(-2)^2 - 3(-2)\right](-2 - 2)$

$= (4 + 6)(-4) = 10(-4) = \mathbf{-40}$

18. $(4x - 3)(12x + 2) = 48x^2 + 8x - 36x - 6$

$= \mathbf{48x^2 - 28x - 6}$

19. $(3x - 2)(5x - 2) = 15x^2 - 6x - 10x + 4$
$$= \mathbf{15x^2 - 16x + 4}$$

20. $\dfrac{\dfrac{x}{x}}{\dfrac{x}{y}} = \dfrac{\dfrac{x}{1} \cdot \dfrac{y}{x}}{\dfrac{x}{y} \cdot \dfrac{y}{x}} = \dfrac{\dfrac{xy}{x}}{1} = \dfrac{y}{1} = \mathbf{y}$

21. $ax^{-2}y^{-1} + bxy^{-1} = \dfrac{a}{x^2 y} + \dfrac{bx}{y} = \dfrac{a}{x^2 y} + \dfrac{bx^3}{x^2 y}$
$$= \dfrac{\mathbf{a + bx^3}}{\mathbf{x^2 y}}$$

22. $40x^4 ym^7 z - 20x^5 y^5 m^2 z + 20xy^2 m$
$$= \mathbf{20xym\left(2x^3 m^6 z - x^4 y^4 mz + y\right)}$$

23. $\dfrac{4x + 4x^2}{4x} = \dfrac{4x(1 + x)}{4x} = \mathbf{1 + x}$

24. $\dfrac{kp^{-2}k\left(p^0\right)^2}{kp(k)\left(p^{-2}\right)^2} = \dfrac{k^2 p^{-2}}{k^2 pp^{-4}} = \dfrac{p^{-2}}{p^{-3}} = \mathbf{p}$

25. $\left(\dfrac{3m^2}{y^{-4}}\right)^2 \left(\dfrac{m}{y}\right) = \dfrac{9m^4 m}{y^{-8} y} = \dfrac{9m^5}{y^{-7}} = \mathbf{9m^5 y^7}$

26. $-\dfrac{3x^2 y^{-2}}{x^{-2} y^{-2}} - 2x^4 yy^{-1} + 4x^3 xyy^{-1} - \dfrac{2x^2}{x^{-2}}$
$$= -3x^4 - 2x^4 + 4x^4 - 2x^4 = -3x^4 = \mathbf{-\dfrac{3}{x^{-4}}}$$

27. $-\dfrac{x^{-2}}{y^4}\left(x^2 y^4 - \dfrac{3x^{-2}}{y^4} - \dfrac{x^2}{y^{-4}}\right)$
$$= -1 + \dfrac{3x^{-4}}{y^8} + 1 = \mathbf{\dfrac{3}{x^4 y^8}}$$

28.
$$2x + 6 = -4 \qquad\qquad 4 - 3y = 13$$
$$\underline{-6 \quad -6} \qquad \underline{-4 -4}$$
$$2x = -10 \qquad\quad -3y = 9$$
$$x = -5 \qquad\qquad\quad y = -3$$

$x - \left(x^2\right)^0 (x - y) - |x - y|$
$= -5 - [-5 - (-3)] - |-5 - (-3)|$
$= -5 - (-2) - 2 = -5 + 2 - 2 = \mathbf{-5}$

29. $P = \left(14 + 8 + \dfrac{2\pi(4)}{2} + 6 + \dfrac{2\pi(4)}{2}\right)$ cm
$$= (28 + 8\pi) \text{ cm} = \mathbf{53.12 \text{ cm}}$$

30. $V = \left(\text{Area}_{\text{base}}\right)(\text{Height})$
$$= \left(40 \text{ m}^2\right)(14 \text{ m}) = \mathbf{560 \text{ m}^3}$$

Practice 65

a. $3\sqrt{3} - 2\sqrt{2} + 5\sqrt{3} = \mathbf{8\sqrt{3} - 2\sqrt{2}}$

b. $12\sqrt{7} + 6\sqrt{7} - 20\sqrt{7} = 18\sqrt{7} - 20\sqrt{7}$
$$= \mathbf{-2\sqrt{7}}$$

c. $\sqrt{2} + 3\sqrt{2} - 4\sqrt{2} + 6\sqrt{3}$
$$= 4\sqrt{2} - 4\sqrt{2} + 6\sqrt{3} = \mathbf{6\sqrt{3}}$$

d. Weighted average $= \dfrac{1(70) + 5(80) + 7(100)}{1 + 5 + 7}$
$$= \dfrac{1170}{13} = \mathbf{90}$$

Problem Set 65

1. $W.A. = \dfrac{1(75) + 2(80) + 3(88) + 4(93)}{1 + 2 + 3 + 4}$
$$= \dfrac{871}{10} = \mathbf{87.1}$$

2. $\qquad\qquad \dfrac{18}{100} \cdot G = 45$
$$\dfrac{100}{18} \cdot \dfrac{18}{100} \cdot G = 45 \cdot \dfrac{100}{18}$$
$$G = \mathbf{250}$$

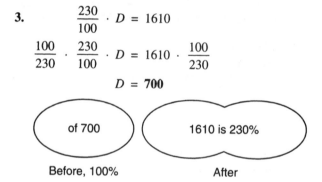

Before, 100%   After

3. $\qquad\qquad \dfrac{230}{100} \cdot D = 1610$
$$\dfrac{100}{230} \cdot \dfrac{230}{100} \cdot D = 1610 \cdot \dfrac{100}{230}$$
$$D = \mathbf{700}$$

of 700   1610 is 230%

Before, 100%   After

4. $7\sqrt{5} - \sqrt{5} + 5\sqrt{3} - 3\sqrt{3} = \mathbf{6\sqrt{5} + 2\sqrt{3}}$

5. $8\sqrt{7} - 4\sqrt{11} - 3\sqrt{7} + 7\sqrt{11}$
$$= \mathbf{5\sqrt{7} + 3\sqrt{11}}$$

6. $\sqrt{196} - \sqrt{49} - \sqrt{121} + \sqrt{256}$
$$= 14 - 7 - 11 + 16 = \mathbf{12}$$

7. $x + 3 > 5; \; D = \{\text{Positive Integers}\}$
$$x + 3 > 5$$
$$\underline{ -3 \quad -3}$$
$$x > 2$$

8. $x < 0; \; D = \{\text{Reals}\}$

9. (a) **Rational**

    (b) **Irrational**

    (c) **Rational**

10. (a) **Irrationals, reals**

    (b) **Rationals, reals**

11. (a) **False. None of the natural numbers are irrational.**

    (b) **True. Every whole number is an integer.**

12. $\begin{cases} x + y = 10 \\ -x + y = 0 \end{cases}$

$$x + y = 10$$
$$x = -y + 10$$
$$-x + y = 0$$
$$-(-y + 10) + y = 0$$
$$y - 10 + y = 0$$
$$2y - 10 = 0$$
$$2y = 10$$
$$y = 5$$

$$x + y = 10$$
$$x + 5 = 10$$
$$x = 5$$

Thus the solution is the ordered pair **(5, 5)**.

13. $\begin{cases} 3x - 3y = 3 \\ x - 5y = -3 \end{cases}$

$$x - 5y = -3$$
$$x = 5y - 3$$

$$3x - 3y = 3$$
$$3(5y - 3) - 3y = 3$$
$$15y - 9 - 3y = 3$$
$$12y - 9 = 3$$
$$12y = 12$$
$$y = 1$$

$$x - 5y = -3$$
$$x - 5(1) = -3$$
$$x - 5 = -3$$
$$x = 2$$

Thus the solution is the ordered pair **(2, 1)**.

14. $y = -\dfrac{1}{2}x$

x	0	4	-4
y	0	-2	2

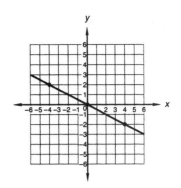

15. $\dfrac{1}{2}y = x - 1$

$$y = 2x - 2$$

x	0	1	-1
y	-2	0	-4

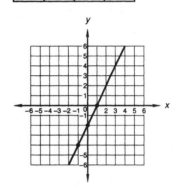

16. $\dfrac{a}{x + y} + \dfrac{5}{x^2} = \dfrac{ax^2}{x^2(x + y)} + \dfrac{5(x + y)}{x^2(x + y)}$

$$= \dfrac{ax^2 + 5(x + y)}{x^2(x + y)}$$

17. $1 + \dfrac{a}{b} - \dfrac{a^3}{b^2} = \dfrac{b^2}{b^2} + \dfrac{ab}{b^2} - \dfrac{a^3}{b^2}$

$$= \dfrac{b^2 + ab - a^3}{b^2}$$

18. $x + \dfrac{1}{x} + \dfrac{1}{x^2} = \dfrac{x^3}{x^2} + \dfrac{x}{x^2} + \dfrac{1}{x^2} = \dfrac{x^3 + x + 1}{x^2}$

19. $cz^{-1}x^2 + dx^{-1}z = \dfrac{cx^2}{z} + \dfrac{dz}{x} = \dfrac{cx^3}{xz} + \dfrac{dz^2}{xz}$

$$= \dfrac{cx^3 + dz^2}{xz} = \dfrac{cx^3 + dz^2}{zx}$$

20. $\dfrac{\frac{a}{x}}{\frac{1}{a^2}} = \dfrac{\frac{a}{x} \cdot \frac{a^2}{1}}{\frac{1}{a^2} \cdot \frac{a^2}{1}} = \dfrac{\frac{a^3}{x}}{1} = \dfrac{a^3}{x}$

21. $(3p - 4)(2p + 5) = 6p^2 + 15p - 8p - 20$

$$= \mathbf{6p^2 + 7p - 20}$$

22. $-3x^{-2}y^2\left(\dfrac{y^{-2}}{x^{-2}} + 4x^2y - \dfrac{2y^{-2}}{x^{-1}}\right)$

$= -3 - 12y^3 + \dfrac{6x^{-2}}{x^{-1}} = -3 - 12y^3 + \dfrac{6}{x}$

23. $\dfrac{4kx - 4kx^2}{4kx} = \dfrac{4kx(1-x)}{4kx} = 1 - x$

24. $\dfrac{x^2 x^{-2} x^0 y^2}{y^2\left(x^{-4}\right)^2} = \dfrac{y^2}{y^2 x^{-8}} = x^8$

25. $\left(\dfrac{2x^{-2}y}{p}\right)^2\left(\dfrac{p^2 x}{2}\right)^{-2} = \dfrac{4x^{-4}y^2}{p^2}\left(\dfrac{p^{-4}x^{-2}}{2^{-2}}\right)$

$= 16x^{-6}y^2 p^{-6}$

26. $\dfrac{3a^2 x}{m} + \dfrac{5xm^{-1}}{a^{-2}} - \dfrac{4aax^{-1}}{x^{-2}m}$

$= \dfrac{3a^2 x}{m} + \dfrac{5a^2 x}{m} - \dfrac{4a^2 x}{m} = \dfrac{4a^2 x}{m}$

27. $-10 - 3x = 2x \qquad m + 3 = 6$

$\dfrac{+3x \quad +3x}{-10 \quad = 5x} \qquad \dfrac{-3 \quad -3}{m = 3}$

$x = -2$

$-x^{-4} - x^2(x - m) = -(-2)^{-4} - (-2)^2(-2 - 3)$

$= -\dfrac{1}{16} - 4(-5) = 20 - \dfrac{1}{16} = 19\dfrac{15}{16} = \dfrac{319}{16}$

28. $-3^0 - 3\left(-2 - 2^0\right)\left(-8^0 - 5\right) - \sqrt[4]{16}$

$= -1 - 3(-3)(-6) - 2 = -1 - 54 - 2 = -57$

29. $A = \dfrac{1}{2}(20 \text{ in.} \times 13 \text{ in.}) + \dfrac{1}{2}(20 \text{ in.} \times 13 \text{ in.})$

$= 130 \text{ in.}^2 + 130 \text{ in.}^2$

$= 260 \text{ in.}^2$

30. Lateral $S.A. = \left(\text{Perimeter}_{\text{base}}\right)(\text{Height})$

$= (10 \text{ ft} + 10 \text{ ft} + 10 \text{ ft} + 10 \text{ ft}$
$+ 10 \text{ ft})(18 \text{ ft})$

$= (50 \text{ ft})(18 \text{ ft})$

$= 900 \text{ ft}^2$

Practice 66

a. $\sqrt{24} + \sqrt{48}$

$= \sqrt{2 \cdot 2 \cdot 2 \cdot 3} + \sqrt{2 \cdot 2 \cdot 2 \cdot 2 \cdot 3}$

$= \sqrt{2}\sqrt{2}\sqrt{2}\sqrt{3} + \sqrt{2}\sqrt{2}\sqrt{2}\sqrt{2}\sqrt{3}$

$= (2)\sqrt{2}\sqrt{3} + (2)(2)\sqrt{3} = 2\sqrt{6} + 4\sqrt{3}$

b. $2\sqrt{18} - \sqrt{27} = 2\sqrt{2 \cdot 3 \cdot 3} - \sqrt{3 \cdot 3 \cdot 3}$

$= 2\sqrt{2}\sqrt{3}\sqrt{3} - \sqrt{3}\sqrt{3}\sqrt{3} = (2)\sqrt{2}(3) - (3)\sqrt{3}$

$= 6\sqrt{2} - 3\sqrt{3}$

c. $\sqrt{50,000,000} = \sqrt{1,000,000 \cdot 50}$

$= \sqrt{1,000,000}\sqrt{50} = 1000\sqrt{50}$

$= 1000\sqrt{5 \cdot 5 \cdot 2} = 1000\sqrt{5}\sqrt{5}\sqrt{2}$

$= 1000(5)\sqrt{2} = 5000\sqrt{2}$

Problem Set 66

1. $3(-N) - 7 = 2N + 3$

$-3N - 7 = 2N + 3$

$\dfrac{-2N + 7 \quad -2N + 7}{-5N \quad = \quad 10}$

$N = -2$

2. $\dfrac{80}{100} \cdot E = 60$

$\dfrac{100}{80} \cdot \dfrac{80}{100} \cdot E = 60 \cdot \dfrac{100}{80}$

$E = 75$

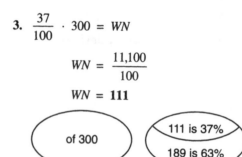

Before, 100%   After

of 75 | 15 is 20% / 60 is 80%

3. $\dfrac{37}{100} \cdot 300 = WN$

$WN = \dfrac{11,100}{100}$

$WN = 111$

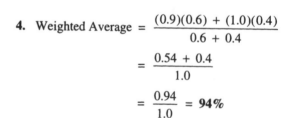

Before, 100%   After

of 300 | 111 is 37% / 189 is 63%

4. Weighted Average $= \dfrac{(0.9)(0.6) + (1.0)(0.4)}{0.6 + 0.4}$

$= \dfrac{0.54 + 0.4}{1.0}$

$= \dfrac{0.94}{1.0} = 94\%$

5. Range $= 96 - 60 = 36$

Median $= 89$

Mode $= 92$

Mean $= \dfrac{60 + 78 + 85 + 89 + 92 + 92 + 96}{7}$

$= \dfrac{592}{7} = 84.57$

6. $4\frac{2}{5}(WN) = 7\frac{7}{10}$

$$\frac{4\frac{2}{5}WN}{4\frac{2}{5}} = \frac{7\frac{7}{10}}{4\frac{2}{5}}$$

$$WN = \frac{77}{10} \cdot \frac{5}{22}$$

$$WN = 1\frac{3}{4}$$

7. $2\frac{1}{8}x - \frac{1}{5} = (5^2)(2^{-3})$

$$2\frac{1}{8}x - \frac{1}{5} = \frac{25}{8}$$

$$\underline{\quad +\frac{1}{5} \qquad +\frac{1}{5}\quad}$$

$$2\frac{1}{8}x \qquad = 3\frac{13}{40}$$

$$\frac{2\frac{1}{8}x}{2\frac{1}{8}} = \frac{3\frac{13}{40}}{2\frac{1}{8}}$$

$$x = \frac{133}{40} \cdot \frac{8}{17}$$

$$x = \frac{\mathbf{133}}{\mathbf{85}}$$

8. $0.003k + 0.188 - 0.001k = 0.2k - 0.01$

$$3k + 188 - k = 200k - 10$$

$$2k + 188 = 200k - 10$$

$$2k - 200k = -10 - 188$$

$$-198k = -198$$

$$k = \mathbf{1}$$

9. $5\sqrt{20} - 6\sqrt{32}$

$= 5\sqrt{2 \cdot 2 \cdot 5} - 6\sqrt{2 \cdot 2 \cdot 2 \cdot 2 \cdot 2}$

$= 5\sqrt{2}\sqrt{2}\sqrt{5} - 6\sqrt{2}\sqrt{2}\sqrt{2}\sqrt{2}\sqrt{2}$

$= 5(2)\sqrt{5} - 6(2)(2)\sqrt{2} = \mathbf{10\sqrt{5} - 24\sqrt{2}}$

10. $2\sqrt{45} - 3\sqrt{20}$

$= 2\sqrt{3 \cdot 3 \cdot 5} - 3\sqrt{2 \cdot 2 \cdot 5}$

$= 2\sqrt{3}\sqrt{3}\sqrt{5} - 3\sqrt{2}\sqrt{2}\sqrt{5}$

$= 2(3)\sqrt{5} - 3(2)\sqrt{5}$

$= 6\sqrt{5} - 6\sqrt{5} = \mathbf{0}$

11. $\sqrt{70,000,000} = \sqrt{1,000,000 \cdot 70}$

$= \sqrt{1,000,000}\sqrt{70} = \mathbf{1000\sqrt{70}}$

12. $x - 3 \not< -5;\ D = \{\text{Positive Integers}\}$

$$x - 3 \not< -5$$

$$\underline{\quad +3 \qquad +3\quad}$$

$$x \not< -2$$

13. (a) **Naturals, wholes, integers, rationals, reals**

(b) **Integers, rationals, reals**

14. (a) **True. Every integer is a rational number.**

(b) **False. Negative integers are not whole numbers.**

15. $\begin{cases} x + 2y = 0 \\ 3x + y = -10 \end{cases}$

$$x + 2y = 0$$

$$x = -2y$$

$$3x + y = -10$$

$$3(-2y) + y = -10$$

$$-6y + y = -10$$

$$-5y = -10$$

$$y = 2$$

$$x + 2y = 0$$

$$x + 2(2) = 0$$

$$x + 4 = 0$$

$$x = -4$$

Thus the solution is the ordered pair **(−4, 2).**

16. $\begin{cases} 5x + 4y = -28 \\ x - y = -2 \end{cases}$

$$x - y = -2$$

$$x = y - 2$$

$$5x + 4y = -28$$

$$5(y - 2) + 4y = -28$$

$$5y - 10 + 4y = -28$$

$$9y - 10 = -28$$

$$9y = -18$$

$$y = -2$$

$$x - y = -2$$

$$x - (-2) = -2$$

$$x + 2 = -2$$

$$x = -4$$

Thus the solution is the ordered pair **(−4, −2).**

17. $\dfrac{a}{x^2 y} + \dfrac{b}{x + y} = \dfrac{a(x + y)}{x^2 y(x + y)} + \dfrac{bx^2 y}{x^2 y(x + y)}$

$= \dfrac{\mathbf{a(x + y) + bx^2 y}}{\mathbf{x^2 y(x + y)}}$

18. $m + \dfrac{1}{m^2} = \dfrac{m^3}{m^2} + \dfrac{1}{m^2} = \dfrac{m^3 + 1}{m^2}$

19. $y = 2x + 2$

x	0	1	–2
y	2	4	–2

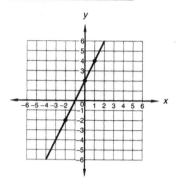

20. $y = 2x - 2$

x	0	1	2
y	–2	0	2

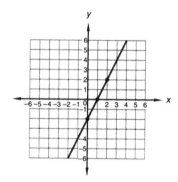

21. $(4x + 5)^2 = (4x + 5)(4x + 5)$
$= 16x^2 + 20x + 20x + 25 = \mathbf{16x^2 + 40x + 25}$

22. $(5x - 3)(3x - 1) = 15x^2 - 5x - 9x + 3$
$= \mathbf{15x^2 - 14x + 3}$

23. $px^{-1} + q^{-2}xy = \dfrac{p}{x} + \dfrac{xy}{q^2} = \dfrac{pq^2}{xq^2} + \dfrac{x^2y}{xq^2}$

$= \dfrac{pq^2 + x^2y}{xq^2}$

24. $\dfrac{\dfrac{x}{1}}{\dfrac{1}{xy + b}} = \dfrac{\dfrac{x}{1} \cdot \dfrac{xy + b}{1}}{\dfrac{1}{xy + b} \cdot \dfrac{xy + b}{1}} = \dfrac{x(xy + b)}{1}$

$= \mathbf{x(xy + b)}$

25. $\dfrac{\dfrac{a}{1}}{\dfrac{1}{x}} = \dfrac{\dfrac{a}{1} \cdot \dfrac{x}{1}}{\dfrac{1}{x} \cdot \dfrac{x}{1}} = \dfrac{ax}{1} = \mathbf{ax}$

26. $12x^2y^3p^4 - 4x^3y^2p^6 + 16x^4y^4p^4$
$= \mathbf{4x^2y^2p^4(3y - xp^2 + 4x^2y^2)}$

27. $\left[(-3 - 4^0) - (-3 - 2)\right] - \sqrt{25}$
$= [(-3 - 1) - (-5)] - 5$
$= -4 + 5 - 5 = \mathbf{-4}$

28. $\dfrac{(3x^3y^5m^2)^2(x^2y)^{-2}}{x^2y^0y^{-4}} = \dfrac{9x^6y^{10}m^4x^{-4}y^{-2}}{x^2y^{-4}}$
$= \mathbf{9y^{12}m^4}$

29. $P = \left(12 + 20 + \dfrac{2\pi(6)}{2} + 8 + \dfrac{2\pi(6)}{2}\right)$ cm
$= \mathbf{(40 + 12\pi)}$ cm $= \mathbf{77.68}$ cm

30. Volume $= \left(\text{Area}_{\text{base}}\right)(\text{Height})$
$= \left[(20 \text{ m} \times 20 \text{ m}) + \dfrac{1}{2}(20 \text{ m} \times 15 \text{ m})\right]$
$\times 2 \text{ m}$
$= \left(400 \text{ m}^2 + 150 \text{ m}^2\right)(2 \text{ m})$
$= \left(550 \text{ m}^2\right)(2 \text{ m})$
$= \mathbf{1100 \text{ m}^3}$

Practice 67

a. (a) $\begin{cases} 3x + 4y = -7 \\ 2x + 3y = -6 \end{cases}$
(b)

(3)(a) $\quad 9x + 12y = -21$
(–4)(b) $\quad \underline{-8x - 12y = 24}$
$\qquad\qquad\qquad x = 3$

(a) $\quad 3x + 4y = -7$
$\qquad 3(3) + 4y = -7$
$\qquad 9 + 4y = -7$
$\qquad\qquad 4y = -16$
$\qquad\qquad\ y = -4$

Thus the solution is the ordered pair $\mathbf{(3, -4)}$.

b. (a) $\begin{cases} 5x + 2y = -3 \\ 2x + 3y = -10 \end{cases}$
(b)

(3)(a) $\quad 15x + 6y = -9$
(–2)(b) $\quad \underline{-4x - 6y = 20}$
$\qquad\quad 11x \qquad\ = 11$
$\qquad\qquad\quad x = 1$

(a) $\quad 5x + 2y = -3$
$\qquad 5(1) + 2y = -3$
$\qquad 5 + 2y = -3$
$\qquad\qquad 2y = -8$
$\qquad\qquad\ y = -4$

Thus the solution is the ordered pair $\mathbf{(1, -4)}$.

Problem Set 67

1. $\dfrac{P}{T} = \dfrac{2}{9}$

$\dfrac{P}{9180} = \dfrac{2}{9}$

$9P = 2 \cdot 9180$

$P = \dfrac{2 \cdot 9180}{9}$

$P = \mathbf{2040}$

2. $\dfrac{80}{100} \cdot A = 2{,}300{,}000$

$\dfrac{100}{80} \cdot \dfrac{80}{100} \cdot A = 2{,}300{,}000 \cdot \dfrac{100}{80}$

$A = \mathbf{2{,}875{,}000}$

3. Weighted Average $= \dfrac{1(88) + 2(93)}{1 + 2}$

$= \dfrac{274}{3} = \mathbf{91.33}$

4. $200 \text{ m} \cdot \text{m} \cdot \text{m} \times \dfrac{100 \text{ cm}}{1 \text{ m}} \times \dfrac{100 \text{ cm}}{1 \text{ m}}$

$\times \dfrac{100 \text{ cm}}{1 \text{ m}} \times \dfrac{1 \text{ in.}}{2.54 \text{ cm}} \times \dfrac{1 \text{ in.}}{2.54 \text{ cm}} \times \dfrac{1 \text{ in.}}{2.54 \text{ cm}}$

$= \dfrac{200(100)^3}{(2.54)^3} \text{ in.}^3 = \mathbf{12{,}204{,}748.82 \text{ in.}^3}$

5. $\dfrac{1}{2}x + 0.75 = \dfrac{43}{4}$

$50x + 75 = 1075$

$50x = 1000$

$x = \mathbf{20}$

6. (a) $\begin{cases} x + y = 4 \\ x - y = 2 \end{cases}$
(b)

(1)(a) $x + y = 4$
(1)(b) $\underline{x - y = 2}$
$\quad 2x \quad\;\; = 6$
$\qquad\quad x = 3$

(a) $x + y = 4$
$\quad 3 + y = 4$
$\qquad\quad y = 1$

Thus the solution is the ordered pair **(3, 1)**.

7. (a) $\begin{cases} 2x + 3y = 7 \\ 2x - y = 3 \end{cases}$
(b)

(1)(a) $\quad 2x + 3y = \;\; 7$
(−1)(b) $\underline{-2x + \;\; y = -3}$
$\qquad\qquad\; 4y = \;\; 4$
$\qquad\qquad\;\; y = 1$

(a) $2x + 3y = 7$
$\quad 2x + 3(1) = 7$
$\quad 2x + 3 = 7$
$\qquad\quad 2x = 4$
$\qquad\qquad x = 2$

Thus the solution is the ordered pair **(2, 1)**.

8. (a) $\begin{cases} 2x - 4y = -4 \\ 3x + 2y = 18 \end{cases}$
(b)

(1)(a) $\quad 2x - 4y = -4$
(2)(b) $\underline{6x + 4y = 36}$
$\quad\; 8x \qquad\;\; = 32$
$\qquad\qquad x = 4$

(a) $\quad 2x - 4y = -4$
$\quad\; 2(4) - 4y = -4$
$\qquad\; 8 - 4y = -4$
$\qquad\quad\; -4y = -12$
$\qquad\qquad\;\; y = 3$

Thus the solution is the ordered pair **(4, 3)**.

9. $6\sqrt{45} + \sqrt{180{,}000}$

$= 6\sqrt{3 \cdot 3 \cdot 5} + \sqrt{10{,}000 \cdot 18}$

$= 6\sqrt{3}\sqrt{3}\sqrt{5} + \sqrt{10{,}000}\sqrt{2 \cdot 3 \cdot 3}$

$= 6(3)\sqrt{5} + 100\sqrt{2}\sqrt{3}\sqrt{3}$

$= 18\sqrt{5} + 100\sqrt{2}(3) = \mathbf{18\sqrt{5} + 300\sqrt{2}}$

10. $2\sqrt{8} - 3\sqrt{32}$

$= 2\sqrt{2 \cdot 2 \cdot 2} - 3\sqrt{2 \cdot 2 \cdot 2 \cdot 2 \cdot 2}$

$= 2\sqrt{2}\sqrt{2}\sqrt{2} - 3\sqrt{2}\sqrt{2}\sqrt{2}\sqrt{2}\sqrt{2}$

$= 2(2)\sqrt{2} - 3(2)(2)\sqrt{2}$

$= 4\sqrt{2} - 12\sqrt{2} = \mathbf{-8\sqrt{2}}$

11. $2\sqrt{12} - 3\sqrt{18} = 2\sqrt{2 \cdot 2 \cdot 3} - 3\sqrt{2 \cdot 3 \cdot 3}$

$= 2\sqrt{2}\sqrt{2}\sqrt{3} - 3\sqrt{2}\sqrt{3}\sqrt{3}$

$= 2(2)\sqrt{3} - 3\sqrt{2}(3) = \mathbf{4\sqrt{3} - 9\sqrt{2}}$

12. $x - 3 > 1; \; D = \{\text{Reals}\}$

$x - 3 > 1$
$\underline{+3 \quad +3}$
$\quad x > 4$

13. (a) **Rational**

(b) **Irrational**

(c) **Rational**

(d) **Rational**

14. (a) **True. Every natural number is also a rational number.**

(b) **False. No integer is a member of the set of irrational numbers.**

15. (a) Since $12^2 = 144$ and $13^2 = 169$, the number whose square is 145 is closest to **12**.

(b) $\sqrt{145} = \mathbf{12.0416}$

16. $\begin{cases} 4x + y = 25 \\ x - 3y = -10 \end{cases}$

$$x - 3y = -10$$
$$x = 3y - 10$$

$$4x + y = 25$$
$$4(3y - 10) + y = 25$$
$$12y - 40 + y = 25$$
$$13y - 40 = 25$$
$$13y = 65$$
$$y = 5$$

$$x - 3y = -10$$
$$x - 3(5) = -10$$
$$x - 15 = -10$$
$$x = 5$$

Thus the solution is the ordered pair **(5, 5)**.

17. $x = -2$

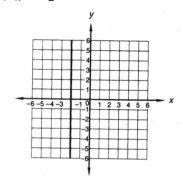

18. $y = -\dfrac{1}{2}x + 3$

x	0	2	-2
y	3	2	4

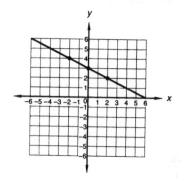

19. $f(x) = x^4 - x^3 + 2x - 5$

$$f(-1) = (-1)^4 - (-1)^3 + 2(-1) - 5$$
$$= 1 - (-1) - 2 - 5$$
$$= 1 + 1 - 2 - 5$$
$$= \mathbf{-5}$$

20. $\dfrac{m}{x^2 a} + \dfrac{3}{a(a + x)}$

$$= \dfrac{m(a + x)}{x^2 a(a + x)} + \dfrac{3x^2}{x^2 a(a + x)}$$

$$= \dfrac{m(a + x) + 3x^2}{ax^2(a + x)}$$

21. $4x + \dfrac{1}{y} = \dfrac{4xy}{y} + \dfrac{1}{y} = \dfrac{4xy + 1}{y}$

22. $\dfrac{\frac{1}{a}}{a} = \dfrac{\frac{1}{a} \cdot \frac{1}{a}}{\frac{a}{1} \cdot \frac{1}{a}} = \dfrac{\frac{1}{a^2}}{1} = \dfrac{1}{a^2}$

23. $\dfrac{\frac{a}{1}}{\frac{a^2}{a + b}} = \dfrac{\frac{a}{1} \cdot \frac{a + b}{a^2}}{\frac{a^2}{a + b} \cdot \frac{a + b}{a^2}} = \dfrac{\frac{a(a + b)}{a^2}}{1}$

$$= \dfrac{a + b}{a}$$

24. $\dfrac{12mx + 12mxy}{12mx} = \dfrac{12mx(1 + y)}{12mx} = \mathbf{1 + y}$

25. $(2^2 y^3 p^4)^3 = 2^6 y^9 p^{12} = \mathbf{64 y^9 p^{12}}$

26. $\left(\dfrac{y^{-5}}{x^2} - \dfrac{3y^5 x^{-2}}{p} + \dfrac{y^5}{x^{-2}} \right) \dfrac{x^{-2}}{y^5}$

$$= \dfrac{y^{-5} x^{-2}}{x^2 y^5} - \dfrac{3x^{-4}}{p} + 1$$

$$= \dfrac{1}{x^4 y^{10}} - \dfrac{3}{x^4 p} + 1$$

27. $2x - 8 = 4x$
$$-2x = 8$$
$$x = -4$$

$$-x^0 - x^2 - a(x - a) - |x^2|$$
$$= -1 - (-4)^2 - 4(-4 - 4) - |(-4)^2|$$
$$= -1 - 16 + 32 - 16 = \mathbf{-1}$$

28. $-2\left\{ \left[(-2 - 3) - (-2^0 - 2) - 2 \right] - 2 \right\} \pm \sqrt{4}$

$$= -2\left\{ [-5 - (-3) - 2] - 2 \right\} \pm 2$$
$$= -2(-4 - 2) \pm 2 = -2(-6) \pm 2$$
$$= 12 \pm 2 = \mathbf{10, 14}$$

29. $\text{Area} = \text{Area}_{\text{parallelogram}} - \text{Area}_{\text{triangle}}$

$= \left[\dfrac{1}{2}\left(12\dfrac{1}{2} \text{ in.} \times 9 \text{ in.}\right) \right.$

$\left. + \dfrac{1}{2}\left(12\dfrac{1}{2} \text{ in.} \times 9 \text{ in.}\right)\right] - \dfrac{1}{2}(9 \text{ in.} \times 5 \text{ in.})$

$= \left(56\dfrac{1}{4} \text{ in.}^2 + 56\dfrac{1}{4} \text{ in.}^2\right) - 22\dfrac{1}{2} \text{ in.}^2$

$= 112\dfrac{1}{2} \text{ in.}^2 - 22\dfrac{1}{2} \text{ in.}^2 = \textbf{90 in.}^2$

30. $S.A. = 2\left(\text{Area}_{\text{triangle}}\right) + \text{Area}_{\text{bottom}} + \text{Area}_{\text{side}}$

$\quad + \text{Area}_{\text{top}}$

$= 2\left[\dfrac{1}{2}(20 \text{ ft} \times 15 \text{ ft})\right] + (10 \text{ ft} \times 15 \text{ ft})$

$\quad + (20 \text{ ft} \times 10 \text{ ft}) + (25 \text{ ft} \times 10 \text{ ft})$

$= 2(150 \text{ ft}^2) + 150 \text{ ft}^2 + 200 \text{ ft}^2 + 250 \text{ ft}^2$

$= 300 \text{ ft}^2 + 600 \text{ ft}^2$

$= \textbf{900 ft}^2$

Practice 68

a. $\dfrac{\dfrac{1}{w} + \dfrac{c}{w}}{\dfrac{1}{c}} = \dfrac{\dfrac{1+c}{w}}{\dfrac{1}{c}} = \dfrac{\dfrac{1+c}{w} \cdot \dfrac{c}{1}}{\dfrac{1}{c} \cdot \dfrac{c}{1}} = \dfrac{(1+c)c}{w}$

b. $\dfrac{\dfrac{1}{m} + 5}{\dfrac{2}{m} - \dfrac{x}{m}} = \dfrac{\dfrac{1}{m} + \dfrac{5m}{m}}{\dfrac{2-x}{m}} = \dfrac{\dfrac{1+5m}{m} \cdot \dfrac{m}{2-x}}{\dfrac{2-x}{m} \cdot \dfrac{m}{2-x}}$

$= \dfrac{1+5m}{2-x}$

c. $\dfrac{ax^{-1} + by^{-1}}{x^{-1}} = \dfrac{\dfrac{a}{x} + \dfrac{b}{y}}{\dfrac{1}{x}} = \dfrac{\dfrac{ay}{xy} + \dfrac{bx}{xy}}{\dfrac{1}{x}}$

$= \dfrac{\dfrac{ay+bx}{xy} \cdot \dfrac{x}{1}}{\dfrac{1}{x} \cdot \dfrac{x}{1}} = \dfrac{ay+bx}{y}$

Problem Set 68

1. $7N + 42 = 2(-N) + 87$

$7N + 42 = -2N + 87$

$\underline{+2N - 42 \quad\quad +2N - 42}$

$9N \quad\quad = \quad\quad 45$

$N = \textbf{5}$

2. $\dfrac{230}{100} \cdot C = 345$

$\dfrac{100}{230} \cdot \dfrac{230}{100} \cdot C = 345 \cdot \dfrac{100}{230}$

$C = \textbf{150}$

| of 150 | 345 is 230% |
| Before, 100% | After |

3. $\dfrac{37}{100} \cdot P = 1110$

$\dfrac{100}{37} \cdot \dfrac{37}{100} \cdot P = 1110 \cdot \dfrac{100}{37}$

$P = \textbf{3000}$

of 3000	1110 is 37%
	1890 is 63%
Before, 100%	After

4. $\text{Overall Average} = \dfrac{(3 \times 4) + (27 \times 8)}{3 + 27}$

$= \dfrac{228}{30} = \textbf{7.6}$

5. $\text{Range} = 170 - 119 = \textbf{51}$

$\text{Median} = \textbf{134}$

$\text{Mode} = \textbf{134}$

$\text{Mean} = (119 + 122 + 133 + 134 + 134 + 152$

$\quad + 170) \div 7$

$= 964 \div 7 = \textbf{137.71}$

6. $12{,}000 \text{ m} \cdot \text{m} \cdot \text{m} \times \dfrac{100 \text{ cm}}{1 \text{ m}} \times \dfrac{100 \text{ cm}}{1 \text{ m}}$

$\times \dfrac{100 \text{ cm}}{1 \text{ m}} \times \dfrac{1 \text{ in.}}{2.54 \text{ cm}} \times \dfrac{1 \text{ in.}}{2.54 \text{ cm}} \times \dfrac{1 \text{ in.}}{2.54 \text{ cm}}$

$\times \dfrac{1 \text{ ft}}{12 \text{ in.}} \times \dfrac{1 \text{ ft}}{12 \text{ in.}} \times \dfrac{1 \text{ ft}}{12 \text{ in.}} \times \dfrac{1 \text{ yd}}{3 \text{ ft}} \times \dfrac{1 \text{ yd}}{3 \text{ ft}}$

$\times \dfrac{1 \text{ yd}}{3 \text{ ft}} = \dfrac{12{,}000(100)^3}{(2.54)^3 (12)^3 (3)^3} \text{ yd}^3 = \textbf{15,695.41 yd}^3$

7. $WF(105) = 5\dfrac{1}{3}$

$WF = \dfrac{5\dfrac{1}{3}}{105}$

$WF = \dfrac{16}{3} \cdot \dfrac{1}{105}$

$WF = \dfrac{\textbf{16}}{\textbf{315}}$

8. $\dfrac{3 - \dfrac{a}{b}}{\dfrac{1}{b} + b} = \dfrac{\dfrac{3b}{b} - \dfrac{a}{b}}{\dfrac{1}{b} + \dfrac{b^2}{b}} = \dfrac{\dfrac{3b - a}{b}}{\dfrac{1 + b^2}{b}} \cdot \dfrac{\dfrac{b}{1 + b^2}}{\dfrac{b}{1 + b^2}}$

$= \dfrac{3b - a}{1 + b^2}$

9. $\dfrac{x^{-1} + y^{-1}}{x^{-1}} = \dfrac{\dfrac{1}{x} + \dfrac{1}{y}}{\dfrac{1}{x}} = \dfrac{\dfrac{y}{xy} + \dfrac{x}{xy}}{\dfrac{1}{x}}$

$= \dfrac{\dfrac{y + x}{xy} \cdot \dfrac{x}{1}}{\dfrac{1}{x} \cdot \dfrac{x}{1}} = \dfrac{y + x}{y}$

10. $4\sqrt{8} - 3\sqrt{12} + \sqrt{30{,}000}$

$= 4\sqrt{2 \cdot 2 \cdot 2} - 3\sqrt{2 \cdot 2 \cdot 3} + \sqrt{10{,}000 \cdot 3}$

$= 4\sqrt{2}\sqrt{2}\sqrt{2} - 3\sqrt{2}\sqrt{2}\sqrt{3} + \sqrt{10{,}000}\sqrt{3}$

$= 4(2)\sqrt{2} - 3(2)\sqrt{3} + 100\sqrt{3}$

$= 8\sqrt{2} - 6\sqrt{3} + 100\sqrt{3}$

$= \mathbf{8\sqrt{2} + 94\sqrt{3}}$

11. $2\sqrt{75} - 4\sqrt{243}$

$= 2\sqrt{3 \cdot 5 \cdot 5} - 4\sqrt{3 \cdot 3 \cdot 3 \cdot 3 \cdot 3}$

$= 2\sqrt{3}\sqrt{5}\sqrt{5} - 4\sqrt{3}\sqrt{3}\sqrt{3}\sqrt{3}\sqrt{3}$

$= 2\sqrt{3}(5) - 4(3)(3)\sqrt{3} = 10\sqrt{3} - 36\sqrt{3}$

$= \mathbf{-26\sqrt{3}}$

12. $20\dfrac{1}{4}x + 5\dfrac{1}{2} = 7\dfrac{1}{16}$

$\dfrac{\; -5\dfrac{1}{2} \quad -5\dfrac{1}{2}}{20\dfrac{1}{4}x \qquad = 1\dfrac{9}{16}}$

$\dfrac{20\dfrac{1}{4}x}{20\dfrac{1}{4}} = \dfrac{1\dfrac{9}{16}}{20\dfrac{1}{4}}$

$x = \dfrac{\dfrac{25}{16}}{\dfrac{81}{4}}$

$x = \dfrac{25}{16} \cdot \dfrac{4}{81}$

$x = \dfrac{\mathbf{25}}{\mathbf{324}}$

13. $-(-3)^3 - 2^2 = -2(-3k - 4)$

$27 - 4 = 6k + 8$

$6k + 8 = 23$

$\dfrac{-8 \qquad -8}{6k \qquad = 15}$

$k = \dfrac{15}{6}$

$k = \dfrac{5}{2}$

14. (a) $\begin{cases} 5x + 3y = 1 \\ 7x + 3y = 5 \end{cases}$
    (b)

(1)(a) $\quad 5x + 3y = 1$
(−1)(b) $\dfrac{-7x - 3y = -5}{-2x \qquad\quad = -4}$
$\qquad\qquad\quad x = 2$

(a) $\quad 5x + 3y = 1$
$\quad 5(2) + 3y = 1$
$\quad 10 + 3y = 1$
$\qquad\quad 3y = -9$
$\qquad\quad\ y = -3$

Thus the solution is the ordered pair **(2, −3)**.

15. (a) $\begin{cases} 5x - 2y = 10 \\ 7x - 3y = 13 \end{cases}$
    (b)

(3)(a) $\quad 15x - 6y = 30$
(−2)(b) $\dfrac{-14x + 6y = -26}{x = 4}$

(a) $\quad 5x - 2y = 10$
$\quad 5(4) - 2y = 10$
$\quad 20 - 2y = 10$
$\qquad\quad -2y = -10$
$\qquad\qquad y = 5$

Thus the solution is the ordered pair **(4, 5)**.

16. $x - 3 < -2; \ D = \{\text{Negative Integers}\}$

$x - 3 < -2$

$\dfrac{+3 \qquad +3}{x < 1}$

17. (a) **False. Some real numbers are not members of the set of irrational numbers.**

(b) **True. Every whole number is a member of the set of real numbers.**

18. $\begin{cases} x + 2y = 15 \\ 3x - y = 10 \end{cases}$

$x + 2y = 15$

$x = -2y + 15$

$$3x - y = 10$$
$$3(-2y + 15) - y = 10$$
$$-6y + 45 - y = 10$$
$$-7y + 45 = 10$$
$$-7y = -35$$
$$y = 5$$

$$x + 2y = 15$$
$$x + 2(5) = 15$$
$$x + 10 = 15$$
$$x = 5$$

Thus the solution is the ordered pair **(5, 5)**.

19. $y = -2x + 4$

x	0	1	4
y	4	2	-4

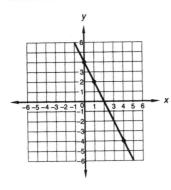

20. $y - \dfrac{1}{3}x = 2$

$$y = \dfrac{1}{3}x + 2$$

x	0	3	-3
y	2	3	1

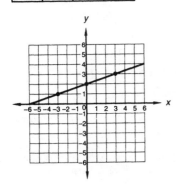

21. $\dfrac{1}{x^2} + \dfrac{m}{x^3 y} + \dfrac{c}{y} = \dfrac{xy}{x^3 y} + \dfrac{m}{x^3 y} + \dfrac{cx^3}{x^3 y}$

$= \dfrac{xy + m + cx^3}{x^3 y}$

22. $2a^{-1}b - a^{-2}b + 1 = \dfrac{2b}{a} - \dfrac{b}{a^2} + 1$

$= \dfrac{2ab}{a^2} - \dfrac{b}{a^2} + \dfrac{a^2}{a^2} = \dfrac{2ab - b + a^2}{a^2}$

23. $\left(4x^{-2}y^2 m\right)^{-2} y = 4^{-2} x^4 y^{-4} m^{-2} y = \dfrac{x^4 y^{-3} m^{-2}}{16}$

$= \dfrac{x^4}{16 y^3 m^2}$

24. $\left(\dfrac{x^{-1}}{y^{-1}}\right)^{-2} \left(\dfrac{y^2}{x^2}\right)^{-4} = \dfrac{x^2}{y^2} \cdot \dfrac{y^{-8}}{x^{-8}} = \dfrac{x^{10}}{y^{10}}$

25. $\dfrac{x^{-2} y^{-2} (p^0)^2}{(x^2 y^2 p^3)^{-2}} = \dfrac{x^{-2} y^{-2}}{x^{-4} y^{-4} p^{-6}} = x^2 y^2 p^6$

26. $-3^2 - \dfrac{1}{(-3)^{-3}} + (-3)^0 = -9 - (-27) + 1$

$= -9 + 27 + 1 = \mathbf{19}$

27. $3m + 7 = 1$

$\dfrac{-7 \quad -7}{3m \quad = -6}$

$m = -2$

$m - |-m + n^{-2}| + n^2 - \sqrt{m^2}$
$= -2 - \left|-(-2) + (-1)^{-2}\right| + (-1)^2 - \sqrt{(-2)^2}$
$= -2 - |2 + 1| + 1 - 2$
$= -2 - 3 + 1 - 2 = \mathbf{-6}$

28. $-x^2 y + 3yx^2 - \dfrac{4y^3 x}{y^2 x^{-1}} - \dfrac{7x^{-2}}{x^{-4} y^{-1}}$

$= -x^2 y + 3yx^2 - 4x^2 y - 7x^2 y = \mathbf{-9x^2 y}$

29. $P = \left(6 + 4 + 6 + \dfrac{2\pi(2)}{2}\right)$ cm

$= (16 + 2\pi)$ cm $= \mathbf{22.28\ cm}$

30. $V = \left(\text{Area}_{\text{base}}\right)(\text{Height})$

$= \left[\dfrac{1}{2}(4\ m \times 3\ m)\right](12\ m)$

$= \left(6\ m^2\right)(12\ m)$

$= \mathbf{72\ m^3}$

Practice 69

a. $x^2 - x - 42$

$(6)(-7) = -42$ and $(6) + (-7) = -1$

$x^2 - x - 42 = (x - 7)(x + 6)$

b. $x^2 + x - 42$

$(7)(-6) = -42$ and $(7) + (-6) = 1$

$x^2 + x - 42 = (x + 7)(x - 6)$

c. $x^2 - 6x - 16$

$(-8)(2) = -16$ and $(-8) + (2) = -6$

$x^2 - 6x - 16 = (x - 8)(x + 2)$

Problem Set 69

1. $\quad \dfrac{18}{100} \cdot S = 720$

$\dfrac{100}{18} \cdot \dfrac{18}{100} \cdot S = 720 \cdot \dfrac{100}{18}$

$S = \textbf{4000}$

of 4000

720 is 18%

3280 is 82%

Before, 100%   After

2. Weighted Average

$= \dfrac{(0.8)(0.2) + (0.9)(0.2) + (1.0)(0.2) + (0.8)(0.4)}{0.2 + 0.2 + 0.2 + 0.4}$

$= \dfrac{0.16 + 0.18 + 0.2 + 0.32}{1.0}$

$= \dfrac{0.86}{1.0} = \textbf{86\%}$

3. (a) **Rational. Every repeating decimal number is a rational number.**

(b) **Rational. Every whole number is a rational number and $\sqrt[3]{27}$ equals 3, which is a whole number.**

(c) **Irrational. The square root of any whole number that is not a perfect square is an irrational number.**

4. $x^2 + 6x - 16$

$(8)(-2) = -16$ and $(8) + (-2) = 6$

$x^2 + 6x - 16 = (x + 8)(x - 2)$

5. $x^2 - 6x + 9$

$(-3)(-3) = 9$ and $(-3) + (-3) = -6$

$x^2 - 6x + 9 = (x - 3)(x - 3)$

6. $x^2 - 6x - 27$

$(-9)(3) = -27$ and $(-9) + (3) = -6$

$x^2 - 6x - 27 = (x - 9)(x + 3)$

7. $p^2 - p - 20$

$(4)(-5) = -20$ and $(4) + (-5) = -1$

$p^2 - p - 20 = (p - 5)(p + 4)$

8. $x^2 - 2x - 15$

$(-5)(3) = -15$ and $(-5) + (3) = -2$

$x^2 - 2x - 15 = (x - 5)(x + 3)$

9. $p^2 - 4p - 21$

$(-7)(3) = -21$ and $(-7) + (3) = -4$

$p^2 - 4p - 21 = (p - 7)(p + 3)$

10. $p^2 + p - 20$

$(5)(-4) = -20$ and $(5) + (-4) = 1$

$p^2 + p - 20 = (p + 5)(p - 4)$

11. $k^2 - 3k - 40$

$(-8)(5) = -40$ and $(-8) + (5) = -3$

$k^2 - 3k - 40 = (k - 8)(k + 5)$

12. $m^2 + 9m + 20$

$(4)(5) = 20$ and $(4) + (5) = 9$

$m^2 + 9m + 20 = (m + 5)(m + 4)$

13. $x^2 + 33 + 14x = x^2 + 14x + 33$

$(11)(3) = 33$ and $(11) + (3) = 14$

$x^2 + 14x + 33 = (x + 11)(x + 3)$

14. $-13p + p^2 + 36 = p^2 - 13p + 36$

$(-4)(-9) = 36$ and $(-4) + (-9) = -13$

$p^2 - 13p + 36 = (p - 9)(p - 4)$

15. $-30 + m^2 - m = m^2 - m - 30$

$(-6)(5) = -30$ and $(-6) + (5) = -1$

$m^2 - m - 30 = (m - 6)(m + 5)$

16. $11n + n^2 + 18 = n^2 + 11n + 18$

$(2)(9) = 18$ and $(2) + (9) = 11$

$n^2 + 11n + 18 = (n + 9)(n + 2)$

17. $x^2 + 27 + 12x = x^2 + 12x + 27$

$(3)(9) = 27$ and $(3) + (9) = 12$

$x^2 + 12x + 27 = (x + 9)(x + 3)$

18. $x^2 + 90 - 19x = x^2 - 19x + 90$

$(-9)(-10) = 90$ and $(-9) + (-10) = -19$

$x^2 - 19x + 90 = (x - 9)(x - 10)$

19. $\dfrac{1 + \dfrac{1}{y}}{\dfrac{1}{y}} = \dfrac{\dfrac{y}{y} + \dfrac{1}{y}}{\dfrac{1}{y}} = \dfrac{\dfrac{y + 1}{y} \cdot \dfrac{y}{1}}{\dfrac{1}{y} \cdot \dfrac{y}{1}} = y + 1$

20. $\dfrac{\dfrac{a}{b} - 4}{\dfrac{x}{b} - b} = \dfrac{\dfrac{a}{b} - \dfrac{4b}{b}}{\dfrac{x}{b} - \dfrac{b^2}{b}} = \dfrac{\dfrac{a - 4b}{b}}{\dfrac{x - b^2}{b}} \cdot \dfrac{b}{x - b^2} = \dfrac{a - 4b}{b} \cdot \dfrac{b}{x - b^2}$

$= \dfrac{a - 4b}{x - b^2}$

21. $7\sqrt{20} - 5\sqrt{32} - \sqrt{45} - 5\sqrt{8}$

$= 7\sqrt{2 \cdot 2 \cdot 5} - 5\sqrt{2 \cdot 2 \cdot 2 \cdot 2 \cdot 2}$
$\quad - \sqrt{3 \cdot 3 \cdot 5} - 5\sqrt{2 \cdot 2 \cdot 2}$

$= 7\sqrt{2}\sqrt{2}\sqrt{5} - 5\sqrt{2}\sqrt{2}\sqrt{2}\sqrt{2}\sqrt{2}$
$\quad - \sqrt{3}\sqrt{3}\sqrt{5} - 5\sqrt{2}\sqrt{2}\sqrt{2}$

$= 7(2)\sqrt{5} - 5(2)(2)\sqrt{2} - (3)\sqrt{5} - 5(2)\sqrt{2}$

$= 14\sqrt{5} - 20\sqrt{2} - 3\sqrt{5} - 10\sqrt{2}$

$= \mathbf{11\sqrt{5} - 30\sqrt{2}}$

22. $2\sqrt{18} - 5\sqrt{28} + 4\sqrt{300} - \sqrt{72}$

$= 2\sqrt{2 \cdot 3 \cdot 3} - 5\sqrt{2 \cdot 2 \cdot 7} + 4\sqrt{100 \cdot 3}$
$\quad - \sqrt{2 \cdot 2 \cdot 2 \cdot 3 \cdot 3}$

$= 2\sqrt{2}\sqrt{3}\sqrt{3} - 5\sqrt{2}\sqrt{2}\sqrt{7} + 4\sqrt{100}\sqrt{3}$
$\quad - \sqrt{2}\sqrt{2}\sqrt{2}\sqrt{3}\sqrt{3}$

$= 2\sqrt{2}(3) - 5(2)\sqrt{7} + 4(10)\sqrt{3} - (2)\sqrt{2}(3)$

$= 6\sqrt{2} - 10\sqrt{7} + 40\sqrt{3} - 6\sqrt{2}$

$= \mathbf{-10\sqrt{7} + 40\sqrt{3}}$

23. $f(x) = 7\sqrt{x + 18} - 5\sqrt{8x}$

$f(2) = 7\sqrt{2 + 18} - 5\sqrt{8(2)}$

$= 7\sqrt{20} - 5\sqrt{16}$

$= 7\sqrt{2 \cdot 2 \cdot 5} - 5(4)$

$= 7\sqrt{2}\sqrt{2}\sqrt{5} - 20$

$= 7(2)\sqrt{5} - 20$

$= \mathbf{14\sqrt{5} - 20}$

24. (a) $\begin{cases} 3x + 4y = -7 \\ 3x - 3y = 21 \end{cases}$

$\quad$ (b)

$\begin{array}{ll}(1)(a) & 3x + 4y = -7 \\ (-1)(b) & \underline{-3x + 3y = -21} \\ & 7y = -28 \\ & y = -4 \end{array}$

(a) $\quad 3x + 4y = -7$

$3x + 4(-4) = -7$

$3x - 16 = -7$

$3x = 9$

$x = 3$

Thus the solution is the ordered pair $(\mathbf{3, -4})$.

25. (a) $\begin{cases} 2x - 2y = -2 \\ 4x - 5y = -9 \end{cases}$
$\quad$ (b)

$\begin{array}{ll}(-2)(a) & -4x + 4y = 4 \\ (1)(b) & \underline{4x - 5y = -9} \\ & -y = -5 \\ & y = 5 \end{array}$

(a) $\quad 2x - 2y = -2$

$2x - 2(5) = -2$

$2x - 10 = -2$

$2x = 8$

$x = 4$

Thus the solution is the ordered pair $(\mathbf{4, 5})$.

26. $\begin{cases} 3x + y = 9 \\ x - 4y = -10 \end{cases}$

$x - 4y = -10$

$x = 4y - 10$

$3x + y = 9$

$3(4y - 10) + y = 9$

$12y - 30 + y = 9$

$13y - 30 = 9$

$13y = 39$

$y = 3$

$x - 4y = -10$

$x - 4(3) = -10$

$x - 12 = -10$

$x = 2$

Thus the solution is the ordered pair $(\mathbf{2, 3})$.

27. $ab^2 - \dfrac{3ab}{b^{-1}} + \dfrac{2a^0 b^2}{a^{-1}} - \dfrac{4a^2}{b^2} + 2a^2 b^{-2}$

$= ab^2 - 3ab^2 + 2ab^2 - \dfrac{4a^2}{b^2} + \dfrac{2a^2}{b^2} = \mathbf{-\dfrac{2a^2}{b^2}}$

28. $\begin{array}{l} x - 5 = -8 \\ \underline{+5 \quad\quad +5} \\ x = -3 \end{array}$

$(x^2 - 6)(x^{-3} - x) = [(-3)^2 - 6][(-3)^{-3} - (-3)]$

$= (9 - 6)\left(-\dfrac{1}{27} + 3\right) = 3\left(2\dfrac{26}{27}\right) = \dfrac{\mathbf{80}}{\mathbf{9}}$

29. $A = \dfrac{1}{2}(60 \text{ in.} \times 20 \text{ in.}) + \dfrac{1}{2}(20 \text{ in.} \times 20 \text{ in.})$

$= 600 \text{ in.}^2 + 200 \text{ in.}^2$

$= \mathbf{800 \text{ in.}^2}$

30. S.A. = $2(\text{Area}_{base})$ + Lateral Surface Area

    = $2[\pi(4 \text{ ft})^2]$ + $(\text{Perimeter}_{base})(\text{Height})$

    = $2(16\pi \text{ ft}^2)$ + $[2\pi(4 \text{ ft})](14 \text{ ft})$

    = $32\pi \text{ ft}^2$ + $(8\pi \text{ ft})(14 \text{ ft})$

    = $32\pi \text{ ft}^2$ + $112\pi \text{ ft}^2$

    = **$144\pi \text{ ft}^2$** = **452.16 ft^2**

Practice 70

a. $P(H, H, H) = P(H) \cdot P(H) \cdot P(H)$

    $= \dfrac{1}{2} \cdot \dfrac{1}{2} \cdot \dfrac{1}{2} = \dfrac{1}{8}$

b. $P(> 3) = \dfrac{3}{6} = \dfrac{1}{2}$

c. The number of ways to obtain a sum of 6 is 5.

    $P(6) = \dfrac{5}{36}$

d. $P(\text{pink marble}) = \dfrac{6}{13}$

e. $P(2, 4, 3) = P(2) \cdot P(4) \cdot P(3)$

    $= \dfrac{1}{4} \cdot \dfrac{1}{4} \cdot \dfrac{1}{4} = \dfrac{1}{64}$

Problem Set 70

1. $P(> 4) = \dfrac{2}{6} = \dfrac{1}{3}$

2. (a) The number of ways to obtain 4 is 3.

    $P(4) = \dfrac{3}{36} = \dfrac{1}{12}$

   (b) There are 6 ways to obtain a sum greater than 9.

    $P(> 9) = \dfrac{6}{36} = \dfrac{1}{6}$

3. $P(H, T, T) = P(H) \cdot P(T) \cdot P(T)$

    $= \dfrac{1}{2} \cdot \dfrac{1}{2} \cdot \dfrac{1}{2} = \dfrac{1}{8}$

4. $P(4, 1) = P(4) \cdot P(1)$

    $= \dfrac{1}{4} \cdot \dfrac{1}{4} = \dfrac{1}{16}$

5. $P(\text{green marble}) = \dfrac{5}{14}$

6. W. A. $= \dfrac{1(70) + 3(80) + 5(80) + 4(90)}{1 + 3 + 5 + 4}$

    $= \dfrac{1070}{13}$ = **82.31**

7. (a) Since $9^2 = 81$ and $10^2 = 100$, the number whose square is 99 is closest to **10**.

   (b) $\sqrt{99}$ = **9.9499**

8. $m^2 - m - 2$

    $(-2)(1) = -2$ and $(-2) + (1) = -1$

    $m^2 - m - 2 = (m - 2)(m + 1)$

9. $y^2 + 2y - 15$

    $(5)(-3) = -15$ and $(5) + (-3) = 2$

    $y^2 + 2y - 15 = (y + 5)(y - 3)$

10. $p^2 + 4p - 5$

    $(5)(-1) = -5$ and $(5) + (-1) = 4$

    $p^2 + 4p - 5 = (p + 5)(p - 1)$

11. $a^2 - 10a + 9$

    $(-9)(-1) = 9$ and $(-9) + (-1) = -10$

    $a^2 - 10a + 9 = (a - 9)(a - 1)$

12. $b^2 - 2b - 3$

    $(-3)(1) = -3$ and $(-3) + (1) = -2$

    $b^2 - 2b - 3 = (b - 3)(b + 1)$

13. $p^2 - 11p + 10$

    $(-10)(-1) = 10$ and $(-10) + (-1) = -11$

    $p^2 - 11p + 10 = (p - 10)(p - 1)$

14. $a^2 + 32 + 18a = a^2 + 18a + 32$

    $(16)(2) = 32$ and $(16) + (2) = 18$

    $a^2 + 18a + 32 = (a + 16)(a + 2)$

15. $12b + b^2 + 27 = b^2 + 12b + 27$

    $(9)(3) = 27$ and $(9) + (3) = 12$

    $b^2 + 12b + 27 = (b + 9)(b + 3)$

16. $16 + x^2 + 10x = x^2 + 10x + 16$

    $(8)(2) = 16$ and $(8) + (2) = 10$

    $x^2 + 10x + 16 = (x + 8)(x + 2)$

17. $15x + 50 + x^2 = x^2 + 15x + 50$

    $(5)(10) = 50$ and $(5) + (10) = 15$

    $x^2 + 15x + 50 = (x + 5)(x + 10)$

18. $18 + x^2 + 11x = x^2 + 11x + 18$

    $(9)(2) = 18$ and $(9) + (2) = 11$

    $x^2 + 11x + 18 = (x + 9)(x + 2)$

19. $3x - 18 + x^2 = x^2 + 3x - 18$

    $(6)(-3) = -18$ and $(6) + (-3) = 3$

    $x^2 + 3x - 18 = (x + 6)(x - 3)$

20. $20 - 9x + x^2 = x^2 - 9x + 20$

$(-4)(-5) = 20$ and $(-4) + (-5) = -9$

$x^2 - 9x + 20 = (x - 5)(x - 4)$

21. $x^2 + 42 - 13x = x^2 - 13x + 42$

$(-6)(-7) = 42$ and $(-6) + (-7) = -13$

$x^2 - 13x + 42 = (x - 7)(x - 6)$

22. $-3 - 2x + x^2 = x^2 - 2x - 3$

$(-3)(1) = -3$ and $(-3) + (1) = -2$

$x^2 - 2x - 3 = (x - 3)(x + 1)$

23. $f(x) = -2x^2 + 3x - 7$

$f(-3) = -2(-3)^2 + 3(-3) - 7$

$= -2(9) - 9 - 7$

$= -18 - 9 - 7 = -34$

24. $2\sqrt{18} - 5\sqrt{8} + 4\sqrt{500} - \sqrt{125}$

$= 2\sqrt{2 \cdot 3 \cdot 3} - 5\sqrt{2 \cdot 2 \cdot 2} + 4\sqrt{100 \cdot 5}$

$\quad - \sqrt{5 \cdot 5 \cdot 5}$

$= 2\sqrt{2}\sqrt{3}\sqrt{3} - 5\sqrt{2}\sqrt{2}\sqrt{2} + 4\sqrt{100}\sqrt{5}$

$\quad - \sqrt{5}\sqrt{5}\sqrt{5}$

$= 2\sqrt{2}(3) - 5(2)\sqrt{2} + 4(10)\sqrt{5} - (5)\sqrt{5}$

$= 6\sqrt{2} - 10\sqrt{2} + 40\sqrt{5} - 5\sqrt{5}$

$= -4\sqrt{2} + 35\sqrt{5}$

25. (a) $\begin{cases} 2x + 5y = 7 \\ x + 3y = 4 \end{cases}$
(b)

$(1)(a) \quad 2x + 5y = 7$
$(-2)(b) \quad \underline{-2x - 6y = -8}$
$\qquad\qquad\quad -y = -1$
$\qquad\qquad\qquad y = 1$

(a) $\quad 2x + 5y = 7$

$2x + 5(1) = 7$

$2x + 5 = 7$

$2x = 2$

$x = 1$

Thus the solution is the ordered pair **(1, 1)**.

26. $\begin{cases} x + y = 10 \\ x + 2y = 15 \end{cases}$

$x + y = 10$

$x = -y + 10$

$x + 2y = 15$

$(-y + 10) + 2y = 15$

$y + 10 = 15$

$y = 5$

$x + y = 10$

$x + 5 = 10$

$x = 5$

Thus the solution is the ordered pair **(5, 5)**.

27. $\dfrac{\dfrac{m}{y} - y}{\dfrac{1}{y} - 1} = \dfrac{\dfrac{m}{y} - \dfrac{y^2}{y}}{\dfrac{1}{y} - \dfrac{y}{y}} = \dfrac{\dfrac{m - y^2}{y} \cdot \dfrac{y}{1 - y}}{\dfrac{1 - y}{y} \cdot \dfrac{y}{1 - y}}$

$= \dfrac{m - y^2}{1 - y}$

28. $\dfrac{x^{-2} + yx^{-1}}{x^{-1}y^2} = \dfrac{\dfrac{1}{x^2} + \dfrac{y}{x}}{\dfrac{y^2}{x}} = \dfrac{\dfrac{1}{x^2} + \dfrac{yx}{x^2}}{\dfrac{y^2}{x}}$

$= \dfrac{\dfrac{1 + yx}{x^2} \cdot \dfrac{x}{y^2}}{\dfrac{y^2}{x} \cdot \dfrac{x}{y^2}} = \dfrac{1 + yx}{xy^2}$

29. $\dfrac{\dfrac{a}{b} + \dfrac{1}{b}}{\dfrac{a}{b} - \dfrac{1}{b}} = \dfrac{\dfrac{a + 1}{b} \cdot \dfrac{b}{a - 1}}{\dfrac{a - 1}{b} \cdot \dfrac{b}{a - 1}} = \dfrac{a + 1}{a - 1}$

30. $V = (\text{Area}_{\text{base}})(\text{Height})$

$= [\pi(6 \text{ cm})^2](24 \text{ cm})$

$= 864\pi \text{ cm}^3 = 2712.96 \text{ cm}^3$

Practice 71

a. $-4x^3 - 28x^2 - 48x = -4x(x^2 + 7x + 12)$

$= -4x(x + 4)(x + 3)$

b. $-x^2 + 24 + 2x = -x^2 + 2x + 24$

$= -(x^2 - 2x - 24) = -(x - 6)(x + 4)$

c. $\begin{cases} 6N_N + 24N_Q = 360 \\ N_Q = N_N + 5 \end{cases}$

$6N_N + 24N_Q = 360$

$6N_N + 24(N_N + 5) = 360$

$6N_N + 24N_N + 120 = 360$

$30N_N + 120 = 360$

$30N_N = 240$

$N_N = 8$

$N_Q = N_N + 5$

$N_Q = 8 + 5$

$N_Q = 13$

d. (a) $\begin{cases} 6N_N + 12N_D = 180 \\ (b) \ N_N + N_D = 12 \end{cases}$

$\quad$ (1)(a) $\quad 6N_N + 12N_D = 180$

$\quad$ (−6)(b) $\ \underline{-6N_N - 6N_D = -72}$

$\qquad\qquad\qquad\qquad 6N_D = 108$

$\qquad\qquad\qquad\qquad\ N_D = \mathbf{18}$

$\quad$ (b) $\ N_N + N_D = 12$

$\qquad\quad N_N + 18 = 12$

$\qquad\qquad\quad N_N = \mathbf{-6}$

Problem Set 71

1. $P(H) = \dfrac{1}{2}$

2. $P(3, 4, 2) = \dfrac{1}{4} \cdot \dfrac{1}{4} \cdot \dfrac{1}{4} = \dfrac{\mathbf{1}}{\mathbf{64}}$

3. $P(\text{black marble}) = \dfrac{3}{13}$

4. (a) The number of ways to obtain a sum of 7 is 6.

$\quad P(7) = \dfrac{6}{36} = \dfrac{\mathbf{1}}{\mathbf{6}}$

$\quad$ (b) The number of ways to get a sum greater than 7 is 15.

$\quad P(>7) = \dfrac{15}{36} = \dfrac{\mathbf{5}}{\mathbf{12}}$

5. Range $= 8 - 2 = \mathbf{6}$

$\quad$ Median $= \mathbf{6}$

$\quad$ Mode $= \mathbf{6}$

$\quad$ Mean $= \dfrac{2 + 4 + 5 + 6 + 6 + 7 + 8}{7}$

$\qquad\quad\ = \dfrac{38}{7} = \mathbf{5.43}$

6. Weighted Average $= \dfrac{2(90) + 1(72)}{1 + 2}$

$\qquad\qquad\qquad\quad = \dfrac{252}{3} = \mathbf{84}$

7. $10{,}000 \text{ km} \cdot \text{km} \times \dfrac{1000 \text{ m}}{1 \text{ km}} \times \dfrac{1000 \text{ m}}{1 \text{ km}}$

$\quad \times \dfrac{100 \text{ cm}}{1 \text{ m}} \times \dfrac{100 \text{ cm}}{1 \text{ m}} \times \dfrac{1 \text{ in.}}{2.54 \text{ cm}} \times \dfrac{1 \text{ in.}}{2.54 \text{ cm}}$

$\quad \times \dfrac{1 \text{ ft}}{12 \text{ in.}} \times \dfrac{1 \text{ ft}}{12 \text{ in.}} \times \dfrac{1 \text{ mi}}{5280 \text{ ft}} \times \dfrac{1 \text{ mi}}{5280 \text{ ft}}$

$\quad = \dfrac{10{,}000(1000)^2 (100)^2}{(2.54)^2 (12)^2 (5280)^2} \text{ mi}^2 = \mathbf{3861.02 \text{ mi}^2}$

8. $2x^2 + 10x + 12 = 2(x^2 + 5x + 6)$

$\qquad\qquad\qquad\quad = \mathbf{2(x + 3)(x + 2)}$

9. $5x^2 + 30x + 40 = 5(x^2 + 6x + 8)$

$\qquad\qquad\qquad\quad = \mathbf{5(x + 4)(x + 2)}$

10. $x^3 - x^2 - 20x = x(x^2 - x - 20)$

$\qquad\qquad\qquad\quad = \mathbf{x(x - 5)(x + 4)}$

11. $ax^2 + 6ax + 9a = a(x^2 + 6x + 9)$

$\qquad\qquad\qquad\quad = \mathbf{a(x + 3)(x + 3)}$

12. $-b^3 + 5b^2 + 24b = -b(b^2 - 5b - 24)$

$\qquad\qquad\qquad\quad = \mathbf{-b(b - 8)(b + 3)}$

13. $-3m^2 - 30m - 48 = -3(m^2 + 10m + 16)$

$\qquad\qquad\qquad\quad = \mathbf{-3(m + 8)(m + 2)}$

14. (a) $\begin{cases} 5N_N + 10N_D = 135 \\ (b) \ N_N + N_D = 17 \end{cases}$

$\quad$ (1)(a) $\quad 5N_N + 10N_D = 135$

$\quad$ (−5)(b) $\ \underline{-5N_N - 5N_D = -85}$

$\qquad\qquad\qquad\qquad 5N_D = 50$

$\qquad\qquad\qquad\qquad\ N_D = \mathbf{10}$

$\quad$ (b) $\ N_N + N_D = 17$

$\qquad\quad N_N + 10 = 17$

$\qquad\qquad\quad N_N = \mathbf{7}$

15. $\begin{cases} 5N_N + 25N_Q = 340 \\ N_Q = N_N + 4 \end{cases}$

$\qquad\qquad 5N_N + 25N_Q = 340$

$\qquad 5N_N + 25(N_N + 4) = 340$

$\qquad 5N_N + 25N_N + 100 = 340$

$\qquad\qquad 30N_N + 100 = 340$

$\qquad\qquad\qquad 30N_N = 240$

$\qquad\qquad\qquad\quad N_N = \mathbf{8}$

$\quad N_Q = N_N + 4$

$\quad N_Q = 8 + 4$

$\quad N_Q = \mathbf{12}$

16. $x^2 - 10 - 3x = x^2 - 3x - 10 = \mathbf{(x - 5)(x + 2)}$

17. $x^2 + 12 + 7x = x^2 + 7x + 12$

$\qquad\qquad\qquad = \mathbf{(x + 3)(x + 4)}$

18. $4 - 4x + x^2 = x^2 - 4x + 4 = \mathbf{(x - 2)(x - 2)}$

19. $x^2 + 14 + 9x = x^2 + 9x + 14$

$\qquad\qquad\qquad = \mathbf{(x + 7)(x + 2)}$

20. $12 + x^2 + 8x = x^2 + 8x + 12$

$= (x + 6)(x + 2)$

21. $-3x - 18 + x^2 = x^2 - 3x - 18$

$= (x - 6)(x + 3)$

22. $\dfrac{mx^{-1} + nz^{-3}}{y} = \dfrac{\dfrac{m}{x} + \dfrac{n}{z^3}}{y} = \dfrac{\dfrac{mz^3}{xz^3} + \dfrac{nx}{xz^3}}{y}$

$= \dfrac{\dfrac{mz^3 + nx}{xz^3} \cdot \dfrac{1}{y}}{\dfrac{y}{1} \cdot \dfrac{1}{y}} = \dfrac{mz^3 + nx}{xz^3 y}$

23. $\dfrac{\dfrac{a}{x} + x}{\dfrac{1}{x} - 1} = \dfrac{\dfrac{a}{x} + \dfrac{x^2}{x}}{\dfrac{1}{x} - \dfrac{x}{x}} = \dfrac{\dfrac{a + x^2}{x} \cdot \dfrac{x}{1 - x}}{\dfrac{1 - x}{x} \cdot \dfrac{x}{1 - x}}$

$= \dfrac{a + x^2}{1 - x}$

24. $5\sqrt{27} - 14\sqrt{12} + 3\sqrt{200} - 4\sqrt{300} + 6\sqrt{72}$

$= 5\sqrt{3 \cdot 3 \cdot 3} - 14\sqrt{2 \cdot 2 \cdot 3} + 3\sqrt{100 \cdot 2}$

$\quad - 4\sqrt{100 \cdot 3} + 6\sqrt{2 \cdot 2 \cdot 2 \cdot 3 \cdot 3}$

$= 5\sqrt{3}\sqrt{3}\sqrt{3} - 14\sqrt{2}\sqrt{2}\sqrt{3} + 3\sqrt{100}\sqrt{2}$

$\quad - 4\sqrt{100}\sqrt{3} + 6\sqrt{2}\sqrt{2}\sqrt{2}\sqrt{3}\sqrt{3}$

$= 5(3)\sqrt{3} - 14(2)\sqrt{3} + 3(10)\sqrt{2} - 4(10)\sqrt{3}$

$\quad + 6(2)\sqrt{2}(3)$

$= 15\sqrt{3} - 28\sqrt{3} + 30\sqrt{2} - 40\sqrt{3} + 36\sqrt{2}$

$= \mathbf{-53\sqrt{3} + 66\sqrt{2}}$

25. **0, 1, 4, 9, 16, 25, 36, 49, 64, 81, 100, 121, 144, 169, 196, 225**

26. (a) **Irrational**

(b) **Rational**

(c) **Rational**

(d) **Irrational**

27. (a) **True. Every whole number is a member of the set of rational numbers.**

(b) **True. Every natural number is an integer.**

28. $x + 24 = 21$

$x = -3$

$x^2 - 9x^{-2} - 4 - |-x| + x^0$

$= (-3)^2 - 9(-3)^{-2} - 4 - |-(-3)| + (-3)^0$

$= 9 - \dfrac{9}{9} - 4 - 3 + 1$

$= 9 - 1 - 4 - 3 + 1 = \mathbf{2}$

29. Area $=$ Area$_{\text{trapezoid}}$ $-$ Area$_{\text{circle}}$

$= \dfrac{1}{2}(20 \text{ in.} \times 10 \text{ in.}) + \dfrac{1}{2}(24 \text{ in.} \times 10 \text{ in.})$

$\quad - \pi(5 \text{ in.})^2$

$= 100 \text{ in.}^2 + 120 \text{ in.}^2 - 25\pi \text{ in.}^2$

$= \mathbf{(220 - 25\pi) \text{ in.}^2 = 141.5 \text{ in.}^2}$

30. S.A. $= 2\left(\text{Area}_{\text{triangle}}\right) + 2\left(\text{Area}_{\text{side}}\right) + \text{Area}_{\text{bottom}}$

$= 2\left[\dfrac{1}{2}(12 \text{ ft} \times 8 \text{ ft})\right] + 2(7 \text{ ft} \times 10 \text{ ft})$

$\quad + (12 \text{ ft} \times 7 \text{ ft})$

$= 2(48 \text{ ft}^2) + 2(70 \text{ ft}^2) + 84 \text{ ft}^2$

$= 96 \text{ ft}^2 + 140 \text{ ft}^2 + 84 \text{ ft}^2$

$= \mathbf{320 \text{ ft}^2}$

Practice 72

a. $(a + b)x^2 + 8x(a + b) + 15(a + b)$

$= (a + b)\left(x^2 + 8x + 15\right)$

$= \mathbf{(a + b)(x + 5)(x + 3)}$

b. $(m - b)x^2c - 2xc(m - b) - 24c(m - b)$

$= c(m - b)\left(x^2 - 2x - 24\right)$

$= \mathbf{c(m - b)(x - 6)(x + 4)}$

c. $V = \dfrac{1}{3}\left(\text{Area}_{\text{base}}\right)(\text{Height})$

$= \dfrac{1}{3}(10 \text{ cm} \times 8 \text{ cm})(12 \text{ cm})$

$= \dfrac{1}{3}(80 \text{ cm}^2)(12 \text{ cm})$

$= \mathbf{320 \text{ cm}^3}$

d. S.A. $=$ Area$_{\text{base}}$ $+$ Lateral Surface Area

$= \pi r^2 + \pi r l$

$= \pi(9 \text{ m})^2 + \pi(9 \text{ m})(15 \text{ m})$

$= 81\pi \text{ m}^2 + 135\pi \text{ m}^2$

$= \mathbf{216\pi \text{ m}^2 = 678.24 \text{ m}^2}$

Problem Set 72

1. $P(2, 4, 2) = \dfrac{1}{4} \cdot \dfrac{1}{4} \cdot \dfrac{1}{4} = \dfrac{1}{64}$

2. $P(\text{orange marble}) = \dfrac{7}{15}$

3. $P(T) = \dfrac{1}{2}$

4. (a) There are exactly 4 ways to obtain a sum of 5.

$$P(5) = \frac{4}{36} = \frac{1}{9}$$

(b) The number of ways to obtain a sum greater than 5 is $5 + 6 + 5 + 4 + 3 + 2 + 1 = 26$.

$$P(> 5) = \frac{26}{36} = \frac{13}{18}$$

5. Weighted Average $= \dfrac{5(9) + 4(8) + 5(9) + 2(7)}{5 + 4 + 5 + 2}$

$$= \frac{136}{16} = 8.5$$

6.
$$\frac{125}{100} \cdot W = 310$$

$$\frac{100}{125} \cdot \frac{125}{100} \cdot W = 310 \cdot \frac{100}{125}$$

$$W = 248 \text{ lb}$$

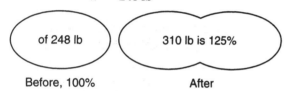

of 248 lb   310 lb is 125%

Before, 100%   After

7. $(x - 1)x^2 + 7x(x - 1) + 10(x - 1)$

$= (x - 1)(x^2 + 7x + 10)$

$= (x - 1)(x + 2)(x + 5)$

8. $m(y + 1)x^2 + 4(y + 1)mx + 4(y + 1)m$

$= m(y + 1)(x^2 + 4x + 4)$

$= m(y + 1)(x + 2)(x + 2)$

9. $(z - 5)x^2 + 5(z - 5)x + 6(z - 5)$

$= (z - 5)(x^2 + 5x + 6)$

$= (z - 5)(x + 2)(x + 3)$

10. $(x + y)m^2 + 12(x + y)m + 35(x + y)$

$= (x + y)(m^2 + 12m + 35)$

$= (x + y)(m + 7)(m + 5)$

11. $2x^3 + 16x^2 + 30x = 2x(x^2 + 8x + 15)$

$= 2x(x + 3)(x + 5)$

12. $abx^2 - 5abx - 24ab = ab(x^2 - 5x - 24)$

$= ab(x - 8)(x + 3)$

13. $m^2 + 10m + 16 = (m + 8)(m + 2)$

14. $-48 - 8n + n^2 = n^2 - 8n - 48$

$= (n - 12)(n + 4)$

15. $y^2 + 56 - 15y = y^2 - 15y + 56$

$= (y - 8)(y - 7)$

16. $p^2 - 55 - 6p = p^2 - 6p - 55$

$= (p - 11)(p + 5)$

17. $12t + 35 + t^2 = t^2 + 12t + 35$

$= (t + 7)(t + 5)$

18. $y^2 + 50 + 51y = y^2 + 51y + 50$

$= (y + 50)(y + 1)$

19. $-0.003k - 0.03k - 0.3k - 666 = 0$

$-3k - 30k - 300k - 666,000 = 0$

$-333k = 666,000$

$k = -2000$

20. $-5 < x \le 2;\ D = \{\text{Reals}\}$

21.
$$\frac{\dfrac{m}{p} + p}{\dfrac{1}{p} - x} = \frac{\dfrac{m}{p} + \dfrac{p^2}{p}}{\dfrac{1}{p} - \dfrac{xp}{p}} = \frac{\dfrac{m + p^2}{p}}{\dfrac{1 - xp}{p}} \cdot \frac{p}{1 - xp}$$

$$= \frac{m + p^2}{1 - xp} = \frac{m + p^2}{1 - px}$$

22.
$$\frac{a + \dfrac{b}{a}}{\dfrac{1}{a} - 4} = \frac{\dfrac{a^2}{a} + \dfrac{b}{a}}{\dfrac{1}{a} - \dfrac{4a}{a}} = \frac{\dfrac{a^2 + b}{a}}{\dfrac{1 - 4a}{a}} \cdot \frac{a}{1 - 4a}$$

$$= \frac{a^2 + b}{1 - 4a}$$

23.
$$\frac{x^{-1} + y^{-1}}{(xy)^{-1}} = \frac{\dfrac{1}{x} + \dfrac{1}{y}}{\dfrac{1}{xy}} = \frac{\dfrac{y}{xy} + \dfrac{x}{xy}}{\dfrac{1}{xy}}$$

$$= \frac{\dfrac{y + x}{xy} \cdot \dfrac{xy}{1}}{\dfrac{1}{xy} \cdot \dfrac{xy}{1}} = \frac{y + x}{1} = y + x$$

24. $g(x) = \sqrt[3]{x^2 - 1} + 2\sqrt{x + 1}$

$g(3) = \sqrt[3]{3^2 - 1} + 2\sqrt{3 + 1}$

$= \sqrt[3]{8} + 2\sqrt{4}$

$= 2 + 2(2)$

$= 2 + 4$

$= 6$

25. (a) $\begin{cases} 5x - 2y = 9 \\ 3x - y = 6 \end{cases}$
(b)

$(1)(a)\quad 5x - 2y = 9$
$(-2)(b)\quad \underline{-6x + 2y = -12}$
$\qquad\qquad -x \quad\quad = -3$
$\qquad\qquad\qquad x = 3$

(b) $3x - y = 6$

$3(3) - y = 6$

$9 - y = 6$

$-y = -3$

$y = 3$

Thus the solution is the ordered pair **(3, 3)**.

26. $\begin{cases} 10N_D + 25N_Q = 495 \\ N_Q = N_D + 10 \end{cases}$

$10N_D + 25N_Q = 495$

$10N_D + 25(N_D + 10) = 495$

$10N_D + 25N_D + 250 = 495$

$35N_D + 250 = 495$

$35N_D = 245$

$N_D = 7$

$N_Q = N_D + 10$

$N_Q = 7 + 10$

$N_Q = 17$

27. (a) **Irrational**

(b) **Rational**

(c) **Rational**

(d) **Rational**

28. $3\sqrt{18} - 7\sqrt{8} + 3\sqrt{50} + \sqrt{32}$

$= 3\sqrt{2 \cdot 3 \cdot 3} - 7\sqrt{2 \cdot 2 \cdot 2} + 3\sqrt{2 \cdot 5 \cdot 5}$
$+ \sqrt{2 \cdot 2 \cdot 2 \cdot 2 \cdot 2}$

$= 3\sqrt{2}\sqrt{3}\sqrt{3} - 7\sqrt{2}\sqrt{2}\sqrt{2} + 3\sqrt{2}\sqrt{5}\sqrt{5}$
$+ \sqrt{2}\sqrt{2}\sqrt{2}\sqrt{2}\sqrt{2}$

$= 3\sqrt{2}(3) - 7(2)\sqrt{2} + 3\sqrt{2}(5) + (2)(2)\sqrt{2}$

$= 9\sqrt{2} - 14\sqrt{2} + 15\sqrt{2} + 4\sqrt{2} = \mathbf{14\sqrt{2}}$

29. $P = \left(12 + 8 + 12 + \dfrac{2\pi(4)}{2}\right)$ cm

$= (32 + 4\pi)$ cm $= \mathbf{44.56\ cm}$

30. $V = \dfrac{1}{3}\left(\text{Area}_{base}\right)(\text{Height})$

$= \dfrac{1}{3}(8\ m \times 6\ m)(7\ m)$

$= \dfrac{1}{3}\left(48\ m^2\right)(7\ m)$

$= \mathbf{112\ m^3}$

Practice 73

a. $64x^2 - 81y^2 = (8x)^2 - (9y)^2$

$= \mathbf{(8x - 9y)(8x + 9y)}$

b. $-25 + 100m^2 = 100m^2 - 25 = (10m)^2 - (5)^2$

$= \mathbf{(10m - 5)(10m + 5)}$

c. $y^4x^2 - 169z^{10} = \left(y^2x\right)^2 - \left(13z^5\right)^2$

$= \mathbf{\left(y^2x - 13z^5\right)\left(y^2x + 13z^5\right)}$

d. (1) $P(\text{both purple}) = \dfrac{4}{7} \cdot \dfrac{4}{7} = \dfrac{\mathbf{16}}{\mathbf{49}}$

(2) $P(\text{both purple}) = \dfrac{4}{7} \cdot \dfrac{3}{6} = \dfrac{12}{42} = \dfrac{\mathbf{2}}{\mathbf{7}}$

e. (1) $P(\text{orange, then blue}) = \dfrac{5}{11} \cdot \dfrac{6}{11} = \dfrac{\mathbf{30}}{\mathbf{121}}$

(2) $P(\text{orange, then blue}) = \dfrac{5}{11} \cdot \dfrac{6}{10}$

$= \dfrac{30}{110} = \dfrac{\mathbf{3}}{\mathbf{11}}$

Problem Set 73

1. $P(\text{both purple}) = \dfrac{6}{10} \cdot \dfrac{5}{9} = \dfrac{30}{90} = \dfrac{\mathbf{1}}{\mathbf{3}}$

2. $P(\text{orange, then blue}) = \dfrac{2}{7} \cdot \dfrac{5}{7} = \dfrac{\mathbf{10}}{\mathbf{49}}$

3. $P(T, T, H) = \dfrac{1}{2} \cdot \dfrac{1}{2} \cdot \dfrac{1}{2} = \dfrac{\mathbf{1}}{\mathbf{8}}$

4. (a) There are only 2 ways to obtain a sum of 3.

$P(3) = \dfrac{2}{36} = \dfrac{\mathbf{1}}{\mathbf{18}}$

(b) There is only one way to obtain a sum less than 3.

$P(<3) = \dfrac{\mathbf{1}}{\mathbf{36}}$

5. $\dfrac{250}{100} \cdot N = 900$

$\dfrac{100}{250} \cdot \dfrac{250}{100} \cdot N = 900 \cdot \dfrac{100}{250}$

$N = \mathbf{360}$

of 360	900 is 250%
Before, 100%	After

6. Overall Average $= \dfrac{(4 \times 2000) + (96 \times 100)}{4 + 96}$

$= \dfrac{17,600}{100} = \mathbf{176\ lb}$

7. $4p^2x^2 - k^2 = (2px)^2 - (k)^2$

$\quad = (2px - k)(2px + k)$

8. $-4m^2 + 25p^2x^2 = 25p^2x^2 - 4m^2$

$\quad = (5px)^2 - (2m)^2 = (5px - 2m)(5px + 2m)$

9. $-9x^2 + 4y^2 = 4y^2 - 9x^2 = (2y)^2 - (3x)^2$

$\quad = (2y - 3x)(2y + 3x)$

10. $9k^2a^2 - 49 = (3ka)^2 - (7)^2$

$\quad = (3ka + 7)(3ka - 7)$

11. $p^2 - 4k^2 = (p)^2 - (2k)^2 = (p + 2k)(p - 2k)$

12. $36a^2x^2 - k^2 = (6ax)^2 - (k)^2$

$\quad = (6ax + k)(6ax - k)$

13. $x^2 - x - 20 = (x - 5)(x + 4)$

14. $4x^2 - 4x - 80 = 4(x^2 - x - 20)$

$\quad = 4(x - 5)(x + 4)$

15. $2b^2 - 48 - 10b = 2b^2 - 10b - 48$

$\quad = 2(b^2 - 5b - 24) = 2(b - 8)(b + 3)$

16. $-90 - 39x + 3x^2 = 3x^2 - 39x - 90$

$\quad = 3(x^2 - 13x - 30) = 3(x - 15)(x + 2)$

17. $(a + b)x^2 + 7(a + b)x + 10(a + b)$

$\quad = (a + b)(x^2 + 7x + 10)$

$\quad = (a + b)(x + 2)(x + 5)$

18. $pm^2 + 9pm + 20p = p(m^2 + 9m + 20)$

$\quad = p(m + 5)(m + 4)$

19. $5k^2 + 30 + 25k = 5k^2 + 25k + 30$

$\quad = 5(k^2 + 5k + 6) = 5(k + 3)(k + 2)$

20. $-x^2 - 8x - 7 = -(x^2 + 8x + 7)$

$\quad = -(x + 7)(x + 1)$

21. $-6 \le x \le 3;\ D = \{\text{Integers}\}$

22. (a) **Irrational**

(b) **Rational**

(c) **Irrational**

(d) **Rational**

23. $25{,}000 \text{ mi} \cdot \text{mi} \times \dfrac{5280 \text{ ft}}{1 \text{ mi}} \times \dfrac{5280 \text{ ft}}{1 \text{ mi}} \times \dfrac{12 \text{ in.}}{1 \text{ ft}}$

$\times \dfrac{12 \text{ in.}}{1 \text{ ft}} \times \dfrac{2.54 \text{ cm}}{1 \text{ in.}} \times \dfrac{2.54 \text{ cm}}{1 \text{ in.}} \times \dfrac{1 \text{ m}}{100 \text{ cm}}$

$\times \dfrac{1 \text{ m}}{100 \text{ cm}} \times \dfrac{1 \text{ km}}{1000 \text{ m}} \times \dfrac{1 \text{ km}}{1000 \text{ m}}$

$= \dfrac{25{,}000(5280)^2 (12)^2 (2.54)^2}{(100)^2 (1000)^2} \text{ km}^2$

$= \mathbf{64{,}749.70 \text{ km}^2}$

24. (a) $\begin{cases} 5x - 2y = 3 \\ 2x - 3y = -1 \end{cases}$
(b)

$(3)(a)\quad 15x - 6y = 9$

$\underline{(-2)(b)\quad -4x + 6y = 2}$

$\qquad\quad 11x \qquad\quad = 11$

$\qquad\qquad\qquad\qquad x = 1$

(a) $\quad 5x - 2y = 3$

$\qquad 5(1) - 2y = 3$

$\qquad\quad 5 - 2y = 3$

$\qquad\qquad -2y = -2$

$\qquad\qquad\quad y = 1$

Thus the solution is the ordered pair **(1, 1)**.

25. $\begin{cases} N_P + N_N = 175 \\ N_P + 5N_N = 475 \end{cases}$

$N_P + N_N = 175$

$\qquad N_P = 175 - N_N$

$\qquad\quad N_P + 5N_N = 475$

$\quad (175 - N_N) + 5N_N = 475$

$\qquad\qquad 175 + 4N_N = 475$

$\qquad\qquad\qquad 4N_N = 300$

$\qquad\qquad\qquad\quad N_N = 75$

$N_P + N_N = 175$

$N_P + 75 = 175$

$\qquad \mathbf{N_P = 100}$

26. $\dfrac{x}{x(x + y)} + \dfrac{1}{x} - \dfrac{y}{x + y}$

$= \dfrac{x}{x(x + y)} + \dfrac{x + y}{x(x + y)} - \dfrac{xy}{x(x + y)}$

$= \dfrac{x + (x + y) - xy}{x(x + y)} = \dfrac{2x + y - yx}{x(x + y)}$

27. $3\sqrt{125} + 2\sqrt{45} - \sqrt{50{,}000}$

$= 3\sqrt{5 \cdot 5 \cdot 5} + 2\sqrt{3 \cdot 3 \cdot 5} - \sqrt{10{,}000 \cdot 5}$

$= 3\sqrt{5}\sqrt{5}\sqrt{5} + 2\sqrt{3}\sqrt{3}\sqrt{5} - \sqrt{10{,}000}\sqrt{5}$

$= 3(5)\sqrt{5} + 2(3)\sqrt{5} - (100)\sqrt{5}$

$= 15\sqrt{5} + 6\sqrt{5} - 100\sqrt{5} = \mathbf{-79\sqrt{5}}$

28. $\dfrac{x^{-1} + 1}{yx^{-1} + x} = \dfrac{\frac{1}{x} + 1}{\frac{y}{x} + x} = \dfrac{\frac{1}{x} + \frac{x}{x}}{\frac{y}{x} + \frac{x^2}{x}}$

$= \dfrac{\frac{1 + x}{x} \cdot \frac{x}{y + x^2}}{\frac{y + x^2}{x} \cdot \frac{x}{y + x^2}} = \dfrac{1 + x}{y + x^2} = \dfrac{\boldsymbol{x + 1}}{\boldsymbol{y + x^2}}$

29. $-[2(-3 - k)] = -4(-3) - |-3|k$

$-2(-3 - k) = 12 - 3k$

$6 + 2k = 12 - 3k$

$\underline{ +3k \qquad\qquad +3k}$

$6 + 5k = 12$

$\underline{-6 \qquad\qquad -6}$

$5k = 6$

$k = \dfrac{\boldsymbol{6}}{\boldsymbol{5}}$

30. $V = \dfrac{1}{3}\left(\text{Area}_{\text{base}}\right)(\text{Height})$

$= \dfrac{1}{3}\left[\pi(3\text{ in.})^2\right](4\text{ in.})$

$= \dfrac{1}{3}\left(9\pi\text{ in.}^2\right)(4\text{ in.})$

$= 12\pi\text{ in.}^3 = \boldsymbol{37.68\text{ in.}^3}$

Practice 74

a. $49{,}900 = \boldsymbol{4.99 \times 10^4}$

b. $49{,}900 \times 10^{-11} = 4.99 \times 10^4 \times 10^{-11}$
$= \boldsymbol{4.99 \times 10^{-7}}$

c. $0.000499 \times 10^3 = 4.99 \times 10^{-4} \times 10^3$
$= \boldsymbol{4.99 \times 10^{-1}}$

Problem Set 74

1. (a) $P(\text{green, then yellow}) = \dfrac{6}{12} \cdot \dfrac{6}{12}$

$= \dfrac{36}{144} = \dfrac{\boldsymbol{1}}{\boldsymbol{4}}$

(b) $P(\text{green, then yellow}) = \dfrac{6}{12} \cdot \dfrac{6}{11}$

$= \dfrac{36}{132} = \dfrac{6}{22} = \dfrac{\boldsymbol{3}}{\boldsymbol{11}}$

2. $P(\text{both gold}) = \dfrac{7}{13} \cdot \dfrac{6}{12} = \dfrac{42}{156} = \dfrac{\boldsymbol{7}}{\boldsymbol{26}}$

3. $P(H, H, H, H) = \dfrac{1}{2} \cdot \dfrac{1}{2} \cdot \dfrac{1}{2} \cdot \dfrac{1}{2} = \dfrac{\boldsymbol{1}}{\boldsymbol{16}}$

4. $\dfrac{\text{Withs}}{\text{Total}} = \dfrac{3}{14}$

$\dfrac{\text{Withs}}{5600} = \dfrac{3}{14}$

$14\text{ Withs} = 3 \cdot 5600$

$\text{Withs} = \dfrac{3 \cdot 5600}{14}$

$\text{Withs} = \boldsymbol{1200}$

5. $\dfrac{120}{100} \cdot 74{,}000 = WN$

$WN = \dfrac{8{,}880{,}000}{100}$

$WN = \boldsymbol{\$88{,}800}$

6. Overall Average $= \dfrac{(6 \times 7.80) + (4 \times 11.2)}{6 + 4}$

$= \dfrac{91.6}{10} = \boldsymbol{9.16}$

7. $x - 3 \not> 4$; $D = \{\text{Integers}\}$

$x - 3 \not> 4$

$\underline{ +3 \quad +3}$

$x \qquad \not> 7$

8. $0.000478 = \boldsymbol{4.78 \times 10^{-4}}$

9. $0.000478 \times 10^6 = 4.78 \times 10^{-4} \times 10^6$
$= \boldsymbol{4.78 \times 10^2}$

10. $0.000478 \times 10^{-8} = 4.78 \times 10^{-4} \times 10^{-8}$
$= \boldsymbol{4.78 \times 10^{-12}}$

11. $5x^2 - 5y^2 = 5\left(x^2 - y^2\right) = \boldsymbol{5(x + y)(x - y)}$

12. $45x^2 - 20m^2 = 5\left(9x^2 - 4m^2\right)$
$= 5\left[(3x)^2 - (2m)^2\right] = \boldsymbol{5(3x + 2m)(3x - 2m)}$

13. $4a^2 - 9b^2 = (2a)^2 - (3b)^2$
$= \boldsymbol{(2a - 3b)(2a + 3b)}$

14. $49a^2p^2 - a^2 = a^2\left(49p^2 - 1\right) = a^2\left[(7p)^2 - (1)^2\right]$
$= \boldsymbol{a^2(7p + 1)(7p - 1)}$

15. $x^2 + 9x + 20 = \boldsymbol{(x + 5)(x + 4)}$

16. $-20 + x^2 + x = x^2 + x - 20 = \boldsymbol{(x + 5)(x - 4)}$

17. $x^2(a + b) + 28(a + b) + 11x(a + b)$
$= x^2(a + b) + 11x(a + b) + 28(a + b)$
$= (a + b)(x^2 + 11x + 28)$
$= \mathbf{(a + b)(x + 7)(x + 4)}$

18. $(x - a)y^2 - 28(x - a) + 3y(x - a)$
$= (x - a)y^2 + 3y(x - a) - 28(x - a)$
$= (x - a)(y^2 + 3y - 28)$
$= \mathbf{(x - a)(y - 4)(y + 7)}$

19. $x^3 + 10x^2 + 24x = x(x^2 + 10x + 24)$
$= \mathbf{x(x + 6)(x + 4)}$

20. $ax^2 - 2ax - 15a = a(x^2 - 2x - 15)$
$= \mathbf{a(x - 5)(x + 3)}$

21. $\dfrac{1}{xc} + \dfrac{b}{x(c + x)} + \dfrac{5}{c + x} - \dfrac{2}{c}$

$= \dfrac{c + x}{xc(c + x)} + \dfrac{bc}{xc(c + x)} + \dfrac{5xc}{xc(c + x)}$

$\quad - \dfrac{2x(c + x)}{xc(c + x)}$

$= \mathbf{\dfrac{c + x + bc + 5xc - 2x(c + x)}{xc(c + x)}}$

22. $\begin{cases} 7x + y = -18 \\ 4x - 2y = 0 \end{cases}$

$7x + y = -18$
$\quad\quad y = -7x - 18$

$\quad\quad 4x - 2y = 0$
$4x - 2(-7x - 18) = 0$
$4x + 14x + 36 = 0$
$\quad\quad 18x + 36 = 0$
$\quad\quad\quad 18x = -36$
$\quad\quad\quad\quad x = -2$

$\quad 7x + y = -18$
$7(-2) + y = -18$
$-14 + y = -18$
$\quad\quad\quad y = -4$

Thus the solution is the ordered pair **(-2, -4)**.

23. (a) $\begin{cases} N_D + N_Q = 40 \\ \end{cases}$
    (b) $\begin{cases} 10N_D + 25N_Q = 475 \end{cases}$

$(-10)(a)\;\; -10N_D - 10N_Q = -400$
$\underline{(1)(b)\quad 10N_D + 25N_Q = \quad 475}$
$\quad\quad\quad\quad\quad\quad 15N_Q = \quad 75$
$\quad\quad\quad\quad\quad\quad\;\; N_Q = 5$

(a) $N_D + N_Q = 40$
$\quad N_D + 5 = 40$
$\quad\quad\quad N_D = 35$

24. $y = -2x - 1$

x	0	1	-2
y	-1	-3	3

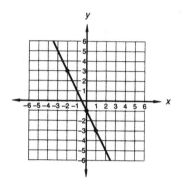

25. $4\sqrt{80} + 8\sqrt{45} - 4\sqrt{48} + \sqrt{30{,}000}$
$= 4\sqrt{2 \cdot 2 \cdot 2 \cdot 2 \cdot 5} + 8\sqrt{3 \cdot 3 \cdot 5}$
$\quad - 4\sqrt{2 \cdot 2 \cdot 2 \cdot 2 \cdot 3} + \sqrt{10{,}000 \cdot 3}$
$= 4\sqrt{2}\sqrt{2}\sqrt{2}\sqrt{2}\sqrt{5} + 8\sqrt{3}\sqrt{3}\sqrt{5}$
$\quad - 4\sqrt{2}\sqrt{2}\sqrt{2}\sqrt{2}\sqrt{3} + \sqrt{10{,}000}\sqrt{3}$
$= 4(2)(2)\sqrt{5} + 8(3)\sqrt{5} - 4(2)(2)\sqrt{3} + (100)\sqrt{3}$
$= 16\sqrt{5} + 24\sqrt{5} - 16\sqrt{3} + 100\sqrt{3}$
$= \mathbf{40\sqrt{5} + 84\sqrt{3}}$

26. $\dfrac{x^{-3}xy^2(y)^{-2}x^{-4}}{(x^0yy^{-2})^2(x^2y^{-3})^{-2}} = \dfrac{x^{-6}}{y^{-2}(x^{-4}y^6)}$

$= \dfrac{x^{-6}}{x^{-4}y^4} = \mathbf{\dfrac{1}{x^2y^4}}$

27. $\dfrac{2x^2}{y^2}\left(\dfrac{-x^2}{2y^{-3}} + \dfrac{x^2a^4}{a^{-2}y^{-2}}\right) = \dfrac{-2x^4}{2y^{-1}} + \dfrac{2x^4a^4}{a^{-2}}$
$= \mathbf{-x^4y + 2x^4a^6}$

28. $f(x) = 2x^2 - 3x - 4$
$f(-2) = 2(-2)^2 - 3(-2) - 4$
$\quad\quad\;\; = 2(4) + 6 - 4$
$\quad\quad\;\; = 8 + 6 - 4 = \mathbf{10}$

29. $A = \dfrac{1}{2}(2\text{ cm} \times 6\text{ cm}) + \dfrac{1}{2}(15\text{ cm} \times 6\text{ cm})$
$\quad\;\; = 6\text{ cm}^2 + 45\text{ cm}^2 = \mathbf{51\text{ cm}^2}$

30. $S.A. = \text{Area}_{\text{base}} + \text{Lateral Surface Area}$
$\quad\quad = (8\text{ m} \times 8\text{ m}) + 4\left[\dfrac{1}{2}(8\text{ m} \times 5\text{ m})\right]$
$\quad\quad = 64\text{ m}^2 + 4(20\text{ m}^2)$
$\quad\quad = 64\text{ m}^2 + 80\text{ m}^2$
$\quad\quad = \mathbf{144\text{ m}^2}$

Practice 75

a. $y = -3$

b. The desired equation is $y = mx + b$.

By inspection, $b = +3$.

By inspection, the sign of m is $-$.

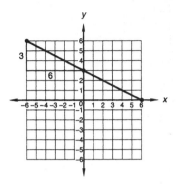

$$|m| = \frac{3}{6} = \frac{1}{2}$$

So $b = +3$ and $m = -\frac{1}{2}$.

$$y = -\frac{1}{2}x + 3$$

c. $x = 3$

d. The desired equation is $y = mx + b$.

By inspection, $b = +3$.

By inspection, the sign of m is $+$.

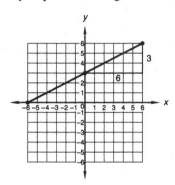

$$|m| = \frac{3}{6} = \frac{1}{2}$$

So $b = +3$ and $m = +\frac{1}{2}$.

$$y = \frac{1}{2}x + 3$$

e. $y = -\frac{2}{3}x + 2$

$$y = \frac{-2}{+3}x + 2$$

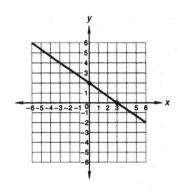

f. $5 + 3y = x$

$$3y = x - 5$$

$$y = \frac{1}{3}x - \frac{5}{3}$$

$$y = \frac{+1}{+3}x - \frac{5}{3}$$

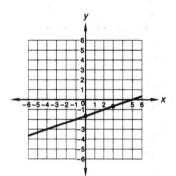

Problem Set 75

1. $P(\text{red, then white}) = \frac{7}{12} \cdot \frac{5}{12} = \frac{35}{144}$

2. $P(4, 2, 3, 1) = \frac{1}{4} \cdot \frac{1}{4} \cdot \frac{1}{4} \cdot \frac{1}{4} = \frac{1}{256}$

3. $P(\text{both white}) = \frac{9}{14} \cdot \frac{8}{13} = \frac{72}{182} = \frac{36}{91}$

4.
$$\frac{3}{100} \cdot C = 120$$

$$\frac{100}{3} \cdot \frac{3}{100} \cdot C = 120 \cdot \frac{100}{3}$$

$$C = \mathbf{4000}$$

of 4000

Before, 100%

120 is 3%

3880 is 97%

After

5. $\dfrac{34}{100} \cdot 4800 = WN$

$$WN = \dfrac{163,200}{100}$$

$$WN = \mathbf{1632}$$

of 4800

1632 is 34%

3168 is 66%

Before, 100%   After

6. $\dfrac{WP}{100} \cdot 1400 = 784$

$$\dfrac{100}{1400} \cdot \dfrac{WP}{100} \cdot 1400 = 784 \cdot \dfrac{100}{1400}$$

$$WP = \dfrac{78,400}{1400}$$

$$WP = \mathbf{56\%}$$

of 1400

616 is 44%

784 is 56%

Before, 100%   After

7. $x = \mathbf{-3}$

8. The desired equation is $y = mx + b$.

By inspection, $b = +2$.

By inspection, the sign of m is $-$.

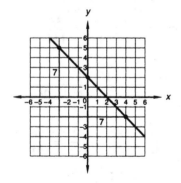

$$|m| = \dfrac{7}{7} = 1$$

So $b = +2$ and $m = -1$.

$$y = \mathbf{-x + 2}$$

9. $y = -\dfrac{3}{2}x + 3$

$$y = \dfrac{-3}{+2}x + 3$$

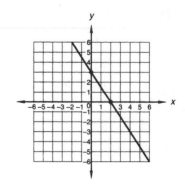

10. $2y = -x + 2$

$$y = -\dfrac{1}{2}x + 1$$

$$y = \dfrac{-1}{+2}x + 1$$

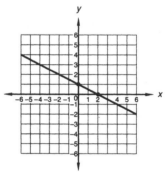

11. $0.00123 \times 10^{-5} = 1.23 \times 10^{-3} \times 10^{-5}$
$$= \mathbf{1.23 \times 10^{-8}}$$

12. $0.00123 \times 10^{8} = 1.23 \times 10^{-3} \times 10^{8}$
$$= \mathbf{1.23 \times 10^{5}}$$

13. $b^3x^2 - 4b^3 = b^3(x^2 - 4) = b^3[(x)^2 - (2)^2]$
$$= \mathbf{b^3(x + 2)(x - 2)}$$

14. $16x^2 - a^2 = (4x)^2 - (a)^2 = \mathbf{(4x - a)(4x + a)}$

15. $-m^2 + 9p^2 = 9p^2 - m^2 = (3p)^2 - (m)^2$
$$= \mathbf{(3p + m)(3p - m)}$$

16. $x^2 + 3x - 10 = \mathbf{(x + 5)(x - 2)}$

17. $4x + x^2 - 21 = x^2 + 4x - 21 = \mathbf{(x + 7)(x - 3)}$

18. $5x^2 - 15x - 50 = 5(x^2 - 3x - 10)$
$$= \mathbf{5(x - 5)(x + 2)}$$

19. $x^3 - 3x^2 + 2x = x(x^2 - 3x + 2)$
$$= \mathbf{x(x - 2)(x - 1)}$$

20. $18(x + y) + 9z(x + y) + z^2(x + y)$

$= z^2(x + y) + 9z(x + y) + 18(x + y)$

$= (x + y)(z^2 + 9z + 18)$

$= (x + y)(z + 6)(z + 3)$

21. $(m + a)x^2 + 3(m + a)x - 18(m + a)$

$= (m + a)(x^2 + 3x - 18)$

$= (m + a)(x + 6)(x - 3)$

22. (a) $\begin{cases} 4x - 5y = -1 \\ 2x + 3y = 5 \end{cases}$
(b)

$\begin{array}{ll} (1)(a) & 4x - 5y = -1 \\ (-2)(b) & \underline{-4x - 6y = -10} \\ & -11y = -11 \\ & y = 1 \end{array}$

(a) $4x - 5y = -1$

$4x - 5(1) = -1$

$4x - 5 = -1$

$4x = 4$

$x = 1$

Thus the solution is the orderd pair **(1, 1)**.

23. $\begin{cases} N_Q + N_D = 25 \\ N_Q = N_D + 3 \end{cases}$

$N_Q + N_D = 25$

$(N_D + 3) + N_D = 25$

$2N_D + 3 = 25$

$2N_D = 22$

$N_D = \textbf{11}$

$N_Q = N_D + 3$

$N_Q = 11 + 3$

$N_Q = \textbf{14}$

24. $15\sqrt{12} - 30\sqrt{18} + 2\sqrt{300}$

$= 15\sqrt{2 \cdot 2 \cdot 3} - 30\sqrt{2 \cdot 3 \cdot 3} + 2\sqrt{100 \cdot 3}$

$= 15\sqrt{2}\sqrt{2}\sqrt{3} - 30\sqrt{2}\sqrt{3}\sqrt{3} + 2\sqrt{100}\sqrt{3}$

$= 15(2)\sqrt{3} - 30\sqrt{2}(3) + 2(10)\sqrt{3}$

$= 30\sqrt{3} - 90\sqrt{2} + 20\sqrt{3} = \textbf{50}\sqrt{\textbf{3}} - \textbf{90}\sqrt{\textbf{2}}$

25. $\dfrac{5}{-3^{-2}} - \sqrt[5]{-32} = \dfrac{5(3^2)}{-1} - (-2)$

$= -45 + 2 = \textbf{-43}$

26. $\dfrac{x^{-2}y^0(x^{-2})^{-2}y^2}{(y^2x^{-4})^2(y^3x^2)^{-1}} = \dfrac{x^{-2}x^4y^2}{y^4x^{-8}y^{-3}x^{-2}}$

$= \dfrac{x^2y^2}{x^{-10}y} = \textbf{x}^{\textbf{12}}\textbf{y}$

27. $\dfrac{a^{-1} + b^{-1}}{a^{-1}b^{-1}} = \dfrac{\dfrac{1}{a} + \dfrac{1}{b}}{\dfrac{1}{ab}} = \dfrac{\dfrac{b}{ab} + \dfrac{a}{ab}}{\dfrac{1}{ab}}$

$= \dfrac{\dfrac{b + a}{ab} \cdot \dfrac{ab}{1}}{\dfrac{1}{ab} \cdot \dfrac{ab}{1}} = \textbf{b} + \textbf{a}$

28. $2.2x - 0.1x + 0.02x = -2 - 0.12$

$220x - 10x + 2x = -200 - 12$

$212x = -212$

$x = -1$

29.

$A = (4 \text{ in.} \times 2 \text{ in.}) + (2 \text{ in.} \times 4 \text{ in.})$

$ + (2 \text{ in.} \times 4 \text{ in.})$

$= 8 \text{ in.}^2 + 8 \text{ in.}^2 + 8 \text{ in.}^2$

$= \textbf{24 in.}^2$

30. $S.A. = \text{Area}_{\text{base}} + \text{Lateral Surface Area}$

$= \pi r^2 + \pi r l$

$= \pi(4 \text{ ft})^2 + \pi(4 \text{ ft})(5 \text{ ft})$

$= 16\pi \text{ ft}^2 + 20\pi \text{ ft}^2$

$= \textbf{36}\pi \textbf{ ft}^2 = \textbf{113.04 ft}^2$

Practice 76

a. $N, N + 1, N + 2$

$N + (N + 2) = 142$

$2N + 2 = 142$

$2N = 140$

$N = 70$

Thus the integers are **70, 71,** and **72.**

b. $N, N + 1, N + 2, N + 3$

$8(N + N + 2) = 10(N + 3) + 40$

$8(2N + 2) = 10N + 30 + 40$

$16N + 16 = 10N + 70$

$6N = 54$

$N = 9$

Thus the integers are **9, 10, 11,** and **12.**

Problem Set 76

1. $N, N + 1, N + 2, N + 3$

$2(N + N + 2) = 3(N + 1) + 11$

$2(2N + 2) = 3N + 3 + 11$

$4N + 4 = 3N + 14$

$N = 10$

Thus the integers are **10, 11, 12,** and **13.**

2. $\dfrac{78}{100} \cdot 18{,}400 = WN$

$WN = \dfrac{1{,}435{,}200}{100}$

$WN = \mathbf{14{,}352}$

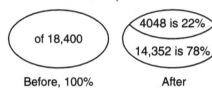

Before, 100%   After

3. $P(\text{gold, then silver}) = \dfrac{8}{15} \cdot \dfrac{7}{14} = \dfrac{56}{210} = \dfrac{\mathbf{4}}{\mathbf{15}}$

4. (a) The number of ways to obtain a sum greater than 6 is $6 + 5 + 4 + 3 + 2 + 1 = 21$.

$P(> 6) = \dfrac{21}{36} = \dfrac{\mathbf{7}}{\mathbf{12}}$

(b) The number of ways to obtain a sum less than 6 is $4 + 3 + 2 + 1 = 10$.

$P(< 6) = \dfrac{10}{36} = \dfrac{\mathbf{5}}{\mathbf{18}}$

5. (a) $x = \mathbf{5}$

(b) The desired equation is $y = mx + b$.

By inspection, $b = 0$.

By inspection, the sign of m is $-$.

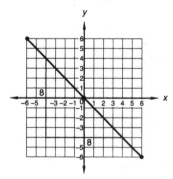

$|m| = \dfrac{8}{8} = 1$

So $b = 0$ and $m = -1$.

$y = -x$

6. $y = -\dfrac{1}{3}x + 2$

$y = \dfrac{-1}{+3}x + 2$

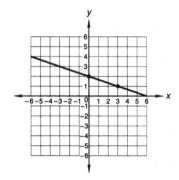

7. $y - 2x = 1$

$y = 2x + 1$

$y = \dfrac{+2}{+1}x + 1$

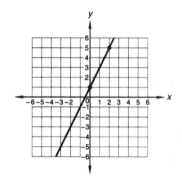

8. $430{,}000 \times 10^{-2} = 4.3 \times 10^{5} \times 10^{-2} = \mathbf{4.3 \times 10^{3}}$

9. $4300 \times 10^{7} = 4.3 \times 10^{3} \times 10^{7} = \mathbf{4.3 \times 10^{10}}$

10. $-9x^{2} + m^{2} = m^{2} - 9x^{2} = (m)^{2} - (3x)^{2}$
$= \mathbf{(m + 3x)(m - 3x)}$

11. $4x^{2} - 9m^{2} = (2x)^{2} - (3m)^{2}$
$= \mathbf{(2x + 3m)(2x - 3m)}$

12. $125m^{2} - 5x^{2} = 5\left(25m^{2} - x^{2}\right) = 5\left[(5m)^{2} - (x)^{2}\right]$
$= \mathbf{5(5m + x)(5m - x)}$

13. $-72k^{2} + 2x^{2} = 2x^{2} - 72k^{2} = 2\left(x^{2} - 36k^{2}\right)$
$= 2\left[(x)^{2} - (6k)^{2}\right] = \mathbf{2(x + 6k)(x - 6k)}$

14. $x^{2} - 5x - 14 = \mathbf{(x - 7)(x + 2)}$

15. $-x^{3} + 4x^{2} + 12x = -x\left(x^{2} - 4x - 12\right)$
$= \mathbf{-x(x - 6)(x + 2)}$

16. $ax^{2} + 7xa + 10a = a\left(x^{2} + 7x + 10\right)$
$= \mathbf{a(x + 5)(x + 2)}$

17. $24x + 2x^2 + 70 = 2x^2 + 24x + 70$
$= 2(x^2 + 12x + 35) = \mathbf{2(x + 7)(x + 5)}$

18. $24 + 27x + 3x^2 = 3x^2 + 27x + 24$
$= 3(x^2 + 9x + 8) = \mathbf{3(x + 8)(x + 1)}$

19. $-px + px^2 - 2p = px^2 - px - 2p$
$= p(x^2 - x - 2) = \mathbf{p(x - 2)(x + 1)}$

20. $\begin{cases} N_N = N_Q + 15 \\ 5N_N + 25N_Q = 525 \end{cases}$

$5N_N + 25N_Q = 525$
$5(N_Q + 15) + 25N_Q = 525$
$5N_Q + 75 + 25N_Q = 525$
$30N_Q = 450$
$\mathbf{N_Q = 15}$

$N_N = N_Q + 15$
$N_N = 15 + 15$
$\mathbf{N_N = 30}$

21. (a) $\begin{cases} 2x + 2y = 14 \\ 3x - 2y = -4 \end{cases}$
(b)

(1)(a) $2x + 2y = 14$
(1)(b) $\underline{3x - 2y = -4}$
$ 5x = 10$
$ x = 2$

(a) $2x + 2y = 14$
$2(2) + 2y = 14$
$4 + 2y = 14$
$2y = 10$
$y = 5$

Thus the solution is the ordered pair **(2, 5)**.

22. (a) **False. Some rational numbers are not integers.**

(b) **False. No integer is an irrational number.**

23. $\dfrac{a}{x^2} + \dfrac{2}{ax^2} + \dfrac{b}{x^3} - \dfrac{1}{a^2}$

$= \dfrac{a(a^2 x)}{a^2 x^3} + \dfrac{2ax}{a^2 x^3} + \dfrac{ba^2}{a^2 x^3} - \dfrac{x^3}{a^2 x^3}$

$= \dfrac{\mathbf{a^3 x + 2ax + ba^2 - x^3}}{\mathbf{a^2 x^3}}$

24. $f(x) = x^{-5} + x^{-4} + x^{-3} + x^{-2} + x^{-1}$
$f(1) = (1)^{-5} + (1)^{-4} + (1)^{-3} + (1)^{-2} + (1)^{-1}$
$= 1 + 1 + 1 + 1 + 1 = \mathbf{5}$

25. $3\sqrt{20} - 2\sqrt{80} + 2\sqrt{125} - \sqrt{500}$
$= 3\sqrt{2 \cdot 2 \cdot 5} - 2\sqrt{2 \cdot 2 \cdot 2 \cdot 2 \cdot 5}$
$ + 2\sqrt{5 \cdot 5 \cdot 5} - \sqrt{100 \cdot 5}$
$= 3\sqrt{2}\sqrt{2}\sqrt{5} - 2\sqrt{2}\sqrt{2}\sqrt{2}\sqrt{2}\sqrt{5}$
$ + 2\sqrt{5}\sqrt{5}\sqrt{5} - \sqrt{100}\sqrt{5}$
$= 3(2)\sqrt{5} - 2(2)(2)\sqrt{5} + 2(5)\sqrt{5} - (10)\sqrt{5}$
$= 6\sqrt{5} - 8\sqrt{5} + 10\sqrt{5} - 10\sqrt{5}$
$= \mathbf{-2\sqrt{5}}$

26. $\dfrac{1}{(-3)^{-2}} + 3^0 - \sqrt[3]{-8} - \dfrac{1}{-3^{-2}}$

$= \dfrac{9}{1} + 1 - (-2) - \dfrac{9}{-1} = 9 + 1 + 2 + 9 = \mathbf{21}$

27. $\dfrac{a^2 x^5}{y} - 3aax^6 x^{-1} y^{-1} + \dfrac{4a^2 y^{-1}}{x^{-5}} - \dfrac{3aax^3 y^{-2}}{y}$

$= \dfrac{a^2 x^5}{y} - \dfrac{3a^2 x^5}{y} + \dfrac{4a^2 x^5}{y} - \dfrac{3a^2 x^3}{y^3}$

$= \dfrac{\mathbf{2a^2 x^5}}{\mathbf{y}} - \dfrac{\mathbf{3a^2 x^3}}{\mathbf{y^3}}$

28. $\dfrac{3x^2 y^{-2}}{ax^{-1}}\left(\dfrac{x^3}{y^2} - \dfrac{2x^{-2} a}{y^{-2}} + \dfrac{4x^{-2} y^2}{a^{-1} x} \right)$

$= \dfrac{3x^5 y^{-2}}{ax^{-1} y^2} - \dfrac{6y^{-2} a}{ax^{-1} y^{-2}} + \dfrac{12}{1}$

$= \dfrac{\mathbf{3x^6}}{\mathbf{ay^4}} - \mathbf{6x + 12}$

29. $-x + 4 - (-2)(-x - 5) = -(-2x - |4|)$
$-x + 4 + 2(-x - 5) = 2x + 4$
$-x + 4 - 2x - 10 = 2x + 4$
$-3x - 6 = 2x + 4$
$\underline{-2x + 6 \quad -2x + 6}$
$-5x = 10$
$ x = \mathbf{-2}$

30. Volume $= (\text{Area}_{\text{base}})(\text{Height})$

$= \left[\dfrac{1}{2}(12\text{ cm} \times 8\text{ cm}) \right](7\text{ cm})$

$= (48\text{ cm}^2)(7\text{ cm})$

$= \mathbf{336\text{ cm}^3}$

Practice 77

a. $N, N + 2, N + 4$

$N + (N + 4) = (N + 2) - 14$
$2N + 4 = N - 12$
$N = -16$

Thus the integers are **−16, −14,** and **−12**.

b. $\dfrac{5}{6}RD = 180$

$RD = \textbf{216 yd}$

c. $\dfrac{1}{8}T = 560$

$T = \textbf{4480}$

Problem Set 77

1. $N,\ N + 2,\ N + 4,\ N + 6$

$(N + 2) + (N + 4) = (N + 6) + 19$

$2N + 6 = N + 25$

$N = 19$

Thus the integers are **19, 21, 23,** and **25.**

2. $6.4T = 46.08$

$T = \dfrac{46.08}{6.4}$

$T = \textbf{7.2}$

3. $\dfrac{7}{8}F = 42{,}000$

$F = \textbf{48,000}$

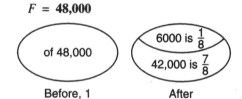

Before, 1　　　　　　　After

4. $P(7) = \dfrac{6}{36} = \dfrac{\textbf{1}}{\textbf{6}}$

5. $P(\text{both black}) = \dfrac{4}{11} \cdot \dfrac{4}{11} = \dfrac{\textbf{16}}{\textbf{121}}$

6. $P(T, T, T, T, T) = \dfrac{1}{2} \cdot \dfrac{1}{2} \cdot \dfrac{1}{2} \cdot \dfrac{1}{2} \cdot \dfrac{1}{2} = \dfrac{\textbf{1}}{\textbf{32}}$

7. The average is simply $\dfrac{495}{3}$ or **165.**

8. (a) The desired equation is $y = mx + b$.

By inspection, $b = 3$.

By inspection, the sign of m is +.

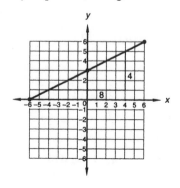

$|m| = \dfrac{4}{8} = \dfrac{1}{2}$

So $b = 3$ and $m = \dfrac{1}{2}$.

$y = \dfrac{1}{2}x + 3$

(b) $x = 3$

9. $2x + y + 2 = 0$

$y = -2x - 2$

$y = \dfrac{+2}{-1}x - 2$

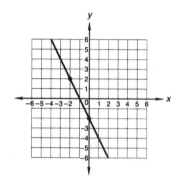

10. $y = -4$

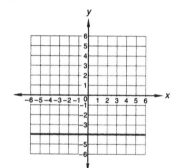

11. $7000 \times 10^{-7} = 7.0 \times 10^3 \times 10^{-7} = \textbf{7.0} \times \textbf{10}^{-4}$

12. $0.000007 \times 10^{-3} = 7.0 \times 10^{-6} \times 10^{-3}$

$= \textbf{7.0} \times \textbf{10}^{-9}$

13. $4x^2 - 49 = (2x)^2 - (7)^2 = \textbf{(2x + 7)(2x - 7)}$

14. $x^2 - 9x^2y^2 = x^2(1 - 9y^2) = x^2[(1)^2 - (3y)^2]$

$= \textbf{x}^2\textbf{(1 - 3y)(1 + 3y)}$

15. $3p^2 - 12k^2 = 3(p^2 - 4k^2) = 3[(p)^2 - (2k)^2]$

$= \textbf{3(p + 2k)(p - 2k)}$

16. $-4m^2 + k^2 = k^2 - 4m^2 = (k)^2 - (2m)^2$

$= \textbf{(k + 2m)(k - 2m)}$

17. $x^2 - 6x + 9 = \textbf{(x - 3)(x - 3)}$

18. $2x^2 - 8x + 8 = 2(x^2 - 4x + 4)$

$\quad\quad = 2(x - 2)(x - 2)$

19. $2x^2 + 8x + 8 = 2(x^2 + 4x + 4)$

$\quad\quad = 2(x + 2)(x + 2)$

20. $2x^2 + 20x + 50 = 2(x^2 + 10x + 25)$

$\quad\quad = 2(x + 5)(x + 5)$

21. $3x^2 - 30x + 75 = 3(x^2 - 10x + 25)$

$\quad\quad = 3(x - 5)(x - 5)$

22. $ax^2 - 12ax + 36a = a(x^2 - 12x + 36)$

$\quad\quad = a(x - 6)(x - 6)$

23. $\begin{cases} x + 3y = 16 \\ 2x - y = 4 \end{cases}$

$x + 3y = 16$

$\quad x = -3y + 16$

$\quad\quad 2x - y = 4$

$\quad 2(-3y + 16) - y = 4$

$\quad\quad -6y + 32 - y = 4$

$\quad\quad\quad -7y + 32 = 4$

$\quad\quad\quad\quad -7y = -28$

$\quad\quad\quad\quad\quad y = 4$

$x + 3y = 16$

$x + 3(4) = 16$

$x + 12 = 16$

$\quad\quad x = 4$

Thus the solution is the ordered pair **(4, 4)**.

24. (a) $\begin{cases} N_N + N_D = 500 \\ 5N_N + 10N_D = 3000 \end{cases}$
(b)

$\quad (-5)(a) \quad -5N_N - 5N_D = -2500$
$\quad (1)(b) \quad \underline{\;\;5N_N + 10N_D = \;\;3000\;\;}$
$\quad\quad\quad\quad\quad\quad\quad 5N_D = \quad 500$
$\quad\quad\quad\quad\quad\quad\quad N_D = \mathbf{100}$

(a) $N_N + N_D = 500$

$\quad N_N + 100 = 500$

$\quad\quad\quad N_N = \mathbf{400}$

25. (a) **Integers, rationals, reals**

(b) **Rationals, reals**

26. $4 \le x < 10$; $D = \{$Integers$\}$

27. $\dfrac{x + y^{-1}}{x^2 y^{-1} - 5} = \dfrac{x + \dfrac{1}{y}}{\dfrac{x^2}{y} - 5} = \dfrac{\dfrac{xy}{y} + \dfrac{1}{y}}{\dfrac{x^2}{y} - \dfrac{5y}{y}}$

$= \dfrac{\dfrac{xy + 1}{y}}{\dfrac{x^2 - 5y}{y}} \cdot \dfrac{\dfrac{y}{x^2 - 5y}}{\dfrac{y}{x^2 - 5y}} = \dfrac{xy + 1}{x^2 - 5y}$

28. $2\sqrt{75} - 6\sqrt{27} + \sqrt{30{,}000}$

$= 2\sqrt{3 \cdot 5 \cdot 5} - 6\sqrt{3 \cdot 3 \cdot 3} + \sqrt{10{,}000 \cdot 3}$

$= 2\sqrt{3}\sqrt{5}\sqrt{5} - 6\sqrt{3}\sqrt{3}\sqrt{3} + \sqrt{10{,}000}\sqrt{3}$

$= 2\sqrt{3}(5) - 6(3)\sqrt{3} + (100)\sqrt{3}$

$= 10\sqrt{3} - 18\sqrt{3} + 100\sqrt{3} = \mathbf{92\sqrt{3}}$

29. $-2|-2| - 2^2 - 3(-2 - x) = -2(x - 3 - 2)$

$\quad\quad -4 - 4 + 6 + 3x = -2x + 10$

$\quad\quad\quad\quad\quad 3x - 2 = -2x + 10$

$\quad\quad\quad\quad \underline{+2x + 2 \quad\quad +2x + 2}$

$\quad\quad\quad\quad\quad 5x \quad = \quad\quad 12$

$\quad\quad\quad\quad\quad x = \dfrac{12}{5}$

30. $S.A. = 2(\text{Area}_{\text{base}}) + \text{Lateral Surface Area}$

$= 2[\pi(8 \text{ in.})^2] + (\text{Perimeter}_{\text{base}})(\text{Length})$

$= 2(64\pi \text{ in.}^2) + [2\pi(8 \text{ in.})](40 \text{ in.})$

$= 128\pi \text{ in.}^2 + (16\pi \text{ in.})(40 \text{ in.})$

$= 128\pi \text{ in.}^2 + 640\pi \text{ in.}^2$

$= \mathbf{768\pi \text{ in.}^2 = 2411.52 \text{ in.}^2}$

Practice 78

a. $\quad \dfrac{z}{4} - \dfrac{1}{3} = \dfrac{z}{2}$

$(12)\dfrac{z}{4} - (12)\dfrac{1}{3} = (12)\dfrac{z}{2}$

$\quad\quad 3z - 4 = 6z$

$\quad\quad\quad -3z = 4$

$\quad\quad\quad\quad z = -\dfrac{4}{3}$

b. $\quad \dfrac{y + 2}{3} - \dfrac{5}{2} = \dfrac{2y - 4}{8}$

$24 \cdot \dfrac{(y + 2)}{3} - 24 \cdot \dfrac{5}{2} = 24 \cdot \dfrac{(2y - 4)}{8}$

$\quad 8(y + 2) - 12(5) = 3(2y - 4)$

$\quad\quad 8y + 16 - 60 = 6y - 12$

$\quad\quad\quad\quad 8y - 44 = 6y - 12$

$\quad\quad\quad\quad\quad 2y = 32$

$\quad\quad\quad\quad\quad y = \mathbf{16}$

Problem Set 78

1. $N, N + 2, N + 4$

$$3(N + N + 2) = (N + 4) - 48$$
$$3(2N + 2) = N - 44$$
$$6N + 6 = N - 44$$
$$5N = -50$$
$$N = -10$$

Thus the integers are **–10, –8,** and **–6.**

2. $N, N + 2, N + 4, N + 6$

$$4(N + N + 4) = 4(N + 6) + 4$$
$$4(2N + 4) = 4N + 24 + 4$$
$$8N + 16 = 4N + 28$$
$$4N = 12$$
$$N = 3$$

Thus the integers are **3, 5, 7,** and **9.**

3. $P(\text{white, then black}) = \dfrac{8}{18} \cdot \dfrac{10}{17} = \dfrac{80}{306} = \dfrac{\mathbf{40}}{\mathbf{153}}$

4. $P(> 2) = \dfrac{4}{6} = \dfrac{\mathbf{2}}{\mathbf{3}}$

5. $\dfrac{x + 80.2 + 91.6 + 123 + 204.7}{5} = \text{Average}$

$$\dfrac{x + 499.5}{5} = 790.6$$
$$x + 499.5 = \mathbf{3953}$$

6. $\dfrac{228}{100} \cdot C = 9120$

$$\dfrac{100}{228} \cdot \dfrac{228}{100} \cdot C = 9120 \cdot \dfrac{100}{228}$$
$$C = \mathbf{4000}$$

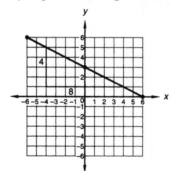

Before, 100%　　　　　　After

7. $\dfrac{7}{10} \cdot F = 4200$

$$\dfrac{10}{7} \cdot \dfrac{7}{10} \cdot F = 4200 \cdot \dfrac{10}{7}$$
$$F = \mathbf{6000}$$

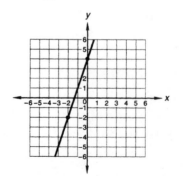

Before, 1　　　　　　After

8. $\dfrac{y}{7} + \dfrac{y + 1}{4} = 6$

$$28 \cdot \dfrac{y}{7} + 28 \cdot \dfrac{(y + 1)}{4} = 28 \cdot 6$$
$$4y + 7(y + 1) = 168$$
$$4y + 7y + 7 = 168$$
$$11y = 161$$
$$y = \dfrac{\mathbf{161}}{\mathbf{11}}$$

9. $\dfrac{x}{2} - \dfrac{1}{3} = \dfrac{x}{4}$

$$(12)\dfrac{x}{2} - (12)\dfrac{1}{3} = (12)\dfrac{x}{4}$$
$$6x - 4 = 3x$$
$$3x - 4 = 0$$
$$3x = 4$$
$$x = \dfrac{\mathbf{4}}{\mathbf{3}}$$

10. (a) $y = -3$

(b) The desired equation is $y = mx + b$.
By inspection, $b = 3$.
By inspection, the sign of m is –.

$$|m| = \dfrac{4}{8} = \dfrac{1}{2}$$

So $b = 3$ and $m = -\dfrac{1}{2}$.

$$y = -\dfrac{1}{2}x + 3$$

11. $y = 3x + 4$

$$y = \dfrac{+3}{+1}x + 4$$

12. $0.0003 \times 10^{-3} = 3.0 \times 10^{-4} \times 10^{-3}$

$\quad = \mathbf{3.0 \times 10^{-7}}$

13. $4000 \times 10^4 = 4.0 \times 10^3 \times 10^4 = \mathbf{4.0 \times 10^7}$

14. $x^2 - 9x + 20 = \mathbf{(x - 4)(x - 5)}$

15. $2ax^2 - 20ax + 42a = 2a(x^2 - 10x + 21)$

$\quad = \mathbf{2a(x - 7)(x - 3)}$

16. $13mx + 42m + mx^2 = mx^2 + 13mx + 42m$

$\quad = m(x^2 + 13x + 42) = \mathbf{m(x + 6)(x + 7)}$

17. $32x^2 - 18a^2 = 2(16x^2 - 9a^2)$

$\quad = 2[(4x)^2 - (3a)^2] = \mathbf{2(4x - 3a)(4x + 3a)}$

18. $25m^2a^2 - 4a^2 = a^2(25m^2 - 4)$

$\quad = a^2[(5m)^2 - (2)^2] = \mathbf{a^2(5m + 2)(5m - 2)}$

19. $-36k^2 + 9m^2y^2 = 9m^2y^2 - 36k^2$

$\quad = 9(m^2y^2 - 4k^2) = 9[(my)^2 - (2k)^2]$

$\quad = \mathbf{9(my - 2k)(my + 2k)}$

20. $\begin{cases} N_Q = N_D + 300 \\ 10N_D + 25N_Q = 8200 \end{cases}$

$\qquad 10N_D + 25N_Q = 8200$

$\qquad 10N_D + 25(N_D + 300) = 8200$

$\qquad 10N_D + 25N_D + 7500 = 8200$

$\qquad 35N_D + 7500 = 8200$

$\qquad\qquad\quad 35N_D = 700$

$\qquad\qquad\qquad N_D = \mathbf{20}$

$N_Q = N_D + 300$

$N_Q = 20 + 300$

$N_Q = \mathbf{320}$

21. (a) $\begin{cases} 4x - 3y = -3 \\ 2x + 4y = -18 \end{cases}$
    (b)

(1)(a) $\quad 4x - 3y = -3$
(−2)(b) $\underline{-4x - 8y = 36}$
$\qquad\qquad -11y = 33$
$\qquad\qquad\qquad y = -3$

(a) $\quad 4x - 3y = -3$

$\qquad 4x - 3(-3) = -3$

$\qquad\quad 4x + 9 = -3$

$\qquad\qquad 4x = -12$

$\qquad\qquad\quad x = -3$

Thus the solution is the ordered pair **(–3, –3).**

22. (a) **Irrationals, reals**

(b) **Rationals, reals**

23. $\dfrac{a}{x^2y} + \dfrac{b}{x^2y^2} + \dfrac{c}{x^2y^3} - \dfrac{d}{x^3y^3}$

$= \dfrac{axy^2}{x^3y^3} + \dfrac{bxy}{x^3y^3} + \dfrac{cx}{x^3y^3} - \dfrac{d}{x^3y^3}$

$= \dfrac{\mathbf{axy^2 + bxy + cx - d}}{\mathbf{x^3y^3}}$

24. $2\sqrt{54} - 3\sqrt{24} + 8\sqrt{600} - \sqrt{96}$

$= 2\sqrt{2 \cdot 3 \cdot 3 \cdot 3} - 3\sqrt{2 \cdot 2 \cdot 2 \cdot 3}$

$\quad + 8\sqrt{100 \cdot 2 \cdot 3} - \sqrt{2 \cdot 2 \cdot 2 \cdot 2 \cdot 2 \cdot 3}$

$= 2\sqrt{2}\sqrt{3}\sqrt{3}\sqrt{3} - 3\sqrt{2}\sqrt{2}\sqrt{2}\sqrt{3}$

$\quad + 8\sqrt{100}\sqrt{2}\sqrt{3} - \sqrt{2}\sqrt{2}\sqrt{2}\sqrt{2}\sqrt{2}\sqrt{3}$

$= 2\sqrt{2}(3)\sqrt{3} - 3(2)\sqrt{2}\sqrt{3} + 8(10)\sqrt{2}\sqrt{3}$

$\quad - (2)(2)\sqrt{2}\sqrt{3}$

$= 6\sqrt{6} - 6\sqrt{6} + 80\sqrt{6} - 4\sqrt{6}$

$= \mathbf{76\sqrt{6}}$

25. $\dfrac{x^0 x^2 y^{-2} (x^0)^{-2}}{(x^2)^{-3}(y^{-2})^3 y^0} = \dfrac{x^2 y^{-2}}{x^{-6}y^{-6}} = \mathbf{x^8 y^4}$

26. $\left(\dfrac{\sqrt[3]{x}}{4}\right)^{-2}(x^{-1}x)\left(\dfrac{\sqrt{y}}{\sqrt[4]{y}}\right) = \left(\dfrac{\sqrt[3]{8}}{4}\right)^{-2}\left(\dfrac{\sqrt{16}}{\sqrt[4]{16}}\right)$

$= \left(\dfrac{2}{4}\right)^{-2} \cdot \dfrac{4}{2} = \left(\dfrac{4}{2}\right)^2 \cdot 2 = 4 \cdot 2 = \mathbf{8}$

27. $\left(\dfrac{ax^2}{y^2} - \dfrac{3x}{xy^2} + \dfrac{2y^2}{x^{-2}}\right)\left(\dfrac{2x^{-2}}{y^2}\right)$

$= \dfrac{2a}{y^4} - \dfrac{6x^{-1}}{xy^4} + 4 = \dfrac{\mathbf{2a}}{\mathbf{y^4}} - \dfrac{\mathbf{6}}{\mathbf{x^2y^4}} + \mathbf{4}$

28. $x + 5 \not< 2; \ D = \{\text{Reals}\}$

$\quad x + 5 \not< 2$

$\quad \underline{-5 \qquad -5}$

$\qquad x \not< -3$

29. $P = (30 + 30 + 30 + 20 + 11 + 21)$ cm

$\quad = \mathbf{142 \ cm}$

30. $V = (\text{Area}_{base})(\text{Height})$

$\quad = [\pi(6 \text{ m})^2](18 \text{ m})$

$\quad = (36\pi \text{ m}^2)(18 \text{ m})$

$\quad = \mathbf{648\pi \ m^3} = \mathbf{2034.72 \ m^3}$

Practice 79

a. $R_A T_A + R_P T_P = 460$

$R_A(2) + (50)(4) = 460$

$2R_A + 200 = 460$

$2R_A = 260$

$R_A = \textbf{130}$

b. $R_T T_T + 200 = R_R T_R$

$(10)T_T + 200 = 15(T_T + 10)$

$10T_T + 200 = 15T_T + 150$

$-5T_T + 200 = 150$

$-5T_T = -50$

$T_T = \textbf{10}$

$T_R = T_T + 10$

$T_R = 10 + 10$

$T_R = \textbf{20}$

Problem Set 79

1. $N, N + 2, N + 4, N + 6$

$4(N + N + 6) = 12(N + 4) + 8$

$4(2N + 6) = 12N + 48 + 8$

$8N + 24 = 12N + 56$

$-4N + 24 = 56$

$-4N = 32$

$N = -8$

Thus the integers are **−8, −6, −4,** and **−2.**

2. $P(\text{Greek, then Roman}) = \dfrac{7}{12} \cdot \dfrac{5}{11} = \dfrac{\textbf{35}}{\textbf{132}}$

3. (a) $P(9) = \dfrac{4}{36} = \dfrac{1}{9}$

(b) The number of ways to get a sum less than 9 is
$1 + 2 + 3 + 4 + 5 + 6 + 5 = 26.$

$P(<9) = \dfrac{26}{36} = \dfrac{\textbf{13}}{\textbf{18}}$

4. $\dfrac{1}{8}N = 400$

$N = \textbf{3200}$

5. $W.A. = \dfrac{2(80) + 4(85) + 3(75) + 2(92)}{2 + 4 + 3 + 2}$

$= \dfrac{909}{11} = \textbf{82.64}$

6. $\dfrac{67}{100} \cdot A = 268$

$\dfrac{100}{67} \cdot \dfrac{67}{100} \cdot A = 268 \cdot \dfrac{100}{67}$

$A = \textbf{400 acres}$

Before, 100%   After

7. $R_A T_A + R_P T_P = 500$

$R_A(5) + (25)(9) = 500$

$5R_A + 225 = 500$

$5R_A = 275$

$R_A = \textbf{55}$

8. $R_H T_H = R_X T_X$

$(3)T_H = 6(T_H - 3)$

$3T_H = 6T_H - 18$

$-3T_H = -18$

$T_H = \textbf{6}$

$T_X = T_H - 3$

$T_X = 6 - 3$

$T_X = \textbf{3}$

9. $\dfrac{x}{4} - \dfrac{x + 2}{3} = 12$

$12 \cdot \dfrac{x}{4} - 12 \cdot \dfrac{(x + 2)}{3} = 12 \cdot 12$

$3x - 4(x + 2) = 144$

$3x - 4x - 8 = 144$

$-x - 8 = 144$

$-x = 152$

$x = \textbf{−152}$

10. $\dfrac{2y}{4} - \dfrac{y}{7} = \dfrac{y - 3}{2}$

$28 \cdot \dfrac{2y}{4} - 28 \cdot \dfrac{y}{7} = 28 \cdot \dfrac{(y - 3)}{2}$

$7(2y) - 4y = 14(y - 3)$

$14y - 4y = 14y - 42$

$-4y = -42$

$y = \dfrac{-42}{-4}$

$y = \dfrac{\textbf{21}}{\textbf{2}}$

11.
$$\frac{p}{6} - \frac{2p}{5} = \frac{4p - 5}{15}$$

$$30 \cdot \frac{p}{6} - 30 \cdot \frac{2p}{5} = 30 \cdot \frac{(4p - 5)}{15}$$

$$5p - 6(2p) = 2(4p - 5)$$

$$5p - 12p = 8p - 10$$

$$-7p = 8p - 10$$

$$-15p = -10$$

$$p = \frac{-10}{-15}$$

$$p = \frac{2}{3}$$

12. $y = -\frac{1}{2}x + 2$

$y = \frac{-1}{+2}x + 2$

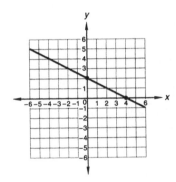

13. $0.000135 \times 10^{-17} = 1.35 \times 10^{-4} \times 10^{-17}$

$\quad = \mathbf{1.35 \times 10^{-21}}$

14. $135{,}000 \times 10^{-17} = 1.35 \times 10^{5} \times 10^{-17}$

$\quad = \mathbf{1.35 \times 10^{-12}}$

15. $-30 - 13x + x^2 = x^2 - 13x - 30$

$\quad = \mathbf{(x + 2)(x - 15)}$

16. $2m^2 - 24m + 70 = 2\left(m^2 - 12m + 35\right)$

$\quad = \mathbf{2(m - 7)(m - 5)}$

17. $-x^3 + 14x^2 - 40x = -x\left(x^2 - 14x + 40\right)$

$\quad = \mathbf{-x(x - 10)(x - 4)}$

18. $4m^2n^2 - 49x^2n^2p^2 = n^2\left(4m^2 - 49x^2p^2\right)$

$\quad = n^2\left[(2m)^2 - (7xp)^2\right]$

$\quad = \mathbf{n^2(2m + 7xp)(2m - 7xp)}$

19. $x^2(r + 2) + 10(r + 2) + 7x(r + 2)$

$\quad = x^2(r + 2) + 7x(r + 2) + 10(r + 2)$

$\quad = (r + 2)\left(x^2 + 7x + 10\right)$

$\quad = \mathbf{(r + 2)(x + 2)(x + 5)}$

20. $4z^2(x + y) - 21z(x + y) + (x + y)z^3$

$\quad = (x + y)z^3 + 4z^2(x + y) - 21z(x + y)$

$\quad = z(x + y)\left(z^2 + 4z - 21\right)$

$\quad = \mathbf{z(x + y)(z + 7)(z - 3)}$

21. $\begin{cases} x + 3y = 16 \\ 2x - 3y = -4 \end{cases}$

$x + 3y = 16$

$\quad x = -3y + 16$

$2x - 3y = -4$

$2(-3y + 16) - 3y = -4$

$-6y + 32 - 3y = -4$

$-9y + 32 = -4$

$-9y = -36$

$y = 4$

$x + 3y = 16$

$x + 3(4) = 16$

$x + 12 = 16$

$x = 4$

Thus the solution is the ordered pair **(4, 4)**.

22. (a) $\begin{cases} N_N + N_D = 22 \\ 5N_N + 10N_D = 135 \end{cases}$
(b)

$(-5)(a)\quad -5N_N - 5N_D = -110$

$(1)(b)\quad \dfrac{5N_N + 10N_D = 135}{5N_D = 25}$

$\qquad\qquad N_D = 5$

(a) $N_N + N_D = 22$

$\quad N_N + 5 = 22$

$\quad N_N = 17$

23. (a) **Irrational**

(b) **Rational**

(c) **Rational**

(d) **Rational**

24. $\dfrac{a}{xy} + \dfrac{4}{x(x + y)} - \dfrac{1}{y}$

$= \dfrac{a(x + y)}{xy(x + y)} + \dfrac{4y}{xy(x + y)} - \dfrac{x(x + y)}{xy(x + y)}$

$= \dfrac{a(x + y) + 4y - x(x + y)}{xy(x + y)}$

25. $5\sqrt{45} - 3\sqrt{180} + 2\sqrt{20}$

$= 5\sqrt{3 \cdot 3 \cdot 5} - 3\sqrt{2 \cdot 2 \cdot 3 \cdot 3 \cdot 5}$
$\quad + 2\sqrt{2 \cdot 2 \cdot 5}$

$= 5\sqrt{3}\sqrt{3}\sqrt{5} - 3\sqrt{2}\sqrt{2}\sqrt{3}\sqrt{3}\sqrt{5}$
$\quad + 2\sqrt{2}\sqrt{2}\sqrt{5}$

$= 5(3)\sqrt{5} - 3(2)(3)\sqrt{5} + 2(2)\sqrt{5}$

$= 15\sqrt{5} - 18\sqrt{5} + 4\sqrt{5} = \mathbf{\sqrt{5}}$

26. $\dfrac{x - 21}{5} = 20 \qquad \dfrac{y + 27}{27} = 4$

$\quad x - 21 = 100 \qquad y + 27 = 108$

$\qquad x = 121 \qquad\qquad y = 81$

$\dfrac{\sqrt{x}}{11} - y^0 + \dfrac{\sqrt[4]{7}}{3} + \sqrt[3]{-1}$

$= \dfrac{\sqrt{121}}{11} - 1 + \dfrac{\sqrt[4]{7}}{3} - 1$

$= 1 - 1 + \dfrac{\sqrt[4]{7}}{3} - 1$

$= \dfrac{\sqrt[4]{7}}{3} - \mathbf{1}$

27. $23,000\ \text{m} \cdot \text{m} \cdot \text{m} \times \dfrac{100\ \text{cm}}{1\ \text{m}} \times \dfrac{100\ \text{cm}}{1\ \text{m}}$

$\times \dfrac{100\ \text{cm}}{1\ \text{m}} \times \dfrac{1\ \text{in.}}{2.54\ \text{cm}} \times \dfrac{1\ \text{in.}}{2.54\ \text{cm}} \times \dfrac{1\ \text{in.}}{2.54\ \text{cm}}$

$\times \dfrac{1\ \text{ft}}{12\ \text{in.}} \times \dfrac{1\ \text{ft}}{12\ \text{in.}} \times \dfrac{1\ \text{ft}}{12\ \text{in.}} = \dfrac{\mathbf{23{,}000(100)^3}}{\mathbf{(2.54)^3(12)^3}}\ \mathbf{ft^3}$

$= \mathbf{812{,}237.33\ ft^3}$

28. $-\big[-2(x - 4) - |-3|\big] = -2x - 8$

$\qquad 2(x - 4) + 3 = -2x - 8$

$\qquad 2x - 8 + 3 = -2x - 8$

$\qquad\qquad 2x + 3 = -2x$

$\qquad\qquad\quad 4x = -3$

$\qquad\qquad\qquad x = -\dfrac{3}{4}$

29. $\text{Area} = \text{Area}_{\text{rectangle}} - \text{Area}_{\text{trapezoid}}$

$= (12\ \text{in.})(6\ \text{in.})$

$\quad - \left[\dfrac{1}{2}(10\ \text{in.} \times 2\ \text{in.}) + \dfrac{1}{2}(8\ \text{in.} \times 2\ \text{in.})\right]$

$= 72\ \text{in.}^2 - \left(10\ \text{in.}^2 + 8\ \text{in.}^2\right)$

$= 72\ \text{in.}^2 - 18\ \text{in.}^2$

$= \mathbf{54\ in.^2}$

30. $S.A. = 2\left(\text{Area}_{\text{base}}\right) + \text{Lateral Surface Area}$

$= 2\left[(12\ \text{ft} \times 20\ \text{ft}) + \dfrac{1}{2}\pi(6\ \text{ft})^2\right]$

$\quad + \left(\text{Perimeter}_{\text{base}}\right)(\text{Height})$

$= 2\left(240\ \text{ft}^2 + 18\pi\ \text{ft}^2\right)$

$\quad + \left(20\ \text{ft} + 12\ \text{ft} + 20\ \text{ft} + \dfrac{2\pi(6\ \text{ft})}{2}\right)$

$\qquad \times 25\ \text{ft}$

$= 480\ \text{ft}^2 + 36\pi\ \text{ft}^2 + (52\ \text{ft} + 6\pi\ \text{ft})(25\ \text{ft})$

$= 480\ \text{ft}^2 + 36\pi\ \text{ft}^2 + 1300\ \text{ft}^2 + 150\pi\ \text{ft}^2$

$= \mathbf{(1780 + 186\pi)\ ft^2 = 2364.04\ ft^2}$

Practice 80

a. $\dfrac{(0.07 \times 10^2)(800{,}000)}{(10{,}000)(0.0000004)} = \dfrac{(7 \times 10^0)(8 \times 10^5)}{(1 \times 10^4)(4 \times 10^{-7})}$

$= \dfrac{7 \cdot 8}{1 \cdot 4} \times \dfrac{10^0 \cdot 10^5}{10^4 \cdot 10^{-7}} = \dfrac{56}{4} \times \dfrac{10^5}{10^{-3}}$

$= 14 \times 10^8 = \mathbf{1.4 \times 10^9}$

b. $\dfrac{(0.04 \times 10^{-9})(50 \times 10^{16})}{(0.000004)(50{,}000)}$

$= \dfrac{(4 \times 10^{-11})(5 \times 10^{17})}{(4 \times 10^{-6})(5 \times 10^4)}$

$= \dfrac{4 \cdot 5}{4 \cdot 5} \times \dfrac{10^{-11} \cdot 10^{17}}{10^{-6} \cdot 10^4}$

$= \dfrac{20}{20} \times \dfrac{10^6}{10^{-2}} = \mathbf{1 \times 10^8}$

Problem Set 80

1. $N,\ N + 2,\ N + 4$

$3(N + N + 2 + N + 4) = 8(N + 4) + 20$

$\qquad\qquad 3(3N + 6) = 8N + 32 + 20$

$\qquad\qquad\quad 9N + 18 = 8N + 52$

$\qquad\qquad\qquad N + 18 = 52$

$\qquad\qquad\qquad\qquad N = 34$

Thus the integers are **34, 36,** and **38.**

2. (a) $P(\text{red marble}) = \dfrac{6}{15} = \dfrac{2}{5}$

(b) $P(\text{purple marble}) = \dfrac{5}{15} = \dfrac{1}{3}$

(c) $P(\text{green marble}) = \dfrac{4}{15}$

3. $P(T, T, T, H, H) = \dfrac{1}{2} \cdot \dfrac{1}{2} \cdot \dfrac{1}{2} \cdot \dfrac{1}{2} \cdot \dfrac{1}{2} = \dfrac{1}{32}$

4.
$$\frac{230}{100} \cdot H = 460$$
$$\frac{100}{230} \cdot \frac{230}{100} \cdot H = 460 \cdot \frac{100}{230}$$
$$H = \mathbf{200}$$

5. $\frac{5}{13}N = 4125$

$N = \mathbf{10{,}725 \ pounds}$

6. $\dfrac{(0.08 \times 10^7)(900{,}000)}{(20{,}000)(0.000003)} = \dfrac{(8 \times 10^5)(9 \times 10^5)}{(2 \times 10^4)(3 \times 10^{-6})}$

$= \dfrac{8 \cdot 9}{2 \cdot 3} \times \dfrac{10^5 \cdot 10^5}{10^4 \cdot 10^{-6}} = \dfrac{72}{6} \times \dfrac{10^{10}}{10^{-2}}$

$= 12 \times 10^{12} = \mathbf{1.2 \times 10^{13}}$

7. $\dfrac{(0.0006 \times 10^{-31})(8000 \times 10^9)}{(0.0000002)(400{,}000)}$

$= \dfrac{(6 \times 10^{-35})(8 \times 10^{12})}{(2 \times 10^{-7})(4 \times 10^5)}$

$= \dfrac{6 \cdot 8}{2 \cdot 4} \times \dfrac{10^{-35} \cdot 10^{12}}{10^{-7} \cdot 10^5}$

$= \dfrac{48}{8} \times \dfrac{10^{-23}}{10^{-2}}$

$= \mathbf{6 \times 10^{-21}}$

8.
$$R_F T_F = R_S T_S$$
$$(R_S + 16)5 = R_S(6)$$
$$5R_S + 80 = 6R_S$$
$$R_S = \mathbf{80}$$

$$R_F = 16 + R_S$$
$$R_F = 16 + 80$$
$$\mathbf{R_F = 96}$$

9.
$$R_M T_M = R_R T_R$$
$$8T_M = 2(5 - T_M)$$
$$8T_M = 10 - 2T_M$$
$$10T_M = 10$$
$$\mathbf{T_M = 1}$$

$$T_R = 5 - T_M$$
$$T_R = 5 - 1$$
$$\mathbf{T_R = 4}$$

10.
$$R_G T_G + R_B T_B = 100$$
$$4T_G + 10(T_G + 3) = 100$$
$$4T_G + 10T_G + 30 = 100$$
$$14T_G = 70$$
$$\mathbf{T_G = 5}$$

$$T_B = T_G + 3$$
$$T_B = 5 + 3$$
$$\mathbf{T_B = 8}$$

11.
$$\frac{3x}{2} - \frac{5 - x}{3} = 7$$
$$6 \cdot \frac{3x}{2} - 6 \cdot \frac{(5 - x)}{3} = 6 \cdot 7$$
$$3(3x) - 2(5 - x) = 42$$
$$9x - 10 + 2x = 42$$
$$11x = 52$$
$$x = \frac{52}{11}$$

12.
$$\frac{2x - 3}{5} - \frac{2x}{10} = \frac{1}{2}$$
$$10 \cdot \frac{(2x - 3)}{5} - 10 \cdot \frac{2x}{10} = 10 \cdot \frac{1}{2}$$
$$2(2x - 3) - 2x = 5$$
$$4x - 6 - 2x = 5$$
$$2x = 11$$
$$x = \frac{11}{2}$$

13.
$$3\frac{1}{8}x - 4\frac{2}{5} = 7\frac{1}{2}$$
$$\frac{25}{8}x - \frac{22}{5} = \frac{15}{2}$$
$$(40)\frac{25}{8}x - (40)\frac{22}{5} = (40)\frac{15}{2}$$
$$5(25x) - 8(22) = 20(15)$$
$$125x - 176 = 300$$
$$125x = 476$$
$$x = \frac{476}{125}$$

14. $y = \dfrac{3}{5}x - 1$

$y = \dfrac{+3}{+5}x - 1$

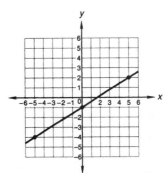

15. $x \nleq 2; \ D = \{\text{Positive Integers}\}$

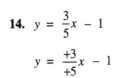

16. $x^3 + 9x^2 + 8x = x(x^2 + 9x + 8)$

$= \mathbf{x(x + 8)(x + 1)}$

17. $-ax^2 + 48a - 13xa = -ax^2 - 13xa + 48a$
$= -a(x^2 + 13x - 48) = -a(x + 16)(x - 3)$

18. $bcx^2 - a^2cb = bc(x^2 - a^2) = bc(x + a)(x - a)$

19. $(x - a)y^2 - 16(x - a) = (x - a)(y^2 - 16)$
$= (x - a)[(y)^2 - (4)^2] = (x - a)(y + 4)(y - 4)$

20. $\begin{cases} N_N = N_D + 12 \\ 5N_N + 10N_D = 510 \end{cases}$

$5N_N + 10N_D = 510$
$5(N_D + 12) + 10N_D = 510$
$5N_D + 60 + 10N_D = 510$
$15N_D = 450$
$N_D = 30$

$N_N = N_D + 12$
$N_N = 30 + 12$
$N_N = 42$

21. (a) $\begin{cases} 7x - 4y = 29 \\ 3x + 5y = -1 \end{cases}$
(b)

(5)(a) $\quad 35x - 20y = 145$
(4)(b) $\quad \dfrac{12x + 20y = \quad -4}{47x \qquad\quad = 141}$

$x = 3$

(a) $\quad 7x - 4y = 29$
$7(3) - 4y = 29$
$21 - 4y = 29$
$-4y = 8$
$y = -2$

Thus the solution is the ordered pair **(3, –2)**.

22. (a) **Irrationals, reals**

(b) **Integers, rationals, reals**

23. $\dfrac{3}{a} + \dfrac{4}{a^2} + \dfrac{7}{a^2(a + x)} - \dfrac{1}{a(a + x)}$

$= \dfrac{3a(a + x)}{a^2(a + x)} + \dfrac{4(a + x)}{a^2(a + x)} + \dfrac{7}{a^2(a + x)}$

$\quad - \dfrac{a}{a^2(a + x)}$

$= \dfrac{3a(a + x) + 4(a + x) + 7 - a}{a^2(a + x)}$

24. $\dfrac{a^{-1}b^{-1} + ab}{(ab)^{-1}} = \dfrac{\dfrac{1}{ab} + ab}{\dfrac{1}{ab}} = \dfrac{\dfrac{1}{ab} + \dfrac{a^2b^2}{ab}}{\dfrac{1}{ab}}$

$= \dfrac{\dfrac{1 + a^2b^2}{ab}}{\dfrac{1}{ab}} \cdot \dfrac{ab}{1} = 1 + a^2b^2$

25. $\dfrac{\left[x^2(y^5)^{-2}\right]^{-3}}{(x^0y^2)y^{-2}} = \dfrac{x^{-6}y^{30}}{1} = \dfrac{y^{30}}{x^6}$

26. $\dfrac{4 + \dfrac{1}{y^2}}{\dfrac{x}{y} + \dfrac{m}{y^2}} = \dfrac{\dfrac{4y^2}{y^2} + \dfrac{1}{y^2}}{\dfrac{xy}{y^2} + \dfrac{m}{y^2}} = \dfrac{\dfrac{4y^2 + 1}{y^2}}{\dfrac{xy + m}{y^2}} \cdot \dfrac{\dfrac{y^2}{xy + m}}{\dfrac{y^2}{xy + m}}$

$= \dfrac{4y^2 + 1}{xy + m}$

27. $\dfrac{x^{-2}}{y^2a}\left(\dfrac{y^2a^{-3}}{x^{-2}} + \dfrac{3x^{-4}}{y^{-2}a^{-4}} - \dfrac{x^2}{a^{-1}y^{-2}}\right)$

$= \dfrac{a^{-3}}{a} + \dfrac{3x^{-6}}{a^{-3}} - \dfrac{1}{1} = \dfrac{1}{a^4} + \dfrac{3a^3}{x^6} - 1$

28. $3 \cdot \dfrac{(x - 9)}{3} = 3 \cdot 21$

$x - 9 = 63$

$x = 72$

$\sqrt[4]{x + 9} + \left(\dfrac{\sqrt{x - 8}}{2}\right) - \sqrt[3]{\dfrac{x}{9}}$

$= \sqrt[4]{72 + 9} + \left(\dfrac{\sqrt{72 - 8}}{2}\right) - \sqrt[3]{\dfrac{72}{9}}$

$= \sqrt[4]{81} + \dfrac{\sqrt{64}}{2} - \sqrt[3]{8}$

$= 3 + 4 - 2 = 5$

29. $P = 10\,\text{cm} + 10\,\text{cm} + 10\,\text{cm} + 10\,\text{cm}$

$\quad + \dfrac{2\pi(10\ \text{cm})}{2} + \dfrac{2\pi(10\ \text{cm})}{2}$

$= (40 + 20\pi)\ \text{cm} = 102.8\ \text{cm}$

30. $V = (\text{Area}_{\text{base}})(\text{Height})$
$= (38\ \text{m}^2)(15\ \text{m})$
$= 570\ \text{m}^3$

Practice 81

a. $\begin{cases} y = x - 1 \\ y = -2x + 5 \end{cases}$

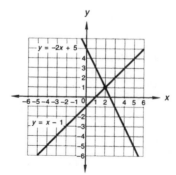

$$y = x - 1 \qquad y = -2x + 5$$
$$1 = 2 - 1 \qquad 1 = -2(2) + 5$$
$$1 = 1 \qquad\quad 1 = 1$$

The solution to the linear equations is **(2, 1)**.

b. $\begin{cases} y = x \\ y = 4 \end{cases}$

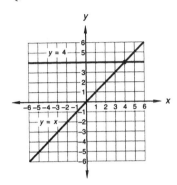

$$y = x \qquad y = 4$$
$$4 = 4 \qquad 4 = 4$$

The solution to the linear equations is **(4, 4)**.

c. (a) $\begin{cases} x + y = 7 \\ x + y = 9 \end{cases}$
(b)

(b) $x + y = 9$
$$x = 9 - y$$

(a) $\quad x + y = 7 \qquad (-1)(a) \;\; -x - y = -7$
$\quad 9 - y + y = 7 \qquad (1)(b) \;\; \dfrac{x + y = 9}{0 \neq 2}$
$\qquad\qquad 9 \neq 7$

Therefore, the linear equations are **inconsistent**.

Problem Set 81

1. $N, N + 2, N + 4$

$$4(N + N + 4) = 7(N + 2) + 16$$
$$4(2N + 4) = 7N + 14 + 16$$
$$8N + 16 = 7N + 30$$
$$N = 14$$

Thus the integers are **14, 16**, and **18**.

2. $N, N + 1, N + 2, N + 3$

$$N + N + 2 + 10 = 4(N + 3) + 6$$
$$2N + 12 = 4N + 18$$
$$-2N + 12 = 18$$
$$-2N = 6$$
$$N = -3$$

Thus the integers are **−3, −2, −1**, and **0**.

3. (a) $P(2) = \dfrac{1}{36}$

(b) $P(> 10) = \dfrac{3}{36} = \dfrac{1}{12}$

4. $\dfrac{WP}{100} \cdot 55 = 33$

$$\dfrac{100}{55} \cdot \dfrac{WP}{100} \cdot 55 = 33 \cdot \dfrac{100}{55}$$

$$WP = \dfrac{3300}{55}$$

$$WP = \mathbf{60\%}$$

5. $\dfrac{7}{5} \times 300 = \mathbf{420\ lb}$

6. $\dfrac{35}{100} \cdot N = 105$

$$\dfrac{100}{35} \cdot \dfrac{35}{100} \cdot N = 105 \cdot \dfrac{100}{35}$$

$$N = \mathbf{300}$$

7. $WF\left(7\dfrac{2}{5}\right) = 49\dfrac{1}{3}$

$$\dfrac{WF \cdot 7\dfrac{2}{5}}{7\dfrac{2}{5}} = \dfrac{49\dfrac{1}{3}}{7\dfrac{2}{5}}$$

$$WF = \dfrac{\dfrac{148}{3}}{\dfrac{37}{5}}$$

$$WF = \dfrac{148}{3} \cdot \dfrac{5}{37}$$

$$WF = \dfrac{20}{3}$$

8. $\begin{cases} y = x - 6 \\ y = -x \end{cases}$

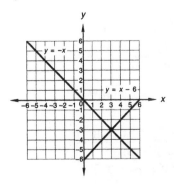

$$y = x - 6 \qquad y = -x$$
$$-3 = 3 - 6 \qquad -3 = -3$$
$$-3 = -3$$

The solution to the linear equations is **(3, −3)**.

9. $\begin{cases} y = x + 1 \\ y = -x - 1 \end{cases}$

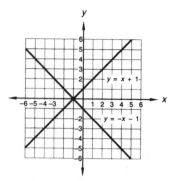

$y = x + 1 \qquad y = -x - 1$

$0 = -1 + 1 \qquad 0 = -(-1) - 1$

$0 = 0 \qquad\qquad 0 = 0$

The solution to the linear equations is **(–1, 0)**.

10. (a) $\begin{cases} y = x + 5 \\ y = x \end{cases}$
(b)

(b) $\quad y = x \qquad (-1)(a)\ -y = -x - 5$

$x + 5 = x \qquad (1)(b)\ \ \underline{\quad y = x \quad}$

$\qquad 0 \neq 5 \qquad\qquad\qquad 0 \neq -5$

Therefore, the linear equations are **inconsistent**.

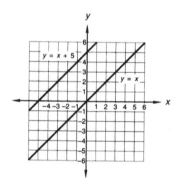

11. $\dfrac{(0.003 \times 10^7)(700{,}000)}{(5000)(0.0021 \times 10^{-6})}$

$= \dfrac{(3 \times 10^4)(7 \times 10^5)}{(5 \times 10^3)(2.1 \times 10^{-9})}$

$= \dfrac{3 \cdot 7}{5 \cdot 2.1} \times \dfrac{10^4 \cdot 10^5}{10^3 \cdot 10^{-9}}$

$= \dfrac{21}{10.5} \times \dfrac{10^9}{10^{-6}} = 2 \times 10^{15}$

12. $\dfrac{(0.0007 \times 10^{-10})(4000 \times 10^5)}{(0.0004)(7000)}$

$= \dfrac{(7 \times 10^{-14})(4 \times 10^8)}{(4 \times 10^{-4})(7 \times 10^3)}$

$= \dfrac{7 \cdot 4}{4 \cdot 7} \times \dfrac{10^{-14} \cdot 10^8}{10^{-4} \cdot 10^3}$

$= \dfrac{28}{28} \times \dfrac{10^{-6}}{10^{-1}} = 1 \times 10^{-5}$

13.
$$R_G T_G + R_B T_B = 120$$
$$4(T_B + 2) + 10(T_B) = 120$$
$$4T_B + 8 + 10T_B = 120$$
$$14T_B = 112$$
$$T_B = 8$$

$$T_G = T_B + 2$$
$$T_G = 8 + 2$$
$$T_G = 10$$

14.
$$R_K T_K = R_N T_N$$
$$6(T_N - 8) = 3T_N$$
$$6T_N - 48 = 3T_N$$
$$3T_N = 48$$
$$T_N = 16$$

$$T_K = T_N - 8$$
$$T_K = 16 - 8$$
$$T_K = 8$$

15.
$$\frac{x}{3} + \frac{5x + 3}{2} = 5$$
$$6 \cdot \frac{x}{3} + 6 \cdot \frac{(5x + 3)}{2} = 6 \cdot 5$$
$$2x + 3(5x + 3) = 30$$
$$2x + 15x + 9 = 30$$
$$17x = 21$$
$$x = \frac{21}{17}$$

16.
$$\frac{y + 3}{2} - \frac{4y}{3} = \frac{1}{6}$$
$$6 \cdot \frac{(y + 3)}{2} - 6 \cdot \frac{4y}{3} = 6 \cdot \frac{1}{6}$$
$$3(y + 3) - 2(4y) = 1$$
$$3y + 9 - 8y = 1$$
$$-5y = -8$$
$$y = \frac{8}{5}$$

17. $ax^2 + 6a - 7ax = ax^2 - 7ax + 6a$
$= a(x^2 - 7x + 6) = a(x - 6)(x - 1)$

18. $-mx^2 - 8m - 6mx = -mx^2 - 6mx - 8m$
$= -m(x^2 + 6x + 8) = -m(x + 4)(x + 2)$

19. $mx^2 - 9ma^2 = m(x^2 - 9a^2) = m[(x)^2 - (3a)^2]$
$= m(x - 3a)(x + 3a)$

20. $b^2(x + a) + 2b(x + a) - 24(x + a)$
$= (x + a)(b^2 + 2b - 24)$
$= (x + a)(b + 6)(b - 4)$

146

21. $\begin{cases} x + 5y = 17 \\ 2x - 4y = -8 \end{cases}$

$x + 5y = 17$

$\quad x = -5y + 17$

$\quad\quad 2x - 4y = -8$

$\quad 2(-5y + 17) - 4y = -8$

$\quad -10y + 34 - 4y = -8$

$\quad\quad\quad\quad -14y = -42$

$\quad\quad\quad\quad\quad y = 3$

$\quad x + 5y = 17$

$\quad x + 5(3) = 17$

$\quad x + 15 = 17$

$\quad\quad\quad x = 2$

Thus the solution is the ordered pair **(2, 3)**.

22. (a) $\begin{cases} N_N + N_D = 30 \\ 5N_N + 10N_D = 250 \end{cases}$
(b)

$(-5)(a)\quad -5N_N - 5N_D = -150$

$(1)(b)\quad \underline{5N_N + 10N_D = 250}$

$\quad\quad\quad\quad\quad 5N_D = 100$

$\quad\quad\quad\quad\quad\quad N_D = \mathbf{20}$

(a) $N_N + N_D = 30$

$\quad N_N + 20 = 30$

$\quad\quad\quad N_N = \mathbf{10}$

23. $4\sqrt{28} - 3\sqrt{63} + \sqrt{175} - 9\sqrt{7}$

$= 4\sqrt{2 \cdot 2 \cdot 7} - 3\sqrt{3 \cdot 3 \cdot 7} + \sqrt{5 \cdot 5 \cdot 7}$
$\quad - 9\sqrt{7}$

$= 4\sqrt{2}\sqrt{2}\sqrt{7} - 3\sqrt{3}\sqrt{3}\sqrt{7} + \sqrt{5}\sqrt{5}\sqrt{7}$
$\quad - 9\sqrt{7}$

$= 4(2)\sqrt{7} - 3(3)\sqrt{7} + (5)\sqrt{7} - 9\sqrt{7}$

$= 8\sqrt{7} - 9\sqrt{7} + 5\sqrt{7} - 9\sqrt{7} = \mathbf{-5\sqrt{7}}$

24. (a) $3 \pm \sqrt{169} = 3 \pm 13 = \mathbf{-10, 16}$

(b) $9 \pm \sqrt{144} = 9 \pm 12 = \mathbf{-3, 21}$

(c) $2 \pm \sqrt{361} = 2 \pm 19 = \mathbf{-17, 21}$

25. $\dfrac{\dfrac{x}{y} - 1}{\dfrac{x}{y} + m} = \dfrac{\dfrac{x}{y} - \dfrac{y}{y}}{\dfrac{x}{y} + \dfrac{my}{y}} = \dfrac{\dfrac{x - y}{y} \cdot \dfrac{y}{x + my}}{\dfrac{x + my}{y} \cdot \dfrac{y}{x + my}}$

$= \dfrac{x - y}{x + my}$

26. $\dfrac{x^2(2y^{-2})^{-3}}{(4x^2)^{-2}} = \dfrac{16x^2y^6}{8x^{-4}} = \mathbf{2x^6y^6}$

27. $\dfrac{1}{-3^{-2}} - 3 - (-3)^2 = -9 - 3 - 9 = \mathbf{-21}$

28. $\dfrac{x - 22}{5} = 8 \qquad 2y = 8$

$\quad\quad\quad\quad\quad\quad\quad\quad y = 4$

$\quad x - 22 = 40$

$\quad\quad\quad x = 62$

$\dfrac{\sqrt[3]{x + 2} + 11}{3} + \sqrt{y^3} = \dfrac{\sqrt[3]{62 + 2} + 11}{3} + \sqrt{64}$

$= \dfrac{4 + 11}{3} + 8 = 5 + 8 = \mathbf{13}$

29. $\dfrac{x^{-2}}{a^2y^{-2}}\left(\dfrac{x^4a^5}{y^4} - \dfrac{3x^{-4}}{a^{-4}y^2} + \dfrac{x^2}{a^{-2}y^2}\right)$

$= \dfrac{x^2a^5}{a^2y^2} - \dfrac{3x^{-6}}{a^{-2}} + \dfrac{1}{1} = \dfrac{x^2a^3}{y^2} - \dfrac{3a^2}{x^6} + \mathbf{1}$

30. Volume $= (\text{Area}_{\text{base}})(\text{Height})$

$= \left[\dfrac{1}{2}(17 \text{ in.} \times 6 \text{ in.})\right](20 \text{ in.})$

$= (51 \text{ in.}^2)(20 \text{ in.})$

$= \mathbf{1020 \text{ in.}^3}$

Practice 82

a. $f(x) = 2x^2 + 3x - 5$

$f(m^2) = 2(m^2)^2 + 3m^2 - 5 = \mathbf{2m^4 + 3m^2 - 5}$

b. $\quad g(x) = x^2 - 4$

$g(m + 2) = (m + 2)^2 - 4$

$\quad\quad\quad\quad = m^2 + 4m + 4 - 4$

$\quad\quad\quad\quad = \mathbf{m^2 + 4m}$

c. $D = \{x \in \mathbb{R}\}; R = \{y \in \mathbb{R}\}$

d. $D = \{x \in \mathbb{R}\}; R = \{2\}$

e. $D = \{x \in \mathbb{R} \mid -1 < x \leq 5\}$
$\quad R = \{y \in \mathbb{R} \mid -1 \leq y \leq 3\}$

f. $D = \{x \in \mathbb{R} \mid x \leq 3\}$

Problem Set 82

1. $N, N + 2, N + 4, N + 6$

$6(N + N + 4) = 5[-(N + 6)] + 3$

$\quad 6(2N + 4) = -5N - 30 + 3$

$\quad 12N + 24 = -5N - 27$

$\quad\quad\quad 17N = -51$

$\quad\quad\quad\quad N = -3$

Thus the integers are **-3, -1, 1, and 3.**

2. $P(\text{both pennies}) = \dfrac{20}{29} \cdot \dfrac{19}{28} = \dfrac{380}{812} = \dfrac{95}{203}$

3. (a) $P(8) = \dfrac{5}{36}$

(b) $P(<8) = \dfrac{1 + 2 + 3 + 4 + 5 + 6}{36}$

$= \dfrac{21}{36} = \dfrac{7}{12}$

4. Overall average $= \dfrac{(5 \times 30) + (15 \times 50)}{5 + 15}$

$= \dfrac{900}{20} = \textbf{45 cm}$

5. Range $= 6 - 2 = \textbf{4 mi}$

Median $= \textbf{5 mi}$

Mode $= \textbf{5 mi}$

Mean $= \dfrac{2 + 3 + 4 + 5 + 5 + 5 + 6}{7}$

$= \dfrac{30}{7} = \textbf{4.29 mi}$

6. $\dfrac{15}{17}T = 3000$

$T = \textbf{3400}$

7. $f(x) = x^2 + 1$

$f(x + 1) = (x + 1)^2 + 1$

$= x^2 + 2x + 1 + 1$

$= \boldsymbol{x^2 + 2x + 2}$

8. $D = \left\{x \in \mathbb{R} \mid x \leq 4\right\}$

9. $D = \left\{x \in \mathbb{R}\right\}; \ R = \{-1\}$

10. $D = \left\{x \in \mathbb{R} \mid -4 \leq x < 4\right\}$
$R = \left\{y \in \mathbb{R} \mid -1 \leq y \leq 3\right\}$

11. $R_M T_M + R_S T_S = 170$

$20\left(T_S + 1\right) + (30)T_S = 170$

$20T_S + 20 + 30T_S = 170$

$50T_S = 150$

$T_S = \textbf{3}$

$T_M = T_S + 1$

$T_M = 3 + 1$

$T_M = \textbf{4}$

12. $\begin{cases} y = x + 4 \\ y = -x + 2 \end{cases}$

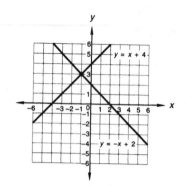

$y = x + 4 \qquad y = -x + 2$

$3 = -1 + 4 \qquad 3 = -(-1) + 2$

$3 = 3 \qquad\qquad 3 = 3$

The solution to the linear equations is **(–1, 3)**.

13. $\begin{cases} y = 2 \\ x = -3 \end{cases}$

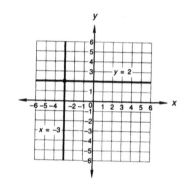

$y = 2 \qquad x = -3$

$2 = 2 \qquad -3 = -3$

The solution to the linear equations is **(–3, 2)**.

14. $\begin{cases} y = x + 2 \\ y = -x - 1 \end{cases}$

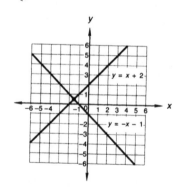

$y = x + 2 \qquad\quad y = x + 2$

$-x - 1 = x + 2 \qquad y = -\dfrac{3}{2} + 2$

$-2x = 3$

$x = -\dfrac{3}{2} \qquad\qquad y = \dfrac{1}{2}$

Therefore the linear equations are **consistent**.

15.
$$\frac{(0.0056 \times 10^{-5})(100{,}000 \times 10^{-14})}{8000 \times 10^{15}}$$

$$= \frac{(5.6 \times 10^{-8})(1 \times 10^{-9})}{8 \times 10^{18}}$$

$$= \frac{5.6 \cdot 1}{8} \times \frac{10^{-8} \cdot 10^{-9}}{10^{18}}$$

$$= \frac{5.6}{8} \times \frac{10^{-17}}{10^{18}} = 0.7 \times 10^{-35} = \mathbf{7 \times 10^{-36}}$$

16.
$$\frac{x+2}{5} - \frac{x}{10} = \frac{3}{20}$$

$$20 \cdot \frac{(x+2)}{5} - 20 \cdot \frac{x}{10} = 20 \cdot \frac{3}{20}$$

$$4(x+2) - 2x = 3$$

$$4x + 8 - 2x = 3$$

$$2x = -5$$

$$x = -\frac{5}{2}$$

17.
$$\frac{3x-4}{2} + \frac{1}{5} = \frac{x}{10}$$

$$10 \cdot \frac{(3x-4)}{2} + 10 \cdot \frac{1}{5} = 10 \cdot \frac{x}{10}$$

$$5(3x-4) + 2 = x$$

$$15x - 20 + 2 = x$$

$$14x = 18$$

$$x = \frac{18}{14}$$

$$x = \frac{9}{7}$$

18. $4a^2 - 160 + 12a = 4a^2 + 12a - 160$
$= 4(a^2 + 3a - 40) = \mathbf{4(a+8)(a-5)}$

19. $-m^3 + k^2 m = k^2 m - m^3 = m(k^2 - m^2)$
$= \mathbf{m(k+m)(k-m)}$

20. $x^4(y+1) + 2(y+1)x^3 + x^2(y+1)$
$= x^2(y+1)(x^2 + 2x + 1)$
$= \mathbf{x^2(y+1)(x+1)(x+1)}$

21.
$$\begin{cases} 5N_N + 10N_D = 450 \\ N_D = N_N + 30 \end{cases}$$

$$5N_N + 10N_D = 450$$
$$5N_N + 10(N_N + 30) = 450$$
$$5N_N + 10N_N + 300 = 450$$
$$15N_N = 150$$
$$N_N = 10$$

$$N_D = N_N + 30$$
$$N_D = 10 + 30$$
$$N_D = \mathbf{40}$$

22. (a) $\begin{cases} 5x - 2y = 7 \\ 4x + y = 3 \end{cases}$
(b)

(1)(a) $\quad 5x - 2y = 7$
(2)(b) $\quad \underline{8x + 2y = 6}$
$\qquad\quad 13x \qquad = 13$
$\qquad\qquad\quad x = 1$

(a) $\quad 5x - 2y = 7$
$\qquad 5(1) - 2y = 7$
$\qquad\quad 5 - 2y = 7$
$\qquad\quad -2y = 2$
$\qquad\qquad y = -1$

Thus the solution is the ordered pair **(1, –1)**.

23. (a) **Rational**

(b) **Rational**

(c) **Rational**

24.
$$\frac{1}{xc^2} + \frac{b}{x(c+x)} + \frac{5}{x^2c^2}$$

$$= \frac{x(c+x)}{x^2c^2(c+x)} + \frac{bxc^2}{x^2c^2(c+x)} + \frac{5(c+x)}{x^2c^2(c+x)}$$

$$= \frac{x(c+x) + bxc^2 + 5(c+x)}{x^2c^2(c+x)}$$

25.
$$\frac{4}{x+y} + \frac{6}{x} - \frac{4}{ax}$$

$$= \frac{4ax}{ax(x+y)} + \frac{6a(x+y)}{ax(x+y)} - \frac{4(x+y)}{ax(x+y)}$$

$$= \frac{4ax + 6a(x+y) - 4(x+y)}{ax(x+y)}$$

26. $7\sqrt{20} - 5\sqrt{32} + 2\sqrt{45} - 2\sqrt{180}$
$= 7\sqrt{2 \cdot 2 \cdot 5} - 5\sqrt{2 \cdot 2 \cdot 2 \cdot 2 \cdot 2}$
$\quad + 2\sqrt{3 \cdot 3 \cdot 5} - 2\sqrt{2 \cdot 2 \cdot 3 \cdot 3 \cdot 5}$
$= 7\sqrt{2}\sqrt{2}\sqrt{5} - 5\sqrt{2}\sqrt{2}\sqrt{2}\sqrt{2}\sqrt{2}$
$\quad + 2\sqrt{3}\sqrt{3}\sqrt{5} - 2\sqrt{2}\sqrt{2}\sqrt{3}\sqrt{3}\sqrt{5}$
$= 7(2)\sqrt{5} - 5(2)(2)\sqrt{2} + 2(3)\sqrt{5} - 2(2)(3)\sqrt{5}$
$= 14\sqrt{5} - 20\sqrt{2} + 6\sqrt{5} - 12\sqrt{5}$
$= \mathbf{8\sqrt{5} - 20\sqrt{2}}$

27. $\dfrac{x^{-2}a}{y^2}\left(\dfrac{a^4 y^{-2}}{x} - \dfrac{3x^2 a}{y^2}\right) = \dfrac{x^{-2}a^5 y^{-2}}{xy^2} - \dfrac{3a^2}{y^4}$

$= x^{-3}a^5 y^{-4} - \dfrac{3a^2}{y^4} = \dfrac{a^5}{x^3 y^4} - \dfrac{3a^2}{y^4}$

28. $\dfrac{x^2y^{-1} + y}{a - xy^{-1}} = \dfrac{\dfrac{x^2}{y} + y}{a - \dfrac{x}{y}} = \dfrac{\dfrac{x^2}{y} + \dfrac{y^2}{y}}{\dfrac{ay}{y} - \dfrac{x}{y}}$

$= \dfrac{\dfrac{x^2 + y^2}{y}}{\dfrac{ay - x}{y}} \cdot \dfrac{\dfrac{y}{ay - x}}{\dfrac{y}{ay - x}} = \dfrac{x^2 + y^2}{ay - x}$

29. $A = \dfrac{\pi(10 \text{ cm})^2}{2} + \dfrac{\pi(10 \text{ cm})^2}{2}$

$= 100\pi \text{ cm}^2 = \textbf{314 cm}^2$

30. Lateral $S.A. = \left(\text{Perimeter}_{\text{base}}\right)(\text{Height})$

$= (13 \text{ m} + 13 \text{ m} + 13 \text{ m} + 13 \text{ m}$
$+ 13 \text{ m})(20 \text{ m})$

$= (65 \text{ m})(20 \text{ m})$

$= \textbf{1300 m}^2$

Practice 83

a. (a) $N_N + N_D = 36$

(b) $5N_N + 10N_D = 290$

(a) $N_N + N_D = 36$

$N_N = -N_D + 36$

(b) $\qquad 5N_N + 10N_D = 290$

$5(-N_D + 36) + 10N_D = 290$

$-5N_D + 180 + 10N_D = 290$

$5N_D = 110$

$N_D = \textbf{22}$

(a) $N_N + N_D = 36$

$N_N + 22 = 36$

$N_N = \textbf{14}$

b. (a) $N_Q = N_D + 9$

(b) $25N_Q + 10N_D = 645$

(b) $\qquad 25N_Q + 10N_D = 645$

$25(N_D + 9) + 10N_D = 645$

$25N_D + 225 + 10N_D = 645$

$35N_D = 420$

$N_D = \textbf{12}$

(a) $N_Q = N_D + 9$

$N_Q = 12 + 9$

$N_Q = \textbf{21}$

Problem Set 83

1. (a) $N_D + N_N = 51$

(b) $10N_D + 5N_N = 410$

$(-5)(a) \quad -5N_D - 5N_N = -255$

$(1)(b) \quad \underline{10N_D + 5N_N = 410}$

$5N_D \qquad = 155$

$N_D = \textbf{31}$

(a) $N_D + N_N = 51$

$31 + N_N = 51$

$N_N = \textbf{20}$

2. (a) $N_D + N_Q = 40$

(b) $10N_D + 25N_Q = 475$

(a) $N_D + N_Q = 40$

$N_D = -N_Q + 40$

(b) $\qquad 10N_D + 25N_Q = 475$

$10(-N_Q + 40) + 25N_Q = 475$

$-10N_Q + 400 + 25N_Q = 475$

$15N_Q = 75$

$N_Q = \textbf{5}$

(a) $N_D + N_Q = 40$

$N_D + 5 = 40$

$N_D = \textbf{35}$

3. $O.A. = \dfrac{(10 \times \$650.50) + (20 \times \$874.75)}{10 + 20}$

$= \dfrac{\$24,000}{30} = \textbf{\$800}$

4. $\dfrac{17}{19} = \dfrac{S}{7600}$

$19S = 17 \cdot 7600$

$S = \dfrac{17 \cdot 7600}{19}$

$S = \textbf{6800}$

5. $P(\text{chocolate, then peanut}) = \dfrac{10}{15} \cdot \dfrac{5}{14}$

$= \dfrac{50}{210} = \dfrac{\textbf{5}}{\textbf{21}}$

6. $P(2, 3, 2) = \dfrac{1}{4} \cdot \dfrac{1}{4} \cdot \dfrac{1}{4} = \dfrac{\textbf{1}}{\textbf{64}}$

7. $f(x) = x^3 + 2$

$f(3) = (3)^3 + 2 = 27 + 2 = \textbf{29}$

8. $g(x) = x^2 - 7x$

$g(a + b) = (a + b)^2 - 7(a + b)$

$\qquad = a^2 + 2ab + b^2 - 7a - 7b$

9. $D = \{x \in \mathbb{R} \mid x \le 9\}$

10. $D = \{x \in \mathbb{R}\};\ R = \{-5\}$

11. $D = \{x \in \mathbb{R} \mid -4 \le x \le 4\}$

$R = \{y \in \mathbb{R} \mid -3 \le y \le 3\}$

12. (a) $x = 4$

(b) The desired equation is $y = mx + b$.

By inspection, $b = 0$.

By inspection, the sign of m is +.

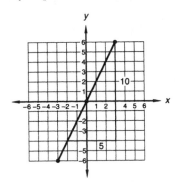

$|m| = \dfrac{10}{5} = 2$

So $b = 0$ and $m = 2$.

$y = 2x$

13. $\begin{cases} y = x + 2 \\ y = -x \end{cases}$

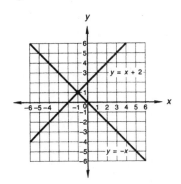

$y = x + 2 \qquad y = -x$

$1 = -1 + 2 \qquad 1 = -(-1)$

$1 = 1 \qquad\qquad 1 = 1$

The solution to the linear equations is **(−1, 1)**.

14. $\begin{cases} y = 2x + 1 \\ y = -2x + 1 \end{cases}$

$\quad y = -2x + 1 \qquad y = 2x + 1$

$2x + 1 = -2x + 1 \qquad y = 0 + 1$

$\qquad 4x = 0 \qquad\qquad y = 1$

$\qquad\ x = 0$

Therefore, the linear equations are **consistent**.

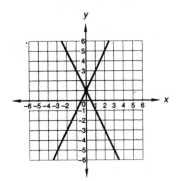

15. $\dfrac{(0.0016 \times 10^{-7})(3000 \times 10^5)}{1{,}200{,}000}$

$= \dfrac{(1.6 \times 10^{-10})(3 \times 10^8)}{1.2 \times 10^6}$

$= \dfrac{1.6 \cdot 3}{1.2} \times \dfrac{10^{-10} \cdot 10^8}{10^6}$

$= \dfrac{4.8}{1.2} \times \dfrac{10^{-2}}{10^6}$

$= \mathbf{4 \times 10^{-8}}$

16. $\dfrac{(0.003 \times 10^{-5})(700 \times 10^{14})}{21{,}000{,}000}$

$= \dfrac{(3 \times 10^{-8})(7 \times 10^{16})}{2.1 \times 10^7}$

$= \dfrac{3 \cdot 7}{2.1} \times \dfrac{10^{-8} \cdot 10^{16}}{10^7}$

$= \dfrac{21}{2.1} \times \dfrac{10^8}{10^7} = 10 \times 10^1 = 10^2 = \mathbf{100}$

17. $\qquad R_P T_P = R_M T_M$

$45(T_M - 8) = 15T_M$

$45T_M - 360 = 15T_M$

$\qquad 30T_M = 360$

$\qquad\quad \mathbf{T_M = 12}$

$T_P = T_M - 8$

$T_P = 12 - 8$

$\mathbf{T_P = 4}$

18. $R_G T_G + 10 = R_P T_P$

$R_G(4) + 10 = (R_G + 45)(2)$

$4R_G + 10 = 2R_G + 90$

$2R_G = 80$

$\mathbf{R_G = 40}$

$R_P = R_G + 45$

$R_P = 40 + 45$

$\mathbf{R_P = 85}$

19.

$$\frac{x}{3} - 2 = \frac{4 - x}{5}$$

$$15 \cdot \frac{x}{3} - 15 \cdot 2 = 15 \cdot \frac{(4 - x)}{5}$$

$$5x - 30 = 3(4 - x)$$

$$5x - 30 = 12 - 3x$$

$$8x = 42$$

$$x = \frac{42}{8}$$

$$x = \frac{21}{4}$$

20.

$$\frac{x}{4} - \frac{1}{2} = \frac{2 - x}{8}$$

$$8 \cdot \frac{x}{4} - 8 \cdot \frac{1}{2} = 8 \cdot \frac{(2 - x)}{8}$$

$$2x - 4 = 2 - x$$

$$3x = 6$$

$$x = 2$$

21. $28x + 11x^2 + x^3 = x^3 + 11x^2 + 28x$

$= x(x^2 + 11x + 28) = \mathbf{x(x + 7)(x + 4)}$

22. $-xy^2 + 4a^2x = 4a^2x - xy^2 = x(4a^2 - y^2)$

$= \mathbf{x(2a + y)(2a - y)}$

23. $x^2(z + 1) - (z + 1)y^2 = (z + 1)(x^2 - y^2)$

$= \mathbf{(z + 1)(x + y)(x - y)}$

24. (a) $\begin{cases} 3x + 2y = 11 \\ 2x - 3y = 16 \end{cases}$

(b)

(3)(a) $9x + 6y = 33$

(2)(b) $\underline{4x - 6y = 32}$

          $13x \quad\quad = 65$

                $x = 5$

(a) $3x + 2y = 11$

     $3(5) + 2y = 11$

      $15 + 2y = 11$

          $2y = -4$

           $y = -2$

Thus the solution is the ordered pair **(5, –2)**.

25. $-3 \le x < 2$; $D = \{\text{Reals}\}$

26. (a) **False. Zero, a member of the set of whole numbers, is not a member of the set of natural numbers.**

(b) **True. Every integer is a rational number.**

27. $\dfrac{1}{a^2} + \dfrac{2b}{a^3} - \dfrac{3b}{4a^3} = \dfrac{4a}{4a^3} + \dfrac{8b}{4a^3} - \dfrac{3b}{4a^3}$

$= \dfrac{4a + 8b - 3b}{4a^3} = \dfrac{\mathbf{4a + 5b}}{\mathbf{4a^3}}$

28. $\dfrac{abc^{-1} - c^{-2}}{4 - ac^2} = \dfrac{\dfrac{ab}{c} - \dfrac{1}{c^2}}{4 - ac^2} = \dfrac{\dfrac{abc}{c^2} - \dfrac{1}{c^2}}{4 - ac^2}$

$= \dfrac{abc - 1}{c^2} \cdot \dfrac{1}{4 - ac^2} = \dfrac{\mathbf{abc - 1}}{\mathbf{c^2(4 - ac^2)}}$

29. $y + 3 = \sqrt{81} - 3$

$y + 3 = 9 - 3$

$y = 3$

$x(x^{-5} - y) - x^2 = -2[(-2)^{-5} - 3] - (-2)^2$

$= -2\left(\dfrac{1}{-32} - 3\right) - 4 = \dfrac{1}{16} + 6 - 4$

$= 2\dfrac{1}{16} = \dfrac{\mathbf{33}}{\mathbf{16}}$

30. $V = (\text{Area}_{\text{base}})(\text{Height})$

$= \left[(10 \text{ in.} \times 18 \text{ in.}) + \dfrac{1}{2}\pi(5 \text{ in.})^2\right](23 \text{ in.})$

$= \left(180 \text{ in.}^2 + \dfrac{25\pi}{2}\text{in.}^2\right)(23 \text{ in.})$

$= \left(4140 + \dfrac{575\pi}{2}\right) \text{in.}^3 = \mathbf{5042.75 \text{ in.}^3}$

Practice 84

a. $5\sqrt{12} \cdot 4\sqrt{3} = 5 \cdot 4\sqrt{12}\sqrt{3} = 20\sqrt{36}$

$= 20(6) = \mathbf{120}$

b. $3\sqrt{2}(4\sqrt{3} + 5\sqrt{6})$

$= 3\sqrt{2} \cdot 4\sqrt{3} + 3\sqrt{2} \cdot 5\sqrt{6}$

$= 3 \cdot 4\sqrt{2}\sqrt{3} + 3 \cdot 5\sqrt{2}\sqrt{6}$

$= 12\sqrt{6} + 15\sqrt{12}$

$= 12\sqrt{6} + 15(2)\sqrt{3} = \mathbf{12\sqrt{6} + 30\sqrt{3}}$

c. Function

d. Not a function

e. $\{a, 6, 7\}$

f. $\{p, a, 7\}$

g. (2), (4)

Problem Set 84

1. (a) $5N_N + N_P = 475$

   (b) $N_N + N_P = 175$

   (1)(a) $5N_N + N_P = \quad 475$
   (−1)(b) $\underline{-N_N - N_P = -175}$
   $\qquad 4N_N \qquad\quad = \quad 300$
   $\qquad\qquad\quad N_N = \mathbf{75}$

   (b) $N_N + N_P = 175$
   $\quad 75 + N_P = 175$
   $\qquad\quad N_P = \mathbf{100}$

2. (a) $N_N = N_D + 12$
   (b) $5N_N + 10N_D = 510$

   (b) $\qquad\quad 5N_N + 10N_D = 510$
   $\quad 5(N_D + 12) + 10N_D = 510$
   $\quad\; 5N_D + 60 + 10N_D = 510$
   $\qquad\qquad 15N_D + 60 = 510$
   $\qquad\qquad\quad\; 15N_D = 450$
   $\qquad\qquad\qquad N_D = \mathbf{30}$

   (a) $N_N = N_D + 12$
   $\quad N_N = 30 + 12$
   $\quad N_N = \mathbf{42}$

3. $\qquad \dfrac{80}{100} \cdot T = 128$

   $\dfrac{100}{80} \cdot \dfrac{80}{100} \cdot T = 128 \cdot \dfrac{100}{80}$

   $\qquad\qquad\quad T = \mathbf{160}$

4. $N, N + 2, N + 4$

   $3(N + N + 2) = 14[-(N + 4)] - 58$
   $\quad 3(2N + 2) = -14N - 56 - 58$
   $\quad\;\; 6N + 6 = -14N - 114$
   $\qquad\;\; 20N = -120$
   $\qquad\qquad N = -6$

   Thus the integers are **−6, −4,** and **−2.**

5. $N, N + 1, N + 2$

   $5(N + N + 1) = -(N + 2) + 7$
   $\quad\; 5(2N + 1) = -N - 2 + 7$
   $\quad 10N + 5 = -N + 5$
   $\qquad\;\; 11N = 0$
   $\qquad\qquad N = 0$

   Thus the integers are **0, 1,** and **2.**

6. (a) $P(11) = \dfrac{2}{36} = \dfrac{1}{\mathbf{18}}$

   (b) $P(\geq 5) = \dfrac{4 + 5 + 6 + 5 + 4 + 3 + 2 + 1}{36}$

   $\qquad\qquad = \dfrac{30}{36} = \dfrac{\mathbf{5}}{\mathbf{6}}$

7. **(a), (d)**

8. **(b), (c), (d)**

9. $\qquad f(x) = 2x^2 - 3x + 2$
   $f(a + 1) = 2(a + 1)^2 - 3(a + 1) + 2$
   $\qquad\quad\;\; = 2(a^2 + 2a + 1) - 3a - 3 + 2$
   $\qquad\quad\;\; = 2a^2 + 4a + 2 - 3a - 3 + 2$
   $\qquad\quad\;\; = \mathbf{2a^2 + a + 1}$

10. $D = \left\{ x \in \mathbb{R} \mid x \leq 11 \right\}$

11. $D = \left\{ x \in \mathbb{R} \mid -4 \leq x \leq 4 \right\}$
    $R = \left\{ y \in \mathbb{R} \mid -1 \leq y \leq 2 \right\}$

12. (a) $y = 4$

    (b) The desired equation is $y = mx + b$.

    By inspection, $b = -2$.

    By inspection, the sign of m is −.

    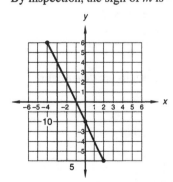

    $|m| = \dfrac{10}{5} = 2$

    So $b = -2$ and $m = -2$.

    $\mathbf{y = -2x - 2}$

13. $\begin{cases} y = -2x - 2 \\ y = -4 \end{cases}$

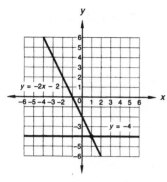

$$y = -2x - 2 \qquad y = -4$$
$$-4 = -2(1) - 2 \qquad -4 = -4$$
$$-4 = -4$$

The solution to the linear equations is **(1, –4)**.

14. (a) $\begin{cases} 4x + 3y = -14 \\ 3x + 2y = -10 \end{cases}$
   (b)

$$\begin{array}{ll} (2)(a) & 8x + 6y = -28 \\ (-3)(b) & \underline{-9x - 6y = 30} \\ & -x = 2 \\ & x = -2 \end{array}$$

(a) $4x + 3y = -14$
$$4(-2) + 3y = -14$$
$$-8 + 3y = -14$$
$$3y = -6$$
$$y = -2$$

Thus the solution is the ordered pair **(–2, –2)**.

15. $\begin{cases} x + y + 2 = 0 \\ 2x + 2y + 4 = 0 \end{cases}$

$$x + y + 2 = 0$$
$$x = -y - 2$$

$$2x + 2y + 4 = 0$$
$$2(-y - 2) + 2y + 4 = 0$$
$$-2y - 4 + 2y + 4 = 0$$
$$0 = 0$$

Therefore the equations are **dependent.**

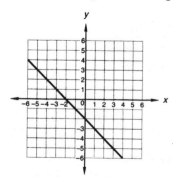

16. $\dfrac{(0.00032 \times 10^{-5})(4000 \times 10^7)}{(160{,}000)(0.00002)}$

$$= \frac{(3.2 \times 10^{-9})(4 \times 10^{10})}{(1.6 \times 10^5)(2 \times 10^{-5})}$$

$$= \frac{3.2 \cdot 4}{1.6 \cdot 2} \times \frac{10^{-9} \cdot 10^{10}}{10^5 \cdot 10^{-5}}$$

$$= \frac{12.8}{3.2} \times \frac{10^1}{10^0}$$

$$= 4 \times 10^1 = \mathbf{40}$$

17. $\dfrac{(a^{-3})^0 (a^2)^0 (a^{-2})^{-2}}{a^4 (x^{-5})^{-2} x x^2} = \dfrac{a^4}{a^4 x^{10} x^3} = \dfrac{1}{x^{13}}$

18. $x \geq -3$; $D = \{\text{Integers}\}$

19. $$R_M T_M = R_K T_K$$
$$30(16 - T_K) = 10T_K$$
$$480 - 30T_K = 10T_K$$
$$-40T_K = -480$$
$$\mathbf{T_K = 12}$$

$$T_M = 16 - T_K$$
$$T_M = 16 - 12$$
$$\mathbf{T_M = 4}$$

20. $$\frac{3 + x}{4} - \frac{x}{3} = 5$$
$$12 \cdot \frac{(3 + x)}{4} - 12 \cdot \frac{x}{3} = 12 \cdot 5$$
$$3(3 + x) - 4x = 60$$
$$9 + 3x - 4x = 60$$
$$-x = 51$$
$$\mathbf{x = -51}$$

21. $$-0.2 - 0.02 - 0.02x = 0.4(1 - x) - 0.012$$
$$-0.22 - 0.02x = 0.4 - 0.4x - 0.012$$
$$-220 - 20x = 400 - 400x - 12$$
$$380x = 608$$
$$\mathbf{x = 1.6}$$

22. $x^3 + 20x + 9x^2 = x^3 + 9x^2 + 20x$
$$= x(x^2 + 9x + 20) = x(x + 5)(x + 4)$$

23. $abx^2 - 6ab + abx = abx^2 + abx - 6ab$
$$= ab(x^2 + x - 6) = ab(x + 3)(x - 2)$$

24. $\dfrac{1}{x^2} - \dfrac{3a}{x - a} - \dfrac{2}{x}$

$$= \frac{x - a}{x^2(x - a)} - \frac{3ax^2}{x^2(x - a)} - \frac{2x(x - a)}{x^2(x - a)}$$

$$= \frac{x - a - 3ax^2 - 2x(x - a)}{x^2(x - a)}$$

25. $(4 + x)(x^2 + 2x + 3)$
$= 4x^2 + 8x + 12 + x^3 + 2x^2 + 3x$
$= x^3 + 6x^2 + 11x + 12$

26. $\sqrt[3]{26.981}$ **is less than 3 because 26.981 is less than 3^3.**

27. $-x^2(x^{-2} - y) - |x - y^4|$
$= -(-3)^2[(-3)^{-2} - (-2)] - |-3 - (-2)^4|$
$= -9\left(\dfrac{1}{9} + 2\right) - |-3 - 16|$
$= -1 - 18 - 19 = \mathbf{-38}$

28. $WF\left(3\dfrac{1}{8}\right) = 1\dfrac{1}{8}$

$\dfrac{WF \cdot 3\frac{1}{8}}{3\frac{1}{8}} = \dfrac{1\frac{1}{8}}{3\frac{1}{8}}$

$WF = \dfrac{\frac{9}{8}}{\frac{25}{8}}$

$WF = \dfrac{9}{8} \cdot \dfrac{8}{25}$

$WF = \dfrac{\mathbf{9}}{\mathbf{25}}$

29. $A = \dfrac{1}{2}(18 \text{ cm} \times 14 \text{ cm})$

$\quad + \dfrac{1}{2}(18 \text{ cm} \times 14 \text{ cm})$

$= 126 \text{ cm}^2 + 126 \text{ cm}^2$

$= \mathbf{252 \text{ cm}^2}$

30. $S.A. = 2\left(\text{Area}_{\text{triangle}}\right) + 2\left(\text{Area}_{\text{top}}\right) + \text{Area}_{\text{bottom}}$
$= 2\left[\dfrac{1}{2}(24 \text{ in.} \times 9 \text{ in.})\right] + 2(8 \text{ in.} \times 15 \text{ in.})$
$\quad + (8 \text{ in.} \times 24 \text{ in.})$
$= 2(108 \text{ in.}^2) + 2(120 \text{ in.}^2) + 192 \text{ in.}^2$
$= 216 \text{ in.}^2 + 240 \text{ in.}^2 + 192 \text{ in.}^2$
$= \mathbf{648 \text{ in.}^2}$

Practice 85

a.

STEM	LEAF
11	1, 8
12	8, 3, 7, 9
13	2, 6, 0, 5, 9
14	2, 5, 8, 9, 2, 9
15	1, 0, 0

b. Range $= 151 - 111 = \mathbf{40}$

c. Median $= \dfrac{136 + 139}{2} = \mathbf{137.5}$

d. Mode $= \mathbf{142, 149, 150}$

e. Mean $= \dfrac{\text{Sum of the 20 numbers}}{20}$

$\quad = \dfrac{2734}{20} = \mathbf{136.7}$

f.

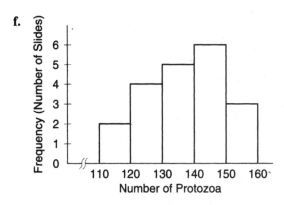

g. $4 + 5 + 6 = \mathbf{15}$

h. $\dfrac{4 + 2}{20} = \dfrac{6}{20} = \dfrac{3}{10} = \mathbf{30\%}$

Problem Set 85

1. (a) $N_P + 5N_N = 1450$
(b) $N_P + N_N = 450$

(1)(a) $\quad N_P + 5N_N = 1450$
(−1)(b) $\quad \underline{-N_P - N_N = -450}$
$\quad\quad\quad\quad\quad 4N_N = 1000$
$\quad\quad\quad\quad\quad\quad N_N = \mathbf{250}$

(b) $N_P + N_N = 450$
$\quad N_P + 250 = 450$
$\quad\quad\quad N_P = \mathbf{200}$

2. $\quad\quad \dfrac{86}{100} \cdot P = 3440$

$\dfrac{100}{86} \cdot \dfrac{86}{100} \cdot P = 3440 \cdot \dfrac{100}{86}$

$\quad\quad\quad\quad P = 4000$

The **original price = \$4000.**
The **price** was **reduced by** $4000 - 3440 = \mathbf{\$560.}$

3. $N, N + 2, N + 4, N + 6$

$$3(N + N + 2) = 5(N + 4) + 18$$
$$3(2N + 2) = 5N + 20 + 18$$
$$6N + 6 = 5N + 38$$
$$N = 32$$

Thus the integers are **32, 34, 36,** and **38.**

4. $\dfrac{E}{T} = \dfrac{3}{17}$

$$\dfrac{E}{102} = \dfrac{3}{17}$$
$$17E = 3 \cdot 102$$
$$E = \dfrac{3 \cdot 102}{17}$$
$$E = \mathbf{18}$$

5. $P(H, T, T, H) = \dfrac{1}{2} \cdot \dfrac{1}{2} \cdot \dfrac{1}{2} \cdot \dfrac{1}{2} = \dfrac{1}{\mathbf{16}}$

6. (a)

STEM	LEAF
3	5, 8, 1, 9
4	1, 3, 8, 5, 7, 2, 0
5	2, 1, 4, 4, 3, 9
6	3, 5, 2

(b) Range $= 65 - 31 = \mathbf{34}$

(c) Median $= \dfrac{47 + 48}{2} = \mathbf{47.5}$

(d) Mode $= \mathbf{54}$

(e) Mean $= \dfrac{\text{Sum of the 20 numbers}}{20} = \dfrac{962}{20} = \mathbf{48.1}$

7. (a)

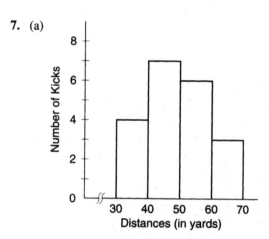

(b) **40–50 interval**

(c) $\dfrac{7 + 4}{20} = \dfrac{11}{20} = \dfrac{55}{100} = \mathbf{55\%}$

8. $P(\text{diamond, then sapphire}) = \dfrac{10}{18} \cdot \dfrac{8}{17} = \dfrac{80}{306} = \dfrac{\mathbf{40}}{\mathbf{153}}$

9. **(a), (c), (d)**

10. $3\sqrt{2} \cdot 4\sqrt{12} - 6\sqrt{54}$

$$= 3 \cdot 4\sqrt{2}\sqrt{12} - 6\sqrt{2}\sqrt{3}\sqrt{3}\sqrt{3}$$
$$= 12\sqrt{2}\sqrt{2}\sqrt{2}\sqrt{3} - 6(3)\sqrt{6}$$
$$= 12(2)\sqrt{6} - 18\sqrt{6} = 24\sqrt{6} - 18\sqrt{6} = \mathbf{6\sqrt{6}}$$

11. $3\sqrt{2}\left(5\sqrt{12} - 8\sqrt{8}\right)$

$$= 3\sqrt{2} \cdot 5\sqrt{12} - 3\sqrt{2} \cdot 8\sqrt{8}$$
$$= 3 \cdot 5\sqrt{2}\sqrt{12} - 3 \cdot 8\sqrt{2}\sqrt{8}$$
$$= 15\sqrt{2}\sqrt{2}\sqrt{2}\sqrt{3} - 24\sqrt{2}\sqrt{2}\sqrt{2}\sqrt{2}$$
$$= 15(2)\sqrt{6} - 24(2)(2) = \mathbf{30\sqrt{6} - 96}$$

12. $D = \left\{x \in \mathbb{R} \mid -3 \le x \le 3\right\}$
$R = \left\{y \in \mathbb{R} \mid -2 \le y \le 2\right\}$

13. $\begin{cases} y = x \\ y = -\dfrac{1}{2}x + 3 \end{cases}$

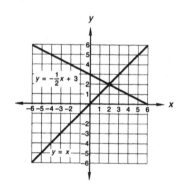

$$y = x \qquad y = -\dfrac{1}{2}x + 3$$
$$2 = 2 \qquad\qquad 2 = -\dfrac{1}{2}(2) + 3$$
$$\qquad\qquad\qquad 2 = 2$$

The solution to the linear equations is **(2, 2).**

14. (a) $\begin{cases} 3x + 4y = 32 \\ 5x - 4y = 0 \end{cases}$
(b)

$$
\begin{array}{rl}
(1)(a)\ & 3x + 4y = 32 \\
(1)(b)\ & \underline{5x - 4y = 0} \\
& 8x \qquad\quad = 32 \\
& \quad x = 4
\end{array}
$$

(a) $\quad 3x + 4y = 32$
$$3(4) + 4y = 32$$
$$12 + 4y = 32$$
$$4y = 20$$
$$y = 5$$

Thus the solution is the ordered pair **(4, 5).**

15. $\begin{cases} 10N_D + 25N_Q = 495 \\ N_Q = N_D + 10 \end{cases}$

$$10N_D + 25N_Q = 495$$
$$10N_D + 25(N_D + 10) = 495$$
$$10N_D + 25N_D + 250 = 495$$
$$35N_D = 245$$
$$N_D = 7$$

$$N_Q = N_D + 10$$
$$N_Q = 7 + 10$$
$$N_Q = 17$$

16. (a) $\begin{cases} 3x + 4y = 7 \\ 6x + 8y = 13 \end{cases}$
(b)

$$(-2)(a) \quad -6x - 8y = -14$$
$$(1)(b) \quad \underline{6x + 8y = 13}$$
$$0 \neq -1$$

Inconsistent. Using the elimination method yields a false equality, so the equations have no point in common.

17. $\dfrac{(4000 \times 10^{-23})(0.00035 \times 10^{15})}{5000 \times 10^5}$

$$= \dfrac{(4 \times 10^{-20})(3.5 \times 10^{11})}{5 \times 10^8}$$

$$= \dfrac{4 \cdot 3.5}{5} \times \dfrac{10^{-20} \cdot 10^{11}}{10^8}$$

$$= \dfrac{14}{5} \times \dfrac{10^{-9}}{10^8} = \mathbf{2.8 \times 10^{-17}}$$

18. $R_K + R_M = 125$
$$R_K = -R_M + 125$$

$$R_K T_K + 60 = R_M T_M$$
$$(-R_M + 125)3 + 60 = R_M(2)$$
$$-3R_M + 375 + 60 = 2R_M$$
$$-3R_M + 435 = 2R_M$$
$$-5R_M = -435$$
$$R_M = 87$$

$$R_K + R_M = 125$$
$$R_K + 87 = 125$$
$$R_K = 38$$

19. $-2p^2 + 110 + 12p = -2p^2 + 12p + 110$
$$= -2(p^2 - 6p - 55) = \mathbf{-2(p - 11)(p + 5)}$$

20. $-49 + t^2 = t^2 - 49 = \mathbf{(t + 7)(t - 7)}$

21. $30a^2b^3c^4 - 15ab^4c^5 + 45ab^4c^4$
$$= \mathbf{15ab^3c^4(2a - bc + 3b)}$$

22.
$$-\dfrac{x + 2}{3} - \dfrac{2x + 8}{7} = 4$$

$$21 \cdot -\dfrac{(x + 2)}{3} - 21 \cdot \dfrac{(2x + 8)}{7} = 21 \cdot 4$$

$$-7(x + 2) - 3(2x + 8) = 84$$
$$-7x - 14 - 6x - 24 = 84$$
$$-13x - 38 = 84$$
$$-13x = 122$$
$$x = -\dfrac{122}{13}$$

23.
$$4\dfrac{2}{3}x - \dfrac{1}{5} = 3\dfrac{2}{3}$$

$$\dfrac{14}{3}x - \dfrac{1}{5} = \dfrac{11}{3}$$

$$(15)\dfrac{14}{3}x - (15)\dfrac{1}{5} = (15)\dfrac{11}{3}$$

$$5(14x) - 3 = 5(11)$$
$$70x - 3 = 55$$
$$70x = 58$$
$$x = \dfrac{58}{70}$$
$$x = \dfrac{29}{35}$$

24. (a) **Naturals, wholes, integers, rationals, reals**
(b) **Integers, rationals, reals**

25. (a) $\dfrac{1}{-3^{-3}} = \dfrac{3^3}{-1} = \mathbf{-27}$

(b) $-3^{-3} = \dfrac{-1}{3^3} = -\dfrac{1}{27}$

(c) $-(-3)^{-3} = -\left(\dfrac{1}{(-3)^3}\right) = -\left(\dfrac{1}{-27}\right) = \dfrac{1}{27}$

26. $x^{-2}y^{-1}\left(\dfrac{x^{-1}}{y^{-1}} - \dfrac{4x^2y^0}{(y^{-3})^2} + \dfrac{1}{x^{-2}y^{-1}}\right)$

$$= x^{-3} - \dfrac{4y^{-1}}{y^{-6}} + 1 = \dfrac{1}{x^3} - 4y^5 + 1$$

27. $x \not> 4$; $D = \{$Integers$\}$

28. $-x^0 - x(x - y^2) = -(-3)^0 - (-3)\left[-3 - (-4)^2\right]$
$$= -1 + 3(-3 - 16) = -1 + 3(-19)$$
$$= -1 - 57 = \mathbf{-58}$$

29. $\dfrac{ax^{-4}}{(x^{-2})^2} + \dfrac{3a^{-2}a^3}{a^0} - \dfrac{6a^5}{(a^{-2})^{-2}} + 3a$

$$= \dfrac{ax^{-4}}{x^{-4}} + \dfrac{3a}{a^0} - \dfrac{6a^5}{a^4} + 3a$$

$$= a + 3a - 6a + 3a = \mathbf{a}$$

30. $V = \frac{1}{3}(\text{Area}_{\text{base}})(\text{Height})$

$\quad\quad = \frac{1}{3}(6\text{ cm} \times 9\text{ cm})(12\text{ cm})$

$\quad\quad = \frac{1}{3}(54\text{ cm}^2)(12\text{ cm})$

$\quad\quad = \textbf{216 cm}^3$

Practice 86

a. $(5x^3 - 9x^2 + x) \div x = \dfrac{5x^3}{x} - \dfrac{9x^2}{x} + \dfrac{x}{x}$

$\quad = \textbf{5}x^2 - \textbf{9}x + \textbf{1}$

b. $(-3x^2 + 6x^3 + x - 40) \div (-2 + x)$

$$
\begin{array}{r}
6x^2 + 9x + 19 \\
x - 2\,\overline{\smash{)}\,6x^3 - 3x^2 + x - 40} \\
\underline{6x^3 - 12x^2} \\
9x^2 + x \\
\underline{9x^2 - 18x} \\
19x - 40 \\
\underline{19x - 38} \\
-2
\end{array}
$$

$6x^2 + 9x + 19 - \dfrac{2}{x - 2}$

c. $\dfrac{x^3 - 5}{x - 2}$

$$
\begin{array}{r}
x^2 + 2x + 4 \\
x - 2\,\overline{\smash{)}\,x^3 + 0x^2 + 0x - 5} \\
\underline{x^3 - 2x^2} \\
2x^2 + 0x \\
\underline{2x^2 - 4x} \\
4x - 5 \\
\underline{4x - 8} \\
3
\end{array}
$$

$x^2 + 2x + 4 + \dfrac{3}{x - 2}$

d. $(3x^3 - 5x + 4) \div (x - 4)$

$$
\begin{array}{r}
3x^2 + 12x + 43 \\
x - 4\,\overline{\smash{)}\,3x^3 + 0x^2 - 5x + 4} \\
\underline{3x^3 - 12x^2} \\
12x^2 - 5x \\
\underline{12x^2 - 48x} \\
43x + 4 \\
\underline{43x - 172} \\
176
\end{array}
$$

$3x^2 + 12x + 43 + \dfrac{176}{x - 4}$

1. (a) $N_S = N_Q + 143$

(b) $100N_S + 25N_Q = 15,300$

(b) $\quad\quad\quad\quad\quad 100N_S + 25N_Q = 15,300$

$\quad\quad\quad 100(N_Q + 143) + 25N_Q = 15,300$

$\quad\quad\quad 100N_Q + 14,300 + 25N_Q = 15,300$

$\quad\quad\quad\quad\quad\quad\quad\quad\quad 125N_Q = 1000$

$\quad\quad\quad\quad\quad\quad\quad\quad\quad\quad N_Q = 8$

(a) $N_S = N_Q + 143$

$\quad N_S = 8 + 143$

$\quad N_S = \textbf{151}$

2. (a) $N_N + N_D = 60$

(b) $5N_N + 10N_D = 500$

$(-5)\text{(a)} \quad -5N_N - 5N_D = -300$

$(1)\text{(b)} \quad \underline{5N_N + 10N_D = 500}$

$\quad\quad\quad\quad\quad\quad 5N_D = 200$

$\quad\quad\quad\quad\quad\quad\quad N_D = 40$

(a) $N_N + N_D = 60$

$\quad N_N + 40 = 60$

$\quad\quad\quad N_N = \textbf{20}$

3. $N,\ N + 1,\ N + 2$

$-4(N + N + 2) = 7[-(N + 1)] - 13$

$\quad -4(2N + 2) = -7(N + 1) - 13$

$\quad\quad -8N - 8 = -7N - 7 - 13$

$\quad\quad -8N - 8 = -7N - 20$

$\quad\quad\quad\quad -N = -12$

$\quad\quad\quad\quad\quad N = 12$

Thus the integers are **12, 13,** and **14.**

4. $\dfrac{40}{100} \cdot 570 = WN$

$\quad\quad WN = \dfrac{22,800}{100}$

$\quad\quad WN = \textbf{228}$

5. $7N - 8 = 2N + 12$

$\quad\quad 5N = 20$

$\quad\quad\ N = \textbf{4}$

6. (a) Range $= 98 - 46 = \textbf{52}$

Median $= \textbf{82}$

Mode $= \textbf{85}$

Mean $= \dfrac{\text{sum of the 15 numbers}}{15} = \dfrac{1203}{15} = \textbf{80.2}$

(b)

STEM	LEAF
4	6
5	
6	8, 5
7	9, 5, 3
8	5, 5, 7, 2, 1
9	3, 5, 1, 8

(c)

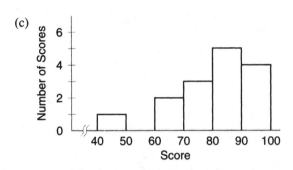

(d) **80–90 interval**

7. $(20x^4 + 5x^3 - 10x^2 + 30x) \div 5x$

$= \dfrac{20x^4}{5x} + \dfrac{5x^3}{5x} - \dfrac{10x^2}{5x} + \dfrac{30x}{5x}$

$= \mathbf{4x^3 + x^2 - 2x + 6}$

8. $(x^3 - 3x^2 + 2x + 5) \div (x + 2)$

$$
\begin{array}{r}
x^2 - 5x + 12 \\
x + 2 \overline{\smash{)}\, x^3 - 3x^2 + 2x + 5} \\
\underline{x^3 + 2x^2} \\
-5x^2 + 2x \\
\underline{-5x^2 - 10x} \\
12x + 5 \\
\underline{12x + 24} \\
-19
\end{array}
$$

$\mathbf{x^2 - 5x + 12 - \dfrac{19}{x + 2}}$

9. $(x^3 - 1) \div (x + 3)$

$$
\begin{array}{r}
x^2 - 3x + 9 \\
x + 3 \overline{\smash{)}\, x^3 + 0x^2 + 0x - 1} \\
\underline{x^3 + 3x^2} \\
-3x^2 + 0x \\
\underline{-3x^2 - 9x} \\
9x - 1 \\
\underline{9x + 27} \\
-28
\end{array}
$$

$\mathbf{x^2 - 3x + 9 - \dfrac{28}{x + 3}}$

10. $(-5x^3 + 14x^2 - x + 10) \div (x + 2)$

$$
\begin{array}{r}
-5x^2 + 24x - 49 \\
x + 2 \overline{\smash{)}\, -5x^3 + 14x^2 - x + 10} \\
\underline{-5x^3 - 10x^2} \\
24x^2 - x \\
\underline{24x^2 + 48x} \\
-49x + 10 \\
\underline{-49x - 98} \\
108
\end{array}
$$

$\mathbf{-5x^2 + 24x - 49 + \dfrac{108}{x + 2}}$

11. (a), (b), (d)

12. $4\sqrt{3} \cdot 6\sqrt{6} \cdot 3\sqrt{3} \cdot 2\sqrt{2}$

$= 4 \cdot 6 \cdot 3 \cdot 2 \cdot \sqrt{3}\sqrt{3}\sqrt{6}\sqrt{2} = 144(3)\sqrt{12}$

$= 144(3)\sqrt{2}\sqrt{2}\sqrt{3} = 144(3)(2)\sqrt{3}$

$= \mathbf{864\sqrt{3}}$

13. $3\sqrt{2}(7\sqrt{2} - \sqrt{6}) = 3 \cdot 7\sqrt{2}\sqrt{2} - 3\sqrt{2}\sqrt{6}$

$= 21(2) - 3\sqrt{2}\sqrt{2}\sqrt{3} = 42 - 3(2)\sqrt{3}$

$= \mathbf{42 - 6\sqrt{3}}$

14. $D = \{x \in \mathbb{R} \mid x \le 11\}$

15. $\quad f(x) = x^2 - 2x + 3$

$f(x + 4) = (x + 4)^2 - 2(x + 4) + 3$

$= x^2 + 8x + 16 - 2x - 8 + 3$

$= \mathbf{x^2 + 6x + 11}$

16. (a) The desired equation is $y = mx + b$.

By inspection, $b = +4$.

By inspection, the sign of m is $-$.

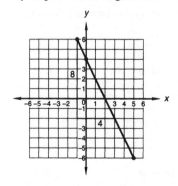

$|m| = \dfrac{8}{4} = 2$

So $b = +4$ and $m = -2$.

$\mathbf{y = -2x + 4}$

(b) $\mathbf{x = -3}$

17. $\begin{cases} y = 3x - 2 \\ y = -x + 2 \end{cases}$

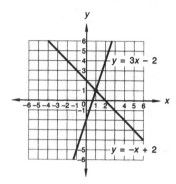

$y = 3x - 2$ $y = -x + 2$

$1 = 3(1) - 2$ $1 = -(1) + 2$

$1 = 3 - 2$ $1 = -1 + 2$

$1 = 1$ $1 = 1$

The solution to the linear equations is **(1, 1)**.

18. $\begin{cases} 4x - 5y = -26 \\ x - y = -6 \end{cases}$

$x - y = -6$

$\quad x = y - 6$

$\quad\quad 4x - 5y = -26$

$\quad 4(y - 6) - 5y = -26$

$\quad 4y - 24 - 5y = -26$

$\quad\quad -y - 24 = -26$

$\quad\quad\quad -y = -2$

$\quad\quad\quad\quad y = 2$

$x - y = -6$

$x - 2 = -6$

$\quad x = -4$

Thus the solution is the ordered pair **(-4, 2)**.

19. (a) $\begin{cases} 3x + 4y = 9 \\ 3x - 4y = 9 \end{cases}$
    (b)

$\begin{array}{ll} (1)(a) & 3x + 4y = 9 \\ (1)(b) & \underline{3x - 4y = 9} \\ & 6x \quad\quad = 18 \\ & \quad x = 3 \end{array}$

(a) $3x + 4y = 9$

$\quad 3(3) + 4y = 9$

$\quad\quad 9 + 4y = 9$

$\quad\quad\quad 4y = 0$

$\quad\quad\quad\quad y = 0$

Consistent. The equations intersect at only one point.

20. $\dfrac{(0.0003 \times 10^{-8})(8000 \times 10^{6})}{0.004 \times 10^{5}}$

$= \dfrac{(3 \times 10^{-12})(8 \times 10^{9})}{4 \times 10^{2}}$

$= \dfrac{3 \cdot 8}{4} \times \dfrac{10^{-12} \cdot 10^{9}}{10^{2}}$

$= \dfrac{24}{4} \times \dfrac{10^{-3}}{10^{2}} = \mathbf{6 \times 10^{-5}}$

21. $\quad R_M T_M + 6 = R_D T_D$

$\quad 3(4 + T_D) + 6 = 12 T_D$

$\quad 12 + 3T_D + 6 = 12 T_D$

$\quad\quad\quad 18 = 9 T_D$

$\quad\quad\quad \mathbf{T_D = 2}$

$T_M = 4 + T_D$

$T_M = 4 + 2$

$\mathbf{T_M = 6}$

22. $ax^2 + 4ax + 4a = a(x^2 + 4x + 4)$

$= \mathbf{a(x + 2)(x + 2)}$

23. $-10 - 3x + x^2 = x^2 - 3x - 10$

$= \mathbf{(x - 5)(x + 2)}$

24. $-4ax^2 + 9a = 9a - 4ax^2 = a(9 - 4x^2)$

$= \mathbf{a(3 + 2x)(3 - 2x)}$

25. $20x + 12x^2 + x^3 = x^3 + 12x^2 + 20x$

$= x(x^2 + 12x + 20) = \mathbf{x(x + 10)(x + 2)}$

26. $\quad \dfrac{x}{2} - \dfrac{3 + x}{4} = \dfrac{1}{6}$

$12 \cdot \dfrac{x}{2} - 12 \cdot \dfrac{(3 + x)}{4} = 12 \cdot \dfrac{1}{6}$

$\quad\quad 6x - 3(3 + x) = 2$

$\quad\quad 6x - 9 - 3x = 2$

$\quad\quad\quad\quad 3x = 11$

$\quad\quad\quad\quad x = \dfrac{11}{3}$

27. $\dfrac{5}{x^2 + y} + \dfrac{3}{x^2} - \dfrac{2}{y}$

$= \dfrac{5x^2 y}{x^2 y(x^2 + y)} + \dfrac{3y(x^2 + y)}{x^2 y(x^2 + y)}$

$\quad - \dfrac{2x^2(x^2 + y)}{x^2 y(x^2 + y)}$

$= \dfrac{5x^2 y + 3y(x^2 + y) - 2x^2(x^2 + y)}{x^2 y(x^2 + y)}$

$= \dfrac{5x^2 y + 3x^2 y + 3y^2 - 2x^4 - 2x^2 y}{x^2 y(x^2 + y)}$

$= \dfrac{\mathbf{6x^2 y + 3y^2 - 2x^4}}{\mathbf{x^2 y(x^2 + y)}}$

28. $\dfrac{\sqrt[3]{x - a}}{2} = \dfrac{\sqrt[3]{-100 - (-127)}}{2} = \dfrac{\sqrt[3]{27}}{2} = \dfrac{3}{2}$

29. $A = \dfrac{1}{2}(5 \text{ cm} \times 6 \text{ cm}) + \dfrac{1}{2}(13 \text{ cm} \times 6 \text{ cm})$

$= 15 \text{ cm}^2 + 39 \text{ cm}^2 = \textbf{54 cm}^2$

30. $S.A. = 2\left(\text{Area}_{\text{base}}\right) + \text{Lateral Surface Area}$

$= 2\left[\dfrac{1}{2}(3 \text{ m} \times 4 \text{ m}) + \dfrac{\pi(2 \text{ m})^2}{2}\right]$

$\qquad + \left(\text{Perimeter}_{\text{base}}\right)(\text{Height})$

$= 2\left(6 \text{ m}^2 + 2\pi \text{ m}^2\right)$

$\qquad + \left(3 \text{ m} + 5 \text{ m} + \dfrac{2\pi(2 \text{ m})}{2}\right)(6 \text{ m})$

$= 12 \text{ m}^2 + 4\pi \text{ m}^2 + (8 \text{ m} + 2\pi \text{ m})(6 \text{ m})$

$= 12 \text{ m}^2 + 4\pi \text{ m}^2 + 48 \text{ m}^2 + 12\pi \text{ m}^2$

$= (60 + 16\pi) \text{ m}^2 = \textbf{110.24 m}^2$

Practice 87

a. $T_1 + T_2 = 60$

$\qquad T_1 = -T_2 + 60$

$\qquad R_1 T_1 = R_2 T_2$

$3(-T_2 + 60) = 6T_2$

$-3T_2 + 180 = 6T_2$

$\qquad 180 = 9T_2$

$\qquad\quad T_2 = 20$

$T_1 + T_2 = 60$

$T_1 + 20 = 60$

$\qquad T_1 = 40$

b. $R_O + R_S = -1$

$\qquad R_O = -R_S - 1$

$\qquad R_O T_O = R_S T_S + 16$

$8(-R_S - 1) = 4R_S + 16$

$-8R_S - 8 = 4R_S + 16$

$\qquad -12R_S = 24$

$\qquad\quad R_S = -2$

$R_O + R_S = -1$

$R_O - 2 = -1$

$\qquad R_O = 1$

c. Function

d. Not a function

e. Function

Problem Set 87

1. (a) $N_N + N_D = 500$

(b) $5N_N + 10N_D = 3000$

$(-5)\text{(a)} \quad -5N_N - 5N_D = -2500$

$(1)\text{(b)} \quad \underline{5N_N + 10N_D = 3000}$

$\qquad\qquad\qquad 5N_D = 500$

$\qquad\qquad\qquad N_D = 100$

(a) $N_N + N_D = 500$

$\qquad N_N + 100 = 500$

$\qquad\qquad N_N = 400$

2. (a) $N_N = N_Q + 15$

(b) $5N_N + 25N_Q = 525$

(b) $\qquad 5N_N + 25N_Q = 525$

$\qquad 5\left(N_Q + 15\right) + 25N_Q = 525$

$\qquad 5N_Q + 75 + 25N_Q = 525$

$\qquad\qquad\qquad 30N_Q = 450$

$\qquad\qquad\qquad N_Q = 15$

(a) $N_N = N_Q + 15$

$\qquad N_N = 15 + 15$

$\qquad N_N = 30$

3. $N, N + 1, N + 2, N + 3$

$3(N + N + 2) = -(N + 1) + 84$

$\qquad 3(2N + 2) = -N - 1 + 84$

$\qquad\quad 6N + 6 = -N + 83$

$\qquad\qquad 7N = 77$

$\qquad\qquad N = 11$

Thus the integers are **11, 12, 13,** and **14.**

4. $\dfrac{90}{100} \cdot 1930 = S$

$\qquad S = \dfrac{173,700}{100}$

$\qquad S = 1737$

5. (a) $P(\text{both red}) = \dfrac{10}{17} \cdot \dfrac{10}{17} = \dfrac{100}{289}$

(b) $P(\text{both red}) = \dfrac{10}{17} \cdot \dfrac{9}{16} = \dfrac{90}{272} = \dfrac{45}{136}$

6. (a)

STEM	LEAF
4	9, 8
5	7, 7, 7, 8, 7, 4, 1, 0
6	1, 1, 8, 4, 5

(b)

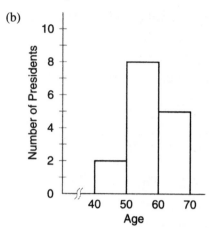

(c) Range = 68 − 48 = **20**

Median = **57**

Mode = **57**

Mean = $\dfrac{\text{sum of 15 numbers}}{15} = \dfrac{857}{15} =$ **57.13**

7. $R_T + R_J = 20$

$\qquad R_T = -R_J + 20$

$\qquad R_T T_T + R_J T_J = 180$

$8(-R_J + 20) + 10R_J = 180$

$-8R_J + 160 + 10R_J = 180$

$\qquad\qquad\qquad 2R_J = 20$

$\qquad\qquad\qquad\quad R_J = \mathbf{10}$

$R_T + R_J = 20$

$R_T + 10 = 20$

$\qquad R_T = \mathbf{10}$

8. (a) **Function**

(b) **Function**

(c) **Not a function**

(d) **Function**

9. $\left(x^3 - 2x^2 + 4\right) \div (x + 2)$

$$
\begin{array}{r}
x^2 - 4x + 8 \\
x + 2 \overline{\smash{\big)}\, x^3 - 2x^2 + 0x + 4} \\
\underline{x^3 + 2x^2} \\
-4x^2 + 0x \\
\underline{-4x^2 - 8x} \\
8x + 4 \\
\underline{8x + 16} \\
-12
\end{array}
$$

$x^2 - 4x + 8 - \dfrac{12}{x + 2}$

10. $\left(2x^3 - 3x^2 + 2x - 4\right) \div (x - 3)$

$$
\begin{array}{r}
2x^2 + 3x + 11 \\
x - 3 \overline{\smash{\big)}\, 2x^3 - 3x^2 + 2x - 4} \\
\underline{2x^3 - 6x^2} \\
3x^2 + 2x \\
\underline{3x^2 - 9x} \\
11x - 4 \\
\underline{11x - 33} \\
29
\end{array}
$$

$2x^2 + 3x + 11 + \dfrac{29}{x - 3}$

11. $\left(32x^4 + 16x^3 - 4x^2 + 8x\right) \div (4x)$

$= \dfrac{32x^4}{4x} + \dfrac{16x^3}{4x} - \dfrac{4x^2}{4x} + \dfrac{8x}{4x}$

$= \mathbf{8x^3 + 4x^2 - x + 2}$

12. (a), (b)

13. $3\sqrt{2}\left(4\sqrt{2} + 6\sqrt{6}\right)$

$= 3 \cdot 4\sqrt{2}\sqrt{2} + 3 \cdot 6\sqrt{2}\sqrt{6}$

$= 12(2) + 3 \cdot 6\sqrt{2}\sqrt{2}\sqrt{3} = 24 + 3 \cdot 6(2)\sqrt{3}$

$= \mathbf{24 + 36\sqrt{3}}$

14. $\qquad f(x) = 9 - 2x - x^2$

$f(y + 1) = 9 - 2(y + 1) - (y + 1)^2$

$\qquad\quad = 9 - 2y - 2 - \left(y^2 + 2y + 1\right)$

$\qquad\quad = 9 - 2y - 2 - y^2 - 2y - 1$

$\qquad\quad = \mathbf{6 - 4y - y^2}$

15. $D = \left\{x \in \mathbb{R} \mid -5 \le x \le 5\right\}$

$\quad\, R = \left\{y \in \mathbb{R} \mid -3 \le y \le 3\right\}$

16. (a) $y = \mathbf{3}$

(b) The desired equation is $y = mx + b$.

By inspection, $b = -4$.

By inspection, the sign of m is −.

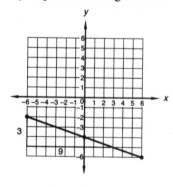

$|m| = \dfrac{3}{9} = \dfrac{1}{3}$

So $b = -4$ and $m = -\dfrac{1}{3}$.

$y = -\dfrac{1}{3}x - 4$

17. $\begin{cases} y = -2 \\ y = 2x - 2 \end{cases}$

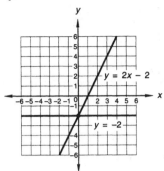

$y = -2$	$y = 2x - 2$
$-2 = -2$	$-2 = 2(0) - 2$
	$-2 = -2$

The solution to the linear equations is **(0, –2)**.

18. (a) $\begin{cases} 3x - y = 8 \\ (b) \quad x + 2y = 12 \end{cases}$

(2)(a) $6x - 2y = 16$
(1)(b) $\underline{\quad x + 2y = 12}$
$\qquad 7x \qquad = 28$
$\qquad\qquad x = 4$

(a) $\quad 3x - y = 8$
$\qquad 3(4) - y = 8$
$\qquad 12 - y = 8$
$\qquad -y = -4$
$\qquad y = 4$

Thus the solution is the ordered pair **(4, 4)**.

19. $\begin{cases} y = x \\ y = 3x \end{cases}$

Consistent. The only ordered pair that is a solution to both equations is (0, 0).

20. $\dfrac{(0.0072 \times 10^{-4})(100,000)}{6000 \times 10^{-24}}$

$= \dfrac{(7.2 \times 10^{-7})(1 \times 10^5)}{6 \times 10^{-21}}$

$= \dfrac{7.2}{6} \times \dfrac{10^{-7} \cdot 10^5}{10^{-21}}$

$= 1.2 \times \dfrac{10^{-2}}{10^{-21}}$

$= \mathbf{1.2 \times 10^{19}}$

21. $max^2 + 9xma + 14ma = ma(x^2 + 9x + 14)$
$\qquad = \mathbf{ma(x + 2)(x + 7)}$

22. $-x^3 - 35x - 12x^2 = -x^3 - 12x^2 - 35x$
$\qquad = -x(x^2 + 12x + 35) = \mathbf{-x(x + 7)(x + 5)}$

23. $(3x)^0(-2 - 3x) - x = -3(-2 - 3)$
$\qquad\qquad -2 - 4x = 6 + 9$
$\qquad\qquad -2 - 4x = 15$
$\qquad\qquad -4x = 17$
$\qquad\qquad x = -\dfrac{17}{4}$

24. $b - 40 = \sqrt{81}$
$\qquad b - 40 = 9$
$\qquad\quad b = 49$

$-b \pm \sqrt{b} = -(49) \pm \sqrt{49} = -49 \pm 7$
$\qquad = \mathbf{-56, -42}$

25. (a) $\sqrt{11} = \mathbf{3.31662}$

(b) $\sqrt{17} = \mathbf{4.12311}$

(c) $\sqrt{54} = \mathbf{7.34847}$

(d) $\sqrt{30} = \mathbf{5.47723}$

26. $\dfrac{\dfrac{x}{y} - 1}{\dfrac{a}{y} + b} = \dfrac{\dfrac{x}{y} - \dfrac{y}{y}}{\dfrac{a}{y} + \dfrac{yb}{y}} = \dfrac{\dfrac{x - y}{y}}{\dfrac{a + yb}{y}} \cdot \dfrac{y}{a + yb}$

$= \dfrac{x - y}{a + yb}$

27. $\dfrac{(x^2)^{-2}(y^0)^2 yy^3}{(y^{-2})^3 yy^4 y^{-1}x} = \dfrac{x^{-4}y^4}{y^{-2}x} = \dfrac{y^6}{x^5}$

28. $\left(\dfrac{x^{-2}}{y} + x^2 y - \dfrac{3x^{-4}a}{y} \right) \dfrac{x^{-2}}{y}$

$= \dfrac{x^{-4}}{y^2} + 1 - \dfrac{3x^{-6}a}{y^2} = \dfrac{1}{x^4 y^2} + 1 - \dfrac{3a}{x^6 y^2}$

29. $P = 14 \text{ in.} + 14 \text{ in.} + \dfrac{2\pi(7 \text{ in.})}{2} + \dfrac{2\pi(7 \text{ in.})}{2}$

$= \mathbf{(28 + 14\pi) \text{ in.}} = \mathbf{71.96 \text{ in.}}$

30. $V = \dfrac{1}{3}(\text{Area}_{\text{base}})(\text{Height})$

$= \dfrac{1}{3}[\pi(8 \text{ ft})^2](6 \text{ ft})$

$= \dfrac{1}{3}(384\pi \text{ ft}^3)$

$= \mathbf{128\pi \text{ ft}^3} = \mathbf{401.92 \text{ ft}^3}$

Practice 88

a.
$$x^2 = -5x + 24$$
$$x^2 + 5x - 24 = 0$$
$$(x + 8)(x - 3) = 0$$

If $x + 8 = 0$ \qquad If $x - 3 = 0$

$\quad x = -8$ \qquad\qquad $x = 3$

$(-8)^2 = -5(-8) + 24$ \qquad $(3)^2 = -5(3) + 24$

$64 = 40 + 24$ \qquad\qquad $9 = -15 + 24$

$64 = 64$ \quad Check \qquad $9 = 9$ \quad Check

b.
$$-48 + x^2 = -8x$$
$$x^2 + 8x - 48 = 0$$
$$(x + 12)(x - 4) = 0$$

If $x + 12 = 0$ \qquad If $x - 4 = 0$

$\quad x = -12$ \qquad\qquad $x = 4$

$-48 + (-12)^2 = -8(-12)$ \qquad $-48 + (4)^2 = -8(4)$

$-48 + 144 = 96$ \qquad\qquad $-48 + 16 = -32$

$96 = 96$ \qquad\qquad\qquad $-32 = -32$

Check \qquad\qquad\qquad\qquad Check

Problem Set 88

1. (a) $\begin{cases} N_P + N_N = 150 \\ N_P + 5N_N = 270 \end{cases}$

(b)

(1)(a) $\quad N_P + N_N = 150$

(-1)(b) $\underline{-N_P - 5N_N = -270}$

$\qquad\qquad -4N_N = -120$

$\qquad\qquad\quad N_N = 30$

(a) $N_P + N_N = 150$

$\quad N_P + 30 = 150$

$\qquad N_P = 120$

2. (a) $N_P = N_N + 54$

(b) $N_P + 5N_N = 270$

(b) $\qquad N_P + 5N_N = 270$

$(N_N + 54) + 5N_N = 270$

$\qquad\qquad 6N_N = 216$

$\qquad\qquad\quad N_N = 36$

(a) $N_P = N_N + 54$

$\quad N_P = 36 + 54$

$\quad N_P = 90$

3.
$$\frac{22}{100} \cdot T = 8800$$
$$\frac{100}{22} \cdot \frac{22}{100} \cdot T = 8800 \cdot \frac{100}{22}$$
$$T = 40{,}000$$

Total Crowd = 40,000

Stood and Cheered = 40,000 − 8800 = **31,200**

4. $N, N + 2, N + 4, N + 6$

$4(N + N + 6) = 7(N + 4) + 3$

$\quad 4(2N + 6) = 7N + 28 + 3$

$\quad 8N + 24 = 7N + 31$

$\qquad\qquad N = 7$

Thus the integers are **7, 9, 11,** and **13.**

5. $P(\text{not peppermint}) = \dfrac{4}{11}$

6. Average $= \dfrac{\text{Sum of 4 numbers}}{4}$

$= \dfrac{396.80}{4} = \mathbf{99.2}$

7. Answers will vary.

8.
$$28 = x^2 - 3x$$
$$x^2 - 3x - 28 = 0$$
$$(x - 7)(x + 4) = 0$$

If $x - 7 = 0$ \qquad If $x + 4 = 0$

$\quad x = 7$ \qquad\qquad $x = -4$

$28 = (7)^2 - 3(7)$ \qquad $28 = (-4)^2 - 3(-4)$

$28 = 49 - 21$ \qquad\qquad $28 = 16 + 12$

$28 = 28$ \quad Check \qquad $28 = 28$ \quad Check

9.
$$x^2 = 25$$
$$x^2 - 25 = 0$$
$$(x + 5)(x - 5) = 0$$

If $x + 5 = 0$ \qquad If $x - 5 = 0$

$\quad x = -5$ \qquad\qquad $x = 5$

$(5)^2 = 25$ \qquad\qquad $(-5)^2 = 25$

$25 = 25$ \quad Check \qquad $25 = 25$ \quad Check

10.
$$x^2 - 6 = x$$
$$x^2 - x - 6 = 0$$
$$(x - 3)(x + 2) = 0$$

If $x - 3 = 0$ \qquad If $x + 2 = 0$

$\quad x = 3$ \qquad\qquad $x = -2$

$(3)^2 - 6 = 3$ \qquad\qquad $(-2)^2 - 6 = -2$

$9 - 6 = 3$ \qquad\qquad $4 - 6 = -2$

$3 = 3$ \quad Check \qquad $-2 = -2$ \quad Check

11.
$$-x^2 - 8x = 16$$
$$-x^2 - 8x - 16 = 0$$
$$-1(x^2 + 8x + 16) = 0$$
$$-1[(x + 4)(x + 4)] = 0$$
$$(x + 4)(x + 4) = 0$$
$$x + 4 = 0$$
$$x = -4$$
$$-(-4)^2 - 8(-4) = 16$$
$$-16 + 32 = 16$$
$$16 = 16 \quad \text{Check}$$

12.
$$R_P T_P + R_K T_K = 170$$
$$2(R_K + 10) + 3R_K = 170$$
$$2R_K + 20 + 3R_K = 170$$
$$5R_K = 150$$
$$\boldsymbol{R_K = 30}$$
$$R_P = R_K + 10$$
$$R_P = 30 + 10$$
$$\boldsymbol{R_P = 40}$$

13. (a), (c), (d)

14. $(2x^3 - 5x + 4) \div (x + 2)$

$$
\begin{array}{r}
2x^2 - 4x + 3 \\
x + 2 \overline{\smash{\big)}\, 2x^3 + 0x^2 - 5x + 4} \\
\underline{2x^3 + 4x^2} \\
-4x^2 - 5x \\
\underline{-4x^2 - 8x} \\
3x + 4 \\
\underline{3x + 6} \\
-2
\end{array}
$$

$$\boldsymbol{2x^2 - 4x + 3 - \frac{2}{x + 2}}$$

15. $(3x^3 - 4) \div (x - 5)$

$$
\begin{array}{r}
3x^2 + 15x + 75 \\
x - 5 \overline{\smash{\big)}\, 3x^3 + 0x^2 + 0x - 4} \\
\underline{3x^3 - 15x^2} \\
15x^2 + 0x \\
\underline{15x^2 - 75x} \\
75x - 4 \\
\underline{75x - 375} \\
371
\end{array}
$$

$$\boldsymbol{3x^2 + 15x + 75 + \frac{371}{x - 5}}$$

16. $(2x^4 - 3x^3 + 2x^2 - x) \div (x)$
$$= \frac{2x^4}{x} - \frac{3x^3}{x} + \frac{2x^2}{x} - \frac{x}{x}$$
$$= \boldsymbol{2x^3 - 3x^2 + 2x - 1}$$

17. $D = \{x \in \mathbb{R} \mid x \geq -1\}$

18. (a) $y = -2$

(b) The desired equation is $y = mx + b$.

By inspection, $b = +3$.

By inspection, the sign of m is $-$.

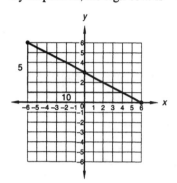

$$|m| = \frac{5}{10} = \frac{1}{2}$$

So $b = +3$ and $m = -\dfrac{1}{2}$.

$$\boldsymbol{y = -\frac{1}{2}x + 3}$$

19. $5\sqrt{5}\left(2\sqrt{10} - 3\sqrt{3}\right)$
$$= 5 \cdot 2\sqrt{5}\sqrt{10} - 5 \cdot 3\sqrt{5}\sqrt{3}$$
$$= 10\sqrt{5}\sqrt{2}\sqrt{5} - 15\sqrt{15}$$
$$= 10(5)\sqrt{2} - 15\sqrt{15}$$
$$= \boldsymbol{50\sqrt{2} - 15\sqrt{15}}$$

20. $4\sqrt{7}\left(2\sqrt{7} - 3\sqrt{14}\right)$
$$= 4 \cdot 2\sqrt{7}\sqrt{7} - 4 \cdot 3\sqrt{7}\sqrt{14}$$
$$= 8(7) - 12\sqrt{7}\sqrt{2}\sqrt{7}$$
$$= 56 - 12(7)\sqrt{2}$$
$$= \boldsymbol{56 - 84\sqrt{2}}$$

21.
$$g(x) = 7 - 3x^2 + 2x$$
$$g(x + 1) = 7 - 3(x + 1)^2 + 2(x + 1)$$
$$= 7 - 3(x^2 + 2x + 1) + 2x + 2$$
$$= 7 - 3x^2 - 6x - 3 + 2x + 2$$
$$= \boldsymbol{-3x^2 - 4x + 6}$$

22. $\begin{cases} y = 2x + 3 \\ x = -3 \end{cases}$

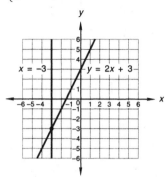

$$y = 2x + 3 \qquad\qquad x = -3$$
$$-3 = 2(-3) + 3 \qquad -3 = -3$$
$$-3 = -6 + 3$$
$$-3 = -3$$

The solution to the linear equations is **(–3, –3)**.

23. (a) $\begin{cases} 3x + 5y = 16 \\ 4x - 3y = 2 \end{cases}$

$$\begin{array}{ll} (3)(a) & 9x + 15y = 48 \\ (5)(b) & 20x - 15y = 10 \\ \hline & 29x \qquad\;\; = 58 \\ & \qquad\quad x = 2 \end{array}$$

(a) $3x + 5y = 16$

$$3(2) + 5y = 16$$
$$6 + 5y = 16$$
$$5y = 10$$
$$y = 2$$

Thus the solution is the ordered pair **(2, 2)**.

24. $\dfrac{(0.016 \times 10^{-5})(300 \times 10^{6})}{(20,000 \times 10^{4})(400 \times 10^{-8})}$

$$= \frac{(1.6 \times 10^{-7})(3 \times 10^{8})}{(2 \times 10^{8})(4 \times 10^{-6})}$$

$$= \frac{1.6 \cdot 3}{2 \cdot 4} \times \frac{10^{-7} \cdot 10^{8}}{10^{8} \cdot 10^{-6}}$$

$$= \frac{4.8}{8} \times \frac{10^{1}}{10^{2}}$$

$$= 0.6 \times 10^{-1} = \mathbf{6 \times 10^{-2}}$$

25. $x + 2 \not\leq 4;\ D = \{\text{Positive Integers}\}$

$$\begin{array}{c} x + 2 \not\leq 4 \\ \underline{-2 \quad -2} \\ x \not\leq 2 \end{array}$$

2   3   4   5

26. $\qquad 1\dfrac{3}{5}x - 2^{-2} = \dfrac{1}{10}$

$$\frac{8}{5}x - \frac{1}{4} = \frac{1}{10}$$

$$20\left(\frac{8}{5}x\right) - 20\left(\frac{1}{4}\right) = 20\left(\frac{1}{10}\right)$$

$$4(8x) - 5 = 2$$

$$32x = 7$$

$$x = \frac{7}{32}$$

27. $\dfrac{1}{a} + \dfrac{2}{a^2} + \dfrac{3}{a + x}$

$$= \frac{a(a + x)}{a^2(a + x)} + \frac{2(a + x)}{a^2(a + x)} + \frac{3a^2}{a^2(a + x)}$$

$$= \frac{a(a + x) + 2(a + x) + 3a^2}{a^2(a + x)}$$

$$= \frac{a^2 + ax + 2a + 2x + 3a^2}{a^2(a + x)}$$

$$= \frac{\mathbf{4a^2 + ax + 2a + 2x}}{a^2(a + x)}$$

28. $\begin{array}{ll} b - 5 = 17 & a = \dfrac{b}{2} \\ b = 22 & \\ & a = \dfrac{22}{2} \\ & a = 11 \end{array}$

$$\frac{-b \pm \sqrt{b^2}}{2a} = \frac{-22 \pm \sqrt{22^2}}{2(11)}$$

$$= \frac{-22 \pm 22}{22}$$

$$= -1 \pm 1$$

$$= \mathbf{-2, 0}$$

29. $-(-4 - 2^{0}) - |-2| + \dfrac{1}{-2^{-3}}$

$$= -(-5) - 2 - 2^{3}$$

$$= 5 - 2 - 8 = \mathbf{-5}$$

30. $S.A. = \text{Area}_{\text{base}} + \text{Lateral Surface Area}$

$$= (12\text{ yd} \times 12\text{ yd}) + 4\left[\frac{1}{2}(12\text{ yd} \times 10\text{ yd})\right]$$

$$= 144\text{ yd}^2 + 4(60\text{ yd}^2)$$

$$= 144\text{ yd}^2 + 240\text{ yd}^2$$

$$= \mathbf{384\text{ yd}^2}$$

Practice 89

a. (a) $N_G + N_O = 18$

(b) $8N_G + 3N_O = 119$

(-3)(a) $-3N_G - 3N_O = -54$

(1)(b) $\underline{8N_G + 3N_O = 119}$

$\quad 5N_G \qquad = 65$

$\qquad N_G = \mathbf{13}$

b. (a) $N_A + N_C = 175$

(b) $5N_A + 2N_C = 686$

(-2)(a) $-2N_A - 2N_C = -350$

(1)(b) $\underline{5N_A + 2N_C = \; 686}$

$\quad 3N_A \qquad = 336$

$\qquad N_A = \mathbf{112}$

(a) $N_A + N_C = 175$

$\quad 112 + N_C = 175$

$\qquad N_C = \mathbf{63}$

Problem Set 89

1. (a) $N_C = N_F - 7$

(b) $45N_C + 30N_F = 735$

(b) $\qquad 45N_C + 30N_F = 735$

$\quad 45\left(N_F - 7\right) + 30N_F = 735$

$\qquad 75N_F - 315 = 735$

$\qquad\qquad 75N_F = 1050$

$\qquad\qquad N_F = 14$

(a) $N_C = N_F - 7$

$\quad N_C = 14 - 7$

$\quad N_C = \mathbf{7}$

2. (a) $N_Q = N_D + 300$

(b) $25N_Q + 10N_D = 8200$

(b) $\qquad 25N_Q + 10N_D = 8200$

$\quad 25\left(N_D + 300\right) + 10N_D = 8200$

$\qquad\qquad 35N_D + 7500 = 8200$

$\qquad\qquad\qquad 35N_D = 700$

$\qquad\qquad\qquad N_D = \mathbf{20}$

(a) $N_Q = N_D + 300$

$\quad N_Q = 20 + 300$

$\quad N_Q = \mathbf{320}$

3. $N,\ N + 2,\ N + 4$

$4(N + N + 2) = -30(N + 4) - 62$

$4(2N + 2) = -30N - 182$

$8N + 8 = -30N - 182$

$38N = -190$

$N = -5$

Thus the integers are **–5, –3,** and **–1.**

4. $\qquad \dfrac{23}{100} \cdot M = 1610$

$\dfrac{100}{23} \cdot \dfrac{23}{100} \cdot M = 1610 \cdot \dfrac{100}{23}$

$\qquad M = \mathbf{7000}$

5. $\qquad \dfrac{14}{17} \cdot T = 2800$

$\dfrac{17}{14} \cdot \dfrac{14}{17} \cdot T = 2800 \cdot \dfrac{17}{14}$

$\qquad T = 200 \cdot 17$

$\qquad T = \mathbf{3400}$

6. (a) $P(\not< 7) = P(\geq 7) = \dfrac{21}{36} = \dfrac{\mathbf{7}}{\mathbf{12}}$

(b) $P(\not> 7) = P(\leq 7) = \dfrac{21}{36} = \dfrac{\mathbf{7}}{\mathbf{12}}$

7.
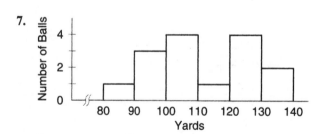

8. (a) Range $= 137 - 85 = \mathbf{52\ yd}$

Median $= \mathbf{109\ yd}$

Mode $= \mathbf{125\ yd}$

Mean $= \dfrac{\text{sum of 15 numbers}}{15}$

$= \dfrac{1678}{15} = \mathbf{111.87\ yd}$

(b) $\dfrac{4}{15} = 0.2667 = \mathbf{26.67\%}$

9. $x^2 - 12x + 35 = 0$

$(x - 7)(x - 5) = 0$

If $x - 7 = 0$ If $x - 5 = 0$

$x = 7$ $x = 5$

$(7)^2 - 12(7) + 35 = 0$ $(5)^2 - 12(5) + 35 = 0$

$49 - 84 + 35 = 0$ $25 - 60 + 35 = 0$

$0 = 0$ $0 = 0$

Check   Check

10. $4x^2 - 9 = 0$

$(2x - 3)(2x + 3) = 0$

If $2x - 3 = 0$ If $2x + 3 = 0$

$2x = 3$ $2x = -3$

$x = \dfrac{3}{2}$ $x = -\dfrac{3}{2}$

$4\left(\dfrac{3}{2}\right)^2 - 9 = 0$ $4\left(-\dfrac{3}{2}\right)^2 - 9 = 0$

$4\left(\dfrac{9}{4}\right) - 9 = 0$ $4\left(\dfrac{9}{4}\right) - 9 = 0$

$9 - 9 = 0$ $9 - 9 = 0$

$0 = 0$ $0 = 0$

Check   Check

11. $-49 = -9p^2$

$9p^2 - 49 = 0$

$(3p - 7)(3p + 7) = 0$

If $3p - 7 = 0$ If $3p + 7 = 0$

$3p = 7$ $3p = -7$

$p = \dfrac{7}{3}$ $p = -\dfrac{7}{3}$

$-49 = -9\left(\dfrac{7}{3}\right)^2$ $-49 = -9\left(-\dfrac{7}{3}\right)^2$

$-49 = -9\left(\dfrac{49}{9}\right)$ $-49 = -9\left(\dfrac{49}{9}\right)$

$-49 = -49$ Check $-49 = -49$ Check

12. $17x = -x^2 - 60$

$x^2 + 17x + 60 = 0$

$(x + 12)(x + 5) = 0$

If $x + 12 = 0$ If $x + 5 = 0$

$x = -12$ $x = -5$

$17(-12) = -(-12)^2 - 60$ $17(-5) = -(-5)^2 - 60$

$-204 = -144 - 60$ $-85 = -25 - 60$

$-204 = -204$ $-85 = -85$

Check   Check

13. $x^2 = 12x - 32$

$x^2 - 12x + 32 = 0$

$(x - 8)(x - 4) = 0$

If $x - 8 = 0$ If $x - 4 = 0$

$x = 8$ $x = 4$

$(8)^2 = 12(8) - 32$ $(4)^2 = 12(4) - 32$

$64 = 96 - 32$ $16 = 48 - 32$

$64 = 64$ Check $16 = 16$ Check

14. $-9x^2 + 4 = 0$

$4 - 9x^2 = 0$

$(2 - 3x)(2 + 3x) = 0$

If $2 - 3x = 0$ If $2 + 3x = 0$

$-3x = -2$ $3x = -2$

$x = \dfrac{2}{3}$ $x = -\dfrac{2}{3}$

$-9\left(\dfrac{2}{3}\right)^2 + 4 = 0$ $-9\left(-\dfrac{2}{3}\right)^2 + 4 = 0$

$-9\left(\dfrac{4}{9}\right) + 4 = 0$ $-9\left(\dfrac{4}{9}\right) + 4 = 0$

$-4 + 4 = 0$ $-4 + 4 = 0$

$0 = 0$ $0 = 0$

Check   Check

15. $T_M + T_T = 7$

$T_M = -T_T + 7$

$R_M T_M + 10 = R_T T_T$

$20(-T_T + 7) + 10 = 55T_T$

$-20T_T + 150 = 55T_T$

$-75T_T = -150$

$T_T = 2$

$T_M + T_T = 7$

$T_M + 2 = 7$

$T_M = 5$

16. **(b), (c), (f)**

17. (b) $D = \{x, y, m\}, \ R = \{p, 5\}$

(f) $D = \{1, 3, 6\}, \ R = \{-2\}$

18. $(x^2 - x - 6) \div (x + 2)$

$$
\begin{array}{r}
x - 3 \\
x + 2 \overline{\smash{\big)}\ x^2 - x - 6} \\
\underline{x^2 + 2x} \\
-3x - 6 \\
\underline{-3x - 6} \\
0
\end{array}
$$

$x - 3$

19. $\left(3x^3 - 1\right) \div (x + 4)$

$$
\begin{array}{r}
3x^2 - 12x + 48 \\
x + 4 \overline{\smash{\big)}\ 3x^3 + 0x^2 + 0x - 1} \\
\underline{3x^3 + 12x^2} \\
-12x^2 + 0x \\
\underline{-12x^2 - 48x} \\
48x - 1 \\
\underline{48x + 192} \\
-193
\end{array}
$$

$$3x^2 - 12x + 48 - \frac{193}{x + 4}$$

20. $f(x) = 3x^2 - 6x + 20$

$f(2 - a) = 3(2 - a)^2 - 6(2 - a) + 20$

$\qquad = 3\left(4 - 4a + a^2\right) - 12 + 6a + 20$

$\qquad = 12 - 12a + 3a^2 - 12 + 6a + 20$

$\qquad = \mathbf{3a^2 - 6a + 20}$

21. (a) $y = 4$

(b) The desired equation is $y = mx + b$.

By inspection, $b = -2$.

By inspection, the sign of m is $-$.

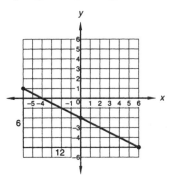

$$|m| = \frac{6}{12} = \frac{1}{2}$$

So $b = -2$ and $m = -\frac{1}{2}$.

$$y = -\frac{1}{2}x - 2$$

22. $\begin{cases} y = 2x - 2 \\ y = -x + 4 \end{cases}$

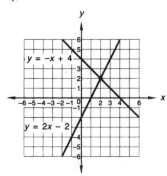

$\begin{array}{ll} y = 2x - 2 & y = -x + 4 \\ 2 = 2(2) - 2 & 2 = -2 + 4 \\ 2 = 4 - 2 & 2 = 2 \\ 2 = 2 & \end{array}$

The solution to the linear equations is $(\mathbf{2, 2})$.

23. (a) $\begin{cases} 3x + 4y = 28 \\ 2x - 3y = -4 \end{cases}$

$\begin{array}{ll} (3)(a) & 9x + 12y = 84 \\ (4)(b) & 8x - 12y = -16 \\ \hline & 17x \qquad = 68 \\ & x = 4 \end{array}$

(a) $\quad 3x + 4y = 28$

$\qquad 3(4) + 4y = 28$

$\qquad 12 + 4y = 28$

$\qquad\qquad 4y = 16$

$\qquad\qquad\ y = 4$

Thus the solution is the ordered pair $(\mathbf{4, 4})$.

24. $3\sqrt{5}\left(5\sqrt{10} - 2\sqrt{5}\right)$

$\qquad = 3 \cdot 5\sqrt{5}\sqrt{10} - 3 \cdot 2\sqrt{5}\sqrt{5}$

$\qquad = 15\sqrt{5}\sqrt{5}\sqrt{2} - 6(5)$

$\qquad = 15(5)\sqrt{2} - 30$

$\qquad = \mathbf{75\sqrt{2} - 30}$

25. (a) **Irrational**

(b) **Rational**

(c) **Rational**

(d) **Rational**

26. $\dfrac{\left(0.0006 \times 10^{-23}\right)\left(300 \times 10^{14}\right)}{90{,}000 \times 10^{25}}$

$= \dfrac{\left(6 \times 10^{-27}\right)\left(3 \times 10^{16}\right)}{9 \times 10^{29}}$

$= \dfrac{6 \cdot 3}{9} \times \dfrac{10^{-27} \cdot 10^{16}}{10^{29}}$

$= \dfrac{18}{9} \times \dfrac{10^{-11}}{10^{29}}$

$= \mathbf{2 \times 10^{-40}}$

27. $\dfrac{xya^{-1} + y^{-1}}{xy^{-1} - a^{-1}} = \dfrac{\dfrac{xy}{a} + \dfrac{1}{y}}{\dfrac{x}{y} - \dfrac{1}{a}} = \dfrac{\dfrac{xy^2}{ay} + \dfrac{a}{ay}}{\dfrac{ax}{ay} - \dfrac{y}{ay}}$

$= \dfrac{\dfrac{xy^2 + a}{ay}}{\dfrac{ax - y}{ay}} = \dfrac{\dfrac{xy^2 + a}{ay} \cdot \dfrac{ay}{ax - y}}{\dfrac{ax - y}{ay} \cdot \dfrac{ay}{ax - y}} = \dfrac{xy^2 + a}{xa - y}$

28. $-|-x^2| + (-x)(-y) + \sqrt[4]{y^2}$

$= -|-(-3)^2| + [-(-3)](-4) + \sqrt[4]{4^2}$

$= -9 - 12 + 2 = \mathbf{-19}$

29. (a) $\dfrac{1}{-3^{-2}} = \dfrac{3^2}{-1} = \mathbf{-9}$

(b) $\dfrac{1}{(-3)^{-2}} = (-3)^2 = \mathbf{9}$

(c) $-(-3)^{-2} = \dfrac{-1}{(-3)^2} = -\dfrac{1}{9}$

30. $V = \left(\text{Area}_{\text{base}}\right)(\text{Height})$

$= \left[(30 \text{ cm} \times 10 \text{ cm}) + \dfrac{1}{2}(30 \text{ cm} \times 12 \text{ cm}) \right]$

$\times 19 \text{ cm}$

$= \left(300 \text{ cm}^2 + 180 \text{ cm}^2\right)(19 \text{ cm})$

$= \left(480 \text{ cm}^2\right)(19 \text{ cm})$

$= \mathbf{9120 \text{ cm}^3}$

Practice 90

a. (a) $L + S = 98$

(b) $L - S = 40$

(1)(a) $\quad L + S = \quad 98$
(1)(b) $\quad \underline{L - S = \quad 40}$
$\qquad 2L \qquad = 138$
$\qquad\qquad L = \mathbf{69}$

(a) $\quad L + S = 98$

$\qquad 69 + S = 98$

$\qquad\qquad S = \mathbf{29}$

b. (a) $N_G = N_B + 11$

(b) $N_G + N_B = 37$

(b) $\qquad N_G + N_B = 37$

$\qquad \left(N_B + 11\right) + N_B = 37$

$\qquad\qquad 2N_B + 11 = 37$

$\qquad\qquad\qquad 2N_B = 26$

$\qquad\qquad\qquad\quad N_B = \mathbf{13}$

(a) $N_G = N_B + 11$

$\quad N_G = 13 + 11$

$\quad N_G = \mathbf{24}$

Problem Set 90

1. (a) $L + S = 48$

(b) $L - S = 24$

(1)(a) $\quad L + S = 48$
(1)(b) $\quad \underline{L - S = 24}$
$\qquad 2L \qquad = 72$
$\qquad\qquad L = \mathbf{36}$

(a) $\quad L + S = 48$

$\qquad 36 + S = 48$

$\qquad\qquad S = \mathbf{12}$

2. (a) $N_G = N_B + 8$

(b) $N_G + N_B = 36$

(b) $\qquad N_G + N_B = 36$

$\qquad \left(N_B + 8\right) + N_B = 36$

$\qquad\qquad 2N_B + 8 = 36$

$\qquad\qquad\qquad 2N_B = 28$

$\qquad\qquad\qquad\quad N_B = \mathbf{14}$

(a) $N_G = N_B + 8$

$\quad N_G = 14 + 8$

$\quad N_G = \mathbf{22}$

3. (a) $L = S + 12$

(b) $L + S = 76$

(b) $\qquad L + S = 76$

$\qquad (S + 12) + S = 76$

$\qquad\qquad 2S + 12 = 76$

$\qquad\qquad\qquad 2S = 64$

$\qquad\qquad\qquad\quad S = \mathbf{32 \text{ m}}$

(a) $L = S + 12$

$\quad L = 32 + 12$

$\quad L = \mathbf{44 \text{ m}}$

4. (a) $N_G + N_P = 210$

(b) $5N_G + 2N_P = 660$

(-2)(a) $\quad -2N_G - 2N_P = -420$
(1)(b) $\quad \underline{5N_G + 2N_P = \quad 660}$
$\qquad 3N_G \qquad\quad = 240$
$\qquad\qquad N_G = \mathbf{80}$

5. Weighted Average $= \dfrac{10(92.4) + 4(84)}{10 + 4}$

$= \dfrac{924 + 336}{14}$

$= \dfrac{1260}{14} = \mathbf{90}$

6. Answers will vary.

7. $1000 \text{ yd} \cdot \text{yd} \cdot \text{yd} \times \dfrac{3 \text{ ft}}{1 \text{ yd}} \times \dfrac{3 \text{ ft}}{1 \text{ yd}} \times \dfrac{3 \text{ ft}}{1 \text{ yd}}$

$\times \dfrac{12 \text{ in.}}{1 \text{ ft}} \times \dfrac{12 \text{ in.}}{1 \text{ ft}} \times \dfrac{12 \text{ in.}}{1 \text{ ft}} \times \dfrac{2.54 \text{ cm}}{1 \text{ in.}}$

$\times \dfrac{2.54 \text{ cm}}{1 \text{ in.}} \times \dfrac{2.54 \text{ cm}}{1 \text{ in.}} \times \dfrac{1 \text{ m}}{100 \text{ cm}} \times \dfrac{1 \text{ m}}{100 \text{ cm}}$

$\times \dfrac{1 \text{ m}}{100 \text{ cm}} = \dfrac{1000(3)^3 (12)^3 (2.54)^3}{(100)^3} \text{ m}^3$

$= \mathbf{764.55 \text{ m}^3}$

8. $2x^2 + 20x + 50 = 0$

$2(x^2 + 10x + 25) = 0$

$x^2 + 10x + 25 = 0$

$(x + 5)(x + 5) = 0$

$x + 5 = 0$

$x = \mathbf{-5}$

$2(-5)^2 + 20(-5) + 50 = 0$

$2(25) - 100 + 50 = 0$

$50 - 50 = 0$

$0 = 0$ Check

9. $3x^2 = -33x - 90$

$3x^2 + 33x + 90 = 0$

$3(x^2 + 11x + 30) = 0$

$x^2 + 11x + 30 = 0$

$(x + 6)(x + 5) = 0$

If $x + 6 = 0$ If $x + 5 = 0$

$x = \mathbf{-6}$ $x = \mathbf{-5}$

$3(-6)^2 = -33(-6) - 90$ $3(-5)^2 = -33(-5) - 90$

$3(36) = 198 - 90$ $3(25) = 165 - 90$

$108 = 108$ Check $75 = 75$ Check

10. $2x^2 - 18 = 0$

$2(x^2 - 9) = 0$

$x^2 - 9 = 0$

$(x + 3)(x - 3) = 0$

If $x + 3 = 0$ If $x - 3 = 0$

$x = \mathbf{-3}$ $x = \mathbf{3}$

$2(-3)^2 - 18 = 0$ $2(3)^2 - 18 = 0$

$2(9) - 18 = 0$ $2(9) - 18 = 0$

$18 - 18 = 0$ $18 - 18 = 0$

$0 = 0$ $0 = 0$

Check   Check

11. $27 - 3p^2 = 0$

$3(9 - p^2) = 0$

$9 - p^2 = 0$

$(3 - p)(3 + p) = 0$

If $3 - p = 0$ If $3 + p = 0$

$p = \mathbf{3}$ $p = \mathbf{-3}$

$27 - 3(3)^2 = 0$ $27 - 3(-3)^2 = 0$

$27 - 3(9) = 0$ $27 - 3(9) = 0$

$27 - 27 = 0$ $27 - 27 = 0$

$0 = 0$ $0 = 0$

Check   Check

12. $T_M + T_B = 18$

$T_M = -T_B + 18$

$R_M T_M = R_B T_B$

$4(-T_B + 18) = 5T_B$

$-4T_B + 72 = 5T_B$

$-9T_B = -72$

$T_B = \mathbf{8}$

$T_M + T_B = 18$

$T_M + 8 = 18$

$T_M = \mathbf{10}$

13. **(a), (d), (f)**

14. $(3x^3 - 2x - 4) \div (x + 1)$

$$\require{enclose}\begin{array}{r} 3x^2 - 3x + 1 \\ x + 1 \enclose{longdiv}{3x^3 + 0x^2 - 2x - 4} \\ \underline{3x^3 + 3x^2} \\ -3x^2 - 2x \\ \underline{-3x^2 - 3x} \\ x - 4 \\ \underline{x + 1} \\ -5 \end{array}$$

$\mathbf{3x^2 - 3x + 1 - \dfrac{5}{x + 1}}$

15. $(2x^3 - 2x^2 - 4) \div (x + 1)$

$$\begin{array}{r} 2x^2 - 4x + 4 \\ x + 1 \enclose{longdiv}{2x^3 - 2x^2 + 0x - 4} \\ \underline{2x^3 + 2x^2} \\ -4x^2 + 0x \\ \underline{-4x^2 - 4x} \\ 4x - 4 \\ \underline{4x + 4} \\ -8 \end{array}$$

$\mathbf{2x^2 - 4x + 4 - \dfrac{8}{x + 1}}$

16. $f(x) = 3x^3 - 4x^2 + 7x - 9$

$f(4) = 3(4)^3 - 4(4)^2 + 7(4) - 9$

$= 192 - 64 + 28 - 9 = \mathbf{147}$

17. $3\sqrt{27} - 2\sqrt{3}\left(4\sqrt{3} - 5\sqrt{12}\right)$

$= 3\sqrt{3}\sqrt{3}\sqrt{3} - 2 \cdot 4\sqrt{3}\sqrt{3} + 2 \cdot 5\sqrt{3}\sqrt{12}$

$= 3(3)\sqrt{3} - 8(3) + 10\sqrt{3}\sqrt{2}\sqrt{2}\sqrt{3}$

$= 9\sqrt{3} - 24 + 10(3)(2)$

$= 9\sqrt{3} - 24 + 60 = \mathbf{9\sqrt{3} + 36}$

18. $2\sqrt{2} \cdot 3\sqrt{3} \cdot 5\sqrt{12} = 2 \cdot 3 \cdot 5\sqrt{2}\sqrt{3}\sqrt{12}$

$= 30\sqrt{2}\sqrt{3}\sqrt{2}\sqrt{2}\sqrt{3} = 30\sqrt{2}\,(3)(2) = \mathbf{180\sqrt{2}}$

19. (a) The desired equation is $y = mx + b$.

By inspection, $b = 0$.

By inspection, the sign of m is $-$.

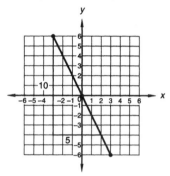

$|m| = \dfrac{10}{5} = 2$

So $b = 0$ and $m = -2$.

$\mathbf{y = -2x}$

(b) $\mathbf{y = -3}$

20. $\begin{cases} y = \dfrac{2}{3}x - 3 \\ y = -x + 2 \end{cases}$

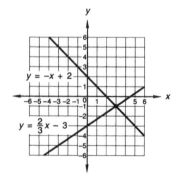

$y = \dfrac{2}{3}x - 3 \qquad\qquad y = -x + 2$

$\qquad\qquad\qquad\qquad -1 = -(3) + 2$

$-1 = \dfrac{2}{3}(3) - 3 \qquad -1 = -1$

$-1 = 2 - 3$

$-1 = -1$

The solution to the linear equations is $\mathbf{(3, -1)}$.

21. $\begin{cases} y = -3x + 10 \\ 2x + 2y = 8 \end{cases}$

$2x + 2y = 8$

$2x + 2(-3x + 10) = 8$

$2x - 6x + 20 = 8$

$-4x = -12$

$x = 3$

$y = -3x + 10$

$y = -3(3) + 10$

$y = -9 + 10$

$y = 1$

Thus the solution is the ordered pair $\mathbf{(3, 1)}$.

22. $\dfrac{\left(3000 \times 10^{-5}\right)\left(0.004 \times 10^{10}\right)}{\left(200 \times 10^{14}\right)(0.000002)}$

$= \dfrac{\left(3 \times 10^{-2}\right)\left(4 \times 10^{7}\right)}{\left(2 \times 10^{16}\right)\left(2 \times 10^{-6}\right)}$

$= \dfrac{3 \cdot 4}{2 \cdot 2} \times \dfrac{10^{-2} \cdot 10^{7}}{10^{16} \cdot 10^{-6}} = \dfrac{12}{4} \times \dfrac{10^{5}}{10^{10}}$

$= \mathbf{3 \times 10^{-5}}$

23. (a) **Naturals, wholes, integers, rationals, reals**

(b) **Integers, rationals, reals**

24. $x + 4 \not> 2; \; D = \{\text{Reals}\}$

$x + 4 \not> 2$

$ \underline{-4 \quad\; -4}$

$x \qquad\; \not> -2$

```
  ┼────┼────┼────●────┼
 -5   -4   -3   -2   -1
```

25. $\dfrac{3x + 2}{5} - \dfrac{x}{2} = 5$

$10 \cdot \dfrac{(3x + 2)}{5} - 10 \cdot \dfrac{x}{2} = 10 \cdot 5$

$2(3x + 2) - 5x = 50$

$6x + 4 - 5x = 50$

$x = \mathbf{46}$

26. $-3x^{0}(-2 - 3)4x = -2(x + 2)$

$-3(-5)4x = -2x - 4$

$60x = -2x - 4$

$62x = -4$

$x = \dfrac{-4}{62}$

$x = -\dfrac{2}{31}$

27. $y = \sqrt[3]{64} - 8$

$y = 4 - 8$

$y = -4$

$|-x| - x^0 - x^2(x - y)$

$= |-(-2)| - (-2)^0 - (-2)^2[-2 - (-4)]$

$= 2 - 1 - 4(2) = 1 - 8 = \mathbf{-7}$

28. $\dfrac{x}{x+1} + \dfrac{x^2}{x(x+1)} - \dfrac{2}{x}$

$= \dfrac{x^2}{x(x+1)} + \dfrac{x^2}{x(x+1)} - \dfrac{2(x+1)}{x(x+1)}$

$= \dfrac{2x^2 - 2(x+1)}{x(x+1)}$

29. (a) $-3^{-2} = \dfrac{-1}{3^2} = -\dfrac{1}{9}$

(b) $(-3)^{-2} = \dfrac{1}{(-3)^2} = \dfrac{1}{9}$

(c) $-(-3)^{-2} = -\dfrac{1}{(-3)^2} = -\dfrac{1}{9}$

30. $S.A. = \text{Area}_{\text{base}} + \text{Lateral Surface Area}$

$= \pi r^2 + \pi r l$

$= \pi(12 \text{ in.})^2 + \pi(12 \text{ in.})(20 \text{ in.})$

$= 144\pi \text{ in.}^2 + 240\pi \text{ in.}^2$

$= \mathbf{384\pi \text{ in.}^2 = 1205.76 \text{ in.}^2}$

Practice 91

a. $-x \geq 5; D = \{\text{Reals}\}$

$x \leq -5$

b. $2 - x \nleq 1; D = \{\text{Integers}\}$

$2 - x > 1$

$-x > -1$

$x < 1$

c. $-3x + 5 > 1; D = \{\text{Integers}\}$

$-3x > -4$

$x < \dfrac{4}{3}$

d. $V = \dfrac{4}{3}\pi r^3$

$= \dfrac{4}{3}\pi(4 \text{ in.})^3$

$= \dfrac{256\pi}{3} \text{ in.}^3 = 267.95 \text{ in.}^3$

e. $S.A. = 4\pi r^2$

$= 4\pi(5 \text{ ft})^2$

$= 100\pi \text{ ft}^2 = 314 \text{ ft}^2$

Problem Set 91

1. (a) $N_F = N_S + 90$

(b) $N_F + N_S = 630$

(b) $N_F + N_S = 630$

$(N_S + 90) + N_S = 630$

$2N_S = 540$

$N_S = \mathbf{270}$

(a) $N_F = N_S + 90$

$N_F = 270 + 90$

$N_F = \mathbf{360}$

2. (a) $N_C + N_F = 50$

(b) $5N_C + 3N_F = 190$

$(-5)(a) \quad -5N_C - 5N_F = -250$

$(1)(b) \quad \underline{5N_C + 3N_F = 190}$

$-2N_F = -60$

$N_F = \mathbf{30}$

3. (a) $N_Q = N_D + 5$

(b) $25N_Q + 10N_D = 650$

(b) $25N_Q + 10N_D = 650$

$25(N_D + 5) + 10N_D = 650$

$35N_D + 125 = 650$

$35N_D = 525$

$N_D = \mathbf{15}$

(a) $N_Q = N_D + 5$

$N_Q = 15 + 5$

$N_Q = \mathbf{20}$

4. $\dfrac{280}{100} \cdot N = 5600$

$\dfrac{100}{280} \cdot \dfrac{280}{100} \cdot N = 5600 \cdot \dfrac{100}{280}$

$N = \mathbf{2000}$

5. Range = 54 − 47 = **7**

Median = **50**

Mode = **50**

Mean = $\dfrac{47 + 48 + 49 + 50 + 50 + 52 + 54}{7}$

$= \dfrac{350}{7} = \mathbf{50}$

6. $-x \geq 3$; D = {Reals}

$x \leq -3$

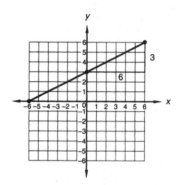

7. $4 \leq x < 7$; D = {Integers}

8. $3 - x \nleq 1$; D = {Reals}

$3 - x > 1$

$-x > -2$

$x < 2$

9. $21 = 10x - x^2$

$x^2 - 10x + 21 = 0$

$(x - 7)(x - 3) = 0$

If $x - 7 = 0$ If $x - 3 = 0$

$x = \mathbf{7}$ $x = \mathbf{3}$

10. $-49 = -4x^2$

$4x^2 - 49 = 0$

$(2x - 7)(2x + 7) = 0$

If $2x - 7 = 0$ If $2x + 7 = 0$

$2x = 7$ $2x = -7$

$x = \dfrac{\mathbf{7}}{\mathbf{2}}$ $x = -\dfrac{\mathbf{7}}{\mathbf{2}}$

11. $32 = -x^2 - 12x$

$x^2 + 12x + 32 = 0$

$(x + 8)(x + 4) = 0$

If $x + 8 = 0$ If $x + 4 = 0$

$x = \mathbf{-8}$ $x = \mathbf{-4}$

12. $R_H T_H - 125 = R_O T_O$

$2(-R_O + 85) - 125 = 3R_O$

$-2R_O + 170 - 125 = 3R_O$

$-5R_O = -45$

$R_O = \mathbf{9}$

$R_H + R_O = 85$

$R_H + 9 = 85$

$R_H = \mathbf{76}$

13. **(b), (c)**

14. (b) $D = \left\{ x \in \mathbb{R} \mid -5 \leq x \leq 3 \right\}$

$R = \left\{ y \in \mathbb{R} \mid -2 \leq y \leq 4 \right\}$

(c) $D = \{3, 4, 9\}$; $R = \{2, 7\}$

15. $\left(x^4 - 2x^2 - 4 \right) \div (x + 2)$

$$
\begin{array}{r}
x^3 - 2x^2 + 2x - 4 \\
x + 2 \overline{\smash{\big)}\ x^4 + 0x^3 - 2x^2 + 0x - 4} \\
\underline{x^4 + 2x^3} \\
-2x^3 - 2x^2 \\
\underline{-2x^3 - 4x^2} \\
2x^2 + 0x \\
\underline{2x^2 + 4x} \\
-4x - 4 \\
\underline{-4x - 8} \\
4
\end{array}
$$

$x^3 - 2x^2 + 2x - 4 + \dfrac{4}{x + 2}$

16. (a) $y = -3$

(b) The desired equation is $y = mx + b$.

By inspection, $b = 3$.

By inspection, the sign of m is $+$.

$|m| = \dfrac{3}{6} = \dfrac{1}{2}$

So $b = 3$ and $m = \dfrac{1}{2}$.

$y = \dfrac{1}{2}x + 3$

17. $5\sqrt{75} - 2\sqrt{108} + 5\sqrt{12}$

$= 5\sqrt{3 \cdot 5 \cdot 5} - 2\sqrt{2 \cdot 2 \cdot 3 \cdot 3 \cdot 3}$

$+ 5\sqrt{2 \cdot 2 \cdot 3}$

$= 5\sqrt{3}\sqrt{5}\sqrt{5} - 2\sqrt{2}\sqrt{2}\sqrt{3}\sqrt{3}\sqrt{3} + 5\sqrt{2}\sqrt{2}\sqrt{3}$

$= 5\sqrt{3}(5) - 2(2)(3)\sqrt{3} + 5(2)\sqrt{3}$

$= 25\sqrt{3} - 12\sqrt{3} + 10\sqrt{3} = \mathbf{23\sqrt{3}}$

18. $2\sqrt{6}\left(3\sqrt{6} - 2\sqrt{12}\right) = 6\sqrt{36} - 4\sqrt{72}$

$= 36 - 4\sqrt{2}\sqrt{2}\sqrt{2}\sqrt{3}\sqrt{3} = 36 - 4(2)\sqrt{2}\,(3)$

$= \mathbf{36 - 24\sqrt{2}}$

19. $\begin{cases} y = -x + 1 \\ y = 2x + 4 \end{cases}$

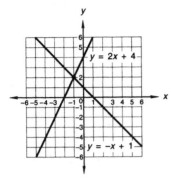

$y = -x + 1$ $y = 2x + 4$

$2 = -(-1) + 1$ $2 = 2(-1) + 4$

$2 = 1 + 1$ $2 = -2 + 4$

$2 = 2$ $2 = 2$

The solution to the linear equations is **(–1, 2)**.

20. (a) $\begin{cases} 4x - 3y = 14 \\ 5x - 4y = 18 \end{cases}$
   (b)

    (4)(a) $16x - 12y = 56$

(–3)(b) $\underline{-15x + 12y = -54}$

                  $x = 2$

  (a) $4x - 3y = 14$

        $4(2) - 3y = 14$

         $8 - 3y = 14$

           $-3y = 6$

             $y = -2$

Thus the solution is the ordered pair **(2, –2)**.

21. $\dfrac{\left(0.00004 \times 10^{15}\right)\left(700 \times 10^{-5}\right)}{14{,}000 \times 10^{-21}}$

$= \dfrac{\left(4 \times 10^{10}\right)\left(7 \times 10^{-3}\right)}{1.4 \times 10^{-17}}$

$= \dfrac{4 \cdot 7}{1.4} \times \dfrac{10^{10} \cdot 10^{-3}}{10^{-17}}$

$= \dfrac{28}{1.4} \times \dfrac{10^{7}}{10^{-17}}$

$= 20 \times 10^{24} = \mathbf{2 \times 10^{25}}$

22. (a) **Rationals, reals**

    (b) **Rationals, reals**

23. $\dfrac{4x}{3} - \dfrac{x+1}{5} = 10$

$15 \cdot \dfrac{4x}{3} - 15 \cdot \dfrac{(x+1)}{5} = 15 \cdot 10$

      $5(4x) - 3(x+1) = 150$

         $20x - 3x - 3 = 150$

               $17x = 153$

                 $x = \mathbf{9}$

24. $3x^{0} - 2x^{0} - 3\left(x^{0} - 2x\right) = -2x(4 - 3)$

       $3 - 2 - 3(1 - 2x) = -2x$

           $1 - 3 + 6x = -2x$

              $-2 + 6x = -2x$

                 $-2 = -8x$

                   $x = \dfrac{1}{4}$

25. $b + 5 = \sqrt{16}$

    $b + 5 = 4$

        $b = -1$

$\dfrac{-b \pm \sqrt{b^{2} - 4ac}}{}$

$= -(-1) \pm \sqrt{(-1)^{2} - 4(-3)(4)}$

$= 1 \pm \sqrt{1 + 48}$

$= 1 \pm \sqrt{49}$

$= 1 \pm 7 = \mathbf{-6, 8}$

26. $\dfrac{\dfrac{3x}{y} - 2}{a - \dfrac{4}{y}} = \dfrac{\dfrac{3x}{y} - \dfrac{2y}{y}}{\dfrac{ay}{y} - \dfrac{4}{y}} = \dfrac{\dfrac{3x - 2y}{y}}{\dfrac{ay - 4}{y}} \cdot \dfrac{y}{ay - 4}$

$= \dfrac{\mathbf{3x - 2y}}{\mathbf{ay - 4}}$

27. $\dfrac{ab^{-1} + a^{-1}}{a^{-1}b} = \dfrac{\dfrac{a}{b} + \dfrac{1}{a}}{\dfrac{b}{a}} = \dfrac{\dfrac{a^{2}}{ab} + \dfrac{b}{ab}}{\dfrac{b}{a}}$

$= \dfrac{\dfrac{a^{2} + b}{ab}}{\dfrac{b}{a}} \cdot \dfrac{a}{b} = \dfrac{\mathbf{a^{2} + b}}{\mathbf{b^{2}}}$

28. $x = \sqrt{16} - \sqrt[4]{16} - \sqrt{4} - \sqrt[3]{8}$

     $= 4 - 2 - 2 - 2 = -2$

  (a) $-x^{-3} = -(-2)^{-3} = \dfrac{-1}{(-2)^{3}} = \dfrac{-1}{-8} = \dfrac{1}{8}$

  (b) $\dfrac{1}{-(-x)^{-3}} = \dfrac{1}{-[-(-2)]^{-3}} = \dfrac{2^{3}}{-1} = \mathbf{-8}$

29. $V = \frac{4}{3}\pi r^3$

$= \frac{4}{3}\pi(1 \text{ cm})^3$

$= \frac{4\pi}{3} \text{ cm}^3 = \textbf{4.19 cm}^3$

30. $V = (\text{Area}_{\text{base}})(\text{Height})$
$= (60 \text{ m}^2)(13 \text{ m}) = \textbf{780 m}^3$

Practice 92

a. $D_W = D_J$

$R_W T_W = R_J T_J$

$T_W = 9$

$T_J = 3$

$R_J = R_W + 4$

$R_W T_W = R_J T_J$

$R_W(9) = (R_W + 4)(3)$

$9R_W = 3R_W + 12$

$6R_W = 12$

$R_W = 2$

$R_J = R_W + 4$

$R_J = 2 + 4$

$R_J = 6$

$D_J = R_J T_J = (6)(3) = \textbf{18 mi}$

b. $D_M = D_T$

$R_M T_M = R_T T_T$

$R_M = 60$

$R_T = 40$

$T_M + T_T = 15$

$R_M T_M = R_T T_T$

$60T_M = 40(-T_M + 15)$

$60T_M = -40T_M + 600$

$100T_M = 600$

$T_M = 6$

$D_M = R_M T_M = (60)(6) = \textbf{360 mi}$

Problem Set 92

1. $D_P = D_F$

$R_P T_P = R_F T_F$

$T_P = 3$

$T_F = 7$

$R_F = R_P - 40$

$R_P T_P = R_F T_F$

$R_P(3) = (R_P - 40)(7)$

$3R_P = 7R_P - 280$

$-4R_P = -280$

$\textbf{R}_P = \textbf{70 mph}$

$R_F = R_P - 40$

$R_F = 70 - 40$

$\textbf{R}_F = \textbf{30 mph}$

2. $D_B = D_W$

$R_B T_B = R_W T_W$

$R_B = 10$

$R_W = 4$

$T_B + T_W = 14$

$R_B T_B = R_W T_W$

$10T_B = 4(-T_B + 14)$

$10T_B = -4T_B + 56$

$14T_B = 56$

$T_B = 4 \text{ hr}$

$D_B = R_B T_B = (10)(4) = \textbf{40 km}$

3. Average $= \dfrac{\text{Sum of 4 numbers}}{4}$

$= \dfrac{12,000.16}{4}$

$= \textbf{3000.04}$

4. (a) $N_W = N_I - 5$

(b) $30N_I + 50N_W = 1350$

(b) $30N_I + 50N_W = 1350$

$30N_I + 50(N_I - 5) = 1350$

$80N_I - 250 = 1350$

$80N_I = 1600$

$N_I = 20$

(a) $N_W = N_I - 5$

$N_W = 20 - 5$

$N_W = \textbf{15}$

5. $(0.38)(50) = WN$

$WN = \textbf{19}$

6. $P(\text{both soccer balls}) = \dfrac{7}{16} \cdot \dfrac{6}{15}$

$= \dfrac{42}{240} = \dfrac{21}{120} = \dfrac{\textbf{7}}{\textbf{40}}$

7. $-4x + 4 \geq 8; \; D = \{\text{Reals}\}$

$-4x \geq 4$

$x \leq -1$

8. $4 - x \not\geq 3$; $D = \{\text{Integers}\}$

$4 - x < 3$

$-x < -1$

$x > 1$

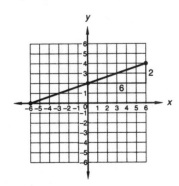

9. $x^2 = -6x - 8$

$x^2 + 6x + 8 = 0$

$(x + 4)(x + 2) = 0$

If $x + 4 = 0$ If $x + 2 = 0$

     $x = -4$ $x = -2$

10. $9 = 4x^2$

$9 - 4x^2 = 0$

$(3 - 2x)(3 + 2x) = 0$

If $3 - 2x = 0$ If $3 + 2x = 0$

$-2x = -3$ $2x = -3$

$x = \dfrac{3}{2}$ $x = -\dfrac{3}{2}$

11. $x^2 = -12x - 32$

$x^2 + 12x + 32 = 0$

$(x + 8)(x + 4) = 0$

If $x + 8 = 0$ If $x + 4 = 0$

     $x = -8$ $x = -4$

12. $D = \left\{x \in \mathbb{R} \mid -8 \leq x \leq -2\right\}$
$R = \left\{y \in \mathbb{R} \mid -2 \leq y \leq 6\right\}$

13. (a) $x = -3$

(b) The desired equation is $y = mx + b$.

By inspection, $b = 2$.

By inspection, the sign of m is +.

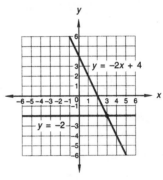

$|m| = \dfrac{2}{6} = \dfrac{1}{3}$

So $b = 2$ and $m = \dfrac{1}{3}$.

$y = \dfrac{1}{3}x + 2$

14. $(x^3 - 4) \div (x - 5)$

$$
\begin{array}{r}
x^2 + 5x + 25 \\
x - 5 \overline{\smash{\big)}\, x^3 + 0x^2 + 0x - 4} \\
\underline{x^3 - 5x^2} \\
5x^2 + 0x \\
\underline{5x^2 - 25x} \\
25x - 4 \\
\underline{25x - 125} \\
121
\end{array}
$$

$x^2 + 5x + 25 + \dfrac{121}{x - 5}$

15. $3\sqrt{45} - 2\sqrt{180} + 2\sqrt{80{,}000}$

$= 3\sqrt{3 \cdot 3 \cdot 5} - 2\sqrt{2 \cdot 2 \cdot 3 \cdot 3 \cdot 5}$
$\quad + 2\sqrt{2 \cdot 2 \cdot 2 \cdot 10{,}000}$

$= 3(3)\sqrt{5} - 2(2)(3)\sqrt{5} + 2(2)\sqrt{2}(100)$

$= 9\sqrt{5} - 12\sqrt{5} + 400\sqrt{2}$

$= -3\sqrt{5} + 400\sqrt{2}$

16. $3\sqrt{2}\left(4\sqrt{20} - 3\sqrt{2}\right) = 12\sqrt{40} - 9\sqrt{4}$
$= 12\left(2\sqrt{10}\right) - 9(2) = 24\sqrt{10} - 18$

17. $\begin{cases} y = -2x + 4 \\ y = -2 \end{cases}$

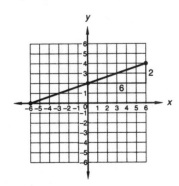

$y = -2x + 4$ $y = -2$

$-2 = -2(3) + 4$ $-2 = -2$

$-2 = -6 + 4$

$-2 = -2$

The solution to the linear equations is **(3, –2)**.

18. (a) $\begin{cases} 3x + y = 20 \\ 2x - 3y = -5 \end{cases}$
(b)

$(3)(a)$ $9x + 3y = 60$
$(1)(b)$ $\underline{2x - 3y = -5}$
$\;\; 11x = 55$
$\; x = 5$

(a) $3x + y = 20$

$3(5) + y = 20$

$15 + y = 20$

$y = 5$

Thus the solution is the ordered pair **(5, 5)**.

19. $\dfrac{0.000030 \times 10^{-18}}{(5000 \times 10^{-14})(300 \times 10^5)}$

$= \dfrac{3 \times 10^{-23}}{(5 \times 10^{-11})(3 \times 10^7)}$

$= \dfrac{3}{5 \cdot 3} \times \dfrac{10^{-23}}{10^{-11} \cdot 10^7}$

$= \dfrac{3}{15} \times \dfrac{10^{-23}}{10^{-4}}$

$= 0.2 \times 10^{-19} = \mathbf{2 \times 10^{-20}}$

20. (a) **False. Some real numbers are not members of the set of rational numbers.**

(b) **False. Zero, a member of the set of whole numbers, is not a member of the set of natural numbers.**

21. $10{,}000 \text{ yd} \cdot \text{yd} \cdot \text{yd} \times \dfrac{3 \text{ ft}}{1 \text{ yd}} \times \dfrac{3 \text{ ft}}{1 \text{ yd}} \times \dfrac{3 \text{ ft}}{1 \text{ yd}}$

$\times \dfrac{12 \text{ in.}}{1 \text{ ft}} \times \dfrac{12 \text{ in.}}{1 \text{ ft}} \times \dfrac{12 \text{ in.}}{1 \text{ ft}} \times \dfrac{2.54 \text{ cm}}{1 \text{ in.}}$

$\times \dfrac{2.54 \text{ cm}}{1 \text{ in.}} \times \dfrac{2.54 \text{ cm}}{1 \text{ in.}} \times \dfrac{1 \text{ m}}{100 \text{ cm}} \times \dfrac{1 \text{ m}}{100 \text{ cm}}$

$\times \dfrac{1 \text{ m}}{100 \text{ cm}} = \dfrac{10{,}000(3)^3 (12)^3 (2.54)^3}{(100)^3} \text{ m}^3$

$= \mathbf{7645.55 \text{ m}^3}$

22. $\dfrac{x}{5} - \dfrac{4+x}{7} = 5$

$35 \cdot \dfrac{x}{5} - 35 \cdot \dfrac{(4+x)}{7} = 35 \cdot 5$

$7x - 5(4+x) = 175$

$7x - 20 - 5x = 175$

$2x = 195$

$x = \dfrac{195}{2}$

23. $2\dfrac{1}{8}x - 3\dfrac{1}{4} = 2\dfrac{1}{16}$

$\dfrac{17}{8}x - \dfrac{13}{4} = \dfrac{33}{16}$

$16 \cdot \dfrac{17}{8}x - 16 \cdot \dfrac{13}{4} = 16 \cdot \dfrac{33}{16}$

$2(17x) - 4(13) = 33$

$34x - 52 = 33$

$34x = 85$

$x = \dfrac{85}{34}$

$x = \dfrac{5}{2}$

24. $p - (-p) - 5(p - 3) - (2p - 5) = 3(p + 2p)$

$p + p - 5p + 15 - 2p + 5 = 9p$

$-5p + 20 = 9p$

$-14p = -20$

$p = \dfrac{-20}{-14}$

$p = \dfrac{10}{7}$

25. $x = -\sqrt{9} \qquad 5y = 20$

$x = -3 \qquad\quad y = 4$

$\left|-x^2\right| - |x| + x(x - y^0)$

$= \left|-(-3)^2\right| - |-3| + (-3)(-3 - 1)$

$= 9 - 3 + 12 = \mathbf{18}$

26. $-3^0 - [(-3 + 5) - (-2 - 5)] = -1 - [2 - (-7)]$

$= -1 - 9 = \mathbf{-10}$

27. (a) $-2^{-2} = \dfrac{-1}{2^2} = -\dfrac{1}{4}$

(b) $\dfrac{1}{-2^{-3}} = \dfrac{2^3}{-1} = \mathbf{-8}$

(c) $-(-2)^{-2} = \dfrac{-1}{(-2)^2} = -\dfrac{1}{4}$

(d) $\sqrt[7]{-128} = \mathbf{-2}$

28. $\left(\dfrac{x^{-1}y}{a^{-2}} + \dfrac{x^4 y}{a^2} - \dfrac{x^{-3}y^2}{ya^{-4}}\right)\dfrac{x^{-4}y}{a^{-2}}$

$= \dfrac{x^{-5}y^2}{a^{-4}} + y^2 - \dfrac{x^{-7}y^3}{ya^{-6}}$

$= \dfrac{a^4 y^2}{x^5} + y^2 - \dfrac{a^6 y^2}{x^7}$

29. $S.A. = 4\pi r^2$

$= 4\pi(2 \text{ in.})^2$

$= 16\pi \text{ in.}^2 = \mathbf{50.24 \text{ in.}^2}$

30. Lateral $S.A. = \left(\text{Perimeter}_{\text{base}}\right)(\text{Height})$

$= (15 \text{ ft} \times 5)(18 \text{ ft})$

$= (75 \text{ ft})(18 \text{ ft})$

$= \mathbf{1350 \text{ ft}^2}$

Practice 93

a. $\dfrac{x^2 - x - 6}{x^2 - 6x - 16} \div \dfrac{x^2 - 3x}{x^2 - 3x - 40}$

$= \dfrac{x^2 - x - 6}{x^2 - 6x - 16} \cdot \dfrac{x^2 - 3x - 40}{x^2 - 3x}$

$= \dfrac{(x - 3)(x + 2)}{(x - 8)(x + 2)} \cdot \dfrac{(x - 8)(x + 5)}{x(x - 3)} = \dfrac{x + 5}{x}$

b. $\dfrac{x^2 + 12x + 36}{x^2 + 13x + 42} \cdot \dfrac{x^2 + 4x - 21}{x^2 + 2x - 24}$

$= \dfrac{(x + 6)(x + 6)}{(x + 7)(x + 6)} \cdot \dfrac{(x + 7)(x - 3)}{(x + 6)(x - 4)} = \dfrac{x - 3}{x - 4}$

Problem Set 93

1. $D_C = D_H$
    $R_C T_C = R_H T_H$

    $R_C = 300$
    $R_H = 400$
    $T_C + T_H = 7$

    $R_C T_C = R_H T_H$
    $300 T_C = 400(-T_C + 7)$
    $300 T_C = -400 T_C + 2800$
    $700 T_C = 2800$
    $T_C = \textbf{4 min}$

    $D_C = R_C T_C = 300(4) = 1200$
    $D = \textbf{1200 cm}$

2. $D_1 = D_2$
    $R_1 T_1 = R_2 T_2$

    $T_1 = 4$
    $T_2 = 3$
    $R_2 = R_1 + 11$

    $R_1 T_1 = R_2 T_2$
    $4 R_1 = 3(R_1 + 11)$
    $4 R_1 = 3 R_1 + 33$
    $R_1 = \textbf{33 mph}$

    $R_2 = R_1 + 11$
    $R_2 = 33 + 11$
    $R_2 = \textbf{44 mph}$

3. (a) $N_A + N_K = 77$
    (b) $3 N_A + 2 N_K = 209$

    $(-3)(a)$ $\quad -3 N_A - 3 N_K = -231$
    $(1)(b)$ $\quad \underline{3 N_A + 2 N_K = 209}$
    $\qquad\qquad\qquad -N_K = -22$
    $\qquad\qquad\qquad N_K = \textbf{22}$

4. (a) $N_B + N_G = 179$
    (b) $N_B = N_G + 13$

    (a) $\qquad N_B + N_G = 179$
    $\qquad (N_G + 13) + N_G = 179$
    $\qquad\qquad 2 N_G + 13 = 179$
    $\qquad\qquad\qquad 2 N_G = 166$
    $\qquad\qquad\qquad N_G = \textbf{83}$

(b) $N_B = N_G + 13$
$\quad N_B = 83 + 13$
$\quad N_B = \textbf{96}$

5. $WP(460) = 92$

    $WP = \dfrac{92}{460}$

    $WP = \dfrac{2}{10}$

    $WP = \textbf{20\%}$

6. $\dfrac{8}{13} T = 400$

    $T = \textbf{650}$

7. $P(H, T, H, T, H) = \dfrac{1}{2} \cdot \dfrac{1}{2} \cdot \dfrac{1}{2} \cdot \dfrac{1}{2} \cdot \dfrac{1}{2} = \dfrac{1}{32}$

8. $\dfrac{x^2 - 16}{x^2 + x - 12} \cdot \dfrac{x^2 + 5x + 6}{x^2 - 2x - 8}$

    $= \dfrac{(x - 4)(x + 4)}{(x + 4)(x - 3)} \cdot \dfrac{(x + 2)(x + 3)}{(x - 4)(x + 2)} = \dfrac{x + 3}{x - 3}$

9. $\dfrac{x^3 - 4x}{x^2 + 7x + 10} \div \dfrac{x^2 - 2x}{x^2 - 25}$

    $= \dfrac{x^3 - 4x}{x^2 + 7x + 10} \cdot \dfrac{x^2 - 25}{x^2 - 2x}$

    $= \dfrac{x(x - 2)(x + 2)}{(x + 2)(x + 5)} \cdot \dfrac{(x + 5)(x - 5)}{x(x - 2)} = \textbf{\textit{x} - 5}$

10. $-x - 3 \not> 2; \; D = \{\text{Reals}\}$
    $-x - 3 \le 2$
    $\qquad -x \le 5$
    $\qquad\quad x \ge -5$

11. $-3 < x < 2; \; D = \{\text{Reals}\}$

12. $\qquad\qquad 40 = -x^2 - 14x$
    $\qquad x^2 + 14x + 40 = 0$
    $\qquad (x + 10)(x + 4) = 0$

    If $x + 10 = 0 \qquad$ If $x + 4 = 0$
    $\qquad x = \textbf{-10} \qquad\qquad x = \textbf{-4}$

13. $\qquad 4x^2 - 16 = 0$
    $\qquad 4(x^2 - 4) = 0$
    $\qquad\quad x^2 - 4 = 0$
    $\qquad (x - 2)(x + 2) = 0$

    If $x - 2 = 0 \qquad$ If $x + 2 = 0$
    $\qquad x = \textbf{2} \qquad\qquad x = \textbf{-2}$

14. (a), (b), (c), (d), (e)

15. $\left(3x^3 - 4\right) \div (x + 3)$

$$
\begin{array}{r}
3x^2 - 9x + 27 \\
x + 3 \overline{\smash{\big)}\ 3x^3 + 0x^2 + 0x - 4} \\
\underline{3x^3 + 9x^2} \\
-9x^2 + 0x \\
\underline{-9x^2 - 27x} \\
27x - 4 \\
\underline{27x + 81} \\
-85
\end{array}
$$

$$3x^2 - 9x + 27 - \frac{85}{x + 3}$$

16. $3\sqrt{6} \cdot 2\sqrt{5} - \sqrt{120}$
$= 6\sqrt{30} - \sqrt{2 \cdot 2 \cdot 2 \cdot 3 \cdot 5}$
$= 6\sqrt{30} - 2\sqrt{30} = \mathbf{4\sqrt{30}}$

17. $4\sqrt{12}\left(3\sqrt{2} - 4\sqrt{3}\right) = 12\sqrt{24} - 16\sqrt{36}$
$= 12\left(2\sqrt{6}\right) - 16(6) = \mathbf{24\sqrt{6} - 96}$

18. $D = \left\{x \in \mathbb{R} \mid -2 < x \le 4\right\}$
$R = \left\{y \in \mathbb{R} \mid -2 \le y < 3\right\}$

19. (a) $x = -5$

(b) The desired equation is $y = mx + b$.
By inspection, $b = 0$.
By inspection, the sign of m is $-$.

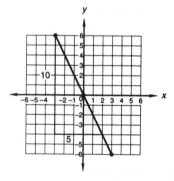

$|m| = \dfrac{10}{5} = 2$

So $b = 0$ and $m = -2$.

$y = -2x$

20. $\begin{cases} y = 2x - 4 \\ y = -x + 2 \end{cases}$

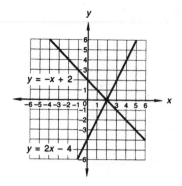

$y = 2x - 4 \qquad y = -x + 2$
$0 = 2(2) - 4 \qquad 0 = -(2) + 2$
$0 = 4 - 4 \qquad\quad 0 = -2 + 2$
$0 = 0 \qquad\qquad 0 = 0$

The solution to the linear equations is **(2, 0)**.

21. $\begin{cases} 3x + 5y = -14 \\ -2x + y = 5 \end{cases}$

$-2x + y = 5$
$\qquad y = 5 + 2x$

$\qquad\quad 3x + 5y = -14$
$3x + 5(5 + 2x) = -14$
$3x + 25 + 10x = -14$
$\qquad\qquad 13x = -39$
$\qquad\qquad\quad x = -3$

$\qquad -2x + y = 5$
$-2(-3) + y = 5$
$\qquad 6 + y = 5$
$\qquad\qquad y = -1$

Thus the solution is the ordered pair **(-3, -1)**.

22. $\dfrac{(0.000004)\left(0.003 \times 10^{21}\right)}{\left(20{,}000 \times 10^8\right)\left(0.002 \times 10^{15}\right)}$

$= \dfrac{\left(4 \times 10^{-6}\right)\left(3 \times 10^{18}\right)}{\left(2 \times 10^{12}\right)\left(2 \times 10^{12}\right)} = \dfrac{4 \cdot 3}{2 \cdot 2} \times \dfrac{10^{-6} \cdot 10^{18}}{10^{12} \cdot 10^{12}}$

$= \dfrac{12}{4} \times \dfrac{10^{12}}{10^{24}} = \mathbf{3 \times 10^{-12}}$

23. $\qquad\qquad \dfrac{x - 5}{7} + \dfrac{x}{4} = \dfrac{1}{2}$

$28 \cdot \dfrac{(x - 5)}{7} + 28 \cdot \dfrac{x}{4} = 28 \cdot \dfrac{1}{2}$

$\qquad\quad 4(x - 5) + 7x = 14$

$\qquad\quad 4x - 20 + 7x = 14$

$\qquad\qquad\qquad 11x = 34$

$\qquad\qquad\qquad\quad x = \dfrac{34}{11}$

24. $-2(3x - 4^0) + 3x - 2^0 = -(x - 3^2)$

$$-6x + 2 + 3x - 1 = -x + 9$$
$$-3x + 1 = -x + 9$$
$$-2x = 8$$
$$x = -4$$

25. $y = -\sqrt[4]{16}$ $a = \sqrt[3]{-125}$

$y = -2$ $a = -5$

$-y^0(-y^2 - 4y) - ay$

$= -1\left[-(-2)^2 - 4(-2)\right] - (-5)(-2)$

$= -(-4 + 8) - 10$

$= -4 - 10$

$= -14$

26. $(3x + 3y)^2 = (3x + 3y)(3x + 3y)$

$= 9x^2 + 9xy + 9xy + 9y^2 = 9x^2 + 18xy + 9y^2$

27. $\dfrac{x}{ya^2} + \dfrac{xa}{a^2y^2} - \dfrac{3}{ay} - \dfrac{a}{ay^2}$

$= \dfrac{xy}{a^2y^2} + \dfrac{xa}{a^2y^2} - \dfrac{3ay}{a^2y^2} - \dfrac{a^2}{a^2y^2}$

$= \dfrac{xy + xa - 3ay - a^2}{a^2y^2}$

28. (a) $\dfrac{1}{-3^{-3}} = \dfrac{3^3}{-1} = -27$

(b) $\dfrac{1}{(-3)^{-3}} = (-3)^3 = -27$

(c) $-(-3)^{-3} = \dfrac{-1}{(-3)^3} = \dfrac{1}{27}$

(d) $\sqrt[3]{-64} = -4$

29. $P = \left(10 + \dfrac{2\pi(5)}{2} + \dfrac{2\pi(5)}{2} + \dfrac{2\pi(5)}{2}\right)$cm

$= (10 + 15\pi)$ cm $= 57.1$ cm

30. $V = \left(\text{Area}_{\text{base}}\right)(\text{Height})$

$= [(30 \text{ m} \times 13 \text{ m}) + (10 \text{ m} \times 15 \text{ m})$

$+ 0.5(20 \text{ m} \times 15 \text{ m})](14 \text{ m})$

$= \left(390 \text{ m}^2 + 150 \text{ m}^2 + 150 \text{ m}^2\right)(14 \text{ m})$

$= \left(690 \text{ m}^2\right)(14 \text{ m}) = \mathbf{9660 \text{ m}^3}$

Practice 94

a.

$D_E + D_W = 500$

$R_ET_E + R_WT_W = 500$

$R_E = R_W$

$T_E = 6$

$T_W = 4$

$R_ET_E + R_WT_W = 500$

$6R_E + 4R_E = 500$

$10R_E = 500$

$R_E = 50 \dfrac{\text{km}}{\text{hr}}$

$R_W = R_E$

$R_W = 50 \dfrac{\text{km}}{\text{hr}}$

b.

$D_1 + D_2 = 750$

$R_1T_1 + R_2T_2 = 750$

$R_2 = 85$

$T_1 = 3$

$T_2 = 3$

$R_1T_1 + R_2T_2 = 750$

$3R_1 + 3(85) = 750$

$3R_1 = 495$

$R_1 = 165 \dfrac{\text{km}}{\text{hr}}$

Problem Set 94

1.

$D_1 + D_2 = 700$

$R_1T_1 + R_2T_2 = 700$

$T_1 = 10$

$T_2 = 10$

$R_1 = R_2 + 30$

$R_1T_1 + R_2T_2 = 700$

$10(R_2 + 30) + 10R_2 = 700$

$10R_2 + 300 + 10R_2 = 700$

$20R_2 = 400$

$R_2 = 20$ mph

$R_1 = R_2 + 30$

$R_1 = 20 + 30$

$R_1 = 50$ mph

2. $D_D = D_W$

$R_D T_D = R_W T_W$

$R_D = 30$

$R_W = 4$

$T_D + T_W = 17$

$$R_D T_D = R_W T_W$$
$$30(-T_W + 17) = 4T_W$$
$$-30T_W + 510 = 4T_W$$
$$510 = 34T_W$$
$$T_W = \textbf{15 hr}$$

$D_W = R_W T_W$

$D_W = (4)(15)$

$\textbf{\textit{D}}_{\textbf{\textit{W}}} = \textbf{60 mi}$

3. (a) $N_B + N_P = 192$

(b) $7N_B + 5N_P = 1140$

$(-5)(a)\ \ -5N_B - 5N_P = -960$

$(1)(b)\ \ \ \ \ 7N_B + 5N_P = 1140$

$$\overline{2N_B= 180}$$
$$N_B = \textbf{90}$$

(a) $N_B + N_P = 192$

$90 + N_P = 192$

$N_P = \textbf{102}$

4. $\dfrac{7}{16} \cdot N = 700$

$N = 1600$

$1600 - 700 = \textbf{900}$

5. $W.A. = \dfrac{70 + 75 + 80 + 85 + 90 + 3(80)}{5 + 3}$

$= \dfrac{640}{8} = \textbf{80}$

6. $\dfrac{63}{100} \cdot N = 2520$

$\dfrac{100}{63} \cdot \dfrac{63}{100} \cdot N = 2520 \cdot \dfrac{100}{63}$

$N = \textbf{4000}$

7. (a) $P(\not< 8) = \dfrac{5 + 4 + 3 + 2 + 1}{36} = \dfrac{15}{36} = \dfrac{\textbf{5}}{\textbf{12}}$

(b) $P(\not> 8) = \dfrac{5 + 6 + 5 + 4 + 3 + 2 + 1}{36}$

$= \dfrac{26}{36} = \dfrac{\textbf{13}}{\textbf{18}}$

8. $\dfrac{1}{N} = -\dfrac{1}{9}$

$N = -9$

Then the additive inverse is **9.**

9. $\dfrac{4x + 12}{x^2 + 11x + 30} \cdot \dfrac{4x^2 + 20x}{x^3 - 4x^2 - 21x}$

$= \dfrac{4(x + 3)}{(x + 6)(x + 5)} \cdot \dfrac{4x(x + 5)}{x(x - 7)(x + 3)}$

$= \dfrac{16}{(x + 6)(x - 7)}$

10. $\dfrac{x^2 + 11x + 24}{x^2 + 3x} \div \dfrac{x^2 + 13x + 40}{4x^2 + 20x}$

$= \dfrac{x^2 + 11x + 24}{x^2 + 3x} \cdot \dfrac{4x^2 + 20x}{x^2 + 13x + 40}$

$= \dfrac{(x + 8)(x + 3)}{x(x + 3)} \cdot \dfrac{4x(x + 5)}{(x + 8)(x + 5)} = \dfrac{4}{1} = \textbf{4}$

11. $\textbf{\textit{D}} = \left\{ x \in \mathbb{R} \mid -4 \leq x < 4 \right\}$

$\textbf{\textit{R}} = \left\{ y \in \mathbb{R} \mid -4 < y \leq 3 \right\}$

12. (a) $\textbf{\textit{y}} = \textbf{--2}$

(b) The desired equation is $y = mx + b$.

By inspection, $b = 3$.

By inspection, the sign of m is +.

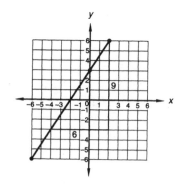

$|m| = \dfrac{9}{6} = \dfrac{3}{2}$

So $b = 3$ and $m = \dfrac{3}{2}$.

$\textbf{\textit{y}} = \dfrac{\textbf{3}}{\textbf{2}}\textbf{\textit{x}} + \textbf{3}$

13. $-4 \leq x < 1;\ D = \{\text{Integers}\}$

14.
$$x^2 = 7x + 30$$
$$x^2 - 7x - 30 = 0$$
$$(x - 10)(x + 3) = 0$$

If $x - 10 = 0$ If $x + 3 = 0$
$$x = \mathbf{10} \qquad\qquad x = \mathbf{-3}$$

15.
$$100 = 9p^2$$
$$100 - 9p^2 = 0$$
$$(10 + 3p)(10 - 3p) = 0$$

If $10 + 3p = 0$ If $10 - 3p = 0$
$$3p = -10 \qquad\qquad -3p = -10$$
$$p = -\frac{10}{3} \qquad\qquad p = \frac{10}{3}$$

16. $D = \left\{ x \in \mathbb{R} \mid x \leq \dfrac{17}{2} \right\}$

17.
$$f(x) = 10x^2 - 7x + 3$$
$$f(x - 2) = 10(x - 2)^2 - 7(x - 2) + 3$$
$$= 10\left(x^2 - 4x + 4\right) - 7x + 14 + 3$$
$$= 10x^2 - 40x + 40 - 7x + 14 + 3$$
$$= \mathbf{10x^2 - 47x + 57}$$

18. $\left(2x^3 + 5x^2 - 1\right) \div (2x + 1)$

$$
\begin{array}{r}
x^2 + 2x - 1 \\
2x + 1 \overline{\smash{\big)}\ 2x^3 + 5x^2 + 0x - 1} \\
\underline{2x^3 + \ x^2} \\
4x^2 + 0x \\
\underline{4x^2 + 2x} \\
-2x - 1 \\
\underline{-2x - 1} \\
0
\end{array}
$$

$$\mathbf{x^2 + 2x - 1}$$

19. $4\sqrt{3} \cdot 5\sqrt{6} + \sqrt{5} \cdot 2 = 20\sqrt{18} + 2\sqrt{5}$
$$= 20(3\sqrt{2}) + 2\sqrt{5} = \mathbf{60\sqrt{2} + 2\sqrt{5}}$$

20. $4\sqrt{12}\left(3\sqrt{2} - 3\sqrt{12}\right) = 12\sqrt{24} - 12(12)$
$$= 12(2\sqrt{6}) - 144 = \mathbf{24\sqrt{6} - 144}$$

21. $\begin{cases} y = x \\ x = -3 \end{cases}$

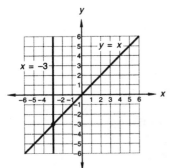

22. $\begin{cases} y = 2x + 4 \\ 2y - x = -1 \end{cases}$

$$2y - x = -1$$
$$2(2x + 4) - x = -1$$
$$4x + 8 - x = -1$$
$$3x = -9$$
$$x = -3$$

$$y = 2x + 4$$
$$y = 2(-3) + 4$$
$$y = -6 + 4$$
$$y = -2$$

Thus the solution is the ordered pair **(–3, –2)**.

23.
$$\frac{(0.00035 \times 10^{15})(200{,}000)}{(1000 \times 10^{-45})(0.00007)}$$
$$= \frac{(3.5 \times 10^{11})(2 \times 10^5)}{(1 \times 10^{-42})(7 \times 10^{-5})}$$
$$= \frac{3.5 \cdot 2}{1 \cdot 7} \times \frac{10^{11} \cdot 10^5}{10^{-42} \cdot 10^{-5}}$$
$$= \frac{7}{7} \times \frac{10^{16}}{10^{-47}}$$
$$= \mathbf{1 \times 10^{63}}$$

24. (a) **Rationals, reals**

    (b) **Wholes, integers, rationals, reals**

25.
$$\frac{x - 7}{4} - \frac{x}{2} = \frac{1}{8}$$
$$8 \cdot \frac{(x - 7)}{4} - 8 \cdot \frac{x}{2} = 8 \cdot \frac{1}{8}$$
$$2(x - 7) - 4x = 1$$
$$2x - 14 - 4x = 1$$
$$-2x = 15$$
$$x = -\frac{15}{2}$$

26. $-p^0(p - 4) - \left(-p^0\right)p + 3^0(p - 2) = -p - 6^0$
$$-p + 4 + p + p - 2 = -p - 1$$
$$p + 2 = -p - 1$$
$$2p = -3$$
$$p = -\frac{3}{2}$$

27. $-3\left[(-2^0 - 5^0) - 2 - (4 - 6)(-2)\right]$
$- |-(-6 + 2)|$
$= -3[(-2) - 2 - 4] - 4$
$= -3(-8) - 4 = 24 - 4 = \mathbf{20}$

28. $4x^2y^{-1}\left(\dfrac{p^0y}{x^2} - 3x^{-2}y^4 - \dfrac{2}{x^{-2}y^{-1}}\right)$

$= \dfrac{4x^2}{x^2} - 12y^3 - \dfrac{8x^2y^{-1}}{x^{-2}y^{-1}} = \mathbf{4 - 12y^3 - 8x^4}$

29. $V = \dfrac{4}{3}\pi r^3$

$= \dfrac{4}{3}\pi(3 \text{ in.})^3$

$= 36\pi \text{ in.}^3 = \mathbf{113.04 \text{ in.}^3}$

30. $S.A. = 2(\text{Area}_{\text{base}}) + \text{Lateral Surface Area}$
$= 2\left[\pi(18 \text{ ft})^2\right] + (\text{Perimeter}_{\text{base}})(\text{Height})$
$= 2(324\pi \text{ ft}^2) + [2\pi(18 \text{ ft})](9 \text{ ft})$
$= 648\pi \text{ ft}^2 + 324\pi \text{ ft}^2$
$= 972\pi \text{ ft}^2 = \mathbf{3052.08 \text{ ft}^2}$

Practice 95

a. (1) $k(x) = \sqrt{x}$

(2) $h(x) = x^3 + 1$

(3) $g(x) = -|x| - 1$

(4) $f(x) = x^2 + 2$

b. (1) $k(x) = -(x + 1)^2$

(2) $h(x) = \sqrt{x}$

(3) $f(x) = |x|$

(4) $g(x) = -x^3 + 1$

Problem Set 95

1. $D_G = D_S$
$R_GT_G = R_ST_S$
$R_G = 12$
$R_S = 8$
$T_G = T_S - 5$

$R_GT_G = R_ST_S$
$12(T_S - 5) = 8T_S$
$12T_S - 60 = 8T_S$
$4T_S = 60$
$T_S = \mathbf{15 \text{ hr}}$

$T_G = T_S - 5$
$T_G = 15 - 5$
$T_G = \mathbf{10 \text{ hr}}$

2. $D_F + D_S = 300$
$R_FT_F + R_ST_S = 300$
$T_F = 3 \text{ hr}$
$T_S = 3 \text{ hr}$
$R_F = R_S + 10$

$R_FT_F + R_ST_S = 300$
$3(R_S + 10) + 3R_S = 300$
$6R_S + 30 = 300$
$6R_S = 270$
$R_S = \mathbf{45 \text{ mph}}$

$R_F = R_S + 10$
$R_F = 45 + 10$
$R_F = \mathbf{55 \text{ mph}}$

3. (a) $N_L + N_S = 30$
(b) $N_L - N_S = 12$

(1)(a) $N_L + N_S = 30$
(1)(b) $\underline{N_L - N_S = 12}$
$2N_L \qquad = 42$
$N_L = \mathbf{21}$

(a) $N_L + N_S = 30$
$21 + N_S = 30$
$N_S = \mathbf{9}$

4. $N, N + 2, N + 4, N + 6$
$-3(N + N + 6) = 10[-(N + 4)] - 30$
$-3(2N + 6) = -10(N + 4) - 30$
$-6N - 18 = -10N - 40 - 30$
$-6N - 18 = -10N - 70$
$4N = -52$
$N = -13$

Thus the integers are **-13, -11, -9,** and **-7.**

5. $\dfrac{20}{100} \cdot T = 300$

$\dfrac{100}{20} \cdot \dfrac{20}{100} \cdot T = 300 \cdot \dfrac{100}{20}$

$T = 1500$

$\dfrac{80}{100} \cdot 1500 = WN$

$WN = \dfrac{120,000}{100}$

$WN = \mathbf{1200}$

6. $\dfrac{87}{100} \cdot 3000 = WN$

$$WN = \dfrac{261,000}{100}$$

$$WN = \mathbf{2610}$$

7. (a) $P(\text{purple, then pink}) = \dfrac{10}{19} \cdot \dfrac{9}{19} = \mathbf{\dfrac{90}{361}}$

(b) $P(\text{purple, then pink}) = \dfrac{10}{19} \cdot \dfrac{9}{18} = \dfrac{90}{342} = \mathbf{\dfrac{5}{19}}$

8. (a)

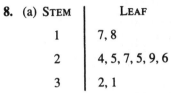

STEM	LEAF
1	7, 8
2	4, 5, 7, 5, 9, 6
3	2, 1

(b)

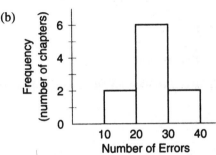

(c) Range = $32 - 17 = \mathbf{15}$

Median = $\dfrac{25 + 26}{2} = \mathbf{25.5}$

Mode = **25**

Mean = $\dfrac{\text{Sum of 10 numbers}}{10} = \dfrac{254}{10} = \mathbf{25.4}$

9. (a) $f(x) = -x^2 + 5$

(b) $k(x) = x^3$

(c) $g(x) = |x| + 5$

(d) $h(x) = \sqrt{x}$

10. (a) $k(x) = (x - 5)^2$

(b) $f(x) = -|x|$

(c) $h(x) = -x^3$

(d) $g(x) = -\sqrt{x}$

11. $\dfrac{x^2 + 5x + 6}{-x^2 - 3x} \div \dfrac{x^2 + 7x + 10}{x^3 + 8x^2 + 15x}$

$= \dfrac{x^2 + 5x + 6}{-x^2 - 3x} \cdot \dfrac{x^3 + 8x^2 + 15x}{x^2 + 7x + 10}$

$= \dfrac{(x + 2)(x + 3)}{-x(x + 3)} \cdot \dfrac{x(x + 5)(x + 3)}{(x + 5)(x + 2)}$

$= -(x + 3)$

12. $\dfrac{4x^2 + 8x}{x^2 + 8x + 12} \div \dfrac{4x^2 - 16}{x^2 + 3x - 18}$

$= \dfrac{4x^2 + 8x}{x^2 + 8x + 12} \cdot \dfrac{x^2 + 3x - 18}{4x^2 - 16}$

$= \dfrac{4x(x + 2)}{(x + 6)(x + 2)} \cdot \dfrac{(x + 6)(x - 3)}{4(x + 2)(x - 2)}$

$= \dfrac{x(x - 3)}{(x + 2)(x - 2)}$

13. $-x + 4 \le 2;\ D = \{\text{Integers}\}$

$-x \le -2$

$x \ge 2$

14. $24 = -x^2 - 10x$

$x^2 + 10x + 24 = 0$

$(x + 6)(x + 4) = 0$

If $x + 6 = 0$ If $x + 4 = 0$

$x = \mathbf{-6}$ $x = \mathbf{-4}$

15. $-4 + 9x^2 = 0$

$9x^2 - 4 = 0$

$(3x - 2)(3x + 2) = 0$

If $3x - 2 = 0$ If $3x + 2 = 0$

$3x = 2$ $3x = -2$

$x = \mathbf{\dfrac{2}{3}}$ $x = \mathbf{-\dfrac{2}{3}}$

16. $f(x) = 12x - x^2 + 6$

$f(x - 5) = 12(x - 5) - (x - 5)^2 + 6$

$= 12x - 60 - (x^2 - 10x + 25) + 6$

$= 12x - 60 - x^2 + 10x - 25 + 6$

$= \mathbf{-x^2 + 22x - 79}$

17. $\left(x^4 - x - 4\right) \div (x - 1)$

$$\begin{array}{r} x^3 + x^2 + x \\ x - 1 \overline{\smash{)}\, x^4 + 0x^3 + 0x^2 - x - 4} \\ \underline{x^4 - x^3} \\ x^3 + 0x^2 \\ \underline{x^3 - x^2} \\ x^2 - x \\ \underline{x^2 - x} \\ -4 \end{array}$$

$x^3 + x^2 + x - \dfrac{4}{x - 1}$

18. $D = \left\{ x \in \mathbb{R} \mid -3 < x \le 4 \right\}$

$R = \left\{ y \in \mathbb{R} \mid -2 \le y \le 3 \right\}$

19. (a) $y = -2$

(b) The desired equation is $y = mx + b$.

By inspection, $b = 5$.

By inspection, the sign of m is $-$.

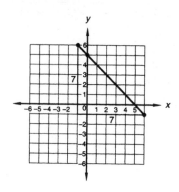

$|m| = \dfrac{7}{7} = 1$

So $b = 5$ and $m = -1$.

$y = -x + 5$

20. $3\sqrt{2} \cdot 4\sqrt{3} \cdot 4\sqrt{6} - 3\sqrt{2} = 48\sqrt{36} - 3\sqrt{2}$

$= 48(6) - 3\sqrt{2} = \mathbf{288 - 3\sqrt{2}}$

21. $3\sqrt{2}\left(5\sqrt{12} - 6\sqrt{36}\right) = 15\sqrt{24} - 3\sqrt{2}(36)$

$= 15\left(2\sqrt{6}\right) - 108\sqrt{2} = \mathbf{30\sqrt{6} - 108\sqrt{2}}$

22. $\begin{cases} y = x + 2 \\ y = -x \end{cases}$

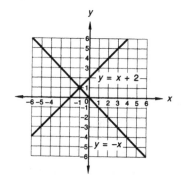

$y = x + 2 \qquad\qquad y = -x$

$1 = -1 + 2 \qquad\quad 1 = -(-1)$

$1 = 1 \qquad\qquad\quad 1 = 1$

The solution to the linear equations is $(-1, 1)$.

23. (a) $\begin{cases} 5x - 2y = 18 \\ 3x + y = 24 \end{cases}$ (b)

$\begin{aligned}(1)(a)\quad & 5x - 2y = 18 \\ (2)(b)\quad & \underline{6x + 2y = 48} \\ & 11x = 66 \\ & x = 6\end{aligned}$

(a) $\quad 5x - 2y = 18$

$5(6) - 2y = 18$

$30 - 2y = 18$

$-2y = -12$

$y = 6$

Thus the solution is the ordered pair $\mathbf{(6, 6)}$.

24. $\dfrac{\left(0.00042 \times 10^{-15}\right)(300{,}000)}{\left(180{,}000 \times 10^{-14}\right)\left(7000 \times 10^{-23}\right)}$

$= \dfrac{\left(4.2 \times 10^{-19}\right)\left(3 \times 10^{5}\right)}{\left(1.8 \times 10^{-9}\right)\left(7 \times 10^{-20}\right)}$

$= \dfrac{4.2 \cdot 3}{1.8 \cdot 7} \times \dfrac{10^{-19} \cdot 10^{5}}{10^{-9} \cdot 10^{-20}}$

$= \dfrac{12.6}{12.6} \times \dfrac{10^{-14}}{10^{-29}}$

$= \mathbf{1 \times 10^{15}}$

25. (a) **Irrationals, reals**

(b) **Naturals, wholes, integers, rationals, reals**

26. $\dfrac{xy - y^{-1}}{xy^{-1} - 4} = \dfrac{xy - \dfrac{1}{y}}{\dfrac{x}{y} - 4} = \dfrac{\dfrac{xy^2}{y} - \dfrac{1}{y}}{\dfrac{x}{y} - \dfrac{4y}{y}}$

$= \dfrac{\dfrac{xy^2 - 1}{y}}{\dfrac{x - 4y}{y}} \cdot \dfrac{y}{x - 4y} \cdot \dfrac{y}{x - 4y} = \dfrac{xy^2 - 1}{x - 4y}$

27. (a) $\dfrac{1}{-3^{-2}} = \dfrac{3^2}{-1} = \mathbf{-9}$

(b) $\dfrac{1}{(-3)^{-2}} = (-3)^2 = \mathbf{9}$

(c) $-(-2)^{-2} = \dfrac{-1}{(-2)^2} = \mathbf{-\dfrac{1}{4}}$

28. $\dfrac{3x}{2} - \dfrac{x - 5}{6} = 3$

$6 \cdot \dfrac{3x}{2} - 6 \cdot \dfrac{(x - 5)}{6} = 6 \cdot 3$

$9x - (x - 5) = 18$

$8x + 5 = 18$

$8x = 13$

$x = \dfrac{13}{8}$

29. $S.A. = 4\pi r^2$

$= 4\pi(3\text{ cm})^2$

$= \mathbf{36\pi \text{ cm}^2} = \mathbf{113.04 \text{ cm}^2}$

30. $V = (\text{Area}_{base})(\text{Height})$

$\quad = \left[\dfrac{1}{2}(9 \text{ m} \times 24 \text{ m})\right](8 \text{ m})$

$\quad = (108 \text{ m}^2)(8 \text{ m})$

$\quad = \mathbf{864 \text{ m}^3}$

Practice 96

a. $p^2 = 169$

$\quad p = \pm\sqrt{169}$

$\quad p = \mathbf{\pm 13}$

b. $q^2 = 23$

$\quad q = \mathbf{\pm\sqrt{23}}$

c. $w^2 = 14$

$\quad w = \mathbf{\pm\sqrt{14}}$

Problem Set 96

1. $D_N + D_S = 340$

$R_N T_N + R_S T_S = 340$

$R_N = 30$

$R_S = 40$

$T_N = T_S + 2$

$\qquad R_N T_N + R_S T_S = 340$

$\quad 30(T_S + 2) + 40T_S = 340$

$\qquad\qquad 70T_S + 60 = 340$

$\qquad\qquad\qquad 70T_S = 280$

$\qquad\qquad\qquad\quad T_S = 4 \text{ hr}$

$T_N = T_S + 2$

$T_N = 4 + 2$

$T_N = 6 \text{ hr}$

Hence, the time at which they are 340 km apart is $3 + 6 = \mathbf{9 \text{ p.m.}}$

2. $D_A = D_B$

$R_A T_A = R_B T_B$

$R_A = 30$

$R_B = 60$

$T_B = T_A - 2$

$\quad R_A T_A = R_B T_B$

$\quad 30T_A = 60(T_A - 2)$

$\quad 30T_A = 60T_A - 120$

$-30T_A = -120$

$\quad\;\; T_A = 4$

Thus, they met at **1 p.m.**

3. $D_R = D_W$

$R_R T_R = R_W T_W$

$R_R = 8$

$R_W = 3$

$T_R + T_W = 11$

$\quad R_R T_R = R_W T_W$

$\quad 8T_R = 3(-T_R + 11)$

$\quad 8T_R = -3T_R + 33$

$\;\, 11T_R = 33$

$\quad\; T_R = 3$

$D_R = R_R T_R = (8)(3) = \mathbf{24 \text{ km}}$

4. (a) $N_Q + N_H = 190$

(b) $25N_Q + 50N_H = 7250$

$(-50)(a) \quad -50N_Q - 50N_H = -9500$

$(1)(b) \quad \underline{25N_Q + 50N_H = 7250}$

$\qquad\qquad\; -25N_Q \qquad\qquad = -2250$

$\qquad\qquad\qquad\qquad N_Q = 90$

(a) $N_Q + N_H = 190$

$\quad 90 + N_H = 190$

$\qquad\quad N_H = \mathbf{100}$

5. $\qquad \dfrac{85}{100} \cdot T = 289$

$\dfrac{100}{85} \cdot \dfrac{85}{100} \cdot T = 289 \cdot \dfrac{100}{85}$

$\qquad\qquad\quad T = \mathbf{340}$

6. (a) $N_H = 3N_E + 1800$

(b) $N_H + N_E = 3000$

(b) $\qquad\qquad N_H + N_E = 3000$

$\quad (3N_E + 1800) + N_E = 3000$

$\qquad\qquad\qquad\quad 4N_E = 1200$

$\qquad\qquad\qquad\quad\; N_E = \mathbf{300}$

(b) $N_H + N_E = 3000$

$\quad N_H + 300 = 3000$

$\qquad\quad N_H = \mathbf{2700}$

7. (a) $P(4) = \dfrac{3}{36} = \dfrac{1}{12}$

(b) $P(>4) = \dfrac{4 + 5 + 6 + 5 + 4 + 3 + 2 + 1}{36}$

$\qquad\qquad\; = \dfrac{30}{36} = \dfrac{5}{6}$

8. (a) $p^2 = 49$

$\quad p = \pm\sqrt{49}$

$\quad p = \pm 7$

(b) $p^2 = 39$

$\quad p = \pm\sqrt{39}$

(c) $k^2 = 11$

$\quad k = \pm\sqrt{11}$

9. (a) $b(x) = x^2 + 5$

(b) $a(x) = 3x + 2$

(c) $d(x) = |x| + 4$

(d) $e(x) = -x^3$

(e) $c(x) = \sqrt{x}$

10. $\dfrac{x^3 + 2x^2 - 15x}{x^2 + 5x} \div \dfrac{x^3 - 6x^2 + 9x}{x^2 - 3x}$

$= \dfrac{x^3 + 2x^2 - 15x}{x^2 + 5x} \cdot \dfrac{x^2 - 3x}{x^3 - 6x^2 + 9x}$

$= \dfrac{x(x + 5)(x - 3)}{x(x + 5)} \cdot \dfrac{x(x - 3)}{x(x - 3)(x - 3)} = \mathbf{1}$

11. $-4 - x \not> -2;\ D = \{\text{Negative Integers}\}$

$-4 - x \le -2$

$\quad -x \le 2$

$\quad x \ge -2$

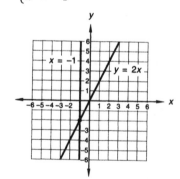

12. $\quad\quad -56 = 15x + x^2$

$x^2 + 15x + 56 = 0$

$(x + 8)(x + 7) = 0$

If $x + 8 = 0$ $\quad$ If $x + 7 = 0$

$\quad x = -8$ $\quad\quad\quad x = -7$

13. $\quad\quad -81 + 4x^2 = 0$

$\quad\quad 4x^2 - 81 = 0$

$(2x - 9)(2x + 9) = 0$

If $2x - 9 = 0$ $\quad$ If $2x + 9 = 0$

$\quad 2x = 9$ $\quad\quad\quad 2x = -9$

$\quad x = \dfrac{9}{2}$ $\quad\quad\quad x = -\dfrac{9}{2}$

14. $D = \left\{ x \in \mathbb{R} \mid x \ge \dfrac{3}{2} \right\}$

15. (a) $x = -5$

(b) The desired equation is $y = mx + b$.

By inspection, $b = 3$.

By inspection, the sign of m is $-$.

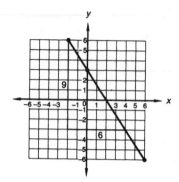

$|m| = \dfrac{9}{6} = \dfrac{3}{2}$

So $b = 3$ and $m = -\dfrac{3}{2}$.

$y = -\dfrac{3}{2}x + 3$

16. $\left(x^3 - x^2 - 2\right) \div (x + 1)$

$$
\begin{array}{r}
x^2 - 2x + 2 \\
x + 1 \overline{\smash{\big)}\ x^3 - x^2 + 0x - 2} \\
\underline{x^3 + x^2} \\
-2x^2 + 0x \\
\underline{-2x^2 - 2x} \\
2x - 2 \\
\underline{2x + 2} \\
-4
\end{array}
$$

$x^2 - 2x + 2 - \dfrac{4}{x + 1}$

17. $4\sqrt{2} \cdot 3\sqrt{3} \cdot 5\sqrt{6} = 60\sqrt{36} = 60(6) = \mathbf{360}$

18. $3\sqrt{2}\left(2\sqrt{2} - 3\sqrt{8}\right) = 6\sqrt{4} - 9\sqrt{16}$

$= 6(2) - 9(4) = 12 - 36 = \mathbf{-24}$

19. $\begin{cases} y = 2x \\ x = -1 \end{cases}$

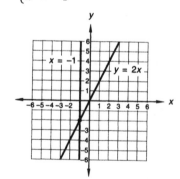

$y = 2x$ $\quad\quad\quad x = -1$

$-2 = 2(-1)$ $\quad\quad -1 = -1$

$-2 = -2$

The solution to the linear equations is $(-1, -2)$.

20. (a) $\begin{cases} 3x + 5y = -13 \\ (b) \end{cases}$
    (b) $\begin{cases} 2x - 3y = 23 \end{cases}$

    (3)(a) $9x + 15y = -39$
    (5)(b) $\underline{10x - 15y = 115}$
           $19x \qquad\quad = 76$
              $x = 4$

    (a) $3x + 5y = -13$
          $3(4) + 5y = -13$
          $12 + 5y = -13$
              $5y = -25$
               $y = -5$

Thus the solution is the ordered pair **(4, –5)**.

21. $\dfrac{(42{,}000{,}000)(0.0001 \times 10^{-5})}{(7000 \times 10^{14})(200{,}000 \times 10^{-8})}$

$= \dfrac{(4.2 \times 10^{7})(1 \times 10^{-9})}{(7 \times 10^{17})(2 \times 10^{-3})}$

$= \dfrac{4.2 \cdot 1}{7 \cdot 2} \times \dfrac{10^{7} \cdot 10^{-9}}{10^{17} \cdot 10^{-3}}$

$= \dfrac{4.2}{14} \times \dfrac{10^{-2}}{10^{14}}$

$= 0.3 \times 10^{-16} = \mathbf{3 \times 10^{-17}}$

22. (a) **Irrational**

    (b) **Irrational**

    (c) **Rational**

    (d) **Rational**

23. $\dfrac{k-4}{2} - \dfrac{k+6}{3} = 5$

     $6 \cdot \dfrac{(k-4)}{2} - 6 \cdot \dfrac{(k+6)}{3} = 6 \cdot 5$

         $3(k-4) - 2(k+6) = 30$

         $3k - 12 - 2k - 12 = 30$

                   $k = \mathbf{54}$

24. $3\dfrac{1}{3}x - \dfrac{1}{6} = \dfrac{5}{12}$

          $\dfrac{10}{3}x - \dfrac{1}{6} = \dfrac{5}{12}$

     $12 \cdot \dfrac{10}{3}x - 12 \cdot \dfrac{1}{6} = 12 \cdot \dfrac{5}{12}$

          $4(10x) - 2 = 5$

               $40x = 7$

                  $x = \dfrac{7}{40}$

25. $m - m^{0}(m - 4) - (-2)m + (-2)(m - 4^{0})$
                                     $= m - 6$

   $m - (m - 4) + 2m - 2m + 2 = m - 6$
            $m - m + 4 + 2 = m - 6$
                     $6 = m - 6$
                    $-m = -12$
                     $m = \mathbf{12}$

26. (a) $\dfrac{ax + a^{2}x^{2}}{ax} = \dfrac{ax(1 + ax)}{ax} = \mathbf{1 + ax}$

    (b) $-(-3)^{-2} = \dfrac{-1}{(-3)^{2}} = \mathbf{-\dfrac{1}{9}}$

27. $-3^{0}\left[(-3^{2} + 4)(-2^{2} - 2) - (-2) + 4\right] - \sqrt[3]{-8}$

     $= -[(-5)(-6) + 2 + 4] + 2$

     $= -36 + 2 = \mathbf{-34}$

28. $-p^{0} - p^{2}(p - a^{0}) - ap + |-ap|$

     $= -1 - (-4)^{2}(-4 - 1) - (-3)(-4) + |-(-3)(-4)|$

     $= -1 - 16(-5) - 12 + 12 = -1 + 80 = \mathbf{79}$

29. $A = \text{Area}_{\text{parallelogram}} - 2\left(\text{Area}_{\text{circle}}\right)$

     $= \left[\dfrac{1}{2}(40 \text{ in.} \times 24 \text{ in.}) + \dfrac{1}{2}(40 \text{ in.} \times 24 \text{ in.})\right]$

       $- 2\left[\pi(5 \text{ in.})^{2}\right]$

     $= \left(480 \text{ in.}^{2} + 480 \text{ in.}^{2}\right) - 2\left(25\pi \text{ in.}^{2}\right)$

     $= (960 - 50\pi) \text{ in.}^{2} = \mathbf{803 \text{ in.}^{2}}$

30. $S.A. = 2\left(\text{Area}_{\text{base}}\right) + \text{Lateral Surface Area}$

     $= 2\left[\dfrac{1}{2}(16 \text{ ft} \times 12 \text{ ft}) + \dfrac{1}{2}\pi(6 \text{ ft})^{2}\right]$

       $+ \left(\text{Perimeter}_{\text{base}}\right)(\text{Height})$

     $= 2\left(96 \text{ ft}^{2} + 18\pi \text{ ft}^{2}\right)$

       $+ \left(16 \text{ ft} + \dfrac{2\pi(6 \text{ ft})}{2} + 20 \text{ ft}\right)(24 \text{ ft})$

     $= 192 \text{ ft}^{2} + 36\pi \text{ ft}^{2} + (36 \text{ ft} + 6\pi \text{ ft})(24 \text{ ft})$

     $= 192 \text{ ft}^{2} + 36\pi \text{ ft}^{2} + 864 \text{ ft}^{2} + 144\pi \text{ ft}^{2}$

     $= (1056 + 180\pi) \text{ ft}^{2} = \mathbf{1621.2 \text{ ft}^{2}}$

Practice 97

a. $p^{2} = 5^{2} + 6^{2}$

    $p^{2} = 25 + 36$

    $p^{2} = 61$

     $p = \pm\sqrt{61}$

     $p = \mathbf{\sqrt{61}}$

b. $15^2 = f^2 + 5^2$

$225 = f^2 + 25$

$f^2 = 200$

$f = \pm\sqrt{200}$

$f = \pm\sqrt{100}\sqrt{2}$

$f = \pm10\sqrt{2}$

$f = \mathbf{10\sqrt{2}}$

c. $q = \mathbf{5}$

d. $r = \mathbf{8}$

Problem Set 97

1. $D_W = D_D$

$R_W T_W = R_D T_D$

$R_W = 60$

$R_D = 50$

$T_W = T_D - 1$

$R_W T_W = R_D T_D$

$60(T_D - 1) = 50T_D$

$60T_D - 60 = 50T_D$

$10T_D = 60$

$T_D = \mathbf{6\ hr}$

$T_W = T_D - 1$

$T_W = 6 - 1$

$T_W = \mathbf{5\ hr}$

$D_W = R_W T_W = (60)(5) = 300$

$D = \mathbf{300\ mi}$

2. $D_B = D_W$

$R_B T_B = R_W T_W$

$T_B = 60$

$T_W = 100$

$R_B = R_W + 2$

$R_W T_W = R_B T_B$

$100R_W = (R_W + 2)(60)$

$100R_W = 60R_W + 120$

$40R_W = 120$

$R_W = 3\ mph$

$D_W = R_W T_W = (3)(100) = \mathbf{300\ mi}$

3. (a) $N_F + N_T = 1250$

(b) $5N_F + 10N_T = 9000$

$(-5)(a)\ -5N_F - 5N_T = -6250$

$(1)(b)\ \underline{\ 5N_F + 10N_T = \ \ 9000}$

$5N_T = \ \ 2750$

$N_T = \mathbf{550}$

(a) $N_F + N_T = 1250$

$N_F + 550 = 1250$

$N_F = \mathbf{700}$

4. $-3(-4 - N) = 2N - 6$

$12 + 3N = 2N - 6$

$N = \mathbf{-18}$

5. $N,\ N + 1,\ N + 2,\ N + 3$

$4(N + N + 3) = 9(N + 2) - 1$

$4(2N + 3) = 9N + 17$

$8N + 12 = 9N + 17$

$-N = 5$

$N = -5$

Thus the integers are **-5, -4, -3,** and **-2.**

6. $\dfrac{(1)(96) + 2(N)}{3} = 120$

$96 + 2N = 360$

$2N = 264$

$N = \mathbf{132}$

7. $\dfrac{20}{100} \cdot T = 32$

$\dfrac{100}{20} \cdot \dfrac{20}{100} \cdot T = 32 \cdot \dfrac{100}{20}$

$T = \mathbf{160}$

8. (a) $a = \mathbf{5}$

(b) $b = \mathbf{10}$

(c) $c = \mathbf{13}$

(d) $d = \mathbf{17}$

9. $k^2 + 4^2 = 6^2$

$k^2 + 16 = 36$

$k^2 = 20$

$k = \sqrt{20}$

$k = \sqrt{4}\sqrt{5}$

$k = \mathbf{2\sqrt{5}}$

10. (a) $x = -2$

(b) The desired equation is $y = mx + b$.

By inspection, $b = -2$.

By inspection, the sign of m is +.

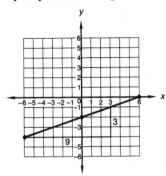

$$|m| = \frac{3}{9} = \frac{1}{3}$$

So $b = -2$ and $m = \frac{1}{3}$.

$$y = \frac{1}{3}x - 2$$

11. (a) $x^2 = 36$

$x = \pm\sqrt{36}$

$x = \pm 6$

(b) $x^2 = 24$

$x = \pm\sqrt{24}$

$x = \pm\sqrt{4}\sqrt{6}$

$x = \pm 2\sqrt{6}$

(c) $x^2 = 17$

$x = \pm\sqrt{17}$

12. (a) $L(x) = -2x + 3$

(b) $f(x) = -x^2 + 5$

(c) $g(x) = x^3$

(d) $p(x) = \sqrt{x}$

(e) $h(x) = -|x|$

13. $\dfrac{x^2 + x - 20}{x^2 + 6x - 16} \div \dfrac{x^2 - 2x - 8}{x^2 + 10x + 16}$

$= \dfrac{x^2 + x - 20}{x^2 + 6x - 16} \cdot \dfrac{x^2 + 10x + 16}{x^2 - 2x - 8}$

$= \dfrac{(x + 5)(x - 4)}{(x + 8)(x - 2)} \cdot \dfrac{(x + 8)(x + 2)}{(x - 4)(x + 2)} = \dfrac{x + 5}{x - 2}$

14. $100 = 25x - x^2$

$x^2 - 25x + 100 = 0$

$(x - 20)(x - 5) = 0$

If $x - 20 = 0$ If $x - 5 = 0$

$x = 20$ $x = 5$

15. $f(x) = 9 - 4x^2$

$f(x + h) = 9 - 4(x + h)^2$

16. (a), (b), (c), (e)

17. $(x^3 - x) \div (x + 2)$

$$
\begin{array}{r}
x^2 - 2x + 3 \\
x + 2 \overline{)\, x^3 + 0x^2 - x + 0} \\
\underline{x^3 + 2x^2} \\
-2x^2 - x \\
\underline{-2x^2 - 4x} \\
3x + 0 \\
\underline{3x + 6} \\
-6
\end{array}
$$

$$x^2 - 2x + 3 - \frac{6}{x + 2}$$

18. $3\sqrt{2} \cdot 5\sqrt{3} + 5\sqrt{54} = 15\sqrt{6} + 5\sqrt{9}\sqrt{6}$

$= 15\sqrt{6} + 15\sqrt{6} = 30\sqrt{6}$

19. $5\sqrt{2}(3\sqrt{6} - 2\sqrt{36}) = 15\sqrt{12} - 10\sqrt{72}$

$= 15\sqrt{4}\sqrt{3} - 10\sqrt{36}\sqrt{2} = 30\sqrt{3} - 60\sqrt{2}$

20. $\begin{cases} y = x + 2 \\ y = -x + 4 \end{cases}$

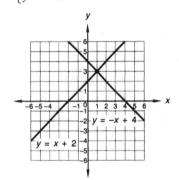

$y = x + 2$ $y = -x + 4$

$3 = 1 + 2$ $3 = -1 + 4$

$3 = 3$ $3 = 3$

The solution to the linear equations is **(1, 3)**.

21. $\dfrac{(36{,}000 \times 10^{-5})(400{,}000)}{(0.0006 \times 10^{-4})(600 \times 10^5)}$

$= \dfrac{(3.6 \times 10^{-1})(4 \times 10^5)}{(6 \times 10^{-8})(6 \times 10^7)}$

$= \dfrac{3.6 \cdot 4}{6 \cdot 6} \times \dfrac{10^{-1} \cdot 10^5}{10^{-8} \cdot 10^7}$

$= \dfrac{14.4}{36} \times \dfrac{10^4}{10^{-1}} = 0.4 \times 10^5 = 4 \times 10^4$

22.
$$\frac{x}{4} - \frac{x-2}{7} = 1$$
$$28 \cdot \frac{x}{4} - 28 \cdot \frac{(x-2)}{7} = 28$$
$$7x - 4(x-2) = 28$$
$$3x + 8 = 28$$
$$3x = 20$$
$$x = \frac{20}{3}$$

23. $-(-3)k^0 - 3^0k + (-2)(2-k) - (-3)(k+2) = 0$
$$3 - k - 4 + 2k + 3k + 6 = 0$$
$$4k + 5 = 0$$
$$4k = -5$$
$$k = -\frac{5}{4}$$

24. (a) $(2m + 2p)^2 = (2m + 2p)(2m + 2p)$
$$= 4m^2 + 4mp + 4mp + 4p^2$$
$$= \mathbf{4m^2 + 8mp + 4p^2}$$

(b) $(2m - 2p)^2 = (2m - 2p)(2m - 2p)$
$$= 4m^2 - 4mp - 4mp + 4p^2$$
$$= \mathbf{4m^2 - 8mp + 4p^2}$$

25.
$$\frac{-b \pm \sqrt{b^2 - 4ac}}{2a} = \frac{-5 \pm \sqrt{25 - 4(2)(2)}}{2(2)}$$
$$= \frac{-5 \pm \sqrt{25 - 16}}{4} = \frac{-5 \pm \sqrt{9}}{4} = \frac{-5 \pm 3}{4}$$
$$= \frac{-5 - 3}{4}, \frac{-5 + 3}{4} = \mathbf{-2, -\frac{1}{2}}$$

26. $\dfrac{x^{-2}}{a^2}\left(x^2 a^2 y^0 - \dfrac{4x^4 y^2}{a^2} - \dfrac{x^{-2}}{a^2 x^2}\right)$
$$= 1 - \frac{4x^2 y^2}{a^4} - \frac{x^{-4}}{a^4 x^2}$$
$$= \mathbf{1 - \frac{4x^2 y^2}{a^4} - \frac{1}{a^4 x^6}}$$

27. $\dfrac{pk^{-1} - 4}{k - k^{-1}} = \dfrac{\dfrac{p}{k} - 4}{k - \dfrac{1}{k}} = \dfrac{\dfrac{p}{k} - \dfrac{4k}{k}}{\dfrac{k^2}{k} - \dfrac{1}{k}}$

$$= \frac{\dfrac{p - 4k}{k}}{\dfrac{k^2 - 1}{k}} \cdot \frac{\dfrac{k}{k^2 - 1}}{\dfrac{k}{k^2 - 1}} = \mathbf{\frac{p - 4k}{k^2 - 1}}$$

28. (a) $\dfrac{-3 - 3x}{3} = \dfrac{-3(1 + x)}{3} = \mathbf{-(1 + x)}$

(b) $\dfrac{-2^2}{-2^{-2}} = \dfrac{-4(2)^2}{-1} = 4(4) = \mathbf{16}$

29. $P = \dfrac{2\pi(6\ \text{cm})}{2} + \dfrac{2\pi(6\ \text{cm})}{2} + \dfrac{2\pi(12\ \text{cm})}{2}$
$$= 6\pi\ \text{cm} + 6\pi\ \text{cm} + 12\pi\ \text{cm}$$
$$= \mathbf{24\pi\ \text{cm} = 75.36\ \text{cm}}$$

30. $V = \left(\text{Area}_{\text{base}}\right)(\text{Height})$
$$= \pi(12\ \text{m})^2(20\ \text{m})$$
$$= \mathbf{2880\pi\ \text{m}^3 = 9043.2\ \text{m}^3}$$

Practice 98

a.

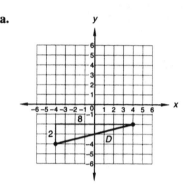

$$D^2 = 8^2 + 2^2$$
$$D^2 = 64 + 4$$
$$D^2 = 68$$
$$D = \sqrt{68}$$
$$D = \sqrt{4}\sqrt{17}$$
$$D = \mathbf{2\sqrt{17}}$$

b. $m = \dfrac{-3 - (-7)}{-8 - (-4)} = \dfrac{-3 + 7}{-8 + 4} = \dfrac{4}{-4} = \mathbf{-1}$

c. $m = \dfrac{-12 - 7}{-14 - 4} = \dfrac{-19}{-18} = \mathbf{\dfrac{19}{18}}$

Problem Set 98

1.
$$D_S + D_J = 332$$
$$R_S T_S + R_J T_J = 332$$
$$R_S = 60$$
$$R_J = 46$$
$$T_S = T_J + 2$$
$$R_S T_S + R_J T_J = 332$$
$$60(T_J + 2) + 46T_J = 332$$
$$106T_J + 120 = 332$$
$$106T_J = 212$$
$$T_J = 2\ \text{hr}$$

So the two met at **4:00 p.m.**

2. $D_D = D_W$

$R_D T_D = R_W T_W$

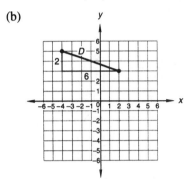

$R_D = 40$

$R_W = 4$

$T_W = T_D + 9$

$R_D T_D = R_W T_W$

$40 T_D = 4(T_D + 9)$

$40 T_D = 4 T_D + 36$

$36 T_D = 36$

$T_D = 1$

$T_W = T_D + 9$

$T_W = 1 + 9$

$\boldsymbol{T_W = 10\ \text{hr}}$

$D_W = R_W T_W = (4)(10) = 40$

$\boldsymbol{D = 40\ \text{mi}}$

3. $3[2(-N) + 7] = 3(-N) + 42$

$-6N + 21 = -3N + 42$

$-3N = 21$

$N = -7$

4. $N,\ N + 2,\ N + 4,\ N + 6$

$3(N + N + 4) = 5(N + 6) + 10$

$3(2N + 4) = 5N + 40$

$6N + 12 = 5N + 40$

$N = 28$

Thus the integers are **28, 30, 32,** and **34.**

5. $\dfrac{350}{100} \times 180 = WN$

$WN = \dfrac{63,000}{100}$

$WN = \boldsymbol{630}$

6. $\dfrac{120}{100} \cdot N = 48$

$\dfrac{100}{120} \cdot \dfrac{120}{100} \cdot N = 48 \cdot \dfrac{100}{120}$

$N = \boldsymbol{40\ \text{hr}}$

7. (a) $P(12) = \dfrac{1}{36}$

(b) $P(< 12) = \dfrac{35}{36}$

8. (a) $a = \boldsymbol{3}$

(b) $b = \boldsymbol{6}$

(c) $c = \boldsymbol{5}$

(d) $d = \boldsymbol{15}$

9. $g^2 + 3^2 = 8^2$

$g^2 + 9 = 64$

$g^2 = 55$

$g = \sqrt{\boldsymbol{55}}$

10. (a) $m = \dfrac{3 - 5}{2 - (-4)} = \dfrac{-2}{6} = -\dfrac{1}{3}$

(b)

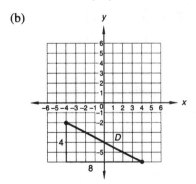

$D^2 = 6^2 + 2^2$

$D^2 = 36 + 4$

$D^2 = 40$

$D = \sqrt{40}$

$D = \sqrt{4}\sqrt{10}$

$D = \boldsymbol{2\sqrt{10}}$

11. (a) $m = \dfrac{-6 - (-2)}{4 - (-4)} = \dfrac{-4}{8} = -\dfrac{1}{2}$

(b)

$D^2 = 8^2 + 4^2$

$D^2 = 64 + 16$

$D^2 = 80$

$D = \sqrt{80}$

$D = \sqrt{16}\sqrt{5}$

$D = \boldsymbol{4\sqrt{5}}$

12. (a) $x^2 = 49$

$\qquad x = \pm\sqrt{49}$

$\qquad x = \pm 7$

(b) $x^2 = 12$

$\qquad x = \pm\sqrt{12}$

$\qquad x = \pm 2\sqrt{3}$

(c) $x^2 = 3$

$\qquad x = \pm\sqrt{3}$

13. (a) $g(x) = \sqrt{x}$

(b) $k(x) = x^3 + 1$

(c) $p(x) = x^2 - 5$

(d) $h(x) = |x|$

(e) $f(x) = 3x + 1$

14. $\dfrac{x^2 + 2x}{4x + 12} \div \dfrac{x^2 - 2x - 8}{x^2 - x - 12}$

$= \dfrac{x^2 + 2x}{4x + 12} \cdot \dfrac{x^2 - x - 12}{x^2 - 2x - 8}$

$= \dfrac{x(x + 2)}{4(x + 3)} \cdot \dfrac{(x - 4)(x + 3)}{(x - 4)(x + 2)} = \dfrac{x}{4}$

15. $3\sqrt{2}\left(6\sqrt{6} - 4\sqrt{12}\right) + 2\sqrt{3}\sqrt{6}$

$= 18\sqrt{12} - 12\sqrt{24} + 2\sqrt{18}$

$= 18\left(2\sqrt{3}\right) - 12\left(2\sqrt{6}\right) + 2\left(3\sqrt{2}\right)$

$= 36\sqrt{3} - 24\sqrt{6} + 6\sqrt{2}$

16. $\qquad\qquad -14 = -x^2 - 5x$

$\qquad x^2 + 5x - 14 = 0$

$\qquad (x + 7)(x - 2) = 0$

If $x + 7 = 0 \qquad$ If $x - 2 = 0$

$\qquad\quad x = -7 \qquad\qquad x = 2$

17. $D = \left\{x \in \mathbb{R} \mid -3 \le x < 4\right\}$

$\quad\; R = \left\{y \in \mathbb{R} \mid -1 \le y < 5\right\}$

18. (a) $y = 3$

(b) The desired equation is $y = mx + b$.

By inspection, $b = -1$.

By inspection, the sign of m is $-$.

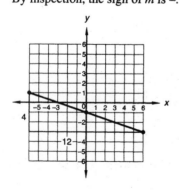

$|m| = \dfrac{4}{12} = \dfrac{1}{3}$

So $b = -1$ and $m = -\dfrac{1}{3}$.

$y = -\dfrac{1}{3}x - 1$

19. $\left(x^3 + 6x^2 + 6x + 5\right) \div (x + 5)$

$$
\begin{array}{r}
x^2 + x + 1 \\
x + 5 \overline{\smash{\big)}\, x^3 + 6x^2 + 6x + 5} \\
\underline{x^3 + 5x^2} \\
x^2 + 6x \\
\underline{x^2 + 5x} \\
x + 5 \\
\underline{x + 5} \\
0
\end{array}
$$

$x^2 + x + 1$

20. $\begin{cases} y = -x \\ y = -4 \end{cases}$

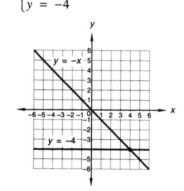

$y = -x \qquad\quad y = -4$

$-4 = -4 \qquad -4 = -4$

The solution to the linear equations is $(4, -4)$.

21. $\dfrac{\left(0.00042 \times 10^8\right)(15,000)}{\left(500 \times 10^7\right)\left(0.02 \times 10^8\right)}$

$= \dfrac{\left(4.2 \times 10^4\right)\left(1.5 \times 10^4\right)}{\left(5 \times 10^9\right)\left(2 \times 10^6\right)}$

$= \dfrac{4.2 \cdot 1.5}{5 \cdot 2} \times \dfrac{10^4 \cdot 10^4}{10^9 \cdot 10^6}$

$= \dfrac{6.3}{10} \times \dfrac{10^8}{10^{15}}$

$= 0.63 \times 10^{-7} = 6.3 \times 10^{-8}$

22. $-x + 2 \not< 3;\; D = \{\text{Integers}\}$

$\qquad -x + 2 \ge 3$

$\qquad\qquad -x \ge 1$

$\qquad\qquad\; x \le -1$

23.
$$\frac{y}{3} - \frac{y-2}{5} = 3$$

$$15 \cdot \frac{y}{3} - 15 \cdot \frac{(y-2)}{5} = 15 \cdot 3$$

$$5y - 3(y-2) = 45$$

$$2y + 6 = 45$$

$$2y = 39$$

$$y = \frac{39}{2}$$

24. $-2k^0 - 4k + 6(-k - 2^0) - (-5k)$

$$= -(2-5)k - 4k$$

$$-2 - 4k - 6k - 6 + 5k = 3k - 4k$$

$$-8 - 5k = -k$$

$$-4k = 8$$

$$k = -2$$

25.
$$\frac{c + 10}{2} = 6$$

$$c + 10 = 12$$

$$c = 2$$

$$x = \sqrt{b^2 - 4ac}$$

$$= \sqrt{11^2 - 4(5)(2)}$$

$$= \sqrt{121 - 40}$$

$$= \sqrt{81}$$

$$= 9$$

26. $-2 - 2^0(-3 - 2) - (-4 + 6)(-5^0 + 2) - 2^2$
$- \sqrt[5]{-243}$

$$= -2 + 5 - 2(1) - 4 - (-3)$$

$$= -2 + 5 - 2 - 4 + 3 = 0$$

27. (a) $\dfrac{5x^2 - 5x}{5x} = \dfrac{5x(x-1)}{5x} = x - 1$

(b) $\dfrac{-3^0}{-3^{-2}} = \dfrac{-1(3^2)}{-1} = 9$

28. $\dfrac{3x - y^{-1}}{2xy^{-1} - 4} = \dfrac{\dfrac{3xy}{y} - \dfrac{1}{y}}{\dfrac{2x}{y} - \dfrac{4y}{y}}$

$$= \dfrac{\dfrac{3xy - 1}{y}}{\dfrac{2x - 4y}{y}} \cdot \dfrac{\dfrac{y}{2x - 4y}}{\dfrac{y}{2x - 4y}} = \dfrac{3xy - 1}{2x - 4y}$$

29. $V = \dfrac{4}{3}\pi r^3$

$$= \dfrac{4}{3}\pi(2 \text{ in.})^3$$

$$= \dfrac{32\pi}{3} \text{ in.}^3 = \textbf{33.49 in.}^3$$

30. $S.A. = 2(\text{Area}_{\text{base}}) + \text{Lateral Surface Area}$

$$= 2\left[\frac{1}{2}(8 \text{ ft} \times 6 \text{ ft}) + \frac{1}{2}(4 \text{ ft} \times 3 \text{ ft})\right]$$

$$+ (\text{Perimeter}_{\text{base}})(\text{Height})$$

$$= 2(24 \text{ ft}^2 + 6 \text{ ft}^2)$$

$$+ (12 \text{ ft} + 5 \text{ ft} + 3 \text{ ft} + 10 \text{ ft})(16 \text{ ft})$$

$$= 2(30 \text{ ft}^2) + (30 \text{ ft})(16 \text{ ft})$$

$$= 60 \text{ ft}^2 + 480 \text{ ft}^2$$

$$= \textbf{540 ft}^2$$

Practice 99

a.
$$D_N + 20 = D_W$$
$$R_N T_N + 20 = R_W T_W$$

$$R_N = 4$$

$$T_N = 9$$

$$T_W = 7$$

$$R_N T_N + 20 = R_W T_W$$

$$(4)(9) + 20 = 7R_W$$

$$36 + 20 = 7R_W$$

$$56 = 7R_W$$

$$R_W = 8 \, \frac{\text{km}}{\text{hr}}$$

b.
$$D_H + 4 = D_P$$
$$R_H T_H + 4 = R_P T_P$$

$$R_H = 6$$

$$R_P = 8$$

$$T_H = T_P$$

$$R_H T_H + 4 = R_P T_P$$

$$6T_P + 4 = 8T_P$$

$$4 = 2T_P$$

$$T_P = 2 \text{ hr}$$

So Paris will catch Helen in **2 hr.**

Problem Set 99

1. $D_F + 500 = D_J$

$R_F T_F + 500 = R_J T_J$

$R_J = 250$

$R_F = 230$

$T_J = T_F$

$R_F T_F + 500 = R_J T_J$

$230 T_J + 500 = 250 T_J$

$-20 T_J = -500$

$T_J = 25$

Therefore, Julia will be a full lap ahead of Ferris in **25** minutes.

2. $D_E = D_A + 60$

$R_E T_E = R_A T_A + 60$

$R_E = 60$

$T_E = 6$

$T_A = 4$

$R_E T_E = R_A T_A + 60$

$60(6) = 4 R_A + 60$

$360 = 4 R_A + 60$

$-4 R_A = -300$

$R_A = \textbf{75 mph}$

3. $5(N - 8) = 2(-N) + 9$

$5N - 40 = -2N + 9$

$7N = 49$

$N = 7$

4. (a) $N_N + N_Q = 450$

(b) $5N_N + 25N_Q = 6250$

$(-5)(a)$ $-5N_N - 5N_Q = -2250$

$(1)(b)$ $\underline{5N_N + 25N_Q = 6250}$

$20N_Q = 4000$

$N_Q = \textbf{200}$

(a) $N_N + N_Q = 450$

$N_N + 200 = 450$

$N_N = \textbf{250}$

5. $\dfrac{66}{100} \cdot T = 3300$

$\dfrac{100}{66} \cdot \dfrac{66}{100} \cdot T = 3300 \cdot \dfrac{100}{66}$

$T = \textbf{5000}$

6. $N, N + 1, N + 2, N + 3$

$5(N + 1 + N + 2) = 7N - 6$

$5(2N + 3) = 7N - 6$

$10N + 15 = 7N - 6$

$3N = -21$

$N = -7$

Thus the integers are **–7, –6, –5,** and **–4.**

7. $d^2 = 7^2 + 4^2$

$d^2 = 49 + 16$

$d^2 = 65$

$d = \sqrt{\textbf{65}}$

8. $a^2 + 9^2 = 12^2$

$a^2 + 81 = 144$

$a^2 = 63$

$a = \sqrt{63}$

$a = \sqrt{9}\sqrt{7}$

$a = \textbf{3}\sqrt{\textbf{7}}$

9. $f^2 + 3^2 = 7^2$

$f^2 + 9 = 49$

$f^2 = 40$

$f = \sqrt{40}$

$f = \sqrt{4}\sqrt{10}$

$f = \textbf{2}\sqrt{\textbf{10}}$

10. (a) $m = \dfrac{-2 - 3}{7 - 4} = -\dfrac{5}{3}$

(b)

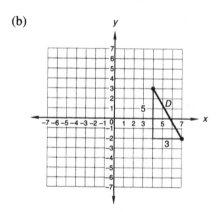

$D^2 = 3^2 + 5^2$

$D^2 = 9 + 25$

$D^2 = 34$

$D = \sqrt{\textbf{34}}$

11. (a) $m = \dfrac{3 - (-2)}{-2 - 4} = -\dfrac{5}{6}$

(b)

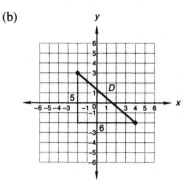

$$D^2 = 6^2 + 5^2$$
$$D^2 = 36 + 25$$
$$D^2 = 61$$
$$D = \sqrt{61}$$

12. (a) $h(x) = x$

(b) $f(x) = x^3$

(c) $p(x) = -x^3$

(d) $g(x) = x^2$

(e) $k(x) = -x^2$

13. (a) $x^2 = 64$

$x = \pm\sqrt{64}$

$x = \pm 8$

(b) $x^2 = 32$

$x = \pm\sqrt{32}$

$x = \pm\sqrt{16}\sqrt{2}$

$x = \pm 4\sqrt{2}$

(c) $x^2 = 11$

$x = \pm\sqrt{11}$

14. $\dfrac{x^2 + 11x + 28}{-x^2 + 5x} \div \dfrac{x^2 + x - 12}{x^3 - 3x^2 - 10x}$

$= \dfrac{x^2 + 11x + 28}{-x^2 + 5x} \cdot \dfrac{x^3 - 3x^2 - 10x}{x^2 + x - 12}$

$= \dfrac{(x + 7)(x + 4)}{-x(x - 5)} \cdot \dfrac{x(x - 5)(x + 2)}{(x + 4)(x - 3)}$

$= -\dfrac{(x + 7)(x + 2)}{x - 3}$

15. $81 = 4x^2$

$81 - 4x^2 = 0$

$(9 + 2x)(9 - 2x) = 0$

If $9 + 2x = 0$ If $9 - 2x = 0$

$2x = -9$ $-2x = -9$

$x = -\dfrac{9}{2}$ $x = \dfrac{9}{2}$

16. (a) **Rational**

(b) **Rational**

(c) **Irrational**

(d) **Rational**

17. $D = \left\{ x \in \mathbb{R} \mid x \geq \dfrac{4}{3} \right\}$

18. (a) $y = 4$

(b) The desired equation is $y = mx + b$.

By inspection, $b = -3$.

By inspection, the sign of m is $-$.

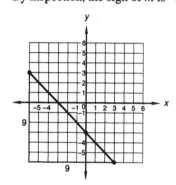

$|m| = \dfrac{9}{9} = 1$

So $b = -3$ and $m = -1$.

$y = -x - 3$

19. $(x^3 - 4) \div (x - 4)$

$$
\begin{array}{r}
x^2 + 4x + 16 \\
x - 4 \overline{)\ x^3 + 0x^2 + 0x - 4\ } \\
\underline{x^3 - 4x^2} \\
4x^2 + 0x \\
\underline{4x^2 - 16x} \\
16x - 4 \\
\underline{16x - 64} \\
60
\end{array}
$$

$x^2 + 4x + 16 + \dfrac{60}{x - 4}$

20. $3\sqrt{2} \cdot 4\sqrt{3} \cdot 5\sqrt{12} + 2\sqrt{8}$

$= 60\sqrt{72} + 2\sqrt{8} = 60(6\sqrt{2}) + 2(2\sqrt{2})$

$= 360\sqrt{2} + 4\sqrt{2} = \mathbf{364\sqrt{2}}$

21. $3\sqrt{2}\left(5\sqrt{2} - 4\sqrt{42}\right) = 15\sqrt{4} - 12\sqrt{84}$

$= 15(2) - 12(2\sqrt{21}) = 30 - 24\sqrt{21}$

22. $\begin{cases} y = x - 4 \\ y = -x + 2 \end{cases}$

$$y = x - 4 \qquad\qquad y = -x + 2$$
$$-1 = 3 - 4 \qquad\quad -1 = -3 + 2$$
$$-1 = -1 \qquad\qquad -1 = -1$$

The solution to the linear equations is **(3, –1)**.

23. $-x - 3 < 2$; $D = \{\text{Reals}\}$

$$-x < 5$$
$$x > -5$$

24. $\dfrac{\left(22{,}000 \times 10^{-7}\right)(500)}{(0.0011)\left(0.002 \times 10^{14}\right)}$

$= \dfrac{\left(2.2 \times 10^{-3}\right)\left(5 \times 10^{2}\right)}{\left(1.1 \times 10^{-3}\right)\left(2 \times 10^{11}\right)}$

$= \dfrac{2.2 \cdot 5}{1.1 \cdot 2} \times \dfrac{10^{-3} \cdot 10^{2}}{10^{-3} \cdot 10^{11}}$

$= \dfrac{11}{2.2} \times \dfrac{10^{-1}}{10^{8}} = \mathbf{5 \times 10^{-9}}$

25. $\dfrac{x}{x + 4} + \dfrac{3}{x} - \dfrac{x + 2}{x^2}$

$= \dfrac{x^3}{x^2(x + 4)} + \dfrac{3x(x + 4)}{x^2(x + 4)} - \dfrac{(x + 2)(x + 4)}{x^2(x + 4)}$

$= \dfrac{x^3 + 3x^2 + 12x - \left(x^2 + 6x + 8\right)}{x^2(x + 4)}$

$= \dfrac{x^3 + 3x^2 + 12x - x^2 - 6x - 8}{x^2(x + 4)}$

$= \dfrac{\mathbf{x^3 + 2x^2 + 6x - 8}}{\mathbf{x^2(x + 4)}}$

26. $\dfrac{p}{6} - \dfrac{p + 2}{4} = \dfrac{1}{3}$

$12 \cdot \dfrac{p}{6} - 12 \cdot \dfrac{(p + 2)}{4} = 12 \cdot \dfrac{1}{3}$

$$2p - 3(p + 2) = 4$$
$$2p - 3p - 6 = 4$$
$$-p - 6 = 4$$
$$-p = 10$$
$$p = \mathbf{-10}$$

27. $2x = -4 \qquad\qquad y = \sqrt[3]{-64}$

$\quad\;\; x = -2 \qquad\qquad y = -4$

$-x^0 y\left(y - x^0\right) - x^2 y^{-1}$

$= -(-4)(-4 - 1) - (-2)^2(-4)^{-1}$

$= 4(-5) - \dfrac{4}{-4} = -20 + 1 = \mathbf{-19}$

28. (a) $\dfrac{-2p^2 a^2 - p^2 a}{-p^2 a} = \dfrac{-p^2 a(2a + 1)}{-p^2 a} = \mathbf{2a + 1}$

(b) $\dfrac{-3^2}{-(-3)^{-2}} = \dfrac{-9(-3)^2}{-1} = \dfrac{-9(9)}{-1} = \mathbf{81}$

29. $S.A. = 4\pi r^2$

$\quad\quad = 4\pi (4\text{ cm})^2$

$\quad\quad = \mathbf{64\pi\ cm^2 = 200.96\ cm^2}$

30. $V = \left(\text{Area}_{\text{base}}\right)(\text{Height})$

$\quad = [(6\text{ m} \times 8\text{ m}) + (4\text{ m} \times 4\text{ m}) + (4\text{ m} \times 8\text{ m})]$

$\quad\quad \times 10\text{ m}$

$\quad = \left(48\text{ m}^2 + 16\text{ m}^2 + 32\text{ m}^2\right)(10\text{ m})$

$\quad = \left(96\text{ m}^2\right)(10\text{ m})$

$\quad = \mathbf{960\ m^3}$

Practice 100

a. 59,7④2,004.012

59,740,000

b. 513.129③47

513.1293

c. 63.01491④9149…

63.014915

Problem Set 100

1. $D_L = D_B + 40$

$R_L T_L = R_B T_B + 40$

$R_L = 10$

$R_B = 6$

$T_L = T_B$

$R_L T_L = R_B T_B + 40$

$10 T_L = 6 T_L + 40$

$4 T_L = 40$

$T_L = 10$

It took Louis **10 seconds** to catch up.

2. $D_R = D_W$

$R_R T_R = R_W T_W$

$R_R = 6$

$R_W = 8$

$T_R = T_W + 2$

$R_R T_R = R_W T_W$

$6(T_W + 2) = 8T_W$

$6T_W + 12 = 8T_W$

$-2T_W = -12$

$T_W = \textbf{6 hr}$

$T_R = T_W + 2$

$T_R = 6 + 2$

$\textbf{\textit{T}}_{\textbf{\textit{R}}} = \textbf{8 hr}$

3. (a) $P_1 + P_2 = 60$

(b) $P_1 = 4P_2 + 10$

(a) $\qquad P_1 + P_2 = 60$

$4P_2 + 10 + P_2 = 60$

$\qquad 5P_2 = 50$

$\qquad \textbf{\textit{P}}_2 = \textbf{10 ft}$

(b) $P_1 = 4P_2 + 10$

$P_1 = 4(10) + 10$

$P_1 = 40 + 10$

$\textbf{\textit{P}}_1 = \textbf{50 ft}$

4. $N, N + 2, N + 4, N + 6$

$5(N + N + 2) = 19(N + 6) - 5$

$5(2N + 2) = 19N + 114 - 5$

$10N + 10 = 19N + 109$

$-9N = 99$

$N = -11$

Thus the integers are **–11, –9, –7,** and **–5.**

5. $\qquad \dfrac{73}{100} \cdot T = 511$

$\dfrac{100}{73} \cdot \dfrac{73}{100} \cdot T = 511 \cdot \dfrac{100}{73}$

$\qquad T = \textbf{700}$

6. $P(3) = \dfrac{1}{6}$

7. (a) $104.062\overset{\downarrow}{\circledad 5}3527$

104.0625

(b) $\overset{\downarrow}{\circled{4}}13.0527$

400

(c) $\dfrac{2}{7} = 0.2\overset{\downarrow}{\circled{8}}5714285...$

0.29

8. (a) $a = \textbf{4}$

(b) $b = \textbf{8}$

(c) $c = \textbf{12}$

(d) $d = \textbf{8}$

9. $s^2 + 4^2 = 6^2$

$s^2 + 16 = 36$

$s^2 = 20$

$s = \sqrt{20}$

$s = \sqrt{4}\sqrt{5}$

$s = \textbf{2}\sqrt{\textbf{5}}$

10. (a) $x = \textbf{5}$

(b) The desired equation is $y = mx + b$.

By inspection, $b = -2$.

By inspection, the sign of m is –.

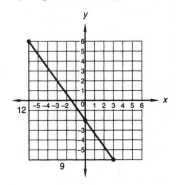

$|m| = \dfrac{12}{9} = \dfrac{4}{3}$

So $b = -2$ and $m = -\dfrac{4}{3}$.

$y = -\dfrac{4}{3}x - 2$

11. (a) $m = \dfrac{-2 - 3}{7 - 4} = -\dfrac{5}{3}$

(b)

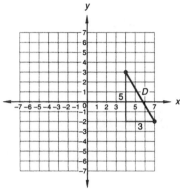

$D^2 = 3^2 + 5^2$

$D^2 = 9 + 25$

$D^2 = 34$

$D = \sqrt{34}$

12. (a) $k(x) = 1 + x^3$

(b) $f(x) = -x^3 + 1$

(c) $g(x) = -(x + 1)^2$

(d) $p(x) = 2x$

(e) $h(x) = x^2$

13. (a) $x^2 = 169$

$x = \pm\sqrt{169}$

$x = \pm 13$

(b) $x^2 = 48$

$x = \pm\sqrt{48}$

$x = \pm\sqrt{16}\sqrt{3}$

$x = \pm 4\sqrt{3}$

(c) $x^2 = 2$

$x = \pm\sqrt{2}$

14. $\dfrac{x^2 + 8x + 15}{x^2 + 3x} \div \dfrac{x^2 + 3x - 10}{x^3 - 6x^2 + 8x}$

$= \dfrac{x^2 + 8x + 15}{x^2 + 3x} \cdot \dfrac{x^3 - 6x^2 + 8x}{x^2 + 3x - 10}$

$= \dfrac{(x + 5)(x + 3)}{x(x + 3)} \cdot \dfrac{x(x - 4)(x - 2)}{(x + 5)(x - 2)} = \boldsymbol{x - 4}$

15. $\qquad\qquad 35 = -12x - x^2$

$x^2 + 12x + 35 = 0$

$(x + 7)(x + 5) = 0$

If $x + 7 = 0$ \qquad If $x + 5 = 0$

$\qquad x = -7 \qquad\qquad x = -5$

16. (a), (b), (d), (e)

17. $\left(x^3 + 12x + 5\right) \div (x + 2)$

$$
\begin{array}{r}
x^2 - 2x + 16 \\
x + 2 \overline{)\ x^3 + 0x^2 + 12x + 5} \\
\underline{x^3 + 2x^2} \\
-2x^2 + 12x \\
\underline{-2x^2 - 4x} \\
16x + 5 \\
\underline{16x + 32} \\
-27
\end{array}
$$

$x^2 - 2x + 16 - \dfrac{27}{x + 2}$

18. $3\sqrt{30{,}000} - 9\sqrt{300} + 3\sqrt{2} \cdot 5\sqrt{6}$

$= 3\sqrt{10{,}000}\sqrt{3} - 9\sqrt{100}\sqrt{3} + 15\sqrt{12}$

$= 300\sqrt{3} - 90\sqrt{3} + 30\sqrt{3} = \boldsymbol{240\sqrt{3}}$

19. $3\sqrt{2}\left(4\sqrt{8} - 3\sqrt{12}\right) = 12\sqrt{16} - 9\sqrt{24}$

$= 12(4) - 9\left(2\sqrt{6}\right) = \boldsymbol{48 - 18\sqrt{6}}$

20. $\begin{cases} y = 2x \\ y = -x + 6 \end{cases}$

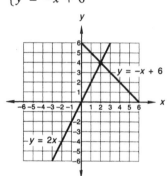

$y = 2x \qquad\qquad y = -x + 6$

$4 = 2(2) \qquad\quad 4 = -2 + 6$

$4 = 4 \qquad\qquad\quad 4 = 4$

The solution to the linear equations is **(2, 4).**

21. $\qquad -2 \geq -2x + 2;\ D = \{\text{Integers}\}$

$2x - 2 \geq 2$

$\quad 2x \geq 4$

$\quad\ x \geq 2$

$$
\begin{array}{ccccc}
\ & \ & \bullet & \bullet & \bullet \\
\hline
0 & 1 & 2 & 3 & 4
\end{array}
$$

22. $\dfrac{\left(400 \times 10^5\right)\left(0.0008 \times 10^{14}\right)}{\left(20{,}000 \times 10^{-30}\right)(0.00002)}$

$= \dfrac{\left(4 \times 10^7\right)\left(8 \times 10^{10}\right)}{\left(2 \times 10^{-26}\right)\left(2 \times 10^{-5}\right)}$

$= \dfrac{4 \cdot 8}{2 \cdot 2} \times \dfrac{10^7 \cdot 10^{10}}{10^{-26} \cdot 10^{-5}}$

$= \dfrac{32}{4} \times \dfrac{10^{17}}{10^{-31}}$

$= \boldsymbol{8 \times 10^{48}}$

23. (a) **Irrationals, reals**

(b) **Naturals, wholes, integers, rationals, reals**

24. $\dfrac{4}{x^2} - \dfrac{x+3}{4x} - \dfrac{2x}{x+1}$

$= \dfrac{16(x+1)}{4x^2(x+1)} - \dfrac{x(x+3)(x+1)}{4x^2(x+1)} - \dfrac{8x^3}{4x^2(x+1)}$

$= \dfrac{16x + 16 - \left[x\left(x^2 + 4x + 3\right)\right] - 8x^3}{4x^2(x+1)}$

$= \dfrac{16x + 16 - x^3 - 4x^2 - 3x - 8x^3}{4x^2(x+1)}$

$= \dfrac{\mathbf{-9x^3 - 4x^2 + 13x + 16}}{\mathbf{4x^2(x+1)}}$

25. $\dfrac{x}{4} - \dfrac{x+2}{6} = 4$

$12 \cdot \dfrac{x}{4} - 12 \cdot \dfrac{(x+2)}{6} = 12 \cdot 4$

$3x - 2(x+2) = 48$

$3x - 2x - 4 = 48$

$x - 4 = 48$

$x = \mathbf{52}$

26. $4(c+2) = 48$

$4c + 8 = 48$

$4c = 40$

$c = 10$

$x = \sqrt{b^2 - 4ac}$

$= \sqrt{12^2 - 4(2)(10)}$

$= \sqrt{144 - 80}$

$= \sqrt{64}$

$= \mathbf{8}$

27. $\dfrac{x^2 - ax^2 - 3x^3}{x^2} = \dfrac{x^2(1 - a - 3x)}{x^2}$

$= \mathbf{1 - a - 3x}$

28. $-2^2 - 2\left[(-3-2)(-5-4)\right]\left[-3^0(-2-5)\right]$

$= -4 - 2(-5)(-9)\left[-(-7)\right]$

$= -4 + 10(-63)$

$= -4 - 630 = \mathbf{-634}$

29. $A = \dfrac{\pi(9 \text{ in.})^2}{2} + \dfrac{\pi(9 \text{ in.})^2}{2}$

$= 81\pi \text{ in.}^2 = \mathbf{254.34 \text{ in.}^2}$

30. $S.A. = 2\left(\text{Area}_{\text{base}}\right) + \text{Lateral Surface Area}$

$= 2\left[(4 \text{ ft} \times 2 \text{ ft}) + (2 \text{ ft} \times 2 \text{ ft}) + (4 \text{ ft} \times 2 \text{ ft})\right]$

$\quad + \left(\text{Perimeter}_{\text{base}}\right)(\text{Height})$

$= 2\left(8 \text{ ft}^2 + 4 \text{ ft}^2 + 8 \text{ ft}^2\right)$

$\quad + (2 \text{ ft} + 4 \text{ ft} + 6 \text{ ft} + 4 \text{ ft} + 2 \text{ ft} + 2 \text{ ft}$

$\quad + 2 \text{ ft} + 2 \text{ ft})(15 \text{ ft})$

$= 2\left(20 \text{ ft}^2\right) + (24 \text{ ft})(15 \text{ ft})$

$= 40 \text{ ft}^2 + 360 \text{ ft}^2$

$= \mathbf{400 \text{ ft}^2}$

Practice 101

a. $\dfrac{9x}{x^2 - 4x - 21} - \dfrac{7}{x-7}$

$= \dfrac{9x}{(x-7)(x+3)} - \dfrac{7}{x-7}$

$= \dfrac{9x}{(x-7)(x+3)} - \dfrac{7(x+3)}{(x-7)(x+3)}$

$= \dfrac{9x - 7x - 21}{(x-7)(x+3)} = \dfrac{\mathbf{2x - 21}}{\mathbf{(x+3)(x-7)}}$

b. $\dfrac{4}{x^2 - 10x + 9} - \dfrac{5}{x^2 - x}$

$= \dfrac{4}{(x-9)(x-1)} - \dfrac{5}{x(x-1)}$

$= \dfrac{4x}{x(x-9)(x-1)} - \dfrac{5(x-9)}{x(x-9)(x-1)}$

$= \dfrac{4x - 5x + 45}{x(x-9)(x-1)} = \dfrac{\mathbf{-x + 45}}{\mathbf{x(x-1)(x-9)}}$

Problem Set 101

1. $D_M = D_F + 40$

$R_M T_M = R_F T_F + 40$

$R_M = 54$

$R_F = 46$

$T_M = T_F$

$R_M T_M = R_F T_F + 40$

$54 T_M = 46 T_M + 40$

$8 T_M = 40$

$T_M = \mathbf{5 \text{ seconds}}$

2. $D_W + D_B = 20$
    $R_W T_W + R_B T_B = 20$

    $R_W = 5$
    $R_B = 15$

    $T_B + T_W = 2$
    $T_W = -T_B + 2$

    $R_W T_W + R_B T_B = 20$
    $5(-T_B + 2) + 15(T_B) = 20$
    $10T_B + 10 = 20$
    $10T_B = 10$
    $T_B = 1 \text{ hr}$

    $D_B = R_B T_B = (15)(1) = \textbf{15 mi}$

3. (a) $N_O + 10N_T = 6750$
    (b) $N_O = N_T + 150$

    (a) $\qquad N_O + 10N_T = 6750$
    $(N_T + 150) + 10N_T = 6750$
    $\qquad\qquad 11N_T = 6600$
    $\qquad\qquad\quad N_T = \textbf{600}$

    (b) $N_O = N_T + 150$
    $N_O = 600 + 150$
    $N_O = \textbf{750}$

4. $N, N + 2, N + 4$

    $4N = 16[(N + 4) + 2]$
    $4N = 16N + 96$
    $-12N = 96$
    $N = -8$

    Thus the integers are **−8, −6,** and **−4.**

5. $\dfrac{4}{5}T = 384$

    $T = 384\left(\dfrac{5}{4}\right)$

    $T = \textbf{480}$

6. (a) $P(\text{both purple}) = \dfrac{9}{12} \cdot \dfrac{8}{11} = \dfrac{18}{33} = \dfrac{\textbf{6}}{\textbf{11}}$

    (b) $P(\text{both purple}) = \dfrac{9}{12} \cdot \dfrac{9}{12} = \dfrac{\textbf{9}}{\textbf{16}}$

7. Range $= 203 - 147 = \textbf{56}$

    Median $= \dfrac{178 + 181}{2} = \textbf{179.5}$

    Mode $= \textbf{172}$

    Mean $= \dfrac{\text{sum of 10 numbers}}{10} = \dfrac{1780}{10} = \textbf{178}$

8. $\dfrac{p}{x^2 - 9} + \dfrac{2x}{x^2 - 3x}$

    $= \dfrac{p}{(x + 3)(x - 3)} + \dfrac{2x}{x(x - 3)}$

    $= \dfrac{p}{(x + 3)(x - 3)} + \dfrac{2(x + 3)}{(x + 3)(x - 3)}$

    $= \dfrac{\textbf{p + 2x + 6}}{\textbf{(x + 3)(x - 3)}}$

9. $\dfrac{8x}{x^2 - 6x + 8} + \dfrac{7}{(x - 2)^2}$

    $= \dfrac{8x}{(x - 2)(x - 4)} + \dfrac{7}{(x - 2)^2}$

    $= \dfrac{8x(x - 2)}{(x - 2)^2(x - 4)} + \dfrac{7(x - 4)}{(x - 2)^2(x - 4)}$

    $= \dfrac{8x^2 - 16x + 7x - 28}{(x - 2)^2(x - 4)} = \dfrac{\textbf{8}x^2 - \textbf{9x} - \textbf{28}}{(x - 2)^2(x - 4)}$

10. (a) $\sqrt{2} = 1.414\,\textcircled{2}\,13\ldots$
    1.4142

    (b) $0.6\,\textcircled{6}\,666\ldots$
    0.67

    (c) $\textcircled{3}\,500.63210$
    4000

11. $a^2 = 8^2 + 4^2$
    $a^2 = 64 + 16$
    $a^2 = 80$
    $a = \sqrt{80}$
    $a = \sqrt{16}\sqrt{5}$
    $a = \textbf{4}\sqrt{\textbf{5}}$

12. (a) **y = −2**

    (b) The desired equation is $y = mx + b$.
    By inspection, $b = 0$.
    By inspection, the sign of m is −.

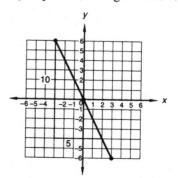

$$|m| = \frac{10}{5} = 2$$

So $b = 0$ and $m = -2$.

$$y = -2x$$

13. (a) $m = \dfrac{-3 - 2}{4 - (-4)} = -\dfrac{5}{8}$

(b)

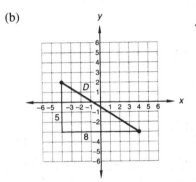

$$D^2 = 8^2 + 5^2$$
$$D^2 = 64 + 25$$
$$D^2 = 89$$
$$D = \sqrt{89}$$

14. (b)

15. (a) $x^2 = 225$
$$x = \pm\sqrt{225}$$
$$x = \pm 15$$

(b) $x^2 = 72$
$$x = \pm\sqrt{72}$$
$$x = \pm\sqrt{36}\sqrt{2}$$
$$x = \pm 6\sqrt{2}$$

(c) $x^2 = 29$
$$x = \pm\sqrt{29}$$

16. $\dfrac{x^3 + 11x^2 + 24x}{x^2 + 10x + 21} \div \dfrac{4x^2 + 32x}{4x + 40}$

$$= \dfrac{x^3 + 11x^2 + 24x}{x^2 + 10x + 21} \cdot \dfrac{4x + 40}{4x^2 + 32x}$$

$$= \dfrac{x(x + 8)(x + 3)}{(x + 3)(x + 7)} \cdot \dfrac{4(x + 10)}{4x(x + 8)} = \dfrac{x + 10}{x + 7}$$

17. $\qquad -81 + 4x^2 = 0$
$$4x^2 - 81 = 0$$
$$(2x + 9)(2x - 9) = 0$$

If $2x + 9 = 0$ If $2x - 9 = 0$
$$2x = -9 \qquad\qquad 2x = 9$$
$$x = -\frac{9}{2} \qquad\qquad x = \frac{9}{2}$$

18. (a) **Irrational**

(b) **Irrational**

(c) **Rational**

(d) **Rational**

19. $2\sqrt{60{,}000} + 3\sqrt{2400}$
$$= 2\sqrt{10{,}000}\sqrt{6} + 3\sqrt{100}\sqrt{4}\sqrt{6}$$
$$= 2(100)\sqrt{6} + 3(10)(2)\sqrt{6}$$
$$= 200\sqrt{6} + 60\sqrt{6}$$
$$= \mathbf{260\sqrt{6}}$$

20. $4\sqrt{5} \cdot 2\sqrt{3} + 5\sqrt{3}(\sqrt{3} + 2\sqrt{5})$
$$= 8\sqrt{15} + 5(3) + 10\sqrt{15} = \mathbf{18\sqrt{15} + 15}$$

21. $\begin{cases} y = -2x \\ y = -2 \end{cases}$

$y = -2x$ $y = -2$
$-2 = -2(1)$ $-2 = -2$
$-2 = -2$

The solution to the linear equations is **(1, −2)**.

22. $-4 - x \not< 2;\ D = \{\text{Reals}\}$
$$-4 - x \geq 2$$
$$-x \geq 6$$
$$x \leq -6$$

$\longleftarrow\!\!\!\!\!-\!\!|\!\!-\!\!|\!\!-\!\!|\!\!-\!\!|\!\!-\!\!|\!\!-\!\!\bullet$
$\quad -12\ -11\ -10\ -9\ -8\ -7\ -6$

23. $\qquad\qquad \dfrac{5x}{3} - \dfrac{x - 5}{2} = 14$

$$6 \cdot \dfrac{5x}{3} - 6 \cdot \dfrac{(x - 5)}{2} = 6 \cdot 14$$
$$10x - 3(x - 5) = 84$$
$$7x + 15 = 84$$
$$7x = 69$$
$$x = \dfrac{69}{7}$$

24. $-2x(4 - 3^0) - (2x - 5) + 3x - 2 = -2^0x$

$$-2x(3) - 2x + 5 + 3x - 2 = -x$$
$$-6x - 2x + 5 + 3x - 2 = -x$$
$$-5x + 3 = -x$$
$$-4x = -3$$
$$x = \frac{3}{4}$$

25. (a) $\dfrac{-4x^2 - 8x^2a}{-4x^2} = \dfrac{-4x^2(1 + 2a)}{-4x^2} = \mathbf{1 + 2a}$

(b) $\dfrac{-3^{-2}}{(-3)^2} = \dfrac{-1}{3^2(-3)^2} = \dfrac{-1}{9(9)} = -\dfrac{1}{\mathbf{81}}$

26. $\dfrac{\dfrac{5p}{x} - 4}{\dfrac{3}{x} - x} = \dfrac{\dfrac{5p}{x} - \dfrac{4x}{x}}{\dfrac{3}{x} - \dfrac{x^2}{x}} = \dfrac{\dfrac{5p - 4x}{x} \cdot \dfrac{x}{3 - x^2}}{\dfrac{3 - x^2}{x} \cdot \dfrac{x}{3 - x^2}}$

$$= \dfrac{\mathbf{5p - 4x}}{\mathbf{3 - x^2}}$$

27. $-x - xk(x - k) = -(-4) - (-4)(5)(-4 - 5)$

$= 4 + 20(-9) = 4 - 180 = \mathbf{-176}$

28. $\dfrac{x^2a(x^2a)(x^{-2})^2 x^0 xa^2}{(a^{-3})^2 ax^{-2}x^4x} = \dfrac{xa^4}{a^{-5}x^3} = \dfrac{\mathbf{a^9}}{\mathbf{x^2}}$

29. $P = \dfrac{2\pi(3 \text{ cm})}{2} + \dfrac{2\pi(5 \text{ cm})}{2} + \dfrac{2\pi(4 \text{ cm})}{2}$

$= 3\pi \text{ cm} + 5\pi \text{ cm} + 4\pi \text{ cm}$

$= \mathbf{12\pi \text{ cm}} = \mathbf{37.68 \text{ cm}}$

30. $V = (\text{Area}_{\text{base}})(\text{Height})$

$= (36 \text{ m}^2)(8 \text{ m}) = \mathbf{288 \text{ m}^3}$

Practice 102

a. $-|x| - 9 > -11$

$-|x| > -2$

$|x| < 2$

b. $|x| > 0$

Problem Set 102

1. $\quad D_N + D_S = 38$

$R_NT_N + R_ST_S = 38$

$R_N = 3$

$R_S = 5$

$T_N = T_S + 2$

$R_NT_N + R_ST_S = 38$

$3(T_S + 2) + 5T_S = 38$

$8T_S + 6 = 38$

$8T_S = 32$

$T_S = 4$

2 p.m. + 4 hr = **6 p.m.**

2. (a) $N_R + N_W = 52$

(b) $N_R = 2N_W + 16$

(a) $\qquad N_R + N_W = 52$

$(2N_W + 16) + N_W = 52$

$3N_W + 16 = 52$

$3N_W = 36$

$N_W = \mathbf{12}$

(b) $N_R = 2N_W + 16$

$N_R = 2(12) + 16$

$N_R = 24 + 16$

$N_R = \mathbf{40}$

3. (a) $N_P + 5N_N = 2950$

(b) $N_P = N_N + 10$

(a) $\qquad N_P + 5N_N = 2950$

$(N_N + 10) + 5N_N = 2950$

$6N_N = 2940$

$N_N = \mathbf{490}$

4. $N, N + 1, N + 2, N + 3$

$5(-N) = -3[(N + 2) + (N + 3)] + 5$

$-5N = -3(2N + 5) + 5$

$-5N = -6N - 15 + 5$

$N = -10$

Thus the integers are **–10, –9, –8,** and **–7.**

5. $\qquad \dfrac{88}{100} \cdot T = 4224$

$\dfrac{100}{88} \cdot \dfrac{88}{100} \cdot T = 4224 \cdot \dfrac{100}{88}$

$T = \mathbf{4800}$

6. $P(H, H, H, H) = \dfrac{1}{2} \cdot \dfrac{1}{2} \cdot \dfrac{1}{2} \cdot \dfrac{1}{2} = \dfrac{\mathbf{1}}{\mathbf{16}}$

7. $|x| > 2$

8. $|x| - 2 \le 0$

$|x| \le 2$

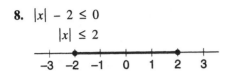

9. $-|x| + 5 > 2$

$-|x| > -3$

$|x| < 3$

10. $\dfrac{4}{x - 4} + \dfrac{5}{x^2 - 16}$

$= \dfrac{4}{x - 4} + \dfrac{5}{(x - 4)(x + 4)}$

$= \dfrac{4(x + 4)}{(x - 4)(x + 4)} + \dfrac{5}{(x - 4)(x + 4)}$

$= \dfrac{4x + 16 + 5}{(x - 4)(x + 4)} = \dfrac{\mathbf{4x + 21}}{\mathbf{(x + 4)(x - 4)}}$

11. $\dfrac{4}{x^2 + 2x + 1} - \dfrac{3}{x + 1}$

$= \dfrac{4}{(x + 1)(x + 1)} - \dfrac{3}{x + 1}$

$= \dfrac{4}{(x + 1)(x + 1)} - \dfrac{3(x + 1)}{(x + 1)(x + 1)}$

$= \dfrac{4 - 3x - 3}{(x + 1)(x + 1)} = \dfrac{\mathbf{-3x + 1}}{\mathbf{(x + 1)(x + 1)}}$

12. (a) $\sqrt{5} = 2.23\,\boxed{6}\,0679...$

2.236

(b) $\boxed{2}\,654$

3000

(c) $572.0\,\boxed{5}\,62...$

572.06

13. (a) $a = \mathbf{5}$

(b) $b = \mathbf{13}$

(c) $c = \mathbf{10}$

(d) $d = \mathbf{17}$

14. $p^2 = 5^2 + 11^2$

$p^2 = 25 + 121$

$p^2 = 146$

$p = \sqrt{\mathbf{146}}$

15. (a) $m = \dfrac{-2 - (-3)}{7 - 5} = \dfrac{1}{2}$

(b)

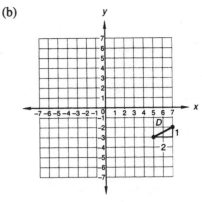

$D^2 = 2^2 + 1^2$

$D^2 = 4 + 1$

$D^2 = 5$

$D = \sqrt{\mathbf{5}}$

16. (a) $g(x) = -|x| + 1$

(b) $k(x) = |x|$

(c) $h(x) = 2x - 1$

(d) $p(x) = -\dfrac{1}{2}x + 1$

(e) $f(x) = x^2$

17. (a) $x^2 = 5$

$x = \pm\sqrt{\mathbf{5}}$

(b) $x^2 = 8$

$x = \pm\sqrt{8}$

$x = \pm\sqrt{4}\sqrt{2}$

$x = \pm\mathbf{2\sqrt{2}}$

(c) $x^2 = 19$

$x = \pm\sqrt{\mathbf{19}}$

18. $\dfrac{x^3 + x^2 - 12x}{x^2 + 4x} \div \dfrac{x^2 - 11x + 24}{x^2 + 2x - 80}$

$= \dfrac{x^3 + x^2 - 12x}{x^2 + 4x} \cdot \dfrac{x^2 + 2x - 80}{x^2 - 11x + 24}$

$= \dfrac{x(x + 4)(x - 3)}{x(x + 4)} \cdot \dfrac{(x + 10)(x - 8)}{(x - 8)(x - 3)}$

$= \mathbf{x + 10}$

19. $\qquad\qquad -80 = x^2 + 18x$

$-x^2 - 18x - 80 = 0$

$(-1)(x^2 + 18x + 80) = 0$

$x^2 + 18x + 80 = 0$

$(x + 10)(x + 8) = 0$

If $x + 10 = 0$ $\qquad$ If $x + 8 = 0$

$\qquad x = \mathbf{-10}$ $\qquad\qquad x = \mathbf{-8}$

20. $D = \{x \in \mathbb{R} \mid -4 \leq x < 5\}$
$R = \{y \in \mathbb{R} \mid -2 \leq y \leq 3\}$

21. (a) $x = -4$

(b) The desired equation is $y = mx + b$.

By inspection, $b = -3$.

By inspection, the sign of m is +.

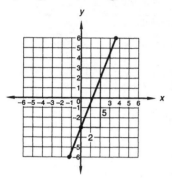

$|m| = \dfrac{5}{2}$

So $b = -3$ and $m = \dfrac{5}{2}$.

$$y = \frac{5}{2}x - 3$$

22. $(2x^3 + x^2 - 3x) \div (2x + 3)$

$$\begin{array}{r} x^2 - x \\ 2x + 3 \overline{\smash{\big)}\ 2x^3 + x^2 - 3x} \\ \underline{2x^3 + 3x^2} \\ -2x^2 - 3x \\ \underline{-2x^2 - 3x} \\ 0 \end{array}$$

$x^2 - x$

23. $3\sqrt{6,000,000} - 5\sqrt{60,000} + 2\sqrt{3}(3\sqrt{2} - 5\sqrt{3})$
$= 3\sqrt{1,000,000}\sqrt{6} - 5\sqrt{10,000}\sqrt{6} + 6\sqrt{6}$
$\quad - 10(3)$
$= 3(1000)\sqrt{6} - 5(100)\sqrt{6} + 6\sqrt{6} - 30$
$= 3000\sqrt{6} - 500\sqrt{6} + 6\sqrt{6} - 30$
$= \mathbf{2506\sqrt{6} - 30}$

24. $\begin{cases} x = 2 \\ y = -\dfrac{1}{2}x + 6 \end{cases}$

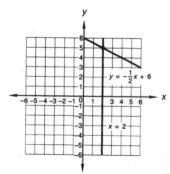

$x = 2 \qquad y = -\dfrac{1}{2}x + 6$
$2 = 2$

$5 = -\dfrac{1}{2}(2) + 6$

$5 = -1 + 6$

$5 = 5$

The solution to the linear equations is **(2, 5)**.

25. $$\frac{5x}{2} - \frac{x-3}{5} = 7$$

$$10 \cdot \frac{5x}{2} - 10 \cdot \frac{(x-3)}{5} = 10 \cdot 7$$

$$25x - 2(x - 3) = 70$$

$$23x + 6 = 70$$

$$23x = 64$$

$$x = \frac{64}{23}$$

26. $\dfrac{(0.0004 \times 10^{15})(0.06 \times 10^{41})}{(30,000,000)(400 \times 10^{-21})}$

$= \dfrac{(4 \times 10^{11})(6 \times 10^{39})}{(3 \times 10^7)(4 \times 10^{-19})}$

$= \dfrac{4 \cdot 6}{3 \cdot 4} \times \dfrac{10^{11} \cdot 10^{39}}{10^7 \cdot 10^{-19}}$

$= \dfrac{24}{12} \times \dfrac{10^{50}}{10^{-12}}$

$= \mathbf{2 \times 10^{62}}$

27. (a) $\dfrac{-3x - 9x^2}{-3x} = \dfrac{-3x(1 + 3x)}{-3x} = \mathbf{1 + 3x}$

(b) $\dfrac{-2^{-2}}{(-2)^2} = \dfrac{-1}{2^2(-2)^2} = \dfrac{-1}{4(4)} = -\dfrac{1}{16}$

28. $x = \dfrac{\sqrt{b^2 - 4ac}}{2a} = \dfrac{\sqrt{13^2 - 4(10)\left(\dfrac{5}{8}\right)}}{2(10)}$

$= \dfrac{\sqrt{169 - 25}}{20} = \dfrac{\sqrt{144}}{20} = \dfrac{12}{20} = \dfrac{3}{5}$

29.

Area $= (10 \text{ in.})(40 \text{ in.}) + \dfrac{1}{2}(40 \text{ in.})(9 \text{ in.})$

$= 400 \text{ in.}^2 + 180 \text{ in.}^2$

$= \mathbf{580 \text{ in.}^2}$

30. $S.A. = 2(\text{Area}_{\text{triangle}}) + 2(\text{Area}_{\text{side}}) + \text{Area}_{\text{bottom}}$

$= 2\left[\dfrac{1}{2}(10 \text{ ft})(12 \text{ ft})\right] + 2[(15 \text{ ft})(13 \text{ ft})]$

$\quad + (15 \text{ ft})(10 \text{ ft})$

$= 2(60 \text{ ft}^2) + 2(195 \text{ ft}^2) + 150 \text{ ft}^2$

$= 120 \text{ ft}^2 + 390 \text{ ft}^2 + 150 \text{ ft}^2$

$= \mathbf{660 \ ft^2}$

Practice 103

a. $(t \neq 0, 3)$

$$\dfrac{5}{t} - \dfrac{2}{t - 3} = 0$$

$$t(t - 3)\left(\dfrac{5}{t}\right) - t(t - 3)\left(\dfrac{2}{t - 3}\right) = 0$$

$$5(t - 3) - 2t = 0$$

$$3t - 15 = 0$$

$$3t = 15$$

$$t = \mathbf{5}$$

b. $(y \neq 0, 3)$

$$\dfrac{8}{y} + \dfrac{5}{y - 3} = 0$$

$$y(y - 3)\left(\dfrac{8}{y}\right) + y(y - 3)\left(\dfrac{5}{y - 3}\right) = 0$$

$$8(y - 3) + 5y = 0$$

$$13y - 24 = 0$$

$$13y = 24$$

$$y = \mathbf{\dfrac{24}{13}}$$

Problem Set 103

1. $\quad D_1 + D_2 = 52$

$R_1T_1 + R_2T_2 = 52$

$R_1 = 3$

$R_2 = 4$

$T_1 + T_2 = 15$

$\quad T_2 = -T_1 + 15$

$\quad R_1T_1 + R_2T_2 = 52$

$3T_1 + 4(-T_1 + 15) = 52$

$\quad -T_1 + 60 = 52$

$\quad -T_1 = -8$

$\quad T_1 = \mathbf{8 \ hr}$

2. $\quad D_W = D_T$

$R_WT_W = R_TT_T$

$R_W = 2$

$R_T = 4$

$T_W = T_T + 2$

$\quad R_WT_W = R_TT_T$

$2(T_T + 2) = 4T_T$

$\quad 2T_T + 4 = 4T_T$

$\quad -2T_T = -4$

$\quad T_T = 2 \text{ hr}$

$D_T = R_TT_T = (4)(2) = \mathbf{8 \ mi}$

3. $5(N + 10) = 7(-N) + 2$

$\quad 5N + 50 = -7N + 2$

$\quad 12N = -48$

$\quad N = \mathbf{-4}$

4. (a) $N_C + N_D = 25$

(b) $10N_C + 20N_D = 350$

$(-10)(a) \quad -10N_C - 10N_D = -250$

$(1)(b) \quad \dfrac{10N_C + 20N_D = \ \ 350}{10N_D = \ \ 100}$

$\quad N_D = \mathbf{10}$

(a) $N_C + N_D = 25$

$\quad N_C + 10 = 25$

$\quad N_C = \mathbf{15}$

5. First hour $= 5(\text{second hour}) = 5(1) = 5$

So, the first hour costs $5 and the other five hours cost $1 a piece.

Cost $= 5 + 1 + 1 + 1 + 1 + 1 = \mathbf{\$10}$

6. $\quad \dfrac{130}{100} \cdot M = 260$

$\dfrac{100}{130} \cdot \dfrac{130}{100} \cdot M = 260 \cdot \dfrac{100}{130}$

$\quad M = 200$

The total number of soldiers is $260 + 200 = \mathbf{460}$.

7. (a) $P(< 6) = \dfrac{1 + 2 + 3 + 4}{36} = \dfrac{10}{36} = \mathbf{\dfrac{5}{18}}$

(b) $P(> 6) = \dfrac{6 + 5 + 4 + 3 + 2 + 1}{36}$

$= \dfrac{21}{36} = \mathbf{\dfrac{7}{12}}$

8. $(p \neq 0)$

$$\frac{p - 4}{p} = \frac{16}{5p} - \frac{1}{5}$$

$$5p \cdot \frac{(p - 4)}{p} = 5p \cdot \frac{16}{5p} - 5p \cdot \frac{1}{5}$$

$$5(p - 4) = 16 - p$$

$$5p - 20 = 16 - p$$

$$6p = 36$$

$$p = \mathbf{6}$$

9. $(n \neq 0, -3)$

$$\frac{3}{4n} = \frac{3}{n + 3}$$

$$4n(n + 3)\left(\frac{3}{4n}\right) = 4n(n + 3)\left(\frac{3}{n + 3}\right)$$

$$3(n + 3) = 12n$$

$$3n + 9 = 12n$$

$$-9n = -9$$

$$n = \mathbf{1}$$

10. $-|x| + 4 \geq -2$

$$-|x| \geq -6$$

$$|x| \leq 6$$

```
 ├───●───┼───┼───┼───┼───┼───●───┼──
   -8  -6  -4  -2   0   2   4   6   8
```

11. $|x| - 4 > -1$

$$|x| > 3$$

```
◄───┼───⊕───┼───┼───┼───┼───⊕───┼───►
   -4  -3  -2  -1   0   1   2   3   4
```

12. $\dfrac{4}{a - 2} + \dfrac{6a}{a^2 - 4}$

$$= \frac{4}{a - 2} + \frac{6a}{(a - 2)(a + 2)}$$

$$= \frac{4(a + 2)}{(a - 2)(a + 2)} + \frac{6a}{(a - 2)(a + 2)}$$

$$= \frac{4a + 8 + 6a}{(a - 2)(a + 2)} = \frac{\mathbf{10a + 8}}{\mathbf{(a - 2)(a + 2)}}$$

13. $\dfrac{5}{x + 4} - \dfrac{3}{x^2 + 2x - 8}$

$$= \frac{5}{x + 4} - \frac{3}{(x + 4)(x - 2)}$$

$$= \frac{5(x - 2)}{(x + 4)(x - 2)} - \frac{3}{(x + 4)(x - 2)}$$

$$= \frac{5x - 10 - 3}{(x + 4)(x - 2)} = \frac{\mathbf{5x - 13}}{\mathbf{(x + 4)(x - 2)}}$$

14. (a) $\sqrt{3} = 1.732\textcircled{0}508\dots$

1.7321

(b) $\dfrac{1}{6} = 0.16\textcircled{6}666\dots$

0.167

(c) $1\textcircled{0}53.7625$

1100

15. $p^2 + 4^2 = 6^2$

$$p^2 + 16 = 36$$

$$p^2 = 20$$

$$p = \sqrt{20}$$

$$p = \sqrt{4}\sqrt{5}$$

$$p = \mathbf{2\sqrt{5}}$$

16. (a) $y = \mathbf{4}$

(b) The desired equation is $y = mx + b$.

By inspection, $b = -3$.

By inspection, the sign of m is $-$.

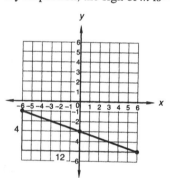

$$|m| = \frac{4}{12} = \frac{1}{3}$$

So $b = -3$ and $m = -\dfrac{1}{3}$.

$$y = -\frac{1}{3}x - 3$$

17. (a) $m = \dfrac{6 - (-3)}{-5 - (-2)} = \dfrac{9}{-3} = \mathbf{-3}$

(b)

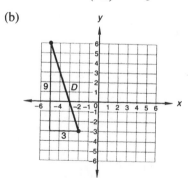

$$D^2 = 3^2 + 9^2$$
$$D^2 = 9 + 81$$
$$D^2 = 90$$
$$D = \sqrt{90}$$
$$D = \sqrt{9}\sqrt{10}$$
$$D = \mathbf{3\sqrt{10}}$$

18. (b)

19. $\dfrac{x^2 + 10x + 25}{x^2 + 5x} \div \dfrac{x^2 + 8x + 15}{x^3 + x^2 - 6x}$

$= \dfrac{x^2 + 10x + 25}{x^2 + 5x} \cdot \dfrac{x^3 + x^2 - 6x}{x^2 + 8x + 15}$

$= \dfrac{(x + 5)(x + 5)}{x(x + 5)} \cdot \dfrac{x(x + 3)(x - 2)}{(x + 5)(x + 3)} = \boldsymbol{x - 2}$

20.
$$4x^2 - 81 = 0$$
$$(2x + 9)(2x - 9) = 0$$

If $2x + 9 = 0$ If $2x - 9 = 0$
$\qquad 2x = -9 \qquad\qquad 2x = 9$
$\qquad x = -\dfrac{9}{2} \qquad\qquad x = \dfrac{9}{2}$

21. (b), (c)

22. $\left(x^3 - 4\right) \div (x + 7)$

$$
\begin{array}{r}
x^2 - 7x + 49 \\
x + 7 \overline{\smash{\big)}\, x^3 + 0x^2 + \ \ 0x - \ \ \ \ 4} \\
\underline{x^3 + 7x^2} \\
-7x^2 + \ \ 0x \\
\underline{-7x^2 - 49x} \\
49x - \ \ \ \ 4 \\
\underline{49x + 343} \\
-347
\end{array}
$$

$x^2 - 7x + 49 - \dfrac{347}{x + 7}$

23. $3\sqrt{2} \cdot 4\sqrt{3} - 4\sqrt{60{,}000} + 2\sqrt{3}\left(3\sqrt{2} - \sqrt{3}\right)$

$= 12\sqrt{6} - 4\sqrt{10{,}000}\sqrt{6} + 6\sqrt{6} - 2(3)$

$= 12\sqrt{6} - 400\sqrt{6} + 6\sqrt{6} - 6$

$= \boldsymbol{-382\sqrt{6} - 6}$

24. $\begin{cases} y = x - 2 \\ y = -\dfrac{1}{2}x + 1 \end{cases}$

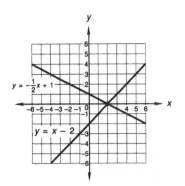

$y = x - 2 \qquad y = -\dfrac{1}{2}x + 1$
$0 = 2 - 2 \qquad\ $
$0 = 0 \qquad\qquad 0 = -\dfrac{1}{2}(2) + 1$
$\qquad\qquad\qquad\quad 0 = -1 + 1$
$\qquad\qquad\qquad\quad 0 = 0$

The solution to the linear equations is $(\mathbf{2, 0})$.

25. (a) Rationals, reals

(b) Integers, rationals, reals

26. (a) $\dfrac{3x - 3x^2}{3x} = \dfrac{3x(1 - x)}{3x} = \mathbf{1 - x}$

(b) $\dfrac{-4^{-2}}{-(-2)^{-2}} = \dfrac{-(-2)^2}{-4^2} = \dfrac{-4}{-16} = \dfrac{\mathbf{1}}{\mathbf{4}}$

27. $\dfrac{a^2 + \dfrac{1}{a}}{ax + \dfrac{b}{a}} = \dfrac{\dfrac{a^3}{a} + \dfrac{1}{a}}{\dfrac{a^2x}{a} + \dfrac{b}{a}} = \dfrac{\dfrac{a^3 + 1}{a} \cdot \dfrac{a}{a^2x + b}}{\dfrac{a^2x + b}{a} \cdot \dfrac{a}{a^2x + b}}$

$= \dfrac{\boldsymbol{a^3 + 1}}{\boldsymbol{a^2x + b}}$

28. $-x - x^2 + (-x)^3(x - y)$

$= -(-3) - (-3)^2 + (3)^3\left[-3 - (-5)\right]$

$= 3 - 9 + 27(2)$

$= -6 + 54 = \mathbf{48}$

29. $P = \dfrac{2\pi(8 \text{ cm})}{2} + 6 \text{ cm} + \dfrac{2\pi(14 \text{ cm})}{2} + 6 \text{ cm}$

$= 22\pi \text{ cm} + 12 \text{ cm}$

$= (\mathbf{12 + 22\pi}) \textbf{ cm} = \mathbf{81.08 \text{ cm}}$

30. $V = \left(\text{Area}_{\text{base}}\right)(\text{Height})$

$= \left[(36 \text{ m})(10 \text{ m}) + \dfrac{1}{2}(36 \text{ m})(10 \text{ m})\right](13 \text{ m})$

$= \left(360 \text{ m}^2 + 180 \text{ m}^2\right)(13 \text{ m})$

$= \left(540 \text{ m}^2\right)(13 \text{ m})$

$= \mathbf{7020 \text{ m}^3}$

Practice 104

a. $(b, m \neq 0)$

$$\frac{3z}{m} + \frac{n}{b} = f$$

$$mb\left(\frac{3z}{m}\right) + mb\left(\frac{n}{b}\right) = mbf$$

$$3bz + mn = mbf$$

$$mn = bmf - 3bz$$

$$mn = b(mf - 3z)$$

$$b = \frac{mn}{mf - 3z}$$

$$b = \frac{nm}{fm - 3z}$$

$(fm - 3z \neq 0)$

b. $(m, y \neq 0)$

$$\frac{3a}{y} - s + \frac{k}{m} = x$$

$$my\left(\frac{3a}{y}\right) - mys + my\left(\frac{k}{m}\right) = myx$$

$$3am - mys + ky = myx$$

$$ky = myx + mys - 3am$$

$$ky = m(xy + sy - 3a)$$

$$m = \frac{ky}{xy + sy - 3a}$$

$(xy + sy - 3a \neq 0)$

Problem Set 104

1. $D_M = D_H$
$R_M T_M = R_H T_H$
$R_M = 8$
$R_H = 16$
$T_M = T_H + 4$

$$R_M T_M = R_H T_H$$
$$8(T_H + 4) = 16T_H$$
$$8T_H + 32 = 16T_H$$
$$32 = 8T_H$$
$$T_H = \mathbf{4\ hr}$$

2. $D_T = D_G$
$R_T T_T = R_G T_G$
$T_T = 4$
$T_G = 48$
$R_T = R_G + 55$

$$R_T T_T = R_G T_G$$
$$(R_G + 55)4 = (R_G)48$$
$$4R_G + 220 = 48R_G$$
$$220 = 44R_G$$
$$R_G = 5$$

$$D_G = R_G T_G = (5)(48) = \mathbf{240\ mi}$$

3. $N, N + 2, N + 4$

$$4N = 2(2 + N + 4) - 14$$
$$4N = 2N + 12 - 14$$
$$2N = -2$$
$$N = -1$$

Thus the integers are **−1, 1,** and **3.**

4. (a) $N_G + N_C = 8$
(b) $422N_G + 4N_C = 2122$

$$\begin{array}{r}(-4)(a)\quad -4N_G - 4N_C = -32 \\ (1)(b)\quad 422N_G + 4N_C = 2122 \\ \hline 418N_G \qquad\quad = 2090 \\ N_G = \mathbf{5}\end{array}$$

5.

$$\frac{30}{100} \cdot T = 81{,}150$$

$$\frac{100}{30} \cdot \frac{30}{100} \cdot T = 81{,}150 \cdot \frac{100}{30}$$

$$T = \mathbf{270{,}500}$$

6. $P(\text{3 green marbles}) = \dfrac{13}{20} \cdot \dfrac{12}{19} \cdot \dfrac{11}{18}$

$$= \frac{1716}{6840} = \mathbf{\frac{143}{570}}$$

7. $(n, x \neq 0)$

$$\frac{a}{n} - m + \frac{5k}{x} = y$$

$$nx\left(\frac{a}{n}\right) - nxm + nx\left(\frac{5k}{x}\right) = nxy$$

$$ax - mnx + 5kn = nxy$$

$$ax = nxy + mnx - 5kn$$

$$ax = n(yx + mx - 5k)$$

$$n = \frac{ax}{yx + mx - 5k}$$

$(yx + mx - 5k \neq 0)$

8. $(a, d \neq 0)$

$$\frac{2c}{a} - x = \frac{b}{d}$$

$$ad\left(\frac{2c}{a}\right) - adx = ad\left(\frac{b}{d}\right)$$

$$2cd - adx = ab$$

$$d(2c - ax) = ab$$

$$d = \frac{ab}{2c - ax}$$

$(2c - ax \neq 0)$

9. $(m \neq 0)$

$$\frac{1 + m}{m} - \frac{3}{m} = 0$$

$$m\left(\frac{1+m}{m}\right) - m\left(\frac{3}{m}\right) = 0$$

$$1 + m - 3 = 0$$

$$m - 2 = 0$$

$$m = 2$$

10. $(x \neq 0, -5)$

$$\frac{3}{4x} = \frac{2}{x+5}$$

$$4x(x+5)\left(\frac{3}{4x}\right) = 4x(x+5)\left(\frac{2}{x+5}\right)$$

$$3(x+5) = 2(4x)$$

$$3x + 15 = 8x$$

$$15 = 5x$$

$$x = 3$$

11.

$$\frac{x}{5} - \frac{3+x}{7} = 0$$

$$35 \cdot \frac{x}{5} - 35 \cdot \frac{(3+x)}{7} = 0$$

$$7x - 5(3+x) = 0$$

$$7x - 15 - 5x = 0$$

$$2x = 15$$

$$x = \frac{15}{2}$$

12. $(x \neq 0, 1)$

$$\frac{2}{x} - \frac{3}{x-1} = 0$$

$$x(x-1)\left(\frac{2}{x}\right) - x(x-1)\left(\frac{3}{x-1}\right) = 0$$

$$2(x-1) - 3x = 0$$

$$2x - 2 - 3x = 0$$

$$-x - 2 = 0$$

$$-x = 2$$

$$x = -2$$

13. $-|x| - 2 < -4$

$$-|x| < -2$$

$$|x| > 2$$

14. $-|x| + 2 \geq 1$

$$-|x| \geq -1$$

$$|x| \leq 1$$

15. $\dfrac{4}{x^2 - 4} + \dfrac{3x}{x-2}$

$$= \frac{4}{(x-2)(x+2)} + \frac{3x}{x-2}$$

$$= \frac{4}{(x-2)(x+2)} + \frac{3x(x+2)}{(x-2)(x+2)}$$

$$= \frac{4 + 3x^2 + 6x}{(x-2)(x+2)} = \mathbf{\frac{3x^2 + 6x + 4}{(x-2)(x+2)}}$$

16. $-\dfrac{x}{x+5} - \dfrac{3x}{x^2 + 3x - 10}$

$$= -\frac{x}{x+5} - \frac{3x}{(x+5)(x-2)}$$

$$= -\frac{x(x-2)}{(x+5)(x-2)} - \frac{3x}{(x+5)(x-2)}$$

$$= \frac{-x^2 + 2x - 3x}{(x+5)(x-2)} = \frac{-x^2 - x}{(x+5)(x-2)}$$

$$= -\mathbf{\frac{x^2 + x}{(x+5)(x-2)}}$$

17. (a) $\sqrt{26} = 5.0\textcircled{9}9019\ldots$

5.10

(b) $3.14159\textcircled{2}654\ldots$

3.141593

(c) $52\textcircled{4}7.6732$

5250

18. $k^2 + 9^2 = 11^2$

$$k^2 + 81 = 121$$

$$k^2 = 40$$

$$k = \sqrt{40}$$

$$k = \sqrt{4}\sqrt{10}$$

$$k = \mathbf{2\sqrt{10}}$$

19. (a) $y = 3$

(b) The desired equation is $y = mx + b$.

By inspection, $b = -3$.

By inspection, the sign of m is +.

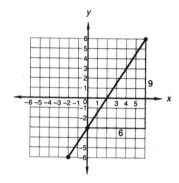

$$|m| = \frac{9}{6} = \frac{3}{2}$$

So $b = -3$ and $m = \frac{3}{2}$.

$$y = \frac{3}{2}x - 3$$

20. (a) $m = \dfrac{6 - 2}{-10 - (-4)} = \dfrac{4}{-6} = -\dfrac{2}{3}$

(b)

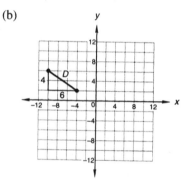

$D^2 = 6^2 + 4^2$

$D^2 = 36 + 16$

$D^2 = 52$

$D = \sqrt{52}$

$D = \sqrt{4}\sqrt{13}$

$D = 2\sqrt{13}$

21. (d)

22.
$$63 = -x^2 - 16x$$
$$x^2 + 16x + 63 = 0$$
$$(x + 9)(x + 7) = 0$$

If $x + 9 = 0$ If $x + 7 = 0$

       $x = -9$ $x = -7$

23. $D = \left\{ x \in \mathbb{R} \mid x \le \dfrac{1}{4} \right\}$

24. $4\sqrt{20{,}000} - 15\sqrt{8} + 3\sqrt{2}\left(4\sqrt{2} - 5\right)$

$= 4\sqrt{10{,}000}\sqrt{2} - 15\sqrt{4}\sqrt{2} + 12(2) - 15\sqrt{2}$

$= 4(100)\sqrt{2} - 15(2)\sqrt{2} + 24 - 15\sqrt{2}$

$= 400\sqrt{2} - 30\sqrt{2} + 24 - 15\sqrt{2}$

$= \mathbf{355\sqrt{2} + 24}$

25. $b - 1 = 2$ $c + 1 = -1$

       $b = 3$ $c = -2$

$$x = \frac{-b \pm \sqrt{b^2 - 4ac}}{2a}$$

$$= \frac{-3 \pm \sqrt{3^2 - 4(2)(-2)}}{2(2)} = \frac{-3 \pm \sqrt{9 + 16}}{4}$$

$$= \frac{-3 \pm \sqrt{25}}{4} = \frac{-3 \pm 5}{4} = \frac{-8}{4}, \frac{2}{4} = \mathbf{-2, \frac{1}{2}}$$

26. $2x^0(x - 2) - 3x - 4 - [-(-2)] - 7^0 = -2x - 4$

       $2x - 4 - 3x - 4 - 2 - 1 = -2x - 4$

                $-x - 11 = -2x - 4$

                      $x = \mathbf{7}$

27. $-x^2 - x(xy - xy^2)$

$= -(-2)^2 - (-2)\left[(-2)(-3) - (-2)(-3)^2\right]$

$= -4 + 2[6 + 2(9)] = -4 + 2(24)$

$= -4 + 48 = \mathbf{44}$

28. (a) $\dfrac{4x^2ay - 4xay}{4xay} = \dfrac{4xay(x - 1)}{4xay} = \mathbf{x - 1}$

(b) $\dfrac{-2^{-2}}{-(-2^0)^{-3}} = \dfrac{-(-2^0)^3}{-2^2} = \dfrac{-(-1)^3}{-4}$

$= \dfrac{-(-1)}{-4} = -\dfrac{1}{4}$

29. Area $=$ Area$_{parallelogram}$ $-$ Area$_{circle}$

$= \left[\dfrac{1}{2}(9 \text{ in.} \times 6 \text{ in.}) + \dfrac{1}{2}(9 \text{ in.} \times 6 \text{ in.}) \right]$

    $- \left[\pi(2 \text{ in.})^2 \right]$

$= (27 \text{ in.}^2 + 27 \text{ in.}^2) - 4\pi \text{ in.}^2$

$= \mathbf{(54 - 4\pi) \text{ in.}^2 = 41.44 \text{ in.}^2}$

30. Lateral $S.A.$ $= \left(\text{Perimeter}_{base} \right)(\text{Height})$

$= (16 \text{ ft} \times 6)(25 \text{ ft})$

$= (96 \text{ ft})(25 \text{ ft})$

$= \mathbf{2400 \text{ ft}^2}$

Practice 105

a. $mba - 7a + mbn - 7n$

$= a(mb - 7) + n(mb - 7)$

$= (a + n)(mb - 7)$

b. $ns + 3nx + 2cs + 6cx$

$\quad = n(s + 3x) + 2c(s + 3x)$

$\quad = (s + 3x)(n + 2c)$

Problem Set 105

1. $\quad D_R = D_W$

$\quad R_R T_R = R_W T_W$

$\quad R_R = 6$

$\quad R_W = 3$

$\quad T_R + T_W = 6$

$\qquad T_R = -T_W + 6$

$\qquad R_R T_R = R_W T_W$

$\quad 6(-T_W + 6) = 3T_W$

$\quad -6T_W + 36 = 3T_W$

$\qquad\qquad -9T_W = -36$

$\qquad\qquad T_W = 4$

$D_W = R_W T_W = (3)(4) = \textbf{12 km}$

2. $\quad D_R + 500 = D_W$

$\quad R_R T_R + 500 = R_W T_W$

$\quad R_W = 40$

$\quad R_R = 20$

$\quad T_R = T_W$

$\quad R_R T_R + 500 = R_W T_W$

$\quad 20T_W + 500 = 40T_W$

$\qquad -20T_W = -500$

$\qquad\qquad T_W = \textbf{25 seconds}$

3. (a) $N_H + N_C = 100$

$\quad$ (b) $4N_H + 6N_C = 540$

$(-6)(a) \quad -6N_H - 6N_C = -600$

$(1)(b) \quad \underline{4N_H + 6N_C = 540}$

$\qquad\qquad -2N_H \qquad\quad = -60$

$\qquad\qquad\qquad N_H = \textbf{30}$

4. $N, N + 2, N + 4, N + 6$

$-6(N + 2 + N + 6) = 11[-(N + 4)] - 8$

$\qquad -6(2N + 8) = -11N - 44 - 8$

$\qquad -12N - 48 = -11N - 52$

$\qquad\qquad\qquad -N = -4$

$\qquad\qquad\qquad\quad N = 4$

Thus the integers are **4, 6, 8,** and **10.**

5. $\qquad \dfrac{73}{100} \cdot T = 438$

$\quad \dfrac{100}{73} \cdot \dfrac{73}{100} \cdot T = 438 \cdot \dfrac{100}{73}$

$\qquad\qquad\qquad T = \textbf{600}$

6. $P(H) = \dfrac{1}{2}$

7. $ac - ad + bc - bd = a(c - d) + b(c - d)$

$\qquad = \textbf{(\textit{c} - \textit{d})(\textit{a} + \textit{b})}$

8. $ab + 4a + 2b + 8 = a(b + 4) + 2(b + 4)$

$\qquad = \textbf{(\textit{b} + 4)(\textit{a} + 2)}$

9. $ab + ac + xb + xc = a(b + c) + x(b + c)$

$\qquad = \textbf{(\textit{b} + \textit{c})(\textit{a} + \textit{x})}$

10. $2mx - 3m + 2pcx - 3pc$

$\qquad = m(2x - 3) + pc(2x - 3) = \textbf{(2\textit{x} - 3)(\textit{m} + \textit{pc})}$

11. $4k - kxy + 4pc - pcxy$

$\qquad = k(4 - xy) + pc(4 - xy) = \textbf{(4 - \textit{xy})(\textit{k} + \textit{pc})}$

12. $ac - axy + dc - dxy$

$\qquad = a(c - xy) + d(c - xy) = \textbf{(\textit{c} - \textit{xy})(\textit{a} + \textit{d})}$

13. $(b, c \neq 0)$

$$\frac{a}{b} + \frac{1}{c} = d$$

$$bc\left(\frac{a}{b}\right) + bc\left(\frac{1}{c}\right) = bcd$$

$$ac + b = bcd$$

$$b - bcd = -ac$$

$$b(1 - cd) = -ac$$

$$b = \frac{-ca}{1 - cd}$$

$$b = \frac{(-1)ca}{(-1)(cd - 1)}$$

$$b = \textbf{\frac{\textit{ca}}{\textit{cd} - 1}}$$

$(cd - 1 \neq 0)$

14. $(c, d, x \neq 0)$

$$\frac{a}{x} - \frac{1}{c} = \frac{b}{d}$$

$$cdx\left(\frac{a}{x}\right) - cdx\left(\frac{1}{c}\right) = cdx\left(\frac{b}{d}\right)$$

$$cda - dx = bcx$$

$$b = \textbf{\frac{\textit{cda} - \textit{xd}}{\textit{xc}}}$$

$(xc \neq 0)$

15. $(x \neq 0, 4)$

$$\frac{4}{x} - \frac{2}{x-4} = 0$$

$$x(x-4)\left(\frac{4}{x}\right) - x(x-4)\left(\frac{2}{x-4}\right) = 0$$

$$4(x-4) - 2x = 0$$

$$4x - 16 - 2x = 0$$

$$2x - 16 = 0$$

$$2x = 16$$

$$x = \mathbf{8}$$

16.
$$\frac{x}{4} - \frac{x+6}{5} = 1$$

$$20 \cdot \frac{x}{4} - 20 \cdot \frac{(x+6)}{5} = 20 \cdot 1$$

$$5x - 4(x+6) = 20$$

$$5x - 4x - 24 = 20$$

$$x = \mathbf{44}$$

17. $|x| + 5 < 2$

$|x| < -3$

```
 ┣━━━┿━━━┿━━━┿━━━┿━━━┿━━━┫
  -3  -2  -1   0   1   2   3
```

No solution

18. $-|x| - 1 \geq 1$

$-|x| \geq 2$

$|x| \leq -2$

```
 ┣━━━┿━━━┿━━━┿━━━┿━━━┿━━━┫
  -3  -2  -1   0   1   2   3
```

No solution

19.
$$\frac{4}{x^2-9} - \frac{3}{x+3}$$

$$= \frac{4}{(x+3)(x-3)} - \frac{3}{x+3}$$

$$= \frac{4}{(x+3)(x-3)} - \frac{3(x-3)}{(x+3)(x-3)}$$

$$= \frac{4-3x+9}{(x+3)(x-3)} = \frac{\mathbf{13-3x}}{\mathbf{(x+3)(x-3)}}$$

20.
$$\frac{5}{x+2} - \frac{3x}{x^2+5x+6}$$

$$= \frac{5}{x+2} - \frac{3x}{(x+2)(x+3)}$$

$$= \frac{5(x+3)}{(x+2)(x+3)} - \frac{3x}{(x+2)(x+3)}$$

$$= \frac{5x+15-3x}{(x+2)(x+3)} = \frac{\mathbf{2x+15}}{\mathbf{(x+3)(x+2)}}$$

21. (a) $\sqrt{13} = 3.6\textcircled{0}55...$

3.61

(b) $2\pi = 6.2831\textcircled{8}5...$

6.28319

(c) $5\textcircled{7},634.679$

58,000

22. $k^2 = 4^2 + 2^2$

$k^2 = 16 + 4$

$k^2 = 20$

$k = \sqrt{20}$

$k = \sqrt{4}\sqrt{5}$

$k = \mathbf{2\sqrt{5}}$

23. $\begin{cases} y = x - 3 \\ y = -x + 3 \end{cases}$

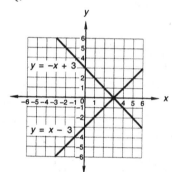

$y = x - 3$	$y = -x + 3$
$0 = 3 - 3$	$0 = -3 + 3$
$0 = 0$	$0 = 0$

The solution to the linear equations is $(\mathbf{3, 0})$.

24. (a) $g(x) = x^2 + 2$

(b) $f(x) = |x + 3|$

(c) $p(x) = -(x+2)^2$

(d) $h(x) = -|x|$

25. (a) $m = \dfrac{8-0}{6-0} = \dfrac{8}{6} = \dfrac{4}{3}$

(b)

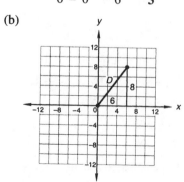

$$D^2 = 6^2 + 8^2$$
$$D^2 = 36 + 64$$
$$D^2 = 100$$
$$D = \sqrt{100}$$
$$D = \mathbf{10}$$

26. $\sqrt{50{,}000} - 25\sqrt{125} + 5\sqrt{5}(5\sqrt{5} - 5)$

$= \sqrt{10{,}000}\sqrt{5} - 25\sqrt{25}\sqrt{5} + 25(5) - 25\sqrt{5}$

$= 100\sqrt{5} - 125\sqrt{5} + 125 - 25\sqrt{5}$

$= \mathbf{-50\sqrt{5} + 125}$

27. $\dfrac{x^2 + 6x + 9}{x^2 + 3x} \div \dfrac{x^3 + 5x^2 + 6x}{x^2 + 2x}$

$= \dfrac{x^2 + 6x + 9}{x^2 + 3x} \cdot \dfrac{x^2 + 2x}{x^3 + 5x^2 + 6x}$

$= \dfrac{(x+3)(x+3)}{x(x+3)} \cdot \dfrac{x(x+2)}{x(x+2)(x+3)} = \dfrac{1}{x}$

28. $x = \dfrac{-b \pm \sqrt{b^2 - 4ac}}{2a}$

$= \dfrac{-(-2) \pm \sqrt{(-2)^2 - 4(3)(-1)}}{2(3)}$

$= \dfrac{2 \pm \sqrt{4 + 12}}{6} = \dfrac{2 \pm \sqrt{16}}{6}$

$= \dfrac{2 \pm 4}{6} = \dfrac{-2}{6}, \dfrac{6}{6} = \mathbf{-\dfrac{1}{3}, 1}$

29. $P = \dfrac{2\pi(8 \text{ cm})}{2} + 8 \text{ cm} + \dfrac{2\pi(4 \text{ cm})}{2}$

$= \mathbf{(8 + 12\pi) \text{ cm} = 45.68 \text{ cm}}$

30. $V = \dfrac{1}{3}\left(\text{Area}_{\text{base}}\right)(\text{Height})$

$= \dfrac{1}{3}(8 \text{ m} \times 12 \text{ m})(16 \text{ m})$

$= \dfrac{1}{3}(96 \text{ m}^2)(16 \text{ m})$

$= (32 \text{ m}^2)(16 \text{ m}) = \mathbf{512 \text{ m}^3}$

Practice 106

a. $m = \dfrac{-1 - (-5)}{2 - 3} = \dfrac{4}{-1} = -4$

Using $(3, -5)$,

$$y = -4x + b$$
$$-5 = -4(3) + b$$
$$-5 = -12 + b$$
$$b = 7$$

$$y = \mathbf{-4x + 7}$$

b. $m = \dfrac{-3 - 5}{-3 - 6} = \dfrac{-8}{-9} = \dfrac{8}{9}$

Using $(-3, -3)$,

$$y = \dfrac{8}{9}x + b$$
$$-3 = \dfrac{8}{9}(-3) + b$$
$$-3 = -\dfrac{8}{3} + b$$
$$b = -\dfrac{1}{3}$$

$$y = \mathbf{\dfrac{8}{9}x - \dfrac{1}{3}}$$

Problem Set 106

1.
$$D_N + D_S = 440$$
$$R_N T_N + R_S T_S = 440$$

$$R_N = 70$$
$$R_S = 30$$
$$T_N = T_S + 2$$

$$R_N T_N + R_S T_S = 440$$
$$70(T_S + 2) + 30T_S = 440$$
$$100T_S + 140 = 440$$
$$100T_S = 300$$
$$T_S = 3$$

$8 \text{ a.m.} + 3 \text{ hr} = \mathbf{11 \text{ a.m.}}$

2.
$$D_S = D_C$$
$$R_S T_S = R_C T_C$$

$$R_S = 30$$
$$R_C = 50$$
$$T_S = T_C + 2$$

$$R_S T_S = R_C T_C$$
$$30(T_C + 2) = 50T_C$$
$$30T_C + 60 = 50T_C$$
$$-20T_C = -60$$
$$T_C = \mathbf{3 \text{ hr}}$$

3. (a) $N_Q + N_D = 64$

(b) $25N_Q + 10N_D = 955$

$(-10)(a) \quad -10N_Q - 10N_D = -640$

$(1)(b) \quad \underline{25N_Q + 10N_D = 955}$

$ 15N_Q = 315$

$ N_Q = \mathbf{21}$

(a) $N_Q + N_D = 64$

$ 21 + N_D = 64$

$ N_D = \mathbf{43}$

4. N, $N + 2$, $N + 4$

$$-7(5 + N + 2) = 5[-(N + 4)] + 11$$
$$-49 - 7N = -5N - 9$$
$$-2N = 40$$
$$N = -20$$

Thus the integers are **–20, –18,** and **–16.**

5.
$$\frac{17}{100} \cdot T = 3825$$
$$\frac{100}{17} \cdot \frac{17}{100} \cdot T = 3825 \cdot \frac{100}{17}$$
$$T = \mathbf{22{,}500}$$

6. (a) $P(2) = \dfrac{1}{36}$

(b) $P(> 2) = \dfrac{36 - 1}{36} = \dfrac{35}{36}$

7. $m = \dfrac{-3 - 5}{-4 - 2} = \dfrac{-8}{-6} = \dfrac{4}{3}$

Using $(2, 5)$,

$$y = \frac{4}{3}x + b$$
$$5 = \frac{4}{3}(2) + b$$
$$5 = \frac{8}{3} + b$$
$$b = \frac{7}{3}$$

$$y = \frac{4}{3}x + \frac{7}{3}$$

8. $m = \dfrac{-2 - 5}{-2 - 5} = \dfrac{-7}{-7} = 1$

Using $(5, 5)$,

$$y = x + b$$
$$5 = 5 + b$$
$$b = 0$$

$$y = x$$

9. $ab + 15 + 5a + 3b = ab + 5a + 3b + 15$
$= a(b + 5) + 3(b + 5) = \mathbf{(a + 3)(b + 5)}$

10. $ay + xy + ac + xc = y(a + x) + c(a + x)$
$= \mathbf{(a + x)(y + c)}$

11. $3mx - 2p + 3px - 2m = 3mx + 3px - 2m - 2p$
$= 3x(m + p) - 2(m + p) = \mathbf{(3x - 2)(m + p)}$

12. $kx - 15 - 5k + 3x = kx - 5k + 3x - 15$
$= k(x - 5) + 3(x - 5) = \mathbf{(x - 5)(k + 3)}$

13. $xpc + pc^2 + 4x + 4c = pc(x + c) + 4(x + c)$
$= \mathbf{(x + c)(pc + 4)}$

14. $acb - ack + 2b - 2k = ac(b - k) + 2(b - k)$
$= \mathbf{(b - k)(ac + 2)}$

15. $(m, y \neq 0)$

$$\frac{x}{y} + \frac{1}{m} = p$$
$$my\left(\frac{x}{y}\right) + my\left(\frac{1}{m}\right) = myp$$
$$mx + y = myp$$
$$y - myp = -mx$$
$$y(1 - mp) = -mx$$
$$y = \frac{(-1)mx}{(-1)(mp - 1)}$$
$$y = \frac{mx}{mp - 1}$$

$(mp - 1 \neq 0)$

16. $(m, c \neq 0)$

$$\frac{k}{m} + \frac{1}{c} = x$$
$$mc\left(\frac{k}{m}\right) + mc\left(\frac{1}{c}\right) = mcx$$
$$ck + m = mcx$$
$$ck - mcx = -m$$
$$c(k - mx) = -m$$
$$c = \frac{(-1)m}{(-1)(mx - k)}$$
$$c = \frac{m}{mx - k}$$

$(mx - k \neq 0)$

17. $(b, x \neq 0)$

$$\frac{1}{b} + \frac{k}{x} = y$$
$$bx\left(\frac{1}{b}\right) + bx\left(\frac{k}{x}\right) = bxy$$
$$x + bk = bxy$$
$$bk - bxy = -x$$
$$b(k - xy) = -x$$
$$b = \frac{(-1)x}{(-1)(xy - k)}$$
$$b = \frac{x}{xy - k}$$

$(xy - k \neq 0)$

18. $(m, c, y \neq 0)$

$$\frac{1}{m} + \frac{b}{c} = \frac{x}{y}$$

$$mcy\left(\frac{1}{m}\right) + mcy\left(\frac{b}{c}\right) = mcy\left(\frac{x}{y}\right)$$

$$cy + bmy = mcx$$

$$bmy - mcx = -cy$$

$$m(by - cx) = -cy$$

$$m = \frac{(-1)cy}{(-1)(cx - yb)}$$

$$m = \frac{cy}{cx - yb}$$

$(cx - yb \neq 0)$

19. $-|x| + 4 > 2$

$$-|x| > -2$$

$$|x| < 2$$

(number line from -3 to 3 with open circles at -2 and 2, segment between)

20. $(x \neq 0)$

$$\frac{12}{x} + \frac{1}{4x} = 7$$

$$4x\left(\frac{12}{x}\right) + 4x\left(\frac{1}{4x}\right) = 4x(7)$$

$$48 + 1 = 28x$$

$$49 = 28x$$

$$x = \frac{49}{28}$$

$$x = \frac{7}{4}$$

21. $(x \neq 0, -11)$

$$\frac{9}{4x} = \frac{5}{x + 11}$$

$$4x(x + 11)\left(\frac{9}{4x}\right) = 4x(x + 11)\left(\frac{5}{x + 11}\right)$$

$$9(x + 11) = 5(4x)$$

$$9x + 99 = 20x$$

$$99 = 11x$$

$$x = 9$$

22.

$$\frac{4}{x^2 - 25} - \frac{x}{x - 5}$$

$$= \frac{4}{(x + 5)(x - 5)} - \frac{x}{x - 5}$$

$$= \frac{4}{(x + 5)(x - 5)} - \frac{x(x + 5)}{(x + 5)(x - 5)}$$

$$= \frac{4 - x(x + 5)}{(x - 5)(x + 5)}$$

23.

$$\frac{3x}{x^2 - x - 6} - \frac{3}{x - 3}$$

$$= \frac{3x}{(x - 3)(x + 2)} - \frac{3}{x - 3}$$

$$= \frac{3x}{(x - 3)(x + 2)} - \frac{3(x + 2)}{(x - 3)(x + 2)}$$

$$= \frac{3x - 3x - 6}{(x - 3)(x + 2)} = -\frac{6}{(x + 2)(x - 3)}$$

24. (a) $\sqrt{11} = 3.31\boxed{6}624...$

3.317

(b) $\boxed{4}5{,}732.654654654...$

50,000

(c) $0.\boxed{5}555...$

0.6

25. $3\sqrt{30{,}000} - 5\sqrt{27} + 5\sqrt{3}(2\sqrt{3} - 2)$

$$= 3\sqrt{10{,}000}\sqrt{3} - 5\sqrt{9}\sqrt{3} + 10(3) - 10\sqrt{3}$$

$$= 300\sqrt{3} - 15\sqrt{3} + 30 - 10\sqrt{3}$$

$$= \mathbf{275\sqrt{3} + 30}$$

26. (a) $\dfrac{6x + 6}{6} = \dfrac{6(x + 1)}{6} = x + 1$

(b) $\dfrac{-3^{-2}}{(-2)^2} = \dfrac{-1}{3^2(-2)^2} = \dfrac{-1}{9(4)} = -\dfrac{1}{36}$

27. $k^2 + 10^2 = 15^2$

$$k^2 + 100 = 225$$

$$k^2 = 125$$

$$k = \sqrt{125}$$

$$k = \sqrt{25}\sqrt{5}$$

$$k = \mathbf{5\sqrt{5}}$$

28.

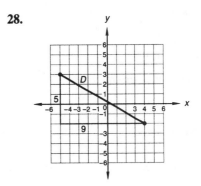

$$D^2 = 9^2 + 5^2$$

$$D^2 = 81 + 25$$

$$D^2 = 106$$

$$D = \sqrt{\mathbf{106}}$$

29. $x = \dfrac{-(-3) \pm \sqrt{(-3)^2 - 4(1)(2)}}{2(1)} = \dfrac{3 \pm \sqrt{9 - 8}}{2}$

$ = \dfrac{3 \pm 1}{2} = \mathbf{1, 2}$

c. $m = -\dfrac{2}{5}$

Using $(2, 3)$,

$$y = -\dfrac{2}{5}x + b$$

$$3 = -\dfrac{2}{5}(2) + b$$

$$3 = -\dfrac{4}{5} + b$$

$$b = \dfrac{19}{5}$$

$$y = -\dfrac{2}{5}x + \dfrac{19}{5}$$

30. *S.A.* $= 2(\text{Area}_{\text{base}}) + \text{Lateral Surface Area}$

$ = 2[(3 \text{ in.} \times 7 \text{ in.}) + (6 \text{ in.} \times 2 \text{ in.})$

$ + (4 \text{ in.} \times 7 \text{ in.})]$

$ + (\text{Perimeter}_{\text{base}})(\text{Height})$

$ = 2(21 \text{ in.}^2 + 12 \text{ in.}^2 + 28 \text{ in.}^2)$

$ + (50 \text{ in.})(17 \text{ in.})$

$ = 2(61 \text{ in.}^2) + 850 \text{ in.}^2$

$ = 122 \text{ in.}^2 + 850 \text{ in.}^2$

$ = \mathbf{972 \text{ in.}^2}$

d. $m = \dfrac{1}{4}$

Using $(-3, 7)$,

$$y = \dfrac{1}{4}x + b$$

$$7 = \dfrac{1}{4}(-3) + b$$

$$7 = -\dfrac{3}{4} + b$$

$$b = \dfrac{31}{4}$$

$$y = \dfrac{1}{4}x + \dfrac{31}{4}$$

Practice 107

a. $y = -3x + 1$

The slopes of parallel lines are equivalent.

Using $(-1, 2)$,

$$y = -3x + b$$

$$2 = -3(-1) + b$$

$$2 = 3 + b$$

$$b = -1$$

$$y = -3x - 1$$

Problem Set 107

1. $D_B = D_T$

$ R_B T_B = R_T T_T$

$ R_B = 20$

$ R_T = 8$

$ T_B + T_T = 14$

$ T_B = -T_T + 14$

$ R_B T_B = R_T T_T$

$ 20(-T_T + 14) = 8T_T$

$ -20T_T + 280 = 8T_T$

$ -28T_T = -280$

$ T_T = 10$

$D_T = R_T T_T = 8(10) = \mathbf{80 \text{ mi}}$

b. $3x + 2y = 5$

$ 2y = -3x + 5$

$ y = -\dfrac{3}{2}x + \dfrac{5}{2}$

The slopes of parallel lines are equivalent.

Using $(-2, -3)$,

$$y = -\dfrac{3}{2}x + b$$

$$-3 = -\dfrac{3}{2}(-2) + b$$

$$-3 = 3 + b$$

$$b = -6$$

$$y = -\dfrac{3}{2}x - 6$$

2. $D_E = D_S + 36$

$R_E T_E = R_S T_S + 36$

$T_E = T_S = 3$

$R_E = 2R_S$

$R_E T_E = R_S T_S + 36$

$3(2R_S) = 3R_S + 36$

$6R_S = 3R_S + 36$

$3R_S = 36$

$R_S = 12$

$R_E = 2R_S = 2(12) = \mathbf{24\ mph}$

3. $\dfrac{40}{100} \cdot T = 20$

$\dfrac{100}{40} \cdot \dfrac{40}{100} \cdot T = 20 \cdot \dfrac{100}{40}$

$T = \mathbf{\$50}$

4. (a) $N_D = 400 + N_Q$

(b) $10N_D + 25N_Q = 7500$

(b) $10N_D + 25N_Q = 7500$

$10(400 + N_Q) + 25N_Q = 7500$

$4000 + 10N_Q + 25N_Q = 7500$

$35N_Q = 3500$

$N_Q = \mathbf{100}$

(a) $N_D = 400 + N_Q$

$N_D = 400 + 100$

$N_D = \mathbf{500}$

5. $N,\ N + 2,\ N + 4$

$-7[N + (N + 4)] = 11[-(N + 2)] + 27$

$-14N - 28 = -11N + 5$

$-3N = 33$

$N = -11$

Thus the integers are **–11, –9,** and **–7.**

6. $y = 2x + 1$

The slopes of parallel lines are equivalent.

Using $(-2, 3)$,

$y = 2x + b$

$3 = 2(-2) + b$

$3 = -4 + b$

$b = 7$

$\mathbf{y = 2x + 7}$

7. $y = -\dfrac{1}{2}x - 3$

The slopes of parallel lines are equivalent.

Using $(0, 1)$,

$y = -\dfrac{1}{2}x + b$

$1 = -\dfrac{1}{2}(0) + b$

$b = 1$

$\mathbf{y = -\dfrac{1}{2}x + 1}$

8. $m = \dfrac{-3 - (-2)}{5 - (-3)} = -\dfrac{1}{8}$

Using $(-3, -2)$,

$y = -\dfrac{1}{8}x + b$

$-2 = -\dfrac{1}{8}(-3) + b$

$-2 = \dfrac{3}{8} + b$

$b = -\dfrac{19}{8}$

$\mathbf{y = -\dfrac{1}{8}x - \dfrac{19}{8}}$

9. $m = \dfrac{0 - (-1)}{0 - 5} = -\dfrac{1}{5}$

Using $(0, 0)$,

$y = -\dfrac{1}{5}x + b$

$0 = -\dfrac{1}{5}(0) + b$

$b = 0$

$\mathbf{y = -\dfrac{1}{5}x}$

10.

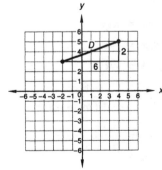

$D^2 = 6^2 + 2^2$

$D^2 = 36 + 4$

$D^2 = 40$

$D = \sqrt{40}$

$D = \sqrt{4}\sqrt{10}$

$D = \mathbf{2\sqrt{10}}$

11. $km^2 + 2c - 2m^2 - kc = km^2 - 2m^2 - kc + 2c$

$= m^2(k - 2) - c(k - 2) = \left(m^2 - c\right)(k - 2)$

12. $6a - xya - xyb + 6b = 6a + 6b - xya - xyb$

$= 6(a + b) - xy(a + b) = (a + b)(6 - xy)$

13. $abx - 2yc + xc - 2yab$

$= abx + xc - 2yab - 2yc$

$= x(ab + c) - 2y(ab + c) = (x - 2y)(ab + c)$

14. $4xn + abn - abm - 4xm$

$= 4xn - 4xm + abn - abm$

$= 4x(n - m) + ab(n - m)$

$= (n - m)(4x + ab)$

15. $(c, x \neq 0)$

$$\frac{a}{c} - \frac{1}{x} = b$$

$$cx\left(\frac{a}{c}\right) - cx\left(\frac{1}{x}\right) = cxb$$

$$ax - c = cxb$$

$$ax = cxb + c$$

$$ax = c(xb + 1)$$

$$c = \frac{xa}{xb + 1}$$

$(xb + 1 \neq 0)$

16. $(m, y \neq 0)$

$$\frac{k}{m} + \frac{x}{y} = p$$

$$my\left(\frac{k}{m}\right) + my\left(\frac{x}{y}\right) = myp$$

$$yk + mx = myp$$

$$mx - myp = -yk$$

$$m(x - yp) = -yk$$

$$m = \frac{(-1)yk}{(-1)(py - x)}$$

$$m = \frac{yk}{py - x}$$

$(py - x \neq 0)$

17. $-4 - |x| \leq -4$

$-|x| \leq 0$

$|x| \geq 0$

18. $(y \neq 0, 2)$

$$\frac{7}{y} + \frac{3}{y - 2} = 0$$

$$y(y - 2)\left(\frac{7}{y}\right) + y(y - 2)\left(\frac{3}{y - 2}\right) = 0$$

$$7(y - 2) + 3y = 0$$

$$7y - 14 + 3y = 0$$

$$10y - 14 = 0$$

$$10y = 14$$

$$y = \frac{14}{10}$$

$$y = \frac{7}{5}$$

19. $(x \neq 0)$

$$\frac{x - 2}{3x} = \frac{4}{x} - \frac{1}{5}$$

$$15x\left(\frac{x - 2}{3x}\right) = 15x\left(\frac{4}{x}\right) - 15x\left(\frac{1}{5}\right)$$

$$5(x - 2) = 15(4) - 3x$$

$$5x - 10 = 60 - 3x$$

$$8x = 70$$

$$x = \frac{70}{8}$$

$$x = \frac{35}{4}$$

20. (a) $\sqrt{30} = 5.4\textcircled{7}722...$

5.48

(b) $4\textcircled{3}49.3766$

4300

(c) $\frac{3}{7} = 0.428\textcircled{5}71...$

0.4286

21. (c)

22. $\dfrac{9}{x^2 - 81} - \dfrac{x}{x - 9}$

$= \dfrac{9}{(x - 9)(x + 9)} - \dfrac{x}{x - 9}$

$= \dfrac{9}{(x - 9)(x + 9)} - \dfrac{x(x + 9)}{(x - 9)(x + 9)}$

$= \dfrac{9 - x(x + 9)}{(x - 9)(x + 9)}$

23.
$$120 = -22x - x^2$$
$$x^2 + 22x + 120 = 0$$
$$(x + 12)(x + 10) = 0$$
If $x + 12 = 0$ If $x + 10 = 0$
$$x = -12 \qquad x = -10$$

24.
$$\frac{(21{,}000 \times 10^{-42})(7{,}000{,}000)}{(0.0003 \times 10^{-21})(700 \times 10^{15})}$$
$$= \frac{(2.1 \times 10^{-38})(7 \times 10^6)}{(3 \times 10^{-25})(7 \times 10^{17})}$$
$$= \frac{2.1 \cdot 7}{3 \cdot 7} \times \frac{10^{-38} \cdot 10^6}{10^{-25} \cdot 10^{17}}$$
$$= \frac{14.7}{21} \times \frac{10^{-32}}{10^{-8}}$$
$$= 0.7 \times 10^{-24} = 7 \times 10^{-25}$$

25.
$$\sqrt{15} + 2\sqrt{3} \cdot 5\sqrt{5} + 2\sqrt{15}(\sqrt{15} - 3)$$
$$= \sqrt{15} + 10\sqrt{15} + 30 - 6\sqrt{15}$$
$$= 5\sqrt{15} + 30$$

26. $x^0 - 3x(2 - 4^0) - (-3) - 2(x - 3) = 3x - (-4)$
$$1 - 6x + 3x + 3 - 2x + 6 = 3x + 4$$
$$-5x + 10 = 3x + 4$$
$$-8x = -6$$
$$x = \frac{-6}{-8}$$
$$x = \frac{3}{4}$$

27. $\dfrac{a}{3} - 3 = 9 \qquad 4c + 11 = 9$
$$\qquad\qquad 4c = -2$$
$$\frac{a}{3} = 12 \qquad c = -\frac{1}{2}$$
$$a = 36$$
$$x = \frac{-b \pm \sqrt{b^2 - 4ac}}{2a}$$
$$= \frac{-7 \pm \sqrt{(7)^2 - 4(36)\left(-\frac{1}{2}\right)}}{2(36)} = \frac{-7 \pm \sqrt{49 + 72}}{72}$$
$$= \frac{-7 \pm \sqrt{121}}{72} = \frac{-7 \pm 11}{72} = \frac{-18}{72}, \frac{4}{72}$$
$$= -\frac{1}{4}, \frac{1}{18}$$

28. (a) $\dfrac{-3^{-2}}{-(-3)^{-3}} = \dfrac{-(-3)^3}{-3^2} = \dfrac{27}{-9} = -3$

(b) $\dfrac{6xy + 6xy^2}{6xy} = \dfrac{6xy(1 + y)}{6xy} = 1 + y$

29. $V = \dfrac{4}{3}\pi r^3$
$$= \frac{4}{3}\pi(5 \text{ cm})^3$$
$$= \frac{500\pi}{3} \text{ cm}^3 = 523.33 \text{ cm}^3$$

30. $V = \dfrac{1}{3}(\text{Area}_{base})(\text{Height})$
$$= \frac{1}{3}\left[\pi(5 \text{ m})^2\right](11 \text{ m})$$
$$= \frac{1}{3}(25\pi \text{ m}^2)(11 \text{ m})$$
$$= \frac{275\pi}{3} \text{ m}^3 = 287.83 \text{ m}^3$$

Practice 108

a. $\sqrt{x - 6} - 3 = 0$
$$\sqrt{x - 6} = 3$$
$$(\sqrt{x - 6})^2 = (3)^2$$
$$x - 6 = 9$$
$$x = 15$$
Check $x = 15$:
$$\sqrt{15 - 6} - 3 = 0$$
$$\sqrt{9} - 3 = 0$$
$$3 - 3 = 0$$
$$0 = 0 \quad \text{Check}$$
$x = 15$

b. $\sqrt{x - 6} - 6 + x = 0$
$$\sqrt{x - 6} = -x + 6$$
$$(\sqrt{x - 6})^2 = (-x + 6)^2$$
$$x - 6 = x^2 - 12x + 36$$
$$-x^2 + 13x - 42 = 0$$
$$(-1)(x^2 - 13x + 42) = 0$$
$$(x - 6)(x - 7) = 0$$
$$x = 6 \quad \text{or} \quad x = 7$$
Check $x = 6$:
$$\sqrt{6 - 6} - 6 + 6 = 0$$
$$\sqrt{0} + 0 = 0$$
$$0 = 0 \quad \text{Check}$$
Check $x = 7$:
$$\sqrt{7 - 6} - 6 + 7 = 0$$
$$\sqrt{1} + 1 = 0$$
$$1 + 1 = 0$$
$$2 \neq 0 \quad \text{Does not check}$$
$x = 6$

Problem Set 108

1. $D_W = D_R$

$R_W T_W = R_R T_R$

$R_W = 2$

$R_R = 10$

$T_W + T_R = 18$

$\qquad T_W = -T_R + 18$

$\qquad R_W T_W = R_R T_R$

$2(-T_R + 18) = 10T_R$

$-2T_R + 36 = 10T_R$

$\qquad -12T_R = -36$

$\qquad T_R = 3$

$D_R = R_R T_R = (10)(3) = \mathbf{30\ mi}$

2. $D_B = D_R + 6$

$R_B T_B = R_R T_R + 6$

$R_B = 10$

$T_B = T_R = 3$

$R_B T_B = R_R T_R + 6$

$10(3) = R_R(3) + 6$

$30 = 3R_R + 6$

$-3R_R = -24$

$\qquad R_R = \mathbf{8\ mph}$

3. (a) $N_G + N_P = 123$

(b) $400N_G + 3N_P = 21{,}013$

$(-3)(a) \quad -3N_G - 3N_P = \quad -369$

$(1)(b) \quad \dfrac{400N_G + 3N_P = 21{,}013}{397N_G \qquad = 20{,}644}$

$\qquad\qquad N_G = \mathbf{52}$

(a) $N_G + N_P = 123$

$52 + N_P = 123$

$\qquad N_P = \mathbf{71}$

4. (a) $N_R + N_G = 178$

(b) $N_R = N_G + 8$

(a) $\qquad N_R + N_G = 178$

$(N_G + 8) + N_G = 178$

$\qquad 2N_G + 8 = 178$

$\qquad 2N_G = 170$

$\qquad N_G = \mathbf{85}$

5. (a) $P(\text{silver, then gold}) = \dfrac{6}{9} \cdot \dfrac{3}{9} = \dfrac{18}{81} = \dfrac{2}{9}$

(b) $P(\text{silver, then gold}) = \dfrac{6}{9} \cdot \dfrac{3}{8} = \dfrac{18}{72} = \dfrac{1}{4}$

6. Weighted Average $= \dfrac{10(76) + 10(94)}{10 + 10}$

$\qquad\qquad\qquad = \dfrac{1700}{20} = \mathbf{85}$

7. $\sqrt{x^2 + 11} - 9 = 0$

$\qquad \sqrt{x^2 + 11} = 9$

$\qquad \left(\sqrt{x^2 + 11}\right)^2 = (9)^2$

$\qquad x^2 + 11 = 81$

$\qquad x^2 = 70$

$\qquad x = \pm\sqrt{70}$

Check $x = -\sqrt{70}$:

$\sqrt{(-\sqrt{70})^2 + 11} - 9 = 0$

$\sqrt{70 + 11} - 9 = 0$

$\sqrt{81} - 9 = 0$

$9 - 9 = 0$

$0 = 0 \quad$ Check

Check $x = \sqrt{70}$:

$\sqrt{(\sqrt{70})^2 + 11} - 9 = 0$

$\sqrt{70 + 11} - 9 = 0$

$\sqrt{81} - 9 = 0$

$9 - 9 = 0$

$0 = 0 \quad$ Check

$x = \mathbf{-\sqrt{70}, \sqrt{70}}$

8. $\sqrt{x - 3} - 4 = 0$

$\qquad \sqrt{x - 3} = 4$

$\qquad (\sqrt{x - 3})^2 = (4)^2$

$\qquad x - 3 = 16$

$\qquad x = 19$

Check $x = 19$:

$\sqrt{19 - 3} - 4 = 0$

$\sqrt{16} - 4 = 0$

$4 - 4 = 0$

$0 = 0 \quad$ Check

$x = \mathbf{19}$

9. $\sqrt{4x - 5} = \sqrt{x + 4}$

$(\sqrt{4x - 5})^2 = (\sqrt{x + 4})^2$

$4x - 5 = x + 4$

$3x = 9$

$x = 3$

Check $x = 3$:

$\sqrt{4(3) - 5} = \sqrt{3 + 4}$

$\sqrt{12 - 5} = \sqrt{7}$

$\sqrt{7} = \sqrt{7}$ Check

$x = 3$

10. $\sqrt{x + 1} + x - 11 = 0$

$\sqrt{x + 1} = -x + 11$

$(\sqrt{x + 1})^2 = (-x + 11)^2$

$x + 1 = x^2 - 22x + 121$

$-x^2 + 23x - 120 = 0$

$(-1)(x^2 - 23x + 120) = 0$

$(x - 15)(x - 8) = 0$

$x = 15$ or $x = 8$

Check $x = 15$:

$\sqrt{15 + 1} + 15 - 11 = 0$

$\sqrt{16} + 4 = 0$

$4 + 4 = 0$

$8 \neq 0$ Does not check

Check $x = 8$:

$\sqrt{8 + 1} + 8 - 11 = 0$

$\sqrt{9} - 3 = 0$

$3 - 3 = 0$

$0 = 0$ Check

$x = 8$

11. $y = -3x + 1$

The slopes of parallel lines are equivalent.

Using $(-1, 2)$,

$y = -3x + b$

$2 = -3(-1) + b$

$2 = 3 + b$

$b = -1$

$y = -3x - 1$

12. $m = \dfrac{-7 - 2}{-5 - 4} = \dfrac{-9}{-9} = 1$

Using $(4, 2)$,

$y = x + b$

$2 = 4 + b$

$b = -2$

$y = x - 2$

13. $rt^2 + 3m + 3r + t^2m = rt^2 + t^2m + 3r + 3m$

$= t^2(r + m) + 3(r + m) = (m + r)(t^2 + 3)$

14. $6c - xyc - xyd + 6d = 6c + 6d - xyc - xyd$

$= 6(c + d) - xy(c + d) = (c + d)(6 - xy)$

15. $(c, y \neq 0)$

$$\frac{x}{y} - \frac{1}{c} - d = k$$

$$cy\left(\frac{x}{y}\right) - cy\left(\frac{1}{c}\right) - cdy = cky$$

$$cx - y - cdy = cky$$

$$cx = y + cdy + cky$$

$$cx = y(1 + cd + ck)$$

$$y = \frac{cx}{ck + 1 + cd}$$

$(ck + 1 + cd \neq 0)$

16. $\dfrac{x}{3} - \dfrac{2 + x}{5} = -3$

$15 \cdot \dfrac{x}{3} - 15 \cdot \dfrac{(2 + x)}{5} = 15 \cdot (-3)$

$5x - 3(2 + x) = -45$

$2x - 6 = -45$

$2x = -39$

$x = -\dfrac{39}{2}$

17. (a) $\dfrac{\pi}{6} = 0.52\overset{\downarrow}{\textcircled{3}}598\ldots$

0.524

(b) $0.037\overset{\downarrow}{\textcircled{4}}374\ldots$

0.0374

(c) $\sqrt{169} = \overset{\downarrow}{\textcircled{1}}3$

10

18. $c^2 + 5^2 = 9^2$

$\qquad c^2 + 25 = 81$

$\qquad\qquad c^2 = 56$

$\qquad\qquad\; c = \sqrt{56}$

$\qquad\qquad\; c = \sqrt{4}\sqrt{14}$

$\qquad\qquad\; c = \mathbf{2\sqrt{14}}$

19. (a) $y = -4$

(b) The desired equation is $y = mx + b$.

By inspection, $b = 2$.

By inspection, the sign of m is +.

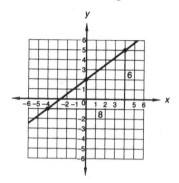

$|m| = \dfrac{6}{8} = \dfrac{3}{4}$

So $b = 2$ and $m = \dfrac{3}{4}$.

$y = \dfrac{3}{4}x + 2$

20. $\dfrac{y^{-1}}{x} + \dfrac{3}{yx} - \dfrac{2}{x+y} = \dfrac{1}{xy} + \dfrac{3}{xy} - \dfrac{2}{x+y}$

$= \dfrac{(x+y)}{xy(x+y)} + \dfrac{3(x+y)}{xy(x+y)} - \dfrac{2xy}{xy(x+y)}$

$= \dfrac{4(x+y) - 2xy}{xy(x+y)}$

21. $\dfrac{3x+2}{x-4} - \dfrac{2x}{x^2-16}$

$= \dfrac{3x+2}{x-4} - \dfrac{2x}{(x-4)(x+4)}$

$= \dfrac{(3x+2)(x+4)}{(x-4)(x+4)} - \dfrac{2x}{(x-4)(x+4)}$

$= \dfrac{3x^2 + 12x + 2x + 8 - 2x}{(x-4)(x+4)}$

$= \dfrac{3x^2 + 12x + 8}{(x-4)(x+4)}$

22. $\begin{cases} y = 3x \\ y = -x + 4 \end{cases}$

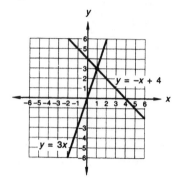

$\begin{array}{ll} y = 3x & y = -x + 4 \\ 3 = 3(1) & 3 = -1 + 4 \\ 3 = 3 & 3 = 3 \end{array}$

The solution to the linear equations is **(1, 3)**.

23. $\dfrac{x^2 - 25}{x^2 - 12x + 35} \div \dfrac{x^2 + x - 6}{x^2 - 4x - 21}$

$= \dfrac{x^2 - 25}{x^2 - 12x + 35} \cdot \dfrac{x^2 - 4x - 21}{x^2 + x - 6}$

$= \dfrac{(x-5)(x+5)}{(x-5)(x-7)} \cdot \dfrac{(x-7)(x+3)}{(x+3)(x-2)} = \dfrac{x+5}{x-2}$

24. $(2x^3 + 3x^2 + 5x + 4) \div (x - 1)$

$$
\begin{array}{r}
2x^2 + 5x + 10 \\
x - 1 \overline{\smash{\big)}\, 2x^3 + 3x^2 + 5x + 4} \\
\underline{2x^3 - 2x^2 } \\
5x^2 + 5x \\
\underline{5x^2 - 5x } \\
10x + 4 \\
\underline{10x - 10} \\
14
\end{array}
$$

$2x^2 + 5x + 10 + \dfrac{14}{x-1}$

25. $D = \{x \in \mathbb{R} \mid -4 < x \le 6\}$

$R = \{y \in \mathbb{R} \mid -3 \le y \le 3\}$

26. $\dfrac{xz^{-1} - z^{-2}}{az^{-1} - 3xz^{-2}} = \dfrac{\dfrac{x}{z} - \dfrac{1}{z^2}}{\dfrac{a}{z} - \dfrac{3x}{z^2}} = \dfrac{\dfrac{xz}{z^2} - \dfrac{1}{z^2}}{\dfrac{az}{z^2} - \dfrac{3x}{z^2}}$

$= \dfrac{\dfrac{xz-1}{z^2} \cdot \dfrac{z^2}{az-3x}}{\dfrac{az-3x}{z^2} \cdot \dfrac{z^2}{az-3x}} = \dfrac{xz-1}{az-3x} = \dfrac{zx-1}{az-3x}$

27. $-\left[\left(-2^0\right)\left(-3^2\right) - (-2) - \sqrt[5]{-32}\right]$
$\quad - [-3(-5 + 7)]$

$= -\left[(-1)(-9) + 2 + 2\right] + 3(2)$

$= -(9 + 2 + 2) + 6$

$= -13 + 6 = \mathbf{-7}$

28. $\dfrac{a}{7} - 3 = 0 \qquad\qquad 8c + 13 = 7$

$\qquad\qquad\qquad\qquad\qquad 8c = -6$

$\qquad \dfrac{a}{7} = 3$

$\qquad\qquad\qquad\qquad\qquad c = -\dfrac{3}{4}$

$\qquad a = 21$

$x = \dfrac{-b \pm \sqrt{b^2 - 4ac}}{2a}$

$= \dfrac{-(-9) \pm \sqrt{(-9)^2 - 4(21)\left(-\dfrac{3}{4}\right)}}{2(21)}$

$= \dfrac{9 \pm \sqrt{81 + 63}}{42} = \dfrac{9 \pm \sqrt{144}}{42} = \dfrac{9 \pm 12}{42}$

$= \dfrac{-3}{42}, \dfrac{21}{42} = \mathbf{-\dfrac{1}{14}, \dfrac{1}{2}}$

29. $A = \dfrac{1}{2}(8 \text{ in.} \times 6 \text{ in.}) + (2 \text{ in.} \times 6 \text{ in.})$

$\qquad + \dfrac{1}{2}\pi(3 \text{ in.})^2$

$= \dfrac{1}{2}\left(48 \text{ in.}^2\right) + 12 \text{ in.}^2 + \dfrac{9\pi}{2} \text{ in.}^2$

$= 24 \text{ in.}^2 + 12 \text{ in.}^2 + \dfrac{9\pi}{2} \text{ in.}^2$

$= \left(36 + \dfrac{9\pi}{2}\right) \text{ in.}^2 = \mathbf{50.13 \text{ in.}^2}$

30. $S.A. = \text{Area}_{\text{base}} + \text{Lateral Surface Area}$

$= (18 \text{ ft} \times 18 \text{ ft}) + 4\left[\dfrac{1}{2}(18 \text{ ft} \times 15 \text{ ft})\right]$

$= 324 \text{ ft}^2 + 4\left(135 \text{ ft}^2\right)$

$= 324 \text{ ft}^2 + 540 \text{ ft}^2$

$= \mathbf{864 \text{ ft}^2}$

Practice 109

a. $-11x - 21 + 2x^2 = 2x^2 - 11x - 21$

$\qquad\qquad\qquad\qquad = (2x \quad)(x \quad)$

$\qquad\qquad\qquad\qquad = (2x + 3)(x - 7)$

b. $3x^2 + 5x - 2$

$= (3x \quad)(x \quad)$

$= (3x - 1)(x + 2)$

Problem Set 109

1. $D_C = D_H$

$R_C T_C = R_H T_H$

$R_C = 8$

$R_H = 6$

$T_C + T_H = 7$

$\qquad T_C = -T_H + 7$

$\qquad R_C T_C = R_H T_H$

$\quad 8\left(-T_H + 7\right) = 6T_H$

$\quad -8T_H + 56 = 6T_H$

$\qquad -14T_H = -56$

$\qquad T_H = 4$

$D_H = R_H T_H = 6(4) = \mathbf{24 \text{ mi}}$

2. $D_N + D_S = 880$

$R_N T_N + R_S T_S = 880$

$R_N = 40$

$R_S = 60$

$T_N = T_S + 2$

$\qquad R_N T_N + R_S T_S = 880$

$\quad 40\left(T_S + 2\right) + 60T_S = 880$

$\qquad\quad 100T_S + 80 = 880$

$\qquad\qquad\quad 100T_S = 800$

$\qquad\qquad\qquad T_S = 8$

6 a.m. + 8 hr = **2 p.m.**

3. (a) $N_S + N_L = 125$

(b) $3N_S + 5N_L = 475$

$(-3)(a) \quad -3N_S - 3N_L = -375$

$(1)(b) \quad \underline{3N_S + 5N_L = \quad 475}$

$\qquad\qquad\qquad 2N_L = \quad 100$

$\qquad\qquad\qquad N_L = \mathbf{50}$

(a) $N_S + N_L = 125$

$\quad N_S + 50 = 125$

$\qquad N_S = \mathbf{75}$

4. $N, N + 2, N + 4$

$-3[N + 2(N + 4)] = 8[-(N + 2)] - 3$

$\qquad -3(3N + 8) = -8N - 16 - 3$

$\qquad -9N - 24 = -8N - 19$

$\qquad\qquad -N = 5$

$\qquad\qquad N = -5$

Thus the integers are **–5, –3,** and **–1.**

5. $\dfrac{N_B}{N_M} = \dfrac{13}{5}$

$\dfrac{N_B}{T} = \dfrac{13}{18}$

$\dfrac{N_B}{2610} = \dfrac{13}{18}$

$18 N_B = 13(2610)$

$N_B = \dfrac{13(2610)}{18}$

$N_B = \mathbf{1885}$

$N_M + N_B = T$

$N_M + 1885 = 2610$

$N_M = \mathbf{725}$

6. $\dfrac{300}{2500} = P$

$P = \dfrac{3}{25}$

$P = \dfrac{12}{100}$

$P = \mathbf{12\%}$

7. $3x^2 - 14x - 5 = \mathbf{(3x + 1)(x - 5)}$

8. $2x^2 + 8 + 10x = 2x^2 + 10x + 8$
$= 2(x^2 + 5x + 4) = \mathbf{2(x + 4)(x + 1)}$

9. $18 - 15x + 2x^2 = 2x^2 - 15x + 18$
$= \mathbf{(2x - 3)(x - 6)}$

10. $-15 + 7x + 2x^2 = 2x^2 + 7x - 15$
$= \mathbf{(2x - 3)(x + 5)}$

11. $8x - 24 + 2x^2 = 2x^2 + 8x - 24$
$= 2(x^2 + 4x - 12) = \mathbf{2(x + 6)(x - 2)}$

12. $2x^2 - 24 - 8x = 2x^2 - 8x - 24$
$= 2(x^2 - 4x - 12) = \mathbf{2(x - 6)(x + 2)}$

13. $2x^2 - 6x + 4 = 2(x^2 - 3x + 2)$
$= \mathbf{2(x - 2)(x - 1)}$

14. $2x^2 - 18 + 9x = 2x^2 + 9x - 18$
$= \mathbf{(2x - 3)(x + 6)}$

15. $2x^2 + 4 + 6x = 2x^2 + 6x + 4$
$= 2(x^2 + 3x + 2) = \mathbf{2(x + 2)(x + 1)}$

16. $\sqrt{x + 3} = x - 3$

$(\sqrt{x + 3})^2 = (x - 3)^2$

$x + 3 = x^2 - 6x + 9$

$-x^2 + 7x - 6 = 0$

$-1(x^2 - 7x + 6) = 0$

$(x - 6)(x - 1) = 0$

$x = 6 \quad$ or $\quad x = 1$

Check $x = 6$:

$\sqrt{6 + 3} = 6 - 3$

$\sqrt{9} = 3$

$3 = 3 \quad$ Check

Check $x = 1$:

$\sqrt{1 + 3} = 1 - 3$

$\sqrt{4} = -2$

$2 \neq -2 \quad$ Does not check

$x = \mathbf{6}$

17. $\sqrt{3x - 3} = \sqrt{x + 7}$

$(\sqrt{3x - 3})^2 = (\sqrt{x + 7})^2$

$3x - 3 = x + 7$

$2x = 10$

$x = 5$

Check $x = 5$:

$\sqrt{3(5) - 3} = \sqrt{5 + 7}$

$\sqrt{15 - 3} = \sqrt{12}$

$\sqrt{12} = \sqrt{12} \quad$ Check

$x = \mathbf{5}$

18. $y = -2x + b$

$-3 = -2(4) + b$

$-3 = -8 + b$

$b = 5$

$\mathbf{y = -2x + 5}$

19. $m = \dfrac{-3 - 5}{-4 - 2} = \dfrac{-8}{-6} = \dfrac{4}{3}$

$y = \dfrac{4}{3}x + b$

$5 = \dfrac{4}{3}(2) + b$

$5 = \dfrac{8}{3} + b$

$b = \dfrac{7}{3}$

$\mathbf{y = \dfrac{4}{3}x + \dfrac{7}{3}}$

20. $(c, x \neq 0)$

$$\frac{a}{c} + \frac{1}{x} = k$$

$$cx\left(\frac{a}{c}\right) + cx\left(\frac{1}{x}\right) = cxk$$

$$xa + c = kcx$$

$$xa - kcx = -c$$

$$x(a - kc) = -c$$

$$x = \frac{-c}{a - kc}$$

$$x = \frac{(-1)c}{(-1)(ck - a)}$$

$$x = \frac{c}{ck - a}$$

$(ck - a \neq 0)$

21. $y^2t - 12m + 3mt - 4y^2$

$= y^2t + 3mt - 4y^2 - 12m$

$= t(y^2 + 3m) - 4(y^2 + 3m)$

$= (t - 4)(y^2 + 3m)$

22. $xm + 4m + xy + 4y = m(x + 4) + y(x + 4)$

$= (m + y)(x + 4)$

23. $f^2 + 7^2 = 11^2$

$f^2 + 49 = 121$

$f^2 = 72$

$f = \sqrt{72}$

$f = \sqrt{36}\sqrt{2}$

$f = 6\sqrt{2}$

24. (a) $y = -4$

(b) The desired equation is $y = mx + b$.

By inspection, $b = 0$.

By inspection, the sign of m is $-$.

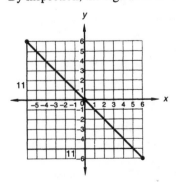

$|m| = \frac{11}{11} = 1$

So $b = 0$ and $m = -1$.

$y = -x$

25. $3 - |x| \geq 1$

$-|x| \geq -2$

$|x| \leq 2$

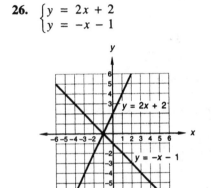

26. $\begin{cases} y = 2x + 2 \\ y = -x - 1 \end{cases}$

$y = 2x + 2 \qquad\qquad y = -x - 1$

$0 = 2(-1) + 2 \qquad 0 = -(-1) - 1$

$0 = -2 + 2 \qquad\qquad 0 = 1 - 1$

$0 = 0 \qquad\qquad\qquad 0 = 0$

The solution to the linear equations is $(-1, 0)$.

27. $(p \neq 0, 4)$

$$\frac{4}{p} - \frac{3}{p - 4} = 0$$

$$p(p - 4)\left(\frac{4}{p}\right) - p(p - 4)\left(\frac{3}{p - 4}\right) = 0$$

$$4(p - 4) - 3p = 0$$

$$4p - 16 - 3p = 0$$

$$p - 16 = 0$$

$$p = 16$$

28. $\dfrac{x^2 + 5x + 6}{x^3 + 7x^2 + 10x} \div \dfrac{x^3 + 11x^2 + 24x}{x^2 + 2x - 15}$

$= \dfrac{x^2 + 5x + 6}{x^3 + 7x^2 + 10x} \cdot \dfrac{x^2 + 2x - 15}{x^3 + 11x^2 + 24x}$

$= \dfrac{(x + 2)(x + 3)}{x(x + 5)(x + 2)} \cdot \dfrac{(x + 5)(x - 3)}{x(x + 8)(x + 3)}$

$= \dfrac{x - 3}{x^2(x + 8)}$

29. $\dfrac{a}{3} = \dfrac{16}{12}$　　　　$c - 9 = -13$

　　　　　　　　　　　$c = -4$

$12a = 3 \cdot 16$

$a = \dfrac{3 \cdot 16}{12}$

$a = 4$

$x = \dfrac{-b \pm \sqrt{b^2 - 4ac}}{2a}$

$= \dfrac{-(-6) \pm \sqrt{(-6)^2 - 4(4)(-4)}}{2(4)}$

$= \dfrac{6 \pm \sqrt{36 + 64}}{8} = \dfrac{6 \pm \sqrt{100}}{8} = \dfrac{6 \pm 10}{8}$

$= \dfrac{-4}{8}, \dfrac{16}{8} = -\dfrac{1}{2}, \mathbf{2}$

30. $V = \left(\text{Area}_{\text{base}}\right)(\text{Height})$

$= \Big[\dfrac{1}{2}(6 \text{ cm} \times 8 \text{ cm}) + (8 \text{ cm} \times 8 \text{ cm})$

$\quad + \dfrac{\pi(4 \text{ cm})^2}{2}\Big](18 \text{ cm})$

$= (24 \text{ cm}^2 + 64 \text{ cm}^2 + 8\pi \text{ cm}^2)(18 \text{ cm})$

$= (88 \text{ cm}^2 + 8\pi \text{ cm}^2)(18 \text{ cm})$

$= \mathbf{(1584 + 144\pi) \text{ cm}^3 = 2036.16 \text{ cm}^3}$

Practice 110

a. $f(x) = x^2 + 3$

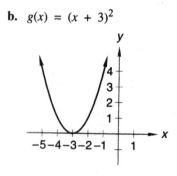

b. $g(x) = (x + 3)^2$

c. $h(x) = -x^2$

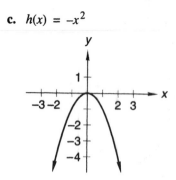

d. (3)

Problem Set 110

1.　$D_L = D_B + 30$

　　$R_L T_L = R_B T_B + 30$

　　$2R_B = R_L$

　　$T_B = T_L = 6$

　　　$R_L T_L = R_B T_B + 30$

　　$(2R_B)(6) = R_B(6) + 30$

　　　$12R_B = 6R_B + 30$

　　　　$6R_B = 30$

　　　　　$R_B = \mathbf{5 \text{ mph}}$

2.　$D_E = D_F + 20$

　　$R_E T_E = R_F T_F + 20$

　　$R_F = 40$

　　$R_E = 60$

　　$T_F = T_E + 2$

　　$R_E T_E = R_F T_F + 20$

　　$60T_E = 40(T_E + 2) + 20$

　　$60T_E = 40T_E + 100$

　　$20T_E = 100$

　　　$T_E = 5$

11 a.m. + 5 hr = **4 p.m.**

3. $N,\ N + 1,\ N + 2$

　$-7(N + N + 2) = 10[-(N + 1)] + 12$

　　$-7(2N + 2) = -10N - 10 + 12$

　　　$-14N - 14 = -10N + 2$

　　　　　$-4N = 16$

　　　　　　$N = -4$

Thus the integers are **−4, −3,** and **−2.**

4. $N, N + 2, N + 4, N + 6$

$$-(N + N + 2) = -4(N + 6) + 4$$
$$-2N - 2 = -4N - 20$$
$$2N = -18$$
$$N = -9$$

Thus the integers are **–9, –7, –5, and –3.**

5.
$$\frac{77}{100} \cdot P = 15{,}400$$

$$\frac{100}{77} \cdot \frac{77}{100} \cdot P = 15{,}400 \cdot \frac{100}{77}$$

$$P = \$20{,}000$$

6.
$$\frac{40}{100} \cdot T = 3000$$

$$\frac{100}{40} \cdot \frac{40}{100} \cdot T = 3000 \cdot \frac{100}{40}$$

$$T = 7500$$

$$\frac{60}{100} \cdot 7500 = F$$

$$F = 4500$$

7. (a) $f(x) = x^2 - 1$

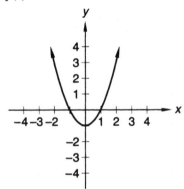

(b) $g(x) = (x - 1)^2$

(c) $h(x) = -x^2$

8. (d)

9. $6y^2 - 15y - 36 = 3(2y^2 - 5y - 12)$
$$= 3(2y + 3)(y - 4)$$

10. $3 + 2z^2 - 7z = 2z^2 - 7z + 3 = (2z - 1)(z - 3)$

11. $2y^2 - 5y - 3 = (2y + 1)(y - 3)$

12.
$$\sqrt{x + 2} - 4 = 1$$
$$\sqrt{x + 2} = 5$$
$$(\sqrt{x + 2})^2 = 5^2$$
$$x + 2 = 25$$
$$x = 23$$

Check $x = 23$:
$$\sqrt{23 + 2} - 4 = 1$$
$$\sqrt{25} - 4 = 1$$
$$5 - 4 = 1$$
$$1 = 1 \quad \text{Check}$$

$x = \mathbf{23}$

13.
$$\sqrt{x - 3} - 5 = 3$$
$$\sqrt{x - 3} = 8$$
$$(\sqrt{x - 3})^2 = (8)^2$$
$$x - 3 = 64$$
$$x = 67$$

Check $x = 67$:
$$\sqrt{67 - 3} - 5 = 3$$
$$\sqrt{64} - 5 = 3$$
$$8 - 5 = 3$$
$$3 = 3 \quad \text{Check}$$

$x = \mathbf{67}$

14. $y = \dfrac{2}{5}x + b$

$$5 = \frac{2}{5}(-2) + b$$

$$5 = -\frac{4}{5} + b$$

$$b = \frac{29}{5}$$

$$y = \frac{2}{5}x + \frac{29}{5}$$

15. $y = -\dfrac{1}{5}x + b$

$-3 = -\dfrac{1}{5}(-2) + b$

$-3 = \dfrac{2}{5} + b$

$b = -\dfrac{17}{5}$

$y = -\dfrac{1}{5}x - \dfrac{17}{5}$

16. $a^2b - 2c^3m + mb - 2a^2c^3$
$= a^2b + mb - 2a^2c^3 - 2c^3m$
$= b(a^2 + m) - 2c^3(a^2 + m)$
$= (b - 2c^3)(a^2 + m)$

17. $6ax + 7am^3 + 12d^3x + 14m^3d^3$
$= a(6x + 7m^3) + 2d^3(6x + 7m^3)$
$= (a + 2d^3)(6x + 7m^3)$

18. $(b, d \neq 0)$

$\dfrac{a}{b} + \dfrac{c}{d} = x$

$bd\left(\dfrac{a}{b}\right) + bd\left(\dfrac{c}{d}\right) = bdx$

$ad + bc = bdx$

$bc = bdx - ad$

$bc = d(bx - a)$

$c = \dfrac{d(bx - a)}{b}$

$(b \neq 0)$

19. $(x \neq 0, 3)$

$\dfrac{4}{x} - \dfrac{3}{x - 3} = 0$

$x(x - 3)\left(\dfrac{4}{x}\right) - x(x - 3)\left(\dfrac{3}{x - 3}\right) = 0$

$4(x - 3) - 3x = 0$

$4x - 12 - 3x = 0$

$x - 12 = 0$

$x = 12$

20.   (a) $9\pi = 28.\textcircled{2}74\ldots$
     28.3

     (b) $\textcircled{0}.50013642$
     1

     (c) $\dfrac{12}{13} = 0.9230\textcircled{7}6923\ldots$
     0.92308

21.   (a) $a = \mathbf{4}$
     (b) $b = \mathbf{8}$
     (c) $c = \mathbf{6}$

22. $-2 - |x| > -5$
        $-|x| > -3$
        $|x| < 3$

23. $\dfrac{x}{4} - \dfrac{x - 2}{3} = 7$

$12 \cdot \dfrac{x}{4} - 12 \cdot \dfrac{(x - 2)}{3} = 12 \cdot 7$

$3x - 4(x - 2) = 84$

$3x - 4x + 8 = 84$

$-x = 76$

$x = \mathbf{-76}$

24. $\dfrac{3x}{\left(x^2 + 7x + 10\right)} - \dfrac{3}{(x + 5)^2}$

$= \dfrac{3x}{(x + 5)(x + 2)} - \dfrac{3}{(x + 5)^2}$

$= \dfrac{3x(x + 5)}{(x + 2)(x + 5)^2} - \dfrac{3(x + 2)}{(x + 2)(x + 5)^2}$

$= \dfrac{3x^2 + 15x - 3x - 6}{(x + 2)(x + 5)^2} = \dfrac{\mathbf{3x^2 + 12x - 6}}{\mathbf{(x + 2)(x + 5)^2}}$

25.   **(a), (d)**

26. $p - 3p^0 - 2\left(p - 4^0\right) - (-3) - 2 = -3^0(2 - p)$

$p - 3 - 2p + 2 + 3 - 2 = -2 + p$

$-p = -2 + p$

$-2p = -2$

$p = 1$

27. $\dfrac{x\left(x^{-2}y\right)^{-2}\left(x^{-2}y\right)x^{-2}}{\left(xy^{-2}\right)^{-2}x^{-2}y^{-4}yy^3x^2} = \dfrac{xy^{-1}}{x^{-2}y^4} = \dfrac{x^3}{y^5}$

28. $4c = 9$

$c = \dfrac{9}{4}$

$x = \dfrac{-b \pm \sqrt{b^2 - 4ac}}{2a}$

$= \dfrac{-7 \pm \sqrt{(7)^2 - 4(5)\left(\dfrac{9}{4}\right)}}{2(5)} = \dfrac{-7 \pm \sqrt{49 - 45}}{10}$

$= \dfrac{-7 \pm \sqrt{4}}{10} = \dfrac{-7 \pm 2}{10} = \dfrac{-9}{10}, \dfrac{-5}{10}$

$= -\dfrac{9}{10}, -\dfrac{1}{2}$

29. $S.A. = 4\pi r^2$

$\qquad = 4\pi(6 \text{ in.})^2$

$\qquad = \mathbf{144\pi \text{ in.}^2 = 452.16 \text{ in.}^2}$

30. $S.A. = \text{Area}_{base} + \text{Lateral Surface Area}$

$\qquad = \pi r^2 + \pi r l$

$\qquad = \pi(7 \text{ ft})^2 + \pi(7 \text{ ft})(19 \text{ ft})$

$\qquad = 49\pi \text{ ft}^2 + 133\pi \text{ ft}^2$

$\qquad = \mathbf{182\pi \text{ ft}^2 = 571.48 \text{ ft}^2}$

Practice 111

a. $6 \leq x - 2 < 7$; $D = \{\text{Reals}\}$

$$
\begin{array}{c}
6 \leq x - 2 < 7 \\
\underline{+2 \qquad +2 \quad +2} \\
8 \leq x \qquad < 9
\end{array}
$$

b. $-x > -3$ or $x \geq 7$; $D = \{\text{Integers}\}$

$\qquad -x > -3 \qquad \text{or} \qquad x \geq 7$

$\qquad x < 3 \qquad \text{or} \qquad x \geq 7$

Problem Set 111

1. $D_H = D_M + 60$

$R_H T_H = R_M T_M + 60$

$R_H = 17$

$T_H = T_M = 20$

$R_H T_H = R_M T_M + 60$

$17(20) = R_M(20) + 60$

$340 = 20R_M + 60$

$-20R_M = -280$

$R_M = \mathbf{14 \text{ mph}}$

2. $D_W = D_B$

$R_W T_W = R_B T_B$

$R_W = 4$

$R_B = 24$

$T_W + T_B = 14$

$T_W = -T_B + 14$

$R_W T_W = R_B T_B$

$4(-T_B + 14) = (24)T_B$

$-4T_B + 56 = 24T_B$

$-28T_B = -56$

$T_B = 2 \text{ hr}$

$D_B = R_B T_B = (24)(2) = \mathbf{48 \text{ mi}}$

3. (a) $N_P = N_A + 29$

(b) $6N_A + 7N_P = 346$

(b) $\qquad 6N_A + 7N_P = 346$

$\qquad 6N_A + 7(N_A + 29) = 346$

$\qquad 13N_A + 203 = 346$

$\qquad 13N_A = 143$

$\qquad N_A = \mathbf{11}$

(a) $N_P = N_A + 29$

$\quad N_P = 11 + 29$

$\quad N_P = \mathbf{40}$

4. $3[13 + (-N)] = 2N - 11$

$\qquad 39 - 3N = 2N - 11$

$\qquad -5N = -50$

$\qquad N = \mathbf{10}$

5. $\qquad \dfrac{80}{100} \cdot \text{Original price} = 120$

$\dfrac{100}{80} \cdot \dfrac{80}{100} \cdot \text{Original price} = 120 \cdot \dfrac{100}{80}$

$\qquad \text{Original price} = \$150$

$P = (\text{Original price})\left(\dfrac{90}{100}\right)$

$P = (\$150)\left(\dfrac{90}{100}\right)$

$P = \mathbf{\$135}$

6. $P(T) = \dfrac{1}{2}$

7. (a) $f(x) = \sqrt{x}$

(b) $g(x) = -\sqrt{x}$

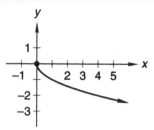

(c) $h(x) = \sqrt{x - 1}$

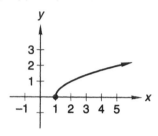

(d) $k(x) = 1 + \sqrt{x}$

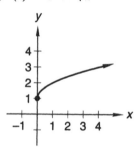

8. (a)

9. $m = \dfrac{-4 - 5}{-3 - 2} = \dfrac{-9}{-5} = \dfrac{9}{5}$

$y = \dfrac{9}{5}x + b$

$5 = \dfrac{9}{5}(2) + b$

$5 = \dfrac{18}{5} + b$

$b = \dfrac{7}{5}$

$y = \dfrac{9}{5}x + \dfrac{7}{5}$

10. $0 \le x + 6 < 11; \ D = \{\text{Integers}\}$

$0 \le x + 6 < 11$

$\dfrac{-6 -6 -6}{-6 \le x < 5}$

-7 -6 -5 -4 -3 -2 -1 0 1 2 3 4 5

11. $x < -1$ or $x \ge 5; \ D = \{\text{Reals}\}$

-2 -1 0 1 2 3 4 5 6

12. $3x^2 - 5 + 14x = 3x^2 + 14x - 5$

$= (3x - 1)(x + 5)$

13. $-27 + 24x + 3x^2 = 3x^2 + 24x - 27$

$= 3(x^2 + 8x - 9) = 3(x + 9)(x - 1)$

14. $9x - 5 + 2x^2 = 2x^2 + 9x - 5$

$= (2x - 1)(x + 5)$

15. $3x^2 - 7 - 20x = 3x^2 - 20x - 7$

$= (3x + 1)(x - 7)$

16. $4\sqrt{y} = 20$

$\sqrt{y} = 5$

$(\sqrt{y})^2 = 5^2$

$y = 25$

Check $y = 25$:

$4\sqrt{25} = 20$

$4(5) = 20$

$20 = 20 \quad \text{Check}$

$y = \mathbf{25}$

17. $\sqrt{x - 4} - 8 = 0$

$\sqrt{x - 4} = 8$

$(\sqrt{x - 4})^2 = (8)^2$

$x - 4 = 64$

$x = 68$

Check $x = 68$:

$\sqrt{68 - 4} - 8 = 0$

$\sqrt{64} - 8 = 0$

$8 - 8 = 0$

$0 = 0 \quad \text{Check}$

$x = \mathbf{68}$

18. $a^2c + bc + 3a^2 + 3b = c(a^2 + b) + 3(a^2 + b)$

$= (a^2 + b)(c + 3)$

19. $(x, c, d \ne 0)$

$$\dfrac{a}{x} - \dfrac{1}{c} = \dfrac{1}{d}$$

$$xcd\left(\dfrac{a}{x}\right) - xcd\left(\dfrac{1}{c}\right) = xcd\left(\dfrac{1}{d}\right)$$

$$acd - dx = cx$$

$$acd = cx + dx$$

$$acd = x(c + d)$$

$$x = \dfrac{acd}{c + d}$$

$(c + d \ne 0)$

20.
$$45 = x^2 + 4x$$
$$-x^2 - 4x + 45 = 0$$
$$(-1)(x^2 + 4x - 45) = 0$$
$$x^2 + 4x - 45 = 0$$
$$(x + 9)(x - 5) = 0$$

If $x + 9 = 0$ If $x - 5 = 0$
$$x = -9 \qquad\qquad x = 5$$

21. $-4 - |x| \leq -4$
$$-|x| \leq 0$$
$$|x| \geq 0$$

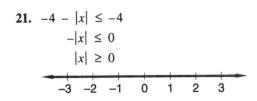

22.

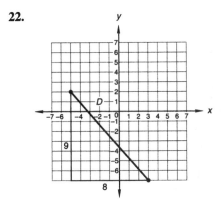

$$D^2 = 8^2 + 9^2$$
$$D^2 = 64 + 81$$
$$D^2 = 145$$
$$D = \sqrt{145}$$

23. $D = \{x \in \mathbb{R} \mid x \leq 6\}$

24. (a) **Irrational**

(b) **Rational**

(c) **Rational**

(d) **Irrational**

25. $4\sqrt{2}\left(5\sqrt{2} - 2\sqrt{12}\right) = 20(2) - 8\sqrt{24}$
$$= 40 - 8\left(2\sqrt{6}\right) = \mathbf{40 - 16\sqrt{6}}$$

26. $\dfrac{-3^{-3}(-3)^{-2}}{3^{-2}} = \dfrac{-1(3^2)}{(3^3)(-3)^2} = \dfrac{-9}{(27)(9)} = -\dfrac{1}{27}$

27. $\dfrac{x^{-2}a^2}{y}\left(\dfrac{ya^{-2}}{x^{-2}} - \dfrac{3x^{-2}a^2}{y} - \dfrac{x^2a^{-2}}{y^{-1}}\right)$
$$= 1 - \dfrac{3x^{-4}a^4}{y^2} - 1 = -\dfrac{3a^4}{x^4y^2}$$

28. $4c + 7 = 37$
$$4c = 30$$
$$c = \frac{30}{4}$$
$$c = \frac{15}{2}$$

$$x = \frac{-b \pm \sqrt{b^2 - 4ac}}{2a}$$

$$= \frac{-(-1) \pm \sqrt{(-1)^2 - 4\left(-\frac{1}{2}\right)\left(\frac{15}{2}\right)}}{2\left(-\frac{1}{2}\right)}$$

$$= \frac{1 \pm \sqrt{1 + 15}}{-1} = \frac{1 \pm \sqrt{16}}{-1} = \frac{1 \pm 4}{-1}$$

$$= \frac{5}{-1}, \frac{-3}{-1} = \mathbf{-5, 3}$$

29. $P = 12 \text{ cm} + \dfrac{2\pi(3 \text{ cm})}{2} + 12 \text{ cm} + \dfrac{2\pi(3 \text{ cm})}{2}$
$$= \mathbf{(24 + 6\pi) \text{ cm} = 42.84 \text{ cm}}$$

30. $V = \left(\text{Area}_{\text{base}}\right)(\text{Height})$
$$= \left[\frac{1}{2}(10 \text{ m})(12 \text{ m})\right](15 \text{ m})$$
$$= \left(60 \text{ m}^2\right)(15 \text{ m})$$
$$= \mathbf{900 \text{ m}^3}$$

Practice 112

a. $\left(5 + \sqrt{2}\right)\left(3 + \sqrt{8}\right)$
$$= 5 \cdot 3 + 5\sqrt{8} + 3\sqrt{2} + \sqrt{2} \cdot \sqrt{8}$$
$$= 15 + 5\left(2\sqrt{2}\right) + 3\sqrt{2} + 4$$
$$= 19 + 10\sqrt{2} + 3\sqrt{2} = \mathbf{19 + 13\sqrt{2}}$$

b. $\left(2 + \sqrt{5}\right)\left(4 - 3\sqrt{5}\right)$
$$= 2 \cdot 4 + 2\left(-3\sqrt{5}\right) + 4\sqrt{5} + \sqrt{5}\left(-3\sqrt{5}\right)$$
$$= 8 - 6\sqrt{5} + 4\sqrt{5} - 15 = \mathbf{-7 - 2\sqrt{5}}$$

c. $\left(\sqrt{2} + \sqrt{5}\right)^2 = \left(\sqrt{2} + \sqrt{5}\right)\left(\sqrt{2} + \sqrt{5}\right)$
$$= 2 + \sqrt{10} + \sqrt{10} + 5 = \mathbf{7 + 2\sqrt{10}}$$

d. $\left(\sqrt{2}x + \sqrt{7}y\right)^2$
$$= \left(\sqrt{2}x + \sqrt{7}y\right)\left(\sqrt{2}x + \sqrt{7}y\right)$$
$$= 2x^2 + \sqrt{14}xy + \sqrt{14}xy + 7y^2$$
$$= \mathbf{2x^2 + 2\sqrt{14}xy + 7y^2}$$

Problem Set 112

1.
$$D_N + D_S = 580$$
$$R_N T_N + R_S T_S = 580$$

$$R_N = 50$$
$$R_S = 45$$
$$T_N = T_S + 4$$

$$R_N T_N + R_S T_S = 580$$
$$50(T_S + 4) + 45T_S = 580$$
$$95T_S + 200 = 580$$
$$95T_S = 380$$
$$T_S = \mathbf{4\ hr}$$

2.
$$D_W = D_B$$
$$R_W T_W = R_B T_B$$

$$R_W = 5$$
$$R_B = 30$$

$$T_W + T_B = 21$$
$$T_B = -T_W + 21$$

$$R_W T_W = R_B T_B$$
$$5T_W = 30(-T_W + 21)$$
$$5T_W = -30T_W + 630$$
$$35T_W = 630$$
$$T_W = 18\ hr$$

$$D_W = R_W T_W = (5)(18) = \mathbf{90\ km}$$

3. (a) $N_F + N_T = 176$
    (b) $5N_F + 20N_T = 1075$

$$(-5)(a)\quad -5N_F - 5N_T = -880$$
$$(1)(b)\quad \underline{5N_F + 20N_T = 1075}$$
$$15N_T = 195$$
$$N_T = \mathbf{13}$$

  (a) $N_F + N_T = 176$
$$N_F + 13 = 176$$
$$N_F = \mathbf{163}$$

4. $\dfrac{900}{1200} = \dfrac{3}{4}$

5. $\dfrac{H}{T} = \dfrac{11}{13}$

$$\dfrac{H}{195} = \dfrac{11}{13}$$
$$13H = 195 \cdot 11$$
$$H = \dfrac{195 \cdot 11}{13}$$
$$H = \mathbf{165}$$

6. $P(\text{red, then blue}) = \dfrac{5}{9} \cdot \dfrac{4}{8} = \dfrac{5}{18}$

7. (a) $f(x) = x^3$

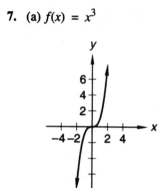

(b) $g(x) = -x^3$

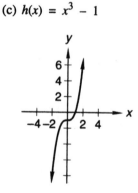

(c) $h(x) = x^3 - 1$

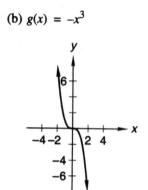

(d) $k(x) = (x + 1)^3$

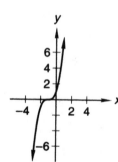

8. (b)

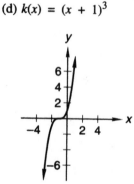

9. (a) $\left(2 - 3\sqrt{12}\right)\left(3 + 2\sqrt{12}\right)$

$= 2 \cdot 3 + 2\left(2\sqrt{12}\right) + 3\left(-3\sqrt{12}\right)$
$\quad + \left(-3\sqrt{12}\right)\left(2\sqrt{12}\right)$

$= 6 + 4\sqrt{12} - 9\sqrt{12} - 72$

$= -66 - 5\sqrt{12}$

$= \mathbf{-66 - 10\sqrt{3}}$

(b) $\left(\sqrt{2a} - \sqrt{3p}\right)^2$

$= \left(\sqrt{2a} - \sqrt{3p}\right)\left(\sqrt{2a} - \sqrt{3p}\right)$

$= 2a - \sqrt{6ap} - \sqrt{6ap} + 3p$

$= \mathbf{2a - 2\sqrt{6ap} + 3p}$

10. $m = \dfrac{-4 - 1}{-2 - 3} = \dfrac{-5}{-5} = 1$

$y = x + b$

$1 = 3 + b$

$b = -2$

$\mathbf{y = x - 2}$

11. $y = -\dfrac{2}{3}x + b$

$-3 = -\dfrac{2}{3}(-2) + b$

$-3 = \dfrac{4}{3} + b$

$b = -\dfrac{13}{3}$

$\mathbf{y = -\dfrac{2}{3}x - \dfrac{13}{3}}$

12. $4 \leq x - 3 < 6$; $D = \{\text{Integers}\}$

$\begin{array}{ccc} 4 \leq & x - 3 & < 6 \\ +3 & +3 & +3 \\ \hline 7 \leq & x & < 9 \end{array}$

13. $x + 2 < 5$ or $x + 2 \geq 6$; $D = \{\text{Reals}\}$

$\begin{array}{ccc} x + 2 < 5 & \text{or} & x + 2 \geq 6 \\ x < 3 & \text{or} & x \geq 4 \end{array}$

14. $2x^2 - 6 - 4x = 2x^2 - 4x - 6$

$= 2\left(x^2 - 2x - 3\right) = \mathbf{2(x - 3)(x + 1)}$

15. $3x^2 - 4 - x = 3x^2 - x - 4 = \mathbf{(3x - 4)(x + 1)}$

16. $3x^2 + 28x - 20 = \mathbf{(3x - 2)(x + 10)}$

17. $2\sqrt{x} - 4 = 3$

$2\sqrt{x} = 7$

$\sqrt{x} = \dfrac{7}{2}$

$\left(\sqrt{x}\right)^2 = \left(\dfrac{7}{2}\right)^2$

$x = \dfrac{49}{4}$

Check $x = \dfrac{49}{4}$:

$2\sqrt{\dfrac{49}{4}} - 4 = 3$

$2\left(\dfrac{7}{2}\right) - 4 = 3$

$7 - 4 = 3$

$3 = 3$ Check

$\mathbf{x = \dfrac{49}{4}}$

18. $\sqrt{x + 5} - 3 = 2$

$\sqrt{x + 5} = 5$

$\left(\sqrt{x + 5}\right)^2 = (5)^2$

$x + 5 = 25$

$x = 20$

Check $x = 20$:

$\sqrt{20 + 5} - 3 = 2$

$\sqrt{25} - 3 = 2$

$5 - 3 = 2$

$2 = 2$ Check

$\mathbf{x = 20}$

19. $xr + ax - br - ab = x(r + a) - b(r + a)$

$= \mathbf{(r + a)(x - b)}$

20. $xy + 3y - x^2 - 3x = y(x + 3) - x(x + 3)$

$= \mathbf{(x + 3)(y - x)}$

21. $-|x| + 2 \geq -1$

$-|x| \geq -3$

$|x| \leq 3$

22. $-2 < x + 1 \leq 2$

$\begin{array}{ccc} -1 & -1 & -1 \\ \hline -3 < & x & \leq 1 \end{array}$

23. $(b, m, c \neq 0)$

$$\frac{a}{b} + \frac{x}{m} - \frac{1}{c} = p$$

$$bcm\left(\frac{a}{b}\right) + bcm\left(\frac{x}{m}\right) - bcm\left(\frac{1}{c}\right) = bcmp$$

$$amc + bcx - bm = bcmp$$

$$amc - bm - bmcp = -bcx$$

$$(-1)[m(bcp + b - ac)] = (-1)bcx$$

$$m = \frac{bcx}{bcp + b - ac}$$

$$(bcp + b - ac \neq 0)$$

24.
$$\begin{cases} y = -x + 3 \\ y = -2 \end{cases}$$

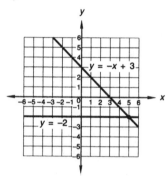

$$y = -x + 3 \qquad\qquad y = -2$$
$$-2 = -5 + 3 \qquad\qquad -2 = -2$$
$$-2 = -2$$

The solution to the linear equations is **(5, –2)**.

25. $D = \left\{ x \in \mathbb{R} \mid -4 < x \leq 4 \right\}$
$R = \left\{ y \in \mathbb{R} \mid -4 < y \leq 3 \right\}$

26. (a) $y = -2$

(b) The desired equation is $y = mx + b$.
By inspection, $b = 0$.
By inspection, the sign of m is –.

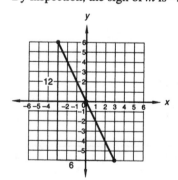

$$|m| = \frac{12}{6} = 2$$

So $b = 0$ and $m = -2$.

$$y = -2x$$

27. $\left(x^3 - 2x - 4\right) \div (x + 2)$

$$\begin{array}{r}
x^2 - 2x + 2 \\
x + 2 \overline{\smash{\big)}\ x^3 + 0x^2 - 2x - 4} \\
\underline{x^3 + 2x^2} \\
-2x^2 - 2x \\
\underline{-2x^2 - 4x} \\
2x - 4 \\
\underline{2x + 4} \\
-8
\end{array}$$

$$x^2 - 2x + 2 - \frac{8}{x + 2}$$

28. $\dfrac{5x + 2}{x - 3} - \dfrac{2x + 2}{x^2 - 9}$

$$= \frac{5x + 2}{x - 3} - \frac{2x + 2}{(x - 3)(x + 3)}$$

$$= \frac{(5x + 2)(x + 3)}{(x - 3)(x + 3)} - \frac{(2x + 2)}{(x - 3)(x + 3)}$$

$$= \frac{5x^2 + 17x + 6 - 2x - 2}{(x + 3)(x - 3)}$$

$$= \frac{5x^2 + 15x + 4}{(x + 3)(x - 3)}$$

29. $A = \dfrac{1}{2}\left(12\dfrac{3}{5}\ \text{in.}\right)\left(14\dfrac{2}{7}\ \text{in.}\right)$

$$+\ \frac{1}{2}\left(12\frac{3}{5}\ \text{in.}\right)\left(14\frac{2}{7}\ \text{in.}\right)$$

$$= 90\ \text{in.}^2 + 90\ \text{in.}^2$$

$$= 180\ \text{in.}^2$$

30. $S.A. = 2\left(\text{Area}_{\text{base}}\right) + \text{Lateral Surface Area}$

$$= 2\left[\frac{1}{2}(3\ \text{ft} \times 4\ \text{ft}) + (4\ \text{ft} \times 4\ \text{ft})\right.$$

$$\left. +\ \frac{\pi(2\ \text{ft})^2}{2}\right] + \left(\text{Perimeter}_{\text{base}}\right)(\text{Height})$$

$$= 2\left(6\ \text{ft}^2 + 16\ \text{ft}^2 + 2\pi\ \text{ft}^2\right)$$

$$+ \left(7\ \text{ft} + 5\ \text{ft} + 4\ \text{ft} + \frac{2\pi(2\ \text{ft})}{2}\right)(9\ \text{ft})$$

$$= 2\left(22\ \text{ft}^2 + 2\pi\ \text{ft}^2\right) + (16\ \text{ft} + 2\pi\ \text{ft})(9\ \text{ft})$$

$$= 44\ \text{ft}^2 + 4\pi\ \text{ft}^2 + 144\ \text{ft}^2 + 18\pi\ \text{ft}^2$$

$$= (188 + 22\pi)\ \text{ft}^2 = 257.08\ \text{ft}^2$$

Practice 113

a. $M = kV$
$$30 = k(6)$$
$$k = 5$$
$$M = 5V$$
$$65 = 5V$$
$$V = 13\ \textbf{liters}$$

b. $P = kT$

$1200 = k(300)$

$k = 4$

$P = 4T$

$300 = 4(T)$

$T = \textbf{75 K}$

c. $P = \dfrac{k}{V}$

$9 = \dfrac{k}{100}$

$k = 900$

$P = \dfrac{900}{V}$

$20 = \dfrac{900}{V}$

$V = \dfrac{900}{20}$

$V = \textbf{45 liters}$

Problem Set 113

1. $R = \dfrac{k}{T}$

$100 = \dfrac{k}{5}$

$k = 500$

$R = \dfrac{500}{T}$

$125 = \dfrac{500}{T}$

$T = \dfrac{500}{125}$

$T = \textbf{4 hr}$

2. $M = kV$

$42 = k(7)$

$k = 6$

$M = 6V$

$63 = 6V$

$V = \textbf{10.5 liters}$

3. $D_R = D_B$

$R_R T_R = R_B T_B$

$R_R = 8$

$R_B = 20$

$T_R + T_B = 7$

$T_R = -T_B + 7$

$R_R T_R = R_B T_B$

$8(-T_B + 7) = 20T_B$

$-8T_B + 56 = 20T_B$

$-28T_B = -56$

$T_B = 2$

$D_B = R_B T_B = (20)(2) = \textbf{40 km}$

4. $D = kT$

$90 = k(9)$

$k = 10$

$D = 10T$

$D = (10)(5)$

$D = \textbf{50 km}$

5. (a) $N_R + N_W = 27$

(b) $50N_R + 40N_W = 1230$

$(-40)(a)\ -40N_R - 40N_W = -1080$

$\underline{(1)(b)\quad 50N_R + 40N_W = \ \ 1230}$

$\qquad\qquad 10N_R \qquad\quad = \ \ 150$

$N_R = \textbf{15}$

(a) $N_R + N_W = 27$

$15 + N_W = 27$

$N_W = \textbf{12}$

6. $P = kA$

$40 = k(120)$

$k = \dfrac{1}{3}$

$P = \dfrac{1}{3}A$

$500 = \dfrac{1}{3}A$

$A = \textbf{1500}$

7. (a) $f(x) = |x|$

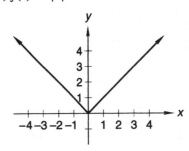

(b) $g(x) = -|x|$

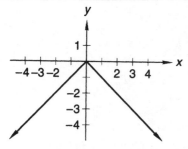

(c) $h(x) = 1 + |x|$

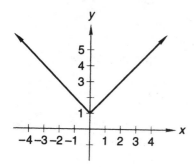

(d) $k(x) = |x + 1|$

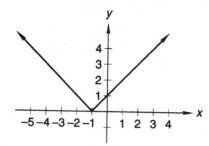

8. (c)

9. $\left(2 + \sqrt{3}\right)\left(4 - 5\sqrt{12}\right)$
$= 8 - 10\sqrt{12} + 4\sqrt{3} - 5\sqrt{36}$
$= 8 - 10\left(2\sqrt{3}\right) + 4\sqrt{3} - 5(6) = \mathbf{-22 - 16\sqrt{3}}$

10. $\left(2 + \sqrt{2}\right)\left(4 - 3\sqrt{8}\right)$
$= 8 - 6\sqrt{8} + 4\sqrt{2} - 3\sqrt{16}$
$= 8 - 6\left(2\sqrt{2}\right) + 4\sqrt{2} - 3(4) = \mathbf{-4 - 8\sqrt{2}}$

11. $\left(5 + \sqrt{6}\right)\left(2 - 3\sqrt{24}\right)$
$= 10 - 15\sqrt{24} + 2\sqrt{6} - 3\sqrt{144}$
$= 10 - 15\left(2\sqrt{6}\right) + 2\sqrt{6} - 3(12)$
$= \mathbf{-26 - 28\sqrt{6}}$

12. $-2 \le x + 5 < 3$; $D = \{\text{Reals}\}$

$$\begin{array}{ccc} -2 \le x + 5 < & 3 \\ \underline{-5 \qquad -5} & \underline{-5} \\ -7 \le x & < -2 \end{array}$$

13. $x + 2 \ge 5$ or $x + 3 \le 0$; $D = \{\text{Reals}\}$

$$\begin{array}{ccc} x + 2 \ge 5 & \text{or} & x + 3 \le 0 \\ x \ge 3 & \text{or} & x \le -3 \end{array}$$

14. $12x^2 + 60x + 72 = 12\left(x^2 + 5x + 6\right)$
$= \mathbf{12(x + 3)(x + 2)}$

15. $40 + 5x^2 - 30x = 5x^2 - 30x + 40$
$= 5\left(x^2 - 6x + 8\right) = \mathbf{5(x - 4)(x - 2)}$

16. $3r^2 - 9r - 390 = 3\left(r^2 - 3r - 130\right)$
$= \mathbf{3(r - 13)(r + 10)}$

17. $2\sqrt{x} + 2 = 5$
$2\sqrt{x} = 3$
$\sqrt{x} = \dfrac{3}{2}$
$\left(\sqrt{x}\right)^2 = \left(\dfrac{3}{2}\right)^2$
$x = \dfrac{9}{4}$

Check $x = \dfrac{9}{4}$:

$2\sqrt{\dfrac{9}{4}} + 2 = 5$

$2\left(\dfrac{3}{2}\right) + 2 = 5$

$3 + 2 = 5$

$5 = 5$ Check

$x = \dfrac{9}{4}$

18. $\sqrt{x - 4} - 2 = 6$
$\sqrt{x - 4} = 8$
$\left(\sqrt{x - 4}\right)^2 = (8)^2$
$x - 4 = 64$
$x = 68$

Check $x = 68$:
$\sqrt{68 - 4} - 2 = 6$
$\sqrt{64} - 2 = 6$
$8 - 2 = 6$
$6 = 6$ Check

$x = 68$

19. $(c, y \neq 0)$

$$\frac{x}{y} - m + \frac{1}{c} = k$$

$$cy\left(\frac{x}{y}\right) - mcy + cy\left(\frac{1}{c}\right) = kcy$$

$$cx - mcy + y = kcy$$

$$y - mcy - kcy = -cx$$

$$y(1 - mc - kc) = -cx$$

$$y = \frac{(-1)cx}{(-1)(ck + cm - 1)}$$

$$y = \frac{cx}{ck + cm - 1}$$

$$(ck + cm - 1 \neq 0)$$

20. $(m \neq 0)$

$$\frac{m + 5}{m} = \frac{3}{2m} - \frac{2}{5}$$

$$10m\left(\frac{m + 5}{m}\right) = 10m\left(\frac{3}{2m}\right) - 10m\left(\frac{2}{5}\right)$$

$$10(m + 5) = 5(3) - 2(2m)$$

$$10m + 50 = 15 - 4m$$

$$14m = -35$$

$$m = \frac{-35}{14}$$

$$m = -\frac{5}{2}$$

21.

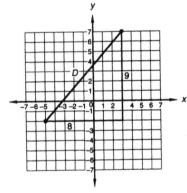

$$D^2 = 8^2 + 9^2$$
$$D^2 = 64 + 81$$
$$D^2 = 145$$
$$D = \sqrt{145}$$

22. $xy - 3y - 2x + 6 = y(x - 3) - 2(x - 3)$

$$= (x - 3)(y - 2)$$

23.
$$-8 = -x^2 + 7x$$
$$x^2 - 7x - 8 = 0$$
$$(x - 8)(x + 1) = 0$$

If $x - 8 = 0$ If $x + 1 = 0$

$\qquad x = 8 \qquad\qquad x = -1$

24.
$$y = 2x + b$$
$$-5 = 2(-2) + b$$
$$-5 = -4 + b$$
$$b = -1$$
$$y = 2x - 1$$

25.
$$k^2 + 5^2 = 8^2$$
$$k^2 + 25 = 64$$
$$k^2 = 39$$
$$k = \sqrt{39}$$

26.
$$\frac{(35,000 \times 10^{-41})(700 \times 10^{14})}{(7000 \times 10^{21})(0.00005 \times 10^{15})}$$

$$= \frac{(3.5 \times 10^{-37})(7 \times 10^{16})}{(7 \times 10^{24})(5 \times 10^{10})}$$

$$= \frac{3.5 \cdot 7}{7 \cdot 5} \times \frac{10^{-37} \cdot 10^{16}}{10^{24} \cdot 10^{10}}$$

$$= \frac{24.5}{35} \times \frac{10^{-21}}{10^{34}}$$

$$= 0.7 \times 10^{-55} = 7 \times 10^{-56}$$

27.
$$\frac{(x^{-2})^{-3}(x^{-2}y^2)}{x^2 y y^0 (x^0 y)^{-2}} = \frac{x^4 y^2}{x^2 y^{-1}} = x^2 y^3$$

28. $a = 3$ $4c = 1$

     $b = 3$ $c = \frac{1}{4}$

$$x = \frac{-b \pm \sqrt{b^2 - 4ac}}{2a}$$

$$= \frac{-3 \pm \sqrt{(3)^2 - 4(3)\left(\frac{1}{4}\right)}}{2(3)}$$

$$= \frac{-3 \pm \sqrt{9 - 3}}{6} = \frac{-3 \pm \sqrt{6}}{6}$$

29. $A = \frac{1}{2}\left(4\frac{3}{4} \text{ cm} \times 2\frac{2}{11} \text{ cm}\right)$

$$+ \frac{1}{2}\left(3\frac{1}{2} \text{ cm} \times 2\frac{2}{11} \text{ cm}\right)$$

$$= \frac{1}{2}\left(\frac{19}{4} \text{ cm} \times \frac{24}{11} \text{ cm}\right) + \frac{1}{2}\left(\frac{7}{2} \text{ cm} \times \frac{24}{11} \text{ cm}\right)$$

$$= \frac{1}{2}\left(\frac{114}{11} \text{ cm}^2\right) + \frac{1}{2}\left(\frac{84}{11} \text{ cm}^2\right)$$

$$= \frac{114}{22} \text{ cm}^2 + \frac{84}{22} \text{ cm}^2$$

$$= \frac{198}{22} \text{ cm}^2$$

$$= 9 \text{ cm}^2$$

30. $S.A. = 2(\text{Area}_{\text{base}}) + \text{Lateral Surface Area}$

$$= 2\left[\frac{1}{2}(8 \text{ m})(6 \text{ m}) + \frac{\pi(5 \text{ m})^2}{2}\right]$$

$$+ (\text{Perimeter}_{\text{base}})(\text{Height})$$

$$= 2\left[\frac{1}{2}(48 \text{ m}^2) + \frac{25\pi \text{ m}^2}{2}\right]$$

$$+ \left(6 \text{ m} + 8 \text{ m} + \frac{2\pi(5 \text{ m})}{2}\right)(3 \text{ m})$$

$$= 2\left(24 \text{ m}^2 + \frac{25\pi \text{ m}^2}{2}\right)$$

$$+ (14 \text{ m} + 5\pi \text{ m})(3 \text{ m})$$

$$= 48 \text{ m}^2 + 25\pi \text{ m}^2 + 42 \text{ m}^2 + 15\pi \text{ m}^2$$

$$= (90 + 40\pi) \text{ m}^2 = 215.6 \text{ m}^2$$

$V = (\text{Area}_{\text{base}})(\text{Height})$

$$= \left(24 \text{ m}^2 + \frac{25\pi \text{ m}^2}{2}\right)(3 \text{ m})$$

$$= \left(72 + \frac{75\pi}{2}\right) \text{ m}^3 = 189.75 \text{ m}^3$$

Practice 114

a. (1) $(2.5)^3 = $ **15.6250**

(2) $(0.5)^{0.5} = $ **0.7071**

(3) $(3.14)^{1/3} = $ **1.4643**

b. (1) $y = 3^x$

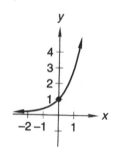

(2) $y = \left(\frac{1}{3}\right)^x$

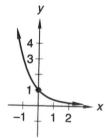

c. $A_n = A_0(1 + r)^n$

$A_n = \$900(1.08)^n$

$A_{12} = 900(1.08)^{12}$

$A_{12} = \$2266.35$

$\$2266.35 - \$900 = \$1366.35$

Problem Set 114

1. (a) $A_t = A_0(y)^t$

$A_t = 1000(4)^t$

(b) $A_{24} = 1000(4)^{24} = $ **2.81 × 10^{17}**

2. (a) $A_n = A_0(1 + r)^n$

$A_n = \$700(1.09)^n$

(b) $A_{11} = 700(1.09)^{11} = $ **$1806.30**

(c) $\$1806.30 - \$700 = $ **$1106.30**

3. (a) $(3.14)^4 = $ **97.2117**

(b) $(3.14)^{2.5} = $ **17.4713**

(c) $(0.25)^{0.5} = $ **0.5000**

4. $y = 2^x$

5. $G = kB$

$21 = 3k$

$k = 7$

$G = 7B$

$G = 7(5)$

$G = 35$

6. $P = \dfrac{k}{D}$

$500 = \dfrac{k}{6}$

$k = 3000$

$P = \dfrac{3000}{D}$

$P = \dfrac{3000}{10}$

$P = 300$

7. $D_A = D_B$

$R_A T_A = R_B T_B$

$R_A = 5$

$R_B = 2$

$T_A + T_B = 28$

$T_A = -T_B + 28$

$R_A T_A = R_B T_B$

$5(-T_B + 28) = 2T_B$

$-5T_B + 140 = 2T_B$

$-7T_B = -140$

$T_B = 20$

$D_B = R_B T_B = (2)(20) =$ **40 mi**

8. (a) $f(x) = -x^2$

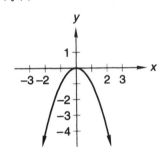

(b) $g(x) = x^2 + 3$

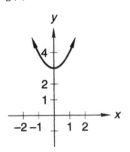

(c) $h(x) = (x + 3)^2$

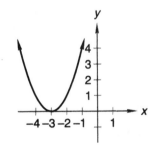

(d) $k(x) = (x - 3)^2$

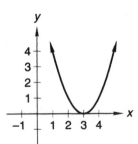

9. $y = -\frac{1}{4}x + b$

$-1 = -\frac{1}{4}(4) + b$

$-1 = -1 + b$

$b = 0$

$y = -\frac{1}{4}x$

10. $m = \frac{4 - (-1)}{-1 - 4} = \frac{5}{-5} = -1$

$y = -x + b$

$4 = -(-1) + b$

$b = 3$

$y = -x + 3$

11. $y = -3x + b$

$-1 = -3(-1) + b$

$-1 = 3 + b$

$b = -4$

$y = -3x - 4$

12. $160{,}000\ \text{m} \cdot \text{m} \cdot \text{m} \times \dfrac{100\ \text{cm}}{1\ \text{m}} \times \dfrac{100\ \text{cm}}{1\ \text{m}}$

$\times \dfrac{100\ \text{cm}}{1\ \text{m}} \times \dfrac{1\ \text{in.}}{2.54\ \text{cm}} \times \dfrac{1\ \text{in.}}{2.54\ \text{cm}} \times \dfrac{1\ \text{in.}}{2.54\ \text{cm}}$

$= \dfrac{160{,}000(100)^3}{(2.54)^3}\ \text{in.}^3 =$ **9,763,799,055 in.^{3}**

13. $x + 4 > 7 \qquad$ or $\qquad x - 2 \le 0$

$\qquad x > 3 \qquad$ or $\qquad\qquad x \le 2$

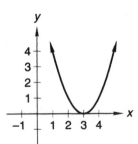

14. $\left(4 + 3\sqrt{5}\right)\left(1 - \sqrt{5}\right)$

$= 4 - 4\sqrt{5} + 3\sqrt{5} - 15 =$ **$-11 - \sqrt{5}$**

15. $\left(3 + 2\sqrt{2}\right)\left(3 - \sqrt{2}\right) = 9 - 3\sqrt{2} + 6\sqrt{2} - 4$

$=$ **$5 + 3\sqrt{2}$**

16. $(p \ne 0)$

$\dfrac{p + 8}{3p} = \dfrac{5}{2p} + \dfrac{1}{4}$

$12p\left(\dfrac{p + 8}{3p}\right) = 12p\left(\dfrac{5}{2p}\right) + 12p\left(\dfrac{1}{4}\right)$

$4(p + 8) = 6(5) + 3p$

$4p + 32 = 30 + 3p$

$p = -2$

17.
$$4\frac{1}{2}x + \frac{3}{5} = \frac{1}{4}$$
$$\frac{9}{2}x + \frac{3}{5} = \frac{1}{4}$$
$$20\left(\frac{9}{2}x\right) + 20\left(\frac{3}{5}\right) = 20\left(\frac{1}{4}\right)$$
$$10(9x) + 4(3) = 5$$
$$90x + 12 = 5$$
$$90x = -7$$
$$x = -\frac{7}{90}$$

18. $\left(7x^3 - 2x - 2\right) \div (x + 2)$

$$
\begin{array}{r}
7x^2 - 14x + 26 \\
x + 2 \overline{\smash{)}\ 7x^3 + 0x^2 - 2x - 2} \\
\underline{7x^3 + 14x^2} \\
-14x^2 - 2x \\
\underline{-14x^2 - 28x} \\
26x - 2 \\
\underline{26x + 52} \\
-54
\end{array}
$$

$$7x^2 - 14x + 26 - \frac{54}{x + 2}$$

19. $5x^2 + 17x + 6 = (5x + 2)(x + 3)$

20. $4x^2 + 4x + 1 = (2x + 1)(2x + 1)$

21. $2x^2l + 6x^2 - 5l - 15$
$$= 2x^2(l + 3) - 5(l + 3) = (l + 3)\left(2x^2 - 5\right)$$

22. $(m, z \neq 0)$

$$\frac{p}{m} - \frac{x}{z} + a = k$$
$$mz\left(\frac{p}{m}\right) - mz\left(\frac{x}{z}\right) + amz = kmz$$
$$pz - mx + amz = kmz$$
$$pz + amz - kmz = mx$$
$$z(p + am - km) = mx$$
$$z = \frac{xm}{p + am - km}$$
$$(p + am - km \neq 0)$$

23.
$$\sqrt{x - 7} + 4 = 9$$
$$\sqrt{x - 7} = 5$$
$$\left(\sqrt{x - 7}\right)^2 = (5)^2$$
$$x - 7 = 25$$
$$x = 32$$

Check $x = 32$:
$$\sqrt{32 - 7} + 4 = 9$$
$$\sqrt{25} + 4 = 9$$
$$5 + 4 = 9$$
$$9 = 9 \quad \text{Check}$$
$$x = \mathbf{32}$$

24. $\begin{cases} y = \dfrac{1}{2}x - 2 \\ x = -4 \end{cases}$

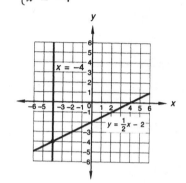

$$y = \frac{1}{2}x - 2 \qquad\qquad x = -4$$
$$\qquad\qquad\qquad\qquad\qquad -4 = -4$$
$$-4 = \frac{1}{2}(-4) - 2$$
$$-4 = -2 - 2$$
$$-4 = -4$$

The solution to the linear equations is **(−4, −4)**.

25.
$$\frac{\dfrac{mp^2}{x} - \dfrac{z}{x^2}}{\dfrac{y}{x^2} - \dfrac{5a}{x}} = \frac{\dfrac{mp^2x}{x^2} - \dfrac{z}{x^2}}{\dfrac{y}{x^2} - \dfrac{5ax}{x^2}}$$

$$= \frac{\dfrac{mp^2x - z}{x^2}}{\dfrac{y - 5ax}{x^2}} \cdot \frac{\dfrac{x^2}{y - 5ax}}{\dfrac{x^2}{y - 5ax}} = \frac{mp^2x - z}{y - 5ax}$$

26.

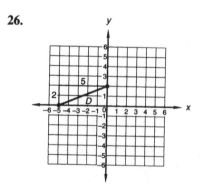

$$D^2 = 5^2 + 2^2$$
$$D^2 = 25 + 4$$
$$D^2 = 29$$
$$D = \sqrt{29}$$

27. $-xy - y^x - x\left(\dfrac{y}{x}\right)$

$= -(-2)(-3) - (-3)^{-2} - (-2)\left(\dfrac{-3}{-2}\right)$

$= -6 - \dfrac{1}{9} + 3 = -3 - \dfrac{1}{9} = -\dfrac{28}{9}$

28. $-3\left[(-3^0 - 3)^2(-3^3 - 3) - (-3)\right] - \sqrt[3]{-27}$

$= -3\left[(-4)^2(-30) + 3\right] - (-3)$

$= -3\left[(16)(-30) + 3\right] + 3$

$= -3(-477) + 3$

$= \mathbf{1434}$

29. $A = (16 \text{ in.} \times 10 \text{ in.}) - \dfrac{1}{2}(6 \text{ in.} \times 8 \text{ in.})$

$= 160 \text{ in.}^2 - \dfrac{1}{2}(48 \text{ in.}^2)$

$= 160 \text{ in.}^2 - 24 \text{ in.}^2$

$= \mathbf{136 \text{ in.}^2}$

30. $S.A. = 2(\text{Area}_{base}) + \text{Lateral Surface Area}$

$= 2\left[(10 \text{ ft} \times 10 \text{ ft}) + 2\left(\dfrac{\pi(5 \text{ ft})^2}{2}\right)\right]$

$\quad + (\text{Perimeter}_{base})(\text{Height})$

$= 2(100 \text{ ft}^2 + 25\pi \text{ ft}^2)$

$\quad + \left[2(10 \text{ ft}) + 2\left(\dfrac{2\pi(5 \text{ ft})}{2}\right)\right](5 \text{ ft})$

$= 200 \text{ ft}^2 + 50\pi \text{ ft}^2 + (20 \text{ ft} + 10\pi \text{ ft})(5 \text{ ft})$

$= 200 \text{ ft}^2 + 50\pi \text{ ft}^2 + 100 \text{ ft}^2 + 50\pi \text{ ft}^2$

$= \mathbf{(300 + 100\pi) \text{ ft}^2 = 614 \text{ ft}^2}$

$V = (\text{Area}_{base})(\text{Height})$

$= (100 \text{ ft}^2 + 25\pi \text{ ft}^2)(5 \text{ ft})$

$= \mathbf{(500 + 125\pi) \text{ ft}^3 = 892.5 \text{ ft}^3}$

Practice 115

a. $x < -2$

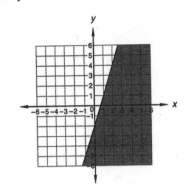

b. $y \le 3x - 2$

c. $y \ge \dfrac{1}{2}x + 1$

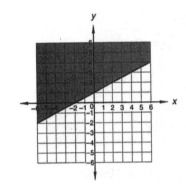

Problem Set 115

1. (a) $A_n = A_0 y^n$

$A_n = 17(2)^n$

(b) $A_n = 17(2)^n$

$A_{30} = 17(2)^{30} = \mathbf{1.83 \times 10^{10}}$

2. $P = \dfrac{k}{V}$

$10 = \dfrac{k}{150}$

$k = 1500$

$P = \dfrac{1500}{V}$

$3 = \dfrac{1500}{V}$

$3V = 1500$

$V = \mathbf{500 \text{ liters}}$

3. $A = \dfrac{k}{W}$

$10 = \dfrac{k}{300}$

$k = 3000$

$A = \dfrac{3000}{W}$

$A = \dfrac{3000}{150}$

$A = \mathbf{20}$

4. $D_R = D_W$

$R_R T_R = R_W T_W$

$R_R = 7$

$R_W = 3$

$T_R + T_W = 20$

$T_R = -T_W + 20$

$R_R T_R = R_W T_W$

$7(-T_W + 20) = 3T_W$

$-7T_W + 140 = 3T_W$

$140 = 10T_W$

$T_W = 14$

$D_W = R_W T_W = 3(14) = \mathbf{42\ miles}$

5. (a) $N_N + N_D = 34$

(b) $5N_N + 10N_D = 270$

$(-5)(a)\ \ -5N_N - 5N_D = -170$

$\underline{(1)(b)\ \ \ 5N_N + 10N_D = \ \ \ 270}$

$\ 5N_D = \ \ \ 100$

$\ \ \ \ \ \ \ \ \ \ \ \ \ \ \ \ \ \ N_D = \mathbf{20}$

(a) $N_N + N_D = 34$

$N_N + 20 = 34$

$N_N = \mathbf{14}$

6. $P(\text{all red}) = \dfrac{7}{12} \cdot \dfrac{6}{11} \cdot \dfrac{5}{10} = \dfrac{\mathbf{7}}{\mathbf{44}}$

7. $y > x$

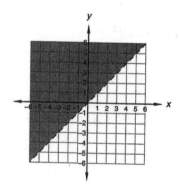

8. $y \le x + 1$

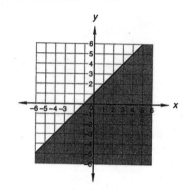

9. $x < -5$

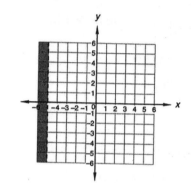

10. $G(x) = \sqrt{x + 1}$

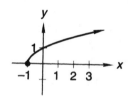

11. $F(x) = -x^2 - 1$

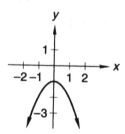

12. $y = \left(\dfrac{1}{2}\right)^x$

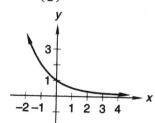

13. $m = \dfrac{-2 - 5}{3 - (-2)} = -\dfrac{7}{5}$

$y = -\dfrac{7}{5}x + b$

$-2 = -\dfrac{7}{5}(3) + b$

$-2 = -\dfrac{21}{5} + b$

$b = \dfrac{11}{5}$

$y = -\dfrac{7}{5}x + \dfrac{11}{5}$

14. $y = -\dfrac{1}{3}x + b$

$5 = -\dfrac{1}{3}(-2) + b$

$5 = \dfrac{2}{3} + b$

$b = \dfrac{13}{3}$

$y = -\dfrac{1}{3}x + \dfrac{13}{3}$

15. $4 \geq |x|;\ D = \{\text{Integers}\}$

$|x| \leq 4$

```
   +--●--●--●--●--●--●--●--●--●--+
  -5 -4 -3 -2 -1  0  1  2  3  4  5
```

16. $4 \leq x + 3 < 7;\ D = \{\text{Reals}\}$

$\begin{array}{ccc} 4 \leq & x + 3 & < 7 \\ -3 & & -3\ -3 \\ \hline 1 \leq & x & < 4 \end{array}$

```
   +--●━━━━━━━━━━━○--+
   0  1  2  3  4  5
```

17. $\left(3 + 2\sqrt{2}\right)\left(5 - 3\sqrt{2}\right)$

$= 15 - 9\sqrt{2} + 10\sqrt{2} - 12 = \mathbf{3 + \sqrt{2}}$

18. $\left(4 + \sqrt{3}\right)\left(2 - 4\sqrt{3}\right)$

$= 8 - 16\sqrt{3} + 2\sqrt{3} - 12 = \mathbf{-4 - 14\sqrt{3}}$

19. $9x^2 + 6x + 1 = (3x + 1)(3x + 1)$

20. $25x^2 - y^2 = (5x + y)(5x - y)$

21. $5z^2 + 2z - 7 = (5z + 7)(z - 1)$

22. $-2\sqrt{x} + 4 = -1$

$-2\sqrt{x} = -5$

$\sqrt{x} = \dfrac{5}{2}$

$\left(\sqrt{x}\right)^2 = \left(\dfrac{5}{2}\right)^2$

$x = \dfrac{25}{4}$

Check $x = \dfrac{25}{4}$:

$-2\sqrt{\dfrac{25}{4}} + 4 = -1$

$-2\left(\dfrac{5}{2}\right) + 4 = -1$

$-5 + 4 = -1$

$-1 = -1$ Check

$x = \dfrac{\mathbf{25}}{\mathbf{4}}$

23. $(k \neq 0)$

$\dfrac{k - 3}{2k} = \dfrac{3}{6k} - \dfrac{1}{4}$

$\dfrac{k - 3}{2k} = \dfrac{1}{2k} - \dfrac{1}{4}$

$4k\left(\dfrac{k - 3}{2k}\right) = 4k\left(\dfrac{1}{2k}\right) - 4k\left(\dfrac{1}{4}\right)$

$2(k - 3) = 2 - k$

$2k - 6 = 2 - k$

$3k = 8$

$k = \dfrac{\mathbf{8}}{\mathbf{3}}$

24. $(m, d \neq 0)$

$\dfrac{x}{m} - \dfrac{c}{d} = d$

$md\left(\dfrac{x}{m}\right) - md\left(\dfrac{c}{d}\right) = md^2$

$dx - cm = md^2$

$dx = md^2 + cm$

$dx = m\left(d^2 + c\right)$

$m = \dfrac{\boldsymbol{dx}}{\boldsymbol{d^2 + c}}$

$\left(d^2 + c \neq 0\right)$

25. **(a), (c), (e), (f)**

26. $y = \sqrt[3]{-125}$

$y = -5$

$xy - a - ya(y - a)$

$= (-2)(-5) - (-1) - (-5)(-1)(-5 + 1)$

$= 10 + 1 - 5(-4) = 10 + 1 + 20 = \mathbf{31}$

27. $\dfrac{4x^2y^{-2}(x^2)^{-2}y^2xy}{(2x^0)^2x^2y^{-2}(xy)} = \dfrac{4x^{-1}y}{4x^3y^{-1}} = \dfrac{y^2}{x^4}$

28. $\dfrac{(21{,}000 \times 10^{-40})(5000 \times 10^{-20})}{(0.0003 \times 10^{14})(0.0007 \times 10^{28})}$

$= \dfrac{(2.1 \times 10^{-36})(5 \times 10^{-17})}{(3 \times 10^{10})(7 \times 10^{24})}$

$= \dfrac{2.1 \cdot 5}{3 \cdot 7} \times \dfrac{10^{-36} \cdot 10^{-17}}{10^{10} \cdot 10^{24}}$

$= \dfrac{10.5}{21} \times \dfrac{10^{-53}}{10^{34}}$

$= 0.5 \times 10^{-87} = \mathbf{5 \times 10^{-88}}$

29. $V = \dfrac{4}{3}\pi r^3$

$= \dfrac{4}{3}\pi(6 \text{ cm})^3$

$= \mathbf{288\pi \text{ cm}^3 = 904.32 \text{ cm}^3}$

30. $V = (\text{Area}_{\text{base}})(\text{Height})$

$= (60 \text{ m}^2)(7.5 \text{ m})$

$= \mathbf{450 \text{ m}^3}$

Practice 116

a. $\sqrt{\dfrac{6}{23}} = \dfrac{\sqrt{6}}{\sqrt{23}} \cdot \dfrac{\sqrt{23}}{\sqrt{23}} = \dfrac{\sqrt{138}}{\mathbf{23}}$

b. $\dfrac{4 + \sqrt{5}}{\sqrt{3}} = \dfrac{4 + \sqrt{5}}{\sqrt{3}} \cdot \dfrac{\sqrt{3}}{\sqrt{3}} = \dfrac{4\sqrt{3} + \sqrt{15}}{\mathbf{3}}$

Problem Set 116

1. (a) $A_n = A_0(1 + r)^n$

$A_n = \mathbf{\$10{,}000(1.08)^n}$

(b) $A_5 = \$10{,}000(1.08)^5 = \mathbf{\$14{,}693.28}$

(c) $\$14{,}693.28 - \$10{,}000 = \mathbf{\$4693.28}$

2. (a) $A_n = A_0(1 + r)^n$

$A_n = \mathbf{\$1100(1.06)^n}$

(b) $A_{20} = \$1100(1.06)^{20} = \mathbf{\$3527.85}$

(c) $\$3527.85 - \$1100 = \mathbf{\$2427.85}$

3. $R = \dfrac{k}{N}$

$10 = \dfrac{k}{100}$

$k = 1000$

$R = \dfrac{1000}{N}$

$R = \dfrac{1000}{25}$

$R = \mathbf{40}$

4. $D_E = D_C$

$R_E T_E = R_C T_C$

$R_E = 2$

$R_C = 10$

$T_E + T_C = 18$

$T_E = -T_C + 18$

$R_E T_E = R_C T_C$

$2(-T_C + 18) = 10T_C$

$-2T_C + 36 = 10T_C$

$-12T_C = -36$

$T_C = 3$

$D_C = R_C T_C = 10(3) = \mathbf{30 \text{ km}}$

5. $\dfrac{60}{100} \cdot P = \$3.60$

$\dfrac{100}{60} \cdot \dfrac{60}{100} \cdot P = \$3.60 \cdot \dfrac{100}{60}$

$P = \mathbf{\$6.00}$

6. (a) $N_C = N_E + 15$

(b) $15N_C + 50N_E = 550$

(b) $\qquad 15N_C + 50N_E = 550$

$15(N_E + 15) + 50N_E = 550$

$65N_E + 225 = 550$

$65N_E = 325$

$N_E = \mathbf{5}$

(a) $N_C = N_E + 15$

$N_C = 5 + 15$

$N_C = \mathbf{20}$

7. $\dfrac{2 + 3\sqrt{6}}{\sqrt{2}} = \dfrac{2 + 3\sqrt{6}}{\sqrt{2}} \cdot \dfrac{\sqrt{2}}{\sqrt{2}} = \dfrac{2\sqrt{2} + 3\sqrt{12}}{2}$

$= \dfrac{2\sqrt{2} + 6\sqrt{3}}{2} = \dfrac{2\sqrt{2}}{2} + \dfrac{6\sqrt{3}}{2}$

$= \mathbf{\sqrt{2} + 3\sqrt{3}}$

8. $\sqrt{\dfrac{2}{5}} = \dfrac{\sqrt{2}}{\sqrt{5}} \cdot \dfrac{\sqrt{5}}{\sqrt{5}} = \dfrac{\sqrt{10}}{5}$

9.
$$\frac{4 + 2\sqrt{10}}{\sqrt{5}} = \frac{4 + 2\sqrt{10}}{\sqrt{5}} \cdot \frac{\sqrt{5}}{\sqrt{5}}$$
$$= \frac{4\sqrt{5} + 2\sqrt{50}}{5} = \frac{4\sqrt{5} + 10\sqrt{2}}{5}$$

10. $y \le x - 3$

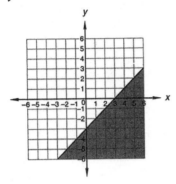

11. $y > \dfrac{1}{2}x + 1$

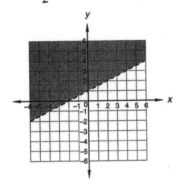

12. $F(x) = |x + 2|$

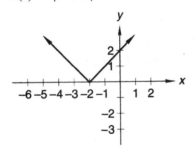

13. $G(x) = (x + 1)^2 + 2$

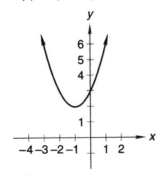

14. $y = 3^x$

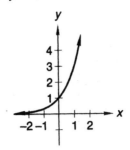

15. $y = \left(\dfrac{1}{3}\right)^x$

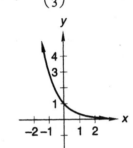

16. $y = -3x + b$

$\quad -2 = -3(5) + b$

$\quad -2 = -15 + b$

$\quad\quad b = 13$

$\quad\quad \mathbf{y = -3x + 13}$

17. $y = -5x + b$

$\quad -3 = -5(-4) + b$

$\quad -3 = 20 + b$

$\quad\quad b = -23$

$\quad\quad \mathbf{y = -5x - 23}$

18. $x + 2 > 6$ or $x - 3 \le -6$; $D = \{\text{Reals}\}$

$\quad x + 2 > 6 \quad$ or $\quad x - 3 \le -6$

$\quad\quad x > 4 \quad$ or $\quad\quad x \le -3$

```
 ◄──●──┼──┼──┼──┼──┼──○──►
   -4 -3 -2 -1  0  1  2  3  4  5
```

19. $\left(3 + 2\sqrt{2}\right)\left(2 - 4\sqrt{2}\right)$

$\quad = 6 - 12\sqrt{2} + 4\sqrt{2} - 8\sqrt{4}$

$\quad = 6 - 8\sqrt{2} - 16 = \mathbf{-10 - 8\sqrt{2}}$

20. $\left(2 + 3\sqrt{3}\right)\left(2 - \sqrt{3}\right)$

$\quad = 4 - 2\sqrt{3} + 6\sqrt{3} - 3\sqrt{9}$

$\quad = 4 + 4\sqrt{3} - 9 = \mathbf{-5 + 4\sqrt{3}}$

21. $\sqrt{x-3} - 2 = 5$

$\sqrt{x-3} = 7$

$(\sqrt{x-3})^2 = (7)^2$

$x - 3 = 49$

$x = 52$

Check $x = 52$:

$\sqrt{52-3} - 2 = 5$

$\sqrt{49} - 2 = 5$

$7 - 2 = 5$

$5 = 5$ Check

$x = \mathbf{52}$

22. $3x^2 + 25x - 18 = \mathbf{(3x - 2)(x + 9)}$

23. $3x^2 - 4 - x = 3x^2 - x - 4 = \mathbf{(3x - 4)(x + 1)}$

24. $ab + 15 + 5a + 3b = ab + 5a + 3b + 15$

$= a(b + 5) + 3(b + 5) = \mathbf{(b + 5)(a + 3)}$

25. $ay + xy + ac + xc = y(a + x) + c(a + x)$

$= \mathbf{(a + x)(y + c)}$

26. $(x, c \neq 0)$

$$\frac{a}{x} - \frac{m}{c} + b = k$$

$$cx\left(\frac{a}{x}\right) - cx\left(\frac{m}{c}\right) + bcx = kcx$$

$$ac - mx + bcx = kcx$$

$$ac + bcx - kcx = mx$$

$$c(a + bx - kx) = mx$$

$$c = \frac{mx}{a + bx - kx}$$

$(a + bx - kx \neq 0)$

27. (a) $(2.718)^2 = \mathbf{7.3875}$

(b) $(1.414)^2 = \mathbf{1.9994}$

(c) $(2.718)^{3.14} = \mathbf{23.0963}$

28. $-2\left[(-2^0 - 2^2)(-2^3 - 2) + (-2)\right]\left[-(-3)(-2)^2\right]$

$= -2[(-5)(-10) + (-2)](12)$

$= -2(48)(12) = \mathbf{-1152}$

29. $S.A. = 4\pi r^2$

$= 4\pi(8 \text{ in.})^2$

$= 256\pi \text{ in.}^2 = \mathbf{803.84 \text{ in.}^2}$

30. $S.A. = 2(\text{Area}_{\text{base}}) + \text{Lateral Surface Area}$

$= 2\left[(12 \text{ ft} \times 30 \text{ ft}) + \frac{1}{2}(18 \text{ ft} \times 24 \text{ ft})\right]$

$+ (\text{Perimeter}_{\text{base}})(\text{Height})$

$= 2(360 \text{ ft}^2 + 216 \text{ ft}^2)$

$+ (36 \text{ ft} + 30 \text{ ft} + 12 \text{ ft} + 12 \text{ ft} + 30 \text{ ft})$

$\times 15 \text{ ft}$

$= 2(576 \text{ ft}^2) + (120 \text{ ft})(15 \text{ ft})$

$= 1152 \text{ ft}^2 + 1800 \text{ ft}^2$

$= \mathbf{2952 \text{ ft}^2}$

$V = (\text{Area}_{\text{base}})(\text{Height})$

$= (576 \text{ ft}^2)(15 \text{ ft})$

$= \mathbf{8640 \text{ ft}^3}$

Practice 117

a. $W = \dfrac{k}{D^2}$

$50,000 = \dfrac{k}{(6000)^2}$

$k = 50,000(6000)^2$

$k = 1.8 \times 10^{12}$

$W = \dfrac{1.8 \times 10^{12}}{D^2}$

$W = \dfrac{1.8 \times 10^{12}}{(25,000)^2}$

$W = \mathbf{2880 \text{ lb}}$

Problem Set 117

1. $D = kV^2$

$1800 = k(30)^2$

$k = 2$

$D = 2V^2$

$D = 2(28)^2$

$D = \mathbf{1568 \text{ m}}$

2. $D = kT^2$

$256 = k(4)^2$

$k = 16$

$D = 16T^2$

$D = 16(13)^2$

$D = \mathbf{2704 \text{ ft}}$

3. $G = kP^2$

$4 = k(2)^2$

$k = 1$

$G = P^2$

$G = (6)^2$

$G = \mathbf{36}$

4. $R = \dfrac{k}{B^2}$

$4 = \dfrac{k}{(20)^2}$

$k = 1600$

$R = \dfrac{1600}{B^2}$

$R = \dfrac{1600}{(4)^2}$

$R = \mathbf{100}$

5. (a) $A_n = A_0(y)^n$

$A_n = \mathbf{2^n}$

(b)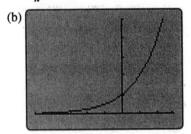

(c) $A_n = 2^n$

$A_9 = 2^9$

$A_9 = \mathbf{512}$

6. $\dfrac{R}{T} = \dfrac{7}{12}$

$\dfrac{R}{16{,}800} = \dfrac{7}{12}$

$R = \dfrac{7 \cdot 16{,}800}{12}$

$R = \mathbf{9800}$

$S = 16{,}800 - 9800$

$S = \mathbf{7000}$

7. $\sqrt{\dfrac{7}{3}} = \dfrac{\sqrt{7}}{\sqrt{3}} \cdot \dfrac{\sqrt{3}}{\sqrt{3}} = \dfrac{\sqrt{\mathbf{21}}}{\mathbf{3}}$

8. $\dfrac{2\sqrt{2} + \sqrt{2}}{\sqrt{2}} = \dfrac{2\sqrt{2} + \sqrt{2}}{\sqrt{2}} \cdot \dfrac{\sqrt{2}}{\sqrt{2}}$

$= \dfrac{2\sqrt{4} + \sqrt{4}}{2} = \dfrac{4 + 2}{2} = \mathbf{3}$

9. $y < 2x + 1$

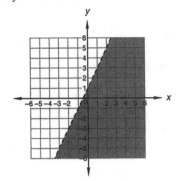

10. $F(x) = -|x| - 3$

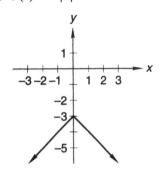

11. $G(x) = \sqrt{x - 1} + 1$

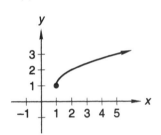

12. $y = 4^x$

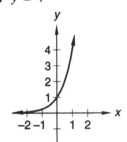

13. $y = \left(\dfrac{1}{4}\right)^x$

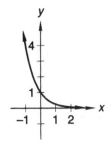

14. $m = \dfrac{-2-5}{3-(-2)} = -\dfrac{7}{5}$

$y = -\dfrac{7}{5}x + b$

$5 = -\dfrac{7}{5}(-2) + b$

$5 = \dfrac{14}{5} + b$

$b = \dfrac{11}{5}$

$y = -\dfrac{7}{5}x + \dfrac{11}{5}$

15. $y = -\dfrac{1}{4}x + b$

$5 = -\dfrac{1}{4}(-2) + b$

$5 = \dfrac{1}{2} + b$

$b = \dfrac{9}{2}$

$y = -\dfrac{1}{4}x + \dfrac{9}{2}$

16. $y = -\dfrac{1}{3}x + b$

$5 = -\dfrac{1}{3}(-2) + b$

$5 = \dfrac{2}{3} + b$

$b = \dfrac{13}{3}$

$y = -\dfrac{1}{3}x + \dfrac{13}{3}$

17. $-2 - |x| > -4$; $D = \{$Reals$\}$

$-|x| > -2$

$|x| < 2$

18. $4 \le x + 2 < 7$; $D = \{$Integers$\}$

$\dfrac{\begin{array}{ccc} 4 & \le\ x + 2 & < 7 \\ -2 & & -2\quad -2 \end{array}}{\quad 2\ \le\ x \qquad\quad < 5}$

19. $x - 1 \le 2$ or $x + 1 > 5$; $D = \{$Reals$\}$

$\begin{array}{lll} x - 1 \le 2 & \text{or} & x + 1 > 5 \\ \quad x \le 3 & \text{or} & \qquad x > 4 \end{array}$

20. $\sqrt{x + 2} - 4 = 1$

$\sqrt{x + 2} = 5$

$(\sqrt{x + 2})^2 = (5)^2$

$x + 2 = 25$

$x = 23$

Check $x = 23$:

$\sqrt{23 + 2} - 4 = 1$

$\sqrt{25} - 4 = 1$

$5 - 4 = 1$

$1 = 1 \qquad$ Check

$x = \mathbf{23}$

21. $2x^2 + 25 + 15x = 2x^2 + 15x + 25$

$= \mathbf{(2x + 5)(x + 5)}$

22. $6x^2 - 40 + 56x = 6x^2 + 56x - 40$

$= 2(3x^2 + 28x - 20) = \mathbf{2(3x - 2)(x + 10)}$

23. $kx - 15 - 5k + 3x = kx - 5k + 3x - 15$

$= k(x - 5) + 3(x - 5) = \mathbf{(k + 3)(x - 5)}$

24. $3mx - 2p + 3px - 2m = 3mx + 3px - 2m - 2p$

$= 3x(m + p) - 2(m + p) = \mathbf{(3x - 2)(m + p)}$

25. $(a, c, k \ne 0)$

$$\dfrac{x}{a} - \dfrac{1}{k} = \dfrac{m}{c}$$

$$akc\left(\dfrac{x}{a}\right) - akc\left(\dfrac{1}{k}\right) = akc\left(\dfrac{m}{c}\right)$$

$$ckx - ac = akm$$

$$-akm - ac = -ckx$$

$$(-1)(akm + ac) = (-1)ckx$$

$$a(km + c) = ckx$$

$$a = \dfrac{kcx}{km + c}$$

$(km + c \ne 0)$

26. $(p \ne 0)$

$$\dfrac{p - 5}{p} = \dfrac{5}{3p} - \dfrac{1}{5}$$

$$15p\left(\dfrac{p - 5}{p}\right) = 15p\left(\dfrac{5}{3p}\right) - 15p\left(\dfrac{1}{5}\right)$$

$$15(p - 5) = 5(5) - 3p$$

$$15p - 75 = 25 - 3p$$

$$18p = 100$$

$$p = \dfrac{100}{18}$$

$$p = \dfrac{50}{9}$$

27. $-3\left[(-2^0 - 3) - (-5 + 7)(-2^2 + 3)\right]$
$\qquad - \left[(-6^0 - 2) + \sqrt[3]{-64}\right]$

$= -3[-4 - (2)(-1)] - (-3 - 4)$

$= -3(-2) + 7$

$= 6 + 7$

$= \mathbf{13}$

28. $b + 4 = 1 \qquad c - 7 = -5$

$\qquad b = -3 \qquad\quad c = 2$

$x = \dfrac{-b \pm \sqrt{b^2 - 4ac}}{2a}$

$\quad = \dfrac{-(-3) \pm \sqrt{(-3)^2 - 4(-2)(2)}}{2(-2)}$

$\quad = \dfrac{3 \pm \sqrt{9 + 16}}{-4}$

$\quad = \dfrac{3 \pm \sqrt{25}}{-4}$

$\quad = \dfrac{3 \pm 5}{-4}$

$\quad = \dfrac{-2}{-4}, \dfrac{8}{-4}$

$\quad = \mathbf{\dfrac{1}{2}, -2}$

29.

$A = A_1 + A_2 - A_3$

$\quad = \dfrac{1}{2}(10 \text{ cm} \times 10 \text{ cm}) + (10 \text{ cm} \times 10 \text{ cm})$

$\qquad - \dfrac{\pi(5 \text{ cm})^2}{2}$

$\quad = 50 \text{ cm}^2 + 100 \text{ cm}^2 - \dfrac{25\pi}{2} \text{ cm}^2$

$\quad = \left(150 - \dfrac{25\pi}{2}\right) \text{ cm}^2$

$\quad = \mathbf{110.75 \text{ cm}^2}$

30. Lateral $S.A. = \left(\text{Perimeter}_{\text{base}}\right)(\text{Height})$

$\qquad\qquad = [6(7 \text{ m})](15 \text{ m})$

$\qquad\qquad = (42 \text{ m})(15 \text{ m})$

$\qquad\qquad = \mathbf{630 \text{ m}^2}$

Practice 118

a. $\qquad\qquad x^2 - 9 = -7x$

$\qquad\quad x^2 + 7x - 9 = 0$

$\qquad\qquad x^2 + 7x = 9$

$x^2 + 7x + \dfrac{49}{4} = 9 + \dfrac{49}{4}$

$\left(x + \dfrac{7}{2}\right)^2 = \left(\sqrt{\dfrac{85}{4}}\right)^2$

$\qquad x + \dfrac{7}{2} = \pm\sqrt{\dfrac{85}{4}}$

$\qquad x + \dfrac{7}{2} = \pm\dfrac{\sqrt{85}}{2}$

$\qquad\qquad x = -\dfrac{7}{2} \pm \dfrac{\sqrt{85}}{2}$

b. $\qquad\qquad x^2 - 5x = 6$

$x^2 - 5x + \dfrac{25}{4} = 6 + \dfrac{25}{4}$

$\left(x - \dfrac{5}{2}\right)^2 = \left(\sqrt{\dfrac{49}{4}}\right)^2$

$\qquad x - \dfrac{5}{2} = \pm\sqrt{\dfrac{49}{4}}$

$\qquad x - \dfrac{5}{2} = \pm\dfrac{7}{2}$

$\qquad\qquad x = \dfrac{5}{2} \pm \dfrac{7}{2}$

$\qquad\qquad x = \dfrac{5 - 7}{2}, \dfrac{5 + 7}{2}$

$\qquad\qquad x = \dfrac{-2}{2}, \dfrac{12}{2}$

$\qquad\qquad x = \mathbf{-1, 6}$

Problem Set 118

1. $R = \dfrac{k}{Y^2}$

$\quad 10 = \dfrac{k}{(100)^2}$

$\quad\; k = 100{,}000$

$\quad R = \dfrac{100{,}000}{Y^2}$

$\quad R = \dfrac{100{,}000}{(5)^2}$

$\quad R = \dfrac{100{,}000}{25}$

$\quad R = \mathbf{4000}$

2. (a) $S(t) = 3(2.71)^t$

$S(0) = 3(2.71)^0$

$S(0) = 3(1) = \mathbf{3}$

(b) $S(10) = 3(2.71)^{10} = \mathbf{64{,}093.53}$

3. $D_F + D_E = 420$

$R_F T_F + R_E T_E = 420$

$T_F = 6$

$T_E = 3$

$R_E = 20 + R_F$

$R_F T_F + R_E T_E = 420$

$6R_F + 3(20 + R_F) = 420$

$9R_F + 60 = 420$

$9R_F = 360$

$\mathbf{R_F = 40\ mph}$

$R_E = 20 + R_F$

$R_E = 20 + 40$

$\mathbf{R_E = 60\ mph}$

4. (a) $N_O = N_T + 293$

(b) $N_O + 10N_T = 2900$

(b) $N_O + 10N_T = 2900$

$(N_T + 293) + 10N_T = 2900$

$11N_T = 2607$

$\mathbf{N_T = 237}$

(a) $N_O = N_T + 293$

$N_O = 237 + 293$

$\mathbf{N_O = 530}$

5. $N, N + 2, N + 4, N + 6$

$-12(N + N + 6) = 19[-(N + 4)] - 6$

$-12(2N + 6) = -19N - 76 - 6$

$-24N - 72 = -19N - 82$

$-5N = -10$

$N = 2$

Thus the integers are **2, 4, 6,** and **8.**

6. $P(H, T) = \dfrac{1}{2} \cdot \dfrac{1}{2} = \dfrac{1}{4}$

7. (a) $A_n = A_0(1 + r)^n$

$A_n = \mathbf{\$50{,}000(1.12)^n}$

(b) $A_{10} = \$50{,}000(1.12)^{10} = \mathbf{\$155{,}292.41}$

(c) $\$155{,}292.41 - \$50{,}000 = \mathbf{\$105{,}292.41}$

8. $x^2 + 2x - 4 = 0$

$x^2 + 2x = 4$

$x^2 + 2x + 1 = 4 + 1$

$(x + 1)^2 = (\sqrt{5})^2$

$x + 1 = \pm\sqrt{5}$

$\mathbf{x = -1 \pm \sqrt{5}}$

9. $x^2 + 3x - 8 = 0$

$x^2 + 3x = 8$

$x^2 + 3x + \dfrac{9}{4} = 8 + \dfrac{9}{4}$

$\left(x + \dfrac{3}{2}\right)^2 = \left(\sqrt{\dfrac{41}{4}}\right)^2$

$x + \dfrac{3}{2} = \pm\sqrt{\dfrac{41}{4}}$

$x + \dfrac{3}{2} = \pm\dfrac{\sqrt{41}}{2}$

$\mathbf{x = -\dfrac{3}{2} \pm \dfrac{\sqrt{41}}{2}}$

10. $x^2 + 2x - 5 = 0$

$x^2 + 2x = 5$

$x^2 + 2x + 1 = 5 + 1$

$(x + 1)^2 = (\sqrt{6})^2$

$x + 1 = \pm\sqrt{6}$

$\mathbf{x = -1 \pm \sqrt{6}}$

11. $x^2 + 4x - 7 = 0$

$x^2 + 4x = 7$

$x^2 + 4x + 4 = 7 + 4$

$(x + 2)^2 = (\sqrt{11})^2$

$x + 2 = \pm\sqrt{11}$

$\mathbf{x = -2 \pm \sqrt{11}}$

12. $\sqrt{\dfrac{2}{7}} = \dfrac{\sqrt{2}}{\sqrt{7}} \cdot \dfrac{\sqrt{7}}{\sqrt{7}} = \dfrac{\sqrt{14}}{7}$

13. $\sqrt{\dfrac{5}{12}} = \dfrac{\sqrt{5}}{\sqrt{12}} \cdot \dfrac{\sqrt{12}}{\sqrt{12}} = \dfrac{\sqrt{60}}{12} = \dfrac{2\sqrt{15}}{12} = \dfrac{\sqrt{15}}{6}$

14. $\dfrac{4 + \sqrt{3}}{\sqrt{6}} = \dfrac{4 + \sqrt{3}}{\sqrt{6}} \cdot \dfrac{\sqrt{6}}{\sqrt{6}} = \dfrac{4\sqrt{6} + \sqrt{18}}{6}$

$= \dfrac{4\sqrt{6} + 3\sqrt{2}}{6}$

15. $\begin{cases} y \le -x + 2 \\ y \ge x \end{cases}$

The solution to this set of inequalities is the region of the graph where both inequalities ($y \le -x + 2$ **and** $y \ge x$) are satisfied. Therefore, this set is simply a conjunction of linear inequalities (see Lessons 111 and 115) which could be written $x \le y \le -x + 2$. Since the solution must satisfy both inequalities, we will shade only the region of the graph that is **both** above the $y = x$ line and below the $y = -x + 2$ line.

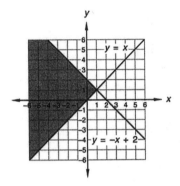

16. $G(x) = x^3 + 1$

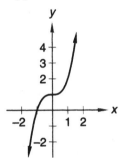

17. $F(x) = -\sqrt{x} - 2$

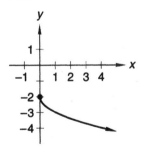

18. (a) $y = 5^x$

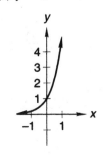

(b) $y = \left(\dfrac{1}{5}\right)^x$

19. $y = \dfrac{1}{5}x + b$

$4 = \dfrac{1}{5}(2) + b$

$4 = \dfrac{2}{5} + b$

$b = \dfrac{18}{5}$

$y = \dfrac{1}{5}x + \dfrac{18}{5}$

20. $m = \dfrac{-3 - 2}{5 - (-3)} = -\dfrac{5}{8}$

$y = -\dfrac{5}{8}x + b$

$2 = -\dfrac{5}{8}(-3) + b$

$2 = \dfrac{15}{8} + b$

$b = \dfrac{1}{8}$

$y = -\dfrac{5}{8}x + \dfrac{1}{8}$

21. $4 \le x - 2 \le 8$; $D = \{$Integers$\}$

$$\begin{array}{ccccc} 4 & \le & x - 2 & \le & 8 \\ +2 & & +2 & & +2 \\ \hline 6 & \le & x & & \le 10 \end{array}$$

22. $3 - |x| > 2$; $D = \{$Reals$\}$

$-|x| > -1$

$|x| < 1$

23. $x + 1 < -2$ or $x - 1 \ge 2$; $D = \{$Reals$\}$

$\quad x + 1 < -2 \quad$ or $\quad x - 1 \ge 2$

$\qquad x < -3 \quad$ or $\qquad x \ge 3$

24. $3x^2 - 35 - 16x = 3x^2 - 16x - 35$
$\quad = (3x + 5)(x - 7)$

25. $-2x + 3x^2 - 5 = 3x^2 - 2x - 5$
$\quad = (3x - 5)(x + 1)$

26. $2x^2 - 5x - 12 = (2x + 3)(x - 4)$

27. $p^2c - ab + p^2b - ac = p^2c + p^2b - ac - ab$
$\quad = p^2(c + b) - a(c + b) = (c + b)(p^2 - a)$

28. $2y + mx^3 + my + 2x^3 = mx^3 + 2x^3 + my + 2y$
$\quad = x^3(m + 2) + y(m + 2) = (m + 2)(x^3 + y)$

29. $\sqrt{4x + 1} - 1 = 2$
$\qquad \sqrt{4x + 1} = 3$
$\qquad (\sqrt{4x + 1})^2 = (3)^2$
$\qquad\qquad 4x + 1 = 9$
$\qquad\qquad\quad 4x = 8$
$\qquad\qquad\quad\ x = 2$

Check $x = 2$:
$\quad \sqrt{4(2) + 1} - 1 = 2$
$\qquad \sqrt{8 + 1} - 1 = 2$
$\qquad\qquad \sqrt{9} - 1 = 2$
$\qquad\qquad\quad 3 - 1 = 2$
$\qquad\qquad\qquad\quad 2 = 2 \quad$ Check

$x = 2$

30. $V = \dfrac{1}{3}(\text{Area}_{\text{base}})(\text{Height})$

$\quad = \dfrac{1}{3}(10 \text{ in.} \times 10 \text{ in.})(12 \text{ in.})$

$\quad = \mathbf{400 \text{ in.}^3}$

$S.A. = \text{Area}_{\text{base}} + \text{Lateral Surface Area}$

$\quad = (10 \text{ in.} \times 10 \text{ in.}) + 4\left[\dfrac{1}{2}(10 \text{ in.} \times 13 \text{ in.})\right]$

$\quad = 100 \text{ in.}^2 + 260 \text{ in.}^2$

$\quad = \mathbf{360 \text{ in.}^2}$

Practice 119

a. $2x^2 - 3x - 7 = 0$

$\quad x = \dfrac{-b \pm \sqrt{b^2 - 4ac}}{2a}$

$\qquad = \dfrac{-(-3) \pm \sqrt{(-3)^2 - 4(2)(-7)}}{2(2)}$

$\qquad = \dfrac{3 \pm \sqrt{9 + 56}}{4} = \dfrac{\mathbf{3 \pm \sqrt{65}}}{\mathbf{4}}$

b. $\qquad\qquad 3x - 1 = -2x^2$
$\qquad 2x^2 + 3x - 1 = 0$

$\quad x = \dfrac{-b \pm \sqrt{b^2 - 4ac}}{2a}$

$\qquad = \dfrac{-(3) \pm \sqrt{(3)^2 - 4(2)(-1)}}{2(2)}$

$\qquad = \dfrac{-3 \pm \sqrt{9 + 8}}{4} = \dfrac{\mathbf{-3 \pm \sqrt{17}}}{\mathbf{4}}$

Problem Set 119

1. $\quad W = \dfrac{k}{D^2}$

$\quad 6000 = \dfrac{k}{(10{,}000)^2}$

$\qquad\quad k = 6000(10{,}000^2)$

$\qquad\quad k = 6 \times 10^{11}$

$\quad W = \dfrac{6 \times 10^{11}}{D^2}$

$\quad W = \dfrac{6 \times 10^{11}}{(5000)^2}$

$\quad W = \mathbf{24{,}000 \text{ lb}}$

2. (a) $A_n = A_0(1 + r)^n$
$\qquad\ A_n = \mathbf{\$19{,}000(1.11)^n}$

(b) $A_8 = \$19{,}000(1.11)^8 = \mathbf{\$43{,}786.22}$

(c) $\$43{,}786.22 - \$19{,}000 = \mathbf{\$24{,}786.22}$

3. $G = \dfrac{k}{B^2}$

$\quad 5 = \dfrac{k}{(50)^2}$

$\quad k = 12{,}500$

$\quad G = \dfrac{12{,}500}{B^2}$

$\quad G = \dfrac{12{,}500}{(10)^2}$

$\quad G = \mathbf{125}$

4. $\quad D_E = D_F$
$\quad R_E T_E = R_F T_F$
$\quad T_E = 20$
$\quad T_F = 25$
$\quad R_E = R_F + 10$

$$R_E T_E = R_F T_F$$
$$(R_F + 10)20 = R_F(25)$$
$$20R_F + 200 = 25R_F$$
$$-5R_F = -200$$
$$\mathbf{R_F = 40\ mph}$$

$$R_E = R_F + 10$$
$$R_E = 40 + 10$$
$$\mathbf{R_E = 50\ mph}$$

5.
$$\frac{130}{100} \cdot P = \$156$$
$$\frac{100}{130} \cdot \frac{130}{100} \cdot P = \$156 \cdot \frac{100}{130}$$
$$\mathbf{P = \$120}$$

6. (a) $N_G = N_S + 2$

(b) $7N_G + 3N_S = 414$

(b)
$$7N_G + 3N_S = 414$$
$$7(N_S + 2) + 3N_S = 414$$
$$10N_S + 14 = 414$$
$$10N_S = 400$$
$$\mathbf{N_S = 40}$$

(a) $N_G = N_S + 2$
$$N_G = 40 + 2$$
$$\mathbf{N_G = 42}$$

7. $N,\ N + 2,\ N + 4$
$$-3(N + N + 4) = 8[-(N + 2)] + 50$$
$$-3(2N + 4) = -8N - 16 + 50$$
$$-6N - 12 = -8N + 34$$
$$2N = 46$$
$$N = 23$$

Thus the integers are **23, 25,** and **27.**

8.
$$-3x = -2x^2 + 10$$
$$2x^2 - 3x - 10 = 0$$
$$x = \frac{-b \pm \sqrt{b^2 - 4ac}}{2a}$$
$$= \frac{-(-3) \pm \sqrt{(-3)^2 - 4(2)(-10)}}{2(2)}$$
$$= \frac{3 \pm \sqrt{9 + 80}}{4}$$
$$= \frac{3 \pm \sqrt{89}}{4}$$

9.
$$-2x = 5 - x^2$$
$$x^2 - 2x - 5 = 0$$
$$x = \frac{-b \pm \sqrt{b^2 - 4ac}}{2a}$$
$$= \frac{-(-2) \pm \sqrt{(-2)^2 - 4(1)(-5)}}{2(1)}$$
$$= \frac{2 \pm \sqrt{4 + 20}}{2} = \frac{2 \pm \sqrt{24}}{2}$$
$$= \frac{2 \pm 2\sqrt{6}}{2} = \mathbf{1 \pm \sqrt{6}}$$

10. $x^2 + 2x - 11 = 0$
$$x = \frac{-b \pm \sqrt{b^2 - 4ac}}{2a}$$
$$= \frac{-(2) \pm \sqrt{(2)^2 - 4(1)(-11)}}{2(1)}$$
$$= \frac{-2 \pm \sqrt{4 + 44}}{2} = \frac{-2 \pm \sqrt{48}}{2}$$
$$= \frac{-2 \pm 4\sqrt{3}}{2} = \mathbf{-1 \pm 2\sqrt{3}}$$

11. $5x^2 - 6x - 4 = 0$
$$x = \frac{-b \pm \sqrt{b^2 - 4ac}}{2a}$$
$$= \frac{-(-6) \pm \sqrt{(-6)^2 - 4(5)(-4)}}{2(5)}$$
$$= \frac{6 \pm \sqrt{36 + 80}}{10} = \frac{6 \pm \sqrt{116}}{10}$$
$$= \frac{6 \pm 2\sqrt{29}}{10} = \mathbf{\frac{3 \pm \sqrt{29}}{5}}$$

12.
$$-3x = -x^2 + 10$$
$$x^2 - 3x = 10$$
$$x^2 - 3x + \frac{9}{4} = 10 + \frac{9}{4}$$
$$\left(x - \frac{3}{2}\right)^2 = \left(\sqrt{\frac{49}{4}}\right)^2$$
$$x - \frac{3}{2} = \pm\sqrt{\frac{49}{4}}$$
$$x - \frac{3}{2} = \pm\frac{7}{2}$$
$$x = \frac{3}{2} \pm \frac{7}{2}$$
$$x = -\frac{4}{2},\ \frac{10}{2}$$
$$x = \mathbf{-2, 5}$$

13.
$$-2x = 5 - x^2$$
$$x^2 - 2x = 5$$
$$x^2 - 2x + 1 = 5 + 1$$
$$(x - 1)^2 = (\sqrt{6})^2$$
$$x - 1 = \pm\sqrt{6}$$
$$x = \mathbf{1 \pm \sqrt{6}}$$

14. $x^2 + 2x - 11 = 0$
$$x^2 + 2x = 11$$
$$x^2 + 2x + 1 = 11 + 1$$
$$(x + 1)^2 = (\sqrt{12})^2$$
$$x + 1 = \pm\sqrt{12}$$
$$x = -1 \pm \sqrt{12}$$
$$x = \mathbf{-1 \pm 2\sqrt{3}}$$

15. $(4 + 2\sqrt{2})(\sqrt{2} + 2)$
$$= 4\sqrt{2} + 8 + 2\sqrt{4} + 4\sqrt{2}$$
$$= 8\sqrt{2} + 8 + 4 = \mathbf{12 + 8\sqrt{2}}$$

16. $\sqrt{\dfrac{3}{8}} = \dfrac{\sqrt{3}}{\sqrt{8}} \cdot \dfrac{\sqrt{8}}{\sqrt{8}} = \dfrac{\sqrt{24}}{8} = \dfrac{2\sqrt{6}}{8} = \dfrac{\sqrt{6}}{\mathbf{4}}$

17. $\dfrac{\sqrt{2} + 1}{\sqrt{2}} = \dfrac{\sqrt{2} + 1}{\sqrt{2}} \cdot \dfrac{\sqrt{2}}{\sqrt{2}} = \dfrac{\mathbf{2 + \sqrt{2}}}{\mathbf{2}}$

18. $\begin{cases} y \geq x \\ y \geq -x + 2 \end{cases}$

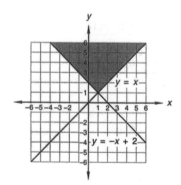

19. $F(x) = -x^3 - 3$

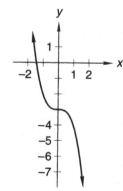

20. $G(x) = (x - 3)^2 + 1$

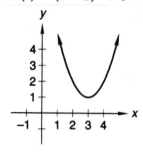

21. (a) $y = 2^x$

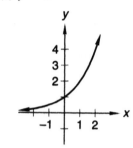

(b) $y = 3^x$

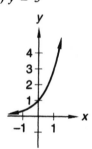

(c) $y = 4^x$

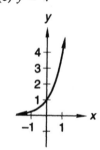

(d) $\mathbf{(0, 1)}$

22. $m = \dfrac{5 - 3}{4 - (-2)} = \dfrac{2}{6} = \dfrac{1}{3}$

$$y = \frac{1}{3}x + b$$
$$5 = \frac{1}{3}(4) + b$$
$$5 = \frac{4}{3} + b$$
$$b = \frac{11}{3}$$
$$y = \frac{1}{3}x + \frac{11}{3}$$

23. $y = -x + b$

$3 = -1 + b$

$b = 4$

$y = -x + 4$

24. $-3 + |x| \geq -2$; $D = \{\text{Reals}\}$

$|x| \geq 1$

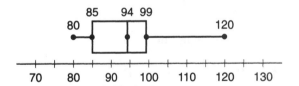

25. $2x^2 - 5x - 25 = (2x + 5)(x - 5)$

26. $acb - ack + 2b - 2k = ac(b - k) + 2(b - k)$

$= (b - k)(ac + 2)$

27.

$$-56 = 15x + x^2$$

$$-x^2 - 15x - 56 = 0$$

$$(-1)(x^2 + 15x + 56) = 0$$

$$x^2 + 15x + 56 = 0$$

$$(x + 8)(x + 7) = 0$$

If $x + 8 = 0$ If $x + 7 = 0$

$\quad x = -8$ $\quad x = -7$

28. $\sqrt{x - 3} + 4 = 5$

$\sqrt{x - 3} = 1$

$(\sqrt{x - 3})^2 = (1)^2$

$x - 3 = 1$

$x = 4$

Check $x = 4$:

$\sqrt{4 - 3} + 4 = 5$

$\sqrt{1} + 4 = 5$

$1 + 4 = 5$

$\quad\quad 5 = 5$ Check

$x = 4$

29. $\dfrac{x + \dfrac{4x}{3y}}{\dfrac{2ax}{y} + 4} = \dfrac{\dfrac{3xy}{3y} + \dfrac{4x}{3y}}{\dfrac{2ax}{y} + \dfrac{4y}{y}}$

$= \dfrac{\dfrac{3xy + 4x}{3y}}{\dfrac{2ax + 4y}{y}} \cdot \dfrac{\dfrac{y}{2ax + 4y}}{\dfrac{y}{2ax + 4y}}$

$= \dfrac{3xy + 4x}{3(2ax + 4y)} = \dfrac{3xy + 4x}{6ax + 12y}$

30. $V = \dfrac{1}{3}(\text{Area}_{\text{base}})(\text{Height})$

$= \dfrac{1}{3}[\pi(5 \text{ cm})^2](12 \text{ cm})$

$= 100\pi \text{ cm}^3 = 314 \text{ cm}^3$

$S.A. = \text{Area}_{\text{base}} + \text{Lateral Surface Area}$

$= \pi r^2 + \pi r l$

$= \pi(5 \text{ cm})^2 + \pi(5 \text{ cm})(13 \text{ cm})$

$= 25\pi \text{ cm}^2 + 65\pi \text{ cm}^2$

$= 90\pi \text{ cm}^2 = 282.6 \text{ cm}^2$

Practice 120

a. (1) Range $= 90 - 45 = $ **45**

Median $=$ **70**

The mode and mean cannot be determined.

(2) **Least $= 45$**

Greatest $= 90$

Median $= 70$

Approximately one fourth of the scores lies between each of the following intervals: 45–60, 60–70, 70–85, and 85–90.

b. 80, 82, 84, 86, 93, 93, 95, 98, 98, 100, 110, 120

Least number $= 80$

Greatest number $= 120$

Median $= \dfrac{93 + 95}{2} = 94$

First Quartile $= \dfrac{84 + 86}{2} = 85$

Third Quartile $= \dfrac{98 + 100}{2} = 99$

Problem Set 120

1. (a) Range $= \$40,000 - \$22,000 = $ **\$18,000**

Median $=$ **\$32,000**

The mode and mean cannot be determined.

(b) **Least $= \$22,000$**

Greatest $= \$40,000$

Median $= \$32,000$

Approximately one fourth of the salaries (in thousands of dollars) lies between each of the following intervals: 22–28, 28–32, 32–35, and 35–40.

2. 7, 10, 13, 19, 21, 23, 25, 27, 33, 35, 37, 45

Least number $= 7$

Greatest number $= 45$

Median $= \dfrac{23 + 25}{2} = 24$

First Quartile $= \dfrac{13 + 19}{2} = 16$

Third Quartile $= \dfrac{33 + 35}{2} = 34$

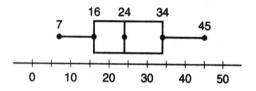

3. $A_t = A_0 y^t$

$A_t = 100(3)^t$

$A_{10} = 100(3)^{10} = \mathbf{5{,}904{,}900}$

4. $W = \dfrac{k}{D^2}$

$25{,}000 = \dfrac{k}{(100{,}000)^2}$

$k = 25{,}000(100{,}000)^2$

$k = 2.5 \times 10^{14}$

$W = \dfrac{2.5 \times 10^{14}}{D^2}$

$W = \dfrac{2.5 \times 10^{14}}{(5000)^2}$

$W = \mathbf{10{,}000{,}000\ lb}$

5. $D_P = D_B$

$R_P T_P = R_B T_B$

$R_P = 11 + R_B$

$T_P = 6$

$T_B = 72$

$R_P T_P = R_B T_B$

$(11 + R_B)6 = R_B(72)$

$66 + 6R_B = 72R_B$

$66 = 66R_B$

$R_B = 1\dfrac{km}{hr}$

$R_P = 11 + R_B$

$R_P = 11 + 1$

$R_P = \mathbf{12\dfrac{km}{hr}}$

$D = R_P T_P$

$D = (12)(6)$

$D = \mathbf{72\ km}$

6. (a) $400N_H + 100N_P = 4500$

(b) $N_H = N_P + 5$

(a) $400N_H + 100N_P = 4500$

$400(N_P + 5) + 100N_P = 4500$

$500N_P + 2000 = 4500$

$500N_P = 2500$

$N_P = 5$

(b) $N_H = N_P + 5$

$N_H = 5 + 5$

$N_H = \mathbf{10}$

7. (a) $A_n = A_0(1 + r)^n$

$A_n = \mathbf{\$500(1.05)^n}$

(b) $A_3 = \$500(1.05)^3 = \mathbf{\$578.81}$

(c) $\$578.81 - \$500 = \mathbf{\$78.81}$

8. $\dfrac{D}{S} = \dfrac{2}{17}$

$\dfrac{S}{T} = \dfrac{17}{19}$

$\dfrac{S}{38{,}000} = \dfrac{17}{19}$

$S = \dfrac{17 \cdot 38{,}000}{19}$

$S = \mathbf{34{,}000}$

9. $4(2N + 7) = N + 70$

$8N + 28 = N + 70$

$7N = 42$

$N = \mathbf{6}$

10. $-2 = x^2 + 6x$

$-x^2 - 6x - 2 = 0$

$(-1)(x^2 + 6x + 2) = 0$

$x^2 + 6x + 2 = 0$

$x = \dfrac{-b \pm \sqrt{b^2 - 4ac}}{2a}$

$= \dfrac{-(6) \pm \sqrt{(6)^2 - 4(1)(2)}}{2(1)}$

$= \dfrac{-6 \pm \sqrt{36 - 8}}{2} = \dfrac{-6 \pm \sqrt{28}}{2}$

$= \dfrac{-6 \pm 2\sqrt{7}}{2} = \mathbf{-3 \pm \sqrt{7}}$

11.
$$-7x = 4 - 2x^2$$
$$2x^2 - 7x - 4 = 0$$
$$x = \frac{-b \pm \sqrt{b^2 - 4ac}}{2a}$$
$$= \frac{-(-7) \pm \sqrt{(-7)^2 - 4(2)(-4)}}{2(2)}$$
$$= \frac{7 \pm \sqrt{49 + 32}}{4} = \frac{7 \pm \sqrt{81}}{4}$$
$$= \frac{7 \pm 9}{4} = -\frac{2}{4}, \frac{16}{4} = \mathbf{-\frac{1}{2}, 4}$$

12.
$$-5 = x^2 - 7x$$
$$x^2 - 7x = -5$$
$$x^2 - 7x + \frac{49}{4} = -5 + \frac{49}{4}$$
$$\left(x - \frac{7}{2}\right)^2 = \left(\sqrt{\frac{29}{4}}\right)^2$$
$$x - \frac{7}{2} = \pm\sqrt{\frac{29}{4}}$$
$$x - \frac{7}{2} = \pm\frac{\sqrt{29}}{2}$$
$$\mathbf{x = \frac{7}{2} \pm \frac{\sqrt{29}}{2}}$$

13.
$$-3x = 4 - x^2$$
$$x^2 - 3x = 4$$
$$x^2 - 3x + \frac{9}{4} = 4 + \frac{9}{4}$$
$$\left(x - \frac{3}{2}\right)^2 = \left(\sqrt{\frac{25}{4}}\right)^2$$
$$x - \frac{3}{2} = \pm\sqrt{\frac{25}{4}}$$
$$x - \frac{3}{2} = \pm\frac{5}{2}$$
$$x = \frac{3}{2} \pm \frac{5}{2}$$
$$x = -\frac{2}{2}, \frac{8}{2}$$
$$\mathbf{x = -1, 4}$$

14.
$$-4 + 9x^2 = 0$$
$$9x^2 - 4 = 0$$
$$(3x + 2)(3x - 2) = 0$$

If $3x + 2 = 0$ If $3x - 2 = 0$
$$3x = -2 \qquad\qquad 3x = 2$$
$$x = -\frac{2}{3} \qquad\qquad x = \frac{2}{3}$$

15.
$$5 = -x^2 - 6x$$
$$x^2 + 6x + 5 = 0$$
$$(x + 1)(x + 5) = 0$$

If $x + 1 = 0$ If $x + 5 = 0$
$$x = \mathbf{-1} \qquad\qquad x = \mathbf{-5}$$

16. $F(x) = |x + 1| - 1$

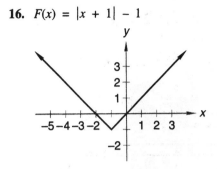

17. $G(x) = -(x - 3)^3$

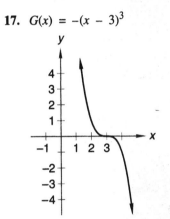

18. $0 \not\leq -x - 3 \not\leq 2$; $D = \{\text{Reals}\}$

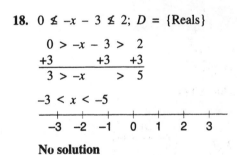

$$0 > -x - 3 > 2$$
$$\underline{+3 \qquad\quad +3 \qquad +3}$$
$$3 > -x \qquad\quad > 5$$

$$-3 < x < -5$$

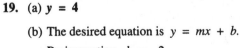

No solution

19. (a) $y = 4$

(b) The desired equation is $y = mx + b$.

By inspection, $b = -2$.

By inspection, the sign of m is $-$.

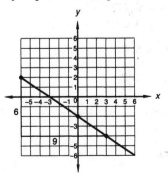

$$|m| = \frac{6}{9} = \frac{2}{3}$$

So $b = -2$ and $m = -\frac{2}{3}$.

$$y = -\frac{2}{3}x - 2$$

20. (a) $y \geq -3x + 2$

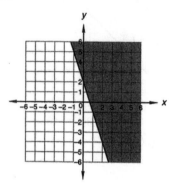

(b) $y < x$

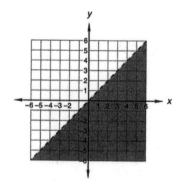

21. $m = \dfrac{3 - 6}{-1 - 8} = \dfrac{-3}{-9} = \dfrac{1}{3}$

$$y = \frac{1}{3}x + b$$

$$6 = \frac{1}{3}(8) + b$$

$$6 = \frac{8}{3} + b$$

$$b = \frac{10}{3}$$

$$y = \frac{1}{3}x + \frac{10}{3}$$

22. (a) $\sqrt{\dfrac{5}{8}} = \dfrac{\sqrt{5}}{\sqrt{8}} \cdot \dfrac{\sqrt{8}}{\sqrt{8}} = \dfrac{\sqrt{40}}{8} = \dfrac{2\sqrt{10}}{8} = \dfrac{\sqrt{10}}{4}$

(b) $\dfrac{\sqrt{5} + 3}{\sqrt{5}} = \dfrac{\sqrt{5} + 3}{\sqrt{5}} \cdot \dfrac{\sqrt{5}}{\sqrt{5}} = \dfrac{5 + 3\sqrt{5}}{5}$

23. $-3\sqrt{12}\left(2\sqrt{6} - 5\sqrt{8}\right)$

$$= -6\sqrt{72} + 15\sqrt{96}$$
$$= -6\sqrt{36}\sqrt{2} + 15\sqrt{16}\sqrt{6}$$
$$= -36\sqrt{2} + 60\sqrt{6}$$

24. $-33 + 30x + 3x^2 = 3x^2 + 30x - 33$
$$= 3\left(x^2 + 10x - 11\right) = \mathbf{3(x + 11)(x - 1)}$$

25. $ax^2 + 5a - 4x^2 - 20$
$$= a\left(x^2 + 5\right) - 4\left(x^2 + 5\right) = \left(x^2 + 5\right)(a - 4)$$

26. (a) **Irrational**

(b) **Rational**

(c) **Rational**

27. **(a), (d), (g)**

28. $f(x) = x^2 - 2x + 3$

$f(x + 2) = (x + 2)^2 - 2(x + 2) + 3$
$$= x^2 + 4x + 4 - 2x - 4 + 3$$
$$= x^2 + 2x + 3$$

29. $x^2 y^{-2} - \dfrac{3x^2}{y^2} + \dfrac{12x^4 x y^{-2}}{x^3} - \dfrac{3x^2 y^2}{x^{-4}}$

$$= \frac{x^2}{y^2} - \frac{3x^2}{y^2} + \frac{12x^2}{y^2} - 3y^2 x^6$$

$$= \frac{10x^2}{y^2} - 3x^6 y^2 = \frac{10}{x^{-2}y^2} - \frac{3}{x^{-6}y^{-2}}$$

30. $S.A. = 2\left(\text{Area}_{\text{base}}\right) + \text{Lateral Surface Area}$

$$= 2\left(\frac{\pi(10 \text{ in.})^2}{2} + \frac{\pi(6 \text{ in.})^2}{2}\right)$$
$$+ \left(\text{Perimeter}_{\text{base}}\right)(\text{Height})$$
$$= 2\left(50\pi \text{ in.}^2 + 18\pi \text{ in.}^2\right)$$
$$+ \left[\left(4 + \frac{2\pi(10)}{2} + 4 + \frac{2\pi(6)}{2}\right)\text{in.}\right](8 \text{ in.})$$
$$= 2\left(68\pi \text{ in.}^2\right) + (8 \text{ in.} + 16\pi \text{ in.})(8 \text{ in.})$$
$$= 136\pi \text{ in.}^2 + 64 \text{ in.}^2 + 128\pi \text{ in.}^2$$
$$= \mathbf{(64 + 264\pi) \text{ in.}^2 = 892.96 \text{ in.}^2}$$

$V = \left(\text{Area}_{\text{base}}\right)(\text{Height})$
$$= \left(68\pi \text{ in.}^2\right)(8 \text{ in.})$$
$$= \mathbf{544\pi \text{ in.}^3 = 1708.16 \text{ in.}^3}$$